# An Appraisal of the 1950 Census Income Data

NATIONAL BUREAU OF ECONOMIC RESEARCH

*CONFERENCE ON RESEARCH IN INCOME AND WEALTH*

# An Appraisal of the 1950 Census Income Data

STUDIES IN INCOME AND WEALTH
VOLUME TWENTY-THREE
BY THE CONFERENCE ON RESEARCH
IN INCOME AND WEALTH

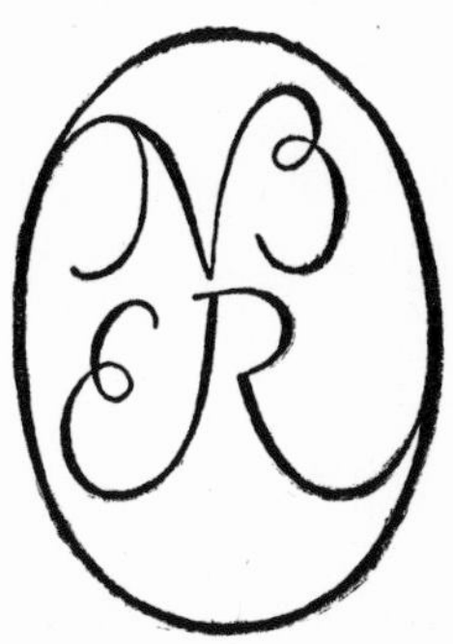

A REPORT OF THE
NATIONAL BUREAU OF ECONOMIC RESEARCH, NEW YORK

PUBLISHED BY
PRINCETON UNIVERSITY PRESS, PRINCETON
1958

L.C. CARD 58-7130

Printed in the United States of America
by Vail-Ballou Press, Inc., Binghamton, New York

Relation of National Bureau Directors to Publications Reporting Conference Proceedings

Since the present volume is a record of conference proceedings, it has been exempted from the rules governing submission of manuscripts to, and critical review by, the Board of Directors of the National Bureau. It has, however, been reviewed and accepted for publication by the Director of Research.

(*Resolution adopted July 6, 1948 and revised November 21, 1949*)

# Prefatory Note

This volume of Studies in Income and Wealth is devoted to the discussion of income data in the 1950 Decennial Census of Population. It is an outcome of the meetings of the Conference on Research in Income and Wealth held in March 1956 at Princeton, New Jersey.

We are indebted to George Garvy who served as chairman of the Program Committee and as editor of this volume; to Dorothy S. Brady, Selma F. Goldsmith, and Herman P. Miller who were members of the committee; and to the Woodrow Wilson School of Public and International Affairs of Princeton University which made its facilities available to the Conference.

Most of the authors and commentators are or were connected with government agencies. Needless to say, all their contributions to this volume represent their own views, which may or may not correspond to those of the organizations with which they are now connected or with which they were associated at the time when the studies reported were undertaken.

Several of the comments compare in scope with the papers to which they relate, and most of them include material not elsewhere available, including results of original research. It was thought particularly appropriate to solicit comments from two especially well qualified experts north of the border, A. H. LeNeveu and Jenny Podoluk, who contribute valuable comparisons between the United States and the Canadian data.

Mildred E. Courtney, Secretary of the Conference, deserves credit for the efficient handling of the organizational chores connected with the Conference and the assembling of the material for this volume. Mary C. Wing's editorial skill contributed materially to its readability and cohesion. H. Irving Forman prepared the charts. Daniel Creamer, Richard A. Easterlin, and Daniel M. Holland made valuable editorial suggestions.

## Contents

# An Appraisal of the 1950 Census Income Data

# Introduction

GEORGE GARVY, FEDERAL RESERVE BANK OF NEW YORK

The 1956 Conference on Research in Income and Wealth dealt with the nature, reliability, and utilization of income data included in the decennial census of population of 1950. The Executive Committee hoped that such a discussion might prove helpful in formulating the income questions in the census of 1960 and in planning the tabulations to be published.

It could not have been the purpose of the Conference to formulate specific suggestions. Instead, it undertook a review of the various studies undertaken to evaluate the statistical quality of the 1950 census income data and an appraisal of their analytical usefulness against the background of similar data available from other sources, including the annual distributions from the Current Population Reports of the Bureau of the Census.

The program of the Conference, held in March 1956, was organized around studies conducted at the request of the Bureau of the Census as a series of cooperative projects involving several agencies. Their object was to match income information from the individual schedules of the 1950 census of population with income data from other sources, including field surveys of other organizations (Survey of Consumer Finances), administrative records (personal income returns of the Internal Revenue Service and wage records of the Bureau of Old-Age and Survivors' Insurance), and a special field survey conducted by the Bureau of the Census itself (the Post-Enumeration Survey) four to six months after the original census was taken.

The matching studies involved a considerable expense of time and money. However, at the time the Conference was planned, no comprehensive reports on any of them were generally available. Several of the key technicians had, in the meantime, left the agencies on behalf of which they had cooperated on these projects. The Conference was designed to help organize the results of the studies and make them available to technicians outside the agencies involved.

Part II of the present volume includes reports on the matching studies. These studies were all initially conceived as integral parts of the Post-Enumeration Survey. The "Census Quality Check" referred to in the paper by Monroe G. Sirken, E. Scott Maynes, and

John A. Frechtling involved the use of the questionnaires, techniques, field organization, and interviewers of the Post-Enumeration Survey in a re-interview of half of the sample employed in the Survey of Consumer Finances. The paper by B. J. Mandel, Irwin Wolkstein, and Marie M. Delaney describes the use of a subsample of the Post-Enumeration Survey sample. The paper by Herman P. Miller and Leon R. Paley refers to still a different subsample of the Post-Enumeration Survey, one for which data collected in the 1950 census were compared with data on income tax returns. Finally, the paper by Leon Pritzker and Alfred Sands discusses the results of the major component of the Post-Enumeration Survey—the "re-enumerative check." A report on the 1949 Audit Control Program of the Treasury Department is also included because the Program Committee thought that a study on the reliability of income data obtained from mandatory reports and involving a penalty for under-reporting would shed light on the quality and limitations of income data collected through the census questionnaire.

Another group of papers deals with substantive findings based on income data, since the most significant appraisal of a body of statistical data must emerge from its actual use in economic and statistical analysis. Part III, therefore, includes several papers using census data analytically. In view of the limited number of projects from which an appraisal of census income distribution data for specific population groups could be obtained for the Conference, the Program Committee did not hesitate to include an analytical paper based on budget data collected by the Bureau of Labor Statistics in the same year.

To give the Conference a proper perspective, three papers of a more general nature were scheduled. In Part I, the first paper surveys some of the frontiers of size-distribution research, thus relating the Conference proceedings to the two earlier conferences on income distribution held in 1943 and 1951. Another establishes a bridge between the census data and other income data. And the third provides a general historical review of income questions in census surveys.

In planning the Conference, the Program Committee had the wholehearted cooperation of the Bureau of the Census and of the various government agencies with which the authors of the several papers are or were associated. All those interested in income size distribution owe a debt of gratitude to the cooperating agencies, but first of all to the Bureau of the Census. Indeed, the initiation of the studies reported in Part II of this volume is an impressive testimonial to the scientific integrity and searching spirit of this veteran of all government organizations concerned with the production of social and economic statistics.

The statistical problems—theoretical as well as operational—encountered in the matching, quality check, and audit programs surpass in interest and significance the limits of the specific projects in which they were encountered. Some of the material presented in Part II, therefore, will be of interest to all who use sample surveys as a tool for the obtaining of analytically significant distributions of economic variables.

The present Conference report differs from all preceding volumes in this series in that it contains a substantial number of statistical tables. Several census tabulations which otherwise would not become generally available, and all original data developed in connection with several of the papers, have been included. This wealth of statistical material—source data, comparative and cross-tabulations, and analytical tables—will, it is hoped, be welcomed by all those who are striving to translate a set of dry statistical records into a dynamic picture of our changing income distribution.

To help the reader in approaching so technical a volume as the present one, it seems useful to summarize here some of the results of the analyses presented in the papers and the related comments and identify some of the problems they raise. Since the authors of the papers were not restricted in the scope of their inquiries, some of the material presented goes far beyond the purely statistical problems that were at the origin of the matching studies around which the Conference program was built.

Indeed, when we probed into the statistical quality of census income data, the question, "How good for what purpose?" emerged immediately. And how good in comparison with what other income data? This question at once opened up the whole issue of the purpose and interpretation of income size distributions in general. From there, it was only a step to probing into the direction and significance of recent changes in size distributions, and to raising some broader questions on the implications and limitations of the personal income concepts now generally used.

The present volume thus takes its place among the several volumes of this series dealing with the broader aspects of the problem of the size distribution of income in the United States.[1] Like its

[1] Volumes Five, two parts (1943), Seven (1946), Nine (1948), Thirteen (1951), and Fifteen (1952) of Studies in Income and Wealth are devoted entirely to the question of size distributions of income. Relevant papers are also included in several other volumes, notably Three (1939), Eight (1946), and Ten (1947). (See list of publications of the Conference at the back of this volume.)

predecessors, it raises more questions than it answers. But, if past experience is a reliable guide, although some seeds take long to germinate, no issue that has been recognized as relevant has ever been permitted to sink into oblivion. The body of empirical data on income structure is in a fluid state. The greater the challenge, the greater the effort required to meet the ever widening needs for factual knowledge of and analytical insight into this vital aspect of economic change and growth.

In consonance with the plan of the Conference, it is proper to begin the summary with a review of the results of the quality check studies, and to pass from there to some more general statistical and analytical issues raised in the Conference reports and the ensuing discussions.

## TESTS OF CONSISTENCY

With the exception of the Audit Control Programs (ACP) of the Treasury Department described by Marius Farioletti, the quality check studies reported on in Part II were undertaken to appraise the quality of the 1950 census income data,[2] not to validate the income distribution it showed, although Miller and Paley seem to take a contrary view (page 200). The appraisals involved comparing answers to income questions in the census with income information obtained independently for the same or "matching" income recipients. The purpose of the Post-Enumeration Survey (PES), according to Pritzker and Sands, was to evaluate the consistency of the replies to income and other questions in successive canvasses by the Census Bureau field staff and to assess improvements obtainable with higher quality interviews and respondents than those of the 1950 census. The survey methods employed by the Bureau of the Census, rather than the income distributions obtained in the 1950 census, were examined. Only the PES and the 1950 census–Internal Revenue Service (IRS) matching study, analyzed in the Miller-Paley paper, involved camparisons with the original census schedules. In the match with Old-Age and Survivors Insurance (OASI) records, the PES schedule was used; this is discussed in the paper by Mandel, Wolkstein, and Delaney. Sirken, Maynes, and Frechtling describe how a special subsample was taken within the

[2] The only important quality check study not reported at the Conference was the 1950 Census–Current Population Survey (CPS) study, the main results of which were already available by the time the Conference was being organized (see Herman P. Miller, "An Appraisal of the 1950 Census Income Data," *Journal of the American Statistical Association,* March 1953)

framework of the Census Quality Check (CQC) sample to study consistency with the Survey of Consumer Finances (SCF).

The schedule for the 1950 census included separate questions on three types of income: wages and salaries, income from self-employment, and income from sources other than earnings. The last catch-all category included property income, rents, and transfer income. For checking purposes only, separate information on nine items of income other than earnings was obtained in the PES schedule. Separate tabulations of persons and families with some income from each of the three major sources were used in the quality check studies. Except for the OASI–PES comparison, all the matching studies involved family units and unattached individuals. In the 1950 census–PES study, however, most comparisons are for persons (Pritzker-Sands, all tables except Tables 14 through 16).

The wide range of empirical data drawn upon in the various papers, together with the lack of a uniform plan of analysis, makes it impossible to cast the results of the matching studies into a uniform mold and to compare them directly. I therefore present merely some of the highlights, focusing, as the underlying studies did, on medians and variability.

In view of the more limited coverage of the IRS data and even more limited coverage of the OASI data, it is not surprising that comparatively few households or individuals could be matched with the census universe. Only about 12 per cent of the 12,000 OASI–PES schedules could be actually matched. Even in the CQC resurvey of part of the SCF sample, 25 per cent of the units could not be matched.

In spite of differences in collection techniques and failure to match a large, but varying, proportion of responding units, median incomes are rather close for all matched units combined as well as for broad subgroups, with the notable exception of farm incomes and of entrepreneurial incomes in general. For the matched schedules, differences between the medians were relatively small, ranging from $24 for all units (families and unattached individuals) in the CQC–SCF match to $77 for persons in the 1950 census–PES study. (No medians were computed for the OASI–PES comparison of wage income because of the various limitations involved.) The 1950 census–IRS comparison occupies an intermediate position, the difference in the medians amounting to $57 (and not exceeding 2 per cent at any given income level). However, the difference between the medians in the IRS and the 1950 census distributions is nearly doubled (increased to $100) when conceptual differences are narrowed down by eliminating individuals reporting nontaxable income in the census. Furthermore, as Farioletti shows, incomes reported to the IRS were lower than those actually received: the full degree of underreporting is not revealed by comparing census reports with IRS returns.[3] The areas of largest underreporting revealed by the matching surveys—income of farmers and of self-employed and professional workers—are precisely where the ACP found the most significant failures to report taxable income.

In the case of CQC–SCF match, a comparison including all schedules, both matched and unmatched units, is of some interest because the CQC undertook a resurvey of about half of the original SCF sample. The medians of the two distributions are only $115 apart, and the largest difference in cumulative percentage distribution is only 2.3 percentage points. The chief explanation for the similarity of means is compensating errors (reporting and enumerative).

Several authors point out that underreporting is larger for families than for persons or one person families. The main reason for missing part of the family income was a failure to inquire about the income of each individual member of the family when obtaining family income data from its head (Pritzker-Sands, page 228; and Goldfield, page 57 ff.).

The response variation was very great for all matched samples even though fairly wide income class intervals were used; narrower intervals would have reduced the percentages of matches considerably. In the 1950 census–IRS match, only 40 to 45 per cent of all families were in the same class. In the 1950 census–PES match, about 60 per cent of the males and 75 per cent of the females fourteen years old or older were assigned to the same income interval. An even lower percentage of persons fourteen years old or older was found in the same income interval in a 1950 census–CPS match (61 per cent),[4] even though in this case the surveys were taken only a month apart and the wording of the questions was practically the same in both. In the CQC–SCF match also (Sirken-Maynes-Frechtling, Table 1), fewer than two-thirds of all consumer units reported income in the same income interval, although the interval used was twice as large ($1,000) as in the other matching studies. Interestingly enough, more women than men reported incomes in the same interval, in part because many more women than men reported no

[3] For the years 1944–1946, Selma F. Goldsmith estimated that tax returns underestimated income by about 14 per cent (see Volume Thirteen (1951) of Studies in Income and Wealth, p. 302).

[4] Miller, *op. cit.,* Table 4.

income. In the OASI–PES match, limited to wage and salary income of $3,000 or less, an identical income was reported by 45 per cent of the covered employees with one employer only; it can be estimated (from Charts 1 and 2 in the Mandel-Wolkstein-Delany paper) that in nearly two-thirds of all cases income reported would have fallen within the same census income interval.

On the whole, the results of the matching studies are consistent with a priori expectations; substantial failure to match units and great response differences are to be expected when matching income information from widely diverse sources. Yet the matching studies reported produced no conclusive results. Because of differences in definitions and technical limitations, it was in no case possible to stipulate in advance what degree of matching was to be expected. Nor are there, as Kaitz points out, any benchmarks to measure response errors (gross), even though there are ways to assess the magnitude of total underreporting (net). Miller and Paley stress that the similarity of over-all distributions masks important differences in their component parts. In analyzing the sources of error, which in their particular case happened largely to offset each other for both the matched and unmatched units, Sirken, Maynes, and Frechtling warn that this may not always be true.

Rather than constituting a validation of any of the distributions compared, the quality check studies contributed to an understanding of the differences among the various types of household surveys and between distributions obtained in such surveys and those derived from other sources. At the same time, they brought into relief the dependence of the results obtained on how the data were collected and processed and on how income, reporting unit, and time period were defined. Matching studies provide no answer on the general superiority of one survey technique over another; a higher reported income does not necessarily mean that a more valid report has been obtained. Indeed, as Goldfield and Grove point out, high incomes reported from self employment may be due to a confusion between gross and net income rather than to a more complete coverage.

## UNDERREPORTING AND RESPONSE VARIABILITY

Much of the Conference discussion was concerned with two important weaknesses of income data from surveys—underreporting and response variability. Both are of particular significance for cross-sectional analyses for which decennial censuses and other survey data provide the income dimension.

Students of survey methods have long been aware of numerous

problems of underreporting and response variation involved in the collection of income data through interview methods. A significant amount of underreporting was revealed by the PES conducted by the Bureau of the Census upon completion of the 1950 census.[5] The PES uncovered nearly 1.7 million additional persons with income, reduced the percentage not reporting income from 6.7 to 2.5 per cent and the percentage reporting no money income from 35.4 to 31.7 per cent. And even though the median income of the additional units was lower than for those reporting in the census ($1,840 versus $1,917), aggregate income covered in the PES was 4.1 per cent higher than in the census. In particular, the census undercounted persons with income other than earnings and those in the highest brackets.

As Peter O. Steiner points out, a proportional understatement of income in all brackets may change the proportion shown in all brackets very little, except at the two extremes. The effect on the extremes explains the relatively large percentage of low-income families shown in census distributions and the corresponding understatement of frequencies at the upper open end. Moreover the evidence presented at the Conference suggests that understatement of income in the 1950 census was not proportional.

The PES and the CQC have given added stress to the importance of obtaining income information from first quality respondents and of using a highly trained and supervised field force. But the large amount of underreporting disclosed by the Audit Control Program of the Treasury Department suggests that underreporting is a serious problem even when reporting is mandatory, penalties are attached to concealment and underreporting, and revenue agents scrutinize the returns. While Farioletti's analysis covers only taxpayers with incomes in 1949 under $10,000 and all returns with business income regardless of total income (but not partnerships), the underreporting disclosed amounted to $4.7 billion. Although this figure represents only a minimum measure of the actual errors, it goes quite far in explaining the gap between Office of Business Economics (OBE) estimates of personal income (adjusted for coverage) and adjusted gross income reported on tax returns, as Pechman shows. He estimates that for 1949, the unexplained portion of the gap was only 3½ per cent of total personal income and suggests that allowing for underreporting of persons with incomes over

[5] For a comparison of the PES with the census distribution, see Herman P. Miller, *Income of the American People,* Wiley, 1955, Table B-15. For a technical description of the PES, see Eli S. Marks, W. Parker Mauldin and Harold Nisselson, "The Post-Enumeration Survey of the 1950 Census: A Case History in Survey Design," *Journal of the American Statistical Association,* June 1953, pp. 220–243.

$10,000 and of some information on persons not required to file will come near to closing this remaining gap.

National aggregates do not provide an entirely independent yardstick for measuring underreporting on tax returns because, as Schwartz points out, the OBE estimates embody some information derived from tax returns. Yet the OBE estimates of total personal income have become so firmly established that the need to reconcile any size distributions of income based on field surveys with national totals becomes inescapable. But reconciliations raise a number of technical questions, such as adjustments for the income concept used, the population covered, and imputations.

Selma F. Goldsmith provides a careful analysis of the underreporting uncovered by comparing the totals derived from distributions from the 1950 census and from the CPS (1944–1954) with corresponding totals from the national income accounts. (She also compares the degree of underreporting in the SCF which gives rise to broadly the same problems of response and enumeration errors as the census distributions.) Her analysis suggests that in the years 1947–1954 the CPS covered between 82 and 84 per cent of the total family money income estimated by the OBE (adjusted to the census concept of money income) and that the last decennial census covered 83 per cent of such income in 1949.[6] (In the first postwar years the percentage covered by the CPS was lower, between 72 and 80 per cent of the OBE income.)

A comparison of aggregate income data from the census and from other sources was made for only one segment of the population—farm families. Similar comparisons with census data could have been made for selected professional groups for which the OBE collects income data through mail questionnaires.

D. Gale Johnson undertook a detailed reconciliation of census aggregates for 1949 with those of the Agricultural Marketing Service (AMS). Grove compared size distributions for selected years between 1945 and 1954 as well. Grove concludes that the 1949 census distribution of farm-operator income was entirely out of line with the CPS distribution and all other distributions summarized in his Table 1. Even though the CPS apparently missed approximately 700,000 farms, between 1947 and 1954, it accounted for between 89 and 99 per cent of the total income of rural farm families as estimated by the AMS, except for 1949, when the percentage fell to 75 per cent (compared with 79 per cent accounted for by the

[6] The Census Bureau estimated from preliminary samples that it covered 92 per cent (see *1950 Census of Population,* Vol. II, *Characteristics of the Population,* Part 1, p. 65).

census). The coverage of the farm income of farm-operator families was lower, apparently in part because the exclusion of transfer income from AMS aggregates tends to reduce their excess over totals obtained from field surveys (which include such income), but does not affect the comparison of farm-operator income.

Grove thinks that underreporting and other response errors may be more serious for farm income than for other types of income. For estimating farm income, he finds the question used in the 1950 census less satisfactory than those asked in the CPS in most years. He considers a separate question on farm self-employment income rather than a single question on total self-employment income, to be preceded by a question on gross income, as an absolute minimum. (The gross income question might prevent the confusion between gross and net income which affected the 1949 census distribution to some extent, in particular at the lower levels.) Indeed, the modification of the census procedure in the PES, which asked for gross and then for net self-employment income, resulted in lowering the median income from self-employment by more than 8 per cent for males and more than 18 per cent for females, according to Pritzker and Sands (Table 17). Grove's conclusions agree with the contention of Sirken, Maynes, and Frechtling that entrepreneurial income is the Achilles' heel of income size distributions, and he endorses their recommendation for carefully controlled experimental surveys to find better techniques to cover this type of income.

While Grove's comparisons of size distributions are limited to farm income, those of Mrs. Goldsmith are for personal family income as a whole. Her findings on differential understatement by source of income in two Census Bureau field surveys (1946 and 1954) are perhaps more significant than her conclusion that about 20 per cent of personal income (after adjustment for conceptual differences) was missed by Census Bureau enumerators. If the underreporting had been systematic and uniform, a single factor could have been used to provide cross-classifications by income levels corresponding to a distribution consistent with personal family aggregates of social accounts.

Since sources and levels of income are correlated, differences among various kinds of income in the percentage unreported must necessarily lead to differential understatements by income level. Indeed, Mrs. Goldsmith finds (Table 4) that family income distributions derived from the 1954 CPS, in which wage and salary income was more fully reported than property and entrepreneurial income, show less inequality than OBE distributions, which fully account for income from all sources. The distribution derived from the SCF for the same year falls between that of the CPS and the OBE for reasons discussed by Mrs. Goldsmith and, in greater detail for 1949, by Sirken, Maynes, and Frechtling.

Comparisons of aggregates (Goldsmith, Tables 2 and 3 and page 75 ff.) as well as matching studies (Pritzker-Sands, Table 18 and Miller-Paley, Table 10) suggest that underreporting was smallest for wage and salary income, although 7½ per cent more families reported such income on income tax returns than to the Census Bureau canvassers. The most serious underreporting occurred for income from sources other than earnings: entrepreneurial and property income as well as social security and other transfer payments. The PES shows that the census missed about one out of three persons with income from "sources other than earnings" (Pritzker-Sands, Table 20), mostly, but not exclusively, in the lowest brackets. When income reported on tax returns is compared with that reported to Census Bureau enumerators (narrowing the definition of income to make it more comparable with "taxable income"), it appears that an even larger proportion of income from "other sources" was missed. For income from self-employment, the PES uncovered relatively few units missed by the decennial census. The matching with tax returns, however, produced substantially larger numbers with such income (including net loss) among nonfarm residents, although substantially the same numbers among farm residents. For both residence categories, however, tax returns showed a considerably larger proportion with net losses, and the median income of units reporting income from self employment was consistently (about one-third) lower in the matched tax returns.

When it is sufficient to rank units by income rather than to associate given characteristics with specific levels of income, a systematic, uniform underreporting of income does not present an insurmountable problem. For example, concentration of underreporting at the extreme upper end of the distribution with fairly uniform rates of underreporting below this would introduce relatively little bias in associating such characteristics as educational levels with income.[7] And Mrs. Goldsmith's analysis suggests that this may be the pattern in field surveys, including the annual CPS and the 1950 census.

However, in other cases differential underreporting by source of

[7] The position of the regression line will be lower than if "true" incomes were used on the ordinate, and most likely its curvature at the upper end of the income scale would be understated; yet for a wide middle range, the curve would portray rather faithfully the nature of the relationship.

income, and consequently by size, may lead to serious errors. For example, the hazard of using census data to appraise or compare the incomes of small geographic areas is obvious. In this connection, Mansfield's comments on city incomes, particularly the inclusion of college students in the size distribution, are relevant. Underreporting would presumably be an important explanatory factor for any differences uncovered in comparing state income totals derived from the 1949 census data with the OBE–state totals. Such a comparison, which would constitute an important guide in appraising census data for smaller areas, is an important gap in the comparisons presented in this volume. The only relevant analysis along these lines developed at the Conference is limited to income data for farm families in a few states. Johnson concluded that some adjustment in census family income data for rural farm areas for inter-area comparability may be required for state to state comparisons.

The matching and quality check studies show that relatively small differences in medians are consistent with a substantial variability in response. Indeed, as an extreme case, one can conceive of a negative correlation between pairs of responses from two samples with an identical median (and mean) income. The Conference did not address itself explicity to the implications of differential underreporting and offsetting response errors detected by the analysis of response variability for the analytical validity of cross-tabulations of socio-economic characteristics by income.

Yet the greatest potentialities of decennial income data lie in the fields of cross-sectional and regional analysis. Schweiger draws attention to one implication of the large variability of income response in field surveys (which presumably would extend to other financial questions, as suggested by the data on savings accounts referred to by him) for any analysis using cross-classifications of income with expenditure, asset holdings, and any other demographic or financial variables. Even if the medians of the "true" population and the survey population are identical, in spite of large gross differences at various income levels, regressions between income and expenditure (or other variables) derived from them may differ significantly.

How gross income response errors are related to errors in reporting other characteristics of the census population was not investigated in the PES. Any interaction of such errors may have resulted in significant net errors, as Pritzker and Sands point out. Furthermore the re-enumerative check revealed that characteristics other than income (age, occupation, and so forth) are also subject to substantial error. Kaitz warns that if response errors on such characteristics as sex, age, and urban or rural residence are not correlated with response errors on income resulting in bracket misclassifications, the comparison of such variables in terms of income must necessarily be impaired.

Schweiger, on the other hand, suggests that misclassification of income tends to smooth out bracket differences in other population characteristics, such as age or family size, because each group reporting in a given income interval includes, in fact, units from a much wider range of incomes. Thus, the $4,000 to $4,999 bracket includes units with actual incomes from $2,000 to $9,999 or even beyond, and the matching surveys suggest that the proportion of the units misclassified is quite substantial. On the other hand, Kaitz sees the presence of random response errors as tending to exaggerate the degree of inequality of a size distribution.

The various cross-classifications of the matched samples suggest that response errors are random, but no detailed test of randomness was made, and the question cannot be considered closed. Kaitz believes that evaluation of the randomness of the empirical response errors would be advanced by the construction of a formal response-error model and by an examination of its properties and implications. Possibly underreporting is not random but instead systematically correlated with the inclusiveness of the income concept. If so, the degree of underreporting would tend to be greatest in the survey using the most inclusive concept.

By bringing the variability of income response into focus, the Conference authors raise a warning signal for the users of these and similar distributions in cross-sectional studies. They also raise the question of what could be done to reduce response variability.

### COORDINATION OF INCOME SIZE DATA

The joint use of income data from several sources may serve purposes other than quality checks. Indeed, in preparing the annual income size distributions, the OBE must do just this. And in Part III, Grove refers to AMS distributions of farm income derived by matching income data from a sample of schedules from the 1950 Census of Population with data on the value of farm products sold and some related cost data from the 1950 Census of Agriculture.

The integration of income information from two or more sources may shed considerable light on the dynamics of income distribution. Coordination of CPS and OASI data, strongly recommended by Mandel, Wolkstein, and Delaney, would provide the basis for a more detailed analysis of wage and salary income. For example, such income could be related to the duration and continuity of an employee's attachment to an industry and to the size and location of the employing firm. Future coordination will be increasingly useful, since the proportion of nonmatches is likely to be reduced by the raising of the limit of taxable wages since the last census, and even more by the substantial extension of the coverage of the social security program, which is now almost universal.

Similarly, coordination of census and IRS data may permit study of sources of unearned income of wage and salary earners, and a more detailed study of patterns of income of taxpayers who receive the bulk of income from sources other than earnings. Pechman urges that the "statistical bridge" technique developed by Hart and Lieblein for integrating field survey and tax return data,[8] expanded to embody corrections for underreporting of tax income, be used to derive size distributions of income in decennial censuses and perhaps even in the CPS.

Some of the difficulties of coordination have been revealed by the quality check studies. Yet, the joint use of census data with other types of data will probably become of increasing importance in analytical studies of income distributions in spite of the differences in coverage and definition. The very existence of several distinct bodies of income data raises the question of their interrelationship; not only of their consistency, but also of their significance for various types of economic analysis.

## CONCEPTUAL PROBLEMS

Several of the papers and comments underline the dependence of size distributions on the income concept, the unit of enumeration, and the income period used, thus confirming the conclusions of earlier investigators. Obviously income distributions based on surveys, including census data, must use income concepts corresponding as closely as possible to the respondent's notions of what constitutes his income. By contrast, in "exhaustive" distributions of total personal income, like those prepared by the OBE from a broad range of sources, various types of income in kind must be imputed to individuals. They will include some types that respondents normally would not report because of failing to recognize them as part of their personal income; for example, investment income of life insurance and pension fund reserves and the undistributed income of personal trust funds.

Clearly, the more complex the income concept used or the larger the number of occasional or part-time workers in the family, the more difficult it becomes to obtain through field surveys complete

[8] Albert Gailord Hart and Julius Lieblein, "Family Income and the Income Tax Base," in Volume Eight (1946) of Studies in Income and Wealth.

and correct information on annual family income. But after all, the need for completeness and exactitude depends on the uses to which the data are to be put. "Are there any essential uses of decennial statistics that require medians to be accurate within $100?" ask Pritzker and Sands. Since for a sample of a given size, errors can be reduced by better training of enumerators, by greater efforts to obtain response from the best qualified respondent, and by better editing, the problem is essentially reduced to one of choice. With given resources, one can either reduce response errors or increase the range of information obtained.

A better synchronization between income and labor status information is necessary, as pointed out by Miller and Teper. Goldfield holds out the prospect that the 1960 census will relate earnings to a person's principal employment status and occupational and industry attachment, as it should, rather than to his work experience during the census week. A corresponding step would be to tabulate family income on the basis of family status during the income period rather than during the census week. Such a reconstruction of families, which, as Mrs. Goldsmith points out, is the first step toward a permanent status approach, involves considerable difficulties. It raises the question to what extent the Bureau of the Census can go beyond the mere publication of tabulations based on edited schedules.

Similarly, tabulation of income by economic families, which is preferable for certain types of economic analysis, would go beyond the concept of biological families on which census reports (including the CPS) are based. SCF and OBE estimates show that the number of separate spending units exceeds that of biological families by about one-seventh. This relationship depends on a variety of factors, including the level of economic activity and wartime influences, and thus is by itself an important explanatory factor of size distributions, as Miss Podoluk suggests. Additional tabulations of census income data by spending units (economic families) seem to involve cost rather than conceptual considerations. But even for biological families, many of the relevant determinants of family income (and in family formation) are lost when family incomes are classified by characteristics of the heads of families only.

## PROBLEMS OF INTERPRETATION

In recent years, rising aggregate income has not merely caused the upward shift of most units along the income scale; it has also changed the way income was produced and consumer income was distributed. An important effect of higher levels of employment has been to raise the incomes of those more or less permanently in the labor force. But increased employment opportunities and higher wages have tended in recent years to draw additional workers into the labor force, including many housewives and very young and very old workers. Some seek only part-time employment, and many of those working normal hours receive lower than average wages because of lack of qualification or work experience. At the same time, some workers who qualify for retirement, including those entitled to private pensions, are encouraged to continue to work because of labor shortages. More students seek vacation employment and even terminate or interrupt their studies to enter the labor force.

Thus, while higher wages, the elimination of short hours, and overtime work tend to increase the income of the core of the labor force, the new entrants tend to be more heavily concentrated on the lower end of the income distribution, the more so in that some casual workers work only part of the year. At the same time, more workers of retirement age, many of whom are relatively good earners, continue to draw producer income rather than transfer payments, normally only a fraction of their earned income. This is likely to be an offsetting influence.

Working housewives and children are mostly supplementary earners. In other cases additional employment may lead to the formation of additional consumer units. Thus the upward movement along the income scale of consumer units with additional earners tends to be obscured by the breaking up of some existing units and the emergence of substantial numbers of additional units, many of which will be ranked near the lower end of the scale. This is particularly likely if they include one person families or units formed during the year and thus with independent income for only part of the report period.

We know by now enough about the income structure in the United States to appreciate the significance of distinguishing between permanent and transitional factors, and units, at both extremes of any distribution. The increased interest in income status (income averaged over a period of years) versus incidence (income in a given year), exemplified by such studies as the one reported by Eleanor M. Snyder, requires the separation of units whose family, and, perhaps, labor force, status has changed during the year.

The problem of distinguishing between income incidence and income status can be approached from several angles. Its importance is put into relief by Miss Snyder's finding of a smaller relative frequency in the lowest income class (under $1,000 in 1950) of unattached individuals and families with low current income but not low economic status than of those with low economic status. Undoubtedly, a companion study would show that there are also considerable numbers of units of low income status who during a given period, because of windfall income and other transient factors, are enumerated in the higher income brackets.

A census-type survey does not necessarily preclude distinguishing between permanent and transient components in family income. Income questions can be expanded to include inquiries about overtime, dual jobs, earnings of members of the family who are not permanent members of the labor force, and other relevant factors. Such a multiplication of income questions would probably be feasible for a relatively small subsample only. Yet an inquiry into the permanent and transient components of income is essential for the understanding of size distributions.

The more the income period is lengthened, the more a size distribution is likely to reflect income status rather than income incidence. Yet it is unlikely that census inquiries could extend the income horizon beyond one year. Furthermore, any lengthening of the income period increases the probability of understatement because of lapses in memory and changes in family composition. But one could conduct successive surveys of an identical sample or accumulate information for successive income periods for an identical group of income recipients.

More generally, interpretation of changes in income distribution requires focusing on mobility. Decennial census data cannot be expected to provide more than a framework into which to fit more frequent and more specific investigations into specific elements making for changes in relative income positions. Some of the main systematic factors are demographic. For the analysis of such data, the population census is the primary and most complete source of data, in particular when geographic factors are taken into consideration or when the analysis is narrowed down to specific regions or communities of certain size or locational characteristics. For most analytical purposes, multivariate tabulations are required, and most census income tabulations are univariate. However the problem is principally one of securing sufficient financial resources to utilize fully the potentialities of the basic information normally collected. In the last two population censuses nothing like a full-scale exploitation of all the possible significant cross-classifications by income was attempted because of budgetary limitations. Even the modest initial plans for basic tabulations had to be subsequently curtailed.

## CENSUS AND OTHER SIZE-DISTRIBUTION DATA

Goldfield reminds us that before the turn of the century the decennial census was the chief avenue open for collecting socio-economic data. Even though a wide variety of financial inquiries was included in most censuses, beginning with the first census of agriculture taken in 1840, the first census to include questions on income was taken a century later.[9]

Population censuses are, indeed, not necessarily the logical vehicle for collecting income data. A recent survey prepared for the Statistical Commission of the Economic and Social Council of the United Nations suggests that the use of population censuses to collect income data is far from universal.[10] Between 1948 and 1953, twelve countries included income questions in their censuses, in most cases for the first time. In addition to the United States and the Philippines, only four Latin American countries and six British Dominions have used censuses to obtain income data, but two of the latter also derive size distributions from income tax returns. By contrast, in eight European countries knowledge of income size distributions is drawn from tabulations of income tax returns. In the United States, income questions were introduced into the decennial census as a significant variable in the demographic and socio-economic analysis of the population structure and not primarily to derive national distributions of income. As suggested by Goldfield, the CPS can be made to carry a good part of the burden of a more detailed probing into the dynamics of income size distribution. He thus raises the question of the respective roles that the decennial census and the CPS should play as primary sources of data on the income structure.

Since the Conference was focused on the quality check of the 1950 census, income data collected by the CPS have been referred to only obliquely, except in the Goldsmith and Grove papers. Yet, in a very real sense, the CPS has developed into a miniature population census. Since in the 1950 population census income information was obtained on a sample basis, and since a large sample (20 per cent) is not necessarily the most efficient one, the question of the specific advantages of including income questions in the decennial censuses was raised at the Conference. Goldfield compares the respective merits of the two bodies of income data collected by the

[9] For a detailed description of the income questions, see A. Ross Eckler, Richard H. Crawford, and Selma F. Goldsmith, "The 1940 Population Census," in Volume Five (1943) of Studies in Income and Wealth.

[10] *Statistics of the Distribution of Income,* Document E/CN.3/208, February 10, 1956.

Bureau of the Census and finds that the miniature census has considerably more advantages than disadvantages. One important shortcoming of CPS is the lack of detailed occupational cross-classification which he thinks could be overcome by expanding the sample. Moreover, Miller's earlier analysis showed great stability in the wage structure by industry and occupation.[11] Similarly, the other major shortcoming—that the CPS sample is too small to provide data for states and smaller areas—could be overcome by expanding the sample. A first attempt in this direction is currently underway in the State of New York, where an expanded CPS sample will provide additional income data to permit a rather detailed analysis of the income structure in that state.

The place of decennial income data within the large structure of income data which has been gradually developed in this country, including size distributions, clearly arises from the Conference discussions. How often are various types of income information desired? How large a sample is needed to obtain each of the most needed types of income distributions and cross-classifications of income with other variables? How precise must the income distribution data be?

Different users of income data will not agree on answers to these and similar questions. Indeed, three ways of looking at income size distributions emerged from the Conference discussion. One way—and perhaps the one which prompted the inclusion of the income question in the census—is to look at income primarily as one of the variables associated with fertility, housing arrangements, or other socio-economic relationships in which income enters as a cause. Another is to look at income distribution as one of the most significant end results of the economic process, with interest centering on explanatory variables accountable for the dynamics of size distributions, such as educational levels, occupation, industry attachments, or ownership of assets. A third and perhaps more novel look, is to regard income as one of the elements in the decision-making process involving issues of economic and social policy.

When income is used as one of the explanatory variables, usually a ranking of units by income level will be sufficient. Where income enters as a datum in the decision-making process, absolute levels rather than ranking will usually be significant. Indeed, dividing lines based on discriminants such as minimum budgets are likely to be drawn on the basis of specific dollar levels, although occasionally they might be drawn at some quintile or similarly defined level.

It is primarily when income is considered as a result that one must

[11] Miller, *Income of the American People,* Chapter 5.

have exhaustive distributions and go beyond what Lampman calls "standard distributions" in order to probe into determinants of income. Analysis of factors making for income inequality and for temporal variability will necessarily focus on sources of income. More detailed information is also needed on the structure of spending units, the work history of the main and supplementary earners, their past earning record, and on family assets.

Mrs. Goldsmith makes a strong case for size distributions by source of income. In discussing Miss Snyder's paper, Miss Podoluk is able to show that in Canada, which distinguishes five income sources, about half of the income in the lowest bracket is derived from transfer payments. No such detail by income level is regularly available in the United States, although an annual breakdown of total family personal income by source is estimated. In the 1950 census, data on three types of income were collected. The published distributions show only the number of persons with each of the three kinds of income, in various combinations,[12] but not the sources of income for all persons in each given income interval. The feasibility of collecting sources of income data through field surveys should be explored further, using the experience of the SCF as well as of the CPS. The analytical importance of data on income by source has been exemplified in recent studies on changes in size distributions of income.[13]

Clearly, a variety of distributions of income by size and numerous types of cross-classifications of income with socio-economic characteristics are required. To evaluate the particular function which decennial benchmarks may play, it would be desirable to obtain a comprehensive analysis of the actual use of the rich and varied array of income data provided by the two last decennial censuses. Yet it is exceedingly difficult to obtain a view of all the analytical uses, legitimate or not, made of census income data. Pritzker and Sands state that the Bureau of the Census itself does not have a clear idea of the extent of the use of these data. The limited use made of the income data from the 1940 census was probably chiefly the result of their wartime publication and their limitation to wage and salary income. And by the time tabulations from the census of 1950 were published, users of income data had become familiar with distributions for several years from the CPS.

Apparently the annual income data from the CPS are more exten-

[12] *1950 Census of Population,* Vol. II, *Characteristics of the Population,* Part 1, Table 143.

[13] Such as Simon Kuznets, *Shares of Upper Income Groups in Income and Savings,* National Bureau of Economic Research, 1953.

sively used than those from the 1950 census, although the CPS offers fewer cross-classifications. Even the census monograph on income includes no general size distribution based on decennial census data.[14] In the monograph the analysis of the determinants of the income distribution (Chapter 3) is based on the CPS and other annual survey data rather than on tabulations from the 1950 census.

However for small geographic areas the decennial census represents the only source of income data. Indeed, the samples of the two other annual field surveys are too small to yield even regional income distributions. Yet in discussing the use of the 1950 census income data for small areas, Edwin Mansfield concludes that their potentialities have scarcely been explored and discusses possible causes of this apparent neglect.

Neither the type of area income data required nor the significance of geographic factors as an explanatory variable of income structure was within the scope of the Conference.[15] Yet the way the need for area income data can best be met deserves attention. Do users of small area income data necessarily need size distributions? Would the total area income and the number of units with income above a given level, which could be varied to reflect differentials in the cost of living, be enough? Perhaps a ranking of counties by average income by family (or per capita, or by income recipient) would meet most of the needs. What is the analytical value of detailed cross-classifications by county in view of the great variability uncovered by the matching studies? And would not county data by source of income, constructed from the OBE state income data by using various allocators, serve more needs, possibly at less cost, than size distributions for the same areas? Which is more limiting, the differential underreporting and response variance in decennial census data or the synthetic nature of county aggregates derived on the basis of allocators? Payrolls, county farm data, and perhaps federal income tax data could be used as allocators. However, to my knowledge, so far the federal income tax data have not been used for this purpose, although state income tax data have.

When geographic factors are used as explanatory variables, the size of the CPS sample can probably be expanded enough to provide all the nationwide breakdowns desirable to compare distributions of the farm, rural, nonfarm, and urban areas, of urban areas

[14] Miller, *Income of the American People.*

[15] Several of the papers in Volume Twenty-one (1957) of this series use census data for states and small areas and deal with some of the questions involving their use.

of different size, and of broad geographic subdivisions of the country. Additional comparisons could be obtained for core and fringe segments of urban areas, or for farm areas classified by the predominant type of farming, product, or farm organization.

Mansfield's suggestions deal with the presentation of census income data for small areas. Lampman makes some more general proposals on the presentation of income size data. He suggests distributions in deciles rather than in fixed dollar intervals, arrayed with the main demographic characteristics of the population falling within each decile, a presentation that would contribute to a better understanding of changes in the degree of inequality. He also suggests the need for size-distribution analysis on the basis of three different concepts. One of these concepts, "producer-contribution income," aims at measuring income shares arising from the participation in the production process (see his Table 1 for the relation of this income concept to the one used in the 1950 census).

More explicitly than Lampman, in commenting on Goldsmith's paper which stresses the stability of the decile distribution of personal incomes since the war, Pechman raises the question whether a complete accounting for economic income of persons should not go beyond the OBE concept of family personal income that served as a bench mark for her estimates of underreporting.[16] A wide range of problems arises from changes in the process of income distribution under the influence of progressive personal income tax legislation combined with high corporate income tax rates and other developments in the institutional framework, some of which the United States shares with other advanced countries. While not quantifying any of these influences, Pechman provides an impressive catalogue of examples of such changes, which tend to increase the gap between economic and family personal income and which are of particular significance in the upper reaches of the income distribution. If it could be assumed that economic income not now measured as part of family personal income is distributed more or less proportionately over the income scale, the analytical significance of the issues raised by Pechman could be minimized. All indications are, however, that the incidence of the types of income now

[16] For this writer's views similar to those expressed by Pechman and Lampman, in addition to the paper quoted by Pechman, see also George Garvy, "Inequality of Income: Causes and Measurement" in Volume Fifteen (1952) of Studies in Income and Wealth; and "A Report on Research on Income Size Distribution in the United States," National Bureau of Economic Research, 1955, mimeographed. See also Selma F. Goldsmith, "Changes in the Distribution of Income Among Economic Groups," *American Economic Association Papers and Proceedings,* March 1957.

disregarded is not proportionate to the size of total income. Furthermore the variation in incidence is more significant for some types of income than for others. Thus family personal money income cannot be taken as a "proxy variable" for the economic income of persons.

The crux of the matter seems to be that as better and better ways of measuring the distribution of personal money income are developed, and as the totals derived from field surveys come closer to national totals obtained by adding distributive shares, money income alone ceases to be fully indicative of either total compensation for productive services or of the purchasing power of the consumer in the market.

The stress is on "fully" and on the direction of change rather than on the amount of divergence between economic and statistical incomes that has already occurred. Yet, as Pechman points out, tax free income disguised as business expense, the transformation of current income into capital gains, the rearrangement of income flows over a lifetime to minimize the tax impact at the peak of earning capacity, and similar devices have considerably diminished the significance of distributions based on definitions that pay too much attention to form and too little to content.

Hardly anybody who has studied recent trends in executive compensation, in collective bargaining contracts, and in the investment policies of individuals can escape the conclusion that a real problem has to be faced. But its statistical dimensions, its differential impact by income level, and its significance for the entire problem of measuring size distributions for limited periods of time within an integrated system of social accounts are unknown. Is a redefinition of personal income needed, or a more complete analysis that would treat accrued and deferred income as changes in assets? But will such a solution meet the challenge of personal income masquerading as business cost, or fully measure the impact of the adaptation of various forms of compensation to minimize income taxes? Yet in a welfare economy where assets are distributed more widely than ever, and where the certain, contractual prospect of delayed payments reduces the need for current income, no picture of income distribution is complete unless it takes account of related changes in assets. At least it must account for assets that embody part of the compensation for productive services and that are a contributing factor in determining current expenditure patterns, including intangible assets like vested pension rights in noncontributory pension plans.

The issue thus raised is broader than income distributions. It is relevant to the definition of total personal income, to the relationship between income and wealth estimates, and to the integration of income and other types of social accounts. The discussion in the present volume thus joins the body of thought developed at several of the preceding meetings of the Conference.

# PART I

## Income Data of the Bureau of the Census

# Some Frontiers of Size-Distribution Research

THOMAS R. ATKINSON, FEDERAL RESERVE BANK OF ATLANTA

Beginning with the 1939 meeting, the size distribution of income has been a recurring subject for the attention of the Conference on Income and Wealth. Generally, the broad outlines of the field have twice been indicated by Simon Kuznets. For the 1941 Conference, Kuznets in his paper "The Why and How of Distribution of Income by Size" suggested that problems for size-distribution studies might logically be divided into three groups: (1) what recipients do with their income; (2) the influence of income on the recipient's other economic and social activities; and (3) non-overt states (attitudes, feelings, and so forth) imputable to income. Again, and more specifically, in June 1950, Kuznets indicated four lines of further inquiry: (1) historical changes and area differences; (2) causal factors in the size distribution of income; (3) factors in the relation between the size and use of income; and (4) normative valuations.

Within these broad subdivisions of inquiry, it is undoubtedly possible to add and compound the detailed questions that Kuznets and others have already suggested. But, as Kuznets has mentioned, the purposes that size distributions may serve are unmanageably numerous, so that any attempt to catalogue and subcatalogue further problems in the field will perhaps also be an unmanageable task. Instead of directing this paper to such a task, therefore, it would seem that a more selective and less comprehensive approach might have some benefits. Specifically, what are some current frontiers of size-distribution research?

Before discussing specific frontiers I would like to point out that the reluctance to consider the size distribution of income that Simon Kuznets, writing in 1939, noted has disintegrated almost to the point of nonexistence. If one attempts to guess the reason for growing interest in the subject of size distribution, one must almost completely reject Kuznets' 1939 prediction that it would come about because of realization of the economic immobility of the individual and the condition of national economic stagnation. Instead, the vast changes in the level and the seemingly vast changes in the distribution of income itself have intruded upon the consciousness of nearly all those old enough to have clear memories of the twenties and thirties and have removed much of the atmosphere of sanctity that previously surrounded the topic of how the fruits of the economy were distributed.

Part of the disintegration of opposition to size-distribution research probably has resulted from the relatively clear view of the workings of supply and demand factors in determining the size distribution of income in the forties and fifties. If pointed remarks have been directed at incomes in some menial occupations, then the influence of demand for the final product, the influence of unions, and the effects of licensing arrangements and building codes were all too clearly seen by those who criticized or ridiculed. The result was certainly the withering of the belief that some sacred force determined one's station in life for all time and the realization that to a considerable extent man-made forces were at work. In addition, as incomes rose generally, the belief that poverty could be eliminated only through redistribution died, removing much of the normative character of discussions of size-distribution topics, together with the almost inevitable opposition to such normative judgments. Lastly, I suspect that the process of collecting and publishing size-distribution data has snowballed and has contributed to the removal of opposition to discussion of the topic. Above all though, it is the existence of changes in the income distribution that catalyzes our interest. What these changes mean in terms of economic effects and how the changes come about provide the major questions around which this paper is oriented.

### *What Does the Income Distribution Determine?*

Awakened interest in size-distribution research seems to stem partly from the belief that changes in the functioning of the economy have been produced, or are capable of being produced, by changes in the distribution of income. This brings us at once to the effect of income distribution upon aggregate consumption.

*Fortune Magazine* had this to say in one of a series of articles on the changing American market:

> Though not a head has been raised aloft on a pikestaff, nor a railway station seized, the U. S. has been for some time now in a revolution. The income explosion of recent years, and the great reshuffling associated with it, have transformed the older American market beyond recognition. This transformation—not to mention the drastic upward revision in living standards—can be construed in no less portentous a word than a revolution. ("The Rich Middle Income Class," *Fortune*, May 1954, p. 95.)

The point of the article, needless to say, was that the increase in the "free spending" middle-income groups had played an important part in the increase in total consumption.

If there has been a fairly widespread acceptance by the public of the doctrine that aggregate consumption has increased over the last twenty years because of greater income equality, it has been generated largely without benefit of statistical support. Some current estimates suggest that the redistribution of after-tax income from 1941 to 1950 amounted to 10 or 11 per cent as measured by the percentage reduction of concentration coefficients between the two years.[1] The effect on consumption of such a redistribution is another matter. Numerous studies of aggregate consumption functions over time seem to have gotten along quite well without income-distribution variables.[2] Even calculations based on static studies of consumption at various income levels suggest an increase in consumption accompanying a 10 per cent redistribution of 0.2 to 2.2 per cent without multiplier effects and from 0.6 to 7.0 per cent with multiplier effects.[3] Clearly this is not the stuff that vast changes in aggregate consumer expenditures are made of. Clearly also, the last word has not been heard on this subject, and, despite the negative results so far, it will remain one of the important frontiers in economic research.

If there is an interest in the effects of changes in the size distribution of income in this and similarly advanced countries, there is even greater interest in this topic in relation to so-called underdeveloped areas. When, as at present, the economies of many of these nations are undergoing rapid change, knowledge is urgently needed about the effects of changes in the size distribution of income. At least two directions of investigation of the effect of size distributions are important in thinking about underdeveloped areas.

First, in many countries economic development has been accompanied by balance-of-payment problems, and the effect of changes in the distribution of income seems of major importance. A recent *Economic Survey of Latin America* by the United Nations stresses this relationship in many of the analyses of individual countries, for the most part focusing attention upon the relation between income distribution and consumption.

Second, there is the question of the relation between income dis-

[1] Calculated from Selma Goldsmith, George Jaszi, Hyman Kaitz, and Maurice Liebenberg, "Size Distribution of Income since the Mid-Thirties," *Review of Economics and Statistics,* February 1954, n. 7, p. 7, and Table 13, p. 25.

[2] Martin Bronfenbrenner, Taro Yamane, and C. H. Lee, "A Study in Redistribution and Consumption," *Review of Economics and Statistics,* May 1955, p. 159.

[3] *Ibid.,* p. 151, and Table 3, p. 155.

tribution and capital formation. Henry Aubrey has suggested in relation to his study of the development of Mexico that a highly unequal income distribution supplied the wherewithal for capital formation, and therefore that "an egalitarian distribution of gains from progress, however desirable socially and politically, is not necessarily the best procedure from a long-term developmental point of view." [4] Despite the apparent logic of this position, Simon Kuznets has warned that the seeming connection between income inequality and capital formation in Western Europe may not hold true for countries presently classified as underdeveloped. On the other hand, he suggests that the lesson of Western Europe cannot be disregarded in favor of development encouraged through inflation or rigid controls instead of a climate favorable to saving and private investment activity.[5] Here then we have a series of frontiers of practical importance to millions of people.

Closely related to the question of how the income distribution affects the level of important economic magnitudes is the problem of how the income distribution affects the stability of the economy. Since World War II, largely without empirical support, the doctrine has developed that a highly equal income distribution provides a measure of resistance to depressions. In 1955 perhaps the most widely recognized version was advanced by Galbraith in his book *The Great Crash.*[6] Galbraith makes the point that the stock market crash of 1929 had such severe impact because, among other things, the deflation of asset values struck at the consumption and investment activities of the high-income groups in whose hands an extreme concentration of income existed at that time. In the fortuitous publication of this book shortly before the September 1955 fall in stock prices, Galbraith pointed out that the greater equality of income distribution since 1929 was a point in support of the belief that such serious effects could not again result from a collapse in equity prices. Despite Galbraith's provocative suggestion about the asset effect on consumption and investment acting on a seemingly constant size distribution, I suspect that cyclical changes in the size distribution which affect these aggregates are closer to the heart of the stability problem. A final aspect of the stability problem is perhaps the relation of cyclical changes in the income distri-

[4] Henry G. Aubrey, "Mexico: Rapid Growth," in *Economic Development: Principles and Patterns,* H. F. Williamson and J. A. Buttrick, editors, Prentice-Hall, 1954, p. 548.

[5] Simon Kuznets, "Economic Growth and Income Inequality," *American Economic Review,* March 1955, pp. 25–26.

[6] John Kenneth Galbraith, *The Great Crash,* Houghton Mifflin, 1955, pp. 182–183.

bution to the mechanism of built-in flexibility. We need to know whether changes in the distribution of income during the business cycle enforce or retard the tendency of the progressive tax system to produce some countercyclical dampening of movements in disposable income.

The topics discussed this far as frontiers in size-distribution research all revolve around the general subject of what people do with their incomes, and more especially how and why they change their ways of spending when their incomes change. More and more we become disenchanted with the belief that we can reason about the effect of income changes by assuming that families moving to a new economic status will adopt the spending pattern of their new position, retain that of their old status, or possibly evolve a compromise between the two with a lag in adjustment. Since most reasoning on the effects of redistribution is still based upon static rather than dynamic studies of income and consumption, it is clear that much remains to be done in studying the behavior of identical spending units over time before satisfactory conclusions can be reached. It is evident that periodic data on consumption and on investment activity of identical consumer units are required. Moreover, to the extent that recent thinking on the determinants of consumption tends to stress both emulation and the retention of previous consumption-saving patterns after incomes have changed, it is necessary to know where the spending unit is in the income pyramid and where it was in the previous periods. The questions of income status (or where in the income pyramid the recipient or spending unit normally finds himself over a period of years), of income incidence (or where he finds himself in a particular year), and of what changes he makes in his behavior as a result, therefore, assume increased importance because of developments in consumption theory.

### *What Determines the Income Distributions?*

We come now to the general topic of what causes the income distribution itself and the closely related subject of the measurement of changes in the size distribution, and causes and permanence of the apparent changes. Herman P. Miller, one of the contributors to this volume, has put in clear focus perhaps the most challenging question for further research into income size distributions. He has set forth two opposing quotations at the head of his chapter on recent changes in income distribution in his book, *Income of the American People.*[7]

[7] Herman P. Miller, *Income of the American People,* Wiley, 1955, p. 97.

> The American economy for many decades has had a rising standard of per capita income, and no evidence exists that the distribution of income during the period was appreciably different from that which now exists. (Testimony of Margaret G. Reid, *Hearings before the Subcommittee on Low-Income Families of the Joint Committee on the Economic Report,* 81st Cong., 1st Sess., December 1949, p. 347.)

> The transformation in the distribution of our national income that has occurred within the past twenty years . . . may already be counted as one of the great social revolutions in history. (Arthur F. Burns, *Looking Forward,* Thirty-first Annual Report of the National Bureau of Economic Research, 1951, p. 3.)

The questions of whether there has, in fact, been a significant change in the distribution of personal incomes, and whether any such change has been in the nature of a cyclical movement or represents a long-term, relatively permanent trend constitute a major frontier in size-distribution research.

As is perhaps inevitable with a significant economic thesis, Kuznets' conclusion that there has been an important decline in the shares going to the upper-income groups has recently come under challenge. Among others, Seers,[8] Lampman,[9] and Perlo [10] suggest, in effect, that the income that Kuznets sought to measure was not actually measured by him and that even if it was, it would have been incomplete or it would have been the wrong income concept to use. Major points in criticism of Kuznets' findings are:

1. The decline in production for home use rather than for market overemphasizes growing income equality, and the possibility exists that price increases have affected the lower-income groups more than the higher-income groups.

2. Income reported on tax returns does not show nonwage income or illegal income, and is subject to evasion and avoidance that favors the upper-income groups.

3. Kuznets' treatment of capital gains and undistributed profits introduces a downward bias into his conclusions.

[8] Dudley Seers, review of Kuznets' *Shares of Upper Income Groups in Income and Savings,* in the *Economic Journal,* June 1955, pp. 315–317.

[9] R. J. Lampman, "Recent Changes in Income Inequality," *American Economic Review,* June 1954, pp. 251–268.

[10] Victor Perlo, "New Findings on Upper Income Shares," Proceedings of the Business and Economics Section, 1955–56, American Statistical Association, p. 292.

Although many of the comments made in criticism of Kuznets' thesis seem relevant, one gets the impression that many of the criticisms are directed less against Kuznets' findings than against the accepted definitions of income. Along this line, the finding by Goldsmith, Jaszi, Kaitz, and Liebenberg that the distribution of national income (rather than personal income) showed little decline in concentration in the upper-income groups from the mid-thirties to 1950 because of the countercyclical movement in undistributed corporate profits, I am sure, makes all of us wonder what we really should be measuring.[11]

It is probably fair to say that the next few years will witness a good many attempts to further measure the changes in the distribution of income that have occurred and are now occurring. Essentially our knowledge of the income distribution upon which we draw our conclusions has come either from income tax data or from sample surveys conducted by personal interviews. In view of the prevailing feelings that the tax materials err most in the lower-income groups and that survey results err most in underestimating incomes in the higher brackets, much remains to be done in discovering ways and means of correcting for the resulting biases in studies based on one or the other methods or, alternatively, in linking the two types of data. Ultimately we may turn for comparison purposes to distributions based on average incomes over several years. One wonders whether the same degree of reduction in inequality would be found between prewar and postwar years if averages for two or more years could be used rather than income for single years.

Closely related to the problem of verifying the view that a change has taken place is the question of the degree of permanence of the changes which our admittedly imperfect data have shown in the over-all distribution. To form valid conclusions on this question requires our knowing more about the determinants of income than we know now.

While there are some reasons to believe that the decline in income inequality may not be as great as our measurements show, there seem to be excellent reasons to believe that the income distribution has become less unequal. A list of the factors tending to make the actual income distribution (as contrasted with the observed distribution) more equal might include the following: [12]

[11] Goldsmith, Jaszi, Kaitz, and Liebenberg, *op. cit.*, pp. 19–20.

[12] See Geoffrey H. Moore, "Secular Changes in the Distribution of Income," *Proceedings of the American Economic Association*, 1952, pp. 527–544; Morris A. Copeland, "Social and Economic Determinants of the Distribution of Income in the United States," *American Economic Review*, March 1947, pp. 56–75; and

1. Shifts in the distribution of income by source caused by changes in the structure of factor prices and in changes in the quantities of factor services supplied
2. Shifts in the distribution of wealth caused by the tax structure
3. Shifts in after-tax income produced by taxation, fiscal policy, and the increased importance of government social programs
4. Shifts in the occupational structure toward occupations with higher incomes and more equal distributions of that income
5. Increased percentage of full-time employees
6. Compacting of wage and salary rates for full-time earners within and between occupations
7. Increase in the number of earners per family; changes in family size and composition
8. Increase in farm incomes in relation to other incomes
9. Changes in the degree of occupational and geographical and rural-urban mobility

Obviously, a considerable frontier exists in drawing up additions to this list and in refining and following back to more basic determinants the factors already recognized. Only then can the existing body of knowledge be sufficient to answer the question of how permanent is the change in the distribution of income.

It is in the field of the determinants of income for the individual that I think the key to many of our size-distribution problems lies. So far we can report little progress beyond the stage reached by Friedman and Kuznets. Recently both Miller [13] and Adams [14] have attempted to look at the influence of various socio-economic variables upon income, and they have widened our knowledge about the influence of the variables they used for analysis. It is interesting to note, however, that each ultimately came upon stumbling blocks that seemed insurmountable because insufficient information appeared to be available. Miller, in noting the differences in incomes between occupations, wondered about occupational mobility both within and between generations. Adams was left to puzzle about whether the differences in abilities between individuals would explain his observed residual variation.

A somewhat different approach to the problem of what determines income is taken by two other recent writers. Robert Summers

---

Miller, *op. cit.;* Lampman, *op. cit.;* and Goldsmith, Jaszi, Kaitz, and Liebenberg, *op. cit.*

[13] Miller, *op. cit.*

[14] F. Gerard Adams, "Some Personal Economic Characteristics and the Size of Wage and Salary Income," unpublished paper presented at the meetings of the Econometric Society, New York, December 1955.

attempts to "generate" mathematically a hypothetical distribution of lifetime incomes utilizing as data the apparent age-income relationship in the postwar years, the relation between this year's and last year's income, and an initial size distribution.[15] Conrad, on the other hand, tackles the problem of relating the income distribution to the structure of production, the supply of factors, and the demand for final products by means of an input-output system.[16] His analysis puts emphasis upon explaining the size distribution in terms of the level and the occupational composition of employment. These studies appear to suggest that the frontiers in research on income determinants will lie in the problems of assessing mobility, ability, the effect of past income on present and future income, factor supply and demand, and, finally, production techniques.

Not only is research going forward on the determinants of the income of the individual and how they relate to the size distribution, but another developing frontier is that of assessing actual and proposed public policy measures in terms of their effects on the distribution of income. Conrad has followed the lead of others in determining the redistributive effects of public budgets in the United States in 1950.[17] Cartter has attempted a somewhat similar task for the central government fiscal program of Britain for 1948 to 1949.[18] Undoubtedly future studies will increase our ability to assess the impact of both single policy measures and broad public programs encompassing many separate measures. Ultimately though, unless we learn the diverse ways that policies with distributive effects manifest themselves in their impact on the individual and how he in turn reacts to a changed economic status, our assessment of policy measures is likely to be somewhat lacking in applicability.

Within the confines of this short paper I have attempted to suggest a few frontiers for research in the size distribution of income. The theme I have chosen to follow is that it is changes in the distribution of income that furnish the greatest challenge for present research. We are not yet out of the woods in knowing how much of a redistribution has occurred over the past two decades—nor do

[15] Robert Summers, "An Econometric Investigation of the Lifetime Size Distribution of Average Annual Income," unpublished paper presented at the meetings of the Econometric Society, New York, December 1955.

[16] Alfred H. Conrad, "Structural Change, Labor Utilization and the Distribution of Incomes," unpublished paper presented at the meetings of the Econometric Society, New York, December 1955.

[17] Alfred H. Conrad, "Redistribution through Government Budgets in the United States, 1950," in *Income Redistribution and Social Policy,* Alan Peacock, editor, London, J. Cape, 1954.

[18] Allan M. Cartter, *The Redistribution of Income in Postwar Britain,* Yale University Press, 1955.

we know what the effect on aggregate consumption, saving, and investment has been. Not knowing this, we do not know how to assess public measures that would alter the distribution of incomes, and we do not know how permanent are past or future changes produced by accident of history or design of public policy. Even so, we are closer to answers to these questions than we were a few years ago, and the pace of our progress seems to be quickening.

# Decennial Census and Current Population Survey Data on Income

EDWIN D. GOLDFIELD, BUREAU OF THE CENSUS

Since 1810, the people of the United States have been answering census questions about their financial status. This long history of collecting financial information in the censuses came about largely because the decennial census was about the only means the Congress had for collecting data in the nineteenth century. Accordingly, the legislators wrote into the census laws long lists of subjects to be covered. These ranged from the physical condition of the people to the amount of capital stock in insurance companies.

Toward the close of the nineteenth century, other government agencies, such as the Department of Agriculture and the Bureau of Labor, began to compile statistical information. Inevitably, the specialized activities of these agencies made it possible to modify the scope of the decennial census.

The Census Bureau collects information from business establishments and other organizations as well as from individuals. The emphasis in this paper, however, will be on the questions asked by the Bureau or its predecessors of individuals—usually in face-to-face interviews—about their own financial status.

## *Financial Subjects other than Income*

### CENSUS OF AGRICULTURE

Since the first census of agriculture was taken in 1840, farmers have reported the value of certain farm products. In the 1850 and subsequent censuses, they also reported the value of their farms. In addition, they have given information on various expenditures and on the amounts received from the sale of selected farm products.

### CENSUS OF POPULATION

Financial inquiries appeared less regularly in the population census. In 1850, enumerators were instructed "to obtain the value of real estate by inquiry of each individual who is supposed to own

Note: Acknowledgment is made of the assistance in the preparation of this paper of Elva Marquard of the Bureau of the Census.

real estate, be the same located where it may, and insert the amount in dollars." But the Superintendent of the Census declared that "The value of real estate is taken loosely, and induces no confidence" [1] and he published only the real estate values that were taken from public records.[2]

The censuses of 1860 and 1870 required a report on the value not only of real estate but also of "all bonds, stocks, mortgages, notes, livestock, plate, jewels, or furniture but exclusive of wearing apparel." The 1880 census law provided that "the inquiries as to the value of real and personal estate owned shall be stricken out."

In 1890, questions on ownership of property again appeared on the population schedule. This investigation, the most ambitious up to that time, was instigated by Single Tax leagues. Because the Superintendent of the Census had some misgivings about collecting these data, he placed only the less objectionable questions on the population schedule and put the more detailed questions in a supplemental schedule.[3] The enumerator asked each family if it owned or rented the home it occupied; if owned, whether the home was free from mortgage encumbrance. He asked similar questions about each farm. The supplemental schedule was then mailed to mortgagors (except in the southern states) asking them to indicate the amount of the mortgage debt, the market value of the farm or home, the annual rate of interest, and the object for which the debt was incurred. Response to the supplemental inquiry was considered good. Less than 1 per cent of those replying refused to give information or gave it with reluctance. Lack of funds—a problem familiar to present-day census-takers—prevented solicitation of some mortgagors for whom reports were needed.[4] The results of this investigation consumed more printed pages (696) than the income statistics in the 1950 census.

The 1890 statistics on property values and mortgages appear to have been complete and convincing.[5] In the next three censuses (1900, 1910, and 1920), the enumerator asked if the home was owned or rented; if owned, whether it was mortgaged; but he did not inquire about the value of the home or the amount of the mortgage.

[1] *1850 Census of the United States,* p. iv.

[2] *1850 Census of the United States, Report of the Superintendent of the Census for December, 1, 1852; to Which is Appended the Report for December 1, 1851,* p. 46.

[3] *1890 Census of the United States, Report on Farms and Homes: Proprietorship and Indebtedness,* pp. 3–6.

[4] *Ibid.,* pp. 5–7.

[5] *1900 Census of the United States,* Vol. II, *Population,* Part 2, p. clxxxvii.

In 1930, financial data were again collected on the population schedule. If the occupant owned his home, he was asked to indicate the value; if he rented it, he was asked to give the monthly rental. These questions also appeared on the 1940 population and housing schedules and on the housing side of the 1950 population and housing schedule. Mortgage data were not collected in 1930, but they were collected in 1940 and 1950 in the housing census.

## *Consumer Income Surveys*

Until the early 1930's, consumer income surveys were limited and infrequent. The Bureau of Labor Statistics, its predecessor (the Bureau of Labor), and the Immigration Commission were among the pioneers in this field.[6] In the main, however, income distributions (especially those on a national basis) had to be estimated from related data. One of the bodies of related data used for this purpose was the information on residential rents and values reported in the 1930 census.[7]

The economic dislocations of the early thirties and the inability of the American people to consume available goods and services brought into sharp focus the distribution of consumer incomes. Accordingly, some of the surveys taken to get other types of data (such as health, consumption, and housing) included questions on income. Prominent among these was the Study of Consumer Purchases conducted by the Bureau of Labor Statistics and the Bureau of Home Economics with funds from the Works Progress Administration.

In the Study of Consumer Purchases, nearly 300,000 families answered detailed questions about their money and nonmoney incomes in 1935–1936. The National Resources Committee regarded the resulting data as far more extensive than those for previous years, although subject to many limitations and shortcomings. Nevertheless, it was able to estimate the distribution of incomes in the United States from these data, supplementing them by other sample data on family and individual incomes, by data on earnings, and by income tax statistics.[8] This income distribution was widely used, and it stimulated the statistical appetites of social scientists.

[6] In one of the early surveys made by the Bureau of Labor, data on income and expenditures were obtained from 25,000 families (see *Eighteenth Annual Report, 1903,* Commissioner of Labor, 1904).

[7] Maurice Leven, Harold G. Moulton, and Clark Warburton, *America's Capacity to Consume,* Brookings, 1934, p. 222.

[8] *Consumer Incomes in the United States: Their Distribution in 1935–36,* National Resources Committee, 1938, p. 2.

## THE 1940 CENSUS

When the 1940 census was planned, many economists were examining the income distribution in their efforts to explain the long depression which the country had experienced. More information on incomes was needed, and suggestions that income questions be included in the census were inevitable. Such a suggestion came from one of the first Conferences on Research in Income and Wealth.[9] By 1940, the Congress had abandoned the practice of writing into the law the questions that were to be asked in each census and had put the selection of the questions in the hands of the Director of the Census.[10] After investigating the need for the data and the possibility of collecting them, the Bureau decided to insert income questions in the 1940 census.

Since some objections could be anticipated despite the need for the data and the legal basis for collecting them, the Census Bureau adopted four methods of lightening the impact of these questions on the public and of getting the information:

1. People were asked to report the amount only of money wages and salaries. Many wage and salary workers knew that such income had been reported to the government for social security purposes, and the Bureau thought they would not object to reporting it in the census. For other types of income, the Bureau asked only "Did this person receive income of $50 or more from sources other than money wages or salary?"

2. The Bureau did not ask for an exact amount if the respondent received more than $5,000 in wages or salary. This device was intended to minimize respondent resistance, but it had a good statistical basis, because a relatively small proportion of the people had more than $5,000 in wage and salary income in 1939.

3. For people who did not wish to reveal the amount of their wages to the local enumerator (who might be a neighbor), the Bureau provided confidential income forms. The enumerator put identifying information on the form and gave it to the respondent who wrote in the answers to the questions and mailed the form to Washington where the information was entered on the schedule.

4. The Bureau put the income question at the end of the schedule so that the enumerator would have obtained the other census information if the respondent protested and refused to cooperate further.

[9] "Report of Committee Three," Conference on Research in Income and Wealth, National Bureau of Economic Research, unpublished, 1936.

[10] 46 Stat. 21 (1929), 13 U.S.C. 201–204.

Despite these precautions, some adverse publicity preceded the enumeration. Some newspapers carried editorials advising people not to give the information, cartoons ridiculing the collection of the data, and articles questioning the legality of the inquiry. Bills were introduced in Congress to prevent the government from asking questions of this kind; the Congress held hearings but took no further action.

In 1940, it must be remembered, the income tax coverage had not been widely extended by either the federal or the state governments. Social security coverage was limited chiefly to wage and salary workers in business establishments. Many people did not report their earnings to any organization or group, and some of them felt that they were not obliged to do so.

However, the Bureau was agreeably surprised by the cooperation of the people. The nonresponse rate was low, and it appeared to represent largely the omission of entries for persons who had no income. Only 2 per cent of the wage and salary workers did not report wage or salary income. Of the 15 million confidential income forms printed, only 200,000 were used.

The coverage of the 1940 census was larger, in terms of number of respondents, than that of any income survey to that time, and it may prove to be the largest ever to be taken. (The 1950 census income questions were on a sample basis.) The 1940 census income questions were directed to all persons fourteen years old and over except those in specified institutions, and there were 100 million people in this category. Of these, 40 million reported some wage or salary income for 1939.

The Bureau made some attempts to appraise the quality of the 1939 statistics. It examined the nonresponse rates, studied the types of people who failed to respond, aggregated the amounts of wages and salaries and compared them with other wage and salary totals, made certain checks to see if the data were internally consistent, and in a small-scale study matched individual reports with social security records. The general conclusions were that the amount of wages and salaries was somewhat underreported and that the persons with other income were somewhat undercounted. (In subsequent surveys, the Bureau has improved its coverage, but the criticisms still apply.) In any event, the 1939 statistics were reasonably accurate, and they provided a wealth of data on income.

The results were subject to several shortcomings:

1. Limiting the data to wage and salary income eliminated some groups, such as farmers and small businessmen, who suffered from

underemployment if not unemployment. But it did cover the main group who had been affected by lack of work, and persons who got most of their income from wages or salaries could be studied in the light of their personal, family, housing, and employment characteristics.

2. Persons with other incomes of $50 or more were excluded from some tabulations on the assumption that they were not primarily dependent on their wage or salary income. This assumption was probably not entirely justified; a higher limit might have been more appropriate.

3. The combination, in some of the wage and salary tabulations, of experienced persons in the labor force with no wage and salary income with those having such incomes of $1 to $99 muddied the statistics of incomes of earners and hampered the comparison of incomes of persons in different groups, such as those in different occupations. This limitation was imposed by procedural difficulties.[11]

Combining data for these two groups highlighted the lack of identity between persons in the experienced labor force at the time of the census (April) and those who had income in the previous year. Experience has shown that appreciable numbers of persons in the labor force in the spring may have had no income in the previous year because they were unemployed, working without pay, or engaged in some activity (such as going to school or running a home) which was outside the labor force. Similarly, some persons who earned wages or salaries during a given year may not be in the labor force in the following spring. They may have lost their jobs, retired, died, or left the labor force for some other activity. The incomes of earners who died or left the country before the census was taken would not be included in the census income distribution because they would not be counted in the census. Such losses from

[11] The main difficulty was that persons with no wage or salary income had been coded in such a way that they could be segregated only with an undue amount of tabulating effort. A secondary difficulty was that the number of counters on the tabulating machines was limited, and a $0 to $99 combination would make the data fit into those available. With the time and funds obtainable, the only way out of the dilemma at this stage appeared to be to combine the two groups. When the 1940 reports were prepared, the sample tabulations showed that 22 per cent of the persons in the experienced labor force in 1940 had no wage or salary income in 1939, and that these persons comprised 87 per cent of the $0 to $99 income group. (*1940 Census of Population,* Vol. III, *The Labor Force,* Part 1, United States Summary, p. 12.) These results were confirmed by the 1950 data, in which persons in the experienced labor force in 1950 with no wage or salary income in 1949 were an even larger proportion (93 per cent) of the $0–99 group. (*1950 Census of Population,* Vol. II, *Characteristics of the Population,* Part 1, United States Summary, Table 144.)

the population account for some of the difference between income aggregated from census figures and income statistics from other sources.

4. Collecting data for persons rather than families necessitated a special procedure to get family data, and it compounded the problem of obtaining total family wage and salary income when the enumerator failed to make an entry for wage or salary income for some person. Family wage or salary income was obtained by transcribing to separate sheets of paper the information for all related persons in the household. The wage or salary income of an entire family had to be classified as "not reported" if information was lacking for only one adult family member who was a wage or salary worker in 1940, or who was not in the labor force in 1940 but who reported one or more weeks worked in 1939.

When the wage or salary income question was not answered for self-employed workers, unpaid family workers, new workers, or persons not in the labor force in 1940 and not working in 1939, the Bureau assumed that they had no wage or salary income. Relatively few such persons worked for wages or salaries in 1939, and it was assumed that the enumerator had probably left the column blank because he believed that the question on wage or salary income did not apply to these persons.

Failure to answer the question on other income raised similar problems, but they were somewhat simpler because amounts were not involved. Thus, an entire family could be classified as "with other income" if only one member reported receiving it. A more difficult problem arose when no family member reported receiving other income and the enumerator left blanks for some family members. Such a family was classified as "without other income" if the blanks were for persons who were engaged in housework in their own homes or who were in school; it was assumed that such persons would not have received other income. But if the blanks were for other persons, the Bureau had to classify the family as "other income not reported." When the data were tabulated, however, the Census Bureau combined the families "with other income not reported" with the families "with other income," so that it would have a clean distribution of families known to be primarily dependent on wage or salary income.

The cross-tabulations were extensive. In the interests of economy and timeliness, some of the tabulations were made on a 5 per cent sample of the returns. Distributions of wage and salary income for persons were cross-classified by the following criteria (an asterisk indicates a distribution was made for the South only):

Class of worker, sex, residence, receipt of other income (for persons in labor force)

Months worked, sex, residence, receipt of other income (for wage or salary workers not on emergency work)

Color, months worked, residence, sex, receipt of other income (for wage or salary workers not on emergency work)

Age, months worked, sex, residence, receipt of other income (for wage or salary workers not on emergency work)

Industry, sex (for experienced persons in labor force not on emergency work)

Industry, months worked, sex (for wage or salary workers not on emergency work)

Family wage and salary income, number of earners in family, receipt of other income in family, color, residence

Wage or salary income of wife, receipt of other income, color*, residence (for nonfarm married men with wife present)

Employment status, sex, months worked, residence (for experienced persons in labor force)

Occupation, sex, months worked (for experienced persons in labor force not on emergency work)

Household relationship, marital status, sex, color, residence, receipt of other income (for experienced persons in labor force not on emergency work)

Years of school completed, age, residence (for native white and Negro males in nonfarm areas)

Sex, residence, receipt of other income, nonworker category (for persons not in the labor force)

Labor force status and age of wife, color, and presence or absence of children under ten years old (for married men without other income, with wives eighteen to sixty-four years old, in specified urban and rural nonfarm areas)

Distributions of family wage and salary income were cross-classified by the following criteria (an asterisk indicates a distribution was made for the South only):

Size of family, residence, receipt of other income, color*, sex, marital status, and age of head

Class-of-worker composition of family, class of worker of head, color*, residence, receipt of other income (for nonfarm families)

Size of family, number of earners, color*, residence, receipt of other income (for nonfarm families with all workers wage and salary workers)

Number of earners in family, months worked in 1939, color*, residence, receipt of other income (for nonfarm families with all workers wage or salary workers)

Employment status and major occupation group of head, color*, residence, receipt of other income (for nonfarm families with all workers wage or salary workers)

Age of head, color*, residence, receipt of other income (for nonfarm families with all workers wage or salary workers)

Sex, marital status and age of head, number of children under eighteen, color*, residence, receipt of other income

Wage or salary income of head, color*, residence, receipt of other income

Tenure, residence, color*, and receipt of other income

Tenure, amount of rent, residence, color*, and receipt of other income (for nonfarm families)

Size of family, amount of rent, tenure, residence, color* (for nonfarm families without other income)

Marital status and sex of head, number of children under twenty-one, tenure, amount of rent, residence, color* (for nonfarm families without other income)

Size of family, tenure, amount of rent, receipt of other income (for families in large metropolitan districts)

Marital status and sex of head, number of children under twenty-one, tenure, amount of rent, receipt of other income (for families in large metropolitan districts)

Number of persons in labor force, tenure, amount of rent, color*, residence (for nonfarm families without other income)

Number of rooms in dwelling unit, tenure, amount of rent, color*, residence (for nonfarm families without other income)

Number of persons in labor force, tenure, amount of rent, receipt of other income (for families in large metropolitan districts)

Number of rooms in dwelling unit, tenure, amount of rent, receipt of other income (for families in large metropolitan districts)

Employment status of head, tenure, amount of rent, color*, residence (for nonfarm families without other income)

Major occupation group of employed head, tenure, amount of

rent, color*, residence (for nonfarm families without other income)

Employment status of head, tenure, amount of rent, receipt of other income (for families in large metropolitan districts)

Major occupation group of employed head, tenure, amount of rent, receipt of other income (for families in large metropolitan districts)

State of repair and plumbing equipment of dwelling unit, tenure, amount of rent, color*, residence (for nonfarm families without other income)

Employment status and major farm occupation group of employed head, tenure, color*, receipt of other income (for farm families)

Size of family, receipt of other income, residence, age, sex, and marital status of head

The publication program was correspondingly extensive. Two volumes were devoted entirely to wage and salary income, and the income data appeared in a number of reports on other subjects. The following reports of the 1940 census include 1939 data on wage and salary income:

*Population,* Vol. III, *The Labor Force*

*Population–The Labor Force* (*Sample Statistics*):

"Employment and Family Characteristics of Women"

"Wage or Salary Income in 1939"

*Population–Families:*

"Family Wage or Salary Income in 1939"

"Size of Family and Age of Head"

"Types of Families"

*Population and Housing–Families:*

"Characteristics of Rural-Farm Families"

"General Characteristics"

"Income and Rent"

"Tenure and Rent"

Wage and salary income data for 1939 were also included in the following special reports:

"Per Capita Income in Wage-Earner Families, by Size of Family: 1939," Series P-44, No. 19, 1944

"Educational Attainment by Wage or Salary Income: 1940," Series P-46, No. 5, 1946

## CURRENT POPULATION SURVEY

After the Census Bureau finished the reports for the 1940 census, economic conditions and administrative decisions combined to put it again in the business of collecting income data. World War II caused incomes to increase sharply and made earlier income statistics obsolete. Businessmen and social scientists were again looking for current income distributions. At the same time, the Government transferred to the Bureau of the Census the Current Population Survey, which the WPA had originally developed as the Monthly Report on Unemployment.

The statistical world looked at the Current Population Survey and saw something more than a monthly survey of unemployment. It saw a miniature population census that could yield any kind of statistics that a census could. Moreover, the CPS had greater flexibility than the census, and it could produce data on a more current basis.

The Bureau had collected some income data in its Consumer Requirements Surveys in 1944, but in May 1945 it took its first sample survey to determine annual incomes of all types of consumers. The inquiry was in the form of a supplement to the Current Population Survey for that month. The survey covered income in 1944, and an earlier month than May would have been better, but in view of the considerable increase in the scope of the inquiries, much time was required for planning. The Bureau studied its previous experience and consulted many experts in the field, particularly those who had worked on the Consumer Purchases Study, including many of the members of the Conference on Research in Income and Wealth. It finally selected nine questions to get the income information, and then proceeded to develop sampling procedures, prepare instructions, and outline tabulations.

Again, the Census Bureau tried to reduce the impact of the income questions on the respondent and to minimize possible damage to the CPS. Instead of asking all households in that survey to answer the income questions, it asked only those that were scheduled to leave the sample in May to do so; then, if any ill feeling developed, it would not affect the CPS response in succeeding months. The income questions were put at the end of the schedule so that the enumerator would have the other information if the respondent refused to cooperate further. Persons with large incomes were not asked to report the exact amount, but the maximum to be reported was raised to $10,000.

Within six months of the time the survey was taken, the Bureau issued a preliminary report of the results. The time required to produce the report seemed to be unreasonable, but a number of years elapsed before it was reduced (see Table 1).

The 1945 survey provided fairly good statistics, it was relatively inexpensive because it was attached to the CPS, and the public cooperated well in providing information. Moreover, government and business groups used the data in various ways and pointed to the advantages of annual income surveys that would provide comparable statistics. In addition, the Bureau needed income surveys to test questions and procedures for the 1950 census, and it saw that it could improve the usefulness of other data by collating them with the income data. Recently, for example, in its statistics on smoking habits, it was able to provide income data for different types of smokers without asking income questions in the smoking survey. As a result of these needs for the data, the Bureau has produced an uninterrupted series covering the years from 1944 to the present.[12]

From time to time, the Bureau has introduced changes in the income survey to improve the income estimates (see Table 1). Some of these changes may have affected the comparability of the data. In the earlier surveys, for example, specific questions were asked about ten or more types of income; in recent surveys, questions were asked about only four types. The intensive inquiry techniques of the earlier surveys may have helped respondents to recall minor or irregular sources of income and thus may have produced more nearly complete results, but evidence on this factor is inconclusive. The change in the maximum to be reported from $10,000 in 1944 to $25,000 in 1954 reflects the change in economic conditions and also the virtual disappearance of objection on the part of the public to furnish income information. Other changes were made in the coverage, the size of the sample, and the time the survey was taken.

The only significant break in the series was occasioned by the elimination of rural-farm households from the 1946 statistics. The Bureau of the Census agreed to exclude this group because the Bureau of Agricultural Economics planned to collect income information from farm households in its January 1947 Quarterly Survey of Agriculture. The two bureaus intended to combine the two sets of statistics, but they were unable to merge them in a satis-

[12] The Census Bureau has issued Current Population Reports on the basis of the annual CPS as Series P-S, Nos. 22 and 22-s and as Series P-60. A list of these can be found in the annual issues of *Catalog of United States Census Publications,* 1947 to 1955. In addition, the *Preliminary Report on Survey of 1944 Consumer Income* was issued in 1945.

factory manner. The Bureau of the Census, therefore, confined its publication of 1946 data to urban and rural-nonfarm persons and families.

The Bureau continues its experimental work and the introduc-

TABLE 1

Selected Characteristics of Income Surveys Taken in the Current Population Survey, 1945–1955

(*number*)

| YEAR COVERED [a] | *Households (thousands)* | CPS *Areas* | *Questions Asked* | *Months from Collection to Publication* |
|---|---|---|---|---|
| 1944 | 6.7 [b] | 68 | 9 | 6 |
| 1945 | 8.7 [b] | 68 | 17 [c] | 13 |
| 1946 | 20.0 [d] | 148 [d] | 20 | 9 |
| 1947 | 25.0 [e] | 68 | [f] | 10 |
| 1948 | 25.0 [e] | 68 | 3 | 10 |
| 1949 | 15.0 [b] | 68 | 4 | 10 |
| 1950 | 25.0 [e] | 68 | 6 | 11 |
| 1951 | 15.0 [b] | 68 | 4 | 13 |
| 1952 | 18.0 [b] | 68 | 4 | 5 |
| 1953 | 15.0 [b] | 230 | 4 | 13 |
| 1954 | 14.0 [b] | 230 | 4 | 4 |

[a] The survey covering 1944 was taken in May 1945; the survey covering 1949, in March 1950; the surveys of all the other years were taken in the April of the year following the year covered.

[b] Subsample of the CPS sample.

[c] Also 39 calculation questions.

[d] Expanded CPS sample.

[e] CPS sample.

[f] Split sample: 1 or 2 questions.

*Coverage:* All persons fourteen years of age and over except (by year covered):

1944–(1) persons living on military reservations; (2) persons in institutions; (3) persons in hotels, YMCA's, fraternity houses, and similar places; and (4) persons in trailer camps, labor camps, logging camps, houseboats, ships, etc.

1945—(1)–(4) same as for 1944, and (5) persons in large lodging houses

1946—(1) persons living on military reservations, (2) inmates of institutions, and (3) residents of rural-farm areas

1947—(1) persons living on military reservations, and (2) inmates of institutions

1948–1954—(1) members of armed forces living in barracks on military reservations, and (2) inmates of institutions

*Maximum income to be reported* (by year covered): 1944–1950—$10,000; 1951–1952—$15,000; and 1953–1954—$25,000

tion of needed changes. In 1956 it related income for 1955 to work experience in that year. Until that time, the Bureau had assumed that the persons who did not answer the income questions had the same characteristics as those who did. In getting information on work experience, it will at least know whether the nonrespondents were paid workers, and hence recipients of earnings, during the year. It will also be able to check the work experience of persons who reported no income to see if they reported paid work. This additional information should increase the reported number of income recipients and, more important, it should increase the reported amount of aggregate income.

### CPS DATA VERSUS CENSUS DATA

Comparing the collection of income data in the 1950 census and in the CPS, the Census Bureau finds that the CPS has a number of advantages and only one or two disadvantages. The advantages are:

1. Since persons are arranged in household groups, income data are collected for all persons in the household, and family income can be tabulated with little difficulty.
2. More questions can be asked because the number of respondents is much smaller and the cost of adding a question is small.
3. Fewer enumerators are employed and they can be better trained.
4. More detailed processing is feasible, because there are fewer schedules. (Income data usually need editing and can be substantially improved in such an operation.)
5. The data can be published within a shorter period of time.
6. Experimentation is easier. Procedures are more flexible, and the CPS sample is large enough so that it can be split into different test groups. (This was done in the April 1948 survey when different questions were tested for the 1950 census.)
7. The data can be obtained without an undue burden on respondents. Not more than 25,000 households have been asked to give income information in any one survey while millions of households are involved in a census.

The major disadvantage of the CPS is that the size of the sample does not permit the detailed cross-classifications that are possible in the census, and it does not provide data for states and smaller areas. This is a severe limitation. Cross-classifications of income and occupation are particularly interesting, but with the CPS sample, the Bureau can cross-classify income by only the major occupation groups. Another possible disadvantage of the CPS is that it lacks the publicity and the mandatory reporting provisions of the census, but it is doubtful whether these shortcomings have had any significant effect.

Costs of CPS and census income data are not easily compared. A comparison of persons enumerated would not yield an exact ratio, because more time is spent on each CPS report than on each census report. A very rough guess is that the income segment of the census costs several hundred times as much as one CPS annual survey. Over a decade, therefore, the ten annual surveys cost much less than the decennial census.

Uses of the two types of data differ somewhat because CPS provides relatively simple national distributions, while the census provides detailed national cross-classifications and also simple distributions for counties and other small areas. The CPS data are utilized mainly by organizations concerned with broad national problems. For example, they are used by Congressional committees to study the problems of low-income families and their effect on economic stability, by labor organizations to determine policies with respect to labor welfare, and by federal government departments to plan programs for the aged, the disabled, the unskilled, and other disadvantaged groups. Census data are also used by organizations concerned with broad national problems, but they are used especially by groups that need income information for counties, cities, suburbs, and other small areas. Census data are used, for example, by marketing experts to analyze potential markets in various parts of the country, by local housing authorities to determine the necessity for public action in slum clearance and new construction, and by utility companies to forecast needs for equipment in newly developed or older areas.

### OTHER SAMPLE SURVEYS

Since 1945, income questions have been included in a considerable number of surveys taken by the Bureau of the Census. In addition to the annual surveys taken with the CPS to obtain income estimates for the general population in the entire country, income surveys have been made for local areas, and income questions have been included in surveys that were made primarily to get information on other subjects.

The first income survey for a local area was made in February 1948 for the District of Columbia. A public housing law required that the District Commissioners determine, "the maximum net family income falling within the lowest 20 per centum by number of all family incomes in the District of Columbia." The National Capital Park and Planning Commission asked the Census Bureau to take the survey, and the Housing and Home Finance Agency and the Bureau of Labor Statistics provided additional funds to extend its scope.

The Bureau has taken a number of "family income and rent" surveys at the request of local housing authorities. In these surveys, data are collected for dwelling units that, at the time of the 1950 census of housing, were renter-occupied and were substandard as defined by the Public Housing Administration. Income distributions were cross-classified with color of the head of the family and with the size of the family. The Bureau also collected income data for renter families in all types of dwelling units (not just substandard) and showed relationships between rent and income. Each of these surveys relates to an individual city.

In studies of certain groups—the aged, veterans, the disabled—the Bureau collected income data to determine their economic status. It also obtained income data in a survey of pension plan coverage in order to segregate the lower-income groups and get further pension information concerning them.

In these surveys, the Bureau has provided materials for a better understanding of the economic situation of special groups and special areas, and it has also derived several technical advantages from them. It has gained experience in compiling income data for special rather than general purposes and thus improved its techniques. In addition, it has discovered relationships between income and other data which will enable it to plan census cross-classifications more intelligently. Among the surveys in which income data were obtained were those on District of Columbia income, family incomes and rents, rents and vacancies, the pension plan coverage in Pennsylvania, aged persons in Rhode Island and in the United States as a whole, disabled persons, and all persons who ever served in the U.S. armed forces.[13]

## THE 1950 CENSUS

The widespread use of the income data provided by the 1940 census and the CPS supplements prepared the Census Bureau for demands for income data in the 1950 census. Government agencies, Congressional committees, business groups, labor organizations,

[13] Some of the data collected in these surveys have been summarized in the following publications: *Income of Families and Persons in Washington, D.C. 1947, Current Population Reports, Series P-60, No. 4, 1948; Family Income and Rent Survey by the U.S. Bureau of the Census for the Local Housing Authority* (separate publication for each city); *Old Age in Rhode Island,* Report of the Governor's Commission to Study Problems of the Aged, 1953; *Selected Employee Benefit Plans,* Report of the Joint State Government Commission to the General Assembly of the Commonwealth of Pennsylvania, Session of 1955; Lenore A. Epstein, "Economic Resources of Persons Aged 65 and Over," *Social Security Bulletin,* June 1955; and Robert Dorfman, "The Labor Force Status of Persons Aged 65 and Over," and Peter O. Steiner, "The Size, Nature, and Adequacy of the Resources of the Aged," both published in the *American Economic Review,* May 1954.

educational and research institutions, and other groups had requested income data throughout the decade. These data had been useful not only in themselves but also in the seasoning which they added to other bodies of data, such as those on occupation, education, types of family, and industry. (Herman P. Miller's paper in this volume is an example of this use.) Accordingly, income was one of the subjects that the Bureau placed on its preliminary schedules and referred to advisory committees for their approval.

Pretests of the income questions began with the District of Columbia income survey taken in February 1948. This survey resulted in changes in the schedule format, in the questions, and in the instructions.[14] In April 1948, three procedures for getting the income data were tested while the regular annual income information was collected.[15] In the same month, the first "full-dress" pretest of the population schedule was made in Missouri. Income questions were included and information was obtained on field costs and operations problems. In October 1948, another full-dress pretest was made in four scattered areas, and in one of these areas the income entries were checked in a re-enumeration survey.

The Bureau presented the experience gained in these pretests to its Technical Advisory Committee on Economic Statistics, and that committee recommended that income data be obtained by asking each person his wage and salary income, his income from self-employment, and his other income.[16] In May 1949, the Bureau took the population schedule to the field for the last full-dress pretest. The final decision was to ask the following questions in the census:

Last year (1949), how much money did he earn working as an employee for wages or salaries?

Last year, how much money did he earn working in his own business, professional practice, or farm?

[14] *The 1950 Censuses—How they Were Taken,* Bureau of the Census, 1955, p. 6.

[15] In the first, the enumerator asked the respondent two questions—one on wages and salaries in 1947, and one on total income in 1947; in the second, only one question—total income in 1947. The third procedure differed from the second only in that the enumerator used a "flashcard." This card showed various income intervals, and the respondent was asked to indicate the class interval of each person's income. The flashcard reduced respondent resistance, but the statistics were not as good.

[16] The following persons served on the Technical Advisory Committee on Economic Statistics: Paul Webbink (Chairman), Wroe Alderson, Dorothy Brady, Ewan Clague, Donald R. G. Cowan, John C. Davis, J. Frederic Dewhurst, Louis J. Ducoff, John D. Durand, Katherine P. Ellickson, Martin Gainsbrugh, Meredith B. Givens, Hildegarde Kneeland, Stanley Lebergott, Howard B. Myers, Gladys L. Palmer, Benedict Saurino, Margaret Scattergood, Samuel Weiss, and Emmett H. Welch.

Last year, how much money did he receive from interest, dividends, veterans' allowances, pensions, rents, or other income (aside from earnings)?

The sample used as a part of the 1950 census was a sample of persons. Every fifth line on each schedule was marked "sample line" and the person enumerated on that line was to be asked the sample questions. The income questions had been moved to the sample section, and the problem arose of obtaining family income data when ordinarily only one person in the family would give income information. The device used to solve this problem was to have two sets of the income questions. If the person on the sample line was not head of a family (and if he was fourteen years of age or over), information for him was entered in the first set of income questions, and the second set was left blank. But if the person on the sample line was head of a family, then the enumerator put the information on his income in the first set of questions and put the information on the income of other family members (as a group) in the second set of questions. This device proved to be a little awkward for both the enumerator and the respondent, but it did provide family income data.

The income inquiries in the 1950 census differed from those in the 1940 census in two important respects: (1) persons were to report on *all* types of money income and not just on wages and salaries; and (2) only one person in five was to answer the income questions (except for the special augmentation when the sample person was a family head).

The income questions were moved from 100 per cent to 20 per cent coverage not because they were unimportant, but because income was one of several items that were shifted to a sample basis as a part of the historical development of census taking. The uses of the statistics for these items did not require 100 per cent enumeration, and money and time were saved by putting the items on a sample basis. The sample was still a very large one compared to those used to collect annual data, and it provided usable income information for relatively small areas.

As in 1940, the Bureau tried to reduce the number of objections in several ways. It did not ask the exact amount of the income if it was over $10,000. It provided confidential income forms for the respondent to send to Washington if he did not want to tell the local enumerator the amount of his income. Again, the Bureau put the income questions near the end of the schedule so that any reaction to them would not affect answers to the other questions. Then too, the Bureau thought the data might be easier to collect on a sample basis, because the respondent would not believe that the Bureau was trying to check on his tax payments or other activities if it asked income information of only one person in five and selected that person entirely by chance.

After ten years of relatively good cooperation from the people who were asked about income, the Bureau was hopeful that the 1940 protests would not be repeated. In 1949, however, objections began to accumulate. Accordingly, the Bureau provided information and explanations for the press, for its own and Commerce Department officials, and for Congressmen. The turmoil diminished and disappeared very much as it had done in 1940. People generally accepted the questions on income as a normal part of the census, and only relatively few of them (300,000) used the confidential income forms. Some of these forms were used not because the respondent was unwilling to give the information to the enumerator, but rather because the enumerator wanted to avoid a return visit to get income information from a particular family member.

The procedure for obtaining information on income provided an unbiased 20 per cent sample of families and persons, but it resulted in some underreporting in family income. If the enumerator had asked about the income received by each member of the family (instead of the combined income received by all family members other than the head), probably a larger amount of income would have been reported.

Another limitation in the 1950 procedure was that sample questions (other than income) were asked only for the person on the sample line. Consequently, when the head of the family fell on the sample line and income was reported for the other members of the family, other sample information was available only for him. For example, it was impossible to get information on weeks worked in 1949 for other members of the family. This information would have enabled the Bureau to judge whether family members other than the head had income in 1949 when the enumerator failed to fill the section for other family members. An assumption that, if the questions for other family members were not answered, these family members had no income, led to some understatement of family income.

In the 1950 census, a family was defined as two or more persons related by blood, marriage, or adoption and living in the same household. This basic definition has been used in the CPS income surveys from their inception. In the 1940 census, however, a family had been defined as a family head and all other persons in the home who were related to the head by blood, marriage, or adoption, and who lived together in a private household. A person living alone was counted as a one-person family. A household head who shared his living accommodations with one or more unrelated persons (but not more than ten) was also counted as a one-person family. In the 1950 census (and the CPS), the one-person family of 1940 was classified as an "unrelated individual." This term also included other persons (except inmates of institutions) who were not living with any relatives. Moreover, the 1950 census definition of a family included not only families in private households but also those in quasi households (hotels, lodging houses, institutions, labor camps, military barracks, etc.).

The Census Bureau planned three groups of tabulations of income data from the 1950 census returns. In the first group were tabulations of income distributions for families and for families plus unrelated individuals for local areas. These were recommended by the Technical Advisory Committee on Economic Statistics. In the second group, income distributions for persons were cross-classified with other data. In this group, the Bureau was forced to choose between detailed data for persons and for families; it chose data for persons because they would supplement and complete occupation, industry, and other labor force data for persons. In the third group of tabulations, family income distributions were to be cross-classified with other family characteristics. Unfortunately, problems developed in preparing the second group of tabulations, and time and money ran out before the third group could be completed. The family tabulations were delayed, and only a small part of them were published.

In addition to providing simple income distributions for families and for families plus unrelated individuals for small areas, the Bureau cross-classified income with the following characteristics in the tabulations for the 1950 Census of Population: [17]

Income of persons:
- Sex, age, color, residence
- Sex, color, family status, residence
- Sex, color, weeks worked in 1949, residence
- Sex, age, color, size of place
- Sex, age, color, marital status, family status, relationship
- Sex, color, age, grade of school completed
- Sex, race, residence
- Sex, age, race

[17] For a complete listing of tabulations and the areas for which they were prepared, see *The 1950 Censuses—How They Were Taken,* Appendix B.

Sex, age, birthplace (or parent's birthplace), residence
Sex, color, type of income, residence (for persons with income)
Sex (for persons in armed forces and persons not in experienced labor force)
Sex, class of worker (for persons in experienced civilian labor force)
Sex, detailed occupation (for persons in experienced civilian labor force)
Sex, detailed industry (for persons in experienced civilian labor force)
Sex, detailed occupation (for persons who worked fifty to fifty-two weeks in 1949)
Sex, detailed occupation (for nonwhite persons in experienced civilian labor force)
Sex, color, detailed industry (for persons in experienced civilian labor force)
Sex, age, type of institution (for inmates of institutions)
Sex, amount of wage and salary income (for persons with income in experienced labor force)
Age, residence in 1949, residence in 1950 (for males living in different county in 1949 and 1950)
Type of family, sex and age of head, residence (for heads of families)
Type of unrelated individual, age, sex, residence (for unrelated individuals)

Wage or salary income of persons:
Sex, detailed occupation (for wage and salary workers)
Sex, detailed industry (for wage and salary workers)

Self-employment income of persons:
Sex, detailed occupation (for self-employed workers)
Sex, detailed industry (for self-employed workers)

Family income:
Sex, color (in selected areas), type of mobility, residence (for family heads living in different house in 1949 and 1950)
Type of family, sex and age of head, residence

Family income was cross-classified with the following characteristics in the tabulations for the 1950 Census of Housing:

For owners of dwelling units in nonfarm areas:
Condition and plumbing facilities

Type of household (husband-wife, etc.)
Number of persons
Persons per room
Number of rooms
Sex and age of household head
Value-income ratio
Value of dwelling unit

For renters of dwelling units in nonfarm areas:
Contract rent
Gross rent
Gross rent as per cent of family income
Number of rooms
Sex and age of household head
Condition and plumbing facilities
Type of household (husband-wife, etc.)
Number of persons
Persons per room

For occupants of dwelling units in farm areas:
Tenure, color, condition and plumbing facilities

The following reports of the 1950 Census of Population include income information:

Vol. II, *Characteristics of the Population*
Vol. III, *Census Tract Statistics*
Vol. IV, *Special Reports:*
"Occupational Characteristics," Part 1, Chap. B
"Industrial Characteristics," Part 1, Chap. D
"General Characteristics of Families," Part 2, Chap. A
"Institutional Population," Part 2, Chap. C
"Marital Status," Part 2, Chap. D
"Nativity and Parentage," Part 3, Chap. A
"Nonwhite Population by Race," Part 3, Chap. B
"Persons of Spanish Surname," Part 3, Chap. C
"Puerto Ricans in Continental United States," Part 3, Chap. D
"Characteristics by Size of Place," Part 5, Chap. A
"Education," Part 5, Chap B

In addition, the following reports were prepared on the basis of income data for families and unrelated individuals obtained in the 1950 census:

*1950 Census of Population—Preliminary Reports,* "Estimated Distribution of Family Income in 1949, for the United States, Regions, and Selected States," Series PC-7, No. 5.

*Farms and Farm People—Population, Income, and Housing Characteristics by Economic Class of Farm,* Bureau of the Census, 1953.

The following reports of the 1950 Census of Housing include income data:

Vol. II. *Nonfarm Housing Characteristics*
Vol. III. *Farm Housing Characteristics*
Vol. IV. *Residential Financing*

## *Plans for the Future*

Looking to future collections of income data, the Census Bureau hopes to increase public acceptance of this kind of collection, to decrease the time between collection of data and publication, to raise the quality of the statistics, and to provide more cross-classifications for family income. It may also investigate the need for data on net worth; some groups want this information to determine the welfare and market status of families with low incomes. Additional cross-classifications of income data have also been recommended. The Bureau will act on such suggestions if the data are given a high priority rating and if available funds are sufficient to provide these and other data of similar priority.

The Bureau will try to increase public acceptance by explaining the need for the data and the precautions it takes to protect the public from disclosure of personal information. In doing so, it is not just trying to create a pleasant atmosphere in which its enumerators can bask. The hard cold fact is that good public relations increase efficiency and reduce costs, because an understanding and cooperative public will provide information more accurately and more quickly.

The Bureau will seek new methods and new equipment to decrease the time span between the date of collecting the information and the date of publishing it. It has already made some advances by using electronic processing equipment, and its growing experience in this field should produce cumulative results. By using electronic tabulating equipment such as the Univac (Universal Automatic Computer) and possibly the Fosdic (Film Optical Sensing Device for Input to Computers), it hopes to reduce considerably the time needed to process the 1960 census data.

The importance of improving quality can be measured by the attention it receives. Many of the papers in this volume are primarily on the topic of quality, and Miller has devoted an entire appendix to this subject in his book on *Income of the American People*.[18] In the future, the Bureau will persist in its attempts to provide better income information, though the reported income may always fall short of the income actually received. In a quick interview with the housewife, some amounts of income are likely to be forgotten, particularly for part-time or casual workers. This bias is sometimes counteracted by the tendency of some self-employed persons to report total receipts instead of net income; but this neutralizing action is not a satisfactory solution to the problem. The Census Bureau's present activities include research on response variation, better training for enumerators, extension of the CPS sample, and efforts to improve public relations. Electronic equipment permits more thorough editing of the schedules, and such processing should result in better statistics.

Some improvement in the significance of some of the income cross-classifications can be effected in the 1960 census if the Bureau relates the employment status, occupation, industry, and class-of-worker questions to the previous year rather than to the previous week. Cross-classifications in the 1950 census had faults caused by the changes that occurred between 1949 (for which income was reported) and a week in the spring of 1950 (for which labor force items were reported). For example, a man may have earned $5,000 on a government job in 1949 but worked as a farm laborer in April 1950. In the cross-classification of income and occupation, the $5,000 income would appear to be earned as a farm laborer. Other types of slippage also occur. Many of these can be eliminated if both the labor force and the income inquiries are directed to the same time interval.

If the point of reference for the labor force questions is changed, it will be done not primarily to improve the income data but to make the labor force data more appropriate for a decennial inventory. Some experts believe that the census (as distinguished from the monthly CPS) should provide a comprehensive view of the normal composition of the labor force over the period of a year and not a snapshot of its composition in a single week. The gainful worker concept used before 1940 enabled the Bureau to provide information of a broad nature, but it was abandoned because it lacked specificity, and it was interpreted differently by different persons at different times. It has been suggested that the Bureau

[18] Herman P. Miller, *Income of the American People*, Wiley, 1955.

seek, for the decennial census, a concept that will have the breadth of the gainful worker concept and the specificity of the labor force concept. If such an approach can be used, and if the income and labor force inquiries are related to the same period, the income statistics will benefit.

To remedy the deficiency in analytical data on family incomes in the census, the Bureau hopes to improve the method of getting data for families in the 1960 census, to put a higher priority on family tabulations, and to develop better equipment for producing them. Just now, the Bureau is considering a sample of households instead of a sample of persons in the population census. If a household sample is used, sample data would be collected for all members of the sample household. With whole family groups and complete information for each member, more cross-classifications of family characteristics will be possible and the housing data collected from the same sample can be used. Moreover, the family income data from a household sample would presumably be more accurate than those obtained with the rather cumbersome 1950 procedure.

Priorities on tabulations are difficult to establish. Each tabulation has the backing of some group which believes it should have a high priority. With the faster equipment available for 1960, however, it may be possible to avoid the 1950 situation where a choice had to be made between tabulations of persons and of families. Presumably, the new electronic equipment will be fully tested by 1960 and will be able to produce the data needed in the time available. We are sure there will be problems, but we hope they will not be as troublesome as the ones in 1950.

In general, the tabulation plans for the 1950 census will serve as a model for the 1960 census. For small areas, the Bureau will probably provide distributions for families and for families plus unrelated individuals. It will plan to cross-classify income of persons with occupation, industry, age, sex, color, and other economic and personal characteristics. Finally, it will cross-classify family income with other family characteristics.

Some of these plans for the future are still only hopes, but others have reached a stage where they can be regarded as expectations. If all its hopes and expectations are realized, the Bureau will produce more and better income statistics in less time, and it may bring in a new era for the recently neglected family data.

# The Relation of Census Income Distribution Statistics to Other Income Data

SELMA F. GOLDSMITH, OFFICE OF BUSINESS ECONOMICS,
DEPARTMENT OF COMMERCE

In 1912 when Frank Streightoff, after an exhaustive analysis of the available data, abandoned his attempt to estimate a distribution of incomes by size for the United States, he argued that the basic material necessary for a satisfactory study was simply not to be found.[1] I wonder how he would react to the multiplicity of global distributions that would be available to him today?

For example, if he wished to group families and unattached individuals into broad income classes in terms of their 1954 incomes, he might place in the "under $2,000" category 14½ million consumer units if he used Census Bureau figures, 10 million if he used the appropriate Survey of Consumer Finances data for families and unattached individuals (rather than those for spending units), or 8 million if he used the figures of the Office of Business Economics. Streightoff was a careful worker so that he would discover quickly that the 10 million figure was relatively low because it excluded the quasi-household population (persons living in lodging houses, hotels, and so forth) but he would raise it by less than 1 million for that reason. He would note, also, that the 8 million figure was lower than the other two partly because it was based on a broader income concept covering certain nonmoney as well as money items of income, while the 14½ million and 11 million totals referred to money incomes, defined, however, in just about the same way in both instances.

But he would be somewhat surprised, when he related these figures to the total of 51 million families and unattached individuals in the nation, to find that the proportion of consumer units with incomes under $2,000 could be any one of the following: almost 3 in 10 (Census Bureau), somewhat over 2 in 10 (Survey of Consumer Finances) or, allowing for nonmoney incomes, 1.7 in 10 (Office of Business Economics).

Note: The views in this paper are those of the author and not of the Office of Business Economics.

[1] Frank H. Streightoff, "The Distribution of Incomes in the United States," *Studies in History, Economics and Public Law,* Columbia University Press, 1912.

To which figures would Streightoff turn if he were interested not so much in the over-all distribution of income but in component income distributions that might help to explain some of the changes in income size distribution that take place over time? For three reasons he would probably decide that his primary source material would be the income data provided by the Census Bureau:

1. The Census Bureau income data are collected and presented for persons as well as for families; the other data sources are available only for "consumer" or "spending" units. The individual rather than the family becomes the significant unit of measurement when attention is focused on the variables determining the distribution of income by size, although how individual income recipients combine into family units is, of course, also of importance.[2]

2. The decennial censuses provide income size-distribution data for persons classified by detailed occupation and industry groupings, by residence, and by age, education, and numerous other variables. For the most part such detailed cross-classifications are not available from other sources.[3]

3. The Census Bureau data are our main source of information on longer-run changes in income distribution. The 1940 and 1950 decennial censuses provide cross-classifications of income data for 1939 and 1949 (although limited in the former case to wages and salaries), and with the 1960 census we hope to have similar and perhaps improved income data for 1959. No other set of income distribution statistics provides detailed cross-classifications of income data for all the population and for the same long span of years.

The Census Bureau data on income size distribution that are presently available are described in detail in other papers in this volume (see particularly Edwin D. Goldfield's paper). Briefly, they include nationwide frequency distributions by total money income level, both for families and unattached individuals, and for persons, for the year 1949 from the 1950 Census of Population, and for each year from 1944 to 1954 from the Current Population Surveys (CPS) of the Census Bureau. In addition, some distributions are available by size of specific types of income, the most important being the frequency distributions for 1939 and 1949 of persons by size of wage and salary income, cross-classified either by detailed occupation or industry, from the two decennial censuses. Both the annual

[2] See Simon Kuznets, "The Why and How of Distributions of Income by Size," in Volume Five (1943) of Studies in Income and Wealth (see the list of publications of the Conference at the back of this volume).

[3] Note should be taken also of the Old-Age and Survivors Insurance (OASI) wage and salary data, which will become increasingly useful in this connection because of the broader coverage of workers introduced in 1951 and 1955.

and decennial census distributions for families and for persons are presented with a variety of other cross-classifications. Separate distributions for states are available from the 1940 and 1950 decennial censuses, and distributions for individual counties and cities from the 1950 census.

### *List of Comparisons with Other Income Data*

Possible comparisons between the Census Bureau income distribution data and other income series prepared in the federal government can be grouped into two main categories: comparisons with other estimates of income size distribution, including data for the United States as a whole, for large component population groups, or for smaller groups for which income data are available, and comparisons of the income totals accounted for by the inflated census surveys with income totals estimated by other governmental agencies.

#### INCOME DISTRIBUTION COMPARISONS

The major sets of data on income size distribution that may be compared with the Census Bureau statistics are the following:

1. Distributions by money income level from the Surveys of Consumer Finances (SCF), which are conducted by the Board of Governors of the Federal Reserve System in cooperation with the Survey Research Center of the University of Michigan and are available annually for 1945 through 1955. Although most tabulations of the data from these surveys are by spending units, special income size distributions for families and unattached individuals comparable in definition with the census data are also available for each year.
2. Distributions of families and unattached individuals by family personal income level prepared in the Office of Business Economics (OBE). In these distributions the consumer unit is defined in the same way as in the CPS series, but the definition of income is broader, covering various nonmoney items in addition to the money income concept used in the CPS and in the SCF. The OBE income distribution series is integrated statistically as well as definitionally with its aggregate personal income series; its money income component is a substantially larger total than the one accounted for in the CPS. OBE distributions are available for 1944, 1946, 1947, and 1950 to 1955; in addition, unofficial estimates with comparable definitions have been prepared for several prewar years.
3. Distributions of workers covered under the Old-Age and Survi-

vors Insurance (OASI) program by size classes of their "covered" wages and salaries or self-employment income. These distributions, which refer to persons rather than families, and to wages and salaries (and to self-employment income for recent years) rather than total income, are available annually since 1937. With the expansion in the coverage of the program in 1951 and again in 1955, difficulties in making comparisons with the OASI data will be much reduced because the noncovered sector has become relatively small. The top limit of $4,200—the total amount of wages subject to tax in any one year—will still be a limiting factor in making comparisons with other wage and salary distributions, such as those of the Census Bureau.

4. Annual distributions of federal individual income tax returns by level of adjusted gross income. The unit of tabulation, the tax return, is not equivalent either to families or persons but is a mixture of both, and the income definition is narrower in some ways and broader in others than that used in the CPS. Nevertheless, with appropriate modification these annual distributions can be compared with the survey data and are particularly important for the period beginning with World War II when the introduction of low filing requirements greatly increased the coverage of the tax-return data.

5. Distributions of urban families and single consumers in 1950 by money income level from the Bureau of Labor Statistics Survey of Consumer Expenditures in 1950. In making comparisons with this set of urban data, allowance must be made for differences in the definition of the consumer unit, particularly with respect to the time period to which the definition refers, as is discussed in a later section.

6. Distributions of selected professional groups by level of professional net earnings (self-employment earnings and professional salaries) from OBE mail-questionnaire surveys. The most recent of the large-scale surveys cover physicians (1949), dentists (1948), and lawyers (1947 and 1954).

### TOTAL INCOME COMPARISONS

Comparisons under the second heading—between amounts of income accounted for in inflated census surveys and aggregate income data from other sources—are listed below. Although the Census Bureau does not publish aggregate amounts of income accounted for in their various surveys, such estimates can be derived by multiplying the frequencies in each income bracket by an estimated mean income for that bracket, including one for the top "and over" bracket where dollar amounts of income were not requested by the Census Bureau enumerators. Each of the comparisons listed below requires numerous special adjustments in the basic series to allow for differences in income definition and coverage between the Census Bureau statistics and those from the specified source.

7. Comparisons of the CPS income totals with the annual OBE personal income series for the United States as a whole, separately for different types of income, for example, wages and salaries, self-employment income, and so forth.

8. Comparisons of the CPS income totals for various types of income with the totals reported on federal individual income tax returns.

9. Comparisons of the decennial census income data for states and regions with the OBE state personal income series.

10. Comparisons of the decennial census data on wages and salaries for separate industry classifications with the OBE series on wages and salaries by industry.

11. Comparisons of the CPS income data for farm families with the series on total net income from farming and from other sources received by farm operators and by all persons on farms, prepared by the Agricultural Marketing Service, Department of Agriculture.

All of these comparisons cannot be covered adequately in a single paper. Moreover, a number of them are the subject matter of other reports in this volume. The present paper will therefore turn first to the items not covered in other papers; to comparisons with the aggregate income figures in the OBE personal income series and with the aggregate amounts reported on federal individual income tax returns—items 7 and 8 above. This is followed by a general discussion of differences among the several sets of family income size distributions, that is, comparisons 1 and 2.[4]

The two comparisons listed above that are not covered in this or other papers in this volume—items 6 and 9—both refer to series prepared in the Office of Business Economics; to OBE income data for selected professional groups and to the OBE state personal income series. Their omission here does not mean that these comparisons are believed to be unimportant but indicates merely that they called for more time or more specialized knowledge than could be furnished by this author. Comparison between the 1950 decennial census income distribution data for states and the OBE state income series, appropriately adjusted to allow for definitional

[4] In connection with this discussion, the reader is referred to the Frechtling-Maynes-Sirken paper in this volume for a more detailed analysis of differences between the CPS and the SCF income distributions.

differences, would be exceedingly interesting as a guide in appraising the Census Bureau income data for smaller geographic areas, for example, for individual counties, for which the 1950 decennial census provides the only official income statistics that are available.

### *Comparison of Income Totals from Field Surveys, Federal Individual Income Tax Returns, and OBE Personal Income Series*

Comparisons of income totals derived from the OBE personal income series with corresponding amounts accounted for in a number of "blown-up" sample field surveys, and with amounts reported on federal individual income tax returns, were summarized in a paper presented at our 1949 Income Conference.[5] The tables shown here bring those earlier comparisons, which extended through 1948, up to date. Parts of the following discussion are necessarily somewhat repetitive of the earlier paper.

#### TOTAL MONEY INCOME COVERED IN FIELD SURVEYS

In Table 1 aggregate family money incomes accounted for in 23 "blown-up" sample field surveys of family income are compared with corresponding estimates derived from the OBE personal income series. Included are the 1941 Survey of Spending and Saving in Wartime (SSSW) conducted jointly by the Bureau of Labor Statistics and the Bureau of Human Nutrition and Home Economics, 11 annual Current Population Surveys of the Census Bureau covering the years 1944 through 1954 (including a farm family survey for 1946 made by the then Bureau of Agricultural Economics), the 1950 Census of Population, and 10 Surveys of Consumer Finances, conducted by the Board of Governors of the Federal Reserve System in cooperation with the Survey Research Center of the University of Michigan, covering 1945 through 1954.

The OBE family money income totals in Table 1, with which the income aggregates from the field surveys are compared, were derived by making two sets of adjustments in the OBE personal income series. The first of these was to subtract income flows included in personal income which are not received by families and unattached individuals. This subtraction yielded the family personal income totals shown in column 2, which are the totals accounted for in the OBE income size-distribution series.

The items subtracted from personal income to derive column 2

[5] Selma F. Goldsmith, "Appraisal of Basic Data Available for Constructing Income Size Distributions," in Volume Thirteen (1951) of Studies in Income and Wealth, pp. 266–372.

TABLE 1

Total Family Money Income as Estimated from OBE Personal Income Series and Covered in Field Surveys, 1941 and 1944–1954

(*billions of dollars, except cols. 7–9*)

| INCOME YEAR | OBE SERIES | | | COVERED IN FIELD SURVEYS | | | PERCENTAGE OF OBE SERIES | | |
|---|---|---|---|---|---|---|---|---|---|
| | *Personal Income* (1) | *Family Personal Income* (2) | *Family Money Income* (3) | SSSW (4) | CPS [a] (5) | SCF [b] (6) | SSSW (4) ÷ (3) (7) | CPS (5) ÷ (3) (8) | SCF (6) ÷ (3) (9) |
| 1941 | 96 | 91 | 86 | 75–78 | | | 87–91 | | |
| 1944 | 166 | 148 | 140 | | 111 | | | 79 | |
| 1945 | 171 | 158 | 151–154 | | 114 | 116 | | 74 | 77 |
| 1946 | 178 | 171 | 166 | | 130 | 135 | | 78 | 81 |
| 1947 | 191 | 185 | 180 | | 148 | 161 | | 82 | 89 |
| 1948 | 209 | 201 | 191 | | 157 | 175 | | 82 | 92 |
| 1949 | 207 | 199 | 190 | | 156 | 171 | | 82 | 90 |
| | | | | | 157 [c] | | | 83 | |
| 1950 | 227 | 217 | 208 | | 171 | 185 | | 82 | 89 |
| 1951 | 255 | 243 | 231 | | 189 | 204 | | 82 | 88 |
| 1952 | 271 | 257 | 245 | | 203 | 219 | | 83 | 89 |
| 1953 | 286 | 272 | 260 | | 216 | 246 | | 83 | 95 |
| 1954 | 288 | 273 | 261 | | 218 | 240 | | 84 | 92 |

[a] Amount accounted for in income distributions of families and unattached individuals from Current Population Surveys, except as noted.

[b] Excluding quasi-household population.

[c] Amount accounted for in 1949 income distribution of families and unattached individuals from 1950 decennial census.

Note: For detailed technical notes on all the tables in this paper, see the Appendix.

The following abbreviations have been used in this and subsequent tables: OBE (Office of Business Economics, Dept. of Commerce); SSSW (1941 Survey of Spending and Saving in Wartime, Bureaus of Labor Statistics and of Human Nutrition and Home Economics); CPS (Current Population Survey, Bureau of the Census); and SCF (Survey of Consumer Finances, Board of Governors of the Federal Reserve System).

included the following estimates: income retained by private pension, trust, and welfare funds, incomes of persons who died or entered the armed forces during the year, and incomes of nonprofit institutions and of institutional residents, including members of the armed forces living on post. In recent years the total amount subtracted to derive family personal income accounted for about 5 per cent of personal income.

The second set of adjustments was to subtract nonmoney items of income not covered in the field surveys and to allow for various other differences in income definition between the family personal income and family money income concepts. The most important items under this heading were the subtraction of the gross value of food and fuel produced and consumed on farms, the gross rental value of farm homes, the net rental value of nonfarm owner-occupied homes, wages in kind, imputed interest (representing the value of free services to individuals by banks and the property income of life insurance companies), the value of farm inventory change, and the noncorporate nonfarm inventory valuation adjustment; and the addition of personal contributions for social insurance, estimated net income from roomers and boarders in private homes, and periodic payments received by consumer units from life insurance companies.

Column 3 of Table 1 shows the resulting estimates of aggregate family money income derived from the personal income series. The totals run about 9 to 10 per cent lower than the personal income series in recent years.

As Table 1 indicates, the amounts covered in the various field surveys are lower than the family money income totals in the OBE series. The 1941 SSSW survey accounted for about 90 per cent of the comparable OBE money income total, and the SCF since 1947 usually accounted for about that proportion. The CPS since 1947 covered some 82 to 84 per cent of the corresponding OBE family money income totals.

In order to avoid misunderstanding, some of the qualifications that attach to comparisons of this type which were discussed at our 1949 Conference, aside from those relating to sampling variability, must be repeated here. These apply not only to Table 1 but to the following tables as well.

In the first place, some understatement of income is to be expected in all field interview studies if only because some respondents are apt to forget minor or irregular amounts of income and because others may purposely understate their incomes for varied reasons. Furthermore, as the Census Bureau states in each of its income reports, not only are the schedule entries for income of the family members in most cases based on memory rather than on records, but "in the majority of instances on the memory or knowledge of some one person, usually the wife of the family head." It would be indeed surprising if the wife could report fully on all items of income for the entire family unit.

The purpose of comparisons between field survey and OBE income aggregates is not merely to point out that understatement exists in the surveys, but to study variations in the extent of undercoverage among different surveys and different types of income. Such comparisons may indicate why various survey income size distributions differ from each other and may suggest areas in which improvements in survey techniques are needed. As the other papers in this volume make abundantly clear, comparisons of income totals represent only one of several methods of appraising the accuracy of survey data.

Second, the comparisons of aggregate income presented in these tables should not be regarded as precise measures of income understatement in the field surveys. In making the adjustments in the personal income series listed above, full allowance could not be made for all the differences in income definition and coverage between the surveys and the OBE series, and a few of the adjustments are necessarily rough approximations of the particular income item (for example, roomer-boarder income). These factors introduce some error in the comparisons for total income in Table 1, and for the separate types of income in Table 2, below.

The income totals accounted for in the "inflated" CPS are also approximate. That is, they were derived by multiplying the number of consumer units in each income bracket by an estimated mean for the bracket, and then summing the results over all income brackets. By varying the estimated means, somewhat different results might have been obtained, but some experimentation indicated that various alternative figures would change the percentage coverage of the CPS in Table 1 by only 1 or at most 2 percentage points.

Finally, there is the question of the extent of possible error in the personal income series itself. In this connection the absolute amount of the difference between the OBE and the survey aggregates is of importance. In each year from 1951 through 1954 the "inflated" CPS accounted for $40-odd billion less family money income than the comparable OBE series. The deficiency in the SCF in this period, except for 1953, was $20 to 25 billion. No serious student of the national income statistics would suggest that the aggregate money income embodied in the OBE personal income series could be overstated by anything like these orders of magnitude. The question, rather, is whether very much smaller errors may attach to the several components of the personal income series, which together may serve to explain some of the excess of the OBE-based series over the totals accounted for in the surveys.

To answer this question fully would require repeating much of the detailed discussion of the reliability of the national income and product estimates set forth by the OBE in the *National Income Supplement, 1954*.[6] The discussion indicates that while the estimates for the components of personal income have various shortcomings, the personal income total itself is believed to be "subject to only a small percentage of error" (page 66). It is most improbable that errors in the personal income series would be large enough to affect to any substantial extent the differences shown in Table 1 for total

[6] *National Income Supplement, 1954;* see pages 62–67, and the detailed descriptions of methodology for each of the major income shares in the various sections of Part III of the *Supplement.*

income, nor would they alter significantly the broad relationships between survey and OBE income totals for the separate types of income in Table 2.

As is indicated in the *National Income Supplement,* estimates of the largest component of personal income, wages and salaries, rank highest in reliability among the income shares mainly because of the adequacy of the social security data on which they are based. The extent of error is relatively small, also, for the important items of government transfer payments and dividends.

Certain of the personal income components are subject to greater error, for example, rent and interest income of persons. The estimates for these income shares are residuals, based on the subtraction of business receipts from total payments in each category, and the source data on rent in particular are far from satisfactory. However, monetary rent and interest account for only a small fraction of total family money income, and inaccuracies in their measurement can have little effect on the over-all estimates in Table 1. In 1954, for example, monetary interest and rent of persons amounted to $13 billion, or only 5 per cent of total family money income. The disparity between this figure and the corresponding amount probably accounted for in the 1954 CPS is so large that the broad pattern of income differences developed in Table 2 would not be significantly affected by any reasonable estimates of the possible error in the OBE series for these shares.

The entrepreneurial income component of personal income is also subject to shortcomings, as is indicated in the *National Income Supplement*. However, for recent years the broadened coverage of the federal income tax, the extensive tabulations of business income made available by the Internal Revenue Service (IRS), and the audit studies of that agency have combined to improve markedly the source material available for constructing the annual entrepreneurial income series.

Net income from nonfarm business is now estimated largely on the basis of data reported on federal individual income tax returns adjusted upward to allow for nonreporting firms and for income understatement as determined from the IRS 1949 audit study.[7] Professional incomes are based on numbers of practitioners as shown in the censuses of population and records of the professional associations, together with average net income data derived mainly from OBE questionnaire surveys. For the farm sector, the net income series is taken directly from the Department of Agriculture, which

[7] For a detailed description of the methods used to develop the noncorporate business income series (separately for about sixty-five industry subgroups) see *National Income Supplement, 1954,* Part III, sec. 3

estimates gross income and production expenses in great detail.

In summary, the figures in Table 1 are open to some error, and differences of a few percentage points in the income coverage of the various surveys should not be regarded as significant. However, the statistics are believed to be entirely adequate for summarizing major differences in income coverage among surveys and (in Tables 2 and 3) among different types of income.

Two points emerge from the comparisons in Table 1. The first is the lower coverage of income in the CPS than in the SCF. This reflects in large part the heavier concentration of consumer units in income brackets below $1,000 and the smaller proportions in the upper income range found in the CPS than in the SCF samples.

The second point is the marked year-to-year stability in relative income coverage shown by the CPS. After ranging between 75 and 80 per cent in the years immediately following World War II, the CPS income coverage increased to 82 per cent in 1947 and has varied only between 82 and 84 per cent ever since. In contrast, the relative amount of income accounted for in the SCF increased sharply in 1953—rising from a level of about 90 per cent of the comparable OBE series to 95 per cent. A marked increase in relative income coverage also occurred in 1947. Such variations in the proportion of income accounted for, which may perhaps reflect commendable improvements in survey techniques, must be kept in mind as a limiting factor in using the survey figures to measure year-to-year changes in income size distribution.

In connection with the 95 per cent coverage figure for 1953, it should be noted that the actual income coverage of the SCF is about 1 to 2 percentage points higher than the figures in Table 1. This is because the quasi-household population (persons living in lodging houses, hotels, and so forth) is not covered in these surveys whereas the income of this population group is included in the OBE series. In view of the very high coverage of SCF income in 1953 it would seem to be a good idea for those concerned both with the SCF and CPS to use that year as a starting point for analyzing the separate amounts of income of various types accounted for in their surveys, and to appraise the reliability and year-to-year comparability of their survey income distribution data in part at least in those terms.

## SEPARATE TYPES OF INCOME REPORTED IN CENSUS BUREAU SURVEYS

Amounts of each of several major types of income covered in the Census Bureau nonfarm plus Bureau of Agricultural Economics farm survey for 1946 and in the CPS for 1954 are compared with the

## TABLE 2

Family Money Income by Type of Income as Estimated from OBE Personal Income Series and Covered in CPS, 1946 and 1954

(*billions of dollars, except col. 5*)

| TYPE OF INCOME | OBE SERIES: *Personal Income* (1) | OBE SERIES: *Adjusted for Comp. with Survey* (2) | COVERED IN CPS [a] (3) | DIFFERENCE (2) — (3) (4) | CPS AS PERCENTAGE OF OBE SERIES (3) ÷ (2) (5) |
|---|---|---|---|---|---|
| | | | *1946* | | |
| Wages and salaries | 109.8 [b] | 101.6 | 92.8 | 8.8 | 91 |
| Nonfarm business and professional income | 21.3 | 22.7 | 13.3 | 9.4 | 59 |
| Farm income | 14.0 | 10.8 | 7.2 | 3.6 | 67 |
| Total earnings | 145.1 | 135.1 | 113.3 | 21.8 | 84 |
| Interest and dividends | 13.4 | 9.4 | 2.2 | 7.2 | 23 |
| Rental income | 6.2 | 5.1 | 3.2 | 1.9 | 63 |
| Military payments | --- | 11.4 | 7.8 | 3.6 | 68 |
| Social security and other | --- | 5.0 | 3.3 | 1.7 | 66 |
| Transfer payments and other labor income | 13.3 | --- | --- | --- | --- |
| Total income other than earnings | 32.9 | 30.9 | 16.5 | 14.4 | 53 |
| Total | 178.0 | 166.0 | 129.8 | 36.2 | 78 |
| | | | *1954* | | |
| Wages and salaries | 191.9 [b] | 185.1 | 168.3 | 16.8 | 91 |
| Nonfarm business and professional income | 25.7 [b] | 25.7 | 22.8 | 2.9 | 89 |
| Farm income | 12.0 | 8.0 | 5.8 | 2.2 | 73 |
| Total earnings | 229.6 | 218.8 | 196.9 | 21.9 | 90 |

continued on next page

TABLE 2, continued

| TYPE OF INCOME | OBE SERIES | | COVERED IN CPS [a] | DIFFERENCE | CPS AS PERCENTAGE OF OBE SERIES |
|---|---|---|---|---|---|
| | *Personal Income* (1) | *Adjusted for Comp. with Survey* (2) | (3) | (2) — (3) (4) | (3) ÷ (2) (5) |
| Interest and dividends | 24.7 | 17.1 | (3.9) [c] | (13.2) [c] | (23) [c] |
| Rental income | 10.5 | 6.2 | (3.9) [c] | (2.3) [c] | (63) [c] |
| Military payments | --- | 6.5 | (4.4) [c] | (2.1) [c] | (68) [c] |
| Social security and other | --- | 12.0 | (7.9) [c] | (4.1) [c] | (66) [c] |
| Transfer payments and other labor income | 22.8 | --- | --- | --- | --- |
| Total income other than earnings | 58.0 | 41.8 | 20.8 | 21.0 | 50 |
| Total | 287.6 | 260.6 | 217.7 | 42.9 | 84 |

[a] Census Bureau nonfarm plus Bureau of Agricultural Economics farm survey for 1946.

[b] Net of personal contributions for social insurance.

[c] Estimated. Amounts were not reported in 1954 CPS for separate types of income other than earnings but only for total income other than earnings. The 1954 estimates shown here for separate types of income other than earnings were derived by multiplying the adjusted OBE aggregate for each type in 1954 (col. 2) by the 1946 percentage coverage for the corresponding type (col. 5).

OBE series in Table 2. The 1946 and 1954 surveys both accounted for 91 per cent of wages or salaries. For the nonfarm entrepreneurial income sector, the 89 per cent coverage in 1954 was markedly higher than the 59 per cent in 1946, whereas for net farm income the coverage was fairly similar, 73 and 67 per cent.

In contrast to these earnings items, only about one-half of total money income other than earnings was accounted for in the 1954 CPS, not greatly different but somewhat less than in 1946. The 1954 CPS schedule did not call for separate reporting of the various types of income other than earnings but only for their total. However to determine the distribution of missing income in the 1954 survey by type of income, rough estimates are included in Table 2 for the survey coverage of each of four major types of income other than earnings. These were based on the assumption that the 1954 percentage coverage for each of these four income types was the same as in 1946, the latest year for which separate survey data are available, that is, that the 1954 survey covered about two-thirds of rent, military payments, and social insurance benefits, and about one-fourth of interest and dividends. The assumption is not unreasonable since estimates of 1954 survey income coverage for the four separate items of income other than earnings, derived in this manner, are found when added together to be approximately equal to the amount of total income other than earnings actually reported in the 1954 survey (column 3 of Table 2).

To summarize, of the $43 billion of income not covered in the 1954 CPS, about $17 billion was wages and salaries, $5 billion business and professional income, $15 billion interest, dividends, and rent, and about $6 billion social insurance and veterans' payments, and miscellaneous income. Since income understatement in the survey appears in all of the various types of income, it probably prevails in all ranges of the income scale though not, of course, in equal proportions in the various income brackets.

## INCOMES REPORTED ON INDIVIDUAL INCOME TAX RETURNS

Comparisons between amounts of income covered on federal individual income tax returns and the OBE series are shown for 1946, 1951, and 1952 in Table 3. Because of the nature of the available data it is simpler to compare the tax-return data with the OBE figures rather than directly with the Census Bureau surveys. Adjustments made in the OBE and tax-return series to achieve as much comparability as possible are described in the technical notes to Table 3, in the Appendix.

Of the major income shares shown in the table, the coverage of tax returns is highest—about 95 per cent—for wages and salaries.

TABLE 3

Family Money Income by Type of Income as Estimated from OBE Personal Income Series and Reported on Federal Individual Income Tax Returns, 1946, 1951, and 1952

*(billions of dollars, except col. 6)*

| TYPE OF INCOME | OBE SERIES | | TAX RETURNS | | DIFFERENCE | TAX RETURNS AS PERCENTAGE OF OBE SERIES |
|---|---|---|---|---|---|---|
| | *Personal Income* (1) | *Adjusted for Comp. with Tax Returns* (2) | *Reported* (3) | *Adjusted* (4) | (2) — (4) (5) | (4) ÷ (2) (6) |
| | | | *1946* | | | |
| Wages and salaries | 109.8 [a] | 105.2 | 99.2 | 98.8 | 6.5 | 94 |
| Business and professional income (including farm) | 35.3 | 32.9 | 23.3 | 23.1 | 9.8 | 70 |
| Total earnings | 145.1 | 138.1 | 122.5 | 121.9 | 16.2 | 88 |
| Interest | 7.6 | 3.2 | 1.1 | 1.1 | 2.1 | 34 |
| Dividends | 5.8 | 4.6 | 3.7 | 3.7 | .9 | 80 |
| Rental income | 6.2 | 3.6 | 1.7 | 1.8 | 1.8 | 50 |
| Subtotal | 19.6 | 11.4 | 6.5 | 6.6 | 4.8 | 58 |
| Other items [b] | 13.3 | | 5.1 | | | |
| Total | 178.0 | 149.5 | 134.1 | 128.5 | 21.0 | 86 |
| | | | *1951* | | | |
| Business and professional income: | | | | | | |
| Nonfarm | 24.8 | 23.4 | 20.1 | 19.9 | 3.5 | 85 |
| Farm | 16.0 | 11.6 | 4.8 | 4.8 | 6.8 | 41 |
| Total | 40.8 | 35.0 | 24.9 | 24.7 | 10.3 | 71 |

continued on next page

TABLE 3, continued

| TYPE OF INCOME | OBE SERIES | | TAX RETURNS | | DIFFERENCE | TAX RETURNS AS PERCENTAGE OF OBE SERIES |
|---|---|---|---|---|---|---|
| | *Personal Income* (1) | *Adjusted for Comp. with Tax Returns* (2) | *Reported* (3) | *Adjusted* (4) | (2) — (4) (5) | (4) ÷ (2) (6) |
| | | | *1952* | | | |
| Wages and salaries | 181.6 [a] | 180.6 | 174.3 | 173.5 | 7.1 | 96 |
| Business and professional income (including farm) | 39.8 [a] | 34.3 | 24.8 | 24.6 | 9.7 | 72 |
| Total earnings | 221.4 | 214.9 | 199.1 | 198.1 | 16.8 | 92 |
| Interest | 12.3 | 5.3 | 1.8 | 1.9 | 3.4 | 36 |
| Dividends | 9.0 | 6.9 | 5.9 | 5.9 | 1.0 | 85 |
| Rental income | 9.9 | 5.4 | 3.1 | 3.2 | 2.2 | 59 |
| Subtotal | 31.2 | 17.6 | 10.8 | 11.0 | 6.6 | 63 |
| Other items [b] | 18.5 | | 5.4 | | | |
| Total | 271.1 | 232.5 | 215.3 | 209.1 | 23.4 | 90 |

[a] Net of personal contributions for social insurance.

[b] Col. 1 includes transfer payments and other labor income; col. 3 includes annuities and pensions, net operating loss deduction (for 1952), gain less loss from sales or exchanges of capital assets, gain less loss from sales or exchanges of property other than capital assets, income from estate and trusts, and miscellaneous income.

This is not surprising in view of the withholding system introduced during World War II and the fact that employer reports on wages and salaries paid serve as a basis both for the reports of individuals on their income tax returns and for a substantial sector of wages and salaries in the personal income series. About 70 per cent of business and professional income is accounted for on tax returns, with relative coverage much higher in the nonfarm than in the farm sector. For the nonfarm, the coverage is about 85 per cent (see the earlier discussion of the relation between the tax return and the OBE series for the nonfarm business sector), whereas for the farm, as nearly as can be measured, it is only around 40 per cent. Monetary interest on tax returns represented about 35 per cent of the comparable OBE figure, and, in 1952, dividends about 85 per cent, and rental income 60 per cent.[8]

These percentages are not to be regarded as precise because the available data did not permit full allowance for all of the definitional differences between the personal income components and the corresponding income concepts in tax returns.[9] This factor is probably relatively most important in the case of farm income for which information is not available to measure certain definitional differences which may be significant. Furthermore, all of the percentage coverage figures are somewhat understated because no allowance is made for amounts received by persons not required to file tax returns. Such amounts, however, are probably relatively small, except for wages and salaries where they have been estimated roughly at about $1½ billion in 1952.[10]

### COMPARISON OF TAX-RETURN AND SURVEY COVERAGE

Turning now to a comparison of Tables 2 and 3, relative income coverage is higher on tax returns than in the Census Bureau surveys for wages and salaries—96 per cent in 1952 tax returns and 91 per cent in the 1954 CPS; here differences of a few percentage points represent large absolute amounts. For interest plus dividends,

[8] In connection with the coverage of tax returns, it should not be inferred that differences between personal income and the amounts shown on tax returns consist entirely of underreporting of *taxable* income on income tax returns. Aside from possible differences in income definition between the two series that may not have been fully allowed for, some of the income omitted from tax returns would not be taxable even if properly reported, inasmuch as it would be offset by the credits and deductions allowable.

[9] For discussion of some of the remaining definitional differences, see Goldsmith, *op. cit.*, pp. 356–358.

[10] Daniel M. Holland and C. Harry Kahn, "Comparison of Personal and Taxable Income," *Federal Tax Policy for Economic Growth and Stability,* Joint Committee on the Economic Report, 1955.

the excess of tax return over survey relative coverage is very large (65 per cent compared with an estimated 23 per cent). For farm income, on the other hand, the survey coverage is much higher than that of tax returns (73 per cent compared with 40 per cent), and for rental income approximately the same proportion (about 60 per cent) is accounted for in the two sets of data. For nonfarm business and professional income, relative income coverage in the 1954 CPS (89 per cent) appears to be slightly higher than on 1951 tax returns (85 per cent), but comparisons for earlier periods indicate that the opposite was true of this income share.

In terms of absolute amounts, total money income not accounted for in the 1954 CPS, as noted earlier, was about $43 billion. By excluding types of income not reportable on income tax returns (military and social security payments and "other" income) the CPS gap is decreased to about $36 billion (based on Table 2). A comparable estimate for income undercoverage on 1954 tax returns is in the order of $24 billion. Thus, undercoverage for corresponding income items is about $12 billion more in the 1954 survey than on tax returns. This figure represents about 5 per cent of total family money income. For 1946, the corresponding figure estimated from Tables 2 and 3 is $10 billion, or about 6 per cent.

Similar comparisons were also made for 1949. They indicated that income coverage on 1949 tax returns was about $5 billion higher than for corresponding income items in the 1949 CPS—about 3 per cent of family money income in that year.[11] Unfortunately it is not possible to make a comparison of this sort with the 1950 decennial census data for families and unattached individuals because data for separate major types of income are not available for these consumer units.[12]

[11] Income unaccounted for in the CPS of 1949 incomes was about $34 billion (Table 1), of which approximately $6 billion referred to income categories not reportable on tax returns. (Since reports for the separate types of income other than earnings were not requested in the 1949 survey, the $6 billion figure is a rough estimate derived as shown for 1954 in Table 2). The remaining $28 billion of income not accounted for in the survey compares with an estimate of $23 billion for the corresponding amount for 1949 tax returns (derived as shown for 1954 in Table 3).

[12] In the 1950 Census of Population, total money income accounted for in the income size distribution of families and unattached individuals for 1949 is estimated by Herman Miller to have amounted to $155–159 billion ("An Appraisal of the 1950 Census Income Data," *Journal of American Statistical Association,* March 1953, p. 40). This agrees closely with the $157 billion coverage of the decennial census and with the $156 billion coverage of the CPS for 1949 estimated here (Table 1). The available data do not make it possible to determine how much of the decennial census income total applied to income categories not reportable on tax returns, because tabulations of families and unattached individuals by size classes of separate major types of income were not made in the 1950

What are the implications of these findings for the income size-distribution data? The comparison suggests that after adjustments to allow for differences in the reporting unit and the definition of income, a distribution of tax returns by income level for any given year will probably be somewhat more heavily concentrated in the upper income ranges than a CPS distribution for families in the same year. Furthermore, the difference in the two distributions will be more marked for nonfarm families than for all families combined. In the case of farm-operator families the reverse will be the case, reflecting the higher coverage of farm income in Table 2 than in Table 3.

### *Family Income Size Distributions from the CPS, the SCF, and OBE Series*

Distributions for the year 1954 of families and unattached individuals by income level from the CPS, the SCF, and the OBE are compared in Table 4. The distributions from the two field surveys are classified by family money income brackets, whereas the classification in the OBE series is by family personal income. The latter includes nonmoney as well as money income items, and—as was explained earlier—its money income component differs from the surveys in income coverage and definition. The concept of family money income is just about the same in the two field surveys.

Definitions of families and unattached individuals (consumer units) agree in all three income size-distribution series, although the universe covered is somewhat narrower in the SCF than in the two other series. Families are defined as units of two or more persons related by blood, marriage, or adoption, and residing together. Unattached individuals ("unrelated individuals" in the CPS reports and "one-person families" in the *Federal Reserve Bulletin* articles) are persons, others than institutional inmates, who are not living with any relatives; for example, they may be living alone or may be lodgers or servants with a private family.

In addition to the consumer-unit distributions shown in Table 4, income distributions are available from the SCF in terms of spending units. The spending unit, the basic interview and tabulating unit in

census. However, the similarity of the figures for total income coverage suggests that the decennial census income distribution of consumer units, like the 1949 CPS, probably accounted for about $5 billion less income than did tax returns.

Miller points out that the income coverage of the 1950 decennial census income distributions is about $9 billion higher for persons fourteen years old and over ($168 billion) than for families and unattached individuals ($155–159 billion) as a result of differences in the collection and editing of income data for persons and families (*ibid.*, pp. 41–43).

these surveys, is defined as related persons living in the same dwelling who pool their incomes for their major expenses. On the basis of this definition, about 5 to 6 million individuals or groups of individuals, who are related to the family head, are treated in recent years as separate units in the spending-unit tabulations. The SCF combines the income data for related spending units living in the same dwelling to obtain the family income distributions shown in Table 4.

TABLE 4

Comparison of Three Distributions of Families and Unattached Individuals by Income Level, 1954

| INCOME LEVEL [a] | FAMILIES AND UNATTACHED INDIVIDUALS CPS (1) | SCF (2) | OBE (3) | FAMILIES CPS (4) | SCF (5) | UNATTACHED INDIVIDUALS CPS (6) | SCF (7) |
|---|---|---|---|---|---|---|---|
| | *Number (millions)* | | | | | | |
| Under $1,000 | 8.1 | 4.3 | 3.1 | 3.7 | 2.2 | 4.4 | 2.1 |
| $ 1,000–$1,999 | 6.5 | 5.8 | 5.4 | 4.6 | 4.3 | 1.9 | 1.5 |
| 2,000– 2,999 | 6.4 | 5.6 | 6.3 | 5.0 | 4.6 | 1.4 | 1.1 |
| 3,000– 3,999 | 7.4 | 7.5 | 7.4 | 6.4 | 6.6 | 1.0 | 0.9 |
| 4,000– 4,999 | 7.0 | 6.8 | 7.6 | 6.5 | 6.4 | 0.5 | 0.4 |
| 5,000– 7,499 | 10.3 | 11.6 | 12.8 | 9.9 | 11.3 | 0.4 | 0.3 |
| 7,500– 9,999 | 3.4 | 3.9 | 4.9 | 3.4 | 3.8 | 0.1 | 0.1 |
| $10,000 and over | 2.5 | 3.5 | 3.7 | 2.4 | 3.4 | 0.1 | 0.1 |
| Total | 51.5 | 49.0 | 51.2 | 41.9 | 42.6 | 9.6 | 6.4 |
| Mean income | $4,223 | $4,900 | $5,344 | $4,765 | $5,310 | $1,850 | $2,195 |
| | *Percentage Distribution* | | | | | | |
| Under $1,000 | 16 | 9 | 6 | 9 | 5 | 45 | 33 |
| $ 1,000–$1,999 | 12 | 12 | 11 | 11 | 10 | 19 | 23 |
| 2,000– 2,999 | 12 | 11 | 12 | 12 | 11 | 14 | 17 |
| 3,000– 3,999 | 14 | 15 | 14 | 15 | 16 | 11 | 14 |
| 4,000– 4,999 | 14 | 14 | 15 | 16 | 15 | 5 | 6 |
| 5,000– 7,499 | 20 | 24 | 25 | 23 | 26 | 4 | 5 |
| 7,500– 9,999 | 7 | 8 | 10 | 8 | 9 | 1 | 1 |
| $10,000 and over | 5 | 7 | 7 | 6 | 8 | 1 | 1 |
| Total | 100 | 100 | 100 | 100 | 100 | 100 | 100 |

[a] Family money income (before income taxes) for all columns except 3; for column 3, family personal income (before income taxes).

In the CPS and OBE series, families and unattached individuals include units living in quasi households (for example, large rooming houses or hotels) as well as households (the usual house or apartment), whereas the former group is excluded from the SCF. The quasi-household population includes about 1¼ million consumer units, of which all but a few hundred thousand are unattached individuals, and of which about 600,000 reported money incomes under $1,000 in the CPS for 1954.

The most striking differences among the three income size distributions appear in the lowest income range, that is, the bracket under $1,000. The proportion of consumer units in this bracket is 16 per cent in the CPS, about 10 per cent in the SCF (when the figures from that survey are roughly adjusted to include quasi-household units), and 6 per cent in the OBE series (where the relatively small proportion reflects in part the inclusion of nonmoney income items in the income definition and in part the more complete allowance for social security payments and other types of money income in the OBE series than in the surveys).

In contrast, the three series are in close agreement in the income range between $1,000 and $5,000. As Table 4 indicates, the proportions vary by at most only one percentage point within any $1,000 bracket in this range.

The counterpart of the differences in figures for the lowest income bracket appears in the income range about $5,000. The CPS shows 32 per cent of consumer units with incomes of $5,000 or more, the SCF 39 per cent, and the OBE series 42 per cent. Above $10,000 the corresponding percentages are 5, 7, and 7.

The conclusion to be drawn from Table 4 is that the OBE and SCF distributions are in reasonable accord. The only noteworthy difference between the two series is in the lower tail of the distribution, and this can be explained in large part by the inclusion of nonmoney items of income in the OBE figures. The major differences that require explanation are those between the CPS and SCF data.

Turning to the separate figures for families and unattached individuals from the two surveys, Table 4 shows that in the under $1,000 income bracket the CPS frequencies exceed those from the SCF by 1½ million for families and by about another 1½ million for unattached individuals (after allowing for quasi-household units). This difference is offset by a deficiency of 3 million in the CPS frequencies for families with incomes above $5,000 compared with the SCF data.

This somewhat oversimplified summary of the differences between the two sets of sample data does not, of course, imply that the explanation of the differences is a simple one, for example, that a sizable group of families classified as having incomes of $6,000 in the SCF are assigned $600 in the CPS, as one reader of Table 4 suggested. Special factors making for the large difference in the survey figures for the under $1,000 income bracket may operate apart from other more general factors that serve, figuratively speaking, to push some of the families in each income bracket in the CPS distribution up the income scale in the SCF.

One of these special factors is the difference between the two surveys shown in Table 4 in the total number of unattached individuals accounted for. The CPS total is 9½ million and the corresponding figure from the SCF about 7½ million (after allowance for quasi-household individuals). Apparently it is this difference that is responsible for the excess of 1½ million in the CPS frequency of unattached individuals in the income bracket under $1,000. For multi-person families, on the other hand, the total number in the SCF is about 1 million higher than in the CPS (after making an allowance for the small number of families in quasi households).

To what extent do the family incomes in the surveys fail to reflect the composition of families during the income year? What effect does this factor have on both the total number of consumer units and the number in the lower ranges of the income scale?

In the CPS no reconstruction of consumer units is attempted. Data on incomes received during the calendar year are obtained only for those persons who constitute the consumer unit at the time of interview, usually April of the following year. For many consumer units this procedure proves satisfactory for family income classification purposes because no changes in composition take place over the period except for the birth of children.

But other changes in family composition are constantly occurring which cause difficulties in reconciling point-of-time figures for the number and size of families and annual income figures.[13] For example, a Mrs. Jones, aged 67, who is living alone in her home in April 1955 because her husband died the preceding month, will report her $600 of dividend income to the CPS enumerator and will be classified as an unattached individual with income under $1,000 in Table 4. No account is taken of the $16,000 earned by Mr. Jones during 1954 prior to his death.

Or a Johnny Smith, aged 23, who is living as a lodger with a private family in April 1955, having left his home town to start on his first full-time job a few months earlier, is also classified by the CPS as an unattached individual with income under $1,000 in Table 4. He reports the $500 he earned during 1954 while attending college in his home town, but no account is taken of the fact that his parents had supplied most of his support while he lived with

[13] This problem is discussed in some detail in Chapter 3 of "Income Distribution in the United States by Size, 1944–1950," a supplement to the *Survey of Current Business,* Dept. of Commerce, 1953.

them during 1954. If his parents' family is enumerated, the family income that is reported will not include the $500 earned by Johnny because he is not living with his parents at the time of interview.

In the SCF the Johnny Smiths are apparently treated in the same way as in the CPS. However, in the case of Mrs. Jones, the SCF enumerator will frequently obtain income information for the deceased Mr. Jones and thereby classify Mrs. Jones in a much higher income bracket than would his enumerator counterpart in the CPS. A discussion by the agencies conducting field surveys of the treatment of these and other instances of changes in family composition and their implication for the income size-distribution series is perhaps in order.

The lack of reconstruction of consumer units as they existed during the income year has probably introduced a net downward bias in the CPS income size-distribution series for the postwar period. Occasionally the bias will be upward, for example, if two groups of relatives (father plus mother, and their son plus his wife) double up after the close of the income year. In such cases the family income total which the CPS credits to one family unit actually represents, from the viewpoint of the income year, the combined income of two separate families. However, in the period of rapid family formation and economic growth following World War II, instances leading to a downward bias were doubtless much more numerous.

Since the bias may be significant, an effort should be made to measure its magnitude. At a minimum the Census Bureau might include questions in the CPS to determine how many of the unattached individuals had a different family status during all or part of the year to which their reports on income pertain. In the case of families a similar determination might be made at least for units reporting incomes of less than $1,000 or $2,000.[14]

A reexamination of the CPS data, particularly for the lower end of the income scale, is suggested also by certain results from the Bureau of Labor Statistics Survey of Consumer Expenditures in 1950, which were discussed by Helen Lamale at the last meetings of the American Statistical Association.[15] In that survey, income and expenditure data were collected for consumer units as they existed during 1950, that is, for reconstructed units. The Johnny Smith

[14] Some questions designed to test the adequacy of the family definition for purposes of income measurement were included in the early Census Bureau surveys but have not been attempted in recent years.

[15] Helen Humes Lamale, "Methodology and Appraisal of Consumer Expenditure Studies," paper presented at 115th Annual Meeting of the American Statistical Association, New York City, December 28, 1955 (mimeographed).

mentioned earlier, who was a newly formed unattached individual, is excluded from the survey, but his income during the time he lived at home is added to that of his parents if they fall in the sample. Similarly, other newly formed units or units dissolved in 1950 were not included in the BLS survey.

As Mrs. Lamale explains, partly as a result of this reconstruction and partly because of differences in the definition of families and single consumers, the BLS survey obtained "substantially fewer urban 1-person units than did the Census Bureau—4.2 million and 6.9 million respectively, and substantially more urban families of smaller average size—27.2 million families averaging 3.34 persons as compared with 25.4 million families averaging 3.49 persons."

Frequency distributions of urban consumer units by income level are not yet available from the BLS survey. There is every reason to believe, however, that the income distribution for the 4.2 million urban unattached individuals from the BLS survey will differ substantially from the CPS distribution of 6.9 million, that is, that the former will show many fewer units in the lower income brackets. The figures may suggest that the CPS definitions of families and unattached individuals, although adequate for other purposes, may require revision with respect to their point-of-time reference when used as a basis for classifying annual income data.

## *Changes in Income Distribution*

### POST-WORLD WAR II DISTRIBUTIONS

How do the various statistical series compare with respect to the changes they show in income distribution over time? Possible comparisons are limited to the post-World War II period because the CPS distributions by family money income level and the OBE distributions by family personal income level extend back only to 1944 (although Census Bureau wage and salary data are available also for 1939), and the SCF begin with 1945.

In Table 5 frequency and percentage distributions of consumer units by income level from the three data sources are compared for 1947 and 1954. By starting with 1947 rather than a year or two earlier, difficulties in income measurement encountered in the earlier surveys that stemmed partly from the large numbers of armed forces personnel returning to civilian life are eliminated. The percentage of total income accounted for in both the CPS and SCF was relatively larger in 1947 and later years than in the first few years of survey experience (see Table 1).

In terms of relative income coverage, survey data for the years

TABLE 5

Comparison of Three Distributions of Families and Unattached Individuals by Income Level, 1947 and 1954

| INCOME LEVEL [a] | CURRENT POPULATION SURVEY | | | SURVEY OF CONSUMER FINANCES | | | OFFICE OF BUSINESS ECONOMICS | | |
|---|---|---|---|---|---|---|---|---|---|
| | *1947* | *1954* | *1954 as percentage of 1947* | *1947* | *1954* | *1954 as percentage of 1947* | *1947* | *1954* | *1954 as percentage of 1947* |
| | | | | | *Number (millions)* | | | | |
| Under $1,000 | 8.0 | 8.1 | 101 | 5.5 | 4.3 | 78 | 3.7 | 3.1 | 84 |
| $ 1,000–$1,999 | 8.1 | 6.5 | 80 | 7.8 | 5.8 | 74 | 7.4 | 5.4 | 73 |
| 2,000– 2,999 | 9.4 | 6.4 | 68 | 8.3 | 5.6 | 67 | 8.5 | 6.3 | 74 |
| 3,000– 3,999 | 7.8 | 7.4 | 95 | 7.1 | 7.5 | 106 | 8.6 | 7.4 | 86 |
| 4,000– 4,999 | 4.5 | 7.0 | 156 | 4.9 | 6.8 | 139 | 5.7 | 7.6 | 133 |
| 5,000– 9,999 | 6.4 | 13.7 | 214 | 7.1 | 15.5 | 218 | 8.8 | 17.7 | 201 |
| $10,000 and over | 1.1 | 2.5 | 227 | 1.8 | 3.5 | 194 | 2.0 | 3.7 | 185 |
| Total | 45.3 | 51.5 | 114 | 42.5 | 49.0 | 115 | 44.7 | 51.2 | 115 |
| Mean income | $3,261 | $4,223 | 130 | $3,780 | $4,900 | 130 | $4,126 | $5,344 | 130 |
| | | | | | *Percentage Distribution* | | | | |
| Under $1,000 | 18 | 16 | 89 | 13 | 9 | 69 | 8 | 6 | 75 |
| $ 1,000–$1,999 | 18 | 12 | 67 | 18 | 12 | 67 | 17 | 11 | 65 |
| 2,000– 2,999 | 21 | 12 | 57 | 20 | 11 | 55 | 19 | 12 | 63 |
| 3,000– 3,999 | 17 | 14 | 82 | 17 | 15 | 88 | 19 | 14 | 74 |
| 4,000– 4,999 | 10 | 14 | 140 | 11 | 14 | 127 | 13 | 15 | 115 |
| 5,000– 9,999 | 14 | 27 | 193 | 17 | 32 | 188 | 20 | 35 | 175 |
| $10,000 and over | 2 | 5 | 250 | 4 | 7 | 175 | 4 | 7 | 175 |
| Total | 100 | 100 | | 100 | 100 | | 100 | 100 | |

[a] Family money income (before income taxes) for all except last three columns; for last three columns, family personal income (before income taxes).

1947 and 1954 are quite comparable. For the CPS this coverage was 82 per cent in 1947 and 84 per cent in 1954, and for the SCF, 89 and 92 per cent (Table 1).

All three series in Table 5 show a 30 per cent increase in the mean income of consumer units between 1947 and 1954.[16] The level of the means, however, is lower in the SCF than in the OBE series, and still lower in the CPS, reflecting the differences discussed above.

[16] OBE mean incomes on a family *money* income basis comparable in definition to that used in the surveys increased by somewhat less (27 per cent). The extra few percentage points of increase shown in the OBE mean family *personal* incomes in Table 5 stem mainly from the inclusion of two items in family personal income excluded from family money income; the value of farm inventory change and the noncorporate nonfarm inventory valuation adjustment. Both were relatively large negative amounts in 1947 and either a positive or a much smaller negative amount in 1954.

Although the pattern of changes in income distribution from 1947 to 1954 shown by the three series in Table 5 is basically similar, some points of difference may be noted. Most striking is the stability between 1947 and 1954 in the number of consumer units in the income range under $1,000 in the CPS in contrast to the decline shown for that range in the SCF and estimated in the OBE series. If the CPS figures portray the actual situation, which seems unlikely, this stability in a period of generally rising incomes would be an exceedingly interesting finding. The very importance of the figures underlines the need for special Census Bureau studies designed to analyze the definitions and meaningfulness of the data for low-income groups.

Another difference in the series is the sharper increase from 1947 to 1954 in the proportion of consumer units in the income range above $4,000 shown by the CPS than by the SCF or the tax-return-based OBE series. The overstatement of the increase in the CPS figures probably reflects a higher relative coverage of business and professional income in the survey for 1954 than for 1947.[17]

All three series show a basic stability in relative income distribution between 1947 and 1954. This is illustrated by the percentage shares of income accruing to families and unattached individuals in each quintile that have been computed for the three series in Table 6. Disregarding small changes in the percentages, the relative income shares show no perceptible trend in the 1947 to 1954 period.

An exception to this statement can, at first glance, be read into the figures in Table 6 in the case of the top quintile, mainly because the SCF shows a decrease in the relative income share of this fifth over the 1947–1954 period. It is likely, however, that the decrease in the survey figure is for the most part merely a reflection of sampling or other survey variations. Table 6 shows that practically all of the decline occurred between 1947 and 1950 and that a decline in that period is refuted by the 1947–1950 stability in the corresponding OBE figure. The OBE distributions through 1952, based in large part on data from federal individual income tax returns, are believed to provide more reliable estimates for the upper

[17] Data for separate major types of earnings are not available from the Census Bureau survey for 1947. However, when a comparison similar to Table 5 is made between 1946 and 1954, the CPS also shows a larger increase in the proportion of consumer units in the income range above $4,000 than the OBE series (i.e. the percentage in that range more than doubled in the CPS and increased by about two-thirds in the OBE distributions). As Table 2 indicates, relative coverage of business income in the CPS was much larger in 1954 than in 1946, and it may be inferred that this was also the case for 1954 versus 1947.

TABLE 6

Percentage Distribution of Total Family Income among Quintiles of Families and Unattached Individuals Ranked by Size of Income, 1947 and 1950–1954

| QUINTILE [a] | *1947* | *1950* | *1951* | *1952* | *1953* | *1954* |
|---|---|---|---|---|---|---|
| | | | *Current Population Survey* | | | |
| Lowest | 3.0 | 2.6 | 3.0 | 3.1 | 2.8 | 2.8 |
| 2 | 10.5 | 10.3 | 11.0 | 10.8 | 10.9 | 10.3 |
| 3 | 16.4 | 17.3 | 17.4 | 17.2 | 17.5 | 17.1 |
| 4 | 23.3 | 23.4 | 24.1 | 24.1 | 24.2 | 24.4 |
| Highest | 46.8 | 46.4 | 44.5 | 44.8 | 44.6 | 45.4 |
| Total | 100.0 | 100.0 | 100.0 | 100.0 | 100.0 | 100.0 |
| | | | *Survey of Consumer Finances* | | | |
| Lowest | 4.2 | 3.8 | 3.8 | 4.0 | 4.1 | 4.2 |
| 2 | 10.3 | 11.1 | 10.5 | 11.3 | 11.1 | 11.3 |
| 3 | 15.3 | 17.1 | 16.9 | 16.9 | 16.8 | 17.0 |
| 4 | 22.1 | 23.2 | 23.0 | 23.0 | 22.1 | 23.0 |
| Highest | 48.1 | 44.8 | 45.8 | 44.8 | 45.9 | 44.5 |
| Total | 100.0 | 100.0 | 100.0 | 100.0 | 100.0 | 100.0 |
| | | | *Office of Business Economics Series* | | | |
| Lowest | 5.0 | 4.8 | 5.0 | 4.9 | 4.9 [b] | 4.9 [b] |
| 2 | 11.0 | 10.9 | 11.3 | 11.4 | 11.4 [b] | 11.4 [b] |
| 3 | 16.0 | 16.1 | 16.5 | 16.6 | 16.6 [b] | 16.6 [b] |
| 4 | 22.0 | 22.1 | 22.3 | 22.4 | 22.4 [b] | 22.4 [b] |
| Highest | 46.0 | 46.1 | 44.9 | 44.7 | 44.7 [b] | 44.7 [b] |
| Total | 100.0 | 100.0 | 100.0 | 100.0 | 100.0 | 100.0 |

[a] Ranking, except for lowest bank of figures, is by family money income (before income taxes); for lowest bank, by family personal income (before income taxes).

[b] Preliminary.

ranges of the income scale than do the small samples from the surveys.

A check on the survey findings for the upper-income groups on the basis of data from individual income tax returns has not yet been made for the period after 1952. This type of check will be conducted by the OBE as tabulations of tax returns for later years become available.

## LONGER-RUN CHANGES IN INCOME DISTRIBUTION

In order to view the postwar income distributions in perspective, they are compared with prewar estimates in Tables 7 and 8. The OBE income distributions are included for selected years since 1944 and prewar estimates are shown for 1941, 1935–1936, and 1929.

Major findings from these tables have been discussed in an article on "Size Distribution of Income since the Mid-Thirties." [18] How-

[18] Selma Goldsmith, George Jaszi, Hyman Kaitz, and Maurice Liebenberg, *Review of Economics and Statistics,* February 1954.

TABLE 7

Percentage Distribution of Total Family Personal Income among Quintiles and Top 5 Per cent of Consumer Units, Selected Years, 1929–1954

| QUINTILE [a] | *1929* [b] | *1935–1936* | *1941* | *1944* | *1946* | *1947* | *1950* | *1951* | *1954* [c] | *Percentage Change* *1929–1954* | *1929–1944* | *1944–1954* | *1941–1944* |
|---|---|---|---|---|---|---|---|---|---|---|---|---|---|
| Lowest } | 12.5 | 4.1 | 4.1 | 4.9 | 5.0 | 5.0 | 4.8 | 5.0 | 4.9 } | 30 } | 26 | 0 | 20 |
| 2 } | | 9.2 | 9.5 | 10.9 | 11.1 | 11.0 | 10.9 | 11.3 | 11.4 } | | | 5 | 15 |
| 3 | 13.8 | 14.1 | 15.3 | 16.2 | 16.0 | 16.0 | 16.1 | 16.5 | 16.6 | 20 | 17 | 2 | 6 |
| 4 | 19.3 | 20.9 | 22.3 | 22.2 | 21.8 | 22.0 | 22.1 | 22.3 | 22.4 | 16 | 15 | 1 | 0 |
| Highest | 54.4 | 51.7 | 48.8 | 45.8 | 46.1 | 46.0 | 46.1 | 44.9 | 44.7 | −18 | −16 | −2 | −6 |
| Total | 100.0 | 100.0 | 100.0 | 100.0 | 100.0 | 100.0 | 100.0 | 100.0 | 100.0 | | | | |
| Top 5 per cent | 30.0 | 26.5 | 24.0 | 20.7 | 21.3 | 20.9 | 21.4 | 20.7 | 20.5 | −32 | −31 | −1 | −14 |

[a] Consumer units are ranked by size of family personal income.
[b] Estimates for 1929 subject to wider margin of error than those for later years; see text.
[c] Preliminary.

TABLE 8

Distribution of Families and Unattached Individuals and of Family Personal Income in 1950 Dollars, by Family Personal Income Level, Selected Years, 1929–1954

| FAMILY PERSONAL INCOME IN 1950 DOLLARS | NUMBER (*thousands*) | | | | | | FAMILY PERSONAL INCOME IN 1950 DOLLARS (*millions of dollars*) | | | | | |
|---|---|---|---|---|---|---|---|---|---|---|---|---|
| | *1929* [a] | *1935–1936* | *1941* | *1944* [b] | *1950* | *1954* | *1929* [a] | *1935–1936* | *1941* | *1944* [b] | *1950* | *1954* |
| Under $1,000 | 5,754 | 7,478 | 6,232 | 2,996 | 3,861 | 3,643 | 2,365 | 4,487 | 4,082 | 1,522 | 1,943 | 1,948 |
| $1,000–$1,999 | 9,239 | 11,231 | 8,236 | 5,588 | 7,464 | 6,191 | 13,845 | 16,846 | 12,412 | 8,548 | 11,333 | 9,381 |
| 2,000– 2,999 | 9,275 | 7,959 | 7,643 | 6,326 | 8,091 | 7,268 | 23,043 | 19,619 | 19,039 | 15,714 | 20,273 | 18,268 |
| 3,000– 3,999 | 4,395 | 4,709 | 6,488 | 7,189 | 8,586 | 8,405 | 15,206 | 16,293 | 22,604 | 24,850 | 29,983 | 29,465 |
| 4,000– 4,999 | 2,590 | 2,806 | 5,069 | 6,004 | 7,054 | 8,006 | 11,551 | 12,502 | 22,657 | 26,973 | 31,533 | 35,927 |
| 5,000– 7,499 | 2,655 | 2,582 | 4,983 | 7,540 | 8,530 | 11,255 | 15,935 | 15,359 | 29,655 | 45,348 | 51,181 | 68,116 |
| 7,500– 9,999 | 1,130 | 686 | 1,304 | 2,853 | 2,758 | 3,326 | 9,750 | 5,877 | 10,998 | 24,281 | 23,364 | 27,958 |
| $10,000 and over | 1,062 | 959 | 1,415 | 2,384 | 2,546 | 3,056 | 29,692 | 21,826 | 30,139 | 42,857 | 47,652 | 55,782 |
| Total | 36,100 | 38,410 | 41,370 | 40,880 | 48,890 | 51,150 | 121,387 | 112,809 | 151,586 | 190,093 | 217,262 | 246,845 |
| Mean income (in 1950 dollars) | $3,363 | $2,937 | $3,664 | $4,650 | $4,444 | $4,826 | | | | | | |
| | | | | | | *Percentage Distribution* | | | | | | |
| Under $1,000 | 15.9 | 19.5 | 15.1 | 7.3 | 7.9 | 7.1 | 2.0 | 4.0 | 2.7 | .8 | .9 | .8 |
| $1,000–$1,999 | 25.6 | 29.2 | 19.9 | 13.7 | 15.3 | 12.1 | 11.4 | 14.9 | 8.2 | 4.5 | 5.2 | 3.8 |
| 2,000– 2,999 | 25.7 | 20.7 | 18.5 | 15.5 | 16.6 | 14.2 | 19.0 | 17.4 | 12.6 | 8.3 | 9.3 | 7.4 |
| 3,000– 3,999 | 12.2 | 12.3 | 15.7 | 17.6 | 17.6 | 16.4 | 12.5 | 14.4 | 14.9 | 13.1 | 13.8 | 11.9 |
| 4,000– 4,999 | 7.2 | 7.3 | 12.3 | 14.7 | 14.4 | 15.7 | 9.5 | 11.1 | 14.9 | 14.2 | 14.5 | 14.6 |
| 5,000– 7,499 | 7.4 | 6.7 | 12.0 | 18.4 | 17.4 | 22.0 | 13.1 | 13.6 | 19.6 | 23.8 | 23.6 | 27.6 |
| 7,500– 9,999 | 3.1 | 1.8 | 3.1 | 7.0 | 5.6 | 6.5 | 8.0 | 5.2 | 7.2 | 12.8 | 10.8 | 11.3 |
| $10,000 and over | 2.9 | 2.5 | 3.4 | 5.8 | 5.2 | 6.0 | 24.5 | 19.4 | 19.9 | 22.5 | 21.9 | 22.6 |
| Total | 100.0 | 100.0 | 100.0 | 100.0 | 100.0 | 100.0 | 100.0 | 100.0 | 100.0 | 100.0 | 100.0 | 100.0 |

[a] Estimates for 1929 subject to wider margin of error than those for later years; see text.
[b] See accompanying text for limitations of price deflater for the war period.

ever, the present tables expand the period for which comparisons are made by adding estimates for recent years for which OBE distributions were not available when the earlier article was written and by including rough estimates for 1929.

Limitations of the family income distribution statistics for 1935–1936 and 1941 were described in the earlier article. Although the estimates for those years, based on data from field surveys and from income tax returns, incorporate a number of adjustments to make them as comparable as possible with the postwar series, full adjustment for definitional and other differences was not feasible.

For 1929, limitations in both the basic data and in the adjustments made here are even greater. Unlike 1935–1936, 1941, and postwar years, there was no nationwide sample field survey of family incomes in 1929 on which to base the income distribution estimates. Instead, the Brookings Institution constructed a 1929 distribution for families and unattached individuals by combining a variety of different sets of income statistics for persons (for example, for wage earners and farmers) and then converting them to a family-unit basis.[19] The Brookings distribution is admittedly rough, particularly for the lower end of the income scale.

At the upper end the Brookings study, like those for later years, incorporated data from federal individual income tax returns. However, capital gains and losses were included in the income definition in that study, in contrast to their exclusion from later estimates. This had the effect of materially exaggerating the relative share of income received by the upper segment of consumer units compared with income-distribution data for following years.

In Tables 7 and 8, the Brookings distribution for 1929 has been adjusted to remove capital gains and losses. This adjustment and a less important one relating to understatement of business income on tax returns are described in the technical notes in the Appendix. The adjustments were necessarily rough, but they serve to make the estimates for 1929 more comparable with those for recent years and thereby make it possible to avoid some mistaken conclusions drawn by students who compared postwar income distributions directly with the Brookings figures. Although the present figures for 1929 are more comparable with respect to capital gains and losses than the unadjusted figures, they are essentially the Brookings figures which, in the absence of basic family income data for that year, are to be regarded as rough approximations to the actual situation.

[19] Maurice Leven, Harold G. Moulton, and Clark Warburton, *America's Capacity to Consume*, Brookings Institution, 1934.

Table 7 presents estimated percentage shares of family personal income accruing to successive quintiles of families and unattached individuals for selected years back to 1929. Most prominent are decreases in the relative shares accruing to the top quintile of consumer units between 1929 and 1944, which were accompanied by increases in the shares of all the other quintiles. For the two lowest fifths, relative gains were largest between 1941 and 1944. The changes in relative income position of the various quintiles prior to 1944 are in marked contrast to the stability of relative income distribution in the postwar period.

The reader is referred to the article on "Size Distribution of Income since the Mid-Thirties" for a discussion of factors underlying these changes in relative income distribution. One of the most important of them—the narrowing of wage differentials since 1939—is discussed in Miller's paper in this volume.

One point from the earlier paper that bears repetition is the warning that the amount of change in relative income distribution depends in part on the particular income definition used. Alternative calculations on a national income basis (differing from personal income by including undistributed corporate profits and corporate profits taxes, and by excluding government transfer payments and government interest) indicate that the decrease from 1929 to the present in the income share of the top 5 per cent was substantially less than is shown on a personal income basis in Table 7.

Another point that should be stressed is that the decline in the relative income share of the top 5 per cent of consumer units over the twenty-five-year period covered by Table 7—which accounted for most of the decline in the relative share of the top quintile—is to a large extent a reflection of a comparable decline shown by statistics from federal individual income tax returns. This can best be illustrated by comparing the 1929 and the postwar mean incomes underlying the figures on the relative income shares of the top income sector.

In 1952, for example, the latest year for which detailed tabulations of tax return statistics are available, the mean family personal income of all consumer units combined, in current dollars, was 2.2 times as large as in 1929 ($5,120 compared with $2,340). For the top 5 per cent of consumer units, the corresponding means that underlie Table 7 are estimated at $21,030 in 1952 and $14,030 in 1929, a ratio of 1.5. The decline in the relative income share of the top 5 per cent of consumer units shown in Table 7 is, of course, simply a reflection of this smaller ratio.

Turning to the income tax return statistics, which were the basic series used in constructing the estimates for the upper-income segment of the consumer-unit distributions in both the prewar and postwar periods, it is immediately apparent that comparisons cannot be made between 1929 and any World War II or postwar year in terms of a "top 5 per cent of income tax returns." The universe of income tax returns differs too radically in the two periods, largely as a result of changes in filing requirements: only 4 million individual income tax returns were filed in 1929, almost 57 million in 1952. Nor can one compare 1929 with a postwar year in terms of the mean incomes reported on those particular income tax returns that underlie the top 5 per cent of consumer units. Aside from other difficulties, the description of the way the Brookings study combined individual income tax returns into family units is not sufficiently detailed to make it possible to determine precisely which income tax returns from which income brackets comprise the top tail of consumer units in the Brookings distribution.

In 1952 the top 5 per cent of families and unattached individuals consisted of consumer units with family personal incomes of approximately $11,480 and over, and in 1929 of those with $5,690 and over. This suggests that the ratio of the mean income reported on individual income tax returns with incomes of $10,000 and over in 1952 to the mean reported on tax returns with incomes of $5,000 and over in 1929 may be taken as roughly equivalent to the corresponding ratio for the top 5 per cent of consumer units. This tax-return ratio is found from *Statistics of Income* to be 1.3 when statutory capital gains are included in income, and 1.5 when such net gains are excluded and the tax returns reranked, as best one can, by size of income exclusive of net capital gains.[20] This latter ratio is the same as that noted above for the top 5 per cent of consumer units.

In other words, a comparison of the top tail of the income distributions developed for postwar years by the OBE with that developed for 1929 by the Brookings authors (as adjusted here) reveals the basic pattern of changes reported in *Statistics of Income* in the structure of the upper-income segment of individual income tax returns. It is in this sense that the statistics in Tables 7 and 8 should be interpreted. A detailed reworking of the 1929 estimates to introduce greater comparability with the family personal income distributions

[20] The reranking is described for 1929 in the notes to Tables 7 and 8, and for 1952 in *Survey of Current Business,* March 1955, p. 10. A further adjustment in 1929, for comparability with 1952, to add statutory deductions to statutory net income exclusive of capital gains raised the estimated mean income of tax returns having incomes of $5,000 or more, but the ratio of the 1952 mean to this adjusted 1929 mean remained at a rounded 1.5.

for later years, particularly with respect to methods of combining tax returns into family units and assumptions relating to income understatement, might result in significant revisions of the figures. The changes since 1929 in mean incomes and income shares of the upper sector of the income distribution might be most affected. Such a reworking of the 1929 figures has not been attempted here.

Frequency distributions of families and unattached individuals by income level, in constant (1950) dollars, are presented in Table 8. The most interesting contrast is between the estimates for 1929 and 1954. Compared with the 12 million consumer units (one-third) with incomes (in 1950 dollars) of $3,000 or more in 1929, 34 million 1954 consumer units (two-thirds) were in that income range. In real income brackets above $4,000, there were 21 per cent of consumer units in 1929 and 50 per cent in 1954, and above $5,000, 13 per cent in the earlier year and 35 per cent in the latter.

Most of the upsweep in real incomes is shown in Table 8 to have occurred in the period up to 1944. However, this is somewhat exaggerated by the price deflators used to derive the constant-dollar figures. The available price indexes do not fully reflect the actual rise in prices that took place during World War II, and hence overstate the price rise in early postwar years.[21] As a result, the actual shift of consumer units up the real income scale is probably somewhat less during the war and somewhat greater in the early postwar period than is shown here.

## *Appendix: Technical Notes to Tables*

### TABLE 1

*Column 1*

From *Survey of Current Business,* Dept. of Commerce, July 1955, Table 3.

*Column 2*

Column 1 minus following items (figures refer to amounts estimated for 1952, in billions of dollars): military nonmoney pay plus money pay of persons not returned to civilian life by end of year who lived on post (6.5); earnings of persons who entered armed forces or died during year (1.2); dividends, interest, rent, and business income received by fiduciaries, less income distributed to individuals by fiduciaries (0.6); interest, dividends, rents, and transfer payments received by nonprofit institutions (1.3); employer contributions to private pension and welfare funds (4.0); miscellaneous items (0.1).

[21] Limitations of the price deflators are discussed in Goldsmith, Jaszi, Kaitz, and Liebenberg, *op. cit.*

*Column 3*

Column 2 minus following items (figures refer to amounts estimated for 1952, in billions of dollars): nonmoney civilian farm and nonfarm wages and salaries (1.8); value of food and fuel produced and consumed on farms by members of farm operator families and gross rental value of farm homes (3.4); net rental values of owner-occupied nonfarm homes (4.2); imputed interest (5.3); noncorporate nonfarm inventory valuation adjustment (0.2); value of change in farm inventories (0.6); accrued interest on unredeemed United States government bonds (0.7); miscellaneous items (1.5); and plus the following items: personal contributions for social insurance (3.8); estimated net income from roomers and boarders in private homes (0.8); and estimated periodic payments received by individuals from life insurance companies (1.0). For 1945, the higher figure in column 3 covers also estimated military pay received in 1945 by persons who returned to civilian life during the first three months of 1946, which is included here to conform in coverage with the census survey conducted in April 1946; the lower figure which excludes the pay of these returnees is comparable to the coverage of the SCF, conducted earlier in 1946.

*Column 4*

Derived from 1941 survey as explained in my paper in Volumn Thirteen (1951) of Studies in Income and Wealth, notes to Table 2.

*Column 5*

Derived from CPS (Census Bureau nonfarm plus Bureau of Agricultural Economics farm survey for 1946) by multiplying tabulated number of consumer units in each income bracket by an estimated average income for the bracket. According to Census Bureau calculations, the aggregate amounts accounted for in these surveys are 1 or 2 percentage points higher than those shown here when CPS distributions of persons (rather than consumer units) are multiplied by estimated means for the several income brackets.

*Column 6*

Product of figures from Board of Governors of the Federal Reserve System on mean income of families and unattached individuals and number of such consumer units in each year. Excludes consumer units in quasi households.

TABLE 2

*Column 1*

From *Survey of Current Business,* July 1955, Tables 1, 3, and 35.

*Column 2*

Column 1 adjusted to subtract or add the appropriate items listed in notes to Table 1, columns 2 and 3, and to transfer certain items from one income category to another to match as closely as possible the definitions in the census field surveys. In accordance with the census income classification, military wages and salaries of persons returned to civilian life are included under military payments in 1946, but under wages and salaries in 1954. For further details, see my paper in Volume Thirteen (1951) of Studies in Income and Wealth, notes to Table 3.

*Column 3*

For 1946, *ibid.,* Table 3. For 1954, figures other than in parentheses derived by multiplying distributions of consumer units by size classes of each of four major types of income (*Current Population Reports—Consumer Income,* Bureau of the Census, Series P-60, No. 20, Table 11) by estimated means for each class. Figures in parentheses derived by multiplying amount for 1954 in column 2 by percentage coverage for 1946 in column 5, as explained in text.

TABLE 3

*Column 1*

From *Survey of Current Business,* July 1955, Tables 1, 3, and 35.

*Column 2*

Column 1 adjusted as follows (figures refer to amounts estimated for 1952, in billions of dollars):

*Wages and salaries.* Column 1 minus military nonmoney pay (1.4), nontaxable items of military money pay (2.9), and nonmoney civilian farm and nonfarm wages and salaries (1.8); and plus employee contributions for social insurance (3.5), directors', jury, etc. fees (0.1), and amount classified as business income in column 1 that is estimated might be reported on individual income tax returns as wages and salaries (1.6).

*Business and professional income.* Column 1 minus value of food and fuel produced and consumed on farms and gross rental value of farm homes (3.9), value of change in farm inventories (0.6), noncorporate nonfarm inventory valuation adjustment (0.2), business income received by fiduciaries (0.1), and amount of nonfarm business income that is estimated might be reported on individual income tax returns as wages or salaries (1.6); plus expenses on owner-occupied farm homes, which are not deductible on individual income tax returns (0.7), and self-employed persons' contributions for social insurance (0.2). Separate amounts for nonfarm and farm business income shown for 1951 were derived by adjusting the OBE amounts for the two separate categories (*Survey of Current Business,* July 1955, Tables 1 and 35), as described above, and transferring patronage refunds and stock dividends paid by farmers' cooperatives from the nonfarm to the farm category.

*Interest.* Column 1 minus imputed interest (5.3), interest received by nonprofit institutions (0.2), by fiduciaries (0.3) and by corporate pension funds (0.2), accrued interest on unredeemed United States government bonds (0.7), and interest on tax-exempt securities (0.3).

*Dividends.* Column 1 minus dividends received by nonprofit institutions (0.2), by fiduciaries (1.7), by corporate pension funds (0.1), and by mutual insurance companies (0.2).

*Rental income.* Column 1 minus imputed net rental value of owner-occupied nonfarm homes (4.2), and rent received by nonprofit institutions and fiduciaries (0.4).

*Column 3*

Reported on federal individual income tax returns, *Statistics of Income,* Treasury Dept., Part 1, 1946, and preliminary report for 1952. For 1951, the figure for farm income is the net amount reported as sole proprietorship income from farming on 1951 tax returns (*ibid.,* 1951) plus an estimate of partnership farm income (derived by extrapolating farm income reported on 1947 partnership tax returns by the reported amounts of proprietorship net income from farming). Nonfarm business and professional income in 1951 was obtained by subtracting the farm income figure from the reported total of business, professional, and partnership net income.

*Column 4*

Column 3 adjusted as follows (figures refer to amounts estimated for 1952, in billions of dollars):

*Wages and salaries.* Column 3 minus reported receipts in Alaska and Hawaii (0.8), and plus reported wages not subject to withholding (less than 0.1).

*Business and professional income.* Column 3 minus reported receipts in Alaska and Hawaii (0.1) and interest, dividends, and rent reported as business income on tax returns that are included under the property-income categories in columns 1 and 2 (0.3); plus depletion not deducted in columns 1 and 2 (0.2).

*Interest.* Column 3 minus reported receipts in Alaska and Hawaii, plus receipts by partnerships that are included under interest in columns 1 and 2, plus interest reported under miscellaneous income on tax returns (each less than 0.1).

*Dividends.* Column 3 minus reported receipts in Alaska and Hawaii (less than 0.1), plus receipts by partnerships that are included under dividends in columns 1 and 2 (0.1), plus dividends reported under miscellaneous income on tax returns (less than 0.1).

*Rental income.* Column 3 minus reported receipts in Alaska and Hawaii (less than 0.1), plus rents reported as business income on tax returns that are included under rents in columns 1 and 2 (0.1).

*Note.* For derivation of most of the adjustments in columns 2 and 4, and for discussion of areas for which full adjustment could not be made, see my paper in Volume Thirteen (1951) of Studies in Income and Wealth, notes to Table 8. In deriving the various items of fiduciary income, the procedures described in Volume Thirteen were revised in all years to incorporate statistics for nontaxable fiduciary income tax returns for 1952. These data are the first available for this category of tax returns since 1939 (see *Statistics of Income,* Part 1, for 1952). The methodology described in Volume Thirteen was also revised to allow for postwar changes in the tax treatment of military pay, and was improved by introducing adjustments (in col. 2) to allow for property income received by corporate pension funds and by eliminating (in col. 2) subtractions which had been made in Volume Thirteen for civilian earnings of persons who died or entered the armed forces during the year.

TABLE 4

*Columns 1, 4, 6*

Derived from *Current Population Reports—Consumer Income,* Series P-60, No. 20, Table 1.

*Columns 2, 5, 7*

From Board of Governors, Federal Reserve System.

*Column 3*

*Survey of Current Business,* June 1956, Table 2, p. 10.

TABLE 5

*1947*

CPS column derived from *Current Population Reports—Consumer Income,* Series P-60, No. 5, Table 1. Survey of Consumer Finances column derived from data from Board of Governors, Federal Reserve System. OBE column from *Survey of Current Business,* June 1956, Table 4, p. 12.

*1954*

See notes to Table 4.

TABLE 6

*CPS*

Interpolated graphically from Lorenz curve of distribution of consumer units by family money income levels. Percentage distributions of consumer units by income level from Table 1 of *Current Population Reports—Consumer Income,* Series P-60, Nos. 5, 9, 12, 15, and 20 (similar data for 1953 furnished by Census Bureau). For each year, aggregate family money income in each income bracket was estimated by multiplying the number of consumer units in the bracket by an estimated mean income. For the highest income bracket in the census tabulations ($10,000 and over in 1947 and 1950, $15,000 and over in 1951, and $25,000 and over in 1952 to 1954, where the census enumerators did not ask for amounts of income) errors of estimation in these means may underlie some of the small changes in income shares shown in the table for the top quintile.

### *SCF*

Interpolated graphically from Lorenz curves. Percentage distributions of consumer units and of aggregate family money income by family money income level from Board of Governors, Federal Reserve System.

### *OBE*

From *Survey of Current Business,* as follows: 1947, *Income Distribution in the United States by Size, 1944–1950,* Supplement, 1953, Table 3, p. 81; 1950–1951, March 1955, Table 9, p. 24; 1952–1954, June 1956, Table 5, p. 12.

## TABLES 7 AND 8

### *1929*

Distribution for 1929 is not part of the official income distribution series of the OBE which begins with 1944. Percentage shares in Table 7 interpolated from income distribution for 1929 which was derived as described below. The 1929 distribution in terms of 1950 prices in Table 8 was obtained by applying the OBE price index used for deflating personal consumption expenditures to the distribution of current dollar incomes, assuming that the same index applied to all income groups. (For statistical procedure, see *Income Distribution in the United States by Size, 1944–1950,* n. 12, p. 38.)

The 1929 distribution of families and unattached individuals by family personal income level was derived by making two adjustments in the Brookings Institution estimates for that year (Maurice Leven, Harold G. Moulton, and Clark Warburton, *America's Capacity to Consume,* The Brookings Institution, 1934). The first of these was to subtract net capital gains from the Brookings figures. Of the total income of $92,950 million accounted for in the Brookings distribution, net capital gains (gains less losses) amounted to $6,200 million or almost 7 per cent (*ibid.,* p. 167). The relative importance of this item was of course very much higher in the upper income ranges. For example, it is estimated that such net gains accounted for 33 per cent of the total income of families and unattached individuals with 1929 incomes over $50,000 in the Brookings figures.

A second adjustment, which also served to lower the income share of top income groups, was to reduce the amount added by the Brookings authors for understatement of business income on income tax returns. The amount that had been added was relatively much higher than the comparable adjustment for later years.

*Capital gains.* The adjustment to remove capital gains was based on the following tabulations of federal individual income tax returns which were available for 1929: (1) aggregate amount of net capital gain segregated for tax at 12½ per cent, by net income classes (net income being defined on tax returns to include net capital gains); (2) number of returns with net capital gain segregated for tax at 12½ per cent, by size classes of such net capital gain (for all returns with net incomes of $5,000 or more); (3) aggregate amount of net capital gain segregated for tax at 12½ per cent, by size classes of such net capital gain (for all returns with net incomes of $5,000 or more); (4), (5), and (6) corresponding tabulations for net capital gain other than segregated for tax at 12½ per cent. (*Statistics of Income for 1929,* pp. 11, 12, 75).

Step 1 was to estimate the number of income tax returns with net capital gains at each net income bracket above $5,000. This was done by constructing, for returns with net capital gain segregated for tax at 12½ per cent, a cross-classification table in which the number of returns with such gain and the aggregate amount of such gain were each distributed by size classes of net capital gain (the columns in the table) and cross-classified by size classes of net income (the rows in the table); and by constructing a corresponding table for returns with net capital gain other than segregated for tax at 12½ per cent. These cross-classification tables were filled in as follows:

a. For the first table, the figures from tabulations 2 and 3 above provided the column totals for numbers of returns and amounts of gain, and those from tabulation 1 the row totals for amounts of gain. Similarly, the margins of the second table were filled in from tabulations 4, 5, and 6.

b. The cells in each of the two tables were filled in, initially, by distributing each column total among the rows in proportion to the corresponding distribution of returns in that capital-gain class in 1950. The 1950 distributions were based on actual cross-classifications of tax returns with capital gain for that year. This yielded preliminary estimates of the number of returns and aggregate amount of net capital gain in each cell. By adding entries within a row, preliminary estimates were obtained of the total number of returns and aggregate amounts of capital gain by net income classes.

c. The latter amounts were compared with the actual row totals from tabulations 1 and 4 and found to be too high in the net income range between $100,000 and $500,000 and too low in most lower and higher income brackets. To correct for this, the amounts of capital gain in the various cells were adjusted, and at the same time the numbers of returns with capital gain in corresponding cells were adjusted proportionately, so that the entries in the cells would total both to the column and the row totals from tabulations 1 through 6.

d. The estimated number of returns with capital gain in each net income class was derived by summing the adjusted numbers in the various cells within each row and adding the results for the two cross-classification tables. It was not possible to allow for instances in which both segregated and unsegregated capital gains may have been reported on the same tax return.

Step 2 was to shift the adjusted number of returns in each cell in c above, i.e. returns within given ranges of net income and of capital gain, to brackets of income exclusive of capital gain. This was done on the basis of formulas for subtracting through a cross-tabulation that had been developed for a corresponding purpose by the OBE (*Income Distribution in the United States by Size, 1944–1950,* n. 9, p. 36). The subtraction yielded a new cross-classification table in which returns with capital gain were classified by net income brackets and, within each such bracket, by size classes of income exclusive of capital gain. This cross-classification covered the various net income brackets above $5,000. On the basis of these figures, corresponding estimates were extrapolated for the lower net income range, which were then adjusted to meet the control totals for this range from tabulations 1 and 4.

Step 3 was to estimate the number of families and unattached individuals with capital gain included in the various family income brackets in the Brookings study. The work of estimating the amounts of capital gain included in total income in corresponding family income brackets had already been done by Simon Kuznets (*Shares of Upper Income Groups in Income and Savings,* National Bureau of Economic Research, 1953, p. 220). The Brookings authors presented estimates of such amounts by brackets of individuals' income (Leven, Moulton, and Warburton, *op. cit.,* pp. 206, 208), and Kuznets, for purposes of his study, transformed these into brackets of family income.

Capital gains included in the Brookings distribution totaled substantially more than was reported on income tax returns because the Brookings authors, in developing the upper tail of the family income distribution from tax returns, had increased capital gains reported in the $5,000 and over net income range by 65 per cent to allow for underreporting; they had also raised the capital gain figures from tax returns in the range below $5,000 to allow for the fact that the coverage of tax returns was incomplete in the lower income range because of the high filing requirements of 1929 (*ibid.,* p. 167). The Brookings authors do not state that the numbers of units with capital gains were raised correspondingly, but it appears from what they say that this must have been the case. Accordingly, the ratio of the amount of capital gain in each income bracket in the Brookings distribution (Kuznets, *op. cit.,* p. 220, columns 1 plus 5) to the amount in the corresponding bracket reported on tax returns (tabulations 1 plus 4 above) was applied to the number of returns with capital gain in the income bracket derived in step 1d above, to obtain the estimated number of consumer units with capital gain in the various family income brackets in the Brookings distribution.

Step 4 was to estimate the number of families and unattached individuals in various size classes of family income exclusive of capital gain. This was done by distributing the number of consumer units in each family income bracket from step 3 in proportion to the distribution of frequencies by size classes of income exclusive of capital gain that had been developed for the corresponding net income bracket in step 2, and then summing the results over all family income brackets.

Step 5 was to adjust the Brookings distribution to remove capital gains. The adjustment in frequencies was made by subtracting the numbers of families and unattached individuals with capital gain in the various family income brackets derived in step 3 from the Brookings frequencies (Leven, Moulton, and Warburton, *op. cit.,* p. 227), and then adding the numbers in the various brackets of family income exclusive of capital gain from step 4. Correspondingly, estimated amounts of aggregate income inclusive of capital gain received by consumer units with capital gain were subtracted from the Brookings total income figures (*ibid.,* p. 229), and aggregate amounts of income exclusive of capital gain received by these units were added, in the appropriate income brackets. Approximately $7 billion of capital gain was subtracted from the Brookings income total by this procedure, $4½ billion of which was subtracted in the income range above $50,000.

*Capital losses.* No adjustment was necessary for capital loss segregated for tax credit at 12½ per cent because such losses had not been deducted by taxpayers in 1929 in determining their net income. (Instead, persons with these losses applied their tax credit directly to their computed tax liability.) The required adjustment for capital loss therefore related only to losses other than those segregated for tax credit.

It was not considered worthwhile to shift the Brookings income distribution to add nonsegregated capital losses except, as noted below, in the deficit class. The losses that were included in the Brookings distribution were relatively small as compared with the gains. Moreover, for the income range under $5,000 the description of methodology in the Brookings study suggests that capital losses may not have been taken into account at all.

In the deficit class, where Brookings included the $0.8 billion of capital losses reported on deficit tax returns, a rough allocation was made of the estimated number of consumer units with capital losses to brackets of family income exclusive of such losses. The allocation was based on a tabulation of 1929 tax returns with nonsegregated capital loss and with incomes of $5,000 or more by size of such capital loss. (*Statistics of Income for 1929,* pp. 11, 16.) The shift of units out of the deficit bracket had the effect of adding $0.8 billion of income to the Brookings figures. As indicated, a similar allocation was not made for consumer units in the income range above $5,000. Instead, the amounts of capital loss reported in these brackets were netted by the Brookings authors and by Kuznets against capital gains in corresponding brackets, and it was these net amounts that were used in steps 3 and 5, above. The omission in this range of an explicit adjustment to remove capital losses, which would have shifted a small proportion of consumer units to higher family income brackets, introduced some error in the estimated income size distribution for 1929, but it is probably small.

*Understatement of business income.* The Brookings authors increased the number of income tax returns reporting net business or partnership earnings in each business earnings bracket above $5,000 by 65 per cent in order to allow for understatement of this type of income on 1929 tax returns (Leven, Moulton, and Warburton, *op. cit.,* p. 187). A correction factor more nearly comparable with that used by the OBE for later years is 15 per cent. Accordingly, an adjustment was made to shift some consumer units down the income scale to introduce closer comparability with the series for later years.

The increase in the number of tax returns that had been introduced in the Brookings study was available for each size class of business earnings above $5,000 (*ibid.,* Table 23, p. 187). Three-fourths of these frequencies—assumed to be the excess in the Brookings adjustment—were shifted to size classes of total income (earnings plus other types of income) on the basis of ratios of total income to earnings available for the various earnings brackets (*ibid.,* Table 35, p. 221). The resulting frequencies were assumed to represent the excess number of consumer units that had been added by the Brookings authors in the several income brackets above about $7,000. (Actually, they represented the excess number of persons, rather than consumer units, with total incomes in these brackets, but the top tail of the Brookings distribution of consumer units was so similar to that for persons—compare Tables 26 and 37 in the Brookings study—that further adjustment was not warranted.) Accordingly, these frequencies were subtracted from the Brookings number of consumer units in those income brackets (*ibid.,* p. 227), and corresponding subtractions were made from the Brookings aggregate income figures. The total number of units subtracted in brackets above $7,000 was then added to the Brookings frequencies in the income range between $5,000 and $7,000, and the aggregate income in that range increased accordingly. The effect of the adjustment was to reduce aggregate income in the Brookings distribution by $1.8 billion.

*Adjustment of 1929 family income distribution to meet control totals.* The Brookings distribution accounted for 36.5 million families and unattached individuals. The control total estimated from revised Census Bureau figures was 36.1 million. The latter figure was distributed in proportion to the adjusted frequencies that had been derived in preceding steps, and multiplied by estimated mean incomes for the various income brackets. The results required only minor adjustment to meet the control total of family personal income derived for 1929 from the OBE personal-income series (see notes to Table 1, columns 1 and 2).

The 1929 distribution that was derived above is presented, after conversion into 1950 prices, in Table 8. Like the estimates for 1935–1936 and 1941, the figures for 1929 in Tables 7 and 8 are not part of the official series of the OBE which covers selected years from 1944 forward.

For the latter period the extension into lower-income brackets of the requirement to file federal individual income tax returns yielded more adequate basic information from tax returns covering a much wider income range than was available for prewar years. For 1929, as is noted in the text, the income distribution presented here is to be regarded as a rough approximation to the actual situation. The adjustments described above serve to make the 1929 distribution more nearly comparable to the income distributions for later years than are the Brookings Institution figures on which they are based. However, a detailed reworking of the 1929 estimates to introduce greater comparability with the distributions for later years might result in significant revisions in the figures.

*1935–1936, 1941*

Selma Goldsmith, George Jaszi, Hyman Kaitz, and Maurice Liebenberg, "Size Distribution of Income since the Mid-Thirties," *Review of Economics and Statistics,* February 1954, Tables 3 and 4.

*1944, 1946, 1947*

Percentages in Table 7 from *Income Distribution in the United States by Size, 1944–1950,* Table 3, p. 81. The 1944 income distribution in terms of 1950 dollars in Table 8 from Goldsmith, Jaszi, Kaitz, and Liebenberg, *op. cit.,* Table 3.

*1950, 1951*

*Survey of Current Business,* March 1955, Tables 9 and 10, pp. 24–25.

*1954*

Table 7 from *Survey of Current Business,* June 1956, Table 5, p. 12. Table 8 was obtained by applying the OBE price index used for deflating personal consumption expenditures to the distribution of current dollar incomes from *ibid.,* Table 16, p. 15. For methodology, see *Income Distribution in the United States by Size, 1944–1950,* p. 38, f. 12.

# COMMENT

JOSEPH A. PECHMAN, COMMITTEE FOR ECONOMIC DEVELOPMENT

Selma F. Goldsmith has covered a great deal of ground with the thoroughness and skill we have learned to expect from her. Although her paper is directed mainly at a comparison of census income distributions with other data, the last section, "Longer-Run Changes in Income Distribution," provides for the first time complete distributions covering the period from 1929 through 1953 on a comparable basis.

## CHANGES IN RELATIVE DISTRIBUTIONS

Table 7 of Mrs. Goldsmith's paper, which summarizes the available estimates, shows that the relative distribution of income changed drastically between 1929 and 1944. The top 20 per cent of the family units received 54 per cent of total family personal income in 1929, and only about 46 per cent in 1944; the share of the top five per cent was cut by almost a third during the same period—from 30 per cent in 1929 to about 21 per cent in 1944. This transformation of the income distribution during the 1930's was so marked that Arthur F. Burns described it as "one of the great social revolutions of history." [1]

According to Mrs. Goldsmith's data, the transformation in the income distribution was completed by 1944; during the following ten years there was no apparent movement toward either greater or less equality, the share of the top 20 per cent of the family units varying between 45 and 46 per cent, and the remaining shares showing equal stability. The Survey of Consumer Finances indicates that the distribution was practically unchanged in 1954 and 1955 as well.

These data confirm the conclusions drawn by Kuznets from income tax returns,[2] and the broad sweep of events—so far as they can be portrayed by the available data on income size distributions—seem reasonably certain. However, before taking the figures at face value, we must not overlook Mrs. Goldsmith's reservation that "the amount of change in the relative distribution of income depends in part on the particular income definition used." [3]

Use of the family personal income concept consistent with the definitions of the Department of Commerce national income accounts for the relatively long period covered by Mrs. Goldsmith would appear to insure comparability of the data. In fact, however, changes in the tax laws and in tax practices have greatly altered the content of family personal income. Methods of employee compensation have been devised to avoid the high tax rates; special tax-relief provisions have lowered reported business or property incomes; advantage has been taken of the preferential capital gains rates by conversion of ordinary income into capital gains; and the practice of

[1] *Looking Forward,* 31st Annual Report, National Bureau of Economic Research, 1951, p. 4.

[2] Simon Kuznets, *Shares of Upper Income Groups in Income and Savings,* National Bureau of Economic Research, 1953.

[3] For an excellent discussion of some of the points presented below, see George Garvy, "Functional and Size Distributions of Income and Their Meaning," *Papers and Proceedings of the American Economic Association,* May 1954, pp. 236–253.

splitting incomes among family members other than the wife has grown. Since the Department of Commerce relies heavily on the bookkeeping and tax records of business firms and individuals for making its estimates, the size distributions of "family personal income" are actually based on income definitions which have undergone considerable change in recent years.

EFFECTS OF CHANGES IN TAX LAWS AND TAX PRACTICES

The precise effect of these changes cannot now be measured, but there is little question about the direction of this effect. Most of the developments noted above, though by no means all, favor the top 1 or 2 per cent of the nation's income recipients. As a consequence, there must be understatement of inequality in the currently available income size distributions for the period since the beginning of World War II if 1929 is used as a basis for comparison. Equally important, the amount of understatement has probably been increasing in recent years as taxpayers become more expert at designing new methods of avoiding the impact of the high tax rates and as Congress continues to enact new relief provisions for the same purpose. This means that the apparent stability in the relative distribution of income since 1944 may conceal a gradual but persistent increase in inequality.

Lest this qualification to Mrs. Goldsmith's conclusions be lightly dismissed, it might be worthwhile to list some important examples of these changes in income accounting. While any one may perhaps have little effect on the distribution of income, their combined effect can hardly be ignored.

Devices for reducing stated earnings have been elaborated during the past fifteen years for the benefit of high-salaried executives and self-employed business and professional men. Deferred-compensation contracts and stock options are arranged in lieu of cash salary increases, and often tax-free expense accounts are used to pay not only legitimate business expenses but also large personal expenditures of the individual and his family. Deferred compensation becomes income to the corporate executive only when he elects to take it rather than when it accrues, while the value of stock options is never included in personal income because it is regarded by the tax laws as a capital gain. As for the so-called business expenses, the Department of Commerce charges them off as nonfactor costs of business operation, and they are therefore not counted as employee compensation or entrepreneurial incomes.

Of these practices, the expense accounts are by far the most important. Individuals have at their disposal company cars, planes, boats, and other company facilities for personal and family use; they charge off as entertainment expenses the cost of theaters, night clubs and restaurants, baseball games, boxing matches and other sports events; and they finance expensive travel and pleasure cruises for themselves and their families.[4] It is impossible to estimate even roughly how much income is distributed to individuals in this form, but clearly the amounts are now much larger than in the 1920's and 1930's, both in absolute and relative terms, and are highly concentrated at the upper end of the income distribution.

The effect of the recent growth in industrial pension plans and other fringe benefits is not reflected in Mrs. Goldsmith's income distributions. Family personal income excludes employer contributions to such plans,[5] an item of accrued income to individuals which has increased many times more than cash wages and salaries. These contributions were over five times larger in 1954 than in 1944 ($5.1 billion as compared with $0.9 billion), while wage and salary disbursements increased by less than 70 per cent during the same period.[6] Other nontaxable fringe benefits (such as life insurance and medical care and health insurance) have also been increasing rapidly in recent years. Although such benefits are less concentrated at the upper end of the income scale than deferred compensation or stock options, they do not extend down to the lowest end. For example, farm workers and employees in service, retail, and other small establishments ordinarily have few wage supplements of this kind, whereas the more skilled and unionized workers have succeeded in obtaining substantial benefits through collective-bargaining agreements. If one could distribute employees' rights in pension and other plans by personal income levels, practically all of the $5 billion of additional income from this source would be added to the upper end of the income distribution in 1954 (perhaps the top half); only a small fraction of this amount would be added in 1944 and earlier years.

The effects of special tax relief on the taxable incomes of industrial organizations and property owners may be illustrated by the provisions applying to the oil and mining industries. Since the 1920's the oil industry has been allowed a deduction for depletion amounting to 27½ per cent of gross income, and it has also been en-

[4] For an interesting account of these and other methods which are used to escape the impact of high tax rates, see *Business Week,* July 16, 1955, p. 45.

[5] *Income Distribution in the United States by Size, 1944–1950,* supplement to *Survey of Current Business,* Dept. of Commerce, 1953, Exhibit 11, p. 53.

[6] *National Income Supplement, 1954, Survey of Current Business,* Dept. of Commerce, Table 34, p. 210; and *Survey of Current Business,* July 1955, Tables 3 and 34, pp. 10 and 20.

titled to deduct currently most of the cost of oil-well development and drilling. Almost every major federal revenue act in recent years has contained some new feature broadening the application of these allowances to other extractive industries. For example, in 1951 percentage depletion was raised from 5 to 10 per cent for coal, and a long list of minerals was added to those already entitled to percentage depletion. In the same year, taxpayers were allowed to deduct currently mineral exploration expenses up to $75,000 per year for a period of four years, in lieu of capitalizing them. In 1954, uranium and several other strategic and critical minerals were granted percentage depletion of 23 per cent, and the $75,000 annual limit on the deduction for mineral exploration expenditures was raised to $100,000.

The Department of Commerce adds back the excess of percentage depletion over cost depletion to net income of unincorporated enterprises, but it does not correct for the additional deductions for development and exploration. Moreover, Mrs. Goldsmith did not distribute the major portion of the excess depletion allowances to the highest income brackets where it belongs.[7] It has been estimated that the special allowances for unincorporated owners of oil and mining interests may have reached a total of $700 million in 1955.[8] Thus, the effect of these allowances on the comparability over time of the incomes of the highest income recipients is by no means small, particularly since the oil industry (which accounts for the major share of the special allowances) has been growing at a faster rate than most other industries.

The definition of key items of business cost—aside from depletion and mineral exploration expenditures—has been liberalized in several respects either by law or through changes in the tax regulations. The use of LIFO, five-year amortization allowances for emergency facilities, more liberal depreciation provisions, and the treatment of expenses for research and development and for soil and water conservation as currently deductible expenses have all had the effect of reducing not only corporate profits (which are not included in a distribution of personal income) but also farm and nonfarm proprietorship and partnership incomes (which are

[7] Apparently excess depletion was distributed by income classes along with other adjustments to the basic tax data on entrepreneurial incomes "in such a manner as to leave the Lorenz curve [based on net incomes as reported on tax returns] in each industry unchanged" (*Income Distribution in the United States by Size, 1944–1950,* p. 44).

[8] William F. Hellmuth, Jr., "Erosion of the Federal Corporation Income Tax Base," *Federal Tax Policy for Economic Growth and Stability,* Papers Submitted by Panelists Appearing before the Subcommittee on Tax Policy, Joint Committee on the Economic Report, 84 Cong., 1st Sess., 1956, p. 914.

included). Since the Department of Commerce follows the tax definitions of these deductions, family personal income and its distribution understate entrepreneurial incomes in the 1940's and 1950's (or, alternatively, overstate them in earlier years).

Prior to 1948, it was common practice among high-income recipients to split their incomes with their wives in order to avoid the high tax rates. After income splitting was universalized by the Revenue Act of 1948, this practice was no longer necessary (since the tax law in effect granted to each married couple the most advantageous split), but the advantage of splitting with children still remained. A married individual with a taxable income of $100,000 and three children would pay $53,640 in tax under present law rates, if he retained ownership to all the income. If, on the other hand, the family financial affairs were so arranged (by gift of property, for example) that each child were the recipient of $20,000 of the $100,000 income (which together with the two $20,000 splits he has on his own joint return with his wife, would yield the lowest possible tax), he would reduce the total tax burden on the family to $36,300, and thus save $17,340 or 32 per cent.[9]

Obviously, it would be difficult for an individual to arrange his affairs so perfectly as to get the maximum advantage from splitting. However he can achieve a major portion of his objective by splitting off only part of his income, since the amounts given to his children would be taxable at the highest rates in his hands. Thus, in the above example, if $10,000 were given to each of the three children, the total tax burden of the family would be $40,740 and they would be realizing almost 75 per cent of the maximum possible savings. We have no basis for judging how far taxpayers have gone in this direction; but, since the incentive is there,[10] it can be stated with a fair degree of certainty that such splitting is taking place, and the likelihood is that it is increasing in importance in view of the continuation of the high surtax rates.[11]

Theoretically, a distribution of income by family units should

[9] The head of the family would be required to pay a gift tax on the property given to his children, but the income tax savings are much larger than the gift tax.

[10] Aside from the income tax incentive, a wealthy individual is well advised to distribute his property to his heirs while he is still living, because the gift tax rates are much lower than the estate tax rates.

[11] The pressure on Congress to validate family partnerships indicates how strong the incentive to split with children really is. An individual would give a gift of property to his child (even if he is a minor) and the child would turn around and "invest" the gift in his parent's business. The parent would then be able to pay part of his entrepreneurial income to the child as a return on the child's investment. This practice had a long and uncertain history in the courts until 1951, when it was made valid for tax purposes.

combine the separate incomes of all members of the family unit. But we do not know whether the field survey data, which must be used for this purpose,[12] are reliable enough at the higher income levels to provide an adequate basis for making the appropriate combinations.

To convert ordinary incomes into capital gains, taxpayers have used two principal methods: arranging their transactions to result in the receipt of capital gains rather than ordinary income and convincing Congress to define their incomes as capital gains. An example of the first method is the device known as the "collapsible" corporation, frequently used by movie stars before the practice was outlawed in 1950.[13] More recently, some court decisions have validated a method of converting oil royalties into capital gains.[14]

As to the second method, the list of incomes formerly considered ordinary incomes that are now defined by law as capital gains includes coal royalties, profits from livestock held for twelve months or more, the value of unharvested crops sold with land, profits from subdividing real estate by persons other than real estate dealers, royalties of an inventor, and profits from the sale of timber. Heavy reliance must be placed on data from tax returns to distribute entrepreneurial and property incomes by income level,[15] and the inclusion of such receipts in individual tax returns as capital gains means that either an inadequate allowance or none is made for the resulting understatement of ordinary incomes.

Finally, the ease with which accumulated corporate savings can be converted into capital gains has important consequences for income distribution analysis. The urge to liquidate these funds in some way other than the dividend route is great, and many tax lawyers spend their time quite profitably devising complex corporate rearrangements to do this very thing. And there are provisions

[12] *Income Distribution in the United States by Size, 1944–1950,* pp. 56–57.

[13] The device operated as follows: A movie star would organize a corporation to film a movie. He and others would purchase stock in the corporation to provide the cash necessary to make the film. After the film was completed, but before any income was realized, the film would be sold. The corporation would then be liquidated and its assets (mainly cash) distributed to the shareholders. The shareholders would pay a tax, at capital gains rates, on the difference between the cost of their stock and the amount they received on liquidation of the corporation. In this way, the shareholders would convert what would ordinarily have been salaries or dividends into capital gains.

[14] This is accomplished by selling the rights to receive a royalty from an oil property for a short term of years at a price roughly equal to the present value of the future stream of royalties. Since the right is regarded as a capital asset, the gain from the sale of the right may be considered as capital gain.

[15] *Income Distribution in the United States by Size, 1944–1950,* pp. 41–42 and 52–55.

in the Internal Revenue Code specifically designed to assist them in these efforts. For example, under the 1954 tax code, a complete redemption by a corporation of a shareholder's stock results in a receipt of a capital gain rather than a dividend if the shareholder does not reacquire an interest in the corporation for a period of ten years thereafter.[16] In 1950, the heirs of a decedent who owned a closely held corporation were permitted to redeem the stock in that corporation *income-tax-free* to pay the estate tax, under conditions which can be met fairly frequently.[17] And there are such esoteric methods as the use of "spin-offs," "split-ups," and "preferred-stock bail-outs," which enable shareholders to cash in on accumulated corporate savings without liability to personal income tax rates on the proceeds. In these and many other instances, stock is redeemed or sold at a value far in excess of its original cost, so that the redemption or sale merely converts corporate savings or potential dividends into capital gains.

Another device which has been used frequently, particularly during the 1950's, is the merger. Although tax reduction is not ordinarily the major motivation, studies by the Harvard Business School have indicated that "the tax structure definitely exerts strong pressure on the owners of many closely-held businesses to sell out or merge with other large companies. . . . The tax incentives to sell are twofold: first, a closely-held business may be sold out to lessen the impact of the estate taxes; and, secondly, the sale may enable the owners of closely-held businesses to take the profits out of their business by the capital gains route rather than to have them distributed as dividends and subjected to the very high bracket individual income tax rates. . . ."[18]

The relative ease with which corporate savings can be distributed to shareholders via the capital gains route raises the question of the validity of size distributions of income which exclude corporate savings or unrealized capital gains. As Mrs. Goldsmith has pointed out, the addition of undistributed corporate profits and corporate profits taxes wipes out a substantial portion of the decline in the income share of the top 5 per cent of the income recipients between 1929 and recent years.[19] She might have added that it could also alter the picture of relative stability that we now have for the years since the end of the war.

[16] *Internal Revenue Code of 1954,* Sec. 302. The purpose of this provision is explained in the *Report of the Committee on Finance, United States Senate, to Accompany H. R. 8300* (Report No. 1622, 83d Cong., 2d sess., p. 45).

[17] *Internal Revenue Code of 1954,* Sec. 303.

[18] J. Keith Butters, John Lintner, and William L. Cary, *Effects of Taxation, Corporate Mergers,* Harvard Business School, 1951, pp. 8–9.

[19] See her paper in this volume, p. 95.

These remarks are not intended to disparage Mrs. Goldsmith's work in any way. We owe a tremendous debt of gratitude to her and to her colleagues at the Department of Commerce for the enormous body of useful statistics on income size distributions which they have made available to us. That they are aware of the shortcomings of their data is evident from the detailed statement of their methodology in *Income Distribution in the United States.* At this stage of their work, they are greatly in need of more information to evaluate the real meaning of their results and to place them in their proper historical perspective. Such information can be obtained from a detailed examination of the supporting schedules submitted by taxpayers with their tax returns. Careful consideration should be given to methods of securing and tabulating this information—even if it means the loss of some of the regular annual tabulations that now appear in *Statistics of Income.*

ROBERT J. LAMPMAN, UNIVERSITY OF WASHINGTON

The papers presented in Part I demonstrate that serious and continuing attempts to find and understand the facts of size distribution have only begun and that those in authority must make positive decisions, plan carefully, and act energetically if the facts are to be forthcoming. My comments will be on three aspects of the problem.

SCHEDULE CHANGES

New questions suggested by a reading of the papers include the following possibilities: one relating the reported income to the recipient's labor-force status of the year in which the income was received, rather than to labor-force status at time of interview; one relating family status and composition to the year for which income is reported; and a series of questions designed to get more complete information on totals of family income (which could, at least, test the widely held belief that extra probing will uncover additional income—especially unearned income—and income recipients). In addition, I suggest trying a question in a small sample study on how the income recipients place themselves on the economic status ladder, thus opening a new "subjective frontier" in income size-distribution research.

CHANGES IN PRESENTATION

How can the 1959 data be organized for improved presentation? Information about differences among the deciles in money income distribution of families and unattached individuals would eliminate certain misleading features of simpler tables and make for better interpretation. I suggest a table set up to show for each decile:

Median income-receiving-unit income

Percentage of all persons to be found in each decile of income-receiving units [1]

Median number of children under eighteen

Percentage of units headed by persons over sixty-five

Percentage of units having rural residence

Median number of earners

Percentage of units headed by women

Percentage of units headed by workers who were in the labor force less than six months

This list is meant to be suggestive rather than exhaustive or necessarily the best.

PROBLEMS OF DEFINITION

It is important that we understand not only the money income distribution and its association with factors such as those noted above, but also how the degree of inequality and changes in it shown in the census money income distributions depend heavily upon the particular definitions of income, income recipient, and income period used. Table 1 offers a beginning toward a reconciliation of all possible size distributions and estimated changes in the degree of inequality shown, starting from the current census definitions of total family money income. Three definitions of income are emphasized: consumer-power income, which is relevant for the welfare judgment; producer-contribution income, which indicates inequality before income redistribution via public and private institutions; and general-market-power income, which is broad enough to cover many shifts in the form that income takes. Some change in the definition of income recipient and income period may be appropriate in working out changes in the definition of income. For example, in drawing up a consumer-power income distribution, it would be reasonable to adjust the income-receiving-unit definition to show the number or percentage of persons in each decile of income-receiving units and to lengthen the time period beyond one year.

Some of the relationships suggested in the table could well be the subject of special sample studies or other methods of inquiry by the Census Bureau and others. But at present, without further inquiry into the facts, some interpretation could be offered of the

[1] I discovered after considerable effort that the top decile of income-receiving units included 12 per cent of the people, the bottom decile 6 per cent in 1949.

TABLE 1

Reconciliation of Income Definitions and Estimate of Effect of Adjustments on the Degree of Inequality Shown in Census Family Income Distributions

| ADJUSTMENT TO DISTRIBUTION | *Estimated Effect on Degree of Inequality Shown* |
|---|---|
| **Part A. Changes in Definition of Income** | |
| Total money income | |
| *Add:* Nonmarketed net product | |
| Net imputed rent of owner-occupied houses | — [a] |
| Home-produced food | — [a] |
| Home-produced services | — [a] |
| Services of consumer durables | + |
| Withheld dividends or corporate savings | + [b] |
| In-kind payments | + (doubtful) |
| Employee fringe benefits | |
| Business expense accounts over and above the "cost of work" | + |
| *Deduct:* Money transfers from government to persons | + [c] |
| *Equals:* Producer-contribution income | |
| *Add:* Money transfers from government to persons | — |
| Personal transfers (gifts, gambling gains and losses, etc.) | |
| *Deduct:* Withheld dividends | — |
| Personal taxes paid | — |
| *Adjust for:* Cost-of-living differences (urban-rural) | — |
| *Equals:* Consumer-power income [d] | |
| *Adjust for:* Changes in value of assets owned (realized and unrealized capital gains) | differ by years |
| *Equals:* General-market-power income | |
| Items which are difficult to assign to individuals: | |
| Indirect taxes | + [c] |
| Government free services | — [c] |
| **Part B. Changes in Definition of Income-Receiving Unit and Income Period** | |
| Convert to distribution by earners (reshuffling) | + [e] |
| Adjust above distribution to exclude part-period earners | — [f] |
| Adjust spending-unit distribution to exclude units having part-period principal earners | — [f] |
| Convert to a per capita income distribution, ranking individuals by per capita income (reshuffling) | + [g] |
| Adjust spending-unit distribution to show percentage of total population represented in each decile of spending units (no reshuffling) | — [h] |
| Include institutionalized population | + [i] |
| Lengthen income period to more than one year | — [j] |
| **Part C. Suggestions Based on Findings of Inadequacies in Census Data** | |
| Adjust for fact that census has: | |
| Greater understatement of self-employment income for farm than nonfarm | — [k] |
| For farm families, assignment of product of unpaid family workers to family head distorting individual earner distribution | no effect on family distribution [l] |
| Differential underreporting of transfer income | — [m] |
| Deficiency of income recipients, particularly secondary family recipients,[n] recipients of income other than earnings,[o] young adult males, nonwhites [o] and urban females.[o] | + [p] |
| Too many small families and unattached individuals [q] | — |

notes to table on next page

Notes to Table 1

[a] Margaret G. Reid, "Distribution of Nonmoney Income" in Volume Thirteen (1951) of Studies in Income and Wealth, pp. 124–178. On the importance of nonmoney income to farm families, see the paper by D. Gale Johnson in this volume, p. 288.

[b] Simon Kuznets, *Shares of Upper Income Groups in Income and Savings,* National Bureau of Economic Research, 1953, Table II, p. 36; also see the distribution of the Office of Business Economics.

[c] John H. Adler, "The Fiscal System, the Distribution of Income, and Public Welfare," *Fiscal Policies and the American Economy,* Kenyon E. Poole, editor, Prentice-Hall, 1950, pp. 359–421, see especially pp. 384–388.

[d] Close to OBE "family personal income."

[e] Kuznets, *op. cit.,* p. 103.

[f] George Garvy, "Some Problems in Measuring Inequality of Income" in Volume Fifteen (1952) of Studies in Income and Wealth, pp. 25–47, 37, 43.

[g] Kuznets, *op. cit.,* pp. 104–107.

[h] For postwar distributions we know there are fewer people per decile below the median than above it.

[i] Most standard distributions exclude the institutionalized population and hence underrepresent the single individuals and low-income units.

[j] Kuznets, *op. cit.,* pp. 139–140. Making adjustments for temporary low income status and size of the spending unit will substantially lessen the number who can be assigned "low economic status" (see the paper by Eleanor M. Snyder in this volume).

[k] Johnson, *op. cit.,* pp. 294 and 299.

[l] *Ibid.,* p. 288.

[m] See the paper by Selma F. Goldsmith in this volume, p. 78.

[n] See the paper by Edwin D. Goldfield in this volume, p. 57.

[o] See the paper by Leon Pritzker and Alfred Sands in this volume, pp. 216 and 231.

[p] Effect on inequality mixed since adding *both* income and income recipients to low-income classes and some income to higher deciles.

[q] Goldsmith, *op. cit.,* p. 86 (contradicts above line in part).

conceptual relationships. Also, users of census income data should be alerted to the determinants of inequality which could be classified in Part C of the table—those arising from errors of questioning, response, and editing.

We now have, of course, the excellent series by the Office of Business Economics estimating something close to the consumer-power income distribution suggested above. It seems to me that there is ample justification for developing two series which would approximate the distribution of producer-contribution income and general-market-power income to place alongside the census total money income and the OBE personal income distributions.

## EDWIN MANSFIELD, CARNEGIE INSTITUTE OF TECHNOLOGY

I have been asked to comment on the census income data for small areas—states, counties, and cities. I shall discuss briefly the nature of these data, some of their uses, and some difficulties that seem to be present in them.

## COMMENT

### CENSUS INCOME DATA FOR SMALL AREAS

The income data published in Volume II of the 1950 census may be classified into two groups.[1] The first deals with the incomes of families and unrelated individuals. Income distributions and medians are provided for them in every state, county, standard metropolitan area, urbanized area, and urban place with more than 2,500 inhabitants. For states, separate data are presented for families and for unrelated individuals; for other areas (except urban places with less than 10,000 inhabitants), separate data are presented for families alone. The state and county data are broken down for the urban, rural nonfarm, and rural farm populations.[2]

The second group of data deals with the income of persons. Income data are given by race and sex; by age and sex; by family status, age, and sex; by weeks worked and sex; by class of worker and sex; and by type of income and sex. These data are published for each state, for the farm and nonfarm populations in each state, and for each large standard metropolitan area. In addition, income data are published for the experienced civilian labor force in each state by occupation and sex, and by industry and sex.[3]

In southern states, some additional information is given on income among nonwhites. Income distributions and medians are presented for nonwhite families and unrelated individuals in each state, county, standard metropolitan area, urbanized area, and urban place with more than 10,000 inhabitants. Separate state data are published for the rural farm, rural nonfarm, and urban populations.

### SOME USES FOR THE DATA

Economists have long been interested in the personal distribution of income because of its welfare implications and its influence on total consumption and resource allocation. In empirical studies, considerable attention has been devoted to income differentials arising among occupations, industries, geographical areas, and other categories. The purpose of much of this work has been to understand more fully the underlying forces that produce an income distribution and that cause temporal changes in such distributions. Presumably, an ultimate objective is the construction of a

[1] Although much of the census income data for small areas is located in Vol. II, other parts of the census contain relevant information. See for example *1950 Census of Population,* Vol. IV, *Special Reports,* Part 5, Chap. A, Table 4.

[2] The urban and rural nonfarm populations are combined in the county data.

[3] Data concerning the wage or salary income of the experienced labor force are also provided for states, large standard metropolitan areas, and large urban places.

model able to explain much of the observed variation in income and one that can be tested empirically.

Studies focusing on interarea income differentials have usually relied on the Department of Commerce state per capita income series, on census data, or on the Study of Consumer Purchases. Although the Commerce series has probably been used most often,[4] the other bodies of data have also been important.[5] Moreover, the 1950 census has provided material, not previously available, for studies of intercity and intercounty differences in income level and interarea differences in the distribution of income. Some work has been done with these data,[6] but they should afford an important basis for further study.

The 1950 census data may also be useful in cross-section analyses. Because statisticians have become increasingly aware of the problems inherent in most time series and because of the increased interest in breaking down the totals, many studies have relied on cross-section data or a combination of cross-section and time-series data.[7] Of course, the usefulness of the census data in this context depends on the purpose of the study, on whether the time interval and coverage correspond with other data, and on other factors.

Finally, the census income data for small areas may be useful to workers in various other fields:

To economists interested in regional development, interregional input-output models, and other matters relating to the spatial structure of the economy.

To economists and statisticians engaged in sampling small areas,

[4] See, for example, papers in *Review of Economics and Statistics:* Frank A. Hanna, "Contributions of Manufacturing Wages to Regional Differences in Per Capita Income," February 1951; Howard G. Schaller, "Veterans Transfer Payments and State Per Capita Incomes, 1929, 1939, and 1949," November 1953.

[5] See, for example, Herbert E. Klarman, "A Statistical Study of Income Differences among Communities" in Volume Six (1943) of Studies in Income and Wealth; D. Gale Johnson, "Some Effects of Region, Community Size, Color and Occupation on Family and Individual Income," and the comment on it by Herman Miller and Edwin Goldfield in Volume Fifteen (1952) of the same series.

[6] See, for example, Thomas R. Atkinson, "Money Income Distribution: South vs. Non-South," presented at the 1954 Southern Economic Association meeting; and my papers, "City Size and Income, 1949" in Volume Twenty-one (1957) of Studies in Income and Wealth; and in *Review of Economics and Statistics,* "Community Size, Region, Labor Force, and Income, 1950," November 1955, and "Some Notes on City Income Levels," November 1956.

[7] For example, two studies where the city is used as a unit are James S. Duesenberry and Helen Kistin, "The Role of Demand in the Economic Structure," in *Studies in the Structure of the American Economy,* Wassily Leontief, editor, Oxford University Press, 1953; and Dorothy Brady, "Family Savings in Relation to Changes in the Level and Distribution of Income" in Volume Fifteen (1952) of Studies in Income and Wealth.

especially, of course, where it seems desirable to stratify the sampling units by income level.

To businessmen interested in marketing studies, as exemplified by the results of a survey (intended to determine the usefulness of census data in marketing) published by the American Marketing Association. Eighty-eight per cent of the respondent firms used census data, and their purposes suggest the value to them of the income estimates for small areas.[8]

To government workers needing information related to economic welfare, to geographical inequality in tax bases and fiscal capacity, and to planning.

To sociologists, city planners, housing experts, and demographers. The data have been used in studies of urban and metropolitan structure and of family income distribution in deficient housing areas.[9]

## SOME DIFFICULTIES PRESENT IN THE DATA

Many of the difficulties confronting an individual user of these data arise because they are collected not for use in a particular model or conceptual framework but for a multitude of uses. Like most general-purpose items, they are sometimes only an approximation to what would be most useful for particular purposes. Others may have become aware of a different set of difficulties. Some of those I have encountered are discussed below.

### *Combination of Data on Families and Unrelated Individuals*

For cities of under 10,000 inhabitants, the 1950 census provides the median income of families and unrelated individuals combined, but it does not provide separate medians for each group. This creates difficulties for persons who must include small cities in their studies.[10]

It is well known that the characteristics of the two groups differ. In particular, the income level among families is substantially higher than that among unrelated individuals,[11] and hence the median in-

[8] N. H. Borden, S. Frame, W. C. Gordon, and C. W. Smith, "An Appraisal of Census Programs for Marketing Uses," *Journal of Marketing,* April 1954.

[9] See, for example, Leo Schnore and David Varley, "Some Concomitants of Metropolitan Size," *American Sociological Review,* August 1955; and Morton Hoffman, "Needed Improvements in the Census for Housing Users," *Land Economics,* November 1955, p. 328.

[10] Apparently, the lack of separate income data for families and unrelated individuals also troubles users of the census tract data (Hoffman, *op. cit.*).

[11] Selma Goldsmith, George Jaszi, Hyman Kaitz, and Maurice Liebenberg, "Size Distribution of Income since the Mid-Thirties," *Review of Economics and Statistics,* February 1954, p. 12.

come of both groups combined may be affected by the proportion of each in a given city. One might suppose that the number of families per unrelated individual is relatively constant from one city to the next and hence that this factor is relatively minor. Instead there appears to be a direct relationship between the number of families per unrelated individual and the median income of families and unrelated individuals.[12] And the variation in the former is often substantial.

Consequently census data for small cities would probably be more useful if distributions and medians were published for families as well as for families and unrelated individuals.[13] This would make possible either separate treatment of the two groups or the use of a combined median based on constant weights for them.[14] Of course, the estimates for families alone would be less precise than the estimates for both groups combined,[15] but it would be useful to have both sets of data.

### *Limited Use of Urbanized-Area Concept*

In many types of economic, business, and sociological research, the urbanized area or standard metropolitan area (a thickly settled, highly integrated urban area) is a more appropriate unit of study than the urban place which includes only the legal limits of a city.[16] It is unfortunate that the urbanized-area concept has been confined to areas surrounding a large central city. Many clusters of smaller urban places may be highly integrated and might be considered urbanized areas. As matters now stand, one must use individual

[12] Among cities of comparable size located in the same region, the number of families per unrelated individual is often higher in those with high incomes than in those with low incomes. There is also a tendency for the number of families per unrelated individual to be higher in standard metropolitan areas than in urban places outside these areas. But there seems to be no tendency for the ratio to be higher among cities of comparable size in high- than in low-income regions. (See my two papers in *Review of Economics and Statistics,* footnote 6.)

[13] If the distributions for families and for families and unrelated individuals were published, it would be possible to derive the distribution for unrelated individuals.

[14] If a large number of cities were included, weighting and combining of the distributions might consume more time than it would be worth. Rougher methods could be used.

[15] All other things being equal, the standard error of the median family incomes will exceed that of the median incomes of families and unrelated individuals because the sample size is smaller in the former case. If the sample is fairly large, the distribution of the median is approximately normal, and its standard deviation is approximately $[2\sqrt{n}\ p\ (\mathrm{E})]^{-1}$ where $p(\mathrm{E})$ is the probability density at the population median and $n$ is sample size.

[16] For definitions of urban place, urbanized area, and standard metropolitan area, see *1950 Census of Population,* Vol. II, *Characteristics of the Population,* Part 1.

median incomes for many urban places that may be parts of larger urban developments rather than independent entities. This is particularly troublesome if city size is used as a variable or a basis for stratification.[17]

Urban places outside standard metropolitan areas located within five miles of some other urban place or standard metropolitan area in the same state (according to 1950 state maps) are shown below (by census division) as a percentage of all urban places located outside standard metropolitan areas.

| | | | |
|---|---|---|---|
| United States | 31 | South Atlantic | 37 |
| New England | 66 | East South Central | 23 |
| Middle Atlantic | 60 | West South Central | 14 |
| East North Central | 30 | Mountain | 27 |
| West North Central | 7 | Pacific | 45 |

Proximity to other cities is of course an extremely rough indicator of the degree of integration with neighboring cities. But this crude indicator suggests that many urban places outside standard metropolitan areas may be candidates for inclusion in urbanized areas.

### *Inclusion of Income of College Students*

Incomes of college students are included in the income distributions provided by the 1950 census; hence the median incomes in cities that contain universities are often quite low. For example, the median incomes in Amherst (Massachusetts), Williamsburg (Virginia), and Ithaca (New York) are $775, $645, and $1,150, respectively. For many purposes, intercity income comparisons are clouded by this factor: the median income in city A may be lower than that in city B merely because the former is the site of some college, and there is no way to determine the weight of this factor or the median income of nonstudent residents. That the effect of student incomes on income levels is fairly widespread is indicated by the following tabulation showing the number of "university cities" (those where college enrollment in 1950 exceeded 10 per cent of families and unrelated individuals) as a percentage of all cities, by region and for particular city-size classes. The city-size classes are: urban places outside standard metropolitan areas (1) 5,000–9,999, and (2) 25,000–49,999; standard metropolitan areas (3) 100,000–249,999.

[17] The Intensive Review Committee for the Appraisal of Census Programs has recommended the extension of the urbanized-area concept to the peripheries of smaller cities (see also Thomas Semon, "The Case for a Broader 'Urbanized Area' Concept," *Journal of Marketing,* October 1954).

| | (1) | (2) | (3) |
|---|---|---|---|
| United States | 16 | 28 | 19 |
| Northeast | 12 | 19 | 0 |
| North Central | 16 | 29 | 17 |
| South | 18 | 30 | 29 |
| Far West | 15 | 27 | 33 |

Although many problems might arise,[18] it would be helpful if data were published from which one could derive income distributions that exclude full-time students.

*Combined Data on Families and Unrelated Individuals, by Color*

The 1950 census provides income distributions for southern nonwhite families and unrelated individuals combined by state, county, and city. But because separate distributions for families or for unrelated individuals are not published, it is impossible to derive separate distributions for white families and white unrelated individuals. Thus, if one is interested in the income level among whites or nonwhites, one must use the median income of families and unrelated individuals combined. The difficulties that surround this figure are outlined above.[19] For some types of research, it may also be unfortunate that no income data for nonwhites are published for cities with less than 10,000 inhabitants.

*Other Difficulties*

Other difficulties—errors and omissions common to all census income data—may often be important in small-area data. For example, data for some areas are collected by only a few enumerators, and it is not so likely that enumerator biases will cancel out. Also the variation in the level of nonmonetary income is probably greater among small areas than among larger ones. These difficulties are present, and every user of the data should be aware of them even though no quick and easy solution is apparent.

[18] For example, difficulties might arise in determining who should be excluded. There seems to be no reason to exclude most students who live at home and who are counted merely as family members. On the other hand, most full-time students who live away from home and who are counted as unrelated individuals should probably be excluded.

[19] Of course, separate estimates of median nonwhite family income would probably be less precise than the estimates of median nonwhite family and unrelated individual income because the sample size would be smaller in the former case. But this might be a relatively minor matter.

# PART II

## The Matching and Quality Check Studies

# The Survey of Consumer Finances and the Census Quality Check

MONROE G. SIRKEN, DEPARTMENT OF HEALTH, EDUCATION, AND WELFARE

E. SCOTT MAYNES, UNIVERSITY OF MINNESOTA

JOHN A. FRECHTLING, FORD MOTOR COMPANY

## *Introduction*

Persistent differences have often been detected in income figures collected in independently conducted household field surveys of about the same population groups. This has been true even when the estimates of the income size distributions were found to be fairly similar. As a recent and striking example of such a difference, proportionately fewer people are usually shown in the upper-income brackets of estimates based on surveys conducted by the Bureau of the Census than on those conducted regularly by the Survey Research Center (SRC) of the University of Michigan for the Board of Governors of the Federal Reserve System (FRB) as the Survey of Consumer Finances (SCF).

Previous comparisons of field surveys have suggested various reasons for the differences found between the resulting income size distributions. But it has been almost impossible to pin down the

Note: At the time the present study was conducted, Mr. Sirken was a member of the staff of the Bureau of the Census; Mr. Maynes, of the Survey Research Center of the University of Michigan; Mr. Frechtling, of the Board of Governors of the Federal Reserve System.

There are many persons in the Survey Research Center, the Bureau of the Census, and the Federal Reserve Board who participated in one phase or another of this study. The authors wish to acknowledge especially the assistance of George Katona, John B. Lansing, Charles Cannell, Leslie Kish, and James N. Morgan of the Survey Research Center; Morris Hansen, William N. Hurwitz, Eli S. Marks, and Leon Pritzker of the Bureau of the Census; and Ralph Young, Homer Jones, and Irving Schweiger of the Federal Reserve Board. Also the authors wish to acknowledge that the analytical work in this report was assisted by a contract with the Office of Naval Research.

Although this report represents the joint effort of the three authors, the major responsibilities for writing the report were divided among them. Mr. Sirken wrote the "Introduction" and "General Differences in Execution"; Mr. Frechtling, "Reporting of Major Components of Income." Mr. Maynes wrote "Improvement of Survey Techniques and of the Interpretation of Survey Data" and also contributed to the "Summary and Conclusions" at the end of each of the two previous sections.

cause and effect relationships because the survey income data being studied were not originally collected with their future comparison in mind. During 1950, the Bureau of the Census, the SRC, and the FRB undertook a joint income study to provide data for this purpose. The plan of the study involved a resurvey by the Bureau of the Census of a subsample of dwelling units contained in the 1950 SCF. In the resurvey, called here the Census Quality Check (CQC), the Bureau used the enumerators and questionnaires it had used in the Post-Enumeration Survey (PES), which was the quality check undertaken to evaluate the completeness and reliability of the 1950 census. Personal income reports for 1949 were collected in both the original survey and the resurvey.

Thus the present paper can offer an analysis of differences between the income reports collected by two survey organizations using an identical sample design. Its authors hope that the discussion of the reasons that were found for the differences between the reports will provide information useful to others—to the survey technician in improving the field survey as a technique for collecting personal income reports, to the income analyst in evaluating data collected in this way, and to the statistician in suggesting what processes cause random and bias errors in the reports of income collected by household surveys.

## THE STUDY PLAN AND ITS IMPLEMENTATION

During January and February of 1950, the SCF collected reports of their 1949 annual money income from persons in a national probability sample of dwelling units. The sample consisted of lists of dwelling units in urban areas and of open-country segments in rural areas.[1] The basic sampling rate was about one in 16,500 dwelling units, and about 3,000 families and unrelated persons were interviewed. High-income families and farmers, however, were oversampled. If occupants of urban dwelling units were believed to have annual incomes of at least $6,000, the units were sampled at six times the basic rate; if between $3,000 and $6,000, at twice the basic rate. Rural farm dwelling units were also sampled at twice the basic rate.

In August and September of 1950, about seven months after the original enumeration by the SCF, the Bureau of the Census conducted a resurvey (CQC) of a random selection of the SCF dwelling units. The CQC enumerators covered about one-half of the addresses in the urban list sample and dwelling units in one-half

[1] A segment is a small area with defined boundaries within which interviews are taken at all dwelling units.

of the open-country segments in each of the sixty-six primary sampling areas in the SCF sample.

The SCF and CQC enumerators had almost the same information to identify the sample dwelling units. In urban areas, enumerators were supplied with the addresses of the sample units and also of the immediately preceding and succeeding units. In rural areas, they were given highway maps or aerial photographs showing the boundaries of the segments.

Persons covered by each survey were assembled into income units of families and unrelated persons. These were weighted so that all had the same probability of selection. Thus, income units in dwelling units sampled at the regular rate in the SCF were counted six times; those in dwellings sampled at twice the regular weight, three times; and those in dwellings sampled at six times the regular weight, only once.

Since the persons covered in the SCF were not identified by name, the demographic characteristics of families and heads of families covered by each survey at the same listed address or within the same rural segment were compared. If the characteristics of the two units were sufficiently similar (according to specified rules), they were taken as the same or "matched" units; if not, as different or "unmatched" units.[2] Almost all the matched units were assigned the same sampling weight in both surveys, although occasionally a matched unit in an open-country segment had different weights in the SCF and in the CQC.[3]

## INTERPRETATION OF THE DATA

To be able to interpret correctly the data obtained in the surveys, various qualifying factors must be taken into account. In addition to limitations resulting from the sample and the study design, two other important qualifying factors and their possible effects on the data will be considered here.

### *The Period between the Surveys*

The long period between the enumeration dates in the SCF and in the CQC probably detracted somewhat from a primary objective of the study, which was to conduct both surveys under essentially the same conditions. In the SCF, persons were asked about their 1949 income about one or two months after the end of the calendar year and about one month before the final date for filing 1949 income tax returns; in the CQC, the enumeration period was about

[2] See Appendix A for a description of the matching procedure.

[3] For an explanation of how this happened, see page 136.

eight or nine months after the end of 1949 or about six months after the final filing date.

What effect the factor of memory had on the size of income reported was not determined in the study. But one likely effect of the long period between the two enumerations was to decrease the correlation between the size of income reported in one and in the other.

The length of the period also affected the matching of units. Since about 20 per cent of the families in the nation moved during 1950, about 12 per cent of the units covered in the SCF could be expected to have moved by the CQC date. The CQC enumerators tried to track down nearby migrants. But under the optimistic assumption that they were successful in finding all within-county migrants, about 8 per cent of the units covered in the SCF would have been missed by the CQC enumerators because they had moved outside the county. Sometimes the CQC enumerators could reconstruct the household composition for units that had migrated too far to be found, and so the CQC units could be matched with the SCF units; sometimes they could not, and so the SCF unit was not matched. Either way, the CQC income of the units was not likely to have been ascertained. Doubtless there were also cases in which the CQC enumerators did not detect that the SCF unit had moved, and so the CQC incomes are for different units from the ones the SCF had found at the sample address.

*The Lack of Names*

The fact that the SCF did not record the names of persons covered increased the chances for making two types of error in matching the SCF and CQC units: (1) different units were erroneously classified as matched units, and (2) the same units were erroneously classified as unmatched units. In view of the rigid matching rules applied, there were probably more matching errors of the second type than of the first. If so, the percentage of units reported as matched represents an undercount of the actual percentage. Matching errors of the first kind would probably reduce the correlation between income reports of matched units in the two surveys.

In view of the limitations of the survey design and its implementation, the data were not inflated to the national level, and sampling errors were not computed. However the data are weighted to a common sampling level to adjust for the oversampling of higher-income households and farmers in the design of the 1950 SCF. Thus the weighted sample sizes referred to in this report are on the average about four times greater than the actual sample sizes.

COMPARISON OF THE TOTAL INCOME REPORTS

All families and unrelated persons covered either in the SCF or CQC, appropriately weighted, are cross-tabulated by total income in Table 1. Unmatched units not covered in the CQC are distributed in line 12 by the total income reported in the SCF, and those not covered in the SCF are distributed in column 12 by the total income reported in the CQC. The matched units are tabulated in the other lines and columns.

Units selected at different sampling rates are distributed in line 11 according to income reported in the SCF and in column 11 according to income reported in the CQC. Matched units sampled at the same rate in both surveys for which total income was not ascertained in the CQC are distributed in line 10 according to the income reported in the SCF and those for which total income was not ascertained in the SCF are distributed in column 10 according to the total income reported in the CQC. Matched units sampled at the same rate and reporting income in both surveys are cross-tabulated in lines 1 to 9 and columns 1 to 9 according to the total income reported in both surveys.

The marginal frequencies in lines 1 to 10 and columns 1 to 10 respectively of Table 1 represent the distributions of CQC and SCF families and unrelated persons by total income size. Percentage distributions based on these frequencies (see Table 2, p. 144) are rather similar for the two surveys, but the distribution of income derived from CQC reports is more heavily weighted at the lower income levels. The median income is about $115 greater in the SCF than in the CQC.

The frequencies in the cells on the main diagonal of lines and columns 1 to 9 in Table 1 represent units which reported income in the same income class to both surveys; the frequencies in all other cells represent units that reported income in different classes. What are the main factors that produced the differences in the reported incomes? How do they operate? And what effect does each factor have on the differences between the two surveys in the percentage distribution by income size? Can findings here be applied generally to the collection of personal income by household surveys? These are the principle questions considered in this report.

## *General Differences in Execution*

The reasons for differences between the SCF and CQC total income size distributions discussed in this section will be those relating to

TABLE 1

Distribution of Families and Unrelated Persons by Total Income Reported to the SCF and the CQC

| INCOME CLASS IN CQC | INCOME CLASS IN SCF — Matched Units: *Loss* (1) | *0– $999* (2) | *$1,000– $1,999* (3) | *$2,000– $2,999* (4) | *$3,000– $3,999* (5) | *$4,000– $4,999* (6) | *$5,000– $7,499* (7) | *$7,500– $9,999* (8) | *$10,000 & over* (9) | *Income Not Ascertained* (10) | *Different Weights in the Two Surveys*[a] (11) | *Unmatched Units Not Covered in SCF* (12) | TOTAL (13) |
|---|---|---|---|---|---|---|---|---|---|---|---|---|---|
| Matched units: | | | | | | | | | | | | | |
| (1) Loss | 3 | 12 | 0 | 6 | 3 | 0 | 1 | 0 | 0 | 0 | 0 | 9 | 34 |
| (2) 0– 999 | 15 | 382 | 93 | 21 | 12 | 7 | 16 | 1 | 0 | 103 | 42 | 229 | 921 |
| (3) $ 1,000–1,999 | 3 | 64 | 411 | 141 | 51 | 9 | 6 | 0 | 3 | 71 | 18 | 257 | 1,034 |
| (4) 2,000–2,999 | 3 | 18 | 106 | 435 | 190 | 31 | 12 | 6 | 0 | 121 | 12 | 286 | 1,220 |
| (5) 3,000–3,999 | 0 | 6 | 33 | 163 | 518 | 87 | 57 | 3 | 0 | 110 | 6 | 149 | 1,132 |
| (6) 4,000–4,999 | 3 | 0 | 12 | 54 | 159 | 338 | 135 | 3 | 3 | 60 | 0 | 92 | 859 |
| (7) 5,000–7,499 | 0 | 0 | 6 | 12 | 42 | 74 | 334 | 53 | 28 | 133 | 0 | 137 | 821 |
| (8) 7,500–9,999 | 0 | 6 | 3 | 3 | 6 | 4 | 64 | 115 | 40 | 37 | 0 | 39 | 317 |
| (9) 10,000 and over | 0 | 0 | 0 | 0 | 3 | 0 | 14 | 12 | 91 | 43 | 0 | 23 | 186 |
| (10) Income not ascertained | 3 | 42 | 66 | 53 | 63 | 36 | 54 | 7 | 42 | 81 | 3 | 405 | 855 |
| (11) Different weights in the two surveys[a] | 0 | 24 | 30 | 3 | 12 | 12 | 6 | 0 | 0 | 9 | 0 | 0 | 96 |
| Unmatched units: | | | | | | | | | | | | | |
| (12) Not covered in CQC | 9 | 145 | 169 | 188 | 118 | 74 | 128 | 34 | 9 | 330 | 0 | 0 | 1,204 |
| Total | 39 | 699 | 929 | 1,075 | 1,177 | 672 | 827 | 236 | 216 | 1,098 | 81 | 1,626 | 8,679 |

[a] These are units in open-country segments in which farmers were sampled at twice the rate of nonfarmers. In each survey, farm status was assigned a unit when most of the total income was farm income. Thus, the same unit was assigned a different weight in each survey, if more than half the reported income was farm income in one survey and nonfarm income in the other survey

Note: Units, that is, families and unrelated persons, are weighted to a least common denominator level to adjust for oversampling of high-income units and farm units.

six differences in the way the two field surveys carried out the sample design. The accompanying tabulation shows what the six differences were and their relative importance.

| Survey Differences | Units Covered in Both Surveys (number) | (per cent) |
|---|---|---|
| Total units [a] | 8,679 | 100.0 |
| Unmatched | –2,830 | 32.6 |
| | 5,849 | |
| Differently weighted | – 177 | 2.0 |
| | 5,672 | |
| No income report in one or both | –1,125 | 12.9 |
| | 4,547 | |
| Differed in number of adults | – 250 | 2.9 |
| | 4,297 | |
| Differed in number of income recipients | – 987 | 11.4 |
| | 3,310 | |
| Not first quality respondent in one or both | – 898 | 10.3 |
| | 2,412 | |
| Units affected by survey differences | 6,186 | 72.1 |
| Units unaffected by survey differences | 2,412 [b] | 27.9 |

[a] Weighted sample size, the actual sample size is 2,201.
[b] The actual number of units is 619.

The effect of each difference will be determined by analysis of the income size distributions of the SCF and CQC units representing the source of difference. Thus the effect of differences in the coverage of units will be studied by an analysis of the income size distributions of the unmatched SCF and CQC units. The effect of other differences will be analyzed successively in the order listed above. The units covered in the analysis of each reason for difference will be eliminated from the subsequent analysis. Consequently, on completion of the analyses contained in this section of the report, the only units not eliminated are those unaffected by the differences between the SCF and CQC considered here, that is, matched units, selected at the same rate in both surveys, for which total income was ascertained in both, and in which the same adults were covered, the same income recipients were reported, and best-quality respondents were interviewed in both.

## DIFFERENCES IN COVERAGE, IN SAMPLING RATE, AND IN NONRESPONSE RATE

### *Unmatched Units*

A weighted total of 8,598 families and unrelated persons (actual sample size, 2,201) was covered by the SCF and CQC.[4] Of these,

[4] Assuming that the matched units sampled at different rates in the two surveys are given the SCF weights.

2,827, or about one-third, were not matched. (This should not be interpreted as one-third of the United States population, since non-matches could be counted as two separate units, but matched units as only one.) The total unmatched units consist of 1,204 SCF units not matched with CQC units and 1,626 CQC units not matched with SQF units. The surplus of CQC units represents about 5 per cent of the units covered in both surveys or about 15 per cent of the unmatched units.

It is not surprising that more units were covered in the CQC than in the SCF. A major CQC objective was to evaluate the coverage of population in the 1950 census, as it had been for the PES, and the enumerators were specifically trained and the questionnaires designed with this goal in mind. Consequently, in the resurvey, a separate coverage questionnaire was completed for each dwelling unit and several pages of questions were included to ensure that sample dwelling units were listed and resident persons were enumerated. There was no equivalent to this coverage questionnaire and coverage questions in the SCF. In the tabulation unmatched income units are distributed by population size of the city of residence.

| CITY SIZE | TOTAL UNITS | UNMATCHED UNITS Covered in: SCF | CQC | PERCENTAGE OF UNITS Un-matched | CQC Surplus |
|---|---|---|---|---|---|
| Total | 8,598 | 1,204 | 1,626 | 32.9 | 4.9 |
| Metropolitan areas [a] | 2,329 | 247 | 323 | 24.5 | 3.3 |
| 50,000 and over | 1,452 | 175 | 329 | 34.7 | 10.6 |
| 2,500–50,000 | 1,852 | 208 | 282 | 26.4 | 4.0 |
| Under 2,500 | 1,376 | 263 | 275 | 39.1 | 0.9 |
| Open-country areas | 1,589 | 311 | 417 | 45.7 | 6.7 |

[a] Urban, suburban, and rural areas surrounding the twelve largest cities in the United States.

Errors in identifying the sample dwelling units probably contributed substantially to the number of unmatched income units. In general, there is a negative correlation between the percentage of unmatched income units and city size. For example, the percentage of unmatched units is about 25 per cent in metropolitan areas and about 46 per cent in open-country areas, where the proportion of unmatched units is about one and a half times greater than in all places where individual sample dwelling units were prelisted.[5]

More income units were always covered in the CQC than in the SCF, but there is no apparent correlation between the percentage surplus of CQC units and city size. Thus the excess of CQC units represents about 7 per cent and 11 per cent of the units covered

[5] The technical problem of matching is more difficult for units in open-country segments. For these one must match not only all the income units at a particular address but also all the dwelling units in a particular segment (about four to eight per segment on the average in this study).

by both surveys in open-country areas and in cities of 50,000 or more, respectively, and ranges between 1 and 4 per cent elsewhere.

In some cases unmatched units were apparently missed in one of the surveys. Many of these units were located in cities of 50,000 and over, which largely explains why this city size has so high a proportion of unmatched units and so large an excess of CQC units. The evidence that the units were missed is that in each case one survey (1) covered more families and unrelated persons in a dwelling unit in which one or more other family units were matched, or (2) detected more occupied dwelling units in a multiple-dwelling-unit structure in which family units in other dwelling units in the same building were matched, or (3) covered family units in a well identified dwelling unit reported vacant in the other survey. Almost all the 368 income units identified as presumably missed were located in urban areas and were missed in the SCF. They account for nearly all the excess of units covered by CQC in nonrural areas. The table shows the unmatched income units distributed by size of total income reported in each survey.

| INCOME CLASS | UNITS COVERED IN SCF ONLY | | UNITS COVERED IN CQC ONLY | | |
|---|---|---|---|---|---|
| | *Total* | *Others* [a] | *Total* | *Missed in* SCF | *Others* |
| | | | *(number)* | | |
| Weighted sample size | 1,204 | 1,162 | 1,626 | 326 | 1,300 |
| Units with income not ascertained | 330 | 330 | 405 | 27 | 378 |
| | | | *(per cent)* | | |
| Income class: | | | | | |
| Total | 100.0 | 100.0 | 100.0 | 100.0 | 100.0 |
| Loss | 0.9 | 0.9 | 0.7 | 0 | 0.8 |
| 0–$ 999 | 15.3 | 15.1 | 17.6 | 27.6 | 15.1 |
| $ 1,000– 1,999 | 18.4 | 17.2 | 19.7 | 16.0 | 20.7 |
| 2,000– 2,999 | 20.6 | 20.3 | 22.3 | 26.7 | 21.2 |
| 3,000– 3,999 | 15.4 | 15.9 | 13.5 | 14.1 | 13.3 |
| 4,000– 4,999 | 9.2 | 9.6 | 8.9 | 8.0 | 9.2 |
| 5,000– 7,999 | 14.6 | 15.1 | 11.6 | 7.1 | 12.7 |
| 7,500– 9,999 | 3.8 | 4.0 | 3.6 | 0 | 4.5 |
| 10,000 and over | 1.8 | 1.9 | 2.2 | 0.6 | 2.5 |
| | | | *(dollars)* | | |
| Median | 2,750 | 2,826 | 2,539 | 2,241 | 2,633 |

[a] There were only 42 units in the weighted sample that were presumably missed in the CQC though covered in the SCF, too few to compute a percentage distribution.

In each survey, the unmatched units are lower-income units, on the average, than the matched units (see Table 2, below). Thus, the median income of matched units is greater than the median income of unmatched units by about $500 in the SCF and by about $675 in the CQC. Also, as might be expected, there is closer agreement between the surveys in the income distributions of matched units than of unmatched units. For example, the median income of the matched units is almost the same in both surveys, but the median income of the unmatched units is over $200 greater in the SCF than in the CQC.

Why is the median income greater for units covered in the SCF only than for units covered in the CQC only? The income distribution of units presumably missed in the SCF provides a clue. These units report less income, on the average, than other unmatched units. That is, the SCF tends to miss a group comprising about 5 per cent of the population whose average income is lower than that of the population as a whole.

### *Units Sampled at Different Rates*

Income units in which farm income comprised at least one-half the total income were oversampled in the SCF. This was accomplished in the following manner. In the SCF, open-country segments were selected at twice the basic sampling rate; in one half all income units were counted, in the other half only farm income units were counted.[6] To compensate, the income reports of farm units were weighted three times and the income reports of nonfarm units, six times. As a result, a matched unit in a farm segment reporting farm income as over half of total income in one survey and as less than half in the other survey did not have the same weighting in both.

The SCF method of oversampling farm units increased somewhat the divergence between the SCF and CQC distributions of total income. Based on the actual weights assigned in each survey, the median income of these units is $854 greater in the SCF than in the CQC. If the units had been sampled at the SCF rate in both surveys, the SCF median would have been $765 higher, if at the CQC rate in both, only $223 higher.

### *Units with Income Not Ascertained*

Income was not ascertained for a higher proportion of matched units in the SCF (16 per cent) than in the CQC (11 per cent). CQC

[6] The procedures for selecting the farm units in open-country segments were somewhat different in the SCF and in the CQC. The SCF enumerators asked a few questions to find out which were farm units, not recording the answers, and then asked the farm income questions only of the farm units. In the CQC, all units were interviewed using the same questionnaire, and the farm units were identified when the schedules were edited. The unmatched CQC nonfarm units in open-country segments were excluded entirely from the study. The matched CQC nonfarm units in these segments were used in some of the following analyses but were assigned a weight of zero in the CQC income distributions.

units in open-country segments were matched with 1950 census enumerations, and, if there was no CQC income report but there was a census income report, it was substituted. However, this use of census reports probably did not materially increase the CQC income response rate.

Reports on total income are missing in either or in both surveys for a weighted total of 1,125 matched units sampled uniformly in both surveys, representing about 69 per cent (SCF) and 53 per cent (CQC) of all units without income reports. Of the 1,125 units, 678 had only a CQC report, 366 only a SCF report, and 81 had no report in either. In the accompanying table, units without total income reports in one survey are distributed by the total income reported in the other. These distributions show a higher percentage of units in the upper-income classes, particularly in the $10,000-and-over class, than distributions of units for which total income was ascertained in both surveys. The median income of units with total income reported only to the CQC is about $100 higher than that of units with total income reported only to the SCF, although the $10,000-and-over class in the SCF is proportionately about twice the size of the same class in the CQC.

| INCOME CLASS | UNITS WITH ONLY SCF INCOME *Total* | UNITS WITH ONLY SCF INCOME *Partial* CQC *Interview* [a] | UNITS WITH ONLY CQC INCOME *Total* | UNITS WITH ONLY CQC INCOME SCF *Non-interview* [b] |
|---|---|---|---|---|
| | | *(number)* | | |
| Weighted sample size | 366 | 305 | 678 | 624 |
| | | *(per cent)* | | |
| Income class: | | | | |
| Total | 100.0 | 100.0 | 100.0 | 100.0 |
| Loss | 0.8 | 1.0 | 0 | 0 |
| 0–$ 999 | 11.5 | 12.8 | 15.2 | 16.0 |
| $ 1,000– 1,999 | 18.0 | 19.7 | 10.5 | 10.4 |
| 2,000– 2,999 | 14.5 | 17.4 | 17.8 | 15.5 |
| 3,000– 3,999 | 17.2 | 15.7 | 16.2 | 17.1 |
| 4,000– 4,999 | 9.8 | 9.8 | 8.8 | 9.0 |
| 5,000– 7,499 | 14.8 | 9.5 | 19.6 | 19.7 |
| 7,500– 9,999 | 1.9 | 0.3 | 5.5 | 5.9 |
| 10,000 and over | 11.5 | 13.8 | 6.3 | 6.2 |
| | | *(dollars)* | | |
| Median | 3,302 | 2,948 | 3,400 | 3,474 |

[a] The sample size of noninterviews in the CQC (61) is too small to compute a percentage distribution.

[b] The sample size of partial interviews in the SCF (54) is too small to compute a percentage distribution.

SCF noninterviews—the income informant was missed or refused to answer—account for about 92 per cent of the matched units without SCF total income reports. Partial interviews—the interview was begun but total income was not recorded—accounted for about 83 per cent of the missing income reports in the CQC. The distributions show that while the noninterviewed represented a higher-income group on the whole, a higher proportion of the partially interviewed were in the $10,000-and-over class. Apparently the CQC enumerators were more successful in initiating interviews, but the SCF enumerators were more successful in obtaining the income for the unit once the interview had been initiated.

### DIFFERENCES IN COVERAGE OF ADULTS, OF INCOME RECIPIENTS, AND IN QUALITY OF RESPONDENT

After eliminating the differing units discussed in the three previous subsections, 4,547 units remain (actual sample size, 1,148). They represent matched families and unrelated persons, sampled at the same rate, for which total income was ascertained in both surveys—the units cross-tabulated by size of total income in columns 1 to 9 and lines 1 to 9 of Table 1. In the following sections the questions to be answered are whether a higher or lower percentage of units would have reported income in the same class in both surveys and whether the SCF and CQC income size distributions would have been more similar if all the units had shown the same number of adults and income recipients and if only first quality respondents had been interviewed. The procedure of a step-by-step elimination of units differing in these respects will be used again.

#### *Units Differing in Number of Adults*

Among the 4,547 units, there are 250 families in which a different number of adults (persons eighteen years of age or older) were covered.[7] In 174 more adults were covered in the CQC, and in 76, more in the SCF.

Differences in the rules for assigning place of residence in the two surveys do not explain why proportionately more units with more adults were covered in the CQC than in the SCF. With one exception, the rules were almost the same in both surveys. The exception was that to determine the place of residence of college students not enumerated at home, the home address was chosen as the place of residence in the SCF; the college address, in the CQC. But this difference favored the enumeration of larger families in the SCF rather than in the CQC.

A more likely explanation is the greater emphasis given to ques-

[7] If the SCF and CQC differed on the number of adults in a family, the units were not considered matched unless there was exceptional agreement on other items.

tions of coverage in the CQC than in the SCF. For example, the CQC enumerator listed the members of the dwelling unit and then asked several questions to make sure that no persons had been missed; for example, they asked whether there were any persons away traveling or visiting friends or relatives. The SCF enumerators also listed the members of the dwelling unit, but they did not ask specifically about who might have been missed.

The median income of the 250 families in which a different number of adults was covered in the two surveys is $3,772 in the SCF, $4,622 in the CQC. About two-thirds (67.6 per cent) did not report total income in the same income class in both surveys. About 42 per cent reported income in a higher class in the CQC than in the SCF; the corresponding percentage for the SCF is 21.6. For all the units, about 25 per cent reported income one class higher in one survey or the other, 42 per cent one or more classes higher, and 17 per cent two or more classes higher.

There is strong evidence that the adults covered in one survey but missed in the other had substantial incomes. Among units in which more adults were covered in the SCF, about 68 per cent reported income in a higher bracket in the SCF and none reported income in a higher bracket in the CQC. The corresponding percentages for the CQC are 60.4 and 6.8. Moreover, of these units, about 32 per cent reported income more than one bracket higher in the SCF and about 40 per cent more than one bracket higher in the CQC.

The matched families in which a different number of adults were covered in the two surveys are shown in the accompanying distribution according to their total incomes. The median CQC income is

| INCOME CLASS | TOTAL | | MORE ADULTS IN SCF | | MORE ADULTS IN CQC | |
|---|---|---|---|---|---|---|
| | SCF | CQC | SCF | CQC | SCF | CQC |
| | | | *(number)* | | | |
| Weighted sample size | 250 | 250 | 76 | 76 | 174 | 174 |
| | | | *(per cent)* | | | |
| Income class: | | | | | | |
| Total | 100.0 | 100.0 | 100.0 | 100.0 | 100.0 | 100.0 |
| Loss | 0 | 0 | 0 | 0 | 0 | 0 |
| 0–$ 999 | 7.2 | 12.0 | 0 | 27.6 | 10.3 | 5.2 |
| $ 1,000– 1,999 | 12.0 | 10.8 | 15.8 | 15.8 | 10.3 | 8.6 |
| 2,000– 2,999 | 13.2 | 5.2 | 11.8 | 9.2 | 13.8 | 3.4 |
| 3,000– 3,999 | 22.8 | 10.8 | 11.8 | 7.9 | 27.6 | 12.1 |
| 4,000– 4,999 | 13.6 | 18.0 | 17.1 | 7.9 | 12.1 | 22.4 |
| 5,000– 7,499 | 15.6 | 21.6 | 15.8 | 15.8 | 15.5 | 24.1 |
| 7,500– 9,999 | 9.6 | 13.2 | 19.8 | 7.9 | 5.2 | 15.5 |
| 10,000 and over | 6.0 | 8.4 | 7.9 | 7.9 | 5.2 | 8.6 |
| | | | *(dollars)* | | | |
| Median | 3,772 | 4,622 | 4,620 | 2,717 | 3,565 | 4,924 |

$1,359 greater than the median SCF income for families in which CQC shows more adults; the median SCF income is $1,903 greater than the median CQC income for families in which the SCF shows more adults. But since there are more than twice as many units in which more adults are shown in the CQC than units with more adults in the SCF, the CQC median income of all units in which the number of adults differ is $1,050 higher than the SCF median for the same units.

*Units Differing in Number of Income Recipients*

After the elimination of families in which a different number of adults were covered in the two surveys, 4,297 matched units are left. In 987 of these the surveys differ on the number of income recipients in the unit, although the identical persons seem to have been included in both surveys in almost all of the units. Consequently the difference in the number of income recipients represents a reporting rather than a coverage difference between the surveys.

Of the 987 units, more than twice as many show more income recipients in the CQC (689) than in the SCF (298). The difference between the interviewing units used in the two surveys may help to explain the greater number of income recipients in the CQC. The basic interviewing unit in the SCF was the spending unit, comprising adults and their dependents in a family receiving $10 per week or more income who pooled their incomes. On the other hand, the individual was the basic unit in the CQC. This difference in the basic unit is reflected in the difference in the type of questionnaire used; a separate questionnaire was completed for each spending unit in the SCF and for each member of the family in the CQC. It seems reasonable to suppose that the CQC interviewing procedure would be likely to detect more income recipients, particularly secondary income recipients, than the SCF procedure.

About 43.5 per cent of the units differing in the number of income recipients shown reported income in a different income class in the two surveys, but the proportion of units reporting more income was about the same in both—about 21.4 per cent in the SCF and 21.9 per cent in the CQC. However, the median income of all 987 units is $3,246 (SCF income) or $3,374 (CQC income).

Unlike the missing adults, persons covered in both surveys but reporting income in only one apparently did not have large incomes. Consequently almost two-thirds of the units with more income recipients either in the SCF or in the CQC reported income in the same income bracket in both surveys. Relatively few reported income more than one income class higher in one survey than in the other.

Of the units with more income recipients in the SCF, 23 and 15 per cent, respectively, reported income one bracket, and more than one bracket, higher in the SCF; and about 4 and 1 per cent, respectively, in higher brackets in the CQC. The corresponding percentages for the CQC units with more income recipients are 20 and 10 per cent (higher CQC income) and about 11 and 4 per cent (higher SCF income).

The matched units in which a different number of income recipients were reported in both surveys are distributed by total income in the accompanying table. The median income of the units in which there are more SCF income recipients is $829 higher in the SCF than in the CQC; the median income of the units in which there are more CQC income recipients is $350 higher in the CQC than in the SCF. Nevertheless, the median income of all units in which a different number of income recipients were reported is $128 higher in the CQC because more than twice as many units reported more income recipients in the CQC than in the SCF.

| INCOME CLASS | TOTAL | | MORE INCOME RECIPIENTS IN SCF | | MORE INCOME RECIPIENTS IN CQC | |
|---|---|---|---|---|---|---|
| | SCF | CQC | SCF | CQC | SCF | CQC |
| | | | *(number)* | | | |
| Weighted sample size | 987 | 987 | 298 | 298 | 689 | 689 |
| | | | *(per cent)* | | | |
| Income class: | | | | | | |
| Total | 100.0 | 100.0 | 100.0 | 100.0 | 100.0 | 100.0 |
| Loss | 0.3 | 1.9 | 1.0 | 6.4 | 0 | 0 |
| 0–$ 999 | 15.0 | 15.1 | 31.2 | 38.9 | 8.0 | 4.6 |
| $ 1,000– 1,999 | 11.9 | 11.9 | 16.1 | 15.1 | 10.0 | 10.4 |
| 2,000– 2,999 | 17.0 | 13.7 | 12.1 | 10.1 | 19.1 | 15.2 |
| 3,000– 3,999 | 23.7 | 20.2 | 11.1 | 9.1 | 29.2 | 25.0 |
| 4,000– 4,999 | 9.6 | 18.5 | 8.1 | 8.0 | 10.3 | 23.1 |
| 5,000– 7,499 | 15.5 | 10.3 | 11.4 | 6.7 | 17.3 | 11.9 |
| 7,500– 9,999 | 4.5 | 6.3 | 6.7 | 4.0 | 3.5 | 7.3 |
| 10,000 and over | 2.5 | 2.2 | 2.3 | 1.7 | 2.6 | 2.5 |
| | | | *(dollars)* | | | |
| Median | 3,246 | 3,374 | 2,140 | 1,311 | 3,442 | 3,792 |

### *Units in Which First-Quality Respondents Were Not Interviewed*

Of the 3,310 weighted sample units remaining after deducting units that differed in the number of income recipients in the two surveys, best-quality respondents were not interviewed in about 24 per cent of the SCF units and in about 13 per cent of the CQC units. There are 898 units in which the respondents were not first quality in either one or both surveys, 457 in the SCF, 119 in the CQC, and 322 in neither.

A stricter definition of first-quality respondent was applied in the CQC than in the SCF. Thus a family was considered to have a first-quality respondent in the SCF if the head of the spending unit answered for the whole unit but in the CQC only if all income recipients answered for themselves. Hence the actual disparity between the surveys in the percentage of units with best-quality respondents may favor the CQC even more than the figures indicate. The differences between the surveys both in the questionnaires and in the instructions given the enumerators probably account for the higher rate of first-quality correspondents in the CQC than in the SCF (for example, the difference in the basic income unit used noted in the previous subsection).

About 47 per cent of the units in which at least one of the respondents was not first quality reported income in different income brackets in the two surveys, and a net of about 10 per cent reported income in a higher bracket in the SCF. The median income of these units is $3,379 in the SCF and $3,267 in the CQC, or $112 higher in the SCF.

The percentages of units in which first-quality respondents were not interviewed in one or both surveys are shown in the accompanying table according to the survey in which income was reported in a higher bracket. The extent of agreement of income reports appears to be greater for units in which first-quality respondents were not interviewed in both surveys than for units in which they were

| INCOME CLASS [a] | FIRST-QUALITY RESPONDENT *In* SCF *Only* | *In* CQC *Only* | *In Neither* | TOTAL ALL UNITS WITH OTHER THAN FIRST-QUALITY RESPONDENTS | FIRST-QUALITY RESPONDENT IN BOTH SURVEYS |
|---|---|---|---|---|---|
| | | | (*number*) | | |
| Weighted sample size | 119 | 457 | 322 | 898 | 2,412 |
| | | | (*per cent*) | | |
| Total | 100.0 | 100.0 | 100.0 | 100.0 | 100.0 |
| Same class | 53.8 | 48.4 | 60.4 | 53.3 | 62.6 |
| Different class | 46.2 | 51.6 | 39.6 | 46.7 | 37.4 |
| Higher class in SCF | 30.2 | 29.5 | 25.7 | 28.3 | 20.8 |
| One higher | 25.2 | 23.6 | 16.4 | 21.3 | 16.1 |
| More than one higher | 5.0 | 5.9 | 9.3 | 7.0 | 4.7 |
| Higher class in CQC | 16.0 | 22.1 | 13.9 | 18.4 | 16.6 |
| One higher | 13.5 | 19.9 | 10.2 | 15.6 | 13.9 |
| More than one higher | 2.5 | 2.2 | 3.7 | 2.8 | 2.7 |
| Net surplus in SCF | 14.2 | 7.4 | 11.8 | 9.9 | 4.2 |

[a] The income classes are those shown in previous tables.

interviewed in only one. Thus about 60 per cent of the units in which first-quality respondents were interviewed in neither reported income in the same bracket in both compared to 54 and 48 per cent, respectively, in which they were interviewed in the SCF only or in the CQC only.

However, as the table indicates, the SCF and CQC income distributions are in closest agreement for units in which first-quality respondents were interviewed in both surveys, although there are still substantial differences—37.4 per cent reported income in a different income bracket in the two surveys and a net surplus of 4.2 per cent reported income in a higher bracket in the SCF than in the CQC. The distribution of the units in which there were not first-quality correspondents is shown in another tabulation according to the SCF and CQC reported income. The agreement is not so close as it is for the units in which first-quality respondents were interviewed in both surveys (see Table 2, below). However the median incomes of the latter are lower. The likely explanation is that a smaller percentage of first-quality respondents are interviewed in high-income than in low-income units.

| INCOME | NOT FIRST QUALITY RESPONDENT IN ONE OR BOTH SURVEYS | |
|---|---|---|
| | SCF | CQC |
| | *(number)* | |
| Weighted sample size | 898 | 898 |
| Income class: | *(per cent)* | |
| Total | 100.0 | 100.0 |
| Loss | 1.3 | 0 |
| 0–$ 999 | 4.7 | 6.7 |
| $ 1,000– 1,999 | 12.5 | 17.5 |
| 2,000– 2,999 | 24.1 | 21.0 |
| 3,000– 3,999 | 19.5 | 18.0 |
| 4,000– 4,999 | 16.7 | 17.5 |
| 5,000– 7,499 | 12.4 | 13.3 |
| 7,500– 9,999 | 5.7 | 3.5 |
| 10,000 and over | 3.2 | 2.6 |
| | *(dollars)* | |
| Median | 3,379 | 3,267 |

SUMMARY AND CONCLUSIONS

On the basis of the six factors just considered, the CQC did a better job than the SCF did in carrying out the survey in the field. Working from the same list of addresses and open country segments, the CQC enumerators found more families and unrelated individuals, more adults per family, more income receivers per family, and more first-quality respondents. How did the differences in the two surveys affect the income size distributions? Table 2 gives the percentage distributions at three stages—before any units were eliminated, after only the unmatched units were eliminated, and the units that remain at the end of all the eliminations, that is, those unaffected by any of the six differences.

TABLE 2

Effect on SCF and CQC Income Distributions of Elimination of Units for the Six Differences

| | *All Units* | | *After Eliminating Unmatched Units* | | *Units Unaffected by Differences* [a] | |
|---|---|---|---|---|---|---|
| INCOME CLASS | SCF | CQC | SCF | CQC | SCF | CQC |
| | | | *(number)* | | | |
| Weighted sample size: [b] | | | | | | |
| Total | 8,679 | | 5,849 | | 2,412 | |
| Each survey | 6,972 | 7,379 | 5,768 | 5,753 | 2,412 | 2,412 |
| | | | *(per cent)* | | | |
| Income class: | | | | | | |
| Total | 100.0 | 100.0 | 100.0 | 100.0 | 100.0 | 100.0 |
| Loss | 0.7 | 0.5 | 0.6 | 0.5 | 0.5 | 0.3 |
| 0–$ 999 | 11.9 | 14.1 | 11.2 | 13.1 | 11.6 | 12.8 |
| $ 1,000– 1,999 | 15.8 | 15.8 | 15.3 | 14.7 | 16.8 | 16.0 |
| 2,000– 2,999 | 18.4 | 18.7 | 17.9 | 17.7 | 17.3 | 19.2 |
| 3,000– 3,999 | 20.0 | 17.4 | 21.0 | 18.4 | 21.5 | 19.9 |
| 4,000– 4,999 | 11.4 | 13.2 | 11.9 | 14.4 | 11.2 | 13.3 |
| 5,000– 7,499 | 14.1 | 12.6 | 14.0 | 12.9 | 13.9 | 11.4 |
| 7,500– 9,999 | 4.0 | 4.9 | 4.1 | 5.2 | 3.2 | 4.8 |
| 10,000 and over | 3.7 | 2.8 | 4.1 | 3.0 | 4.0 | 2.3 |
| Percentage reporting income in same class | 30 | | 45 | | 63 | |
| | | | *(dollars)* | | | |
| Median | 3,162 | 3,047 | 3,238 | 3,214 | 3,177 | 3,085 |
| Excess of SCF over CQC | 115 | | 24 | | 92 | |

[a] That is, matched units, sampled at the same rate, in which both surveys had reports on total income, identified the same adults and income receivers, and interviewed first-quality respondents.

[b] The units are weighted to a least common denominator level to adjust for over-sampling of high-income and farm units. The actual sample size of all units is 2,201; 1,804 in the SCF and 1,928 in the CQC. The remainder, the units unaffected by the differences, is actually 619 units. In the first two sets of distributions the units for which income was not ascertained are distributed proportionately.

On the average, the CQC found 5 per cent more families and unrelated individuals than the SCF did. The excess of CQC units was greatest for large, but not metropolitan, areas (11 per cent) and open-country areas (7 per cent), and least for towns under 2,500 and metropolitan areas. Since units in the areas where the CQC excess was greatest tended to have lower incomes than the average for all areas, this excess lowered the CQC income distribution relative to the SCF one.

Nonmatched units constitute 17 per cent of all units covered by the SCF, 22 per cent of all those covered by the CQC. Nonmatches are units covered in one survey for which almost identical units could not be found in the other survey under the matching rules, though some of the units were actually covered in both surveys. Families or individuals had moved and could not be found (probably 60 per cent of the SCF units, 45 per cent of the CQC units). Or they were living in the same place but were not interviewed in one of the surveys because they were not at home (SCF, about one-third; CQC, about one-quarter), or were missed (the CQC missed fewer). Or the composition of the families had changed substantially between the two survey dates, or the unit was inaccurately described in one of the surveys. (Particular units cannot be assigned to these categories.) The median income of the unmatched units is relatively low in both surveys, $2,750 for the SCF and $2,539 for the CQC.

The SCF and CQC distributions of families and unrelated persons are in closer agreement after eliminating unmatched units from the distributions, and at a generally higher level of income (Table 2). The percentage reporting incomes in the same class rises from 30 to 45 per cent and the median incomes are only $24 apart instead of $115.[8] Thereafter the elimination of units in open-country segments that were not sampled at the same rate and of matched units for which income was not ascertained in either or both surveys have a relatively small effect on the difference in the median income between the two surveys.

Among the matched units, the CQC was more successful than the SCF in obtaining complete income reports. Refusals to answer, respondents not at home or ill, language barriers, and so forth, account for not obtaining such reports in 11 per cent of the CQC units, in 16 per cent of the SCF units. Reports were obtained in the SCF for 53 per cent of the CQC units that lacked them; the median income of these units is $3,302, of which 11.5 per cent reported incomes of $10,000 or more. Similarly, for 69 per cent of the SCF units lacking reports, the CQC obtained them; the median income is $3,400. Only 6.3 per cent of these CQC units reported incomes $10,000 and over, proportionately about half as many as in the SCF group.

[8] The classes referred to throughout this summary are those shown in Table 2 and elsewhere in this section.

Apparently the income distributions would have been in closer agreement if the same units had been covered and sampled at the same rate in the two surveys. But they would have been in greater disagreement if income had been ascertained for all units in both surveys. A result of eliminating units for the three differences is to raise the median income in both (from $3,162 to $3,264 in the SCF and from $3,047 to $3,245 in the CQC).

The two surveys differed in the number of adults shown in a unit in about 3 to 4 per cent of the units remaining after the elimination of those affected by the first three factors. There is evidence that the adults missed had substantial incomes. The number of units differing in the number of income recipients is higher, about 13 to 14 per cent in both surveys. In this factor as in the other coverage factors, the CQC was more successful than the SCF. In 70 per cent of these units the CQC found more recipients, the SCF found more in only 30 per cent. Because it found more, the level of the CQC distribution was affected more than that of the SCF one. Units where the CQC reported a larger number have a higher median income ($3,800) than units where the SCF found a larger number ($2,140). However, supplementary income recipients uncovered by the SCF tended to add more income to the total received by the unit than did those uncovered by the CQC.

In 27 to 28 per cent of the units in both surveys (matched, and with the same number of adults and income recipients) first-quality respondents were not interviewed. Again the CQC was more successful than the SCF, accounting for 51 per cent of this group compared to 13 per cent for the SCF. In 36 per cent of cases neither survey interviewed first-quality respondents.

The percentage of persons reporting income in the same class in both surveys changes with the elimination of the various divergent units. Starting with 30 per cent for all the units covered in both surveys, eliminating the unmatched units raises this to 45 per cent. It falls to 42.8 per cent when units sampled at different rates are removed, rises to 57.2 per cent with the removal of units without reports on total income, and to 59.2, 60.1, and 62.6 per cent with the successive elimination of units differing in the number of adults, and income recipients, and lacking first-quality respondents. But while the elimination of the first three groups raises the median income in both surveys, the elimination of the last three lowers them in both. This is to be expected, since obviously in family units having several adults the chances are greater that differing numbers of adults or income recipients will be reported or that second-quality respondents will be interviewed than in single person units, so a higher proportion of the latter will be left. And single persons tend to have lower incomes than families.

If other factors had been constant, the evidence is that if the same number of adults had been covered in both surveys, the same number of income recipients had reported income, and all income recipients had reported for themselves in both surveys, the SCF and CQC income distributions would probably have been in greater disagreement than they are. But a larger percentage of the units would probably have reported total income in the same income class in both surveys.

All in all, the extent of agreement of the income size distributions in the two surveys was virtually unaffected by the differences arising from the six factors discussed so far. Both before and after eliminating the differing units the distribution based on the SCF reports shows a higher percentage in the upper-income classes than that based on the CQC reports, and a median income about $100 greater. This lack of change came about because better performance by the CQC than by the SCF did not consistently result in larger CQC income reports. The excess of units covered in the CQC and apparently missed in the SCF were below-average-income units. On the other hand, better performance by the CQC on the other criteria discussed resulted in larger income reports in the CQC than in the SCF for the same units, though not enough to remove the bias in the distributions shown by the difference in the medians.

Matched units with identical adults, income recipients, and first-quality respondents constituted about one third of all the CQC and SCF units; a weighted sample of 2,412 units, 619 actual units. Of this select group, 63 per cent reported total income in the same income class in both surveys, 93 per cent in the same or adjacent income classes. The next section of this paper is devoted to an analysis of how the two surveys compared in the reports of major sources of income by these units.

## *Reporting of Major Components of Income*

The examination of how differences between the two surveys in their questionnaires and interviewing situations affected their income reports will be based on the 619 actual units (weighted sample size 2,412) which were matched, sampled at the same rate in both surveys, and in which the same adults and income receivers were identified and first-quality respondents interviewed.[9] The vari-

[9] The SCF questionnaire is given in Appendix B of this paper, the CQC questionnaire, which was the one used in the PES, on page 237 of this volume.

ous forms of income pose widely differing reporting problems, and each will be considered in turn.

The elimination of various categories of unmatched and partially matched units reduced the weighted number of units to 33 per cent of the total CQC units and 35 per cent of the SCF total. As previously indicated, this group cannot be regarded as a random slice of the population. The inconclusive results of our examination of entrepreneurial incomes underlines again the need for the experiments on income reporting by farmers and businessmen. But we believe that for wages and salaries and the various minor sources of income, our 619 cases proved a large enough group to yield fairly firm conclusions on the direction, if not on the precise magnitude, of reporting differences.

### THE INTERVIEWING SITUATION

The "total interviewing situation" is a slippery subject, involving possibilities rather than firm conclusions. The most concrete difference between the surveys is that the SCF interview took place about one and one-half months, the CQC interview about nine months, after the close of the year for which income was being obtained. If people do tend to forget small items more readily than large ones, minor sources of income should be reported more fully in the SCF than in the CQC. This apparently was the case.

Also the attitudes of both interviewers and interviewed may be assumed as different in surveys conducted by private research organizations and governmental agencies. The private interviewers may have to work harder to establish rapport and thus obtain a more complete account of income; the governmental interviewers may receive more cooperation from the interviewed. We can only point out these possibilities. But they indicate the desirability of using the same interviewing corps both times in similar experiments.

All groups should proceed with such projects. For while general principles of questionnaire design may be established, differences in the relationship to respondents such as those encountered by the Bureau of the Census and the Survey Research Center may make modifications desirable. And although much pretesting of questionnaires has already been done, few results have been systematically reported to users of income distribution data.

### NUMBER OF COMPONENTS REPORTED

If wages and salaries, self-employment income, and all other forms of income taken together are considered as the three major income components, an average of 1.42 components was reported to the CQC and of 1.47 to the SCF by the 619 units. Wages and salaries accounted for almost all of the difference, as 76 per cent reported such income to the SCF and only 72 per cent to the CQC (Table 3). The amount of income reported by the additional recipient units tended to be small, so that the median wages and salary income is smaller for the group in the SCF than in the CQC. However for the 70 per cent reporting wages and salaries to both, the amounts reported tended to be larger in the SCF.

It is hard to interpret these results because the CQC asked each income recipient for a detailed job history, but the SCF asked each spending unit only three rather general questions. Possibly the dulling of recall by the passage of an extra seven months more than offset the presumed superiority of the more detailed questionnaire. Or the SCF question on work outside of regular employment may have been more effective than the CQC question on part-time work and odd jobs because the SCF question was one of three, while the single CQC question followed an extended series used to complete the job history. Furthermore, the CQC question appeared overleaf from the job history, and the interviewer had to turn the page to enter any part-time or odd jobs.

Although the discrepancies between the results of the two surveys for wages and salaries are puzzling, they are relatively small compared to the differences for other kinds of income. And the large proportion who reported wages and salaries in the same or adjoining income brackets (66 per cent) or who reported zero wages and salaries to both surveys indicates the stability of the data. Whether asking for a job history rather than for answers to a few questions is a more valid method or yields enough additional income data to be worth the cost is a question that should receive attention in the near future. The length of the period for which income is to be obtained is especially relevant in this connection.

### SELF-EMPLOYMENT INCOME

Self-employment income accounted for only a minor part of the net additional major income sources reported to the SCF. This result is not unexpected since a comparatively small proportion of the population are self-employed.

Reports to only one survey, or, if to both, discrepancies of more than one income class in the amount reported, were much more frequent for self-employment income than for wages and salaries. While 9.0 per cent of the units reported self-employment income in the same class in both surveys, 8.5 per cent reported such income

TABLE 3

Distribution of Similar Families and Unrelated Persons by Major Component of Income Reported to the SCF and CQC

*Income Size Distribution*

| INCOME CLASS [a] | *Wages and Salaries* | | *Self-employment Income* | | | | | | *"Other" Income* [b] | |
|---|---|---|---|---|---|---|---|---|---|---|
| | | | *Total* [c] | | *Farm* | | *Business* | | | |
| | SCF | CQC | SCF | CQC | SCF [d] | CQC | SCF | CQC | SCF | CQC |
| | | | | | *(per cent)* | | | | | |
| Total reporting | 100.0 | 100.0 | 99.2 | 99.2 | 99.6 | 99.6 | 99.2 | 99.2 | 100.5 | 100.5 |
| Amount not ascertained | 0.4 | [e] | 0.1 | [e] | 0.1 | 0.1 | [e] | 0.1 | [e] | [e] |
| Loss | 0 | 0 | 1.1 | 0.7 | 0.5 | 0.3 | 0.5 | 0.3 | 0 | 0 |
| None | 24.0 | 28.0 | 76.2 | 76.9 | 90.5 | 89.9 | 89.9 | 87.5 | 52.0 | 52.1 |
| Positive income | 75.6 | 72.0 [f] | 21.8 | 21.6 [f] | 8.5 | 9.3 [f] | 8.8 | 11.3 [f] | 48.5 | 48.4 [f] |
| Reporting positive income: | | | | | | | | | | |
| $ 1–$ 949 | 11.2 | 8.5 | 6.5 | 6.3 | 2.5 | 2.7 | 1.8 | 3.6 | 34.6 | 38.0 |
| 950– 1,949 | 11.8 | 12.6 | 5.0 | 4.8 | 2.3 | 2.6 | 1.7 | 2.1 | 9.6 | 7.8 |
| 1,950– 2,949 | 16.6 | 15.8 | 3.4 | 3.1 | 1.6 | 1.4 | 1.5 | 1.6 | 2.4 | 1.6 |
| 2,950– 3,949 | 13.2 | 10.6 | 2.5 | 2.5 | 1.0 | 1.3 | 1.3 | 1.1 | 0.6 | 0.5 |
| 3,950– 4,949 | 8.5 | 12.1 | 0.8 | 1.2 | 0.2 | 0.5 | 0.5 | 0.1 | 0.1 | [e] |
| 4,950– 7,449 | 10.3 | 8.5 | 1.7 | 2.3 | 0.5 | 0.7 | 1.0 | 1.7 | 0.8 | 0.4 |
| 7,450– 9,949 | 2.6 | 2.9 | 0.6 | 0.8 | 0.2 | [e] | 0.2 | 1.0 | | |
| 9,950– 14,949 | 1.1 | 0.5 | 1.1 | 0.2 | 0.3 | [e] | 0.5 | [e] | 0.4 | [e] |
| 14,950 and over | 0.3 | 0.3 | 0.2 | 0.4 | [e] | 0.1 | 0.2 | 0.1 | | |
| | | | | | *(dollars)* | | | | | |
| Median | 2,540 | 2,892 | 1,720 | 1,815 | 1,654 | 1,642 | 2,350 | 1,855 | 701 | 637 |

*Income Class Correspondence*

| INCOME CLASS [a] | *Wages and Salaries* | *Self-Employment Income* | | | *"Other" Income* [b] |
|---|---|---|---|---|---|
| | | *Total* [c] | *Farm* | *Business* | |
| | | | *(per cent)* | | |
| Total reporting | 100.0 | 99.2 | 99.6 | 99.2 | 100.5 |
| Zero income | 30.3 | 80.8 | 91.2 | 91.5 | 62.5 |
| To both | 21.7 | 72.3 | 89.2 | 85.9 | 41.6 |
| To SCF only | 2.3 | 3.9 | 1.3 | 4.0 | 10.5 |
| To CQC only | 6.3 | 4.6 | 0.7 | 1.6 | 10.4 |
| Income reported to both | 69.7 | 18.4 | 8.4 | 7.7 | 38.0 |
| Reporting income to both [g] | 69.1 | 17.1 | 7.6 | 7.1 | |
| Same class [h] | 45.0 | 9.0 [i] | 4.6 | 3.7 [j] | 31.3 |
| Different class | 24.1 | 8.1 | 3.0 | 3.4 | |
| Higher class in SCF | 12.7 | 4.6 | 1.6 | 1.6 | 4.8 |
| One higher | 11.2 | 2.6 | 0.8 [k] | 0.9 | 3.8 |
| More than one higher | 1.5 | 2.0 [i] | 0.8 [k] | 0.7 [j] | 1.0 |
| Higher class in CQC | 11.4 | 3.5 | 1.4 | 1.8 | 1.9 |
| One higher | 9.6 | 1.9 | 0.9 | 1.0 | 1.8 |
| More than one higher | 1.8 | 1.6 [i] | 0.5 [k] | 0.8 [j] | 0.1 |

[a] The income classes refer to the amount of each type of income reported, not to total income.

notes continued on next page

Notes to TABLE 3, continued

[b] "Other" income includes rental, dividend and royalty, interest, and transfer payment income, and all additional forms of income other than wages and salaries and self-employment income.

[c] Includes farm, business, professional, and similar self-employment income.

[d] Of farm operators only.

[e] No cases reported or less than 0.05 per cent.

[f] This figure includes units whose income was reported as "$10,000 and over," and therefore they cannot be distributed between the two highest classes shown below. These units constituted 0.2 per cent of those reporting wages and salaries, 0.1 per cent of those reporting "other" income, and either less than 0.05 per cent or none of those reporting income in the other categories.

[g] Excludes units in which the amount was not ascertained and the CQC "$10,000 and over" class.

[h] Based on the income classes shown in this table.

[i] Positive incomes only. In addition, 0.3 per cent reported negative incomes to both, 0.1 per cent negative incomes to the CQC and zero to the SCF, 0.3 per cent negative incomes to the CQC and positive to the SCF, and 0.8 per cent reported negative incomes to the SCF and positive incomes to the CQC.

[j] Positive incomes only. In addition, 0.2 per cent reported negative incomes to both, 0.1 per cent negative incomes to the CQC and zero to the SCF, 0.1 per cent negative income to the SCF and zero to the CQC, and 0.3 per cent negative incomes to the SCF and positive incomes to the CQC.

[k] Positive incomes only. In addition, the 0.5 per cent reporting losses to the SCF and the 0.3 per cent reporting losses to the CQC reported positive incomes to the other survey in all cases.

to only one survey and 3.6 per cent reported income differing by more than one class. Yet the difference in median self-employment income between the two surveys is only $95. An examination of farm and nonfarm self-employment income separately reveals both conceptual and procedural differences between the surveys.

### *Farm Income*

The SCF used two sets of farm income questions. If farm income was a minor source of income, the interviewer asked one question on net income; if a major source, an extended series of questions on cash expenses and cash receipts. (However, the list of expenses was not exhaustive; one obvious omission was property taxes.) In contrast, the CQC interviewer asked only for gross income and for income net of farm expenses but asked this of all units with farm income.

Secondly, the SCF procedure of an extended series of questions seemed better able to prevent certain types of capital expenditures from appearing as expenses than the CQC one. Expenditures on machinery, buildings, and so forth, were obtained specifically in a section devoted to savings. A conceptual difference between the surveys was that the SCF assigned the value of increases in livestock and in privately financed crop inventories to expenses, but the CQC asked that they be excluded from expenses, although it did not provide an explicit check.

The comparison of the farm income data from the two surveys is inconclusive because so few units were involved. The slight excess of units reporting farm incomes to the CQC in part reflects the SCF coding procedure, in which farm income obtained as a secondary source was not coded with farm income obtained from the extended series of questions. Comparison of the distributions indicates that the SCF one tends to be somewhat flatter. However the medians of the two distributions are quite close, a result consistent with the conceptual difference noted, since net income may be expected to vary less widely than net cash flow which excluded changes in inventories.

*Nonfarm Income*

For nonfarm self-employment income, the CQC obtained gross and net receipts by using the same questions described above for farm income, plus a question to find out whether the net income reported included "salary" and other cash withdrawals. If not, these were determined and added to net income.

The SCF used several questions to obtain nonfarm self-employment income. It distinguished between unincorporated business income and professional and other self-employment income which represents payment primarily for the work of persons, with capital playing a minor role. Owners of unincorporated business were asked for their net profit (or loss) and their withdrawals in the income section, and were also asked about the liquidation of all or part of a business in the savings schedule.

A priori, the SCF schedule seems superior to the CQC one on two counts. First, it picks up explicitly income from investments in unincorporated businesses that do not involve the self-employment of the investor. Such income would presumably be reported in answer to the clean-up question at the end of the CQC schedule, but it is not explicitly mentioned in the interview. Secondly, the SCF question on liquidation may have prevented some liquidation from being treated as income. However, it is an open question whether some respondents know enough about accounting to answer accurately this question or many others designed to elicit income as defined by economists.

The net incomes of professional persons and of others of the self-employed not classed as business owners were obtained by a single SCF question, which also obtained any incidental self-employment income, such as payments for work done in home workshops.

As in the case of the two kinds of farm income, the SCF did not combine the incomes of business owners with those of professional persons and others self-employed, so there is no complete, separate SCF coding of nonfarm self-employment income. Again the excess of units reporting such income to the CQC (Table 3) probably reflects this omission. The CQC median is lower than that of the SCF because the omitted SCF self-employment income presumably was dominated by part-time self-employment.

And again like the farm income, the data on nonfarm self-employment income are based on too small a sample to furnish anything except leads for further investigation. For this type of income alone the SCF reported incomes tended to run lower than the CQC incomes for the same units, reflecting perhaps the SCF questions on the net income estimate and a consequent elimination of liquidation proceeds from income.

*Total Self-Employment Income*

The distributions of total self-employment incomes include the SCF secondary farm incomes and nonfarm, nonbusiness self-employment incomes coded separately by the SCF. Probably as a result, the excess of CQC reports disappears. With the inclusion of these usually secondary incomes in the SCF distribution, the SCF median income ($1,720) falls below the CQC median ($1,815). The proportion of units reporting self-employment income to only one survey is as high as the proportion for wages and salaries even though the latter form of income is much more common.

Units reporting self-employment income to both surveys tended to report higher amounts to the SCF than to the CQC, in spite of the slight tendency for the SCF farm incomes to be higher and the SCF nonfarm business incomes to be lower than their CQC counterparts. The cause may be the addition of the income reports of the self-employed professional persons and other self-employed, who may have given gross rather than net incomes in answer to the one question on net income. And the many checks provided by the other financial questions may also have produced higher reports by this group in the SCF.

### "OTHER" INCOME

The findings on "other" income are more in line with received dogma. For the sum of four minor types of income—rents; interest, dividends, and royalties; proceeds from roomers and boarders; and public and private transfers—the SCF median ($701) was higher than the CQC one ($637). In each survey the percentage of units reporting other income to it alone is more than one-fifth of the total reporting other income. For units reporting such income in different classes in the two surveys, the SCF clearly obtained larger amounts.

Turning to the components of other income (Table 4), we find that the CQC obtained more and generally higher reported income from transfer payments, but the reverse was true for the other three components. These results were to be expected in view of the questionnaire design. The CQC devoted six questions to public and private transfer income; the SCF, only two. Similar questions were used in both surveys to obtain interest and other forms of property income, but the SCF also asked questions on ownership and on the value of the related assets in other sections of the questionnaire. This could be expected to improve the reporting of income.

In contrast to the distributions of income from major sources, in these distributions the survey with more units reporting income also had a higher median. This indicates that the extra incomes picked up were not much smaller than the incomes reported to both surveys, although of course all incomes of this sort are marginal for most income recipients.

Despite the indications that a better questionnaire design can improve the reporting of this type of income, the proportion reporting income to only one survey is uncomfortably large. For example, 12 per cent reported interest, dividend, or royalty income to the SCF, but another 4 per cent reported such income to the CQC only. This indicates that these minor forms of income are substantially understated by the surveys.

## SUMMARY AND CONCLUSIONS

Only about one-third of the SCF and CQC units (619) were involved in the comparison of income reporting in the two surveys. These were the matched units, sampled at the same rate, which had identical adults and income recipients and for which there were income reports based on the replies of first quality respondents.

The SCF was more successful than the CQC in obtaining reports of major sources of income; the average number of sources reported to the SCF was 1.47, to the CQC, 1.42. More frequent reports of wages and salaries in the SCF account for most of the difference —76 per cent for the SCF, 72 per cent for the CQC. Among those reporting wage and salary income to both surveys, reports of $7,450 or more occurred with equal frequency. However reports of wages and salaries of $9,950 or more were made almost half again as frequently to the SCF as to the CQC. The 6 per cent of the units that reported wage and salary income to the SCF but zero income to the CQC (the corresponding percentage for units reporting said income to the CQC but none to the SCF was 2) reported relatively small amounts of income on the average.

TABLE 4

Distribution of Similar Families and Unrelated Persons by Component of "Other" Income Reported to the SCF *and* CQC

*Income Size Distribution*

| INCOME CLASS [a] | *Income From Roomers and Boarders* SCF | CQC | *Rent From Property* SCF | CQC | *Interest, Dividends, and Royalties* SCF | CQC | *All Other Types* [b] SCF | CQC |
|---|---|---|---|---|---|---|---|---|
| | | | | *(per cent)* | | | | |
| Total reporting | 99.8 | 99.8 | 99.6 | 99.6 | 99.8 | 99.8 | 99.6 | 99.6 |
| Amount not ascertained | 0.1 | [c] | 0.1 | [c] | 0.3 | [c] | 0.2 | [c] |
| None | 96.0 | 97.5 | 88.3 | 90.8 | 87.7 | 91.5 | 67.6 | 65.7 |
| Positive income | 3.7 | 2.3 | 11.2 | 8.8 | 11.8 | 8.3 | 31.8 | 33.9 |
| Reporting positive income: | | | | | | | | |
| $ 1–$ 99 | 0.5 | 0.3 | 0.1 | 0.6 | 4.7 | 4.0 | 3.4 | 2.7 |
| 100– 499 | 2.7 | 1.3 | 5.9 | 6.2 | 3.7 | 2.1 | 14.2 | 16.5 |
| 500– 999 | 0.2 | 0.6 | 2.1 | 1.0 | 1.7 | 0.9 | 9.0 | 8.8 |
| 1,000– 1,999 | 0.1 | 0.1 | 1.2 | 0.4 | 1.2 | 1.0 | 4.9 | 5.4 |
| 2,000– 2,999 | 0 | 0 | 1.1 | 0.4 | 0.3 | 0.3 | 0.2 | 0.5 |
| 3,000– 4,999 | 0.2 | [c] | 0.5 | [c] | 0.2 | [c] | 0.1 | [c] |
| 5,000 and over | 0 | 0 | 0.3 | 0.2 | 0 | 0 | 0 | 0 |
| | | | | *(dollars)* | | | | |
| Median | [d] | [d] | 500 | 345 | 240 | 185 | 450 | 488 |

*Income Class Correspondence*

| INCOME CLASS | *Income from Roomers and Boarders* | *Rent from Property* | *Interest, Dividends, and Royalties* | *All Other Types* [a] |
|---|---|---|---|---|
| | | *(per cent)* | | |
| Total reporting | 99.8 | 99.6 | 99.8 | 99.6 |
| Zero income | | | | |
| To both | 94.8 | 85.4 | 83.6 | 60.9 |
| To SCF only | 1.2 | 2.9 | 4.1 | 6.7 |
| To CQC only | 2.7 | 5.4 | 7.9 | 4.8 |
| Income reported to both [e] | 1.1 | 5.9 | 4.2 | 27.2 |
| Reporting income to both | 1.1 | 5.8 | 4.2 | 27.0 |
| Same class [f] | 0.9 | 4.0 | 2.9 | 19.9 |
| Different class | 0.2 | 1.8 | 1.3 | 7.1 |
| Higher class in SCF | 0.2 | 1.6 | 0.8 | 2.5 |
| One higher | 0.2 | 1.1 | 0.6 | 2.2 |
| More than one higher | [b] | 0.5 | 0.2 | 0.3 |
| Higher class in CQC | | 0.2 | 0.5 | 4.6 |
| One higher | [c] | 0.1 | 0.4 | 3.7 |
| More than one higher | [c] | 0.1 | 0.1 | 0.9 |

[a] The income classes refer to the amount of each type of income reported, not to total income.
[b] Includes social security benefits, alimony, veterans pensions, and other forms of public and private transfer payments.
[c] No cases reported or less than 0.05 per cent.
[d] Too few cases for computation.
[e] Excludes units in which the amount of income was not ascertained.
[f] Based on income classes shown in this table.

The SCF–CQC differences in reports of farm and nonfarm self-employment income were larger in size than for any other type of income. Of those units reporting such income to both surveys 20 per cent reported amounts differing by more than one income class;[10] the comparable figure for wage and salary income is 5 per cent. Though the median self-employment income reported to the CQC ($1,815) was close to the SCF median ($1,720), twice as many units reported self-employment income of $9,950 or more to the SCF than to the CQC.

"Other" income—all income except wages, salaries, or self-employment income—was reported by 21 per cent of the units to one survey but not to the other. This 21 per cent was evenly divided between the two surveys. The units that reported such income to both surveys reported larger amounts to the SCF one and one-half times as often as to the CQC. Transfer payments alone, however, were reported a little more often to the CQC than to the SCF (34 versus 32 per cent). And when they were reported to both, a higher amount was reported almost twice as often to the CQC as to the SCF.

This examination of the reporting of types of income underscores the dependence of results on the techniques and definitions employed. More work is needed, especially on the reporting of entrepreneurial incomes where new techniques may be in order, unlike the reporting of wages, salaries, and the other nonbusiness, nonfarm incomes, where improvements involve more careful application of known principles. Since for some purposes the return from such efforts may not be worth the cost of the improvements, a clearer specification than any now available of the problems toward whose solution the data are to be used is necessary before a conclusion can be reached. A desire for improvement should not blind us to the usefulness at times of the short questionnaire, which yields quicker if less accurate results than a detailed schedule.

### *Improvement of Survey Techniques and of the Interpretation of Survey Data*

If an original purpose of the research described here is to be fulfilled, what we have learned must be used in the improvement of techniques by survey technicians and of interpretation of survey data by income analysts. The detailed findings have already been summarized. In brief, the CQC enumerators, working from the same list of addresses and open-country segments, found more families

[10] The income classes referred to are those shown in Table 3.

and unrelated individuals, more adults and income receivers per family, and more first-quality respondents than the SCF enumerators did. On the other hand, for the units unaffected by these differences, the SCF interviewers obtained reports of more sources of income and—for most types of income—a higher mean or median income. Both results are consistent with the known emphasis placed by the Census Bureau on enumeration and by the SCF on financial information.

## THE PROBLEM OF VALIDITY

Interpretation of the results confronts us with the problem of validity; we do not have "true" figures with which to compare them.[11] Lacking a valid benchmark, each individual will have to judge for himself what kinds of findings are most valid.

As to coverage, most people think that the more properly identified units, adults, or income receivers there are in a category, the more valid the result. They argue that an interviewer is more likely to find too few than to find too many. He may easily miss a janitor's quarters in an apartment house or an apartment above a garage; miss an adult, especially if enumeration is a small part of his activities; or miss an income receiver, especially if the income is small and a long interview appears necessary. He is less likely to make mistakes in the other direction and include in the sample too many families, adults, or income receivers because he has counted a dwelling unit as 1312 Main Street when in fact it is 1313 Main Street or counted as a member of the family an adult who resides elsewhere most of the time. Still, the common belief that the higher the number of unit, adults, and so forth, the more valid the result, is an assumption, not a tested conclusion.

Similarly, most people think that the higher the income reported, the more valid the report.[12] Here they have several supporting arguments. The income respondent may forget minor sources of income —money a hobby brought in or that his child made selling news-

[11] One could compare the SCF and CQC income reports with reports of total income obtained by the Internal Revenue Service (IRS) on tax returns and compare the wage and salary reports of less than $3,000 with data collected by the Bureau of Old-Age and Survivor's Insurance (OASI). But there are questions on the conceptual comparability and completeness of these reports. In view of these factors and the difficulty of analyzing three-way comparisons, a detailed analysis of this sort was not undertaken in this study. Comparisons of census data with IRS and OASI data are given elsewhere in this volume.

[12] Some evidence is available. Three-way comparisons of SCF, CQC, and IRS data show that in the $3,000–7,499 total income class, CQC total income reports correspond more closely to the IRS one than do the SCF reports; for incomes above $7,500, the SCF reports correspond more closely.

papers. Or he may understate his income because he thinks the survey organization will report the amount to the Internal Revenue Service. To the extent that a report shows higher income because either kind of understatement was avoided, it will be better. A different sort of argument is that since survey aggregates fail to come up to an adjusted personal income total, such as the one calculated by the Department of Commerce, any report that gives a higher income will be better because it will lessen the gap. But this argument applies to the validity of totals not of individual reports, which are our concern here.

On the other hand, a respondent may overstate his income because he forgets to subtract all business or farm expenses from entrepreneurial incomes or because he includes income of another period in "last year's income." Or the concept of the entrepreneurial income to be measured may differ from one survey to another; one survey wanting such income reported on a cash basis, the other on an accrual basis; one including, the other excluding, reinvested profits. If a report shows higher income for any of these reasons, it is less valid. In general, however, people accept as more valid the report with the higher income. Again, this is an assumption, not a tested conclusion.

## LESSONS FROM THE RESULTS

### *The Similarity of the Income Reports*

We have stressed the differences in the various results obtained by the two surveys. Indeed this was necessary since through analysis of the differences we can infer their cause. Yet in some respects the SCF and CQC results are remarkably parallel.

Under optimal coverage (the same unit, adults, income recipients, and first-quality respondents) 63 per cent of the units reported income in the same income class to both surveys, 93 per cent in either the same or an adjacent class. With less satisfactory coverage (the same unit but other conditions not controlled) the corresponding percentages were 57 and 89. Even the SCF and CQC income distributions based on *all* units covered by both surveys (including the 17 to 22 per cent of the units in each survey that were not covered in the other survey) correspond closely. And both these last distributions purport to represent the entire population. The medians are separated by only $115 and the largest difference in the cumulative percentage distributions is 2.3 percentage points. (Table 2 shows the distributions at the three stages.)

The reason for the similarity is that major sources of differences offset one another. First, the income of unmatched units was low on the average in both surveys. Since there were more unmatched units in the CQC than in the SCF, this factor has the effect of lowering the CQC income distribution relative to the SCF one. Another factor producing the same effect was the SCF's more complete coverage of sources of income and higher reported income for completely matched units. On the other hand, the CQC identified more income receivers and more adults and interviewed more first-quality respondents, factors which by and large have the opposite effect; they tend to raise the level of income in the CQC distribution.

The income analyst should be aware of the way one class of error may sometimes counterbalance another, as in this case. He should also be alert to the possibility that this may not always be true in survey comparisons.

*Coverage of Units*

As noted earlier, the SCF missed more units than the CQC did, and these missed units were concentrated in nonmetropolitan cities of 50,000 or more and in the open country. As a result of this finding, several new sampling procedures have been instituted in recent SCF samplings.

The most notable of these is the use of city directories as a source of sample addresses in medium-sized cities. Sample blocks are selected. Interviewers are then sent to each block to see what dwelling units the city directory enumerators may have missed. Finally separate selections of addresses are made from both those initially listed by the city directory and the additional addresses picked up by the SCF interviewers. The theory underlying this procedure is that any single enumerator will miss some dwelling units, perhaps 5 per cent. Different enumerators, however, will miss different dwelling units. To the extent that they do in fact miss different ones, the double listing reduces net misses.

A second innovation is the use, for small towns and open-country areas, of segments whose size is made smaller than before and carefully controlled. According to SCF procedures, interviews are to be taken from all units within a segment. Decreasing its size to an area containing five to seven dwelling units should make possible a more intensive scrutiny of the area for dwelling units, and thus fewer will be missed.

Between 1955 and 1956, presumably as a result of these changes, the relative coverage of the population by the SCF increased by 6 per cent. In 1955 the SCF sample (inflated) accounted for 89.5 per cent of the Current Population Survey's estimate of occupied dwelling units. In 1956 the comparable figure was 95.3 per cent. The reduction of missed units appears to have had the effect of shifting the income distribution downward from what it otherwise would have been.

*Noninterviews and Partial Interviews*

Before looking for applications of the findings of the present study, we will consider the frequency and treatment of noninterviews and partial interviews in the regular Current Population Surveys (CPS) and the annual SCFs. But first, we should point out that the CQC and the CPS differ greatly from each other. The CQC was a special survey in which selected enumerators and an extremely detailed demographic and income questionnaire were used. The CPS uses similar enumerative techniques but a relatively simple questionnaire containing four questions about income. Thus some of the generalizations from the SCF–CQC study cannot be properly applied to the interpretation of the CPS. This is not true of the SCF since data for one-half of the sample of the regular 1950 SCF were analyzed in this study.

In the 1954 CPS and SCF, noninterviews constituted 5 per cent (CPS) and 12 per cent (SCF) of the respective samples; partial interviews, 10 per cent (CPS) and 2 per cent (SCF). Both surveys take account of noninterviews by increasing the weights of sampling strata in which the noninterview rate is highest; decreasing the weights of those in which it is lowest. In the SCF this system of weighting leaves the income distribution almost unaltered though it has important consequences for the distribution of other variables (for example, car ownership). Presumably the effect of the weighting in the CPS is similar.

On the other hand, the CPS excludes partially interviewed units from the tabulations and makes no adjustment for them, on the implicit assumption that partially and completely interviewed units have the same mean income, the same income distribution. In the SCF, where this problem is small, partially interviewed units are assigned the mean income of units defined as "similar" on the basis of occupation, type of spending unit, place of residence, and holdings of liquid assets. The mean income assigned to these partially interviewed units is higher than the mean for those completely interviewed; consequently the income distribution of all the units is raised slightly.

In the SCF–CQC study the incomes of about 69 per cent of the units not interviewed in the SCF were reported to the CQC. If this 69 per cent are similar to units for which there is no report in either survey, then the entire group had a somewhat higher average income (by about $200) than the units whose interviews were completed. This implies that the SCF procedure for the units not interviewed results in some understatement of income.

The ratio of units not interviewed to those partially interviewed in the CQC (1 to 5) is so different from the corresponding ratio in the CPS (1 to 2) that it is doubtful whether the information obtained here can be properly applied to the CPS.

*Coverage within the Family*

The finding that the 1950 SCF was less successful than the CQC in identifying income recipients has already led to improvements in SCF techniques. An analysis showed that to obtain income reports from supplementary income recipients the interviewer had to ask a long series of somewhat ambiguous questions which generally yielded negative answers and which appeared unnecessary to the respondent. The questionnaire was revised to make the interviewer's task easier. Detailed questions on sources of income are now asked of the head of the unit. Supplemental questions follow: "Did your wife have any income during the year? Did your son (or other person) have any income?" "Yes" answers to these lead questions are followed by two other questions: "How much did she (he) receive? Was it from wages, salary, a business, or what?" In this way the psychological hazard of asking many "unnecessary" questions of other possible income recipients is eliminated. This new approach —adopted first in the 1954 SCF—worked. The accompanying tabulation shows that the proportion of units with multiple income receivers increased sharply.

| NUMBER OF INCOME RECIPIENTS | PERCENTAGE OF DISTRIBUTION OF SPENDING UNITS | | |
|---|---|---|---|
| | *New Approach 1954* SCF | *Old Approach 1953* SCF | *1954–1953 Difference* |
| Total | 100.0 | 100.0 | |
| Zero | 0.8 | 0.5 | +0.3 |
| One | 68.3 | 74.3 | −6.0 |
| Two | 27.9 | 23.3 | +4.6 |
| Three | 2.5 | 1.8 | +0.7 |
| Four or more | 0.5 | 0.1 | +0.4 |

This particular problem is not relevant to the CQC or the CPS where standard instructions call for interviews with each person rather than only with the head of the unit.

*First-Quality Respondents*

Both the CQC and the SCF instructed interviewers to deal with first-quality respondents, but the CQC found more of them. And apparently the quality of the respondent does matter. Though units generally reported income in a higher income class to the SCF, the net surplus was highest when the SCF interviewed a first-quality respondent and the CQC did not; lowest when the CQC interviewed a first-quality respondent and the SCF did not. This finding that income reports of first-quality respondents tend to be higher than those of second-quality ones, *ceteris paribus,* is reasonable, as a first-quality respondent is selected as the person most likely to be familiar with the income or other financial transactions of the spending unit.

*Number of Questions and Size of Income Reported*

One operating maxim of the survey technician which found support in this study is the proposition that the total income reported will increase as the number of questions asked about different *sources* of income increases. The CQC asked six questions about transfer payments, the SCF only two. Unlike the results for other components about which the SCF asked more questions, reports of this type of income were made more frequently to the CQC than to the SCF, and the reported amounts were larger. Consequently, in interpreting the results of annual income surveys, the income analyst should expect the survey with the most questions to have the highest reported incomes.

*Reporting of Wages and Salaries*

The CQC and the SCF employed widely differing techniques to obtain reports of wage and salary income. Taking the job history approach, the CQC asked questions about each place and period of employment and then up to seven questions about the income received from each employer. On the other hand the SCF asked only three general questions about wages and salaries. Yet more respondents reported the receipt of wage and salary income to the SCF, and, if they reported it to both surveys, they reported larger amounts to the SCF.

These results indicate that survey technicians should usually prefer the simpler SCF approach to a job history one, since the former requires fewer questions and less time and apparently yields as good or better results. Perhaps the CQC questions suggested regular, well-ordered jobs and the incomes related to such jobs. If so, the CQC may have tended to miss income from irregular or part-time employment, such as income from mowing lawns or from consultations.

*Farm Income*

As noted earlier, analysis of the reports of farm income did not establish the superiority of either the short CQC schedule (three questions) or the detailed SCF farm schedule (nineteen questions). Consequently in the 1954 SCF a separate farm schedule was abandoned, and a simple five-question sequence—similar to the CQC one but with a more explicit control of capital expenses—was adopted as a substitute.

### CONCLUSIONS

At a more general level than the previous discussion, the study has demonstrated once again that differences in survey techniques affect the resulting income distributions of surveys, whether they are conducted by different organizations or by the same organization at different times. Indeed the income analyst should be particularly alert to the effect of changes in procedures in a regularly conducted survey. Whenever possible he should restrict himself to the use of data drawn from only one survey or from surveys that employ similar techniques. And those conducting surveys have a responsibility to inform the public of changes in techniques and of their likely effect on the income distributions they publish.

As to the present study, if a similar one were to be undertaken, interviews should be conducted during approximately the same period in the two surveys. This would remove memory error as a possible explanation of differences between their reports. Also it would be desirable to obtain the names of respondents in both to facilitate matching. Otherwise, as in the present study, the interpretation of the results is obscured. Would the placement of the unmatched units in their proper groups have changed the results obtained? We do not know; we can only bring the problem to the attention of the user of this study.

Finally, research in methods should be executed more rapidly than the present study was. Had our results been available sooner, improvements in survey techniques might have been undertaken sooner, and their benefits passed on to the ultimate consumer of the data.

## *Appendix A: The Matching Procedure*

Since names were not obtained in the 1950 SCF, it was necessary to institute a matching procedure by which families and unrelated individuals interviewed in both SCF and CQC could be designated as identical or nonidentical units.

A review group of four professional persons examined interviews taken at the same address by the SCF and CQC. By comparing the demographic characteristics of the unit as reported to each survey, and other information in the respective interviews, the review group was able to arrive at an agreement on whether the units were "positive matches"

(99 per cent probability that the units were identical), "probable matches" (95 to 99 per cent probability), or "nonmatches" (less than 95 per cent probability). The "matched units" group mentioned in the body of the paper consists of both positive and probable matches.

The demographic characteristics considered in assigning the match status included sex, age, occupation, education, veteran status, length of marriage, home-owning status, number of adults and children, and number of children born in 1949 or 1950. All of the individual characteristics refer to the head of the spending unit.

Special weight in assigning match status was given to agreement on unusual characteristics as, for example, when both surveys reported the head as sixty-five years or more ("very old").

## *Appendix B: Income Questions Asked in the Survey of Consumer Finances*

In the 1950 SCF the following questions were asked of spending units whose heads were primarily engaged in an occupation *other than* farming. (The Post-Enumeration Survey questionnaire, used in the CQC, is shown on page 237 of this volume.) Interviewers were instructed, where possible, to obtain answers from the head of the spending unit.

(In this survey, all over the country we are trying to get an accurate picture of people's financial situation. One thing we need to know is the income of all the people we interview. We start with wages and salaries, yours and those of your. . . . SU)

| | | *Head of SU* | *Wife and others* (List sep.) |
|---|---|---|---|
| | 1. How much did you (R & SU) [1] receive from wages and salaries in 1949? I mean, before they deducted anything such as taxes, social security, and so on? | ....... | ........ |
| If income from wages and salaries | 2. Does that include bonuses, overtime and commissions? (If no) How much was that? | ....... | ........ |
| | 3. Did you (R & SU) have any pay from work outside your regular work? (If yes) How much? | ....... | ........ |
| | 4. Did you (R & SU) receive income from roomers and boarders? (If yes) How much? | ....... | ........ |
| | 5. Did you (R & SU) receive any money from other rent? (If yes) How much was it after allowing for your expenses? | ....... | ........ |

[1] R = respondent; SU = spending unit.

6. Did you (R & SU) receive any money from interest, dividends, a trust fund, or royalties? (If yes) How much was that? ........ .........

If (R & SU) owns or partly owns an unincorporated business (P. 2, Q. 16)

7. What was the profit, or loss, of your business in 1949? I mean, your share, if you have partners, and after deducting expenses?

[PROFIT] ....... .........

[LOSS] ....... .........

8. How much did you take out from your business in 1949, including any salary you paid to yourself or other withdrawals?

$........

9. Is that included in the profit you gave me before?

[Yes] [No]

10. Did you (R & SU) have any income from professional practice or other self-employment or farming (other than what you have already mentioned)? (If yes) What was your net income for the year from your profession (self-employment, farming) considering all the money you took in and deducting your expenses? ....... .........

11. Did you (R & SU) receive veterans' pension, veterans' school allotment, family allotment, or veterans' bonus from a state? (If yes) How much did that amount to? ....... .........

12. How about retirement pay, unemployment compensation, old-age pensions, annuities, alimony, regular contributions, or welfare? Did you (R & SU) receive any income of this sort? (If yes) How much? ....... .........

Just to be sure I didn't get anything wrong, I'll add this up.......................... ....... .........

....... .........

Is that about right?

..........

..........

SCF heads of spending units whose primary occupation was farming were asked the following set of questions:

(Now, we would like to know about your farm expenses)

1. Did you buy any livestock during the year? (If yes) How much did that come to? $........
2. Did you pay out any wages to farm hands? (If yes) How much was that? $........
3. About how much did you pay for insurance on your crops and stock and buildings? $........
4. How much did you spend for feed in 1949? $........
5. How much did you spend for seed? $........
6. What did you spend for lime and fertilizer during the year? $........
7. How much of what you spent for fuel, tires, and repairs to your car was for farm business? $........
8. How much did you spend for fuel, tires, and repairs for your tractor, your truck, and any other farm machinery? $........
9. Are you paying anything on a mortgage or other farm loans? (If yes) What did the interest on these loans come to in 1949? $........
10. Did you pay any cash rent for this farm or for other farm land? (If yes) How much was that? $........
11. Did you have any custom work done by others last year such as combining, plowing, or baling? (If yes) How much did you pay for it? $........
12. Did you have any other expenses? For instance, for storing crops, renting machinery, containers, irrigation, ginning, etc? (If yes) How much did they come to? $........
13. Now adding all of these figures together, I find that your farm expenses in 1949 were ........ $........

........

(Let's consider now what money you took in last year before deducting any of these expenses.)

| | *Product* | *Total Receipts* |
|---|---|---|
| 14. Did you sell any crops during 1949? (If yes) What did you sell? Can you tell me how much you got for each of these? | ................ | $...... |
| | ................ | $...... |
| | ................ | $...... |
| 14a. Were there any other crops you sold last year? (If yes) How much did it (they) bring? | [NOTE: A similar space for computations was allowed for each receipt category.] | |

15. In addition to these, did you in 1949 put any crops under Commodity Credit Loan? (If yes) How much did you get on the loan? $......

16. Did you sell any livestock in 1949? (If yes) What did you sell? How much did you get for them? $......
    16a. Was there any other livestock you sold during 1949? (If yes) How much did they bring? $......
17. Did you sell any butter, milk, cream, poultry or eggs last year? (If yes) What was that? How much did you get for them? $......
    17a. Was there anything else of this sort that you sold in 1949? (If yes) How much did you get for them? $......
18. Did you sell any fruits and vegetables during 1949? (If yes) What did you sell? How much did you get for them? $......
    18a. Were there any other fruits and/or vegetables that you sold last year? (If yes) How much did you get for them? $......
19. Did you sell anything else off the farm last year? (If yes) What else did you sell? What did these bring altogether last year? $......
20. Did you receive any Government Payments during the year, such as soil conservation payments? (If yes) How much did you receive? $......
21. That means you got altogether from your farm last year . . . . . $......

......

    21a. Now deducting your expenses (Q. 13 bottom of previous page) we find that your net income from farming was about . . . . . . . . . . . . . . . . . $......

......

Does that seem about right?

(Enter here the net farm income from bottom of previous page) . . . . . . . . . . . . . . . $......

| ASK EVERYONE | *Head of SU* | *Wife and Others* |
|---|---|---|
| 22. Did you (other members of SU) do any custom work last year? (If yes) How much did you get for it? | $....... | $....... |
| 23. Did you (other members of SU) earn any wages or salary during 1949? (If yes) How much was that? | $....... | $....... |
| 24. Do you have any land or other property that you are renting out? Do you have any investments (mortgages) that you get interest or dividends on? (If yes) How much did you receive during the year in interest, dividends, rent? | $....... | $....... |

| | | | |
|---|---|---|---|
| (If owns an unincorporated business P. 2, Q. 16) | 25. What was your net income from your business? . . . . . . . | $. . . . . . . | $. . . . . . . |
| | 26. Did you (or other members of the SU) receive veterans' pension, veterans' school allotment, family allotment or veterans' bonus from a state? (If yes) How much was that? . . . . . . . . . . . . . . | $. . . . . . . | $. . . . . . . |
| | 27. Did you (or other members of SU) have any income from any other source, such as roomers, retirement pay, old age pensions, and so on? (If yes) How much was that? . . . . . . . . . | $. . . . . . . | $. . . . . . . |
| | 28. Adding these to your net income, we find your total income in 1949 was about . . . . . . . . . . . . . . . . . . . . . . . . . . . . . | $. . . . . . .<br>. . . . . . . | |

# Coordination of Old-Age and Survivors Insurance Wage Records and the Post-Enumeration Survey

B. J. MANDEL, IRWIN WOLKSTEIN, AND MARIE M. DELANEY

BUREAU OF OLD-AGE AND SURVIVORS INSURANCE,

DEPARTMENT OF HEALTH, EDUCATION, AND WELFARE

## *Introduction*

The coordination of the Bureau of the Census's Post-Enumeration Survey (PES) responses with records of the Bureau of Old-Age and Survivors Insurance (OASI), like the other matching studies discussed in this volume, was part of the 1950 census record check program which attempted to provide benchmarks for evaluation of verbal survey responses. The check discussed in this paper consisted of a comparison of data on the number of employers and amount of wages reported to the PES with those reported on 1949 OASI tax returns.

The hope was that recognized deficiencies in comparisons of data from different surveys (since response errors are a function of the different survey conditions, and also some biases are present in all verbal responses) could be evaluated concretely by an actual case-by-case comparison of the most accurate survey material (PES) with tax records required by law from employers. If these records are presumed nearly perfect, differences between the survey responses and the records would be a direct measure of error in the survey responses. Because of inherent differences in the underlying concepts and coverage of the data compared, the wage match was only for a limited group of workers (those with a single employer during the year and less than $3,000 wages reported in both sources). The chief problems arising from the 1949 OASI data were incomplete coverage and limitation of the tax base to $3,000.

These difficulties, making results of the check somewhat inconclusive, appeared in various combinations at each step in the matching process. Briefly, the steps were: search for an OASI record for each of the 12,000 individuals in the PES sample, and matching for identity; comparison for each matched individual of number of

Note: The opinions expressed in this article do not necessarily reflect the views of the Bureau of Old-Age and Survivors Insurance. The writers are indebted to Rena Levine Berman for her assistance in planning the tabulations.

employers reported in each source, and matching single employer for identity; comparison for each single employer individual of annual wages reported in each source. Despite the various limitations of the findings, the procedures and results may be useful beyond the initial purpose of the study.

All users of income statistics would benefit from the improvement in quality of published data which can result from coordination of data from two types of source. When the 1960 Census of Population is taken, OASI coverage of annual taxable earnings will be nearly complete, and the taxable wage base will be higher than that of 1949. The value of future comparisons will then increase.

The statistical program and related research activities of the Bureau of OASI will benefit from use of census earnings records which are more complete, for many workers, and can also provide information not now available to it on characteristics of income recipients (such as relationship to head of family and occupation of earner). In studies of income maintenance, data are needed on the income of the aged; in coverage extension studies, data on earnings in noncovered employment are required to estimate the additional tax yield and ultimate benefit levels. Further, the Bureau of OASI has a general interest in family income levels and occupational earnings, and a specific interest in the income of self-employed persons.

Besides the obvious value of OASI earnings records to the Census Bureau (for studying problems of interview response, possibly improving the accuracy of its data), the benefit payment records should supply an additional means of improving the accuracy of individual income data. OASI benefits are becoming an increasingly important income component—nearly $7½ billion in 1957.

### *Procedural and Technical Problems of Coordination*

Difficulties, already touched upon, of coordinating two such dissimilar sets of data are increased by errors arising in clerical, coding, and tabulating operations, which can usually be eliminated or controlled. But the Bureaus of the Census and of OASI previously had demonstrated the feasibility of coordinating their respective data on employment, industry, and geographic location reported by employers for identical establishments, in their joint publication of *County Business Patterns* statistics.

#### MATCHING RECORDS FOR IDENTITY OF INDIVIDUALS

In this study, the Bureau of OASI received from the Census Bureau its PES records for a sample of 12,000 individuals aged fourteen and over. The only advance information was that 70 to 75 per cent of the population aged fourteen and over had social security account numbers as of January 1, 1950. Approximately 7,800 account numbers were located by name in the OASI records, about two-thirds of the sample. (Because this ratio was calculated from the unweighted total, it cannot be automatically applied to the total population aged fourteen and over.) Possibly an additional 5 to 10 per cent had social security numbers but were not matched. In our judgment, the incompleteness of the match does not seriously detract from the validity of the findings.

Each case located in OASI records was classified as either a positive or probable match depending on the amount of identical information (date of birth, race, sex) in the two records.

### MATCHING EMPLOYERS IN INDIVIDUALLY MATCHED CASES

For each matched case, OASI figures on 1949 annual wages reported by each employer were compared with PES figures to secure matches in the number of employers and annual wages for that year. In addition to a comparison of number of employers reported, an attempt was made to match individual employers. (The employer-matching operation was confined to the major employer on each of the records, that is, the employer that paid the worker the largest amount of wages or salary in the year.)

The case records with matches for major employers were analyzed further to pinpoint discrepancies between PES and OASI records. The resulting classification consisted of five groups with variations in reporting major employer, and twelve subgroups containing variants in wages reported in the two sources (less than $100 difference; $100 or more difference).[1] Presumably, a difference in coverage

[1] 1. Same major employer in PES and OASI records:
   a. Less than $100 difference in wage
   b. $100 or more or n.a. (not ascertainable) difference in wage
2. Employers reported as major to one agency and as nonmajor to the other:
   a. Less than $100 difference in wage between PES and OASI for each given employer
   b. $100 or more or n.a. difference in wage between PES and OASI for each given employer
   c. Less than $100 difference in wage between PES and OASI for PES major employer, and $100 or more n.a. difference for OASI major employer
   d. $100 or more or n.a. difference in wage between PES and OASI for PES major employer, and less than $100 difference for OASI major employer
3. OASI major employer not reported in PES, and PES major employer reported as nonmajor OASI employer:
   a. Less than $100 difference in wage of PES major employer
   b. $100 or more or n.a. difference in wage of PES major employer
4. PES major employer not reported in OASI, and OASI major employer reported as nonmajor in PES:
   a. Less than $100 difference in wage of OASI major employer

accounts for a failure to match a major employer in the census record to the OASI record, while a failure to match a major employer in the OASI record can probably be traced to incomplete response to the PES. But other possibilities must be considered, for example, errors caused by overstatement and nonmatches due to incomplete identifying information, compensated—to an extent difficult to determine—by understatements and false matches.

WAGE MATCHING

Comparison of wages reported in the two sources was necessarily preceded by the employer-matching process just described, because coordination of earnings data obviously could be carried out only when the same job was reported to PES and OASI. Since only about 2,000 individuals, or 30 per cent of the positive matches showed one and the same employer in the two records, the comparative study of total annual earnings had to be confined to this limited group.

### *Results of Coordination Procedure*

The nature of the basic data did not permit a refined quantitative analysis of the accuracy of earnings reports in either source, but a number of qualitative facts became apparent from the comparison of number of employers reported in each source.

EMPLOYER MATCHING

The following table shows how many employers were reported for the approximately 7,800 positively matched workers in the PES and OASI records for 1949:

| NUMBER OF EMPLOYERS | PES *Records* | OASI *Records* | *Same Number in Both* |
|---|---|---|---|
| | (*per cent of positively matched workers*) | | |
| Total | 100.0 | 100.0 | 68.4 |
| None | 32.8 | 48.8 | 29.7 |
| One | 58.9 | 40.7 | 35.7 |
| Two | 7.1 | 7.8 | 2.7 |
| Three | 1.1 | 1.6 | 0.2 |
| Four | 0.1 | 0.7 | [a] |
| Five and over | [a] | 0.5 | 0 |

[a] Less than 0.05 per cent.

In about 68 per cent of the cases the same number of employers was reported in each source. Allowing for compensating errors, em-

b. $100 or more or n.a. difference in wage of OASI major employer

5. Other:

OASI and PES major employers not reported in PES and OASI respectively

No employer in either PES or OASI or both

ployer matching even for the number of employers was probably imperfect in more than a third of the cases. Somewhat surprisingly, the PES records show fewer workers having two or more employers than the OASI records—8.3 per cent compared with 10.6 per cent. Noncovered employment undoubtedly accounts for most of the cases where PES records show more employers than OASI records; presumably response errors account for the fewer cases where the reverse is true. But even when there were more employers in the PES records, the major OASI employer was frequently not among them: [2]

| EMPLOYER AGREEMENT | *Per Cent of Positively Matched Workers* | *Number of Employers Reported:* PES<OASI | PES=OASI | PES>OASI |
|---|---|---|---|---|
| | | *(per cent of workers of a class)* | | |
| Total | 100 | 10 | 68 | 22 |
| Same major employer | 38 | 5 | 85 | 11 |
| Major and minor reversed | 1 | 39 | 47 | 14 |
| OASI major not in PES, PES major a nonmajor in OASI | 1 | 75 | 25 | 0 |
| PES major not in OASI, OASI major a nonmajor in PES | 5 | 4 | 10 | 86 |
| OASI or PES major employer not in other record | 8 | 22 | 70 | 8 |
| None in either or both | 53 | 6 | 58 | 36 |

Nearly 80 per cent of the positively matched records for women agreed on the number of employers, only about 60 per cent of the records for men:

| SEX | *Number of Employers Reported:* PES<OASI | PES=OASI | PES>OASI |
|---|---|---|---|
| | *(per cent of workers of a sex)* | | |
| Both sexes | 9.5 | 68.4 | 22.1 |
| Male | 11.6 | 60.7 | 27.7 |
| Female | 6.8 | 78.6 | 14.6 |

This difference may be explained, in part, by the fact that women change jobs less often than men do, and therefore have fewer jobs to remember.

### WAGE MATCHING

In addition to the limitation of data for employer matching to individuals in the PES who were also (in 1949) covered by OASI, further limitation of this data for use in wage matching was required by the need to prove that the same wages from the same employer were to be compared in the two sources. This reduced our sample for wage matching to 30 per cent of the 7,800 positive matches, or

[2] The complexity of the code may have produced an excessive number of clerical errors which may account for some of the inconsistencies shown.

about 2,240. While this group is obviously not a random sample of all 1949 wage earners, it is, in our opinion, not biased in any obvious manner for the purpose of measuring differences between wages reported in the two records for a given job. Errors due to failure to report an employer cannot, of course, be determined from an analysis of the data for this group.

The following table shows the percentage distribution of the records for positive matches with a single employer, by the amount of 1949 wages recorded in each of the two sources:

| WAGES | PES *Records* | OASI *Records* | *Same in Both* |
|---|---|---|---|
| | *(per cent of all workers)* | | |
| Total | 100.0 | 100.0 | 82.3 |
| $ 1–$ 499 | 9.0 | 10.2 | 8.1 |
| 500– 999 | 7.4 | 7.0 | 5.1 |
| 1,000– 1,499 | 8.1 | 9.0 | 6.0 |
| 1,500– 1,999 | 11.1 | 11.0 | 7.9 |
| 2,000– 2,999 | 27.8 | 27.6 | 22.5 |
| 3,000 and over | 36.6 | 35.2 | 32.7 |

Differences in distribution by earnings shown in the two sources are not significant in spite of different wage classes recorded in the two sources for nearly 18 per cent of the group. Obviously, compensating errors in reporting were responsible for the consistency in distributions. If real differences existed, they were in the direction of higher wages reported for the same employer in PES than in OASI. But, since the employer comparison showed a tendency on the part of PES respondents to omit second or third employers, underreporting in the survey of number of employers is partly compensated for by overreporting of annual earnings from a single job. This analysis of "bias" in survey response was made on the assumption that the OASI record could be used as a standard for comparison.

The analysis of wage differences was subject to the unavoidable restriction of 1949 OASI coverage—and therefore reported earnings—to $3,000 per individual. In the following table, showing the percentage distribution of single employer matched records (about 2,240) by broad wages class and sex, the first line gives the relative size of the class reporting less than $3,000 in each source, 61 per cent of the employer matched records.

| WAGES REPORTED | | *Percentage Distribution* | | |
|---|---|---|---|---|
| OASI | PES | *Total* | *Male* | *Female* |
| Less than $3,000 | Less than $3,000 | 61 | 45 | 92 |
| Less than $3,000 | $3,000 or more | 4 | 5 | 2 |
| $3,000 or more | Less than $3,000 | 3 | 3 | 1 |
| $3,000 or more | $3,000 or more | 33 | 46 | 5 |

If the two classes where less than $3,000 was reported in one source and more than $3,000 in the other source were considered in calculating numerical differences between wages reported in each source, without also including the class reporting more than $3,000 in both sources, a biased presentation would result. Therefore, the analysis of wage differences was restricted to the class reporting less than $3,000 to both PES and OASI, consisting of 61 per cent of the workers in the original wage matching group or less than 1,400. Chart 1 shows the percentage distribution of these workers by the amount of difference in reported wages.

**Chart 1**

**Percentage Distribution of All Persons Having One Employer in PES and OASI, with Agreement on That Employer and on Wage Income under $3,000, by Wage and Salary Difference, 1949**

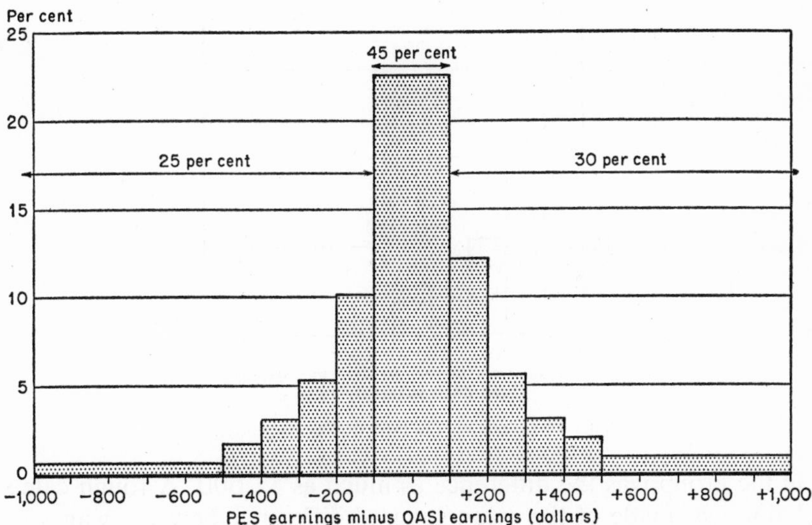


Note: 1.1 per cent were in the minus $1,000 or less class, 2.9 in the plus $1,000 or more class.

This very symmetrical chart supports our previous findings, that is, the existence of a tendency for wage reporting errors to be reciprocally compensating, and our observation that, if any bias does exist for these matched single employer reports, it is in the direction of a slightly higher wage report in the PES. In the analysis of the basic data, tests for differences between reports of men and women and in reports of workers over and under age sixty-five showed that differences associated with sex or age were insufficient to significantly influence the distribution.

Chart 2 shows the percentage distribution of workers by amount of absolute difference in wages regardless of the direction of the difference.

About 45 per cent of the records for workers with earnings of less than \$3,000 in both sources differed by less than \$100, and two-thirds by less than \$200. For less than 5 per cent of the workers

**Chart 2**

**Percentage Distribution of All Persons Having One Employer in PES and OASI, with Agreement on That Employer and on Wage Income under \$3,000, by Absolute Wage and Salary Difference, 1949**

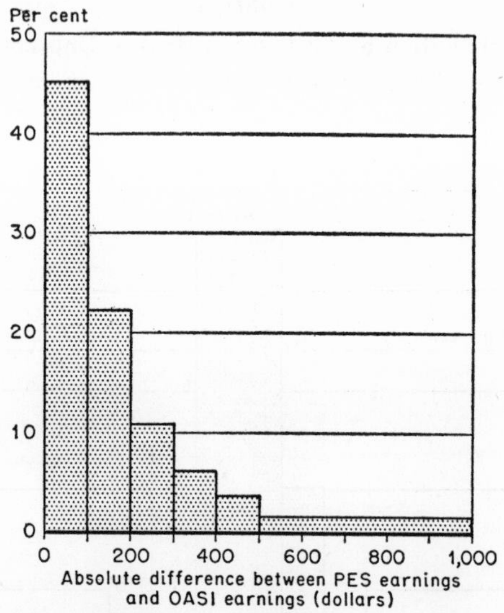


Note: 4.0 per cent were in the \$1,000 or more class.

in the group was the difference as much as \$1,000. A rough calculation was made of the mean squared difference between wages reported by the two sources, and it was compared with the variance of the wage distribution. For the limited area of comparison, the mean square response error appears to be much less than the variance of the wage distribution.

## *Summary and Conclusions*

Chart 3 traces in terms of percentages the number of persons originally identified in the OASI–PES sample through the various stages of analysis.

It is apparent that with successive steps in the analysis, the orig-

**Chart 3**

**Percentage of Workers with OASI Account Numbers Used in Successive Stages of Analysis, 1949**

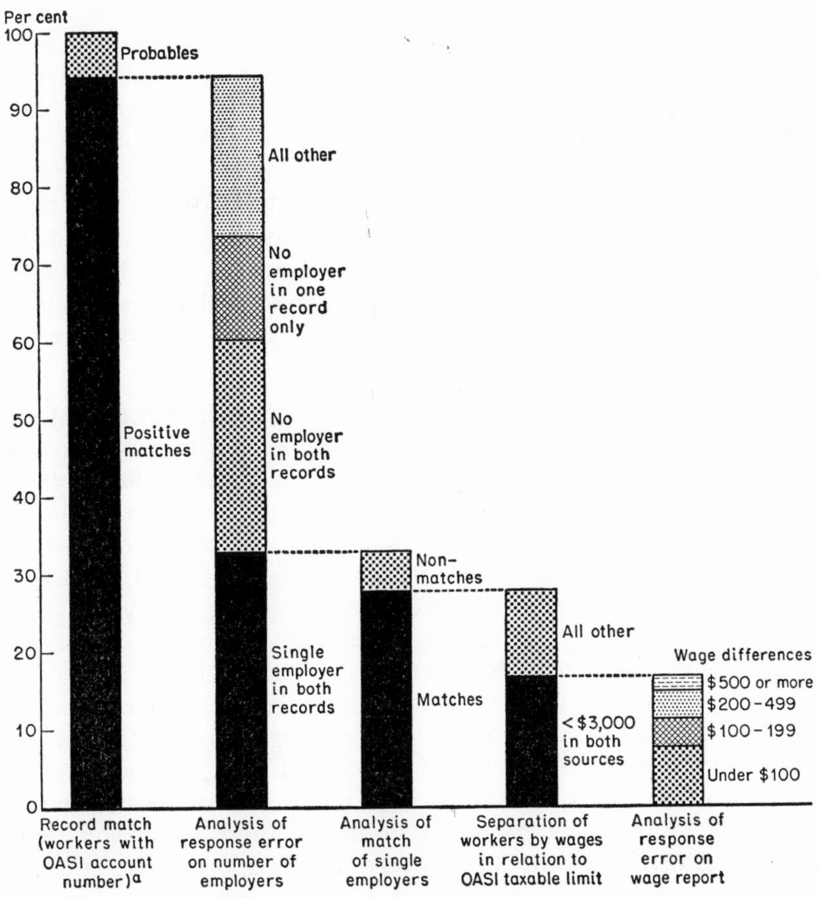


[a] Represents 65 per cent of all workers in PES sample.

inally identified group of 7,800 cases was gradually reduced. These reductions were made because of limitations in scope of operations and the limitations in 1949 of old-age and survivors insurance coverage to only about 70 to 75 per cent of all jobs and the first $3,000 of earnings. Despite the limited nature of the comparisons possible in this study, we believe that the following generalizations can be made:

1. The belief of the Census Bureau that incidental employment is frequently forgotten is confirmed by the finding that some re-

spondents fail to report additional employers if they have more than one job in a year.

2. Amounts reported do not appear to be significantly biased, at least not for workers with less than $3,000 a year.

3. The errors found in PES reported wages which could be compared to those in OASI appear to be small relative to the variance of the wage distribution. For samples small in comparison with the population, the contribution of reporting error to total error of estimate of mean wages for the groups studied is probably negligible, compared with sampling error.

4. For most individuals with records in both census and OASI sources, matches can be achieved with a reasonable expenditure of effort, provided proper identifying information is in the census record. The limited effort devoted to matching in the present study resulted in matching the records for about 90 per cent of the covered persons.

It is appropriate to add some recommendations about the future of coordination of household interview responses with OASI records. We have no doubt that such coordination has value in filling gaps in knowledge about workers and beneficiaries under the old-age and survivors insurance program. As far as the interests of Bureau of the Census and users of census statistics are concerned, accuracy checks and response research are unquestionably necessary and will, therefore, continue. The various checks already made, however, should be reviewed critically, and the combination of sources providing the "best" results with the least expenditure should be chosen. In making this selection the scope of the OASI program by the time of the proposed check will be an added favorable factor, for the four increases in coverage since 1949 will probably be expanded, making results of future wage coordination studies more significant than those obtained from the 1949 study. Furthermore, difficulties in matching procedures may be lessened; with nearly universal coverage of workers under OASI, the necessity for matching employers may be eliminated. One factor to be stressed in the effectiveness of a matching study is the availability of sufficient identifying information, which depends largely on efforts expended to collect it in the enumeration process.

# Income Reported in the 1950 Census and on Income Tax Returns

HERMAN P. MILLER AND LEON R. PALEY,

BUREAU OF THE CENSUS

About forty years ago, a group of economists and statisticians met to discuss, among other things, the adequacy of income statistics in the United States. Papers were presented to this gathering by Allyn Young, who later became president of the American Economic Association, and by Willford King, one of the early pioneers in income analysis.[1] Both authors lamented the poor quality of the scanty income data available at that time, but both were optimistic about the future.

Since that meeting on the eve of our entry into World War I, a considerable volume of statistics on the size distribution of income has been collected in the United States. There is still a pressing need for more income data, but there is also need for analysis and appraisal of the data already at our disposal. We who participate in collecting such information are duty-bound to investigate its reliability. This paper reports on one phase of such an investigation.

Various procedures were designed to check the accuracy of the income statistics collected in the 1950 Census of Population. The one described here was a matching study of the income reported to the census interviewer and to the Internal Revenue Service (IRS) by a representative sample of the population. The study was conducted solely for the purpose of checking the accuracy of income statistics collected in the census. At every stage of the investigation precautions were taken to keep data pertaining to specific individuals confidential; all tabulations dealt with subgroups of the population, never with individual families.

## *Description of Census-Tax Return Match*

The primary vehicle used in the census-tax return matching study was the Post-Enumeration Survey (PES) sample, a probability sample of about 25,000 households created for the specific purpose

[1] Papers presented at a joint meeting of the American Economic and American Statistical Associations in December 1916: Allyn A. Young, "Do the Statistics of the Concentration of Wealth in the United States Mean What They Are Commonly Assumed to Mean?"; and Willford I. King, "Desirable Additions to Statistical Data on Wealth and Income," *Quarterly Publication of the American Statistical Association,* March 1917, pp. 471–501.

of evaluating the 1950 census results.[2] Theoretically, all households in the sample should have been interviewed in the 1950 census; and one-fifth of them, or about 5,000 households, should have reported on income. In September 1950, about four months after completion of the census, these households were reinterviewed, and the more detailed information obtained was compared with the original census data for the identical households to measure the accuracy of the original data.

In November 1951, a year after the completion of the PES, the identifying information for each of the 5,000 households in the income subsample of the PES sample was copied on a separate form. Each household member fourteen years old or over was identified. If there were more than three such members in the household, additional matching forms were used. Each person's name, address, and social security number were copied from the PES schedule, his age from the census schedule. Income information was not copied from either the census or the PES schedule at this time to eliminate the possibility of disclosure of census income information to the IRS, and to minimize the possibility of bias in matching with income tax returns.

Equipped with this information, Census Bureau clerks (sworn in as IRS employees) attempted to locate the tax returns for the specified persons at IRS offices throughout the country, using a manual of instructions prepared for the purpose. Files were searched for the 1949 tax return filed by the head of each household, and for separate returns filed by other members of the household if their names did not appear on the head of the household's return. The results of all searches and the income information from the tax returns were entered on the matching forms, which were then submitted to the Census Bureau for collation with income and other information obtained in the 1950 census and the PES. A separate punch card was made for each family and unrelated individual (as determined by the standard Census Bureau definition).

To minimize the conceptual differences between the census and IRS definitions of income, the clerks were instructed to transcribe from the tax returns:

1. Wage and salary income
2. Net, not gross, income from a business, farm, or profession, or from rents and royalties

[2] For a detailed discussion of the plan of the Post-Enumeration Survey, see Eli S. Marks, W. Parker Mauldin and Harold Nisselson, "The Post-Enumeration Survey of the 1950 Censuses: A Case History in Survey Design," *Journal of the American Statistical Association,* June 1953, pp. 220–243; see also the paper by Leon Pritzker and Alfred Sands in this volume.

3. Gross, not merely taxable, income from annuities and pensions
4. All other income except capital gains or losses

Even so, some elements of difference remained. Certain kinds of income other than earnings, such as unemployment compensation, veterans payments, dependency allotments, and other types described below (page 189) were not reported on tax returns but were reported to the census interviewer. These items could not be deducted from the census reports because they had been recorded as part of a lump sum that included receipts from all sources other than earnings. Using procedures described below (page 189), separate tabulations were made for families roughly classified as "with taxable income only" so that families whose income was reported according to roughly the same concept in both sources could be identified.

How representative was the PES sample with respect to income? And how successful was the attempt to match this sample in the IRS files? The answer to the first question is indicated in the first two tables. Table 1 shows the 1950 census percentage distribution of families and individuals by income class, as estimated from the full 20 per cent sample used to obtain income estimates in the census and as transcribed for all families and individuals in the PES sample. (It should be emphasized that the income distribution for the PES sample is based on information obtained in the census itself and not in the PES interview.) This information was copied from the basic census schedule after the IRS data had been entered. For both families and individuals, the census income distribution based on the PES sample closely approximates the published census results. Differences are statistically insignificant; for all families, there is only a $60 difference between the two medians; for unrelated individuals, only a $3 difference. A closer look at the distributions in Table 1 indicates that in the two samples the proportion of families at each income level varies by no more than 1 percentage point, and the proportions of unrelated individuals at each income level are almost equally close.

While Table 2 presents less detail by income class than Table 1, it provides better insight into the structure of the sample by showing for each group the proportions of families and individuals by color and residence, as well as their median incomes. Unfortunately, the census data for this comparison had to be obtained from Preliminary Sample Tabulations (PST) of census returns rather than from the full 20 per cent census sample, because these data were not included in the final census tabulations. However, since the

TABLE 1

Income Reported in 1950 Census for Families and Unrelated Individuals: 20 Per Cent Sample and PES Sample

| INCOME IN CENSUS | 20 PER CENT SAMPLE [a] Families | 20 PER CENT SAMPLE [a] Unrelated Individuals | PES SAMPLE [b] Families | PES SAMPLE [b] Unrelated Individuals |
|---|---|---|---|---|
| | | *(number)* | | |
| Total in sample | 38,310,980 | 11,051,050 | 7,131 | 1,409 |
| Reporting on income | 36,439,955 | 10,049,135 | 6,730 | 1,328 |
| | | *(per cent)* | | |
| Total reporting | 100.0 | 100.0 | 100.0 | 100.0 |
| Under $ 500 | 8.3 | 31.8 | 8.1 | 29.5 |
| $ 500– 999 | 6.4 | 18.3 | 6.1 | 20.5 |
| 1,000– 1,499 | 7.1 | 12.4 | 6.8 | 13.3 |
| 1,500– 1,999 | 7.5 | 9.2 | 7.7 | 9.2 |
| 2,000– 2,499 | 9.7 | 8.7 | 9.2 | 7.7 |
| 2,500– 2,999 | 9.4 | 6.1 | 9.0 | 5.2 |
| 3,000– 3,499 | 11.0 | 5.0 | 11.6 | 5.7 |
| 3,500– 3,999 | 8.4 | 2.7 | 9.4 | 2.9 |
| 4,000– 4,499 | 7.1 | 1.7 | 6.7 | 1.4 |
| 4,500– 4,999 | 5.0 | 0.9 | 4.6 | 1.1 |
| 5,000– 5,999 | 7.8 | 1.2 | 8.2 | 0.6 |
| 6,000– 6,999 | 4.3 | 0.6 | 4.8 | 1.3 |
| 7,000– 9,999 | 4.9 | 0.6 | 4.4 | 0.2 |
| 10,000 and over | 3.1 | 0.7 | 3.2 | 1.4 |
| | | *(dollars)* | | |
| Median income | 3,073 | 997 | 3,129 | 1,000 |

Note: "Income" in this and the following tables refers to total money income unless otherwise qualified.

[a] *1950 Census of Population,* Vol. II, *Characteristics of the Population,* Part 1, *United States Summary,* Table 57.

[b] Income reported in the 1950 census for families and individuals included in the Post-Enumeration Survey sample. The numbers shown are weighted sample cases and not inflated population estimates, that is, each sample case was weighted by a factor required to make the sample self-weighting, but was not inflated to meet population controls. To cite an unrealistic example, if the rural population was sampled at one-half the rate of the urban population, each rural card would have been counted twice and each urban card once but neither card would have been multiplied by the weight (let us assume 5,000) required to inflate it to the independent estimate of the population. The figures exclude the small number of families and individuals (207 weighted sample cases) who were missed in the census but were interviewed in the PES. However, they include the equally small number of families and individuals (113 weighted sample cases) erroneously included in the census.

PST results were close to the final census results wherever comparisons could be made, there is some justification for the use of these data. The striking fact indicated in Table 2 is that the PES and PST results agree closely in both the proportions and the median incomes for each residence and color subgroup. Almost all the sample proportions differ by less than 1 percentage point, and the greatest

TABLE 2

Median Income in 1950 Census for White and Nonwhite Families and Individuals, by Residence: PST Sample and PES Sample

| COLOR AND RESIDENCE | PST SAMPLE [a] | | PES SAMPLE [b] | |
|---|---|---|---|---|
| | *As % of Sample* | *Median Income* | *As % of Sample* | *Median Income* |
| Families | 100.0 | $3,068 | 100.0 | $3,129 |
| Nonfarm | 85.5 | 3,245 | 86.4 | 3,307 |
| White | 78.4 | 3,379 | 79.6 | 3,427 |
| Nonwhite | 7.1 | 1,658 | 6.8 | 1,681 |
| Farm | 14.5 | 1,733 | 13.6 | 1,648 |
| White | 12.9 | 1,937 | 11.1 | 2,053 |
| Nonwhite | 1.6 | 730 | 2.5 | 605 |
| Unrelated individuals | 100.0 | $ 987 | 100.0 | $1,000 |
| Nonfarm | 94.2 | 1,021 | 93.0 | 1,070 |
| White | 81.2 | 1,079 | 80.1 | 1,115 |
| Nonwhite | 13.0 | 814 | 13.0 | 883 |
| Farm | 5.8 | 651 | 7.0 | [b] |
| White | 5.0 | 702 | 6.4 | [b] |
| Nonwhite | 0.7 | 420 | 0.6 | [b] |

[a] Derived from *1950 Census of Population, Employment and Income in the United States, by Regions, 1950,* Series PC-7, No. 2, Table 9. This report was based on Preliminary Sample Tabulations (PST) of 1950 census returns. In general, the results of this preliminary sample agreed very favorably with the final census tabulations. However, the data by color shown above were never tabulated on the basis of the full 20 per cent sample of census returns which contained income data.

[b] Median not shown where there were fewer than 100 cases in the sample reporting on income in census.

discrepancy between any two medians is about $125—statistically insignificant differences.

The above facts leave little doubt that the PES sample matched with tax returns is an adequate reflection of the universe from which it was drawn. It now remains to be determined how successful the matching was. This question cannot be answered unequivocally because the nonmatched group includes families and individuals whose tax returns could not be located, as well as those not required to file returns because their incomes were too low. The problem is not quite so simple as it was depicted by King Gama in Gilbert and Sullivan's *Princess Ida,* when he said:

> "I know everybody's income and what everybody earns;
> And I carefully compare it with the income tax returns."

### *Results of the Matching Process*

As a first attempt to measure the degree of success in locating tax returns for the appropriate families and individuals we will first consider the number of returns completely matched, partly matched, or not matched at all, without regard to whether or not they should have been matched. A complete match means that each person in the family aged fourteen years or over was identified on a tax return; a partial match, one in which some family member aged fourteen years or over could not be located on tax returns; and a nonmatch, one in which no tax return was located for the family. The actual figures for each of these groups are shown in Table 3.

TABLE 3

Families and Unrelated Individuals by Match Status, Actual and Adjusted, and by Residence

| RESIDENCE | ACTUAL MATCH STATUS *Completely Matched* | *Partly Matched* | *Not Matched* | TOTAL | ADJUSTED MATCH STATUS *Completely Matched* [a] | *Partly Matched* | *Not Matched* |
|---|---|---|---|---|---|---|---|
| | | | | (*number*) | | | |
| Families | 3,903 | 946 | 2,242 | 7,091 [b] | 5,340 | 634 | 1,117 |
| Nonfarm | 3,553 | 805 | 1,762 | 6,120 | 4,539 | 568 | 1,013 |
| Farm | 350 | 141 | 480 | 971 | 801 | 66 | 104 |
| Unrelated individuals | 334 | — | 1,002 | 1,336 [b] | 717 | — | 619 |
| Nonfarm | 321 | — | 923 | 1,244 | [c] | — | [c] |
| Farm | 13 | — | 79 | 92 | [c] | — | [c] |
| | | | | (*per cent*) | | | |
| Families | 55.0 | 13.3 | 31.6 | 100.0 | 75.3 | 8.9 | 15.8 |
| Nonfarm | 58.1 | 13.2 | 28.8 | 100.0 | 74.2 | 9.3 | 16.6 |
| Farm | 36.0 | 14.5 | 49.4 | 100.0 | 82.5 | 6.8 | 10.7 |
| Unrelated individuals | 25.0 | — | 75.0 | 100.0 | 53.7 | — | 46.3 |
| Nonfarm | 25.8 | — | 74.2 | 100.0 | [c] | — | [c] |
| Farm | [d] | — | [d] | 100.0 | [c] | — | [c] |

— Equals zero or less than 0.05 per cent in this and the following tables.

[a] Including those implicitly matched; see the discussion in the text for adjustments made.

[b] These numbers are slightly lower than the comparable numbers shown in Table 1 because the figures in the above table exclude families and individuals who were missed in the census as well as those who were erroneously included in the census. The latter were included in Table 1 because they were part of the universe which the PES sample was designed to approximate; however, because of their relatively small number they are excluded from this table and all later tables.

[c] The breakdown into nonfarm and farm was not calculated for this group.

[d] Percentages not shown where there were fewer than 100 cases in the sample base.

About 55 per cent of all the families were completely matched, 13 per cent partly matched, and 32 per cent not matched at all. The matching rate was much higher for nonfarm families (about 58 per cent) than it was for those living on farms (36 per cent). This difference is probably largely due to the lower incomes of the farm families.[3] The matching rate for individuals (25 per cent) was

[3] Part of this difference may also be attributed to possibly greater compliance with tax laws on the part of the nonfarm population, as suggested by F. D.

below that obtained for families. The main reason for the low rate is that unrelated individuals usually receive low incomes, often below the tax filing requirement. They also may be more dependent on nontaxable income, such as pensions. And finally, they move more often than families do, and so their tax returns are harder to find.

The fact that a rather large proportion of the families and individuals could not be matched with tax returns is not in itself sufficient evidence of a shortcoming in the study. The unmatched group includes families with taxable incomes whose tax returns could not be located, as well as other families who did not file a return, apparently either because their income was below the tax-filing requirement or because it was not high enough to require a tax payment, when allowance was made for dependents. Part of this nonfiling group could be implicitly matched by adopting certain assumptions.

All of the 3,188 families not matched with tax returns reported on size of family in the census and all but 183 reported their income in the census. If the income reported for these families in the census is assumed correct, and if the standard tax exemption of $600 is allowed for each family member, then incompletely matched or unmatched two-person families with incomes under $1,200, three-person families with incomes under $1,800, and so forth, can be regarded as implicitly matched. This is based on the supposition that most of these families did not file a tax return because they did not have to pay a tax or claim a tax refund. In the case of the self-employed, where taxes are not withheld at the source, many farmers and shopkeepers may regard it as relatively unimportant to file a return if no tax payment is required. Even among wage and salary workers, if no taxes are withheld at the source as a result of allowances for dependents, the question of filing a tax return may often become purely a matter of technical compliance with the law.

Under the foregoing assumptions, the adjusted matching rates shown in Table 3 are considerably greater than the unadjusted rates. Whereas 58 per cent of the nonfarm families were completely matched, about 74 per cent were matched when allowance is made for the implicit matches as defined above. Among farm families, the matching rate was increased from 36 to 83 per cent by the adjustment procedure.

Although the adjusted matching rate for unrelated individuals (54 per cent) was about twice the unadjusted rate, it was still much

Stocker, *The Impact of Federal Income Taxes on Farm People,* Dept. of Agriculture, ARS 43–11, July 1955, p. 29.

lower than the rate for families. The rate for unrelated individuals is lower partly because many with total incomes over $600 had lower taxable incomes and could not be readily identified as implicitly matched. Implicit matches were estimated only to provide a more refined index of matching success; however, they are treated as nonmatches or partial matches in the tabulations by income class in Tables 4 through 6.

The validity of the matching study depends not only on how many matched households there are but also on how representative they are, that is, on how large a proportion is successfully matched at each income class. Since the lowest income groups are not required to file tax returns, one would expect the nonmatched families to have lower incomes than the matched and Table 4 clearly shows this was so. About one-third of the nonmatched families had incomes under $1,000 compared with only 5 per cent of the completely matched group. The median income for nonmatched families

TABLE 4

Income in 1950 Census for Families and Individuals by Match Status

(*weighted sample cases*)

| | FAMILIES | | | | UNRELATED INDIVIDUALS | | |
|---|---|---|---|---|---|---|---|
| INCOME IN CENSUS | TOTAL | *Completely Matched* | *Partly Matched* | *Not Matched* | TOTAL | *Matched* | *Not Matched* |
| | | | | (*number*) | | | |
| Total in sample | 7,091 | 3,903 | 946 | 2,242 | 1,336 | 334 | 1,002 |
| Reporting on income | 6,692 | 3,687 | 893 | 2,112 | 1,259 | 311 | 948 |
| | | | | (*per cent*) | | | |
| Total reporting | 100.0 | 100.0 | 100.0 | 100.0 | 100.0 | 100.0 | 100.0 |
| None | 3.9 | 1.5 | 3.4 | 8.2 | 15.9 | 6.4 | 19.0 |
| Loss | 0.1 | 0.1 | — | 0.1 | 0.6 | 0.6 | 0.5 |
| $ 1–$ 499 | 4.2 | 1.6 | 2.6 | 9.3 | 13.6 | 8.4 | 15.3 |
| 500– 999 | 6.1 | 2.1 | 4.7 | 13.4 | 20.6 | 15.1 | 22.4 |
| 1,000– 1,499 | 6.7 | 4.1 | 8.0 | 10.7 | 13.1 | 12.2 | 13.4 |
| 1,500– 1,999 | 7.8 | 5.7 | 8.4 | 11.1 | 8.6 | 10.0 | 8.1 |
| 2,000– 2,499 | 9.2 | 8.9 | 11.8 | 8.8 | 7.8 | 13.5 | 5.9 |
| 2,500– 2,999 | 9.0 | 10.7 | 9.2 | 6.0 | 4.8 | 6.8 | 4.2 |
| 3,000– 3,499 | 11.6 | 14.4 | 10.5 | 7.3 | 5.7 | 6.4 | 5.5 |
| 3,500– 3,999 | 9.4 | 12.4 | 6.7 | 5.3 | 3.1 | 7.7 | 1.6 |
| 4,000– 4,499 | 6.7 | 8.3 | 7.1 | 3.7 | 1.5 | 1.9 | 1.4 |
| 4,500– 4,999 | 4.6 | 5.1 | 4.6 | 3.7 | 1.1 | 3.2 | 0.4 |
| 5,000– 5,999 | 8.2 | 9.6 | 11.1 | 4.6 | 0.6 | 0.6 | 0.6 |
| 6,000– 6,999 | 4.9 | 6.0 | 4.9 | 2.9 | 1.4 | 4.2 | 0.4 |
| 7,000– 9,999 | 4.4 | 5.6 | 4.5 | 2.3 | 0.2 | 1.0 | — |
| 10,000 and over | 3.3 | 3.8 | 2.7 | 2.5 | 1.4 | 1.9 | 1.3 |
| | | | | (*dollars*) | | | |
| Median income | 3,133 | 3,534 | 3,098 | 1,868 | 986 | 1,863 | 840 |

was only $1,868 compared with $3,098 for the partly matched group, and $3,534 for the completely matched. Similarly, the median income for the nonmatched unrelated individuals ($840) was only about one-half that shown for the matched group ($1,863). The matched sample of families had a somewhat higher income than the universe from which it was drawn. This bias, however, is largely eliminated when allowance is made for the fact that a relatively large proportion of the nonmatched group were not required to file tax returns and are therefore implicitly matched. It is more difficult to appraise the representativeness of the matched sample of unrelated individuals because of the large proportion of nonmatched cases, and also because of the difficulty of adjusting the matching rate to include implicitly matched cases.

Another way of examining the income distributions is to compare the proportion of cases matched in each income class. This is done in Table 5. The proportion of completely matched families increased progressively from about 20 per cent for those with incomes under $1,000 to a maximum of 73 per cent for those in the $3,500 to $3,999 income class. In higher income classes the matching rate fluctuated between 60 and 70 per cent. Among families with incomes of $5,000 and over, where there are relatively few

TABLE 5

Match Status of Families by 1950 Census Income Class

*(based on weighted sample cases)*

| INCOME IN CENSUS | TOTAL | *Completely Matched* | *Partly Matched* | *Not Matched* |
|---|---|---|---|---|
| | | | *(per cent)* | |
| Total reporting | 100.0 | 55.0 | 13.3 | 31.7 |
| None | 100.0 | 21.6 | 11.6 | 66.8 |
| Loss | 100.0 | [a] | [a] | [a] |
| $ 1–$ 499 | 100.0 | 20.9 | 8.3 | 70.9 |
| 500– 999 | 100.0 | 19.5 | 10.4 | 70.1 |
| 1,000– 1,499 | 100.0 | 33.5 | 15.8 | 50.7 |
| 1,500– 1,999 | 100.0 | 40.6 | 14.4 | 45.0 |
| 2,000– 2,499 | 100.0 | 53.1 | 17.0 | 29.9 |
| 2,500– 2,999 | 100.0 | 65.6 | 13.6 | 20.9 |
| 3,000– 3,499 | 100.0 | 68.1 | 12.1 | 19.8 |
| 3,500– 3,999 | 100.0 | 72.9 | 9.5 | 17.6 |
| 4,000– 4,499 | 100.0 | 68.4 | 14.0 | 17.6 |
| 4,500– 4,999 | 100.0 | 60.9 | 13.4 | 25.7 |
| 5,000– 5,999 | 100.0 | 64.3 | 18.0 | 17.7 |
| 6,000– 6,999 | 100.0 | 67.7 | 13.5 | 18.8 |
| 7,000– 9,999 | 100.0 | 70.0 | 13.5 | 16.5 |
| 10,000 and over | 100.0 | 64.7 | 11.0 | 24.3 |

[a] Percentages not shown since there were fewer than 100 cases in the sample reporting "Loss" in the census.

implicitly matched cases and where failure to match must be generally attributed to technical difficulties inherent in the matching process, about two-thirds of the families were completely matched. Although the matching rate is not impressively high for any income class, there is no evidence of a bias in the ability to match different groups of families within the income class in which one can reasonably expect to establish a match.

One final factor to be considered in appraising the validity of the matching study is the income level of families and individuals who did not report income in the census, since a marked bias in this group would seriously challenge the representativeness of the matched group. There is little evidence that such a bias exists. The nonresponse rate for income questions in the census as a whole was only 6 per cent, and tax returns were located for 54 per cent of the families in the sample who did not report on income in the census (see Table 6). The median income on tax returns for these families ($3,707) was only slightly higher than that for all matched

TABLE 6

Income on Tax Returns for Families Who Did Not Report on Income in the 1950 Census

(*weighted sample cases*)

| INCOME ON TAX RETURNS | *Families* |
|---|---|
| | (*number*) |
| Total | 399 |
| Completely matched | 216 |
| Not completely matched | 183 |
| | (*per cent*) |
| Total completely matched | 100.0 |
| Loss | 1.9 |
| $ 1–$ 499 | 0.9 |
| 500– 999 | 1.9 |
| 1,000– 1,499 | 2.3 |
| 1,500– 1,999 | 6.5 |
| 2,000– 2,499 | 13.9 |
| 2,500– 2,999 | 6.0 |
| 3,000– 3,499 | 8.8 |
| 3,500– 3,999 | 19.0 |
| 4,000– 4,499 | 8.3 |
| 4,500– 4,999 | 2.8 |
| 5,000– 5,999 | 9.3 |
| 6,000– 6,999 | 6.5 |
| 7,000– 9,999 | 10.2 |
| 10,000 and over | 1.9 |
| | (*dollars*) |
| Median income | 3,707 |

families ($3,591). The number of unrelated individuals in the sample who did not report income in the census was too small to permit comparisons.

### *Comparison of Census and Tax Return Income Distributions for Matched Groups*

Turning from a discussion of the representativeness of the sample and the degree to which the sample households were matched with tax returns, we can now compare the income information reported in the census and on tax returns by those families and individuals who were completely matched in the tax files. To sharpen the analysis, information is shown separately for all matched groups and for those roughly identified as not having reported any "nontaxable" income in the census.

All families and individuals who reported no income other than earnings were immediately classified in the latter category. Then PES schedules were located for families and individuals who, in the census, either did not report on such income or reported receiving one dollar or more of it. The PES schedule contained separate information on each of the following categories of income other than earnings: (1) unemployment or workmen's compensation; (2) social security benefits and government pensions or assistance; (3) other pensions and allowances; (4) veterans payments; (5) dependency allotments; (6) interest, dividends, and income from estates and trusts; (7) receipts from roomers and boarders; (8) rents and royalties; (9) money for support from persons not living in the household. Families and individuals reporting no income from items 1 through 5 and item 9 were classified as "with taxable income only"; all others were classified as having nontaxable income or as not reporting on taxable income.[4] Certain types of income, such as interest from nontaxable securities and Railroad Retirement pensions, may have been correctly reported in the census (the amount actually reported was very small) and correctly omitted from the tax returns. Similarly, the tax returns may include the cash value of certain types of income "in kind," which would have been

[4] The following additional criterion was used in the classification of families and individuals by taxable income. If there was a difference in type and size of family between the census and PES, the family was excluded from the group under analysis—"with taxable income only," in order to retain in this category only those families who reported the same composition in the PES and the census, and for whom all income information should have been reported for all family members in the census and on tax returns. Only 3 per cent of the matched families showed a difference in type or size of family between the PES and the census.

excluded from the census data. But in spite of many inadequacies, the procedure provides a reasonable, objective basis for roughly identifying families and individuals whose income in the census and on the tax returns was based on approximately the same income concept.

As might have been expected, the matching rate for families with taxable income only was higher (about 59 per cent) than that for other families (55 per cent). The same was true for unrelated individuals, 28 per cent, compared with 25 per cent for all individuals in the sample. Table 7 presents a summary picture of the income distributions in the census and on the tax returns for completely matched families and individuals.

There is a marked similarity between the census and tax return distributions for all families by income class; the maximum difference for any given class was only 2 percentage points and for most classes the difference was less than 1 percentage point. The discrepancy of $57 between the medians is not statistically significant. The same conclusions apply to families with taxable income only. Exclusion of families with nontaxable income tended to raise the level slightly for both distributions but had a greater impact on the tax return than on the census distribution. The explanation of this higher level is that nontaxable income, as defined here, consists largely of veterans payments, social security payments, public assistance payments, and other types of income usually received by low income groups.

The differences between the census and tax return income distributions are much greater for unrelated individuals than for families. Although the difference between the medians for all unrelated individuals is not significant ($90), the differences for given income classes are often quite substantial (Table 7). In part, the differences by income class are due to the relatively small number of unrelated individuals in the matched sample, but many are too great to be attributed to sampling error. For example, the census distribution shows about 6 per cent of matched individuals with no income, while none could appear in the tax return distribution. However, if one considers the proportion of individuals with incomes under $1,000, instead of just the "zero-income" group, the two distributions are more comparable—about 31 per cent in the census distribution, 28 per cent in the tax return distribution. This would indicate that while the zero-income individuals were classified at too low an income level in the census, most of this group clearly seems to have received less than $1,000 during 1949.

The similarity of the income distributions in the census and on

Matched Families and Unrelated Individuals by Income in 1950 Census and on Tax Returns

(*weighted sample cases*)

| INCOME IN CENSUS OR ON TAX RETURNS [a] | MATCHED FAMILIES [b] | | | | MATCHED INDIVIDUALS [b] | | | |
|---|---|---|---|---|---|---|---|---|
| | *Total* | | *With Taxable Income Only* [c] | | *Total* | | *With Taxable Income Only* [c] | |
| | *Census* | *Tax Returns* | *Census* | *Tax Returns* | *Census* | *Tax Returns* | *Census* | *Tax Returns* |
| | | | | (*number*) | | | | |
| Total in sample | 3,903 | 3,903 | 3,286 | 3,286 | 334 | 334 | 280 | 280 |
| Reporting on income | 3,687 | 3,903 | 3,118 | 3,286 | 311 | 334 | 266 | 280 |
| | | | | (*per cent*) | | | | |
| Total reporting | 100.0 | 100.0 | 100.0 | 100.0 | 100.0 | 100.0 | 100.0 | 100.0 |
| None | 1.5 | — | 1.7 | — | 6.4 | — | 6.8 | — |
| Loss | 0.1 | 0.4 | 0.1 | 0.5 | 0.6 | 1.5 | 0.8 | 1.8 |
| $ 1–$ 499 | 1.6 | 1.1 | 1.4 | 0.9 | 8.4 | 9.6 | 6.8 | 7.1 |
| 500– 999 | 2.1 | 3.7 | 2.0 | 3.5 | 15.1 | 18.6 | 12.8 | 18.9 |
| 1,000– 1,499 | 4.1 | 4.7 | 3.6 | 3.7 | 12.2 | 11.4 | 11.7 | 10.0 |
| 1,500– 1,999 | 5.7 | 6.7 | 5.3 | 6.4 | 10.0 | 16.5 | 11.7 | 15.0 |
| 2,000– 2,499 | 8.9 | 8.2 | 8.9 | 8.0 | 13.5 | 11.7 | 14.3 | 13.2 |
| 2,500– 2,999 | 10.7 | 10.1 | 10.7 | 10.6 | 6.8 | 9.6 | 7.9 | 10.7 |
| 3,000– 3,499 | 14.4 | 13.3 | 14.6 | 13.2 | 6.4 | 3.3 | 7.1 | 3.6 |
| 3,500– 3,999 | 12.4 | 10.4 | 12.8 | 9.8 | 7.7 | 8.7 | 6.8 | 9.6 |
| 4,000– 4,499 | 8.3 | 7.7 | 7.8 | 8.1 | 1.9 | 2.1 | 2.3 | 2.1 |
| 4,500– 4,999 | 5.1 | 7.0 | 5.3 | 7.5 | 3.2 | 1.2 | 3.0 | 1.4 |
| 5,000– 5,999 | 9.6 | 10.9 | 10.0 | 11.6 | 0.6 | 3.6 | 0.8 | 4.3 |
| 6,000– 6,999 | 6.0 | 6.7 | 6.5 | 7.3 | 4.2 | — | 4.9 | — |
| 7,000– 9,999 | 5.6 | 5.5 | 5.7 | 5.5 | 1.0 | 0.6 | 1.1 | 0.7 |
| 10,000 and over | 3.8 | 3.7 | 3.7 | 3.4 | 1.9 | 1.8 | 1.5 | 1.4 |
| | | | | (*dollars*) | | | | |
| Median income | 3,534 | 3,591 | 3,569 | 3,669 | 1,863 | 1,773 | 1,984 | 1,905 |

[a] The income classes refer to the amount of income in the 1950 census when columns marked *Census* are used, and by the amount of income on tax returns when the columns marked *Tax Returns* are used. (This applies also to Tables 8, 9, and 10.)

[b] In this and the following tables "matched" refers to "completely matched" families or unrelated individuals.

[c] As defined in the text. (This applies also to Table 8.)

tax returns for all families masks important differences in the underlying figures. One is revealed in Table 8, a comparison of the distributions for farm and nonfarm families. The census and tax return income distributions for nonfarm families are very similar. The discrepancy between the medians for all nonfarm families is only about $100, and for nonfarm families with taxable income only, about $150. But the differences between the distributions for farm families are striking. The median income for all farm families was $2,800 in the census compared with about $2,300 on tax returns. If the farm families with taxable income only are considered instead, the medians are closer; $2,700 in the census, $2,300 on tax returns. The differences between the *medians* for farm families are symptomatic of relatively large differences in the underlying distributions. Thus the census data show 8 per cent of all farm families with incomes under $500; the tax returns, 2 per cent. If the group is increased to all under $1,000, the proportions are much closer—12 per cent for the census and 15 per cent on tax returns. However, for the $1,000 to $1,999 income class, the difference is again striking—17 per cent for the census and 27 per cent on tax returns. Equally large differences were found for several other income classes. At the upper end of the farm income distribution ($6,000 and over) the census data show about 7 per cent of the families compared with only 3 per cent on tax returns.

The relatively large difference between the census and tax return income distributions for farm families is consistent, at least in direction, with facts obtained in the Audit Control Program (ACP) conducted by the Internal Revenue Service for a representative sample of tax returns for 1948.[5] One of the striking facts discovered in this study was that "mistakes on erroneous tax returns aggregated about $1.5 billion of tax change, or 10 per cent of the total tax liability voluntarily reported." [6] Even more important for the present discussion is the fact that about one-half of the $1.5 billion was made on returns with income or loss from business, farm, or profes-

[5] A description of the procedures and some preliminary results of the Audit Control Program may be found in: *The Audit Control Program: A Summary of Preliminary Results, May 1951,* Bureau of Internal Revenue; and in three papers by Marius Farioletti, "The 1948 Audit Control Program for Federal Income Tax Returns" (*National Tax Journal,* June 1949); "Some Results of the First Year's Audit Control Program of the Bureau of Internal Revenue" (*National Tax Journal,* March 1952); and the one in this volume.

[6] M. Farioletti, "Some Results of the First Year's Audit Control Program of the Bureau of Internal Revenue," p. 66. This article further notes that "about $1.4 billion or more than nine-tenths of the total tax change is estimated to involve additional assessments, and somewhat less than $100 million involves over assessments."

TABLE 8

Matched Families by Income in 1950 Census and on Tax Returns and by Residence

(*weighted sample cases*)

| INCOME IN CENSUS OR ON TAX RETURNS | MATCHED NONFARM FAMILIES | | | | MATCHED FARM FAMILIES | | | |
|---|---|---|---|---|---|---|---|---|
| | *Total* | | *With Taxable Income Only* | | *Total* | | *With Taxable Income Only* | |
| | *Census* | *Tax Returns* | *Census* | *Tax Returns* | *Census* | *Tax Returns* | *Census* | *Tax Returns* |
| | | | | (*number*) | | | | |
| Total in sample | 3,553 | 3,553 | 3,001 | 3,001 | 350 | 350 | 285 | 285 |
| Reporting on income | 3,351 | 3,553 | 2,845 | 3,001 | 336 | 350 | 273 | 285 |
| | | | | (*per cent*) | | | | |
| Total reporting | 100.0 | 100.0 | 100.0 | 100.0 | 100.0 | 100.0 | 100.0 | 100.0 |
| None | 1.4 | — | 1.5 | — | 2.4 | — | 2.9 | — |
| Loss | 0.1 | 0.4 | 0.1 | 0.4 | 0.6 | 1.1 | 0.7 | 1.4 |
| $ 1–$ 499 | 1.3 | 1.1 | 1.1 | 0.8 | 4.8 | 1.1 | 5.1 | 1.4 |
| 500– 999 | 1.9 | 2.8 | 1.7 | 2.6 | 4.2 | 12.9 | 4.4 | 12.6 |
| 1,000– 1,499 | 3.4 | 3.8 | 2.9 | 2.8 | 10.7 | 13.4 | 10.3 | 12.3 |
| 1,500– 1,999 | 5.6 | 6.0 | 5.1 | 5.6 | 6.5 | 13.7 | 7.0 | 14.0 |
| 2,000– 2,499 | 8.3 | 7.9 | 8.3 | 7.6 | 14.6 | 11.4 | 15.0 | 11.9 |
| 2,500– 2,999 | 10.8 | 9.9 | 10.8 | 10.3 | 10.4 | 12.3 | 9.9 | 13.7 |
| 3,000– 3,499 | 14.1 | 13.5 | 14.2 | 13.4 | 17.6 | 10.9 | 18.7 | 11.2 |
| 3,500– 3,999 | 12.9 | 10.8 | 13.4 | 10.3 | 8.0 | 6.0 | 7.0 | 4.6 |
| 4,000– 4,499 | 8.7 | 7.9 | 8.0 | 8.3 | 5.1 | 5.1 | 5.5 | 5.6 |
| 4,500– 4,999 | 5.5 | 7.2 | 5.8 | 7.8 | 1.2 | 4.6 | 0.7 | 4.9 |
| 5,000– 5,999 | 9.8 | 11.5 | 10.4 | 12.5 | 6.8 | 4.6 | 6.2 | 2.8 |
| 6,000– 6,999 | 6.1 | 7.3 | 6.7 | 7.8 | 4.8 | 1.1 | 3.7 | 1.4 |
| 7,000– 9,999 | 6.1 | 6.0 | 6.1 | 6.0 | 1.2 | 0.6 | 1.5 | 0.7 |
| 10,000 and over | 4.1 | 3.9 | 3.9 | 3.6 | 1.2 | 1.1 | 1.5 | 1.4 |
| | | | | (*dollars*) | | | | |
| Median income | 3,621 | 3,718 | 3,659 | 3,807 | 2,800 | 2,338 | 2,731 | 2,346 |

sional practice.[7] Since nine-tenths of the tax change on returns with business and professional incomes involved additional assessments (probably indicating underreporting of income), it is of interest to compare the census and tax return income distributions for families headed by farm operators and by nonfarm businessmen. In Table 9, all matched families are classified by total income in the census and on tax returns, and by the occupation of the family head.

Although the cross-classification of the sample of matched families by both income and occupation produces distributions with relatively small frequencies and, therefore, relatively large sampling errors, certain significant patterns appear. The medians show very similar income levels in both sources for several groups of families headed by persons who are predominantly wage or salary workers: salaried professional and managerial workers; clerical and sales workers; craftsmen and operatives; laborers and service workers. None of the above pairs of medians were significantly different in a statistical sense (that is, the variations were all within the range of sampling error of the estimates). In contrast, the census median income for farm operator families was about $800 higher than that reported on tax returns, and for families headed by self-employed professional and managerial workers (which includes proprietors of unincorporated businesses), about $500 higher.

The findings noted in the occupation analysis are generally confirmed by the figures in Table 10, which gives the distributions by type of income in the census and on tax returns. The striking similarity between the two distributions of total income and the median incomes for families headed by wage workers is borne out by the wage or salary income data. Furthermore, the sharp disparity between the self-employment income distributions confirms the differences previously noted in the total income distributions for families headed by farm operators or by self-employed professional and managerial workers.

The census and tax returns distributions of income other than earnings received by all families bear a strong resemblance to each other. According to both sets of data, four-fifths of the families received less than $1,000 and about 4 per cent received over $5,000 in unearned income; the median was the same in both cases—$400. This picture is somewhat deceptive, however, because of the marked differences in the definition of income other than earnings in the census and on tax returns. If one looks at families with taxable income only, a weakness in the census data becomes apparent. Only

[7] *Ibid.*, p. 77.

## TABLE 9

Matched Families by Income in 1950 Census and on Tax Returns and by Occupation of Head in April 1950

(*weighted sample cases*)

| TOTAL INCOME IN CENSUS OR ON TAX RETURNS | SELF-EMPLOYED PROFESSIONAL AND MANAGERIAL WORKERS | | SALARIED PROFESSIONAL AND MANAGERIAL WORKERS | | FARMERS AND FARM MANAGERS | | CLERICAL AND SALES WORKERS | | CRAFTSMEN AND OPERATIVES | | LABORERS AND SERVICE WORKERS | |
|---|---|---|---|---|---|---|---|---|---|---|---|---|
| | *Census* | *Tax Returns* | *Census* | *Tax Returns* | *Census* | *Tax Returns* | *Census* | *Tax Returns* | *Census* | *Tax Returns* | *Census* | *Tax Returns* |
| | (*number*) | | | | | | | | | | | |
| Total in sample | 307 | 307 | 557 | 557 | 230 | 230 | 473 | 473 | 1,574 | 1,574 | 413 | 413 |
| Reporting on income | 268 | 307 | 527 | 557 | 216 | 230 | 445 | 473 | 1,521 | 1,574 | 380 | 413 |
| | (*per cent*) | | | | | | | | | | | |
| Total reporting | 100.0 | 100.0 | 100.0 | 100.0 | 100.0 | 100.0 | 100.0 | 100.0 | 100.0 | 100.0 | 100.0 | 100.0 |
| None | 4.9 | — | 0.2 | — | 1.9 | — | — | — | 0.3 | — | 2.1 | — |
| Loss | — | 1.3 | — | 0.2 | — | 2.6 | — | — | — | 0.1 | 0.5 | — |
| $ 1–$ 499 | 0.7 | 1.6 | 0.4 | 0.4 | 4.6 | 0.9 | 0.4 | — | 1.0 | 0.6 | 1.1 | 0.7 |
| 500– 999 | 6.0 | 7.8 | 0.4 | 0.5 | 6.9 | 10.9 | 0.9 | 0.8 | 1.1 | 2.0 | 1.6 | 3.4 |
| 1,000– 1,499 | 2.6 | 3.9 | 1.1 | 1.4 | 10.2 | 14.3 | 2.0 | 1.9 | 2.9 | 4.1 | 6.3 | 3.9 |
| 1,500– 1,999 | 2.6 | 5.9 | 1.5 | 1.1 | 4.2 | 17.0 | 6.5 | 6.6 | 4.7 | 5.1 | 8.7 | 12.1 |
| 2,000– 2,499 | 8.2 | 10.4 | 4.6 | 3.2 | 11.1 | 11.7 | 8.8 | 9.5 | 9.1 | 7.7 | 15.3 | 12.3 |
| 2,500– 2,999 | 6.7 | 10.4 | 6.3 | 5.2 | 11.6 | 11.7 | 10.8 | 8.9 | 12.9 | 11.7 | 16.1 | 11.1 |
| 3,000– 3,499 | 8.2 | 11.1 | 7.0 | 9.2 | 19.0 | 9.6 | 15.7 | 16.7 | 16.8 | 13.7 | 19.2 | 18.2 |
| 3,500– 3,999 | 11.6 | 3.6 | 13.9 | 9.5 | 2.8 | 2.2 | 13.9 | 13.1 | 14.5 | 13.9 | 10.3 | 10.2 |
| 4,000– 4,499 | 9.7 | 3.6 | 5.7 | 5.7 | 5.1 | 4.3 | 12.6 | 8.0 | 9.7 | 10.4 | 5.5 | 7.3 |
| 4,500– 4,999 | 3.0 | 3.6 | 6.8 | 8.8 | 0.9 | 2.6 | 4.5 | 5.1 | 6.3 | 9.3 | 4.5 | 6.3 |
| 5,000– 5,999 | 10.1 | 13.7 | 13.9 | 16.3 | 10.2 | 8.7 | 8.5 | 12.1 | 10.1 | 9.8 | 4.7 | 8.4 |
| 6,000– 6,999 | 3.4 | 3.3 | 11.8 | 19.7 | 7.4 | 0.9 | 7.9 | 6.1 | 4.9 | 5.3 | 3.2 | 3.9 |
| 7,000– 9,999 | 5.2 | 5.9 | 17.5 | 11.0 | 2.3 | 0.9 | 3.8 | 6.8 | 4.7 | 4.9 | 0.5 | 2.2 |
| 10,000 and over | 17.2 | 14.0 | 9.1 | 7.7 | 1.9 | 1.7 | 3.6 | 4.4 | 1.2 | 1.3 | 0.5 | — |
| | (*dollars*) | | | | | | | | | | | |
| Median income | 3,935 | 3,390 | 5,158 | 5,291 | 2,980 | 2,185 | 3,673 | 3,714 | 3,546 | 3,679 | 2,951 | 3,177 |

TABLE 10

Matched Families by Type of Income in 1950 Census and on Tax Returns
(*weighted sample cases*)

| | | | SELF-EMPLOYMENT INCOME | | | | INCOME OTHER THAN EARNINGS | | | |
|---|---|---|---|---|---|---|---|---|---|---|
| | WAGE OR SALARY INCOME | | *Nonfarm Residents* | | *Farm Residents* | | *All Families* | | *Families with Taxable Income Only* | |
| INCOME IN CENSUS OR ON TAX RETURNS | *Census* | *Tax Returns* | *Census* | *Tax Returns* | *Census* | *Tax Returns* | *Census* | *Tax Returns* | *Census* | *Tax Returns* |
| | | | | | (*number*) | | | | | |
| Total in sample | 3,918 | 3,918 | 3,556 | 3,556 | 352 | 352 | 3,908 | 3,908 | 3,290 | 3,290 |
| Reporting on type of income | 3,742 | 3,918 | 3,402 | 3,556 | 348 | 352 | 3,757 | 3,908 | 3,187 | 3,290 |
| Reporting $1 or more | 3,144 | 3,379 | 530 | 642 | 232 | 229 | 1,014 | 1,006 | 525 | 829 |
| | | | | | (*per cent*) | | | | | |
| Total reporting $1 or more | 100.0 | 100.0 | 100.0 | 100.0 | 100.0 | 100.0 | 100.0 | 100.0 | 100.0 | 100.0 |
| Loss | — | — | 2.8 | 10.9 | 0.9 | 5.7 | — | 5.2 | — | 4.1 |
| $ 1–$ 499 | 2.7 | 2.4 | 10.4 | 12.5 | 12.9 | 5.2 | 57.1 | 62.9 | 63.0 | 65.7 |
| 500– 999 | 2.6 | 3.3 | 9.6 | 9.5 | 9.5 | 19.2 | 20.7 | 13.6 | 15.2 | 12.9 |
| 1,000– 1,499 | 4.5 | 4.8 | 6.0 | 10.1 | 9.9 | 14.4 | 9.2 | 5.4 | 7.2 | 5.2 |
| 1,500– 1,999 | 6.6 | 6.2 | 6.4 | 8.7 | 10.3 | 10.9 | 3.8 | 2.2 | 2.3 | 1.9 |
| 2,000– 2,499 | 9.2 | 7.8 | 6.0 | 12.3 | 11.6 | 12.2 | 3.0 | 2.0 | 2.9 | 2.2 |
| 2,500– 2,999 | 11.8 | 10.4 | 8.3 | 7.6 | 3.9 | 11.4 | 1.6 | 0.9 | 1.9 | 0.8 |
| 3,000– 3,499 | 15.3 | 13.5 | 11.1 | 6.1 | 19.0 | 5.2 | 0.1 | 2.4 | 0.2 | 1.7 |
| 3,500– 3,999 | 12.0 | 12.0 | 8.1 | 1.2 | 3.4 | 2.6 | 0.4 | 0.6 | 0.4 | 0.5 |
| 4,000– 4,499 | 7.6 | 8.2 | 5.8 | 4.5 | 3.4 | 4.4 | 0.3 | 0.7 | 0.2 | 0.8 |
| 4,500– 4,999 | 5.7 | 6.3 | 3.0 | 2.8 | 0.9 | — | 0.2 | 0.4 | 0.4 | 0.5 |
| 5,000– 5,999 | 8.7 | 9.6 | 10.4 | 5.5 | 9.1 | 6.1 | 1.1 | 0.8 | 1.7 | 0.7 |
| 6,000– 6,999 | 6.7 | 7.5 | 2.6 | 1.1 | 2.6 | — | 0.8 | 0.4 | 1.1 | 0.5 |
| 7,000– 9,999 | 4.0 | 5.4 | 3.6 | 3.0 | 0.9 | 0.9 | 0.2 | 1.0 | 0.4 | 1.0 |
| 10,000 and over | 2.6 | 2.6 | 5.7 | 4.2 | 1.7 | 1.7 | 1.6 | 1.6 | 3.0 | 1.4 |
| | | | | | (*dollars*) | | | | | |
| Median income for those reporting income of specified type | 3,412 | 3,570 | 3,017 | 1,902 | 2,278 | 1,750 | 439 | 356 | 398 | 350 |

one-sixth reported to the census receipts of one dollar or more of such income, but one-fourth of the families reported such receipts on tax returns. Although the census indicated a smaller proportion of recipients, the level and distribution of income reported was the same as that reported on tax returns.

## *Cross-Classification of Income in Census and on Tax Returns*

The data presented thus far were used primarily in classifications by the amount of income reported by each family and individual either in the census or on tax returns. Cross-classification by the amount of income reported in both of these sources so far has been discussed only in an examination of the income on tax returns for families who did not report on income in the census and an examination of the income reported in the census for families whose tax returns could not be matched. The cross-classification data helped to answer important questions on a potential source of bias in the census income reports and contributed to an evalution of the present matching study.

But these data can also be used to examine the consistency of response for identical families. In the preceding section a marked similarity between the census and tax return distributions was seen particularly for nonfarm families headed by wage or salary workers. This similarity could be the result of reports either of the same income to the census interviewer and on tax returns, or of different incomes but ones that in balance tended to offset each other. If there are offsetting differences, it is important to find out whether they are random errors attributable to faulty memory or if they are systematically related to the economic or demographic characteristics of the families and so may affect some of the cross-classifications of income with other variables.

Table 11, restricted to completely matched families which reported on income in the census, shows the percentage distribution of families in each income class in the census according to the amount of income reported on tax returns. The diagonal cells (indicated by rules) represent families found in the same income class in both sources. Some families in the diagonal cells may have reported relatively large differences, whereas those in adjacent cells may have reported relatively small ones, but here it is assumed that families in the diagonal cells reported their incomes consistently and that the other families did not. Clearly the variation in response for identical families is considerable. Only about 45 per cent of the families were found in the same income class in both the census and on tax returns. Another 24 per cent of the families were either in one higher or lower adjacent class in both sources. The proportion of families in the same class was greatest in the income classes above $5,000, largely because their minimum size was $1,000 compared with the uniform $500 classes used at the lower levels. This

TABLE 11

Matched Families by Income in 1950 Census and by Income on Tax Returns

*(weighted sample cases)*

| INCOME IN CENSUS [a] | INCOME ON TAX RETURNS [a] | | | | | | | | | | | | | | | |
|---|---|---|---|---|---|---|---|---|---|---|---|---|---|---|---|---|
| | *Total* | *Loss* | *$1 to $499* | *$500 to $999* | *$1,000 to $1,499* | *$1,500 to $1,999* | *$2,000 to $2,499* | *$2,500 to $2,999* | *$3,000 to $3,499* | *$3,500 to $3,999* | *$4,000 to $4,499* | *$4,500 to $4,999* | *$5,000 to $5,999* | *$6,000 to $6,999* | *$7,000 to $9,999* | *$10,000 and Over* |
| | *(per cent)* | | | | | | | | | | | | | | | |
| $ 1,000–$1,499 | 100.0 | — | — | 16.0 | 38.7 | 16.0 | 4.0 | 6.0 | 2.7 | 4.7 | 1.3 | — | 1.3 | 8.0 | — | 1.3 |
| 1,500– 1,999 | 100.0 | — | 6.2 | 10.4 | 13.7 | 41.2 | 10.9 | 6.6 | 3.3 | 2.4 | 1.9 | — | 0.5 | — | 2.8 | — |
| 2,000– 2,499 | 100.0 | — | 1.2 | 3.0 | 6.7 | 16.2 | 33.8 | 13.1 | 9.5 | 5.8 | 1.5 | 2.1 | 4.0 | 0.6 | 1.8 | 0.6 |
| 2,500– 2,999 | 100.0 | 1.0 | 0.5 | — | 4.0 | 6.1 | 12.4 | 45.7 | 15.7 | 4.5 | 2.8 | 2.5 | 2.5 | 1.3 | 1.0 | — |
| 3,000– 3,499 | 100.0 | — | 0.4 | 2 8 | 2.6 | 3.6 | 8.1 | 10.2 | 46.6 | 10.4 | 4.7 | 4.3 | 2.8 | 2.3 | 0.8 | 0.4 |
| 3,500– 3,999 | 100.0 | — | — | — | 1.7 | 1.7 | 1.7 | 8.3 | 17.4 | 40.5 | 8.1 | 9.8 | 7.0 | 1.3 | 1.5 | 0.9 |
| 4,000– 4,499 | 100.0 | 0.7 | — | — | 1.3 | 1.0 | 3.3 | 2.6 | 10.7 | 12.4 | 43.3 | 11.4 | 6.5 | 3.6 | 1.3 | 2.0 |
| 4,500– 4,999 | 100.0 | 0.5 | — | — | — | 2.1 | 2.1 | 4.8 | 2.1 | 4.3 | 12.8 | 48.7 | 14.4 | 4.3 | 1.1 | 2.7 |
| 5,000– 5,999 | 100.0 | 0.6 | — | 1.1 | — | 0.3 | 3.7 | 1.1 | 2.8 | 4.5 | 4.8 | 9.6 | 55.8 | 7.9 | 5.9 | 1.7 |
| 6,000– 6,999 | 100.0 | — | — | 1.8 | 0.5 | 2.7 | 1.8 | 3.6 | 0.5 | 2.3 | 2.3 | 3.2 | 20.9 | 45.0 | 13.6 | 1.8 |
| 7,000– 9,999 | 100.0 | — | 1.0 | — | — | 1.0 | 1.4 | 1.0 | 2.4 | — | 3.8 | 1.9 | 9.1 | 30.8 | 47.1 | 0.5 |
| 10,000 and over | 100.0 | — | 0.7 | — | 1.4 | — | 1.4 | — | 1.4 | — | 1.4 | 4.3 | 2.8 | 1.4 | 8.5 | 76.6 |

[a] No percentage shown for the first four census income classes— "none", "loss", $1–499, and $500–999—because there were fewer than 100 matched sample cases in each of these classes in the census.

fact would explain the extent of agreement (77 per cent) in the $10,000 and over class. In most income classes below $5,000, between 40 and 45 per cent of the families were in the same class in the census and on tax returns, the only exception being the $2,000–2,499 class, where only 34 per cent were in agreement.

Table 12 highlights the considerable response variation in income reporting by families headed by persons in different occupational

TABLE 12

Matched Families in Same or Different Income Class in 1950 Census and on Tax Returns by Occupation of Head in April 1950

*(based on weighted sample cases)*

| INCOME CLASS IN CENSUS AND ON TAX RETURNS | TOTAL REPORTING ON INCOME | OCCUPATION OF FAMILY HEAD | | | | | |
|---|---|---|---|---|---|---|---|
| | | *Professional and Managerial Workers* | | *Farmers and Farm Managers* | *Clerical and Sales Workers* | *Craftsmen and Operatives* | *Laborers and Service Workers* |
| | | *Self Employed* | *Salaried* | | | | |
| | | | | *(per cent)* | | | |
| Total reporting | 100.0 | 100.0 | 100.0 | 100.0 | 100.0 | 100.0 | 100.0 |
| Same class | 44.9 | 36.2 | 49.1 | 36.6 | 47.6 | 50.0 | 36.6 |
| Adjacent class | 24.3 | 17.5 | 31.5 | 18.5 | 21.2 | 23.6 | 27.1 |
| Census higher | 13.9 | 12.3 | 22.2 | 10.2 | 13.3 | 11.4 | 13.2 |
| Tax returns higher | 10.4 | 5.2 | 9.3 | 8.3 | 7.9 | 12.2 | 13.9 |
| Difference of 2 or more classes | 30.8 | 46.2 | 19.3 | 44.9 | 31.3 | 26.4 | 36.3 |
| Census higher | 14.4 | 27.2 | 8.3 | 33.3 | 11.7 | 11.7 | 14.2 |
| Tax returns higher | 16.4 | 19.0 | 11.0 | 11.6 | 19.6 | 14.7 | 22.1 |
| | | | | *(dollars)* | | | |
| Median income: | | | | | | | |
| Census | 3,534 | 3,935 | 5,158 | 2,980 | 3,673 | 3,546 | 2,951 |
| Tax returns | 3,591 | 3,390 | 5,291 | 2,185 | 3,714 | 3,679 | 3,177 |

groups. Compared to all families in the same income class or in one higher or lower adjacent class in the census and on tax returns (about 70 per cent), families headed by self-employed persons or by laborers and service workers showed somewhat greater variation. About 35 per cent of these families were in the same income class and another 20 per cent in an adjacent one. In contrast, about 50 per cent of the other families (those headed by salaried professional and managerial workers, clerical and sales workers, and craftsmen and operatives) were in the same class and another 25 per cent in an adjacent one. Occupation groups having the most stable incomes show the least variation in response. However, even in these groups, only one-half of the families were in the same income class in both the census and on tax returns. Despite this extreme variation in response, however, the median incomes reported in the census and on tax returns for most groups were quite similar. Only in the case of the self-employed did the median vary by more than $250.

All income matching studies conducted to date indicate that the variability of response in income surveys is relatively great.[8] Apparently only about half of the income recipients report receipts in the same income class even when asked a given set of income questions only one month apart. Fortunately, the variations in response elicited in repeated interviews appear to be random and do not introduce any systematic bias into the income distribution. The study of variation in response in field surveys of income does not preclude the existence of a systematic downward bias attributable to faulty memory, misunderstanding of the income concept, or misrepresentation. However, if one assumes that a given respondent uses a constant framework of reference from one month to the next, then his failure to report the same amount of income must be laid to random lapses of memory resulting in overstatements of income balanced by understatements.

### *Implications of Findings*

In this study, income reports obtained in the 1950 census were compared with similar information reported by identical families on tax returns, on the premise that such a comparison would validate the census data. The results indicate a high degree of consistency between income distributions for wage or salary workers based on these two sources of data. Also, differences between the distributions for self-employed persons are consistent, in direction at least, with information obtained in field studies conducted by the Internal Revenue Service. On this basis, one could conclude that the census income data are quite accurate. The validity of the conclusion, however, depends entirely on the validity of the assumption that tax returns are accurate.

There may be some understatement of income on tax returns, though its precise amount is difficult to estimate. According to Selma Goldsmith, tax returns contained about a 14 per cent understatement of income in 1944 to 1946.[9] This figure was obtained by estimating both the aggregate income reported on tax returns and

[8] For a more detailed discussion of the variability of response in income surveys, as indicated by income matching studies, see Herman P. Miller, *Income of the American People,* Wiley, 1955, pp. 143–145, 157–164.

[9] Selma F. Goldsmith, "An Appraisal of Basic Data Available for Constructing Size Distributions," in Volume Thirteen (1951) of Studies in Income and Wealth, p. 302, and also her paper in this volume.

the comparable aggregate derived from the personal income series of the Department of Commerce. If Mrs. Goldsmith's analysis is correct, the underlying assumption that tax returns can be used as a validation check for census reports is questionable. The national income estimates may be more nearly correct, since they are among the most important and the most carefully prepared of all our statistical series. Yet as the national income estimators themselves admit, certain segments of the national income totals, such as entrepreneurial income, rental income, and interest, may be subject to substantial margins of error. And adjustment of the basic national income estimates for comparability with tax returns may be subject to even greater error.

# COMMENT

JOSEPH A. PECHMAN, COMMITTEE FOR ECONOMIC DEVELOPMENT

The matching studies summarized in this volume have long been awaited by the income distribution fraternity. This small band of diligent statisticians and economists has been struggling for years to evaluate and to reconcile the several income distributions appearing periodically, and the studies needed for this purpose have at last been made possible by the Census Bureau, the Internal Revenue Service, the Social Security Administration, the Federal Reserve Board, and the Michigan Survey Research Center. The value of the information thus provided has been enhanced by the release in this volume of some of the results of the 1949 IRS audit study. Our small income distribution fraternity can now go to work not only to evaluate the existing data but also to improve those to be obtained in the future.

I shall confine my remarks to the paper prepared by Herman Miller and Leon R. Paley, which compares the 1949 incomes reported by a representative sample of the population to the Census Bureau and to the IRS.

## SUMMARY OF THE MILLER–PALEY FINDINGS

At the risk of condensing too much, I believe that the findings of the study by Miller and Paley may be fairly summarized as follows:

1. There is a marked similarity between the distributions of the matched families as ranked by the income reported to the Census

Bureau and to the IRS, the medians of the IRS being $57 higher (a little more than 1.6 per cent). For unrelated individuals, however, the census median is $90 higher (about 5 per cent).[1] These differences are based on incomes as reported to the two agencies, without correction for differences in income concept.

2. To eliminate the effect of conceptual differences, the sample cases reporting nontaxable income in the census were removed. This increased the medians for both distributions, widened the gap between the medians of families, and narrowed the gap between the medians of unrelated individuals. For families with taxable income only,[2] the IRS median is higher by $100 (2.8 per cent) than the corresponding median based on census reports; the census median for unrelated individuals with taxable income exceeds the corresponding IRS median by only $79 (4.1 per cent).

3. Although the distributions of all families from the census and IRS reports are almost identical, there are marked differences in the distributions for the farm (census median 16 per cent higher) and nonfarm (IRS median 4 per cent higher) sectors and for some of the occupations within the nonfarm sector. Among nonfarm families, the IRS gives higher medians for those headed by wage earners and salaried, professional, and managerial workers, while the census yields higher medians for the self-employed businessmen and professional workers. Miller and Paley note correctly that these results are consistent with what we know about tax returns from the IRS Audit Control Programs for the years 1948 and 1949. The ACP found inaccuracies in reporting income on tax returns by self-employed persons (farm and nonfarm), who tend to overstate deductions and forget receipts, in contrast to the fairly accurate reports of income by wage earners, subject to tax by withholding.[3]

4. One of their most interesting tables (Table 11) distributes the matched families by census incomes and cross-classifies them by IRS incomes. As might be expected, the diagonal cells in this table are the most densely populated, indicating that numerous families report "approximately" equal incomes to the two agencies. But the families in the diagonal cells are by no means the majority

[1] These and subsequent percentage comparisons between census and IRS medians are computed by dividing the absolute difference by the lower of the two figures.

[2] To avoid confusion, I am using the term "taxable" income as it is used by Miller and Paley—i.e., as the income (exclusive of net capital gains) individuals or married couples include in their tax returns, before allowances for deductions and exemptions. The tax law actually defines taxable income as adjusted gross income less deductions and less personal exemptions.

[3] See Marius Farioletti, "Some Results of the First Year's Audit Control Program of the Bureau of Internal Revenue," *National Tax Journal,* March 1952, pp. 65–78, and his paper in this volume, Tables 1–6.

(about 45 per cent below $5,000), and the class intervals in the table are wide enough to mask differences in the two incomes for families in the same cells. This table would have been more revealing if the diagonal cells had been split between those families who reported higher incomes to the census and those who reported higher incomes to the IRS. However, it is quite obvious from the table as it stands that the relatively small net difference previously noted between the medians for families covers up sizeable offsetting differences in reporting.

UNDERREPORTING BY THE CENSUS

The most important facts in the Miller and Paley study are significant for income distribution work, but the conclusions they seem to draw from these facts are questionable. It is hard to pin down their reasoning, but I believe it proceeds somewhat as follows:

A distribution of randomly selected families ranked by census incomes looks a good deal like a distribution of the same families ranked by their IRS incomes (admitting significant differences in the reports by some segments of the population—particularly for self-employed farm and nonfarm groups). However, the results of this matching study, like others, indicate that "the variations in response elicited in repeated interviews appear to be random and *do not introduce any systematic bias into the income distribution*" (italics added). Thus the authors point out that "on this basis" the match between the census and IRS data indicates that "the census income data are quite accurate." But they realize immediately that they have overstated their case for the accuracy of census data, because such a conclusion rests entirely on "the validity of the assumption that tax returns are accurate." Referring to Mrs. Goldsmith's finding that total income calculated from income tax returns is understated compared to national income estimates of total income—which the authors consider "most nearly correct"—they reluctantly conclude that "the underlying assumption that tax returns can be used as a validation check for census reports is questionable."

It is surprising indeed that Miller and Paley suggest that there is no systematic bias in the census distribution, and that they are so reluctant to admit that unaudited tax returns cannot be used to check the census data. Conclusive evidence on this point is given in Farioletti's paper on the IRS Audit Control Program. It is well to recall that the estimates of reporting errors described in this study were based on personal interviews conducted by trained internal revenue agents, that the income concept they used was unambiguous (except in the rare instances where even the income tax law can be variously interpreted), that these agents had the force of law behind them, and that they had in their possession at the time of the interviews as many of the information returns as could be found for each individual in the files of the IRS. Farioletti warns us that, despite these important advantages, the IRS was not able to disclose all the errors in its sample returns. Accordingly, it is not a matter of conjecture that unaudited tax returns understate incomes—we know this to be a fact. Since the census median for families is lower than the IRS median based on unaudited tax returns, it follows that the census distribution understates total family income.

It is abundantly clear that the aggregate income covered by the census distributions falls considerably short of the correct total—$42 billion, or 25 per cent, short of the NID aggregate for 1949.[4] While the national income estimates may not be accurate to the nearest billion dollars, few will challenge Mrs. Goldsmith's statement that "no serious student of the national income statistics would suggest that the aggregate money income embodied in the OBE personal income series could be overstated by anything like these orders of magnitude."[5] The evidence of underreporting by individuals in field surveys is so clear that the national income estimator has no choice but to correct for this underreporting when he distributes total income by size.

To take one example: the national income estimate of dividends paid is based on data reported on corporation income tax returns, but comparison of these estimates with dividends reported by individuals on their tax returns (corrected for the known differences in coverage) reveals a gap of some 15 to 20 per cent.[6] Thus, two sets of data published by the same agency yield substantially different results. When the national income estimator finds that survey data yield about the same amount of dividends as that disclosed on individual tax returns, he must attempt to correct for underreporting in estimating the distribution of total income by size.

One of the major arguments in favor of census data has been that, in spite of the known underreporting, they are useful in disclosing internal relationships in the structure of the income distribution (differences in incomes among cities of different size, relationships between earnings and income other than earnings, and relative distributions of families headed by persons belonging to different population groups). However, underreporting in the census surveys

[4] See the paper by Selma F. Goldsmith, in this volume, Table 1.
[5] *Ibid.*, p. 73. [6] *Ibid.*, Table 3.

is not distributed evenly by size classes, by regions, or by size of city. According to Mrs. Goldsmith's estimates census data cover more than 90 per cent of total wages; 89 per cent of nonfarm entrepreneurial income; 78 per cent of farm income; about two-thirds of rental income, social security, and military payments; and only about 23 per cent of interest and dividends.[7] With such wide variations in coverage, many of the relationships shown by the census surveys must be unreliable. To mention one obvious example, the CPS survey for the year 1954 shows almost fifteen million families and unattached individuals with money incomes of less than $2,000.[8] Since farm families make up a large portion of this group, and since there is more understatement of farm than of urban incomes, it is difficult to judge the magnitude and character of the low-income problem.

## CORRECTING FOR UNDERREPORTING

Unfortunately, although a careful analyst can approximate the amount of underreporting in a field survey, he is rarely able to distribute that amount by income level. He needs both what Hart and Lieblein called a "statistical bridge" [9] between the field survey data and the tax return data and estimates of underreporting on tax returns. The papers by Miller and Paley and by Farioletti indicate that it is technically feasible to obtain such information, and I urge that a concerted effort be made to do so. There is sufficient time between now and 1960, when the next decennial census is to be taken, to plan for the necessary tabulations.

I suggest that the census materials will be useful for classifying the population into family units, but the incomes they report should be regarded as only first approximations of their actual incomes. A subsample of the census sample might be used to obtain the necessary statistical bridge between census incomes and the incomes reported on tax returns. This subsample should be large enough to provide statistically reliable cross-classifications of family units by income size classes and by other characteristics, such as occupation, type of income receipts, and size of family. A matching study between the census and IRS data, similar to the study reported on by Miller and Paley, would provide the data to fill in the cells in the statistical bridge. Once the bridge is available, all that would be needed is an audit study of tax returns (based on an entirely differ-

[7] *Ibid.*, Table 2. [8] *Ibid.*, Table 4.

[9] Albert Gailord Hart and Julius Lieblein, "Family Income and the Income Tax Base," in Volume Eight (1946) of Studies in Income and Wealth, pp. 235–262.

ent sample in order to avoid disclosing the names of census respondents to the IRS) to estimate the underreporting of census incomes. The audit study should be designed to provide estimates of underreporting by type of income throughout the income scale, in addition to the administrative data needed by the IRS for evaluating and improving tax enforcement techniques.[10] These tabulations would, of course, be supplementary to the regular census tabulations and would not supplant them.

This undertaking would be costly, but not prohibitively so. If necessary, the number of annual surveys could be reduced, especially since available evidence suggests that the year-to-year changes in the relative distribution of income are minor. Accurate data on income distributions once every two or five years would be more valuable than incomplete data on annual distributions.

[10] The expenditure of funds for an audit study could be justified on the ground that the data would be useful not only for income size distribution work, but also for administrative purposes by the IRS. A follow-up of the 1948–1950 audit studies once every five years is a minimum requirement for effective income tax enforcement.

# The 1950 Census and the Post-Enumeration Survey

LEON PRITZKER, BUREAU OF THE CENSUS AND
CASE INSTITUTE OF TECHNOLOGY
ALFRED SANDS, BUREAU OF THE CENSUS

## *Introduction*

This paper will describe the Post-Enumeration Survey of the 1950 Censuses of Population, Housing, and Agriculture. We shall be concerned mainly with what the PES has to say about the accuracy of the 1950 census percentage distributions of the population with respect to income. We shall also strive to make clear the methods and techniques of the PES, as well as its assumptions and limitations.

### DEFINITIONS USED

The PES provides a basis for evaluating both the data and the statistics of the 1950 censuses. By a *datum,* we mean an edited and coded recording of an individual response to a census inquiry. By a *statistic,* we mean any result of a tabulating and computing operation carried out on data; a total, a median, or a percentage.

We use the term *gross error* to refer to errors in data; for example, the failure to list a person on the rolls of the census, the erroneous reporting, recording, or coding of income. We use the term *net error* to refer to errors in statistics, deviations from "true values."

### INTERPRETATION OF RESULTS

The PES results can be viewed in two ways: first, as estimates of difference between two enumerations of the same population; second, as estimates of error in the original enumeration. In this paper, we shall in most cases take the latter position. The assumptions on which this view is based are set forth in the next section.

Tables 1 and 2 provide some results relating to the income data of the 1950 Census of Population. There were errors in obtaining in-

Note: The PES was the product of many minds. We would have to list at least fifty names if we were explicitly to acknowledge the contributions of others to the production of the results and of the ideas contained in this paper. We choose instead to acknowledge our own responsibility for the errors and omissions of this particular presentation as well as to disclaim any credit for whatever is included of value.

come data in the PES as well as in the 1950 census. Hence, with regard to the evaluation of data, we take the first position stated above. The PES furnishes estimates of gross difference between the data obtained in two enumerations of the same population, and not of gross error in the 1950 census. Yet we regard the PES as accurate enough to evaluate the net errors of the 1950 census.

### QUANTITATIVE ESTIMATES OF ERROR

At present, only a start has been made by the Bureau of the Census in the development of methods for measuring accuracy. Some of this work has been documented.[1] Beginning in 1945, we have been experimenting with two methods, the record check and the re-enumerative check. The PES incorporated both. The papers in this volume that compare census data with data of the Survey Research Center, the Bureau of Old-Age and Survivors Insurance, and the Internal Revenue Service are based on information derived from the PES. This paper is concerned with the re-enumerative check of the PES.

### THE NATURE OF THE CHECK

Four or five months after the start of the original census enumeration on April 1, 1950, intensive recanvasses were made of samples of small areas designed to represent the United States. The object was to find people, dwellings, and farms that were missed in the original enumeration. At the same time, and mostly in the same areas, intensive reinterviews were conducted with a sample of the population enumerated in the census in the hope of obtaining information of sufficient accuracy to evaluate that obtained in the original enumeration. The check was designed along the following lines:

1. It was as close to a "maximum intensity" procedure as could be designed. Contrast, for example, the probing-type questions used to obtain income data in the PES with the global-type questions of the census enumeration (see the appendix, Exhibits A-1 and A-2). Roughly twenty times more money was spent per case than in the original enumeration. In the census enumeration, a single individual could answer for all members of a household; in the check, the "best" respondent had to be sought out, even at the expense of repeated calls. The "best" respondent was generally regarded as the person for whom the information was required. Thus, in general, each adult was queried about his own income.

[1] A. Ross Eckler and Leon Pritzker, "Measuring the Accuracy of Enumerative Surveys," paper presented before the 27th Session of the International Statistical Institute, New Delhi, India, December 5, 1951.

2. About 250 superior interviewers were obtained, given more training, and provided with closer supervision than was possible for the 130,000 census enumerators.

3. The check provided for case-by-case comparison and, usually, reconciliation. The interviewers, for example, were provided with transcripts of the original income data obtained for 95 out of every 100 persons in the "personal income subsample." They were instructed not to examine these transcripts until they had obtained responses to their questions.

## *Major Assumptions Underlying the PES*

We have stated our view that the PES results provide estimates of net error in the income statistics of the 1950 census. Four major assumptions are required for this position. Not one of them can be accepted unreservedly, and to the extent that they cannot, they limit the validity of the PES results.

### TRUE VALUES EXIST

This is the assumption that there was a precisely defined true value for the income in 1949 of everyone in the United States. In the light of the definitions and instructions provided in the Enumerator's Reference Manual for the 1950 census, however, there was at least one case in which two income analysts, in possession of "all the facts" and employing the same definitions, would differ as to the amount of income. We do not know how common such disagreements would be, but we assume that they would not have any significant effect.

There is a deeper problem, however; the "true values" sought by the Bureau of the Census may not meet the requirements of some users of the statistics. The PES does not furnish any data on this; the census definitions were used as a basis for the PES inquiries.

### "BETTER" METHODS LEAD TO GREATER ACCURACY

Largely on a priori grounds, it has been held that the addition of certain features constitutes "improvement"—features like probing interviews, insistence on the "best" respondent, intensive training and supervision of personnel, in fact all the special features employed in the PES. These improvements, it is held, show up in more accurate data and statistics. Thus, it is argued that the PES was "better" than the census, in fact sufficiently accurate to evaluate the census.

There is an obvious limitation to this assumption. Both the census and the PES made use of interview methods and both were subject to some of the inherent limitations of such methods.

THE TIME LAG DID NOT ADVERSELY AFFECT THE PES RESULTS

In our judgment, this assumption is false, at least as far as the results relating to the number of persons missed in the original enumeration are concerned. The PES check underestimated the extent of underenumeration in the 1950 census. One reason was that the PES interviewers were unable to account for all the missed people who changed their residence during the period between the onset of the census and the onset of the check.

The validity of the assumption in regard to the reporting of income is also important. The census inquiries about income in 1949 were conducted almost entirely in April and May 1950. The PES inquiries, also directed at 1949, were conducted almost entirely in August and September 1950. Was there any significant deterioration in the respondents' memories? We do not know; we assume that there was not, especially since the PES inquires were, at least a priori, better designed to restore or refresh memory.

CERTAIN CENSUS OPERATIONS DID NOT REQUIRE CHECKING

The punching, tabulating, reviewing, and publishing operations of the census were believed sufficiently controlled. The PES results do not indicate any of the errors that may have arisen during these operations. They reflect only the errors arising from three activities of the census; enumeration, editing, and coding.

### *Gross Differences and Net Errors: Total Income of Persons*

The starting points for study of the PES results are tables like Tables 1 and 2. They provide a first view of the sources of error in census statistics. Although we are dealing with gross differences rather than gross errors, we believe that the tables afford a fairly realistic conception of the relative contribution of each source of error. We shall not attempt any detailed description of the sources of error or of the gross differences, but we call attention to two results shown in the tables:

1. If the PES had been conducted on the entire population of the United States, about 40 per cent of the males and about 25 per cent of the females would have been assigned to different income classes from the ones they had been assigned to in the census. (These estimates exclude the contributions of nonresponse and of errors and differences in defining the population; not enumerating

## TABLE 1

### 1949 Income of Males: Estimated PES Distribution by 1950 Census Distribution

(estimates in thousands rounded without adjustment to group totals, which are independently rounded)

| ITEM | Total PES: Adjusted[a] | Total PES: Not adjusted | Not included in census income distribution: Misclassified[b] | Not included in census income distribution: Omitted | Population enumerated in census and PES | Income in census: Total census | None | Under $500[c] | $500–$999 | $1,000–$1,499 | $1,500–$1,999 | $2,000–$2,499 | $2,500–$2,999 | $3,000–$3,499 | $3,500–$3,999 | $4,000–$4,499 | $4,500–$4,999 | $5,000–$5,999 | $6,000–$6,999 | $7,000–$9,999 | $10,000 and over | Income not reported |
|---|---|---|---|---|---|---|---|---|---|---|---|---|---|---|---|---|---|---|---|---|---|---|
| TOTAL CENSUS[d] | | | | | | 54,601 | 6,350 | 4,682 | 4,633 | 4,281 | 4,083 | 5,198 | 4,767 | 5,198 | 3,335 | 2,398 | 1,347 | 1,832 | 818 | 889 | 929 | 3,862 |
| Not included in PES income distribution: | | | | | | | | | | | | | | | | | | | | | | |
| Misclassified[e] | | | | | | 197 | 72 | 20 | 10 | 10 | 0 | 10 | 0 | 0 | 0 | 0 | 9 | 0 | 0 | 0 | 0 | 66 |
| Erroneously included | | | | | | 603 | 112 | 19 | 77 | 76 | 63 | 63 | 41 | 29 | 5 | 0 | 0 | 10 | 0 | 11 | 11 | 86 |
| Population enumerated in census and PES | | | | | | 53,801 | 6,166 | 4,643 | 4,546 | 4,195 | 4,020 | 5,125 | 4,726 | 5,169 | 3,330 | 2,398 | 1,338 | 1,822 | 818 | 878 | 918 | 3,710 |
| Income in PES | | | | | | | | | | | | | | | | | | | | | | |
| Total PES | 55,438 | 55,438 | 233 | 1,404 | 53,801 | | | | | | | | | | | | | | | | | |
| None | 5,435 | 4,999 | 55 | 137 | 4,807 | | 3,475 | 381 | 94 | 61 | 20 | 51 | 41 | 27 | 19 | 11 | 10 | 21 | 0 | 0 | 9 | 587 |
| Under $ 500[c] | 5,089 | 4,664 | 0 | 137 | 4,527 | | 898 | 2,724 | 440 | 122 | 52 | 19 | 11 | 19 | 19 | 20 | 0 | 37 | 0 | 0 | 29 | 137 |
| $ 500– 999 | 5,038 | 4,608 | 0 | 133 | 4,475 | | 461 | 498 | 2,476 | 356 | 175 | 100 | 64 | 29 | 31 | 34 | 11 | 17 | 35 | 0 | 11 | 177 |
| 1,000– 1,499 | 4,542 | 4,093 | 0 | 107 | 3,986 | | 226 | 301 | 597 | 2,055 | 283 | 170 | 55 | 15 | 21 | 19 | 0 | 0 | 0 | 16 | 63 | 165 |
| 1,500– 1,999 | 4,885 | 4,613 | 16 | 103 | 4,494 | | 258 | 113 | 306 | 606 | 2,307 | 468 | 79 | 73 | 60 | 22 | 21 | 5 | 5 | 0 | 9 | 162 |
| 2,000– 2,499 | 5,196 | 4,896 | 0 | 106 | 4,790 | | 143 | 95 | 114 | 274 | 589 | 2,505 | 561 | 183 | 9 | 31 | 5 | 53 | 0 | 0 | 9 | 219 |
| 2,500– 2,999 | 5,410 | 5,188 | 14 | 105 | 5,069 | | 42 | 23 | 37 | 50 | 191 | 985 | 2,831 | 449 | 103 | 47 | 19 | 30 | 21 | 0 | 20 | 221 |
| 3,000– 3,499 | 5,346 | 5,110 | 48 | 91 | 4,971 | | 39 | 0 | 29 | 66 | 58 | 236 | 507 | 3,198 | 323 | 44 | 19 | 137 | 24 | 51 | 0 | 240 |
| 3,500– 3,999 | 3,986 | 3,918 | 5 | 55 | 3,858 | | 34 | 6 | 10 | 90 | 48 | 125 | 143 | 588 | 2,192 | 206 | 105 | 34 | 20 | 0 | 21 | 236 |
| 4,000– 4,499 | 3,076 | 3,028 | 0 | 45 | 2,983 | | 67 | 10 | 0 | 15 | 0 | 50 | 118 | 222 | 333 | 1,678 | 250 | 59 | 82 | 9 | 0 | 90 |
| 4,500– 4,999 | 1,375 | 1,292 | 0 | 15 | 1,277 | | 0 | 9 | 0 | 26 | 10 | 37 | 65 | 26 | 34 | 102 | 659 | 260 | 5 | 0 | 9 | 35 |
| 5,000– 5,999 | 1,721 | 1,635 | 0 | 18 | 1,617 | | 16 | 11 | 9 | 0 | 5 | 10 | 24 | 79 | 46 | 91 | 102 | 933 | 114 | 55 | 20 | 102 |
| 6,000– 6,999 | 695 | 552 | 0 | 17 | 535 | | 0 | 5 | 0 | 0 | 0 | 11 | 0 | 10 | 27 | 23 | 45 | 102 | 214 | 49 | 10 | 39 |
| 7,000– 9,999 | 1,099 | 1,049 | 0 | 16 | 1,033 | | 37 | 9 | 4 | 5 | 10 | 21 | 0 | 10 | 40 | 22 | 9 | 39 | 126 | 534 | 99 | 68 |
| 10,000 and over | 933 | 859 | 0 | 18 | 841 | | 34 | 33 | 0 | 20 | 0 | 37 | 5 | 5 | 5 | 0 | 0 | 9 | 29 | 114 | 535 | 15 |
| Income not reported | 1,613 | 2,929 | 95 | 120 | 2,714 | | 264 | 298 | 194 | 140 | 168 | 116 | 83 | 74 | 19 | 38 | 49 | 39 | 119 | 50 | 60 | 1,003 |
| Age not reported | | 2,006 | | 181 | 1,825 | | 172 | 127 | 236 | 309 | 104 | 184 | 139 | 162 | 49 | 10 | 34 | 47 | 24 | 0 | 14 | 214 |

Note: Figures are for persons fourteen years old and over here and in all subsequent tables unless otherwise noted.
[a] Adjusted by assigning income recorded in census to persons for whom income or age was not reported in PES.
[b] As under fourteen years old in census.
[c] Includes income classes "loss" and "even" here and in all subsequent tables.
[d] Census totals are based on a 20 per cent sample.
[e] As fourteen years old and over in census.

## TABLE 2

1949 Income of Females: Estimated PES Distribution by 1950 Census Distribution

(estimates in thousands rounded without adjustment to group totals, which are independently rounded)

| ITEM | Total PES | | Not included in census income distribution | | Population enumerated in census and PES | Income in census | | | | | | | | | | | | | | | |
|---|---|---|---|---|---|---|---|---|---|---|---|---|---|---|---|---|---|---|---|---|---|
| | Adjusted[a] | Not adjusted | Misclassified[b] | Omitted | | Total census | None | Under $500[c] | $500–$999 | $1,000–$1,499 | $1,500–$1,999 | $2,000–$2,499 | $2,500–$2,999 | $3,000–$3,499 | $3,500–$3,999 | $4,000–$4,499 | $4,500–$4,999 | $5,000–$5,999 | $6,000–$6,999 | $7,000–$9,999 | $10,000 and over | Income not reported |
| TOTAL CENSUS[d] | | | | | | 57,102 | 30,534 | 6,996 | 4,304 | 3,015 | 2,822 | 2,535 | 1,393 | 825 | 346 | 213 | 107 | 148 | 66 | 79 | 97 | 3,623 |
| Not included in PES income distribution: | | | | | | | | | | | | | | | | | | | | | |
| Misclassified[e] | | | | | | 119 | 58 | 0 | 0 | 0 | 0 | 0 | 0 | 0 | 0 | 0 | 0 | 0 | 0 | 0 | 0 | 61 |
| Erroneously included | | | | | | 448 | 206 | 20 | 61 | 0 | 62 | 20 | 10 | 0 | 0 | 11 | 0 | 0 | 0 | 0 | 0 | 58 |
| Population enumerated in census and PES | | | | | | 56,535 | 30,270 | 6,976 | 4,243 | 3,015 | 2,760 | 2,515 | 1,383 | 825 | 346 | 202 | 107 | 148 | 66 | 79 | 97 | 3,504 |
| Income in PES | | | | | | | | | | | | | | | | | | | | | |
| Total PES | 57,932 | 57,932 | 126 | 1,271 | 56,535 | | | | | | | | | | | | | | | | |
| None | 29,625 | 28,037 | 20 | 492 | 27,525 | | 23,868 | 944 | 354 | 162 | 96 | 115 | 74 | 124 | 31 | 24 | 0 | 20 | 0 | 0 | 39 | 1,674 |
| Under $ 500[c] | 8,802 | 8,398 | 0 | 162 | 8,236 | | 2,700 | 4,723 | 379 | 72 | 34 | 34 | 43 | 0 | 0 | 0 | 0 | 11 | 0 | 0 | 10 | 230 |
| $ 500– 999 | 5,134 | 4,908 | 0 | 132 | 4,776 | | 999 | 595 | 2,716 | 251 | 21 | 38 | 10 | 0 | 0 | 0 | 0 | 0 | 0 | 0 | 0 | 146 |
| 1,000– 1,499 | 3,521 | 3,317 | 64 | 64 | 3,189 | | 409 | 70 | 439 | 1,826 | 251 | 69 | 22 | 16 | 9 | 0 | 0 | 9 | 10 | 0 | 10 | 49 |
| 1,500– 1,999 | 3,427 | 3,281 | 0 | 76 | 3,205 | | 315 | 128 | 68 | 362 | 1,846 | 241 | 72 | 0 | 20 | 10 | 0 | 0 | 0 | 10 | 0 | 133 |
| 2,000– 2,499 | 2,663 | 2,555 | 0 | 54 | 2,501 | | 95 | 58 | 46 | 90 | 270 | 1,595 | 133 | 29 | 10 | 0 | 0 | 0 | 0 | 0 | 0 | 175 |
| 2,500– 2,999 | 1,476 | 1,417 | 0 | 29 | 1,388 | | 88 | 0 | 0 | 19 | 45 | 238 | 820 | 76 | 10 | 0 | 0 | 10 | 0 | 10 | 0 | 72 |
| 3,000– 3,499 | 920 | 903 | 0 | 24 | 879 | | 45 | 5 | 0 | 19 | 41 | 58 | 114 | 489 | 68 | 5 | 0 | 15 | 10 | 0 | 0 | 10 |
| 3,500– 3,999 | 345 | 335 | 0 | 1 | 334 | | 19 | 20 | 10 | 0 | 0 | 0 | 10 | 47 | 160 | 38 | 0 | 9 | 0 | 0 | 0 | 21 |
| 4,000– 4,499 | 205 | 105 | 0 | 2 | 103 | | 10 | 0 | 0 | 0 | 0 | 0 | 10 | 18 | 0 | 16 | 29 | 0 | 0 | 0 | 10 | 10 |
| 4,500– 4,999 | 147 | 147 | 0 | 4 | 143 | | 0 | 9 | 0 | 0 | 0 | 0 | 0 | 0 | 28 | 9 | 78 | 19 | 0 | 0 | 0 | 0 |
| 5,000– 5,999 | 115 | 115 | 0 | 5 | 110 | | 32 | 0 | 0 | 0 | 0 | 19 | 11 | 0 | 0 | 0 | 0 | 23 | 0 | 5 | 0 | 20 |
| 6,000– 6,999 | 149 | 129 | 0 | 1 | 128 | | 19 | 5 | 0 | 0 | 0 | 0 | 5 | 0 | 0 | 0 | 0 | 32 | 16 | 10 | 13 | 28 |
| 7,000– 9,999 | 148 | 138 | 0 | 1 | 137 | | 58 | 11 | 5 | 10 | 10 | 0 | 0 | 9 | 0 | 0 | 0 | 0 | 10 | 24 | 0 | 0 |
| 10,000 and over | 67 | 58 | 0 | 3 | 55 | | 25 | 4 | 0 | 0 | 0 | 0 | 0 | 0 | 0 | 0 | 0 | 0 | 0 | 10 | 6 | 10 |
| Income not reported | 1,189 | 2,447 | 42 | 120 | 2,285 | | 920 | 179 | 70 | 133 | 86 | 70 | 40 | 0 | 10 | 100 | 0 | 0 | 10 | 10 | 0 | 657 |
| Age not reported | | 1,643 | | 101 | 1,542 | | 668 | 225 | 156 | 71 | 60 | 38 | 19 | 17 | 0 | 0 | 0 | 0 | 10 | 0 | 9 | 269 |

[a] Adjusted by assigning income recorded in census to persons for whom income or age was not reported in PES.
[b] As under fourteen years old in census.
[c] Includes income classes "loss" and "even" here and in all subsequent tables.
[d] Census totals are based on a 20 per cent sample.
[e] As fourteen years old and over in census.

people, enumerating them in error, or differences in the classification of the population by age.)

2. There were more differences in which the PES income classification was higher than that of the census than vice versa. Of the 18,454,000 males who would have been classified differently, it is estimated that 11,149,000 (60 per cent) were placed in the census in lower income classes than they would have been in the PES. Of the 11,925,000 females classified differently, an estimated 7,781,000 (65 per cent) were placed in lower income classes in the census than they would have been in the PES. The major explanation for the greater difference among the females than among the males lies in the fact that the PES found that a substantial number of females classified as "persons without income" in the census received very small amounts of income in 1949.

These estimates of gross difference are made relative to the class intervals shown in Tables 1 and 2. For grosser intervals, the divergence would be less.

### ACCURACY OF CENSUS STATISTICS

Table 3 contains a comparison of the marginal totals of Tables 1 and 2. Because of the fairly high levels of sampling error in the PES estimates, no single figure in the table can legitimately be used to correct the corresponding census total.[2] It is the general pattern that provides a basis for analysis. It is one of understatement of the number of income recipients in each class. There is estimated to have been a 9 per cent understatement in the total number of male income recipients and an 18 per cent understatement in the number of female recipients; about 4 million persons in each case. If the census and PES "income not reported" totals were to be proportionately distributed among the other classes, then the estimated discrepancy of 8 million recipients for males and females combined would be reduced to about 5 million. There were two major causes for this discrepancy; the underenumeration of the population and the misclassification of persons who actually acquired income in 1949 as "persons without income."

### NONRESPONSE IN THE PES

The PES income distributions were derived from "adjusted PES totals." These totals were derived after substituting the census classifications, where available, for cases in which the PES was not

[2] Because of the great effort that would have been required, estimates of sampling error have not been prepared. Some information on the extent of sampling error can be furnished, on request, by the authors.

TABLE 3

Comparison of the 1950 Census Class Totals with the Estimated PES Class Totals: 1949 Income of Males and Females

(*estimates in thousands*)

| | MALE | | | | FEMALE | | | |
|---|---|---|---|---|---|---|---|---|
| | | | *Difference* | | | | *Difference* | |
| INCOME CLASS | *1950 Census* [a] | *Adjusted* PES *Totals* | *Number* [b] | *Percentage of 1950 Census* | *1950 Census* [a] | *Adjusted* PES *Totals* | *Number* [b] | *Percentage of 1950 Census* |
| Total | 54,601 | 55,438 | —837 | —1.5 | 57,102 | 57,932 | —830 | —1.5 |
| Income reported | 50,739 | 53,825 | —3,086 | —6.1 | 53,479 | 56,743 | —3,264 | —6.1 |
| Income not reported | 3,862 | 1,613 | | | 3,623 | 1,189 | | |
| Total reporting income | 50,739 | 53,825 | —3,086 | —6.1 | 53,479 | 56,743 | —3,264 | —6.1 |
| None | 6,350 | 5,435 | 915 | 14.4 | 30,534 | 29,625 | 909 | 3.0 |
| Some | 44,389 | 48,390 | —4,001 | —9.0 | 22,945 | 27,118 | —4,173 | —18.2 |
| Total reporting some income | 44,389 | 48,390 | —4,001 | —9.0 | 22,945 | 27,118 | —4,173 | —18.2 |
| Under $ 500 | 4,682 | 5,089 | —407 | —8.7 | 6,996 | 8,802 | —1,806 | —25.8 |
| $ 500– 999 | 4,633 | 5,038 | —405 | —8.7 | 4,304 | 5,134 | —830 | —19.3 |
| 1,000– 1,499 | 4,281 | 4,542 | —261 | —6.1 | 3,015 | 3,521 | —506 | —16.8 |
| 1,500– 1,999 | 4,083 | 4,885 | —802 | —19.6 | 2,822 | 3,427 | —605 | —21.4 |
| 2,000– 2,499 | 5,198 | 5,196 | 2 | 0 | 2,535 | 2,663 | —128 | —5.0 |
| 2,500– 2,999 | 4,767 | 5,410 | —643 | —13.5 | 1,393 | 1,476 | —83 | —6.0 |
| 3,000– 3,499 | 5,198 | 5,346 | —148 | —2.8 | 825 | 920 | —95 | —11.5 |
| 3,500– 3,999 | 3,335 | 3,986 | —651 | —19.5 | 346 | 345 | 1 | 0.3 |
| 4,000– 4,499 | 2,398 | 3,076 | —678 | —28.3 | 213 | 205 | 8 | 3.8 |
| 4,500– 4,999 | 1,347 | 1,375 | —28 | —2.1 | 107 | 147 | —40 | —37.4 |
| 5,000– 5,999 | 1,832 | 1,721 | 111 | 6.1 | 148 | 115 | 33 | 22.3 |
| 6,000– 6,999 | 818 | 695 | 123 | 15.0 | 66 | 149 | —83 | —125.8 |
| 7,000– 9,999 | 889 | 1,099 | —210 | —23.6 | 79 | 148 | —69 | —87.3 |
| 10,000 and over | 929 | 933 | —4 | —0.4 | 97 | 67 | 30 | 30.9 |

[a] Census totals are based on a 20 per cent sample.
[b] Census minus PES.

able to obtain responses. We recognize that this is a debatable practice. It was done on the premise that it would provide the best possible response in each case. Actually, as Tables 1 and 2 indicate, the unadjusted PES nonresponse rates were quite substantial, about 8 per cent. The major reason for this level of nonresponse was the insistence on obtaining information from the "best" respondents in the re-enumerative check. If, after repeated calls, a best respondent could not be located, the PES interviewer was instructed to record a nonresponse instead of seeking out an available respondent. Another factor, which also accounts for some of the divergence in the data of the census and the PES, is that more stringent coding rules were used for the responses in the re-enumerative check. In the PES, if one type of income was not reported, total income was coded as "not reported." On the other hand, under certain conditions, the entry for a type of income was assumed in the census to be "none" if it was not reported, thus permitting the assignment of a numerical code for total income.

### *Distributions of Total Income of Persons*

We turn now to the results. Keeping in mind the following facts, we shall first examine Tables 4 through 8:

1. The "1950 census" medians and distributions were transcribed directly from the summary volume of the 1950 census.[3]
2. The "PES" medians and distributions were derived from "adjusted PES totals" obtained from tables like Tables 1 and 2. These totals are based on samples of approximately 10,000 persons enumerated in the 1950 census and 1,800 persons erroneously omitted from the 1950 census.
3. "Persons without income," the zero class, are not reflected in the medians.
4. All of the PES estimates are subject to fairly high sampling errors. For this reason, the medians have been rounded to the tens digit. No single figure is precise enough to be used to "correct" a census statistic; all that we can point to are general tendencies or patterns.

#### MEDIANS

Table 4 compares census medians with those estimated from the re-enumerative check. Results are given for males and females separately, classified by color and by residence.

Despite the levels of gross difference in the data and the levels of

[3] *1950 Census of Population,* Vol. II, *Characteristics of the Population,* Part 1, United States Summary.

net error in the class totals, not one estimated difference between medians is greater than $100. The PES medians are estimated to be higher than those of the census for the nonwhite and urban-male components of the population. For white females and rural males, the PES medians are estimated to be lower. The latter can be explained by the disproportionate addition of recipients of income to the low-income classes.

### INCOME RECIPIENTS

The PES found significantly higher proportions of persons with income than did the census. The understatements in the census appear to be most pronounced for the nonwhite population (estimated at almost 8 percentage points for males and 6 percentage points for females) and for the urban-female population (estimated at almost 6 percentage points).

### DISTRIBUTION

Comparison of the distributions in Tables 4 through 8, class by class, reveals no striking patterns of difference. The addition of income recipients to the low-income classes accounts, in part, for the finding that, for the female population, the relative sizes of the income classes above $2,000 tend to have been overstated in the census. By and large, however, the similarities appear to be more striking than the differences.

### IDENTICAL POPULATION

The differences between the statistics of the 1950 census and the PES, summarized in Tables 4 through 8, result from more than gross differences in the reporting and coding of the amount of income. As Tables 1 and 2 indicate, "coverage" errors, errors in the reporting of age, nonresponse, and errors in the designation of

TABLE 4

Comparison of the 1950 Census Medians with the Estimated PES Medians: 1949 Income of All Males and Females, by Color and by Residence

| | MALE | | | FEMALE | | |
|---|---|---|---|---|---|---|
| GROUP | *1950 Census* | PES | *Difference* [a] | *1950 Census* | PES | *Difference* [a] |
| All males or females | $2,430 | $2,450 | $—20 | $1,030 | $ 960 | $ 70 |
| White | 2,570 | 2,600 | —30 | 1,140 | 1,050 | 90 |
| Nonwhite | 1,340 | 1,350 | —10 | 580 | 640 | —60 |
| Urban | 2,780 | 2,810 | —30 | 1,230 | 1,160 | 70 |
| Rural nonfarm | 2,070 | 2,040 | 30 | 720 | 620 | 100 |
| Rural farm | 1,340 | 1,300 | 40 | 460 | 450 | 10 |

[a] Census minus PES.

TABLE 5

Comparison of the 1950 Census Percentage Distributions with the Estimated PES Percentage Distributions: 1949 Income of All Males, by Color

| INCOME CLASS | TOTAL | | | WHITE | | | NONWHITE | | |
|---|---|---|---|---|---|---|---|---|---|
| | *1950 Census* | PES | *Difference* [a] | *1950 Census* | PES | *Difference* [a] | *1950 Census* | PES | *Difference* [a] |
| Total | 100.0 | 100.0 | 0 | 100.0 | 100.0 | 0 | 100.0 | 100.0 | 0 |
| Income reported | 92.9 | 97.1 | —4.2 | 93.1 | 97.4 | —4.3 | 91.4 | 94.6 | —3.2 |
| Income not reported | 7.1 | 2.9 | 4.2 | 6.9 | 2.6 | 4.3 | 8.6 | 5.4 | 3.2 |
| Total reporting income | 100.0 | 100.0 | 0 | 100.0 | 100.0 | 0 | 100.0 | 100.0 | 0 |
| None | 12.5 | 10.1 | 2.4 | 12.1 | 10.2 | 1.9 | 16.5 | 8.8 | 7.7 |
| Some | 87.5 | 89.9 | —2.4 | 87.9 | 89.8 | —1.9 | 83.5 | 91.2 | —7.7 |
| Total reporting some income | 100.0 | 100.0 | 0 | 100.0 | 100.0 | 0 | 100.0 | 100.0 | 0 |
| Under $ 500 | 10.5 | 10.5 | 0 | 9.6 | 9.3 | 0.3 | 20.2 | 21.6 | —1.4 |
| $ 500– 999 | 10.4 | 10.4 | 0 | 9.6 | 9.5 | 0.1 | 18.7 | 18.6 | 0.1 |
| 1,000– 1,499 | 9.6 | 9.4 | 0.2 | 9.0 | 8.9 | 0.1 | 16.2 | 14.1 | 2.1 |
| 1,500– 1,999 | 9.2 | 10.1 | —0.9 | 8.7 | 9.4 | —0.7 | 14.2 | 16.1 | —1.9 |
| 2,000– 2,499 | 11.7 | 10.7 | 1.0 | 11.5 | 10.6 | 0.9 | 13.3 | 11.9 | 1.4 |
| 2,500– 2,999 | 10.7 | 11.2 | —0.5 | 11.0 | 11.4 | —0.4 | 8.0 | 8.8 | —0.8 |
| 3,000– 3,499 | 11.7 | 11.0 | 0.7 | 12.4 | 11.7 | 0.7 | 5.3 | 4.9 | 0.4 |
| 3,500– 3,999 | 7.5 | 8.2 | —0.7 | 8.1 | 9.0 | —0.9 | 1.9 | 1.1 | 0.8 |
| 4,000– 4,499 | 5.4 | 6.4 | —1.0 | 5.9 | 6.9 | —1.0 | 0.9 | 1.0 | —0.1 |
| 4,500– 4,999 | 3.0 | 2.8 | 0.2 | 3.3 | 3.1 | 0.2 | 0.3 | 0.7 | —0.4 |
| 5,000 and over | 10.0 | 9.2 | 0.8 | 11.0 | 10.1 | 0.9 | 0.8 | 1.1 | —0.3 |

[a] Census minus PES.

TABLE 6

Comparison of the 1950 Census Percentage Distributions with the Estimated PES Percentage Distributions: 1949 Income of All Males, by Residence

| INCOME CLASS | TOTAL | | | URBAN | | | RURAL NONFARM | | | RURAL FARM | | |
|---|---|---|---|---|---|---|---|---|---|---|---|---|
| | *1950 Census* | PES | *Difference* [a] | *1950 Census* | PES | *Difference* [a] | *1950 Census* | PES | *Difference* [a] | *1950 Census* | PES | *Difference* [a] |
| Total | 100.0 | 100.0 | 0 | 100.0 | 100.0 | 0 | 100.0 | 100.0 | 0 | 100.0 | 100.0 | 0 |
| Income reported | 92.9 | 97.1 | —4.2 | 93.0 | 97.8 | —4.8 | 91.3 | 94.9 | —3.6 | 94.6 | 96.9 | —2.3 |
| Income not reported | 7.1 | 2.9 | 4.2 | 7.0 | 2.2 | 4.8 | 8.7 | 5.1 | 3.6 | 5.4 | 3.1 | 2.3 |
| Total reporting income | 100.0 | 100.0 | 0 | 100.0 | 100.0 | 0 | 100.0 | 100.0 | 0 | 100.0 | 100.0 | 0 |
| None | 12.5 | 10.1 | 2.4 | 11.2 | 8.6 | 2.6 | 12.9 | 10.8 | 2.1 | 17.6 | 15.6 | 2.0 |
| Some | 87.5 | 89.9 | —2.4 | 88.8 | 91.4 | —2.6 | 87.1 | 89.2 | —2.1 | 82.4 | 84.4 | —2.0 |
| Total reporting some income | 100.0 | 100.0 | 0 | 100.0 | 100.0 | 0 | 100.0 | 100.0 | 0 | 100.0 | 100.0 | 0 |
| Under $ 500 | 10.5 | 10.5 | 0 | 7.4 | 6.6 | 0.8 | 12.7 | 13.6 | —0.9 | 21.8 | 24.2 | —2.4 |
| $ 500– 999 | 10.4 | 10.4 | 0 | 7.9 | 7.5 | 0.4 | 12.8 | 14.0 | —1.2 | 18.4 | 18.7 | —0.3 |
| 1,000– 1,499 | 9.6 | 9.4 | 0.2 | 7.9 | 8.6 | —0.7 | 11.8 | 10.2 | 1.6 | 14.5 | 11.9 | 2.6 |
| 1,500– 1,999 | 9.2 | 10.1 | —0.9 | 8.3 | 8.9 | —0.6 | 10.8 | 11.1 | —0.3 | 11.0 | 14.1 | —3.1 |
| 2,000– 2,499 | 11.7 | 10.7 | 1.0 | 11.8 | 10.4 | 1.4 | 12.8 | 12.8 | 0 | 10.0 | 9.5 | 0.5 |
| 2,500– 2,999 | 10.7 | 11.2 | —0.5 | 11.8 | 13.0 | —1.2 | 10.4 | 8.6 | 1.8 | 6.3 | 6.2 | 0.1 |
| 3,000– 3,499 | 11.7 | 11.0 | 0.7 | 13.6 | 12.4 | 1.2 | 10.0 | 10.4 | —0.4 | 5.6 | 5.5 | 0.1 |
| 3,500– 3,999 | 7.5 | 8.2 | —0.7 | 8.9 | 9.8 | —0.9 | 6.1 | 7.2 | —1.1 | 3.0 | 2.4 | 0.6 |
| 4,000– 4,499 | 5.4 | 6.4 | —1.0 | 6.5 | 7.9 | —1.4 | 4.0 | 4.5 | —0.5 | 2.5 | 1.7 | 0.8 |
| 4,500– 4,999 | 3.0 | 2.8 | 0.2 | 3.7 | 3.6 | 0.1 | 2.2 | 1.6 | 0.6 | 1.3 | 1.1 | 0.2 |
| 5,000 and over | 10.0 | 9.2 | 0.8 | 12.2 | 11.1 | 1.1 | 6.3 | 5.9 | 0.4 | 5.7 | 4.8 | 0.9 |

[a] Census minus PES.

TABLE 7

Comparison of the 1950 Census Percentage Distributions with the Estimated PES Percentage Distributions: 1949 Income of All Females, by Color

| INCOME CLASS | TOTAL | | | WHITE | | | NONWHITE | | |
|---|---|---|---|---|---|---|---|---|---|
| | *1950 Census* | PES | *Difference* [a] | *1950 Census* | PES | *Difference* [a] | *1950 Census* | PES | *Difference* [a] |
| Total | 100.0 | 100.0 | 0 | 100.0 | 100.0 | 0 | 100.0 | 100.0 | 0 |
| Income reported | 93.7 | 97.9 | —4.2 | 93.7 | 98.0 | —4.3 | 93.1 | 97.7 | —4.6 |
| Income not reported | 6.3 | 2.1 | 4.2 | 6.3 | 2.0 | 4.3 | 6.9 | 2.3 | 4.6 |
| Total reporting income | 100.0 | 100.0 | 0 | 100.0 | 100.0 | 0 | 100.0 | 100.0 | 0 |
| None | 57.1 | 52.2 | 4.9 | 57.9 | 53.2 | 4.7 | 49.4 | 43.4 | 6.0 |
| Some | 42.9 | 47.8 | —4.9 | 42.1 | 46.8 | —4.7 | 50.6 | 56.6 | —6.0 |
| Total reporting some income | 100.0 | 100.0 | 0 | 100.0 | 100.0 | 0 | 100.0 | 100.0 | 0 |
| Under $ 500 | 30.5 | 32.5 | —2.0 | 28.5 | 31.1 | —2.6 | 45.8 | 42.4 | 3.4 |
| $ 500– 999 | 18.8 | 18.9 | —0.1 | 17.9 | 17.7 | 0.2 | 25.1 | 27.8 | —2.7 |
| 1,000– 1,499 | 13.1 | 13.0 | 0.1 | 13.2 | 13.0 | 0.2 | 12.7 | 12.7 | 0 |
| 1,500– 1,999 | 12.3 | 12.6 | —0.3 | 12.9 | 13.3 | —0.4 | 7.7 | 8.0 | —0.3 |
| 2,000– 2,499 | 11.0 | 9.8 | 1.2 | 11.9 | 10.5 | 1.4 | 4.7 | 4.5 | 0.2 |
| 2,500– 2,999 | 6.1 | 5.4 | 0.7 | 6.6 | 5.9 | 0.7 | 2.1 | 2.0 | 0.1 |
| 3,000– 3,499 | 3.6 | 3.4 | 0.2 | 3.9 | 3.8 | 0.1 | 1.0 | 0.5 | 0.5 |
| 3,500– 3,999 | 1.5 | 1.3 | 0.2 | 1.7 | 1.4 | 0.3 | 0.3 | 0.3 | 0 |
| 4,000– 4,499 | 0.9 | 0.8 | 0.1 | 1.0 | 0.9 | 0.1 | 0.2 | 0 | 0.2 |
| 4,500– 4,999 | 0.5 | 0.5 | 0 | 0.5 | 0.6 | —0.1 | 0.1 | 0.1 | 0 |
| 5,000 and over | 1.6 | 1.6 | 0 | 1.9 | 1.8 | 0.1 | 0.4 | 1.9 | —1.5 |

[a] Census minus PES

TABLE 8

Comparison of the 1950 Census Percentage Distributions with the Estimated PES Percentage Distributions: 1949 Income of All Females, by Residence

| INCOME CLASS | TOTAL | | | URBAN | | | RURAL NONFARM | | | RURAL FARM | | |
|---|---|---|---|---|---|---|---|---|---|---|---|---|
| | *1950 Census* | PES | *Difference* [a] | *1950 Census* | PES | *Difference* [a] | *1950 Census* | PES | *Difference* [a] | *1950 Census* | PES | *Difference* [a] |
| Total | 100.0 | 100.0 | 0 | 100.0 | 100.0 | 0 | 100.0 | 100.0 | 0 | 100.0 | 100.0 | 0 |
| Income reported | 93.7 | 97.9 | —4.2 | 93.7 | 98.0 | —4.3 | 93.0 | 97.3 | —4.3 | 94.6 | 98.5 | —3.9 |
| Income not reported | 6.3 | 2.1 | 4.2 | 6.3 | 2.0 | 4.3 | 7.0 | 2.7 | 4.3 | 5.4 | 1.5 | 3.9 |
| Total reporting income | 100.0 | 100.0 | 0 | 100.0 | 100.0 | 0 | 100.0 | 100.0 | 0 | 100.0 | 100.0 | 0 |
| None | 57.1 | 52.2 | 4.9 | 52.7 | 47.0 | 5.7 | 61.1 | 57.7 | 3.4 | 73.6 | 71.2 | 2.4 |
| Some | 42.9 | 47.8 | —4.9 | 47.3 | 53.0 | —5.7 | 38.9 | 42.3 | —3.4 | 26.4 | 28.8 | —2.4 |
| Total reporting some income | 100.0 | 100.0 | 0 | 100.0 | 100.0 | 0 | 100.0 | 100.0 | 0 | 100.0 | 100.0 | 0 |
| Under $ 500 | 30.5 | 32.5 | —2.0 | 25.4 | 27.1 | —1.7 | 41.2 | 45.0 | —3.8 | 54.6 | 55.7 | —1.1 |
| $ 500– 999 | 18.8 | 18.9 | —0.1 | 18.4 | 18.6 | —0.2 | 20.8 | 21.5 | —0.7 | 17.6 | 16.4 | 1.2 |
| 1,000– 1,499 | 13.1 | 13.0 | 0.1 | 13.7 | 13.7 | 0 | 12.4 | 10.6 | 1.8 | 9.9 | 11.6 | —1.7 |
| 1,500– 1,999 | 12.3 | 12.6 | —0.3 | 13.4 | 14.2 | —0.8 | 9.8 | 8.5 | 1.3 | 7.2 | 7.0 | 0.2 |
| 2,000– 2,499 | 11.0 | 9.8 | 1.2 | 12.5 | 11.0 | 1.5 | 7.4 | 7.1 | 0.3 | 5.0 | 4.3 | 0.7 |
| 2,500– 2,999 | 6.1 | 5.4 | 0.7 | 7.1 | 6.5 | 0.6 | 3.6 | 2.2 | 1.4 | 2.2 | 2.2 | 0 |
| 3,000– 3,499 | 3.6 | 3.4 | 0.2 | 4.2 | 3.9 | 0.3 | 2.0 | 2.7 | —0.7 | 1.3 | 0.5 | 0.8 |
| 3,500– 3,999 | 1.5 | 1.3 | 0.2 | 1.8 | 1.5 | 0.3 | 0.8 | 0.2 | 0.6 | 0.6 | 0.9 | —0.3 |
| 4,000– 4,499 | 0.9 | 0.8 | 0.1 | 1.1 | 0.9 | 0.2 | 0.5 | 0.4 | 0.1 | 0.4 | 0.4 | 0 |
| 4,500– 4,999 | 0.5 | 0.5 | 0 | 0.5 | 0.7 | —0.2 | 0.2 | 0.2 | 0 | 0.2 | 0.2 | 0 |
| 5,000 and over | 1.6 | 1.6 | 0 | 1.9 | 1.9 | 0 | 1.2 | 1.5 | —0.3 | 1.2 | 0.8 | 0.4 |

[a] Census minus PES.

persons as "persons with income" all contribute to the differences in Tables 4 through 8.

One major factor was the difference in the reporting and coding of income. To deal with this factor by itself, we had to define an "identical population"; the persons who were classified as "persons with income" in both the 1950 census and the PES. We exclude cases of critical difference in the reporting of age, coverage error, and nonresponse. We thus have a "population" in which there are two reports of income in 1949 for each individual. As we have noted, there is evidence of directional differences between the 1950 census and PES reports of income for this "identical population." The effect of this directional difference on the income distribution is shown in Tables 9 through 13.

TABLE 9

Comparison of the 1950 Census Medians with the Estimated PES Medians: 1949 Income of Identical Males and Females, by Color and by Residence

| GROUP | MALE | | | FEMALE | | |
|---|---|---|---|---|---|---|
| | *1950 Census* | PES | *Difference* [a] | *1950 Census* | PES | *Difference* [a] |
| All males or females | $2,520 | $2,580 | $ −60 | $1,080 | $1,140 | $ −60 |
| White | 2,640 | 2,700 | −60 | 1,190 | 1,250 | −60 |
| Nonwhite | 1,320 | 1,430 | −110 | 620 | 680 | −60 |
| Urban | 2,860 | 2,910 | −50 | 1,280 | 1,340 | −60 |
| Rural nonfarm | 2,150 | 2,200 | −50 | 740 | 740 | 0 |
| Rural farm | 1,400 | 1,420 | −20 | 450 | 480 | −30 |

[a] Census minus PES.

TABLE 10

Comparison of the 1950 Census Percentage Distributions with the Estimated PES Percentage Distributions: 1949 Income of Identical Males, by Color

| INCOME CLASS | TOTAL | | | WHITE | | | NONWHITE | | |
|---|---|---|---|---|---|---|---|---|---|
| | *1950 Census* | PES | *Difference* [a] | *1950 Census* | PES | *Difference* [a] | *1950 Census* | PES | *Difference* [a] |
| Total | 100.0 | 100.0 | 0 | 100.0 | 100.0 | 0 | 100.0 | 100.0 | 0 |
| Under $ 500 | 9.5 | 8.7 | 0.8 | 8.5 | 7.8 | 0.7 | 20.5 | 18.0 | 2.5 |
| $ 500– 999 | 10.0 | 9.5 | 0.5 | 9.2 | 8.6 | 0.6 | 18.6 | 19.2 | −0.6 |
| 1,000– 1,499 | 9.1 | 8.9 | 0.2 | 8.4 | 8.4 | 0 | 16.9 | 14.8 | 2.1 |
| 1,500– 1,999 | 9.2 | 10.1 | −0.9 | 9.0 | 9.7 | −0.7 | 11.6 | 14.5 | −2.9 |
| 2,000– 2,499 | 11.8 | 11.0 | 0.8 | 11.7 | 10.8 | 0.9 | 13.9 | 12.5 | 1.4 |
| 2,500– 2,999 | 11.1 | 11.9 | −0.8 | 11.3 | 12.0 | −0.7 | 8.4 | 11.0 | −2.6 |
| 3,000– 3,499 | 12.2 | 11.6 | 0.6 | 12.8 | 12.2 | 0.6 | 5.8 | 5.7 | 0.1 |
| 3,500– 3,999 | 8.0 | 8.9 | −0.9 | 8.6 | 9.6 | −1.0 | 1.9 | 1.2 | 0.7 |
| 4,000– 4,499 | 5.8 | 7.0 | −1.2 | 6.3 | 7.6 | −1.3 | 1.0 | 1.3 | −0.3 |
| 4,500– 4,999 | 3.1 | 3.1 | 0 | 3.3 | 3.3 | 0 | 0.4 | 1.0 | −0.6 |
| 5,000 and over | 10.1 | 9.2 | 0.9 | 10.9 | 10.0 | 0.9 | 1.0 | 0.9 | 0.1 |

[a] Census minus PES.

TABLE 11

Comparison of the 1950 Census Percentage Distributions with the Estimated PES Percentage Distributions: 1949 Income of Identical Males, by Residence

| | TOTAL | | | URBAN | | | RURAL NONFARM | | | RURAL FARM | | |
|---|---|---|---|---|---|---|---|---|---|---|---|---|
| INCOME CLASS | *1950 Census* | PES | *Difference* [a] | *1950 Census* | PES | *Difference* [a] | *1950 Census* | PES | *Difference* [a] | *1950 Census* | PES | *Difference* [a] |
| Total | 100.0 | 100.0 | 0 | 100.0 | 100.0 | 0 | 100.0 | 100.0 | 0 | 100.0 | 100.0 | 0 |
| Under $ 500 | 9.5 | 8.7 | 0.8 | 6.6 | 5.1 | 1.5 | 11.3 | 11.2 | 0.1 | 20.1 | 21.2 | −1.1 |
| $ 500– 999 | 10.0 | 9.5 | 0.5 | 7.5 | 6.9 | 0.6 | 12.3 | 11.6 | 0.7 | 18.0 | 18.6 | −0.6 |
| 1,000– 1,499 | 9.1 | 8.9 | 0.2 | 7.4 | 8.1 | −0.7 | 10.7 | 9.5 | 1.2 | 14.9 | 12.0 | 2.9 |
| 1,500– 1,999 | 9.2 | 10.1 | −0.9 | 7.9 | 8.4 | −0.5 | 11.8 | 12.0 | −0.2 | 11.9 | 15.5 | −3.6 |
| 2,000– 2,499 | 11.8 | 11.0 | 0.8 | 11.8 | 10.2 | 1.6 | 13.3 | 14.5 | −1.2 | 10.2 | 10.1 | 0.1 |
| 2,500– 2,999 | 11.1 | 11.9 | −0.8 | 12.3 | 13.9 | −1.6 | 10.7 | 9.7 | 1.0 | 6.2 | 6.0 | 0.2 |
| 3,000– 3,499 | 12.2 | 11.6 | 0.6 | 14.3 | 13.2 | 1.1 | 10.0 | 11.0 | −1.0 | 5.4 | 5.4 | 0 |
| 3,500– 3,999 | 8.0 | 8.9 | −0.9 | 9.5 | 10.5 | −1.0 | 6.7 | 8.1 | −1.4 | 3.3 | 2.7 | 0.6 |
| 4,000– 4,499 | 5.8 | 7.0 | −1.2 | 7.0 | 8.8 | −1.8 | 4.4 | 5.0 | −0.6 | 2.5 | 1.9 | 0.6 |
| 4,500– 4,999 | 3.1 | 3.1 | 0 | 3.7 | 3.9 | −0.2 | 2.3 | 1.7 | 0.6 | 1.4 | 1.1 | 0.3 |
| 5,000 and over | 10.1 | 9.2 | 0.9 | 12.1 | 11.1 | 1.0 | 6.3 | 5.8 | 0.5 | 6.0 | 5.5 | 0.5 |

[a] Census minus PES.

TABLE 12

Comparison of the 1950 Census Percentage Distributions with the Estimated PES Percentage Distributions: 1949 Income of Identical Females, by Color

| | TOTAL | | | WHITE | | | NONWHITE | | |
|---|---|---|---|---|---|---|---|---|---|
| INCOME CLASS | *1950 Census* | PES | *Difference* [a] | *1950 Census* | PES | *Difference* [a] | *1950 Census* | PES | *Difference* [a] |
| Total | 100.0 | 100.0 | 0 | 100.0 | 100.0 | 0 | 100.0 | 100.0 | 0 |
| Under $ 500 | 28.9 | 27.3 | 1.6 | 27.1 | 25.7 | 1.4 | 43.2 | 39.6 | 3.6 |
| $ 500– 999 | 18.8 | 18.7 | 0.1 | 17.8 | 17.3 | 0.5 | 27.1 | 29.3 | −2.2 |
| 1,000– 1,499 | 13.6 | 14.0 | −0.4 | 13.6 | 13.9 | −0.3 | 13.7 | 15.3 | −1.6 |
| 1,500– 1,999 | 12.9 | 14.2 | −1.3 | 13.7 | 15.2 | −1.5 | 7.1 | 6.5 | 0.6 |
| 2,000– 2,499 | 11.8 | 11.5 | 0.3 | 12.7 | 12.4 | 0.3 | 4.3 | 4.5 | −0.2 |
| 2,500– 2,999 | 6.4 | 6.3 | 0.1 | 6.9 | 6.8 | 0.1 | 2.6 | 2.7 | −0.1 |
| 3,000– 3,499 | 3.5 | 4.2 | −0.7 | 3.8 | 4.7 | −0.9 | 1.2 | 0.7 | 0.5 |
| 3,500– 3,999 | 1.6 | 1.5 | 0.1 | 1.7 | 1.6 | 0.1 | 0.4 | 0.5 | −0.1 |
| 4,000– 4,499 | 0.4 | 0.4 | 0 | 0.5 | 0.5 | 0 | 0 | 0 | 0 |
| 4,500– 4,999 | 0.5 | 0.7 | −0.2 | 0.6 | 0.8 | −0.2 | 0.1 | 0.1 | 0 |
| 5,000 and over | 1.5 | 1.2 | 0.3 | 1.6 | 1.3 | 0.3 | 0.4 | 0.9 | −0.5 |

[a] Census minus PES.

MEDIANS

Table 9 shows that this difference produced an error of about $60, on the average, in the census medians. This demonstrates the stability of the median as a measure of central tendency.

DISTRIBUTIONS

The gross differences in reporting produced no clear shift in any of the distributions shown in Tables 10 through 13, except that in general, both the lowest and the highest classes were reported in the census as having somewhat too high proportions of the population.

For the "identical" male population, the average absolute deviation between the 1950 census and PES percentages was about 0.7 of a percentage point for the ten income classes from $1 to $4,999. For the female population, the corresponding average absolute deviation was about 0.5 of a percentage point.

## *Distributions of Total Income of Families*

The inquiries used in the 1950 census to obtain information on family income are reproduced in the Appendix. The method of obtaining the data was as follows:

If the head of a family was listed on a sample line on a census schedule, he (or his respondent) was asked three questions. His own total income was computed and coded from the answers. Next,

TABLE 13

Comparison of the 1950 Census Percentage Distributions with the Estimated PES Percentage Distributions: 1949 Income of Identical Females, by Residence

| INCOME CLASS | TOTAL | | | URBAN | | | RURAL NONFARM | | | RURAL FARM | | |
|---|---|---|---|---|---|---|---|---|---|---|---|---|
| | *1950 Census* | PES | *Difference* [a] | *1950 Census* | PES | *Difference* [a] | *1950 Census* | PES | *Difference* [a] | *1950 Census* | PES | *Difference* [a] |
| Total | 100.0 | 100.0 | 0 | 100.0 | 100.0 | 0 | 100.0 | 100.0 | 0 | 100.0 | 100.0 | 0 |
| Under $ 500 | 28.9 | 27.3 | 1.6 | 23.4 | 21.6 | 1.8 | 40.5 | 40.0 | 0.5 | 55.2 | 52.3 | 2.9 |
| $ 500– 999 | 18.8 | 18.7 | 0.1 | 18.7 | 18.5 | 0.2 | 19.8 | 20.6 | —0.8 | 18.1 | 15.9 | 2.2 |
| 1,000– 1,499 | 13.6 | 14.0 | —0.4 | 13.9 | 14.4 | —0.5 | 13.6 | 12.6 | 1.0 | 10.6 | 13.6 | —3.0 |
| 1,500– 1,999 | 12.9 | 14.2 | —1.3 | 14.3 | 15.8 | —1.5 | 10.5 | 10.3 | 0.2 | 6.0 | 7.6 | —1.6 |
| 2,000– 2,499 | 11.8 | 11.5 | 0.3 | 13.3 | 13.0 | 0.3 | 7.8 | 8.0 | —0.2 | 6.1 | 4.3 | 1.8 |
| 2,500– 2,999 | 6.4 | 6.3 | 0.1 | 7.7 | 7.6 | 0.1 | 3.4 | 2.7 | 0.7 | 1.2 | 2.3 | —1.1 |
| 3,000– 3,499 | 3.5 | 4.2 | —0.7 | 4.2 | 4.8 | —0.6 | 2.2 | 3.3 | —1.1 | 0 | 0.7 | —0.7 |
| 3,500– 3,999 | 1.6 | 1.5 | 0.1 | 1.9 | 1.8 | 0.1 | 0.7 | 0.3 | 0.4 | 0.7 | 1.3 | —0.6 |
| 4,000– 4,499 | 0.4 | 0.4 | 0 | 0.4 | 0.4 | 0 | 0.3 | 0.5 | —0.2 | 0.5 | 0.5 | 0 |
| 4,500– 4,999 | 0.5 | 0.7 | —0.2 | 0.6 | 0.9 | —0.3 | 0.3 | 0.3 | 0 | 0.3 | 0.3 | 0 |
| 5,000 and over | 1.5 | 1.2 | 0.3 | 1.6 | 1.2 | 0.4 | 1.1 | 1.4 | —0.3 | 1.4 | 1.1 | 0.3 |

[a] Census minus PES.

essentially the same three questions were asked concerning all the other members of his family. A single figure was recorded as the sum of each type of income for the remaining members of the family. The totals of the three types of income were then added to the total income of the family head to produce a total for family income.

In the PES, a much more elaborate procedure was employed. A complete set of income questions was asked of each member of each family.

The method of tabulation of the data for the approximately 5,500 families in the "family income subsample" precludes any direct evaluation of the family income distributions of the 1950 census. We have not been able to project the sample results to universe figures. The results are based on unadjusted totals derived from the same type of table as Tables 1 and 2. The picture of the family income data is essentially the same as that of the personal income data; a large number of disagreements in classification, of coverage errors, of errors in the definition of families, all leading to sizeable differences in the income class totals.

Again, two sets of results have been prepared, one based on all families in the sample and the other based on "identical" families. In the former case, the differences between the medians and distributions reflect all sources of error detected by the re-enumerative check. In the latter case, the differences reflect only errors arising from the reporting and coding of income. An "identical family" is one that was properly enumerated, received income in 1949, and where the PES and census agree on family type and size.

The available results are presented in Tables 14 through 16. The term "original" is used to describe the tabulation of the census data; the term "recheck" refers to the tabulation of the PES data from the same sample. Results are available only by residence.

TABLE 14

Comparison of Original and Recheck Medians: 1949 Income of Families, by Residence

| GROUP | ALL FAMILIES | | | IDENTICAL FAMILIES | | |
|---|---|---|---|---|---|---|
| | *Original* | *Recheck* | *Difference* [a] | *Original* | *Recheck* | *Difference* [a] |
| All families | $3,210 | $3,480 | $—270 | $3,260 | $3,510 | $—250 |
| Urban | 3,540 | 3,860 | —320 | 3,610 | 3,920 | —310 |
| Rural nonfarm | 2,700 | 3,020 | —320 | 2,710 | 2,990 | —280 |
| Rural farm | 1,820 | 1,950 | —130 | 1,850 | 1,900 | —50 |

[a] Original minus recheck.

TABLE 15

Comparison of Original and Recheck Percentage Distributions: 1949 Income for All Families, by Residence

| INCOME CLASS | TOTAL | | | URBAN | | | RURAL NONFARM | | | RURAL FARM | | |
|---|---|---|---|---|---|---|---|---|---|---|---|---|
| | *Original* | *Recheck* | *Difference* [a] | *Original* | *Recheck* | *Difference* [a] | *Original* | *Recheck* | *Difference* [a] | *Original* | *Recheck* | *Difference* [a] |
| Total | 100.0 | 100.0 | 0 | 100.0 | 100.0 | 0 | 100.0 | 100.0 | 0 | 100.0 | 100.0 | 0 |
| Income reported | 94.4 | 87.5 | 6.9 | 93.6 | 87.2 | 6.4 | 95.9 | 87.8 | 8.1 | 96.3 | 88.5 | 7.8 |
| Income not reported | 5.6 | 12.5 | —6.9 | 6.4 | 12.8 | —6.4 | 4.1 | 12.2 | —8.1 | 3.7 | 11.5 | —7.8 |
| Total reporting income | 100.0 | 100.0 | 0 | 100.0 | 100.0 | 0 | 100.0 | 100.0 | 0 | 100.0 | 100.0 | 0 |
| None | 3.9 | 1.4 | 2.5 | 3.5 | 1.2 | 2.3 | 3.2 | 1.6 | 1.6 | 6.9 | 2.5 | 4.4 |
| Some | 96.1 | 98.6 | —2.5 | 96.5 | 98.8 | —2.3 | 96.8 | 98.4 | —1.6 | 93.1 | 97.5 | —4.4 |
| Total reporting some income | 100.0 | 100.0 | 0 | 100.0 | 100.0 | 0 | 100.0 | 100.0 | 0 | 100.0 | 100.0 | 0 |
| Under $ 500 | 4.4 | 3.5 | 0.9 | 2.4 | 1.6 | 0.8 | 4.7 | 3.5 | 1.2 | 14.1 | 13.1 | 1.0 |
| $ 500– 999 | 6.3 | 5.9 | 0.4 | 3.8 | 3.2 | 0.6 | 9.8 | 9.6 | 0.2 | 13.8 | 14.0 | —0.2 |
| 1,000– 1,499 | 7.1 | 5.9 | 1.2 | 4.5 | 3.9 | 0.6 | 10.7 | 8.3 | 2.4 | 15.1 | 12.4 | 2.7 |
| 1,500– 1,999 | 8.1 | 7.1 | 1.0 | 6.8 | 5.4 | 1.4 | 10.5 | 9.8 | 0.7 | 11.0 | 11.7 | —0.7 |
| 2,000– 2,499 | 9.6 | 8.1 | 1.5 | 9.2 | 7.1 | 2.1 | 10.6 | 8.5 | 2.1 | 10.5 | 12.6 | —2.1 |
| 2,500– 2,999 | 9.3 | 9.0 | 0.3 | 9.5 | 9.1 | 0.4 | 9.5 | 9.8 | —0.3 | 8.1 | 7.8 | 0.3 |
| 3,000– 3,499 | 12.1 | 11.0 | 1.1 | 12.9 | 11.4 | 1.5 | 11.4 | 11.6 | —0.2 | 8.7 | 8.4 | 0.3 |
| 3,500– 3,999 | 9.8 | 10.4 | —0.6 | 11.0 | 11.4 | —0.4 | 8.6 | 10.8 | —2.2 | 5.0 | 5.1 | —0.1 |
| 4,000– 4,499 | 6.9 | 7.7 | —0.8 | 7.4 | 8.5 | —1.1 | 7.9 | 7.0 | 0.9 | 3.1 | 5.0 | —1.9 |
| 4,500– 4,999 | 4.7 | 6.8 | —2.1 | 6.0 | 8.0 | —2.0 | 2.7 | 5.6 | —2.9 | 1.1 | 1.9 | —0.8 |
| 5,000 and over | 21.6 | 24.7 | —3.1 | 26.3 | 30.5 | —4.2 | 13.5 | 15.5 | —2.0 | 9.3 | 8.1 | 1.2 |

[a] Original minus recheck.

TABLE 16

Comparison of Original and Recheck Percentage Distributions: 1949 Income for Identical Families, by Residence

| INCOME CLASS | TOTAL | | | URBAN | | | RURAL NONFARM | | | RURAL FARM | | |
|---|---|---|---|---|---|---|---|---|---|---|---|---|
| | *Original* | *Recheck* | *Difference*[a] | *Original* | *Recheck* | *Difference*[a] | *Original* | *Recheck* | *Difference*[a] | *Original* | *Recheck* | *Difference*[a] |
| Total | 100.0 | 100.0 | 0 | 100.0 | 100.0 | 0 | 100.0 | 100.0 | 0 | 100.0 | 100.0 | 0 |
| Under $ 500 | 3.9 | 3.5 | 0.4 | 2.1 | 1.6 | 0.5 | 4.4 | 2.6 | 1.8 | 12.3 | 14.0 | −1.7 |
| $ 500– 999 | 6.3 | 5.7 | 0.6 | 3.9 | 3.1 | 0.8 | 9.9 | 9.5 | 0.4 | 14.0 | 13.4 | 0.6 |
| 1,000– 1,499 | 6.4 | 5.8 | 0.6 | 3.6 | 3.7 | −0.1 | 10.1 | 8.2 | 1.9 | 15.2 | 13.2 | 2.0 |
| 1,500– 1,999 | 8.0 | 6.9 | 1.1 | 6.5 | 5.1 | 1.4 | 10.2 | 10.1 | 0.1 | 12.1 | 11.8 | 0.3 |
| 2,000– 2,499 | 9.4 | 8.2 | 1.2 | 8.9 | 7.0 | 1.9 | 11.1 | 9.3 | 1.8 | 9.9 | 12.7 | −2.8 |
| 2,500– 2,999 | 9.9 | 9.2 | 0.7 | 10.2 | 9.4 | 0.8 | 10.2 | 10.5 | −0.3 | 7.9 | 6.5 | 1.4 |
| 3,000– 3,499 | 11.5 | 10.4 | 1.1 | 12.2 | 10.4 | 1.8 | 11.0 | 12.1 | −1.1 | 8.8 | 8.3 | 0.5 |
| 3,500– 3,999 | 10.5 | 10.6 | −0.1 | 11.8 | 11.7 | 0.1 | 9.3 | 10.1 | −0.8 | 5.5 | 5.4 | 0.1 |
| 4,000– 4,499 | 7.1 | 7.6 | −0.5 | 7.8 | 8.6 | −0.8 | 7.3 | 5.7 | 1.6 | 2.9 | 4.7 | −1.8 |
| 4,500– 4,999 | 4.8 | 7.0 | −2.2 | 6.0 | 8.4 | −2.4 | 2.7 | 6.1 | −3.4 | 1.1 | 1.7 | −0.6 |
| 5,000 and over | 22.3 | 25.1 | −2.8 | 27.0 | 31.0 | −4.0 | 13.8 | 15.8 | −2.0 | 10.3 | 8.4 | 1.9 |

[a] Original minus recheck.

MEDIANS [4]

For the urban and rural-nonfarm cases, the original medians are about $300 less than the recheck medians, with essentially the same result for identical families as for all families. For the rural-farm cases, the original and recheck medians appear to be somewhat closer together, with a difference of $130 for all families and of $50 for identical families. As in the case of personal income, some of the 1950 census medians for family income were estimated to have been too high because the additional income recipients picked up by the PES appear to have been concentrated in the low income class. We would guess (no direct evidence is available) that failing to include the income of persons other than the family head was an important factor in the understatement of the census medians.[5]

FAMILIES WITHOUT INCOME

In the census tabulations, this group is included in the class "income under $500." The results indicate that about two and one-half times as many families were included in that class in the census (about 4 per cent) as should have been (about 1.5 per cent).

DISTRIBUTIONS

Tables 15 and 16 show evidence of a small but definite directional bias in the census distributions. The proportions in the lowest income classes appear to have been overstated, in general, while the proportions in the income classes beginning with $3,500 appear to have been understated. (There are some differences depending on the residence of the families.) The fact that the results shown in Table 15 (all families) parallel those in Table 16 (identical families) indicates that the underreporting of the amount of income was the most significant source of error in the census distributions.

### *Distributions of Income of Persons, by Type of Income*

Tables 17 through 20 present the PES results relating to income by type; wages and salaries, income from self-employment, and income from all other sources. Again we have not been able to

[4] The medians were defined on a somewhat different basis than the published 1950 census medians for family income. The published figures *include* the "families with no income" in the computation; the figures in this report do *not*.

[5] The editing rules employed in the 1950 census probably had some impact. There were situations in which a nonresponse to a specific inquiry could be treated as a response of "none."

TABLE 17

Comparison of Original and Recheck Medians: 1949 Income of Males and Females, by Type of Income

| URCE OF INCOME | MALE | | | FEMALE | | |
|---|---|---|---|---|---|---|
| | *Original* | *Recheck* | *Difference* [a] | *Original* | *Recheck* | *Difference* [a] |
| tal income [b] | $2,430 | $2,450 | $—20 | $1,030 | $ 960 | $ 70 |
| ages and salaries | 2,460 | 2,540 | —80 | 1,200 | 1,130 | 70 |
| lf-employment | 1,920 | 1,760 | 160 | 930 | 760 | 170 |
| l other income | 470 | 460 | 10 | 450 | 420 | 30 |

[a] Original minus recheck.
[b] Based on actual 1950 census tabulations and projections of PES results to the universal level.

compare the actual census tabulations with the PES data projected to universe levels. As in the case of family income, the comparisons are limited to the sample itself, and thus the terms "original" and "recheck" are used. Also the results relate only to all individuals in the sample; no results are available for "identical" individuals. Thus the results reflect all sources of error and difference, errors in defining the population and nonresponse as well as differences in the reporting of the amount of income.

TABLE 18

omparison of Original and Recheck Percentage Distributions: 1949 Income from Wages or Salary, Males and Females

| INCOME CLASS | MALE | | | FEMALE | | |
|---|---|---|---|---|---|---|
| | *Original* | *Recheck* | *Difference* [a] | *Original* | *Recheck* | *Difference* [a] |
| otal | 100.0 | 100.0 | 0 | 100.0 | 100.0 | 0 |
| Income reported | 94.7 | 93.9 | 0.8 | 94.9 | 94.5 | 0.4 |
| Income not reported | 5.3 | 6.1 | —0.8 | 5.1 | 5.5 | —0.4 |
| otal reporting income | 100.0 | 100.0 | 0 | 100.0 | 100.0 | 0 |
| None | 31.5 | 31.1 | 0.4 | 69.6 | 67.2 | 2.4 |
| Some | 68.5 | 68.9 | —0.4 | 30.4 | 32.8 | —2.4 |
| otal reporting some income | 100.0 | 100.0 | 0 | 100.0 | 100.0 | 0 |
| Under $ 500 | 11.3 | 11.9 | —0.6 | 27.6 | 28.9 | —1.3 |
| $ 500– 999 | 9.0 | 9.0 | 0 | 16.8 | 17.7 | —0.9 |
| 1,000– 1,499 | 8.4 | 7.7 | 0.7 | 14.0 | 12.6 | 1.4 |
| 1,500– 1,999 | 9.4 | 8.9 | 0.5 | 13.3 | 14.1 | —0.8 |
| 2,000– 2,499 | 12.8 | 11.5 | 1.3 | 13.5 | 12.1 | 1.4 |
| 2,500– 2,999 | 11.2 | 12.4 | —1.2 | 8.0 | 7.4 | 0.6 |
| 3,000– 3,499 | 13.5 | 12.2 | 1.3 | 3.3 | 3.9 | —0.6 |
| 3,500– 3,999 | 8.6 | 9.5 | —0.9 | 1.7 | 1.2 | 0.5 |
| 4,000– 4,499 | 4.5 | 5.8 | —1.3 | 0.7 | 0.5 | 0.2 |
| 4,500– 4,999 | 3.1 | 3.1 | 0 | 0.5 | 0.6 | —0.1 |
| 5,000 and over | 8.2 | 8.1 | 0.1 | 0.5 | 0.9 | —0.4 |

[a] Original minus recheck.

TABLE 19

Comparison of Original and Recheck Percentage Distributions: 1949 Income from Self-Employment, Males and Females

| INCOME CLASS | MALE | | | FEMALE | | |
|---|---|---|---|---|---|---|
| | *Original* | *Recheck* | *Difference* [a] | *Original* | *Recheck* | *Difference* [a] |
| Total | 100.0 | 100.0 | 0 | 100.0 | 100.0 | 0 |
| Income reported | 94.4 | 93.4 | 1.0 | 94.6 | 94.1 | 0.5 |
| Income not reported | 5.6 | 6.6 | −1.0 | 5.4 | 5.9 | −0.5 |
| Total reporting income | 100.0 | 100.0 | 0 | 100.0 | 100.0 | 0 |
| None | 83.7 | 82.4 | 1.3 | 96.5 | 96.9 | −0.4 |
| Some | 16.3 | 17.6 | −1.3 | 3.5 | 3.1 | 0.4 |
| Total reporting some income | 100.0 | 100.0 | 0 | 100.0 | 100.0 | 0 |
| Under $ 500 | 17.6 | 20.1 | −2.5 | 37.9 | 40.8 | −2.9 |
| $ 500– 999 | 14.8 | 14.5 | 0.3 | 14.2 | 17.9 | −3.7 |
| 1,000– 1,499 | 10.5 | 10.0 | 0.5 | 5.1 | 7.8 | −2.7 |
| 1,500– 1,999 | 8.5 | 10.6 | −2.1 | 9.4 | 8.0 | 1.4 |
| 2,000– 2,499 | 7.9 | 9.7 | −1.8 | 6.7 | 6.3 | 0.4 |
| 2,500– 2,999 | 5.8 | 6.0 | −0.2 | 4.2 | 1.6 | 2.6 |
| 3,000– 3,499 | 8.8 | 5.7 | 3.1 | 6.1 | 0.7 | 5.4 |
| 3,500– 3,999 | 6.0 | 6.4 | −0.4 | 0.5 | 0.6 | −0.1 |
| 4,000– 4,499 | 4.2 | 3.2 | 1.0 | 5.8 | 5.9 | −0.1 |
| 4,500– 4,999 | 1.9 | 1.8 | 0.1 | 1.1 | 0.5 | 0.6 |
| 5,000 and over | 13.7 | 11.9 | 1.8 | 9.2 | 10.0 | −0.8 |

[a] Original minus recheck.

TABLE 20

Comparison of Original and Recheck Percentage Distributions: 1949 Income from Sources other than Earnings, Males and Females

| INCOME CLASS | MALE | | | FEMALE | | |
|---|---|---|---|---|---|---|
| | *Original* | *Recheck* | *Difference* [a] | *Original* | *Recheck* | *Difference* [a] |
| Total | 100.0 | 100.0 | 0 | 100.0 | 100.0 | 0 |
| Income reported | 94.4 | 93.6 | 0.8 | 94.3 | 94.1 | 0.2 |
| Income not reported | 5.6 | 6.4 | −0.8 | 5.7 | 5.9 | −0.2 |
| Total reporting income | 100.0 | 100.0 | 0 | 100.0 | 100.0 | 0 |
| None | 78.2 | 68.7 | 9.5 | 87.7 | 81.0 | 6.7 |
| Some | 21.8 | 31.3 | −9.5 | 12.3 | 19.0 | −6.7 |
| Total reporting some income | 100.0 | 100.0 | 0 | 100.0 | 100.0 | 0 |
| Under $ 500 | 53.7 | 55.0 | −1.3 | 56.1 | 59.6 | −3.5 |
| $ 500– 999 | 23.2 | 25.8 | −2.6 | 23.8 | 21.1 | 2.7 |
| 1,000– 1,499 | 10.2 | 9.5 | 0.7 | 7.9 | 9.0 | −1.1 |
| 1,500– 1,999 | 4.6 | 4.2 | 0.4 | 2.6 | 3.5 | −0.9 |
| 2,000– 2,499 | 2.5 | 2.2 | 0.3 | 2.4 | 2.0 | 0.4 |
| 2,500– 2,999 | 1.4 | 0.6 | 0.8 | 1.3 | 0.7 | 0.6 |
| 3,000– 3,499 | 0.3 | 0.5 | −0.2 | 1.7 | 0.7 | 1.0 |
| 3,500– 3,999 | 0.3 | 0.3 | 0 | 0 | 0.4 | −0.4 |
| 4,000– 4,499 | 0.5 | 0.1 | 0.4 | 0.3 | 0.3 | 0 |
| 4,500– 4,999 | 0.1 | 0.2 | −0.1 | 0.3 | 0.3 | 0 |
| 5,000 and over | 3.0 | 1.7 | 1.3 | 3.6 | 2.5 | 1.1 |

[a] Original minus recheck.

MEDIANS

The results of the re-enumerative check indicate that the census medians for income from self-employment may have been overstated by about $150. The census medians for income from all other sources may have been very slightly overstated. In the case of wages and salaries, there appears to have been a sex difference, with the original median for males being lower than the recheck median by about $80; while for females the original median is about $70 higher.

INCOME RECIPIENTS

Perhaps the most striking finding of the PES is that the deficiency of income recipients reported in the census was caused primarily by the failure to record income from sources other than earnings. In the case of wages and salaries and of income from self-employment, the evidence from the sample indicates that the understatement of the proportions of income recipients in the census may have been quite small.

In the case of income from sources other than earnings, however, Table 20 shows that the "original" proportion of male income recipients was understated by 9.5 percentage points, and of females by 6.7 percentage points. The additional recipients are concentrated in the low-income classes. This accounts for the PES median being lower than the census median by about $150.

DISTRIBUTIONS

Except for the consistent evidence of understatement in the census of the proportions of persons in the lowest income class ($1 to $500 or loss) for each type of income, there are no clearly discernible patterns in the results.

## *Discussion of Results*

Despite our intentions, we have "interpreted" some of the estimates of error from the standpoint of the consumer. We have labeled some of the errors as "small." But, then, this was primarily an attempt to obtain information. Are there, for example, any essential uses of census income statistics that require the medians to be accurate within $100?

PROBING QUESTIONS

The re-enumerative check uncovered additional recipients of income from sources other than earnings. The PES also found more recipients of wages and salaries than had been identified in the 1950 census. It is conceivable that even more intensive probing might have uncovered larger numbers of recipients of very small amounts of income. Yet, if techniques intensive enough to uncover very small amounts of income had been used in the census, would the statistics have been more useful? Median incomes were based on distributions for persons who received $1 or more of income in 1949. Would it be more desirable to base the medians on distributions beginning with $100 or $500?

### SELF-EMPLOYMENT INCOME

The assumption that individual true values exist is subject to the strongest reservation in the case of income from self-employment. That the PES results are so similar to those of the census attests, however, to the statistical stability of the concept of self-employment income.

It is of interest that the "better" method produced somewhat lower medians in the case of self-employment income. The fairly general belief that the best survey procedure "gets the most income" must be discounted if we are willing to regard a procedure that precedes a question on net income with one on gross income as "better."

### FUTURE CENSUSES

Our rough-and-ready evaluation of the costs and gains suggests that there would be little to be gained by including the PES types-of-income inquiry in a census. The cost would be prohibitive; the improvements in accuracy, marginal. Although the PES does not provide any substantial proof, there may, however, be some merit in obtaining family income data after first determining the income of each family member separately. This plus a single question designed to uncover small amounts of income from sources other than earnings would be the most we would recommend.

### AGGREGATES AND AVERAGES

The effect on the percentage distributions of income caused by underenumeration in the 1950 census was probably trivial. The same can be said for the failure on the part of the PES to find all the people that were missed in the census.

Table 3 indicates that, according to the PES, persons fourteen years old and over were understated by 1.5 per cent in the 1950 census. There is little doubt that this estimate is too low; there is some evidence that the undercount may be 3 per cent.[6]

[6] Ansley J. Coale, "The Population of the United States in 1950 Classified by

We conjecture that it is even disproportionately lower in the low-income classes. This is based on the belief that the PES had the greatest difficulty in finding young adult migrants who were missed in the census, persons typically at the low end of the occupational scale.

The chief impact of underenumeration would arise in estimating family income where an independently determined income aggregate is applied to a census population total. This type of average, if not corrected for underenumeration, would be too high. Averages (and aggregates) based entirely on the 1950 census are, however, probably not seriously affected by underenumeration.

### SHOULD ERRORS BE MEASURED?

The measurement of errors in statistics is a costly business. Suppose techniques of measurement of error were advanced to the point of unquestioned validity. Which would be preferable, measurements of error or more statistics?

## *Appendix: Procedures of the Re-enumerative Check*

The study of income was but a small part of the re-enumerative check phase of the PES. The design of the check represented a compromise to achieve an optimum balance of effort over various subject matter areas.

Two overlapping probability samples were drawn, designed on the one hand to represent the land area of the United States and on the other hand to represent the persons, dwelling units, and farms enumerated in the 1950 censuses.

About 250 specially selected and trained enumerators were employed to canvass the sample of areas intensively in a search for persons, dwelling units, and farms which might have been missed in the original enumeration. These enumerators also conducted probing interviews designed to study the accuracy of the information obtained originally. In addition, these interviews were designed to uncover cases of overenumeration, that is, units listed on the rolls of the censuses that should not have been listed.

This work was carried out under close supervision; the questionnaires obtained were carefully edited both in the field and in Washington. Intensive searches were made of the census schedules before a unit was finally classified as erroneously omitted from or erroneously included in the census. Tabulations were made for selected characteristics of persons, dwelling units, and farms. These tabula-

Age, Sex, and Color—A Revision of Census Figures," *Journal of the American Statistical Association,* March 1955, pp. 16–54.

tions exhibit, category by category, the estimated numbers of content differences and coverage errors that would have occurred had the PES been conducted on the entire universe rather than on a sample.

### THE SAMPLE

The basic sample for the re-enumerative check was a stratified, multistage area sample of the United States. The first stage, consisting of 276 primary sampling units (counties or groups of counties), was drawn with probability proportionate to the population of the United States in 1940.

One of the major tasks of the PES was to discover households and farms which had been missed by census enumerators. To accomplish this, a segment sample was selected. This consisted of about 2,800 urban and about 1,000 rural small areas selected within the primary sample units. These small segments contained about six dwelling units in urban parts of the primary sampling units and about ten dwelling units and five farms in the rural parts.

To determine how many persons were missed in households which were enumerated, to study the extent of overenumeration in the censuses, and to study the content errors of the censuses, samples of households and farms were drawn from the census rolls. These made up what is termed the list sample of the PES. Techniques were devised to make the list sample overlap in urban areas as much as possible with the segment sample. In rural areas, the segment and list samples were drawn from the same primary sampling units but were independent of one another.

To aid the PES enumerators in canvassing the segments for missed dwelling units and farms, a special map or aerial photograph was prepared for each segment. In addition, for many segments, the PES enumerators were supplied either with photostats of the original census schedules or with lists of names and addresses of persons, dwelling units, and farms which were enumerated in or near the designated segments.

In preparing the list sample, an elaborate transcription procedure designated the specific persons, dwelling units, and farms in the list sample and provided transcriptions of the original census data for these units. To cut the cost of the program, subsamples of enumerated persons within dwelling units designated for the list sample were selected. One-half of the sample overlapped the census income sample. Transcriptions of the original census data were provided for 95 per cent of the dwelling units and persons in the sample and for 90 per cent of the farms that were sampled. A control group was set up by not supplying transcriptions for the remainder of the cases.

The combined segment and list samples yielded 11,800 cases for the personal income subsample and 5,500 cases for the family income subsample.

### DESIGN OF THE INTERVIEW

Three major considerations governed the type of interview to be conducted in the PES. The first was that in the PES the respondent be the "best" (usually the person for whom the information was being collected). The procedure in the 1950 censuses permitted the enumerator to interview any responsible member of the household or even under certain conditions to substitute other persons, such as landlords or neighbors.

The second consideration was that a series of detailed questions be supplied for a given topic. It was believed that a more accurate answer would result than that from the single question approach of the 1950 censuses.

The third guiding principle was the belief that an on-the-spot reconciliation of differences in response between the original census enumeration and the PES would produce more accurate data.

To accomplish these objectives, separate questionnaires were designed for the persons, dwelling units, and farms in the sample. In addition, a "coverage questionnaire" was designed to aid the enumerators in identifying missed dwelling units, in identifying missed persons within enumerated dwelling units, in locating farms that might have been missed, and in checking on overenumeration of dwelling units.

### SUPERVISION AND TRAINING

There were fourteen PES supervisors and fourteen assistant supervisors. These people were selected from among the most highly qualified members of the supervisory staff of the census field organization. In addition to the supervisors, working observers were provided from the headquarters of the Bureau of the Census, from other government agencies, and from university groups. The observers shared responsibility with the supervisors for the technical aspects of the PES and also participated in the training of the PES interviewers. The supervisors and observers were given three weeks of training, including a full week of practice enumeration.

About 250 enumerators were selected from among the most highly qualified personnel who worked on the 1950 censuses. No person was assigned to a sample area for which he had any responsibility in the original census enumeration. The PES enumerators were specialized; approximately 160 were selected to work in urban areas and approximately 90 were selected to cover rural areas. Both urban and rural enumerators received a week's training.

In addition, there was a field edit of the questionnaires and other documents of each enumerator as soon as they were received in the area offices. This was primarily designed to return defective work to the field for correction.

PROCESSING

The processing of returns was lengthy and complex. It consisted of:

1. *An initial screening.* To detect and send back to the field defective materials which had slipped through the field-edit procedure.

2. *Editing, coding, and transcription.* To prepare material for the record checks, to identify cases of possible coverage error for which special searching of the census returns was required, and to convert the information for punching and tabulation.

3. *Searching.* Detailed criteria were established for deciding whether or not a given unit of enumeration belonged in the class of "erroneous omissions" or of "erroneous inclusions." This demanded a careful search of the census returns.

4. *Punching and tabulating.* Three punch cards were prepared for every person and three for every family in the subsamples. The basic tabulations, made on a high-speed electronic computer, in practically every case took the form of Tables 1 and 2.

In the family income results and the results for income by type, the frequencies in the basic tables represent cases in the sample adjusted to a self-weighting level. In the personal income results presented above, the frequencies in the basic tables are weighted to represent the population of the United States. To minimize the sampling error of the estimates, a final stage of "difference" estimating was employed in constructing Tables 1 and 2.

This technique is reflected in Table 1. The column totals for the census income classes are the published totals. They were substituted for the totals derived from the sample. To adjust the breakdown in a column to add to the new total, the sum of the nondiagonal elements (the weighted PES estimate of error in the column) was subtracted from the census total. This gave a new diagonal-cell entry (a "difference" estimate of the number of persons for whom no errors were made), which replaced the original sample estimate. After this adjustment, the row totals (the PES estimates) were obtained.

## Exhibit A-1

### Income Questions in the 1950 Census

| FOR PERSONS 14 YEARS OF AGE AND OVER | | | | | | | |
|---|---|---|---|---|---|---|---|
| Income received by this person in 1949 | | | | If this person is a family head (see definition below)—Income received by his relatives in this household | | | |
| **Last year (1949), how much money did he earn working as an employee for wages or salary?** (Enter amount before deductions for taxes, etc.) | **Last year, how much money did he earn working in his own business, professional practice, or farm?** (Enter net income) | **Last year, how much money did he receive from interest, dividends, veteran's allowances, pensions, rents, or other income (aside from earnings)?** | LEAVE BLANK | **Last year (1949), how much money did his relatives in this household earn working for wages or salary?** (Amount before deductions for taxes, etc.) | **Last year, how much money did his relatives in this household earn in own business, professional practice, or farm?** (Net income) | **Last year, how much money did his relatives in this household receive from interest, dividends, veteran's allowances, pensions, rents, or other income (aside from earnings)?** | LEAVE BLANK |
| 31a | 31b | 31c | F | 32a | 32b | 32c | G |

# Exhibit A-2

## Income Questions in the PES

**29. Last year (1949) did you do any work at all, even for a week or two?**

☐ **Yes - Fill out the Table below**

☐ **No** - *Skip to Item 30.*

**TABLE II**

| | | | A |
|---|---|---|---|
| (1) Repeat the questions until job history for entire calendar year, 1949, is completed. If he held more than one job during the period, use a separate column for each period of work and each period of doing something else. | | | **Last December (1949) what were you doing —**<br>☐ **Working or**<br>☐ **Something else?** |
| (2) **If "Working": When did you begin to work?**<br>**If "Something else": When did you leave your last job or business before that?** | | | |
| (3) **If "Working": When did this work end?**<br>**If "Something else": You were not working from........ (2) to when?** | | | **December 31, 1949** |
| **If "Something else"** | (4) **From............. (2) to............. (3), while you were not working, were you getting unemployment or workman's compensation?** | | ☐ Yes<br>☐ No } *Skip to Item (1) B* |
| **If "Working"** | (5) **For whom were you working?** | | Name of employer<br><br>☐ Own farm<br>☐ Own business } *Skip to Item (1) B* |
| **If Working for Someone Else** | (6) **How much money did you make while working for................ (5)?** | | $ __________<br>☐ Don't know - *Skip to Item (8).* |
| | (7) **Is this before deductions for taxes, social security, etc.?** | | ☐ Yes<br>☐ No - *Correct figure in Item (6)* |
| | If Total in Item (6) is not known | (8) **How much did you receive each week before deductions?** | $ __________ |
| | | (9) **How many weeks on this job did you receive this amount?** | |
| | | (10) Total amount received on this job in 1949 - (8) times (9). | $ __________ |
| | (11) **Did you receive any tips, bonuses, or commissions from this job?** | | ☐ Yes<br>☐ No |
| | If "Yes" in Item (11) | (12) **Is this included in the $.......... (6) or (10)?** | ☐ Yes<br>☐ No - *Correct figure in Item (6) or (1* |
| | (13) Total wages and salary earned in 1949 - (6) or (10). | | |

| B | C | D | TOTALS |
|---|---|---|---|
| **Before ..........(2A)....what were you doing —**<br>☐ **Working**<br>☐ **Something else?** | **Before ..........(2B)....what were you doing —**<br>☐ **Working**<br>☐ **Something else?** | **Before ..........(2C)....what were you doing —**<br>☐ **Working**<br>☐ **Something else?** | |
| | | | |
| | | | |
| ☐ Yes<br>☐ No } ***Skip to Item (1) C*** | ☐ Yes<br>☐ No } ***Skip to Item (1) D*** | ☐ Yes<br>☐ No | |
| Name of employer | Name of employer | Name of employer | |
| ☐ Own farm<br>☐ Own business } ***Skip to Item (1) C*** | ☐ Own farm<br>☐ Own business } ***Skip to Item (1) D*** | ☐ Own farm<br>☐ Own business | |
| $ ________<br>☐ Don't know - ***Skip to Item (8)*** | $ ________<br>☐ Don't know - ***Skip to Item (8)*** | $ ________<br>☐ Don't know - ***Skip to Item (8)*** | $ ________ |
| ☐ Yes<br>☐ No - ***Correct figure in Item (6)*** | ☐ Yes<br>☐ No - ***Correct figure in Item (6)*** | ☐ Yes<br>☐ No - ***Correct figure in Item (6)*** | |
| $ ________ | $ ________ | $ ________ | |
| | | | |
| $ ________ | $ ________ | $ ________ | $ ________ |
| ☐ Yes<br>☐ No | ☐ Yes<br>☐ No | ☐ Yes<br>☐ No | |
| ☐ Yes<br>☐ No - ***Correct figure in Item (6) or (10)*** | ☐ Yes<br>☐ No - ***Correct figure in Item (6) or (10)*** | ☐ Yes<br>☐ No - ***Correct figure in Item (6) or (10)*** | |
| | | | $ ________ |

30. Did you do any (other) work during 1949, such as part-time work, odd jobs, etc.?

☐ Yes - *Enter information in Table II*

☐ No

IF SELF-EMPLOYED AT ANY TIME DURING 1949 ANSWER ITEMS 31-33

31. From . . . . to . . . . what was your gross income, that is, the total amount you took in during that period (if farm, include government loans on crops)?

$ ____________

32. What was your net income after deducting business expenses? This is before deducting personal expenses, personal income taxes, and before deducting money spent for capital items such as land and buildings, equipment, machinery (tractors, trucks, etc.)?

$ ____________

33. If nonfarm self-employment:

a. Did you take out a salary or make any other cash withdrawals from your business during 1949?

☐ No

◯ Yes

b. If "Yes": Does the net income figure of......... include all the money you withdrew from the business for yourself as well as any other profits which the business made?

☐ No - *correct figure in Item 32*

☐ *Yes*

34. Last year, during 1949, did you receive any money from other sources such as: | If yes, **HOW MUCH?**

a. Unemployment or workmen's compensation (Include veterans readjustment allowances)? Verify this by referring to Item 29-(4) in Table II. ☐ No ☐ Yes $ ______

b. Social Security benefits and government pensions or assistance? ☐ No ☐ Yes $ ______

c. Any other pensions or allowances? ☐ No ☐ Yes $ ______

d. Veterans' payments, such as education and training subsistence allowances, bonuses or disability pensions? ☐ No ☐ Yes $ ______

e. Dependency allotments (from members of the Armed Forces)? ☐ No ☐ Yes $ ______

f. Interest, cash dividends, and income from estates and trusts? ☐ No ☐ Yes $ ______

g. Receipts from roomers and boarders (net income after expenses)? ☐ No ☐ Yes $ ______

h. Rents and royalties from property (net income after expenses)? ☐ No ☐ Yes $ ______

i. Money for support from persons not living in this household (including alimony)? ☐ No ☐ Yes $ ______

**NOTE:** If amounts from any source are reported in this question or in Question 35 by more than one member of the family, make sure these amounts are not duplicated.

35. a. Last year did you receive any money from any other source?

1 ☐ No

◯ Yes

b. If "Yes," list the types and sources of income and show the amount

(1) ______ $ ______

(2) ______ $ ______

36. Compute the total "other" income for this person by adding all amounts in Items 34 and 35. $ ______

# Some Income Adjustment Results from the 1949 Audit Control Program

MARIUS FARIOLETTI, PLANNING DIVISION,
INTERNAL REVENUE SERVICE

## *Purpose of the Audit Control Programs*

In the broadest sense, the Audit Control Programs were an ambitious and complicated venture into the field of quantitative analysis in the attempt to speed up the audit improvements needed to cope with the vastly greater responsibilities placed on the Internal Revenue Service during World War II and since. The programs used the technique of probability sampling to select representative tax returns for audit. The results were tabulated to produce statistics representing the size and nature of the audit problems of federal taxpayers and administrators.

However, the programs were not merely a fact-collecting project. Through the development of new tax return processing and selection procedures, the objectivity and sharpness inherent in quantitative analysis were, to some extent, combined with the practical knowledge of the experienced audit manager. The programs also made clear the need to develop similar basic information about the regular audit programs. This information is now being gathered, and it shows how far audit problems are actually being covered by the regular examination procedures. Any areas that are being too thinly or heavily covered are brought to light. In this way, by balancing the case experience of examining officers with the facts about the size and relative importance of different audit problems, more effective tax enforcement is being attained.

The stated objectives of the ACP involving the 1948–1950 income years for individual income tax returns, and the 1949 income year for corporations with assets under $250,000 were primarily:

1. To provide a sound basis for estimating the total audit workload for the types of tax returns covered by the programs.

Note: While the writer is responsible for the preparation of this paper, the materials are largely the products of group research and thinking of staff members of the Internal Revenue Service's Planning and Statistics Divisions. Particular credit should be given to C. W. Anderson, T. E. McHold, A. C. Rosander, W. C. Shoup, and J. H. Wilson, Statistics Division; C. B. Fine, Appellate Division; and J. W. Connaughton, Planning Division. Mr. Rosander and Mr. Fine are responsible for the preparation of the appendix materials on sampling and estimating methods.

2. To improve the existing procedures for selecting for regular examination or audit erroneous tax returns with relatively large tax errors.

3. To find out which types of tax errors should be attacked by new laws, new regulations, and, if possible, new ways of explaining tax ideas to mistaken taxpayers, many of whom are willing to comply with the tax laws if they can only be taught how.

4. In addition to exploring the size and nature of the audit problems of the individual and corporate income taxes, the 1949 program was expected to provide information on the feasibility of auditing all federal tax returns of one taxpayer during one examination, including withholding and pay roll taxes and certain excises.

The tax administrator is not primarily in the business of producing statistics. Consequently, when he undertakes a big project such as the ACP he expects practical results rather quickly. Thus none of the stated objectives include the production of income information helpful in evaluating the income estimates made by federal and other agencies.

The 1949 program was designed to permit the tabulation of income adjustments, since this information was considered to be a desirable by-product. However, no additional funds were made available for this purpose. Therefore the estimates of income adjustments to be found if all tax returns of the described types were examined are by-products of tabulations made for the express purpose of attaining the stated objectives. Owing to the limited resources which could be made available for the ACP tabulations and the analyses of the 1949 ACP results, only a limited amount of the income adjustment information collected has been tabulated and no further tabulations are planned.

## *Methods Used in the Programs*

### SELECTING THE SAMPLE RETURNS FOR AUDIT

Even before the results of the 1948 program were received and tabulated, let alone analyzed, it was necessary to start the program for the 1949 returns. The 1949 program included another, but smaller, sample of individual returns, a sample of small corporation returns—largely those with assets under $250,000, and an examination of the pay roll and certain excise tax returns of these same groups. The *Statistics of Income* estimates, which have been produced by the IRS Statistics Division for many years from income tax returns filed, not only indicated the characteristics that the ACP sample should take but also provided a fund of reliable information without which the audit problem could not have been as clearly defined.

In brief, the audit control sample for 1949 individual income tax returns was a subsample of the *Statistics of Income* sample of about 620,000 returns. This subsample involved about 65,000 individual income tax returns stratified by type of return (Forms 1040A versus Forms 1040), size of adjusted gross income, and type of income. Each timely filed individual income tax return had a predetermined probability of inclusion in the sample. A higher sampling rate was used to select returns reporting business incomes than to select returns reporting only nonbusiness incomes. (Detailed explanations of the individual income tax sample and of the estimating methods used are contained in the Appendix.)

In contrast, the 1949 sample of corporation income tax returns filed covers only those returns with assets under $250,000 and those filed without balance sheets, accounting for about 80 per cent of all of the 1949 corporation income tax returns filed. The sample consisted of about 16,000 returns of these small corporations, or about 3 per cent of the total number of returns filed in the four asset classes included in the program. However, the sample was stratified by asset classes and by broad industry classes, and was sampled accordingly.

The corporation audit sample was limited to the mass of small corporations because they seemed to be about the only type of corporate taxpayer that could be thoroughly examined and the results tabulated and analyzed within the time limits of the ACP. The examinations of the larger corporations are frequently so complicated and technical that several years' time is required to complete the investigations, discussions, and conferences needed to reach the final stages of agreement or disagreement within the administrative procedures of the IRS. (The technical details of the sampling and estimating procedures for the corporation income tax returns are also contained in the Appendix.)

To complete the record, the audit sample for 1949 excise and pay roll tax returns was a derivative sample. It was a probability subsample automatically derived from the samples of both individual and corporation returns. Taxpayers with business incomes, whose 1949 income tax returns were selected under the sampling procedures indicated above, were automatically selected for excise and pay roll tax audits if they were required to file returns for withholding, federal insurance contributions, federal unemployment, some of the admissions taxes, and the four retail excise taxes. This derivative sample was believed to be the most appropriate one for analyzing the complex of business-taxpayer problems at the federal level.

### CONTROLLING THE QUALITY OF THE RESULTS

From the beginning, it was believed that the largest potential sources of error lay in the field offices of the Service as compared with sampling and processing errors. As the result of close collaboration among personnel of the Service's then Management Staff, Statistical Division, Accounts and Collections Unit, and Income Tax Unit in Washington, and of regional conferences with the field office staffs, instructions covering the operations of the program were developed. In addition, as new questions were raised during the course of operations, supplements to these instructions were issued on questions of general interest, and individual letters prepared on purely local questions.

At the planning stage of the project it had been concluded that it would not be practicable to establish standards of audit needed to estimate all errors that taxpayers make. Consequently, it was proposed to estimate the errors that experienced Internal Revenue investigators would find if all returns were thoroughly audited.

To implement this decision and to assure geographical uniformity of the results, the following standards of performance were established for the ACP:

1. The examining officers assigned sample returns for examination had to be experienced and capable of performing fully the job intended.

2. The audit had to be conducted by personal interview with the taxpayer or his representative and had to cover the examination of books and records, if any. Correspondence audits, therefore, were not permissible.

3. The sample return had to be intensively investigated to make certain that all taxable income had been reported, that all nontaxable income had been excluded; all deductions, credits, and exemptions claimed were properly allowable; and that all deductions, credits, and exemptions properly allowable had been claimed.

4. When the sample return selected was the separate return of a spouse, the related return of the other spouse also had to be examined. Similarly, when the audit sample return included income from a partnership or fiduciary, these related returns had to be examined to establish the accuracy of the income reported on the sample return.

After the samples of ACP returns were drawn in Washington, they were properly identified and returned to the originating collectors' and agents' offices for examination.[1] After the examination the data desired were entered by the examining officers on special check sheets designed specifically for ACP purposes in accordance with the precise instructions issued. There the officers assigned to review the regular income tax reports of the office auditors, deputy collectors, and Internal Revenue agents were also assigned the responsibility of reviewing the adequacy and accuracy of audit information provided in the check sheets. After the examinations had been concluded and the results accepted by both the field offices and the taxpayers, the 1949 sample returns with the examination file were shipped to Washington for "post-review." There, the responsibility for editing the sample check sheets was placed with the Income Tax Division where the editing work was carried on jointly with the post-review of regular audit reports. Not until after this final post-review were the 1949 check sheets made available to the Statistics Division for statistical processing.

The ACP estimates do not represent all of the errors that taxpayers make, but only the errors that experienced Internal Revenue examining officers would find if all of the returns of the taxpayers were audited with about the same experience and time factors. If more time and more experienced personnel were to be applied to the examination of the same sample of returns, additional errors would probably be found. The reverse is also true, if less experienced examining officers or less time had been spent on the 1949 ACP returns, fewer and smaller errors, on the average, would have been disclosed.

No one really knows the size of the difference between errors disclosed and errors made. Some of the undisclosed errors resulted from oversight, others involved highly technical interpretations of factual and legal situations, and others involved fraud. No one knows the relative proportions of the undisclosed errors by source. It will never be possible to find all of the errors that taxpayers make, since some will be more or less successful in concealing information necessary to the correct determination of tax liability. Consequently, the ACP results are subject to errors one cannot segregate or estimate to establish the total income actually received by the individuals and persons covered by the program.

[1] At that time the Internal Revenue Service divided its individual income tax enforcement work into two parts: (1) the great mass of lower income tax returns with adjusted gross incomes under $7,000 were under the audit jurisdiction of the sixty-four collectors of Internal Revenue; and (2) the much smaller number of individual income tax returns with adjusted gross incomes over $7,000 and all corporation income tax returns were under the audit jurisdiction of the thirty-nine Internal Revenue agents in charge of the field offices of the Income Tax Division.

## *Estimates of Income Changes*

As previously indicated, all of the materials relating to income changes obtained by the 1949 ACP have not been tabulated. The income estimates made have been by-products of tabulations of other tax adjustment data designed to help answer questions pertaining to enforcement programs. Consequently, the estimates presented below do not comprise an integrated whole or neat pattern, and are, in a sense, fragments. We hope, however, that they will help students of income and wealth to evaluate the adequacy of the existing data on income and its distribution.

### WAGE AND SALARY CHANGES ON FORMS 1040A

Table 1 presents estimates of changes found in the amounts of salaries and wages subject to withholding tax that were reported on the 1949 Form 1040A returns filed.[2] These estimates are distributed between returns with changes only in the withheld class of wages and salaries and returns in which other income changes were also made.

About 16.8 million Forms 1040A were filed and, at the time the estimates were made, audit results had been received on sample returns representing 16.1 million or over 96 per cent of the returns filed. The estimates show that about 464,000 returns, or less than 3 per cent of the 16.1 million, would probably have a change in wages and salaries subject to the withholding tax after examination.[3] The total estimated change is $110 million, or 0.3 per cent of the $35.1 billion of adjusted gross income estimated to have been reported on the covered returns. On the average, 1.7 hours of examination time (including official travel [4] and report writing time) was spent per sample Form 1040A return audited.

About 347,000 or 75 per cent, of the 464,000 returns with change in salaries and wages subject to withholding showed change only in such salaries and wages. These returns accounted for $85 million, or over 77 per cent of the $110 million of the total change in salaries and wages subject to withholding. The other 25 per cent of returns with changes in salaries and wages subject to withholding also showed changes in other items on the Form 1040A return.

[2] A Form 1040A may be filed by a wage earner with adjusted gross income under $5,000, provided not more than $100 of such income is from wages not subject to withholding and from dividends and interest.

[3] "Change" means both increases and decreases in the adjusted items. In the case of wages and salaries, the decrease adjustments are relatively unimportant.

[4] Most Form 1040A returns were examined at Internal Revenue offices and very little travel time was involved.

Thus, 22,000, or about 5 per cent, also showed a change in wages and salaries *not* subject to withholding. These returns accounted for $4 million, or less than 4 per cent of the total change in salaries and wages subject to withholding. About 35,000, or less than 8 per cent of the 464,000 change returns, also showed change in interest and dividends. This group of returns accounted for less than $4 million of the change in salaries and wages subject to withholding. In about 41,000, or 9 per cent of the change returns, exemption changes were found, and these returns accounted for about $15 million, or 14 per cent of the total change in salaries and wages subject to withholding.

To explain the reason for this exclusive interest in wages subject to withholding, this tabulation was designed as part of a general project attempting to determine the relative importance among Form 1040A returns filed of misreporting of wages subject to withholding and therefore subject to check by information documents. It also indicated the relative importance of attempts to follow up other potential errors on the Form 1040A tax return when the examination originated from a lead furnished by an unmatched or mismatched information document.

### INCOME CHANGES ON FORMS 1040 WITH INCOMES UNDER $10,000

Table 2 presents estimates of changes found in the amounts of adjusted gross income that were reported on the 1949 Form 1040 returns with adjusted gross incomes under $10,000. These estimates are distributed between returns with no change in tax liability from that originally reported when filed, and returns with change in tax liability.

About 34.1 million Forms 1040 with incomes under $10,000 were filed and, at the time the estimates were made, audit results had been received on sample returns representing 33.4 million or 98 per cent of the returns filed. These returns reported about $101 billion of adjusted gross income, and it is estimated that examination of all of them would have disclosed a change of about $4 billion in the reported income, or 4 per cent of the reported amount. The estimates show that about 11.2 million returns, or almost 34 per cent of the 33.4 million, would probably result in a change in tax liability of $2 or more upon examination. The estimated change in adjusted gross income on this group of returns is $3.8 billion, or almost 10 per cent of the $40.3 billion of adjusted gross income estimated to have been reported. Only $359 million of change in adjusted gross income is estimated for the no tax change returns.

This was about 0.6 per cent of the $60.7 billion of adjusted gross income reported on this group of returns when filed. On the average, 3.1 hours of examination time (including official travel and report writing time) was spent per sample audit of Form 1040 returns with adjusted gross incomes under $10,000. The average was 2.4 hours of examination time on such returns without business income, and 6.3 hours on those with business income.[5]

Table 3 distributes the tax change returns by major source of tax error.[6] It shows about 5.9 million or 52 per cent of the returns with tax error with the major source of error in adjusted gross income. These returns accounted for $3.7 billion, or almost 90 per cent of the $4.1 billion of total change in adjusted gross income from the more than 33 million Form 1040 returns estimated to have been available for examination. The other 48 per cent of returns with tax change accounted for 2 per cent of the total change in adjusted gross income.

Table 4 distributes the estimated income changes likely to be found on the 5.9 million returns with adjusted gross income as the major source of tax error by twelve kinds of major income error.[7] It shows that the 2.2 million returns (or 20 per cent of the 11.2 million with tax change) with the major error in business income or loss accounted for about $2.3 billion of adjusted gross income change, or 59 per cent of the adjusted gross income change on the 11.2 million tax change returns, and 54 per cent of the total adjusted gross income change on the 33.4 million returns that were available for examination. Of the remaining eleven classes of major income error, the three representing income from partnerships, sales or exchanges of capital assets, and rents and royalties each accounted for 6 per cent to 8 per cent of the total adjusted gross income change on the 33.4 million returns. Three more classes, both wages and salaries subject to withholding and those *not* subject, and the residual "other" class, each accounted for 3 per cent to 5 per cent of the total change in adjusted gross income. The adjusted gross income changes accounted for by the other five classes of major income error were all under 2 per cent of the total.

## CHANGES IN BUSINESS INCOMES

Table 5 presents estimates of changes found in the amounts of gross receipts and net profit or loss reported from businesses and

[5] That is, income reportable on Schedule C or Form 1040F.

[6] That is, the largest portion of the tax change is attributable to the indicated source listed in Table 3.

[7] That is, the largest portion of the change in adjusted gross income is attributable to the kind of income specified in Table 4.

professions on all 1949 Forms 1040 with Schedule C and Form 1040F.[8] These estimates are listed by about sixty business groups, along with the sample count for each group.

At the time these estimates were made, audit results had been received on 35,872 sample returns representing about 6.7 million business returns filed. The estimates show that about $105.5 billion of gross receipts was reported on the returns and that examination of all of them would probably have disclosed a total of $107.4 billion in gross receipts, an increase of $1.9 billion or less than 2 per cent of the gross receipts reported on the covered returns when filed. The percentage change in the aggregate gross receipts as reported and as disclosed by audit varies from a —0.2 per cent for returns reporting gross receipts from mining and quarrying to a high of 4.5 per cent from returns reporting gross receipts classifiable into the "other professional and social services" group.[9]

The aggregate net profit less net loss reported on the 6.7 million returns when filed was about $13.6 billion. The estimates indicate that examination of all of the returns filed would increase this aggregate to $16.3 billion, an increase of $2.7 billion, or 20 per cent. The difference between the increase of $1.9 billion of gross receipts and $2.7 billion in aggregate net profit less net loss, or $0.8 billion, is attributable to unallowable and disallowed business deductions. The present increase in aggregate net profits less net loss varies from a low of 2.9 per cent on the returns of accountants to a high of 39.4 per cent on returns listing receipts from the manufacture of lumber and wood products, except furniture. The aggregate net loss in mining and quarrying was decreased 64.4 per cent.

Table 6 also presents estimates of changes found in the amounts of gross receipts reported on all 1949 Forms 1040 with Schedule C and Form 1040F. These gross receipts estimates differ from those in Table 3 in that (1) the aggregate of increases and the aggregate of decreases are shown separately instead of being presented as a net amount, (2) the estimates are listed for 17 instead of 60 business groups, and (3) the sample counts are different.

At the time the Table 6 estimates were made, audit results had been received on 36,176 sample returns representing about 6.9 million business returns filed. The estimates still show that about $105.5 billion of gross receipts was reported on the returns filed and that examination of all of them would probably have disclosed

[8] Partnership income was not covered by this definition of business income because the ACP studies were attempting to identify erroneous returns by, among other things, kinds of income reported on the return as filed.

[9] The percentage increase in gross receipts for the "not allocable or unknown" group was 4.8 per cent.

a net increase of $1.9 billion or 1.8 per cent of the gross receipts originally reported. The estimates indicate that about 1.5 million returns would have shown an increase after examination of $2.1 billion in gross receipts, or an average of $1,414 per return with an increase. About 225,000 returns would have shown a decrease in gross receipts aggregating about $220 million, or an average decrease of $981 per return. Thus, over 1.7 million returns with business income, or 25 per cent of the 1949 population, apparently would have shown a change in gross receipts upon examination. The gross change is estimated to be about $2.4 billion, and the net change is estimated as an increase of about $1.9 billion in gross receipts.

In Table 7 the estimates of total returns and gross receipts reported and the total changes therein disclosable by audit that were presented in Table 6 are now given by size of adjusted gross income reported on the return when filed. In Table 7, $1.5 billion, or 71 per cent of the $2.1 billion increase in gross receipts, is accounted for by the 5.8 million returns (representing about 84 per cent of the population) reporting less than $7,000 of adjusted gross incomes when filed. It shows that the changes in gross receipts disclosable by audit tend to decrease in relative importance as the size of adjusted gross income increases. Thus, in the class of returns with adjusted gross incomes under $7,000, the gross change (i.e. the sum of increases and decreases) in gross receipts was 4.0 per cent (column 8 plus column 9) of the aggregate gross receipts reported. This percentage decreased to 1.2 per cent for the group of returns with adjusted gross incomes between $7,000 and $25,000; to 0.4 per cent for returns with adjusted gross incomes between $25,000 and $100,000; and, to 0.3 per cent in returns reporting adjusted gross incomes of $100,000 and over. The relative importance of decreases in gross receipts, as a proportion of the gross change (i.e. column 9 divided by column 8 plus column 9), apparently increases as the size of adjusted gross income increases. Thus, on returns with incomes under $7,000 the returns with decreases in gross receipts showed an aggregate decrease of $121 million. This was 0.3 per cent of the aggregate gross receipts reported on all returns of this group, but it was over 7 per cent of the gross amount of adjustment aggregating $1,647 million. On the group of returns reporting incomes of $100,000 and over the aggregate decrease in gross receipts on returns showing such decreases was $0.8 million, but 42 per cent of the gross change of $1.9 million.

Table 8 distributes the estimates of returns, gross receipts, and changes therein by size of gross receipts reported on the returns when filed. It shows that $788 million, or 37 per cent of the $2.1 billion increase in gross receipts, is accounted for by the two classes of returns reporting either no gross receipts from business or under $7,000 of such receipts. These two classes accounted for 59 per cent of the "available" returns. An additional $728 million increase in gross receipts is accounted for by the class of returns reporting gross receipts of from $7,000 to $25,000. These three classes of returns accounted for 86 per cent of the returns in the population and 71 per cent of the increases in gross receipts disclosable by audit.

Table 8 also shows that the relative importance of the changes in gross receipts, when measured as a percentage of the gross receipts reported on the return as filed, decreases as the size of gross receipts reported increases. Thus, returns reporting gross receipts under $7,000 averaged a gross change of 5.5 per cent of the gross receipts reported. Those reporting gross receipts of $100,000 and over showed an average gross change of 0.5 per cent of the aggregate gross receipts reported. The relative importance of decreases in gross receipts disclosable by audit, as a percentage of the gross change, increases as the size of total receipts increases. Returns reporting total receipts under $7,000 are estimated to have over-reported their gross receipts by $34 million, or about 5 per cent of the gross change of $630 million. This percentage increases to 24 per cent for returns reporting total receipts of $100,000 and over. In addition, Table 8 estimates that 439,000 returns that should have reported gross receipts from business did not do so. In about 272,000 of these returns the net profit or loss was apparently correctly reported, but in about 167,000 of them there was a change in gross receipts.

### CHANGES IN INCOME AND DEDUCTIONS ON CORPORATE RETURNS

The Table 9 series presents estimates of changes that would be found on examination in the amounts of net income and net loss reported on all 1949 corporation returns filed with balance sheets showing net assets under $250,000 or with incomplete or no balance sheets. Some of these estimates are also shown by the nine administrative regions of the IRS.

Table 9 merely gives the total estimated number of such corporate returns filed for the United States and by region, further distributed between those with current year net income and with net loss. It shows, for example, that an estimated 507,000 of these "small" corporate returns were filed, of which 295,000 reported current year net incomes and 212,000 reported current year net losses.

Table 10 gives United States and regional estimates pertaining to the 295,000 returns reporting current year net incomes. The average examination time spent per sample return of this type was 13.2 hours. The table shows that, for the United States, about $2,272 million of net income was reported on these returns, and that examination of all of them would probably have disclosed a net increase of $225 million or almost 10 per cent of the net income originally reported. The estimates indicate that 141,000 returns would have shown an increase of $249 million in net income upon examination, or an average of $1,767 per return with an increase. About 17,000 returns showed a decrease in net income aggregating about $24 million, or an average decrease of $1,393 per return. Thus, over 158,000 returns with net income, or about 54 per cent of the population, apparently would show a change in net income upon examination. The gross change is estimated to be about $273 million, and the net change is estimated as an increase of $225 million in net income.

Table 11 gives United States and regional estimates regarding the 212,000 returns reporting current year net losses. The average examination time spent per sample return of this type was 11.0 hours. The United States estimates show that about $1,070 million of net loss was reported on these returns, and that examination of all of them would probably have disclosed a net decrease of $174 million or over 16 per cent of the net loss originally reported. The estimates indicate that about 11,000 returns would have shown an increase of $22 million in net loss upon examination, or an average of $1,982 per return with an increase. About 86,000 returns showed a decrease in net loss aggregating about $195 million, or an average decrease of $2,284 per return. Thus, over 96,000 returns with net loss, or almost 46 per cent of the population, apparently would have shown a change in net loss upon examination. The gross change is estimated to be about $217 million, and the net change is estimated as a decrease of about $174 million in net loss.

Tables 12 and 13 present estimates of changes in nine income items that would have been found during the examination of the 1949 net income and net loss corporation returns filed with balance sheets showing net assets under $250,000 or with incomplete or no balance sheets.

Table 12 gives United States estimates pertaining to the 295,000 returns reporting current year net incomes, and shows that 34,900 income changes probably would have been found upon examination.[10] About 26,500, or 76 per cent of the changes in income items,

[10] The total of item changes is not the equivalent of returns, since a return could have more than one item of change.

involved $77 million of increase in net income. About 8,400 items of income change relate to income decreases that would probably have been disclosed, aggregating about $31 million. The estimates indicate that the 295,000 returns would have shown a net increase of $46 million in net income from all changes in income items, and a gross change of $108 million. About 15,000 returns showed a change in gross sales and receipts. This item accounted for about 42 per cent of all of income items changes, for 62 per cent of the $77 million increase in net income, and for 65 per cent of the $31 million decrease in net income. None of the other specific income items listed in Table 12 account for as much as 10 per cent of the income change. In the amount of increase column, "dividends" and "net long term capital gains" are the next largest change classes, and each account for a little less than 9 per cent of the gross increase of $77 million. In the amount of decrease column, "royalties" with 7 per cent of the $31 million gross decrease, and "net long term capital gains" with 9 per cent are the next largest change categories.

Table 13 gives United States estimates pertaining to the 212,000 corporate returns reporting current year net losses, and shows that 23,500 items of income change probably would have been found upon examination. About 19,300, or 82 per cent of the changes in income items, involved $67 million increase in income resulting in that amount of decrease in net loss. About 4,300 of the items of income change relate to income decreases that would probably have been disclosed upon examination. These aggregated about $14 million, resulting in increases in net loss reported. The estimates indicate that the 212,000 net loss returns would have shown a net decrease of about $53 million in net loss from all changes in income items, and a gross change of $81 million. About 13,000 returns showed a change in gross sales and receipts. This item accounted for about 55 per cent of all income items changed, for 75 per cent of the $67 million decrease in net loss, and for 66 per cent of the $14 million increase in net loss. None of the other specific income items listed in Table 13 account for as much as 10 per cent of the income change. In the amount of increase column, "rents" and "net long term capital gains" are the next largest change classes accounting for about 6 per cent and 7 per cent, respectively, of the $67 million gross decrease in net loss. In the amount of decrease column, "net gain from sale or exchange of other property" with 8 per cent of the $14 million gross decrease, and "net long term capital gains" with 9 per cent are the next largest change categories involving increases in net loss.

Tables 14 and 15 present estimates of changes in sixteen deduction items that probably would have been found during the examination of the 1949 net income and net loss corporation returns filed with balance sheets showing net assets under $250,000 or with incomplete or no balance sheets.

Table 14 gives United States estimates pertaining to the 295,000 returns reporting current year net incomes, and shows that over 295,000 changes in deduction items probably would be found upon examination. About 214,000, or 72 per cent of the item changes, involved decreases in taxpayer claims amounting to $221 million increase in net income. About 82,000 of the deduction item changes involved raising taxpayer claims, aggregating $42 million of net income decreases that would probably have been disclosed. The estimates indicate that the 295,000 net income returns would have shown a net increase of about $179 million in net income from all changes in deduction items, and a gross change of $263 million. About 25,000 returns showed a change in cost of goods sold and operations. This item accounted for about 9 per cent of all of deduction items changed, for 35 per cent of the $42 million increase in deduction allowances, and for 24 per cent of the $221 million decrease in deduction allowances. In the amount of increase column, "taxes" and "depreciation" are the next largest change classes and each account for a little more than 15 per cent of the gross increase in deductions allowances. In the amount of decrease column, "depreciation" with almost 14 per cent of the gross decrease in deductions allowances and "compensation of officers" with about 13 per cent are the next largest change categories. None of the other specific deduction items listed in Table 14 account for as much as 10 per cent of the amounts of change.

Table 15 gives United States estimates pertaining to the 212,000 returns reporting current year net losses, and shows that over 179,000 deduction items probably would have been changed upon examination. About 139,000, or 78 per cent of the changes in deduction items, involved about $163 million decrease in deductions claimed, resulting in that amount of decrease in net loss. About 40,000 of the deduction changes relate to allowable increases that would probably have been disclosed. These aggregated about $42 million, resulting in increases in net loss after examination. The estimates indicate that the 212,000 net loss returns would have shown a net decrease of about $121 million in net loss from all changes in deduction items, and a gross change of $204 million. About 21,000 returns showed a change in cost of goods sold and operations. This item accounted for about 12 per cent of all deductions items changed, for 27 per cent of the $163 million decrease in net loss from disallowing deductions claimed, and for 39 per cent of the $42 million increase in net loss from allowing more deductions than were claimed. In the amount of increase column, "depreciation" and "net loss from sale or exchange of other property" are the next largest change classes accounting for about 24 per cent and 10 per cent, respectively, of the $42 million gross increase in net loss. In the amount of decrease column, "depreciation" and "compensation of officers" with a little less than 10 per cent of the $163 million gross decrease in net loss are the next largest change categories. None of the other specific deduction items listed in Table 15 accounts for as much as 10 per cent of the amounts of change.

The following summary table shows that about $179 million or 80 per cent of the estimated $225 million net increase in net income that would have been found upon examination of the 295,000 net income returns is attributable to the estimated net decrease in deduction items. Only 20 per cent of the net income increase derives from disclosed net increases in income items. As shown in Tables 10, 12, and 14, the changes for net income corporations, in millions of dollars, were as follows:

| | *Gross Increase* | *Gross Decrease* | *Net Increase* |
|---|---|---|---|
| Table 10 change in net income | 249.2 | 24.1 | 225.1 |
| Table 12 change in income items | 77.0 | 31.3 | 45.7 |
| Table 14 change in deduction items | 221.4 | 42.0 | 179.4 |
| Sum of Tables 12 and 14 | 298.4 | 73.3 | 225.1 |

The summary table for net loss corporations shows a similar story. About $121 million, or 70 per cent, of the estimated $174 million net decrease in net loss that would have been found upon examination of the 212,000 net loss returns is attributable to the estimated net decrease in deduction items. About $53 million, or 30 per cent, of the net loss decrease derives from increases in income items. As shown in Tables 11, 13, and 15, the changes for net loss corporations, in millions of dollars, were as follows:

| | *Gross Increase* | *Gross Decrease* | *Net Decrease* |
|---|---|---|---|
| Table 11 change in net loss | 21.7 | 195.3 | 173.6 |
| Table 13 change in income items | 14.1 | 66.8 | 52.7 |
| Table 15 change in deduction items | 41.9 | 162.7 | 120.9 |
| Sum of Tables 13 and 15 | 56.0 | 229.6 | 173.6 |

TABLE 1

Estimated Audit Change in Salaries and Wages Subject to Withholding Tax from Amount Reported by Individuals on 1949 Form 1040A Individual Income Tax Returns

(*numbers in thousands, dollars in millions*)

| DESCRIPTION | *Number of Returns* [a] | *Adjusted Gross Income Reported* [a] | *Change in Salaries and Wages* [b] |
|---|---|---|---|
| Total filed | 16,752.0 | $36,435.6 | n.a. |
| Not available for examination | 624.9 [c] | 1,359.2 | n.a. |
| Available for examination | 16,127.2 | 35.076.4 | $109.7 |
| With change in salaries and wages subject to withholding | 463.9 | n.a. | 109.7 |
| With change in these alone | 347.2 | n.a. | 85.0 |
| With change in these and also in: | | | |
| Salaries and wages not subject to withholding | 22.1 | n.a. | 4.0 |
| Interest and dividends | 34.7 | n.a. | 3.7 |
| Exemptions | 41.0 | n.a. | 15.3 |
| Other, including combinations | 18.9 | n.a. | 1.7 |

n.a. = not available.

Figures may not add to totals because of rounding.

[a] Estimated.

[b] Subject to withholding.

[c] Taxpayer could not be located or outside continental United States, sample audits not completed, and final settlements not made in time for inclusion in tabulation.

Source: Audit Control Program for 1949 Individual Income Tax Returns, Internal Revenue Service.

TABLE 2

Estimated Audit Change in Adjusted Gross Income from Amount Reported by Individuals Reporting under $10,000 of Such Income on 1949 Form 1040 Individual Income Tax Returns

(*numbers in thousands, dollars in millions*)

| DESCRIPTION | *Number of Returns* [a] | *Adjusted Gross Income* | |
|---|---|---|---|
| | | *Reported* [a] | *Change* |
| Total filed | 34,105 | n.a. | n.a. |
| Not available for examination | 673 [b] | n.a. | n.a. |
| Available for examination | 33,432 | $100,988 | $4,171 |
| With no change in tax liability | 22,251 | 60,682 | 359 |
| With change in tax liability | 11,181 | 40,306 | 3,812 |

n.a. = not available.

Figures may not add to totals because of rounding.

[a] Estimated.

[b] Taxpayer could not be located or outside continental United States, sample audits not completed, and final settlements not made in time for inclusion in tabulation.

Source: Audit Control Program for 1949 Individual Income Tax Returns, Internal Revenue Service.

TABLE 3

Estimated Audit Change in Adjusted Gross Income from Amount Reported by Individuals Reporting under $10,000 of Such Income on 1949 Form 1040 Individual Income Tax Returns and Whose Returns Indicated a Change in Tax Liability, by Major Source of Tax Error

*(numbers in thousands, dollars in millions)*

| MAJOR SOURCE OF TAX ERROR [a] | *Number of Returns* [b] | *Adjusted Gross Income* | |
|---|---|---|---|
| | | *Reported* [b] | *Change* [b] |
| Total [c] | 11,181 | $40,306 | $3,812 |
| Adjusted gross income | 5,857 | 20,334 | 3,730 |
| Personal deductions | 3,225 | 12,910 | 14 |
| Exemptions | 1,241 | 3,760 | 29 |
| Arithmetic | 526 | 2,228 | 26 |
| Tax table | 251 | 788 | 3 |
| Not specified | 80 | 287 | 10 |

Figures may not add to totals because of rounding.

[a] Major source of tax error means that the largest portion of tax change is attributable to the source listed. [b] Estimated.

[c] Total returns with change in tax liability (last line of Table 2).

Source: Audit Control Program for 1949 Individual Income Tax Returns, Internal Revenue Service.

TABLE 4

Estimated Audit Change in Adjusted Gross Income from Amount Reported by Individuals Reporting under $10,000 of Such Income on 1949 Form 1040 Individual Income Tax Returns Whose Returns Indicated a Change in Tax Liability with the Largest Portion Attributable to Error in Adjusted Gross Income, by Major Income Item in Error

*(numbers in thousands, dollars in millions)*

| MAJOR INCOME ITEM IN ERROR [a] | *Number of Returns* [b] | *Adjusted Gross Income* | |
|---|---|---|---|
| | | *Reported* [b] | *Change* [b] |
| Total [c] | 5,857 | $20,334 | $3,730 |
| Business income or loss | 2,207 | 7,048 | 2,261 |
| Salaries and wages subject to withholding | 561 | 1,866 | 188 |
| Deductions from salaries and wages subject to withholding | 134 | 548 | 72 |
| Salaries and wages not subject to withholding | 422 | 1,116 | 119 |
| Dividends | 220 | 871 | 49 |
| Interest | 522 | 2,116 | 38 |
| Rents and royalties | 822 | 3,110 | 264 |
| Sale or exchange of capital assets | 391 | 1,614 | 286 |
| Partnership | 360 | 1,258 | 329 |
| Annuities and pensions | 25 | 81 | 5 |
| Estates and trusts | 12 | 58 | 7 |
| Other and not specified | 181 | 647 | 112 |

Figures may not add to totals because of rounding.

[a] Major income item in error means that the largest portion of change in adjusted gross income is attributable to the income source listed. [b] Estimated.

[c] Total returns with change in tax liability where the largest portion of tax change is attributable to error in adjusted gross income (second line of Table 3).

Source: Audit Control Program for 1949 Individual Income Tax Returns, Internal Revenue Service.

## TABLE 5

Estimated Audit Net Change in Gross Receipts from Business and Professions and in Net Profit or Loss from Amount Reported on 1949 Individual Income Tax Returns, by Kind of Business Activity

(*numbers in thousands, dollars in millions*)

| KIND OF BUSINESS | NUMBER OF RETURNS | | AGGREGATE GROSS RECEIPTS [b] | | | AGGREGATE NET PROFIT LESS NET LOSS [c] | | | PROFIT AS A PERCENTAGE OF RECEIPTS | |
|---|---|---|---|---|---|---|---|---|---|---|
| | *Sample* | *Population* [a] | *Reported* | *Disclosable by Audit* | *Percentage Increase* | *Reported* | *Disclosable by Audit* | *Percentage Increase* | *Reported* | *Disclosable by Audit* |
| **Total** | 35.872 | 6,686.2 | $105,500.7 | $107,416.6 | 1.8% | $13,578.5 | $16,293.4 | 20.0% | 12.9% | 15.2% |
| Mining and quarrying | 0.331 | 15.8 | 849.2 | 847.3 | −0.2 | −16.8 | −6.0 | 64.4 | −2.0 | −0.7 |
| Manufacturing, total | 1.270 | 162.6 | 4,826.9 | 4,857.5 | 0.6 | 399.7 | 469.8 | 17.5 | 8.3 | 9.7 |
| Food and beverage | 0.220 | 23.2 | 1,365.0 | 1,368.5 | 0.3 | 65.1 | 76.1 | 16.9 | 4.8 | 5.6 |
| Textile and apparel | 0.133 | 15.3 | 802.5 | 804.5 | 0.3 | 35.1 | 42.3 | 20.5 | 4.4 | 5.3 |
| Lumber and wood products except furniture | 0.242 | 36.8 | 652.6 | 664.6 | 1.8 | 47.6 | 66.3 | 39.4 | 7.3 | 10.0 |
| Printing, publishing, and allied industries | 0.193 | 28.9 | 467.8 | 471.8 | 0.9 | 88.4 | 100.3 | 13.5 | 18.9 | 21.3 |
| Other manufacturing | 0.482 | 58.5 | 1,539.0 | 1,548.0 | 0.6 | 163.5 | 184.8 | 13.0 | 10.6 | 11.9 |
| Transportation, communication, and utilities, total | 1.264 | 222.3 | 2,197.1 | 2,270.8 | 3.4 | 334.1 | 420.8 | 25.9 | 15.2 | 18.5 |
| Trucking, warehousing, and storage | 0.950 | 166.5 | 1,712.6 | 1,767.5 | 3.2 | 260.1 | 320.9 | 23.4 | 15.2 | 18.2 |
| Other transportation, communication, and storage | 0.314 | 55.7 | 484.5 | 503.3 | 3.9 | 74.0 | 99.9 | 35.0 | 15.3 | 19.8 |
| Trade, total | 13.158 | 1,625.0 | 58,812.8 | 59,645.4 | 1.4 | 3,696.1 | 4,670.4 | 26.4 | 6.3 | 7.8 |
| Wholesale trade | 1.489 | 158.6 | 10,661.7 | 10,755.3 | 0.9 | 514.4 | 603.5 | 17.3 | 4.8 | 5.6 |
| Retail trade, total | 10.941 | 1,384.1 | 44,182.7 | 44,852.9 | 1.5 | 2,953.7 | 3,789.4 | 28.3 | 6.7 | 8.4 |

continued on next page

TABLE 5, continued

| KIND OF BUSINESS | NUMBER OF RETURNS | | AGGREGATE GROSS RECEIPTS [b] | | | AGGREGATE NET PROFIT LESS NET LOSS [c] | | | PROFIT AS A PERCENTAGE OF RECEIPTS | |
|---|---|---|---|---|---|---|---|---|---|---|
| | *Sample* | *Population* [a] | *Reported* | *Disclosable by Audit* | *Percentage Increase* | *Reported* | *Disclosable by Audit* | *Percentage Increase* | *Reported* | *Disclosable by Audit* |
| Department, general merchandise, and dry goods | 0.614 | 72.5 | 2,319.1 | 2,365.1 | 2.0 | 139.1 | 189.9 | 36.5 | 6.0 | 8.0 |
| Food | 3.051 | 387.4 | 13,050.4 | 13,207.9 | 1.2 | 724.5 | 955.6 | 31.9 | 5.6 | 7.2 |
| Package liquor stores | 0.202 | 23.9 | 826.4 | 847.6 | 2.6 | 62.7 | 86.1 | 37.4 | 7.6 | 10.2 |
| Drug stores and proprietary stores | 0.368 | 35.1 | 1,722.9 | 1,742.6 | 1.1 | 170.6 | 197.7 | 15.9 | 9.9 | 11.3 |
| Wearing apparel and accessories | 0.547 | 65.7 | 2,101.2 | 2,122.7 | 1.0 | 155.9 | 192.4 | 23.4 | 7.4 | 9.1 |
| Furniture, home furnishings, and equipment | 0.404 | 49.5 | 1,745.0 | 1,778.7 | 1.9 | 125.4 | 168.5 | 34.4 | 7.2 | 9.5 |
| Eating and drinking places | 1.971 | 281.0 | 6,135.8 | 6,229.0 | 1.5 | 488.1 | 644.5 | 32.0 | 8.0 | 10.3 |
| Automotive dealers | 0.598 | 50.0 | 4,986.8 | 5,074.4 | 1.8 | 213.4 | 268.1 | 25.6 | 4.3 | 5.3 |
| Gasoline service stations | 1.209 | 149.0 | 4,473.2 | 4,537.2 | 1.4 | 292.4 | 363.4 | 24.3 | 6.5 | 8.0 |
| Hardware and farm equipment | 0.262 | 25.4 | 1,303.8 | 1,319.8 | 1.2 | 101.1 | 124.7 | 23.3 | 7.8 | 9.4 |
| Lumber, building supplies, and coal | 0.124 | 14.0 | 556.1 | 558.8 | 0.5 | 45.4 | 50.6 | 11.5 | 8.2 | 9.1 |
| Jewelry stores | 0.152 | 22.4 | 400.5 | 407.8 | 1.8 | 55.0 | 66.0 | 20.0 | 13.7 | 16.2 |
| Other retail trade | 1.439 | 208.3 | 4,561.4 | 4,661.4 | 2.2 | 380.1 | 482.1 | 26.8 | 8.3 | 10.3 |
| Not allocable trade | 0.728 | 82.3 | 3,968.4 | 4,037.1 | 1.7 | 227.9 | 277.5 | 21.8 | 5.7 | 6.9 |
| Services, total | 8.818 | 1,191.5 | 11,171.2 | 11,409.8 | 2.1 | 3,617.4 | 4,023.9 | 11.2 | 32.4 | 35.3 |
| Hotels | 0.515 | 83.3 | 856.2 | 877.3 | 2.5 | 110.1 | 150.5 | 36.7 | 12.9 | 17.2 |
| Personal services, total | 1.994 | 357.0 | 2,325.5 | 2,379.4 | 2.3 | 609.3 | 692.6 | 13.7 | 26.2 | 29.1 |
| Laundry and laundry services | 0.342 | 56.2 | 683.7 | 690.8 | 1.0 | 101.6 | 120.6 | 18.7 | 14.9 | 17.5 |

continued on next page

TABLE 5, continued

| KIND OF BUSINESS | NUMBER OF RETURNS | | AGGREGATE GROSS RECEIPTS [b] | | | AGGREGATE NET PROFIT LESS NET LOSS [c] | | | PROFIT AS A PERCENTAGE OF RECEIPTS | |
|---|---|---|---|---|---|---|---|---|---|---|
| | *Sample* | *Population* [a] | *Reported* | *Disclosable by Audit* | *Percentage Increase* | *Reported* | *Disclosable by Audit* | *Percentage Increase* | *Reported* | *Disclosable by Audit* |
| Barber and beauty shops | 1.065 | 198.7 | 851.3 | 874.9 | 2.8 | 319.3 | 347.7 | 8.9 | 37.5 | 39.7 |
| Other personal services | 0.587 | 102.1 | 790.5 | 813.7 | 2.9 | 188.4 | 224.2 | 19.0 | 23.8 | 27.6 |
| Business services | 0.376 | 52.4 | 617.7 | 626.6 | 1.4 | 143.9 | 159.1 | 10.5 | 23.3 | 25.4 |
| Automobile repair services and garages | 0.520 | 84.9 | 979.8 | 1,009.0 | 3.0 | 144.9 | 176.0 | 21.4 | 14.8 | 17.4 |
| Amusement services | 0.466 | 56.7 | 800.2 | 813.8 | 1.7 | 42.3 | 79.2 | 87.1 | 5.3 | 9.7 |
| Professional and social services, total | 4.306 | 437.6 | 4,791.3 | 4,875.0 | 1.7 | 2,380.3 | 2,548.6 | 7.1 | 49.7 | 52.3 |
| Accountants | 0.219 | 27.0 | 206.1 | 206.9 | 0.4 | 103.9 | 106.9 | 2.9 | 50.4 | 51.7 |
| Physicians | 1.722 | 133.8 | 2,002.9 | 2,038.8 | 1.8 | 1,080.5 | 1,155.8 | 7.0 | 53.9 | 56.7 |
| Dentists | 0.592 | 72.5 | 814.9 | 832.1 | 2.1 | 414.1 | 447.4 | 8.1 | 50.8 | 53.8 |
| Other medical | 0.357 | 51.7 | 556.7 | 564.7 | 1.4 | 173.0 | 193.3 | 11.7 | 31.1 | 34.2 |
| Legal services | 0.937 | 96.1 | 718.6 | 730.8 | 1.7 | 414.2 | 432.1 | 4.3 | 57.6 | 59.1 |
| Engineering and architectural services | 0.205 | 19.8 | 242.0 | 244.3 | 0.9 | 88.4 | 95.7 | 8.2 | 36.5 | 39.2 |
| Educational services | 0.104 | 16.4 | 105.6 | 106.4 | 0.8 | 32.6 | 35.9 | 10.0 | 30.9 | 33.7 |
| Other professional and social services | 0.170 | 20.4 | 144.5 | 151.0 | 4.5 | 73.7 | 81.6 | 10.7 | 51.0 | 54.0 |
| Miscellaneous repair services | 0.641 | 119.5 | 800.4 | 828.6 | 3.5 | 186.6 | 218.0 | 16.8 | 23.3 | 26.3 |
| Finance, insurance, and real estate, total | 1.037 | 119.3 | 1,449.7 | 1,469.7 | 1.4 | 420.4 | 466.1 | 10.9 | 29.0 | 31.7 |
| Insurance agents | 0.364 | 42.5 | 502.4 | 508.4 | 1.2 | 197.4 | 211.5 | 7.1 | 39.3 | 41.6 |
| Real estate | 0.435 | 52.4 | 669.9 | 682.5 | 1.9 | 132.3 | 160.1 | 21.0 | 19.7 | 23.5 |

continued on next page

TABLE 5, concluded

| KIND OF BUSINESS | NUMBER OF RETURNS | | AGGREGATE GROSS RECEIPTS [b] | | | AGGREGATE NET PROFIT LESS NET LOSS [c] | | | PROFIT AS A PERCENTAGE OF RECEIPTS | |
|---|---|---|---|---|---|---|---|---|---|---|
| | *Sample* | *Population* [a] | *Reported* | *Disclosable by Audit* | *Percentage Increase* | *Reported* | *Disclosable by Audit* | *Percentage Increase* | *Reported* | *Disclosable by Audit* |
| Other finance, insurance, and real estate | 0.238 | 24.5 | 277.4 | 278.8 | 0.5 | 90.7 | 94.6 | 4.2 | 32.7 | 33.9 |
| Construction, total | 2.043 | 276.8 | 6,983.6 | 7,108.1 | 1.8 | 828.4 | 981.5 | 18.5 | 11.9 | 13.8 |
| General contractors | 0.446 | 42.4 | 2,345.2 | 2,376.0 | 1.3 | 162.3 | 194.6 | 19.9 | 6.9 | 8.2 |
| Special trade contractors | 1.426 | 212.7 | 4,093.3 | 4,181.4 | 2.2 | 604.5 | 713.3 | 18.0 | 14.8 | 17.1 |
| Other construction and general contractors | 0.171 | 21.6 | 545.0 | 550.6 | 1.0 | 61.6 | 73.6 | 19.6 | 11.3 | 13.4 |
| Agriculture and related industries, total | 7.402 | 2,946.3 | 18,366.2 | 18,923.4 | 3.0 | 4,181.5 | 5,145.5 | 23.1 | 22.8 | 27.2 |
| Farming | 7.034 | 2,885.1 | 17,651.0 | 18,192.2 | 3.1 | 4,071.1 | 5,010.1 | 23.1 | 23.1 | 27.5 |
| Agriculture and similar services | 0.250 | 39.9 | 600.6 | 615.7 | 2.5 | 83.0 | 105.0 | 26.6 | 13.8 | 17.1 |
| Forestry, fishing, and other related services | 0.118 | 21.3 | 114.6 | 115.6 | 0.8 | 27.5 | 30.4 | 10.6 | 23.9 | 26.3 |
| Not allocable or unknown | 0.549 | 126.6 | 843.9 | 884.6 | 4.8 | 117.6 | 121.2 | 3.1 | 13.9 | 13.7 |

Figures may not add to totals due to rounding.

[a] Estimated.

[b] Total business receipts reported on Schedule C or Form 1040F for all returns in group.

[c] Total net profit reported on all returns in group with net profit, less total net loss reported on all returns with net loss.

Source: Audit Control Program for 1949 Individual Income Tax Returns, Internal Revenue Service.

TABLE 6

Estimated Audit Increase and Decrease in Gross Receipts from Business and Professions from Amount Reported on 1949 Individual Income Tax Returns, by Major Industry Group

(*numbers in thousands, dollars in millions*)

| INDUSTRY GROUP | NUMBER OF RETURNS | | AGGREGATE GROSS RECEIPTS REPORTED [b] | CHANGE IN GROSS RECEIPTS | | | | | |
|---|---|---|---|---|---|---|---|---|---|
| | | | | *Increase* | | *Decrease* | | *Percentage of Amount Reported* | |
| | *Sample* | *Population* [a] | | *Number* | *Amount* | *Number* | *Amount* | *Increase* (5)÷(3) | *Decrease* (7)÷(3) |
| | (1) | (2) | (3) | (4) | (5) | (6) | (7) | (8) | (9) |
| Total | 36.176 | 6,915.0 | $105,515.7 | 1,514.7 | $2,141.7 | 222.8 | $218.6 | 2.0% | 0.2% |
| Mining and quarrying | 0.335 | 15.9 | 849.3 | 2.2 | 2.5 | 0.4 | 4.4 | 0.3 | 0.5 |
| Manufacturing | 1.271 | 165.2 | 4,827.9 | 23.5 | 33.7 | 3.6 | 3.1 | 0.7 | 0.1 |
| Transportation, communication, and other public utilities | 1.267 | 229.9 | 2,197.2 | 45.2 | 83.0 | 5.8 | 9.4 | 3.8 | 0.4 |
| Wholesale trade | 1.494 | 158.7 | 10,663.3 | 28.2 | 109.9 | 3.9 | 16.3 | 1.0 | 0.2 |
| Retail trade, including not allocable trade | 11.681 | 1,487.5 | 48,159.1 | 340.9 | 783.0 | 40.4 | 45.6 | 1.6 | 0.1 |
| Hotels and other lodging places | 0.516 | 83.6 | 856.3 | 14.9 | 21.9 | 2.0 | 0.8 | 2.6 | 0.1 |
| Personal services | 1.999 | 358.2 | 2,326.2 | 70.8 | 59.6 | 8.5 | 5.8 | 2.6 | 0.2 |
| Business services, including accountants | 0.598 | 82.2 | 823.9 | 9.2 | 10.8 | 2.6 | 1.1 | 1.3 | 0.1 |
| Automobile repair services and garages | 0.522 | 87.1 | 979.9 | 16.2 | 30.5 | 3.2 | 1.3 | 3.1 | 0.1 |
| Amusements | 0.469 | 59.7 | 800.3 | 9.1 | 15.3 | 1.9 | 1.7 | 1.9 | 0.2 |
| Medical and health services | 2.679 | 259.3 | 3,375.9 | 51.4 | 63.3 | 6.5 | 2.2 | 1.9 | 0.1 |
| Legal, educational, and other services | 1.422 | 158.7 | 1,210.8 | 21.7 | 23.5 | 2.0 | 1.5 | 1.9 | 0.1 |
| Miscellaneous repair services | 0.641 | 119.5 | 800.4 | 23.3 | 30.7 | 2.6 | 2.5 | 3.8 | 0.3 |
| Finance, insurance, and real estate | 1.051 | 122.9 | 1,450.0 | 15.6 | 25.2 | 2.0 | 5.3 | 1.7 | 0.4 |
| Construction | 2.049 | 282.1 | 6,984.4 | 64.6 | 157.7 | 13.6 | 32.9 | 2.3 | 0.5 |
| Agriculture, forestry, and fisheries | 7.467 | 3,004.3 | 18,366.7 | 720.7 | 634.7 | 111.3 | 75.1 | 3.5 | 0.4 |
| Not allocable | 0.715 | 240.2 | 844.1 | 57.1 | 56.2 | 12.4 | 9.8 | 6.7 | 1.2 |

Figures may not add to totals because of rounding.

[a] Estimated.

[b] Total business receipts reported on Schedule C or Form 1040F for all returns in group.

Source: Audit Control Program for 1949 Individual Income Tax Returns, Internal Revenue Service.

TABLE 7

Estimated Audit Increase and Decrease in Gross Receipts from Business and Professions from Amount Reported on 1949 Individual Income Tax Returns, by Size of Adjusted Gross Income Reported

*(numbers in thousands, dollars in millions)*

| | NUMBER OF RETURNS | | AGGREGATE GROSS RECEIPTS | CHANGE IN GROSS RECEIPTS | | | | | |
|---|---|---|---|---|---|---|---|---|---|
| | | | | *Increase* | | *Decrease* | | *Percentage of Amount Reported* | |
| SIZE OF ADJUSTED GROSS INCOME | *Sample* (1) | *Population*[a] (2) | REPORTED[b] (3) | *Number* (4) | *Amount* (5) | *Number* (6) | *Amount* (7) | *Increase* (5)÷(3) (8) | *Decrease* (7)÷(3) (9) |
| Total | 36.176 | 6,915.0 | $105,515.7 | 1,514.7 | $2,141.7 | 222.8 | $218.6 | 2.0% | 0.2% |
| Under $7,000 | 18.321 | 5,803.9 | 40,901.5 | 1,291.2 | 1,526.4 | 187.3 | 120.7 | 3.7 | 0.3 |
| $7,000 and under $25,000 | 12.906 | 1,054.4 | 56,298.3 | 217.0 | 587.3 | 34.1 | 93.1 | 1.0 | 0.2 |
| $25,000 and under $100,000 | 3.696 | 53.5 | 7,583.2 | 6.2 | 25.9 | 1.4 | 4.1 | 0.3 | 0.1 |
| $100,000 and over | 1.253 | 3.1 | 732.6 | .2 | 1.1 | .1 | .8 | 0.2 | 0.1 |

Figures may not add to totals because of rounding.

[a] Estimated.

[b] Total business receipts reported on Schedule C or Form 1040F for all returns in class.

Source: Audit Control Program for 1949 Individual Income Tax Returns, Internal Revenue Service.

TABLE 8

Estimated Audit Increase and Decrease in Gross Receipts from Business and Professions from Amount Reported on 1949 Individual Income Tax Returns, by Size of Total Receipts Reported

*(numbers in thousands, dollars in millions)*

| SIZE OF TOTAL RECEIPTS | NUMBER OF RETURNS | | AGGREGATE GROSS RECEIPTS REPORTED [b] | CHANGE IN GROSS RECEIPTS | | | | | |
|---|---|---|---|---|---|---|---|---|---|
| | | | | *Increase* | | *Decrease* | | *Percentage of Amount Reported* | |
| | *Sample* (1) | *Population* [a] (2) | (3) | *Number* (4) | *Amount* (5) | *Number* (6) | *Amount* (7) | *Increase* (5)÷(3) (8) | *Decrease* (7)÷(3) (9) |
| Total | 36.176 | 6,915.0 | $105,515.7 | 1,514.7 | $2,141.7 | 222.8 | $218.6 | 2.0% | 0.2% |
| Not reported | 0.601 | 439.0 | | 146.0 | 192.1 | 21.4 | 14.5 | | |
| Under $7,000 | 12.334 | 3,640.9 | 11,470.1 | 677.4 | 596.0 | 102.2 | 34.3 | 5.2 | 0.3 |
| $7,000 and under $25,000 | 9.850 | 1,889.5 | 24,842.1 | 480.7 | 727.9 | 66.0 | 63.4 | 2.9 | 0.3 |
| $25,000 and under $100,000 | 10.223 | 801.2 | 36,554.0 | 184.6 | 493.4 | 27.5 | 65.6 | 1.3 | 0.2 |
| $100,000 and over | 3.168 | 144.5 | 32,649.4 | 26.0 | 132.2 | 5.7 | 40.9 | 0.4 | 0.1 |

Figures may not add to totals because of rounding.

[a] Estimated.

[b] Total business receipts reported on Schedule C or Form 1040F for all returns in class.

Source: Audit Control Program for 1949 Individual Income Tax Returns, Internal Revenue Service.

TABLE 9

Estimated Number of 1949 Corporation Income Tax Returns Filed by Corporations with Assets under $250,000,[a] by Region

(*numbers in thousands*)

| UNITED STATES AND REGIONS | NUMBER OF RETURNS [b] | NUMBER WITH CURRENT YEAR [b] | |
|---|---|---|---|
| | | *Net Income* | *Net Loss* |
| United States | 507.2 | 295.2 | 211.9 |
| Atlanta | 40.5 | 25.3 | 15.2 |
| Boston | 47.5 | 26.5 | 21.0 |
| Chicago | 57.3 | 34.2 | 23.1 |
| Cincinnati | 52.0 | 33.1 | 18.9 |
| Dallas | 25.2 | 15.2 | 10.0 |
| New York | 132.9 | 73.3 | 59.6 |
| Omaha | 43.2 | 28.4 | 14.9 |
| Philadelphia | 64.5 | 37.4 | 27.0 |
| San Francisco | 44.1 | 22.0 | 22.1 |

Figures may not add to totals because of rounding.

[a] Includes corporations filing returns with incomplete or no balance sheets.

[b] Estimated; corporations reporting net income or net loss before net operating loss deduction in the current year.

Source: Audit Control Program for 1949 Corporation Income Tax Returns Filed by Corporations with Assets under $250,000, Internal Revenue Service.

TABLE 10

Estimated Audit Increase and Decrease in Net Income from Amount Reported by Corporations with Assets under $250,000 [a] Reporting Current Year Net Income on 1949 Corporation Income Tax Returns, by Region

(*numbers in thousands, dollars in millions*)

| UNITED STATES AND REGIONS | NUMBER OF RETURNS [b] | NET INCOME REPORTED | CHANGE IN NET INCOME | | | |
|---|---|---|---|---|---|---|
| | | | *Increase* | | *Decrease* | |
| | | | *Number* | *Amount* | *Number* | *Amount* |
| United States | 295.2 | $2,271.6 | 141.0 | $249.2 | 17.3 | $24.1 |
| Atlanta | 25.3 | 237.6 | 10.4 | 21.2 | 1.9 | 4.8 |
| Boston | 26.5 | 176.7 | 15.6 | 27.9 | 1.9 | 1.5 |
| Chicago | 34.2 | 270.6 | 15.1 | 32.5 | 2.2 | 3.3 |
| Cincinnati | 33.1 | 302.5 | 14.1 | 21.7 | 2.0 | 5.1 |
| Dallas | 15.2 | 145.8 | 6.0 | 13.8 | 0.9 | 0.7 |
| New York | 73.3 | 406.3 | 41.8 | 59.3 | 3.0 | 2.1 |
| Omaha | 28.4 | 244.9 | 10.8 | 15.5 | 2.4 | 2.4 |
| Philadelphia | 37.4 | 256.3 | 19.3 | 33.9 | 1.6 | 1.3 |
| San Francisco | 22.0 | 231.0 | 8.0 | 23.3 | 1.4 | 2.9 |

Figures may not add to totals because of rounding.

[a] Includes corporations filing returns with incomplete or no balance sheets.

[b] Estimated; corporations reporting net income before net operating loss deduction in the current year.

Source: Audit Control Program for 1949 Corporation Income Tax Returns Filed by Corporations with Assets under $250,000, Internal Revenue Service.

TABLE 11

Estimated Audit Increase and Decrease in Net Loss from Amount Reported by Corporation with Assets under $250,000[a] Reporting Current Year Net Loss on 1949 Corporation Income Tax Returns, by Region

(*numbers in thousands, dollars in millions*)

| UNITED STATES AND REGIONS | NUMBER OF RETURNS[b] | AMOUNT OF NET LOSS REPORTED | CHANGE IN NET LOSS | | | |
|---|---|---|---|---|---|---|
| | | | *Increase* | | *Decrease* | |
| | | | *Number* | *Amount* | *Number* | *Amount* |
| United States | 211.9 | $1,069.8 | 10.9 | $21.7 | 85.5 | $195.3 |
| Atlanta | 15.2 | 82.3 | 0.9 | 0.6 | 6.0 | 17.1 |
| Boston | 21.0 | 88.6 | 1.2 | 1.4 | 8.5 | 14.8 |
| Chicago | 23.1 | 152.0 | 1.4 | 2.7 | 8.2 | 18.2 |
| Cincinnati | 18.9 | 97.8 | 1.2 | 1.0 | 8.0 | 14.3 |
| Dallas | 10.0 | 51.7 | 0.5 | 0.7 | 3.4 | 6.2 |
| New York | 59.6 | 255.2 | 2.5 | 3.5 | 29.7 | 67.3 |
| Omaha | 14.9 | 80.6 | 1.1 | 0.8 | 4.0 | 11.8 |
| Philadelphia | 27.0 | 122.6 | 0.9 | 1.7 | 12.1 | 21.9 |
| San Francisco | 22.1 | 139.2 | 1.4 | 9.2 | 5.7 | 23.7 |

Figures may not add to totals because of rounding.

[a] Includes corporations filing returns with incomplete or no balance sheets.

[b] Estimated; corporations reporting net loss before net operating loss deduction in the current year.

Source: Audit Control Program for 1949 Corporation Income Tax Returns Filed by Corporations with Assets under $250,000, Internal Revenue Service.

TABLE 12

Estimated Audit Increase and Decrease in Income Items from Amount Reported by Corporations with Assets under $250,000[a] Reporting Current Year Net Income on 1949 Corporation Income Tax Returns, by Income Item

(*dollars in thousands*)

| INCOME ITEM | NUMBER OF ITEMS[b] | CHANGE IN INCOME ITEM | | | |
|---|---|---|---|---|---|
| | | *Increase* | | *Decrease* | |
| | | *Number* | *Amount* | *Number* | *Amount* |
| Total | 34,911 | 26,533 | $77,016 | 8,378 | $31,314 |
| Gross sales and receipts | 14,724 | 11,372 | 47,375 | 3,352 | 20,235 |
| Net long term capital gain | 4,420 | 2,661 | 6,612 | 1,759 | 2,943 |
| Rents | 3,557 | 3,008 | 2,731 | 549 | 400 |
| Interest | 3,196 | 2,786 | 1,461 | 410 | 390 |
| Net gains from sale or exchange of other property | 2,227 | 1,187 | 2,076 | 1,040 | 1,311 |
| Dividends | 303 | 187 | 6,600 | 116 | 22 |
| Net short term capital gain | 194 | 103 | 92 | 91 | 224 |
| Royalties | 184 | 48 | 100 | 136 | 2,258 |
| Other | 6,106 | 5,181 | 9,968 | 925 | 3,532 |

Figures may not add to totals because of rounding.

[a] Includes corporations filing returns with incomplete or no balance sheets.

[b] Estimated; corporations reporting net income before net operating loss deduction in the current year.

Source: Audit Control Program for 1949 Corporation Income Tax Returns Filed by Corporations with Assets under $250,000, Internal Revenue Service.

TABLE 13

Estimated Audit Increase and Decrease in Income Items from Amount Reported by Corporations with Assets under $250,000 [a] Reporting Current Year Net Loss on 1949 Corporation Income Tax Returns, by Income Item

*(dollars in thousands)*

| INCOME ITEM | NUMBER OF ITEMS [b] | CHANGE IN INCOME ITEM | | | |
|---|---|---|---|---|---|
| | | *Increase* | | *Decrease* | |
| | | *Number* | *Amount* | *Number* | *Amount* |
| Total | 23,543 | 19,284 | $66,847 | 4,259 | $14,150 |
| Gross sales and receipts | 12,893 | 10,627 | 50,161 | 2,266 | 9,332 |
| Rents | 2,502 | 2,119 | 3,718 | 383 | 376 |
| Net long term capital gain | 1,927 | 1,503 | 4,982 | 424 | 1,277 |
| Net gains from sale or exchange of other property | 1,568 | 1,176 | 1,573 | 392 | 1,111 |
| Interest | 1,406 | 1,220 | 398 | 186 | 13 |
| Net short term capital gain | 262 | 247 | 1,363 | 15 | 7 |
| Dividends | 46 | 15 | 11 | 31 | 12 |
| Other | 2,939 | 2,377 | 4,641 | 562 | 2,021 |

Figures may not add to totals because of rounding.

[a] Includes corporations filing returns with incomplete or no balance sheets.

[b] Estimated; corporations reporting net loss before net operating loss deduction in the current year.

Source: Audit Control Program for 1949 Corporation Income Tax Returns Filed by Corporations with Assets under $250,000, Internal Revenue Service.

TABLE 14

Estimated Audit Increase and Decrease in Deduction Items from Amount Reported by Corporations with Assets under $250,000 [a] Reporting Current Year Net Income on 1949 Corporation Income Tax Returns, by Deduction Item

*(dollars in thousands)*

| DEDUCTION ITEM | NUMBER OF ITEMS [b] | CHANGE IN DEDUCTION ITEM | | | |
|---|---|---|---|---|---|
| | | *Increase* | | *Decrease* | |
| | | *Number* | *Amount* | *Number* | *Amount* |
| Total | 295,247 | 81,530 | $42,003 | 213,717 | $221,398 |
| Taxes | 61,827 | 30,571 | 6,408 | 31,256 | 9,057 |
| Depreciation | 58,871 | 24,202 | 6,449 | 34,669 | 30,603 |
| Cost of goods sold and operations | 25,184 | 4,026 | 14,502 | 21,158 | 52,628 |
| Contributions or gifts | 20,263 | 11,239 | 760 | 9,024 | 1,208 |
| Repairs | 18,699 | 747 | 352 | 17,952 | 17,239 |
| Compensation of officers | 13,921 | 796 | 3,434 | 13,125 | 29,368 |
| Interest | 7,794 | 1,882 | 718 | 5,912 | 4,780 |
| Bad debts | 7,590 | 728 | 1,203 | 6,862 | 8,190 |
| Salaries and wages | 3,653 | 767 | 506 | 2,886 | 3,987 |
| Advertising | 3,216 | 137 | 157 | 3,079 | 1,319 |
| Rent | 2,187 | 364 | 136 | 1,823 | 1,806 |
| Net loss from sale or exchange of other property | 1,964 | 1,017 | 3,277 | 947 | 928 |
| Depletion | 981 | 502 | 484 | 479 | 939 |

continued on next page

TABLE 14, continued

| DEDUCTION ITEM | NUMBER OF ITEMS [b] | CHANGE IN DEDUCTION ITEM: *Increase* *Number* | *Increase* *Amount* | *Decrease* *Number* | *Decrease* *Amount* |
|---|---|---|---|---|---|
| Contributions under pension, annuity, stock bonus, etc. plans | 432 | 36 | 24 | 396 | 590 |
| Losses by fire, storm, etc. | 180 | 18 | 4 | 162 | 185 |
| Other, including amortization emergency facilities | 68,485 | 4,498 | 3,589 | 63,987 | 58,569 |

Figures may not add to totals because of rounding.

[a] Includes corporations filing returns with incomplete or no balance sheets.

[b] Estimated; corporations reporting net income before net operating loss deduction in the current year.

Source: Audit Control Program for 1949 Corporation Income Tax Returns Filed by Corporations with Assets under $250,000, Internal Revenue Service.

TABLE 15

Estimated Audit Increase and Decrease in Deduction Items from Amount Reported by Corporations with Assets under $250,000 [a] Reporting Current Year Net Loss on 1949 Corporation Income Tax Returns, by Deduction Item

(*dollars in thousands*)

| DEDUCTION ITEM | NUMBER OF ITEMS [b] | CHANGE IN DEDUCTION ITEM: *Increase* *Number* | *Increase* *Amount* | *Decrease* *Number* | *Decrease* *Amount* |
|---|---|---|---|---|---|
| Total | 179,272 | 39,939 | $41,863 | 139,333 | $162,741 |
| Depreciation | 32,461 | 14,616 | 10,025 | 17,845 | 15,462 |
| Taxes | 25,960 | 9,192 | 1,548 | 16,768 | 4,877 |
| Cost of goods sold and operations | 20,657 | 3,496 | 16,326 | 17,161 | 43,481 |
| Contributions or gifts | 17,506 | 2,226 | 97 | 15,280 | 1,672 |
| Repairs | 9,319 | 644 | 391 | 8,675 | 7,613 |
| Compensation of officers | 8,601 | 587 | 1,486 | 8,014 | 16,031 |
| Interest | 5,903 | 1,488 | 392 | 4,415 | 3,095 |
| Bad debts | 4,045 | 676 | 1,212 | 3,369 | 10,064 |
| Salaries and wages | 3,584 | 1,224 | 1,925 | 2,360 | 1,604 |
| Advertising | 2,383 | 255 | 42 | 2,128 | 1,089 |
| Rent | 2,337 | 268 | 204 | 2,069 | 3,330 |
| Net loss from sale or exchange of other property | 2,327 | 930 | 4,101 | 1,397 | 12,804 |
| Depletion | 313 | 49 | 45 | 264 | 1,171 |
| Losses by fire, storm, etc. | 214 | 18 | 7 | 196 | 430 |
| Contributions under pension, annuity, stock bonus, etc. plans | 132 | 49 | 4 | 83 | 275 |
| Other, including amortization emergency facilities | 43,530 | 4,221 | 4,058 | 39,309 | 39,745 |

Figures may not add to totals because of rounding.

[a] Includes corporations filing returns with incomplete or no balance sheets.

[b] Estimated; corporations reporting net loss before net operating loss in the current year.

Source: Audit Control Program for 1949 Corporation Income Tax Returns Filed by Corporations with Assets under $250,000, Internal Revenue Service.

## *Appendix: Sampling and Methods of Estimation*

### INDIVIDUAL INCOME TAX RETURNS

1. *Population.* The population studied consisted of timely filed individual income tax returns for the year 1949. Taxpayers were required to file their returns with the then "Collector of Internal Revenue" for the district in which they resided. Each collector entered a "serial number" on each return filed with him. The use of collection district plus serial number provides a unique identification for each return.

2. *Frame.* The frame described in section 1 was partitioned into broad classes as follows:

.01 Form 1040A returns
.02 Lower income returns on Form 1040, described as "collectors' returns"
.03 Higher income returns on Form 1040, described as "agents' returns"
- .031 Under $25,000
- .032 $25,000 up to $100,000
- .033 $100,000 and over

3. *Sampling rates.* The rates allocated to each partition of the frame were as follows:

| | *Partition* | *Class of Return* | *Sampling Rate (per cent)* |
|---|---|---|---|
| .01 | Form 1040A | all | 0.03 |
| .02 | Collectors' 1040: | nonbusiness | 0.04 |
| | | nonfarm business | 0.50 |
| | | farm | 0.15 |
| .03 | Agents' 1040: | | |
| .031 | Under $25,000 | nonbusiness | 0.30 |
| | | business | 1.20 |
| .032 | $25,000 up to $100,000 | nonbusiness | 2.00 |
| | | business | 5.00 |
| 0.33 | $100,000 and over | nonbusiness | 20.00 |
| | | business | 40.00 |

Note: In the .03 partitions, returns reporting farm income are included with business.

4. *Method of selection.* Serial numbers have at least four digits. The sampling rates allocated above were approximated by selecting returns with the following digit combinations:

| | *Partition and Class* | *Thousands* | *Hundreds* | *Tens* | *Units* |
|---|---|---|---|---|---|
| .01 | Form 1040A | 0 | 0 | 0,1,2 | 0 |
| .02 | Collectors' 1040: | | | | |
| | Nonbusiness | 0 | 0 | 0 | 0,1 |
| | | 0 | 0 | 4 | 8,9 |
| | Nonfarm business | 0 | 0 | 0,1,2,3,4 | all |

continued on next page

Note: This section of the appendix was prepared by C. B. Fine.

| Partition and Class | Thousands | Hundreds | Tens | Units |
|---|---|---|---|---|
| Farm | 0 | 0 | 0 | all |
| | 0 | 0 | 1 | 0,1,2 |
| | 0 | 0 | 4 | 8,9 |
| .03 Agents' 1040: | | | | |
| .031 Under $25,000: | | | | |
| Nonbusiness | all | 0 | 0,1,2 | 0 |
| Business | all | 0 | all | 0 |
| | all | 0 | 2,7 | 5 |
| .032 $25,000 up to $100,000: | | | | |
| Nonbusiness | all | all | 0,2 | 0 |
| Business | all | all | 0,2,4,6,8 | 0 |
| .033 $100,000 and over: | | | | |
| Nonbusiness | all | all | all | 0,5 |
| Business | all | all | all | 0,3,5,7 |

5. *Systematic nature of sample.* It is apparent from the above description that the sample is systematic as well as stratified. Returns were numbered by the collector as an aid to processing the returns in the ordinary business of the Internal Revenue Service. Usually a working group consists of 100 returns, called a "block" and consecutively numbered from 00 to 99. Further, "series" are reserved for similar groups of returns. Usually a series will start with a number ending in four zeros, hence a series with few blocks will be sampled more heavily than one with many blocks if returns with "00" block numbers are chosen. Similarly, a block may contain less than 100 returns. For these reasons, the use of low digits may result in sampling in excess of the allocated rate.

To the extent that characteristics correlated with tax change are used by the collector, the sampling system described above will be more efficient than random sampling.[11]

6. *Method of estimation.* Estimates were derived from each partition separately, viz., .01, .02, .031, .032, and .033 for each collection district. The general formula used was

$$X' = \frac{N}{n} \sum_{j=1}^{3} \frac{1}{r_j} \sum_{k=1}^{n_j} x_{jk}$$

where $N$ = number of returns in the specified partition of the frame

$$n = \sum_{j=1}^{3} \frac{n_j}{r_j}$$

[11] See William G. Madow and Lillian H. Madow, "On the Theory of Systematic Sampling, I," *Annals of Mathematical Statistics,* March 1944, pp. 1–24; Lillian H. Madow, "Systematic Sampling and its Relation to Other Sampling Designs," *Journal of the American Statistical Association,* June 1945, pp. 204–217; and William G. Cochran, "Relative Accuracy of Systematic and Stratified Random Samples for a Certain Class of Populations," *Annals of Mathematical Statistics,* June 1946, pp. 164–177.

$j = 1$ if nonbusiness
2 if nonfarm business
3 if farm
$n_j$ = number of sample returns in the $j^{th}$ class
$r_j$ = sampling rate allocated to $j^{th}$ class
$k = 1, 2, \ldots, n_j$
$x_{jk}$ = the value of a characteristic for the $jk^{th}$ return.

The individual estimate for a single partition was then added within the size group, e.g. Forms 1040A, to obtain a total for all collection districts. In this case, the general formula can be simplified by omitting the $j$ summation to

$$X' = \frac{N}{n} \sum_{k=1}^{n} x_k$$

For example, the partition Alabama (.02) collectors' 1040's contained the following sampled returns:

| *Class* | *Number of Returns in Sample* | *Allocated Rate* | *Weight per Sampled Return* |
|---|---|---|---|
| Nonbusiness | 134 | .0004 | 2,456 |
| Nonfarm business | 176 | .0050 | 196 |
| Farm | 36 | .0015 | 655 |

A total of 387,276 collectors' Form 1040 returns were filed in Alabama for 1949. The computation was as follows:

$$\frac{134}{.0004} + \frac{176}{.005} + \frac{36}{.0015} = 394{,}200$$

$$\frac{387{,}276}{394{,}200} \times \frac{1}{.0004} \doteq 2{,}456$$

$$\frac{387{,}276}{394{,}200} \times \frac{1}{.0050} \doteq 196$$

$$\frac{387{,}276}{394{,}200} \times \frac{1}{.0015} \doteq 655$$

7. *General size of sample.* While space does not permit specifying the size of the sample for each partition and class of return, the following table summarizes the partitions for all collection districts combined:

| | | *Returns in Sample* |
|---|---|---|
| .01 | Form 1040A: | 5,300 |
| .02 | Collectors' 1040: | 29,000 |
| .031 | Agents' under $25,000: | 18,000 |
| .032 | Agents $25,000 up to $100,000: | 8,100 |
| .033 | Agents $100,000 and over: | 3,200 |

## CORPORATION INCOME TAX RETURNS

The Audit Control Program for 1949 included a sample of corporation income tax returns as filed, with assets of $250,000 or less, and returns with incomplete or no balance sheets. It was estimated that resources were available to process a sample of 15,000 returns; actually 16,035 returns were selected in the sample.

All corporation income tax returns filed for the tax year 1949 were tabulated to obtain the data for *Statistics of Income,* Part 2. The total number of returns was about 650,000. The restricted population from which the audit control sample was selected included slightly more than 500,000 of these returns.

The sample design employed was of the stratified random type with optimum allocation. The population from which this sample was selected was stratified by 4 asset classes and by 41 industry groups making a total of 164 strata. The distribution of the population by the asset classes as well as the distribution of the sample, and the corresponding weights, follow:

| *Strata* | *Sample Size* | *Population Size* | *Weight* |
|---|---|---|---|
| Retail furriers and luggage stores | 624 | 678 | 1.0865 |
| Asset size: | | | |
| Under $50,000 | 2,681 | 242,397 | 90.4129 |
| $50,000–$100,000 | 3,248 | 99,728 | 30.7044 |
| $100,000–$250,000 | 5,656 | 104,155 | 18.4149 |
| No balance sheet | 3,826 | 60,216 | 15.4047 [a] |
| Total | 16,035 | 507,174 | |

[a] 16 returns were weighted by 90.4129 and 5 returns by 30.7044

A serious problem arose in connection with the sampling of corporation income tax returns because these returns were not only assembled in bundles of various sizes but they moved through a routine of processing as a continuous flow. It was impossible therefore to accumulate all of the income tax returns in a file and to design a sampling method applicable to a file of returns. The problem of counting all returns and identifying the sample returns in 164 strata was solved by using decks of punch cards which were racked in special built sampling boxes.[12] A separate deck of punch cards was prepared for each of the 164 strata. These cards were punched with the following codes: asset size codes, the industry code, and a sample code to indicate whether the card report was a sample or nonsample return. A punch card was drawn from the boxes for each tax return. White cards were used for nonsample returns while red cards were used to designate the sample returns. The red cards were inter-spaced with the white cards with evenly spaced intervals cor-

Note: This section of the appendix was prepared by A. C. Rosander.

[12] A detailed description of this technique and its operation appears in a paper by Rosander, Blythe, and Johnson entitled "Sampling 1949 Corporation Income Tax Returns," *Journal of the American Statistical Association,* June 1951, pages 233–241.

responding to the proper sampling ratios. The punch cards drawn from the boxes were tabulated daily by asset class and industry. In this way complete control was maintained over the selection of the sample in each of the strata.

Although the sampling procedure gave population counts for the various strata and therefore could be used as a basis of validating the weights, actually the weights were derived by using the *Statistics of Income* totals for each of the four asset classes. (There were only slight differences between the population as estimated from the sample and the population arrived at from the 100 per cent tabulation of corporation income tax returns.) As the accompanying table shows, the original weights for the four strata of 90, 30, 18, and 15 were revised only slightly in our final calculations. The weights shown in the accompanying table by asset classes were applied to all the sample data including counts and money values in each of the strata to which that weight applied.

## COMMENT

CHARLES F. SCHWARTZ, OFFICE OF BUSINESS ECONOMICS, DEPARTMENT OF COMMERCE

The paper by Marius Farioletti is a most valuable contribution containing audit information now made public through the cooperation of the Internal Revenue Service and concise explanations of the purpose, scope, and procedure of the 1949 Audit Control Program. He makes clear that the estimates produced by the ACP represent not all the actual errors but those that would be found if all returns were audited with about the same experience and time factors, concluding, "No one really knows the size of the difference between errors disclosed and errors made."

Farioletti is wholly right, and his statement of the definition of error in the ACP is impeccable. Still, one is prone to wonder how experienced the investigators were who worked on the 1949 study and whether adequate time was made available to them. If the answers to such questions were favorable—as I believe they would be—greater confidence could be attached to the audit estimates than is permitted by a strict interpretation of Farioletti's statement.

### CONTRIBUTION TO NATIONAL INCOME ESTIMATION

For our National Income Division estimates of family personal income by size classes, Tables 2 to 4, 7, and 8 will prove useful, but certain additional information is needed. For instance, Table 4 shows the amount of adjusted gross income disclosed by audit classified by the type of income representing the major source of error. We need to know directly, however, the total amounts of interest, rents, dividends, and so forth disclosed by audit for each adjusted gross income bracket, not just for the under $10,000 class. Also Table 7 would be more useful for our work if the audit changes shown related to net profit from business, instead of to gross receipts from business, and if farm income were tabulated separately.

For our estimates of entrepreneurial nonfarm income included in the national income and personal income series we have used IRS tax-return tabulations extensively in preparing benchmarks for a number of years since 1939. These tabulations are made from unaudited returns, with the amounts of income taken as directly reported by taxpayers. To adjust the tabulations for understatement of income was at first a matter of guesswork and therefore unsatisfactory, particularly on an industry basis. For preparing *National Income Supplement, 1954,* however, Farioletti kindly made available to us the unpublished audit data shown in his Table 5. This essential information shows the amount of additional net income disclosed by audit of a representative sample of returns.

But this information covers only sole proprietorships, not partnerships, for the single year 1949. The 1949 sample audit of individual proprietorships, valuable as it is, had to be used to make an audit correction, industry by industry, of nonfarm proprietors' income over the whole period since 1929. Audit information of the type shown in Table 5, covering partnerships as well, would be highly desirable to have on at least a periodic basis.

The corporate profits component of national income is also based on IRS tax-return tabulations with the same problem of adjusting the original, unaudited returns for understatement. Since direct estimates of the amount of additional corporate profits that would be disclosed by a full audit have never been available, we have had to work with data on additional assessments of tax liability (by methods described in the *National Income Supplement*). The procedure involved a complex problem of timing pattern, difficulties in the treatment of deficit corporations, and of selecting an effective tax rate by which to raise tax liabilities to an estimate of total net profit. For the past few years the information on tax liabilities that was used in this method has not been available from the IRS, and we have had to extend the corporate profits audit adjustment on an informal, judgmental basis.

Farioletti's tables showing audit changes for corporations will prove helpful to us, but their immediate impact is to whet the appetite for similar information on corporations with assets over $250,000. We recognize, of course, that auditing returns for large corporations is a long drawn out process that could not have been accomplished by the 1949 study.

That students of national income need much more information on audit changes is simply the familiar situation of the statistical demand exceeding the available resources. My strong hope is that some means can be found for making additional tabulations from the audit programs already completed, and that audit studies can be conducted on a periodic basis with an eye to the needs of statisticians.

JOSEPH A. PECHMAN, COMMITTEE FOR ECONOMIC DEVELOPMENT

Farioletti's paper will be extremely helpful to national income estimators as a source of information on underreporting of income by individuals and married couples on their tax returns. The unaudited data tabulated by the Internal Revenue Service in *Statistics of Income* are used not only to estimate the movement of specific types of income receipts but also to approximate the distribution of income by income levels. Income statisticians have, of course, been aware that, on balance, taxpayers tend to understate their incomes on tax returns, but they have had to use secondary and less desirable sources to supplement *Statistics of Income* to correct for this underreporting. Although we need to know a great deal more, the information provided thus far from the 1949 Audit Control Program throws considerable light on the so-called gap between the official Department of Commerce estimate of personal income and the amount of income (i.e. adjusted gross income) reported on individual income tax returns.

In the years 1948–1952, adjusted gross income reported on tax returns fell short of personal income by an average of almost $50 billion, or about 20 per cent. Actually, much of this "unadjusted gap" can be accounted for by known conceptual differences between the two totals. On the one hand, numerous receipts in personal income are not included in adjusted gross income, such as transfer payments, other labor income, income in kind, imputed interest, and nontaxable military pay and allowances. On the other, many receipts subject to tax are excluded from personal income, including employee contributions for social insurance, capital gain, annuities, and incomes of residents of Alaska and Hawaii. Most of these adjustments can be estimated fairly accurately, so that we can go fairly readily from personal income to adjusted gross income. The detailed adjustments for 1949—the year for which the new data from the ACP are now available—are shown in Table 1.[1]

Personal income amounted to $206.8 billion in 1949, $46.2 billion more than the adjusted gross income reported on taxable and nontaxable individual income tax returns. As indicated in Table 1, after correction of personal income for conceptual dif-

[1] Data for the years 1948 through 1956 are shown in my paper, "Erosion of the Individual Income Tax," *National Tax Journal,* March 1957, Table 1, p. 4.

TABLE 1

Adjustments of Department of Commerce Estimates of Personal Income to Arrive at Adjusted Gross Income, 1949

(*billions of dollars*)

| *Item* | *Amount* |
|---|---|
| Personal income | 206.8 |
| Portion of personal income not included in adjusted gross income | 28.7 |
| 1. Transfer payments (except fees and military retirement pay) | 12.4 |
| 2. Other labor income (except pay of military reservists) | 2.7 |
| 3. Food and fuel produced and consumed on farms | 2.2 |
| 4. Imputed gross rental value of tenant-occupied farm houses | 0.4 |
| 5. Other personal income in kind except services of financial intermediaries | 5.1 |
| 6. Noncorporate nonfarm inventory valuation adjustment | 0.5 |
| 7. Value of change in farm inventories | —0.9 |
| 8. Imputed interest | 4.0 |
| 9. Nontaxable military pay and allowances | 0.4 |
| 10. Accrued interest on U. S. government bonds | 0.6 |
| 11. Tax-exempt interest | 0.3 |
| 12. Fiduciary income (other than capital gains) not distributed to individuals | 0.6 |
| 13. Property income of nonprofit organizations | 0.4 |
| Portion of adjusted gross income not included in personal income | 5.6 |
| 14. Employee contributions for social insurance | 2.2 |
| 15. Net gains from sale of assets reported on individual income tax returns | 1.5 |
| 16. Adjusted gross income of residents of Alaska and Hawaii reported on individual income tax returns | 0.7 |
| 17. Miscellaneous income (except other income on Form 1040A) reported on individual income tax returns | 1.0 |
| 18. Annuities and pensions reported on individual income tax returns | 0.4 |
| 19. Deductions for net operating loss carryover and depletion | —0.3 |
| Total adjustment for conceptual differences (line 1–19) | 23.1 |
| Estimated adjusted gross income of taxable and nontaxable individuals | 183.7 |

Figures are rounded and will not necessarily add to totals.

Source

Lines 1, 2, 3, 5, 6, 7, 8, and 14—Dept. of Commerce.

Lines 10 and 11—Estimates based on data in the *Annual Report of the Secretary of the Treasury.*

Lines 12, 15, 16, 17, and 18—*Statistics of Income for 1948,* Part 1.

Lines 4, 9, 13, and 19—Based on data supplied by Selma F. Goldsmith.

ferences, adjusted gross income should total $183.7 billion. Thus roughly half of the "unadjusted gap" is accounted for by differences in concept. The remaining gap of $23 billion is the discrepancy to be explained.

Three major items enter into this gap: (1) the incomes of persons not required to file returns, (2) underreporting of income by persons who do file, and (3) errors in the personal income estimates. If the first two items could be measured with certainty, we could verify the official estimates of personal income. Farioletti supplied a few figures covering the second item, and it is of interest to see how much of the gap we can explain with them.

His estimates of underreporting (summarized in Table 2) do not cover the entire income distribution. They include figures only for taxpayers with incomes under $10,000 and all persons who report business income regardless of their total income.

The total of $4.7 billion of underreporting disclosed by the ACP appears at first to explain only a small portion of the $23 billion gap; but on closer examination it explains quite a good deal. It does not include the underreporting of taxpayers with incomes of $10,000 or more who did not report business income. This could be derived directly from the ACP, and the IRS would perform a use-

TABLE 2

Amount of Underreporting of Adjusted Gross Income on Tax Returns Disclosed by the 1949 Audit Control Program

(*millions of dollars*)

| *Taxpayer Category* | | *Amount of Underreporting, 1949* |
|---|---|---|
| Persons filing Forms 1040A | | 109.7 |
| Persons filing Forms 1040 with adjusted gross income under $10,000 | | 4,171.0 |
| Persons reporting business income with adjusted gross income of $10,000 or more: | | |
| Aggregate for all persons reporting business income | 2,714.9 | |
| *Deduct:* Underreported income on 1040 returns with adjusted gross income under $10,000 and major source of error in business income [a] | 2,261.0 | |
| *Equals:* Underreporting of business income on returns with adjusted gross income of $10,000 or more | | 453.9 |
| Total underreporting on all returns with adjusted gross income under $10,000, and on returns with business income and adjusted gross income of $10,000 or more | | 4,734.6 |

[a] Assumes that entire error in adjusted gross income is due to the major source of error.

Source: Marius Farioletti's paper in this volume, Tables 1, 2, 4, and 5.

ful service if it made the tabulation available. In the absence of a direct figure, we can only hazard a guess. According to Farioletti's Table 2, persons filing Form 1040 with adjusted gross income under $10,000 underreported their income by about 4.1 per cent. It is conceivable that the underreporting above $10,000 would be of roughly the same proportion, but it is more likely that the proportion is lower because the returns of higher income taxpayers are subject to closer scrutiny by the revenue agents. If we assume that taxpayers with incomes above the $10,000 level underreport their incomes by 2 per cent (half the percentage of those under $10,000), then the total amount of underreporting not covered by Farioletti would be about $0.4 billion.[2] Adding this to the $4.7 billion shown in Table 2, we arrive at an estimated total of more than $5 billion for the underreporting disclosed by the ACP at all income levels.

Aside from this $5 billion, two other factors enter into the gap. First, there is a large difference between farm income included in the National Income Division's estimates of personal income and the tax return data corrected for Farioletti's audit results. The NID estimates total farm self-employment income as $10 billion; while Farioletti estimates that, if every farm return were subject to a full field audit, we would obtain $5 billion or about 23 per cent more than the amount reported by farmers. Second, Holland and Kahn have estimated that the wages and salaries received by persons not required to file returns probably amounted to about $1.5 billion. Adding these two amounts to the estimated $5 billion of underreporting by persons who file returns, we arrive at a total of $11.5 billion, which is half of the $23 billion gap between total adjusted gross income and adjusted gross income reported on tax returns. The remaining $11.5 billion is the part of the gap which still remains unexplained (see Table 3).

The unexplained portion of the 1949 gap ($11.5 billion) amounts to about 5.5 per cent of total personal income ($206.8 billion). Does this mean that personal income is overestimated by that amount? The answer is obviously no. First, the sample used in the ACP was confined to persons who filed returns, and therefore it failed to pick up the incomes of persons who were required to file and did not. Also, as Farioletti pointed out, it is hardly likely that the field audits disclosed all of the unreported income on the returns examined.

My own view is that these factors are sufficient to account for

[2] This figure was derived by multiplying the 2 per cent estimate by the total income other than business income or loss in the adjusted gross income classes of $10,000 or more ($20.8 billion), as shown in *Statistics of Income for 1949,* Part 1, Table 2.

TABLE 3

Reconciliation of Department of Commerce Estimate of Personal Income with Adjusted Gross Income Reported on Individual Tax Returns, 1949

(*billions of dollars*)

| *Item* | *Amount* |
|---|---|
| 1. Personal income | 206.8 |
| 2. *Deduct:* Conceptual differences | 23.1 |
| 3. *Equals:* Total adjusted gross income | 183.7 |
| 4. *Deduct:* | |
| a. Underreporting disclosed by 1949 ACP | 4.7 |
| b. Underreporting on incomes not covered by 1949 ACP | 0.4 |
| c. Farm entrepreneurial income not disclosed by 1949 ACP | 4.9 |
| d. Wages and salaries of persons not required to file tax returns | 1.6 |
| 5. *Deduct:* Adjusted gross income reported on taxable and nontaxable individual income tax returns | 160.6 |
| 6. *Equals:* Unexplained gap | 11.5 |

Source

Line 1—Dept. of Commerce.
Line 2—Table 1.
Line 3—Table 1.
Line 4a—Table 2.
Line 4b—Computed on the assumption that the percentage underreporting by persons with adjusted gross income of $10,000 or more and incomes other than entrepreneurial incomes is half that of persons with adjusted gross income of less than $10,000.
Line 4c—Difference between Dept. of Commerce estimate of farm entrepreneurial money income and amount of net profit from farming disclosed on audited tax returns (Marius Farioletti's paper in this volume, Table 2).
Line 4d—Estimate by Daniel M. Holland and C. Harry Kahn, "Comparison of Personal Income and Taxable Income," *Federal Tax Policy for Economic Growth and Stability,* Papers Submitted by Panelists appearing before the Subcommittee on Tax Policy, Joint Committee on the Economic Report, 1955, p. 335.
Line 5—*Statistics of Income for 1949,* Part 1, Table 2.
Line 6—Lines 3 to 5, inclusive.

the unexplained $11.5 billion, and perhaps even more. But in any case, the official personal income estimates are probably not subject to a large margin of error and, assuming that the farm income estimate is correct, they may even be a bit low.

In conclusion, we are close to explaining the mysterious gap which has plagued us for so many years. More work on the incomes of persons not filing returns and another table by the IRS on the amount of underreporting by persons with incomes of $10,000 or more would go a long way toward accounting for the part of the gap which remains unexplained.

HYMAN B. KAITZ, DEPARTMENT OF LABOR

The four papers on the matching studies cover hitherto largely unexplored territory and we can, perhaps, only begin to consider certain general patterns which emerge from their findings. At first glance it seems reassuring to find such good agreement between surveys in the distribution of matched units by income level in view of the usual amount of dispersion in any table of consumer units cross-classified by the incomes reported to each of two surveys.

Such reassurance has been expressed about the influence on the results of response errors. For example, Miller and Paley say, "Fortunately, the variations in response elicited in repeated interviews appear to be random and do not introduce any systematic bias into the income distribution." Mandel, Wolkstein, and Delaney consider their analysis of differences in wages reported to the Bureau of Old-Age and Survivors Insurance and to the Post-Enumeration Survey "supports our previous findings, that is, the existence of a tendency for wage reporting errors to be reciprocally compensating. . . ."

And yet, who will discount the intuitive judgment that response errors decrease the accuracy of the results of a single survey—the greater the relative response error, the greater the decrease in accuracy? If two surveys of the same people yield approximately the same income distributions, then what is the effect of the response errors? Some rough idea of the magnitude of these effects can be derived, for units whose incomes were positive in both surveys, from the data in Table 1 of the Sirken, Maynes, and Frechtling paper. I should like to discuss briefly and on a tentative basis some of the possible effects.

## SYSTEMATIC AND RANDOM ERRORS

First there is the notion of response error arising from the hypothetical repetition of the same survey many times on the same group of respondents, with the use of the same interviewers, interview situations, and questionnaires. For present purposes "true" income is defined as the average of all the incomes which would be reported by a unit to an indefinite number of repetitions of a survey. By this definition, true income may differ from the actual income received by the unit and create, in effect, a systematic response error for individual units. This type of response error is ignored here.

Random response error for a unit in a single survey is the difference between its income reported to that survey and the hypothetical average income of the unit for all repeated surveys. This kind of response error is attached to any survey or, in my opinion, to institutional records such as tax returns and OASI cards. If no survey is free of it, then an analysis of error based on a comparison of two surveys of the same people, for which there is no adequate benchmark, requires postulation of a response error model, formal or informal.

TWO RESPONSE ERROR MODELS

The systematic effects of response errors on an income distribution and its inequality will be examined under two simple response error models to test (indirectly) their correspondence with observation and to examine their properties and implications.

The simplest and most familiar model, expressed in terms appropriate to the present context, is that true incomes and errors (differences between true and reported incomes) are uncorrelated with each other. It should be assumed at the same time that error variance increases as true income rises since the usual (implicit) assumption of a uniform absolute error would mean that a person with a true income of $1,000 is as likely to be in error in his reported income on a single survey by $400 as a person with a true income of $100,000—a conclusion which is hard to accept. However, for some illustrative purposes, a uniform absolute error is tentatively assumed in this model.

A second and more reasonable model is a restatement of the first model in terms of the logarithms of true income and income error. It follows from this model that a unit with a true income of $1,000 is as likely to report a figure in error by 10 per cent as one with an income of $100,000. This model makes more sense than the first, and I shall discuss it in more detail.

Under the first model the variance of the true income distribution is less than that of the observed income distribution. The arithmetic mean income is the same for both. Consequently, the coefficient of variation—a good measure of income inequality—is affected; the inequality of the true income distribution must clearly be less than that of the observed distribution. Similarly, under the second model, the logarithmic variance (another measure of inequality) of the true distribution is less than that of the observed distribution.[1]

[1] For the first model, the coefficient of variation is reduced by 10 per cent; for the second model, the logarithmic variance is reduced by 17 per cent. The observed distribution used here is an arithmetic average by income levels of the two marginal distributions, SCF and CQC, of units matched with positive incomes. The estimates are based on computed correlation coefficients between matched incomes (model 1) and matched income logarithms (model 2).

Part of the effect of response errors for each of the models could have been estimated from the cross-tabulation of SCF income by CQC incomes of the matched units, if the tabulation had been sufficiently detailed. Under the second model, for example, if each unit were classified by the geometric mean of its SCF and CQC

While the decrease in inequality of the income distribution is clearly presented by the use of the logarithmic variance, it is always desirable to show, if possible, the effect of response errors on the Lorenz curve of the distribution. For this purpose it was necessary to estimate the true income distribution directly.[2] The Lorenz curves of the true and observed income distributions are given in Chart 1.

**Chart 1**

**Hypothetical Survey and "True" Income Distributions**

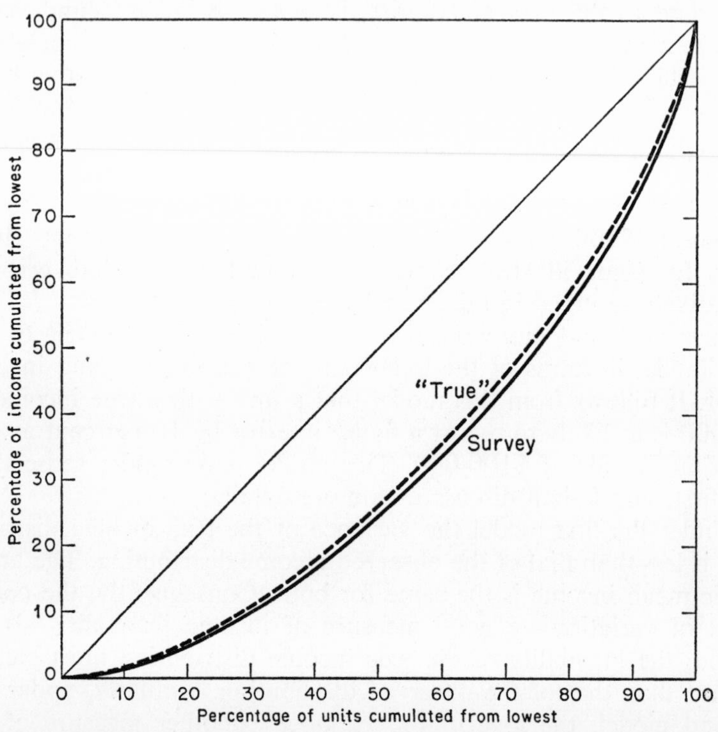


incomes, the resulting income distribution would be partially free of response error, and would in fact show a reduction in inequality (logarithmic variance) of half the total possible 17 per cent. The process of adding through the given cross-tabulation to obtain this intermediate distribution with any reasonable accuracy was a rather formidable prospect.

[2] The true distribution was obtained from the observed distribution by use of a linear transformation in the logarithms of income, with the constants of the transformation chosen so that the desired logarithmic mean and variance were obtained. Just as in the first model, the observed arithmetic mean income is also the true mean income, so in the second model the geometric mean income remains unchanged.

### COMMON IMPLICATIONS OF THE MODELS

Each of the two response error models have some unsatisfactory aspects, the first more than the second. However, even if more satisfactory models are developed, I believe some of their common implications will remain. It is reasonable to think that the inequality of an income distribution must be reduced if its random response errors are removed. Marginal propensities to consume, calculated from survey data on income and expenditures, should tend to increase with a reduction in response errors. This is seen most clearly under the second (logarithmic) model. To the extent that response errors result in the misclassification of units in some category—by family size, urban-rural, age of head, and so forth—and these errors are not correlated with income, the comparisons of such categories in terms of income must necessarily be impaired.

Twice when working on the construction of income size distributions from survey and tax return data, I was impressed by a pattern among the incomes of family members. Once the distributions of survey incomes of subfamilies and of main families were almost independent of those of supplementary income recipients and family heads.[3] Another time I found a marked correspondence between estimated distributions of combined family earnings (assuming independence of earnings in two-earner families) and observed survey distributions of family earnings.[4] This lack of relationship among patterns of income of individual family members or family subunits must be due, at least in part, to the presence of random response errors in the basic survey data.

While response errors can hardly be eliminated entirely, a respectable body of theory can probably be developed for sharpening our tools of analysis. To this end, we must look for help to the people engaged in planning and conducting consumers surveys at the Michigan Center, the Census Bureau, the Bureau of Labor Statistics, and similar organizations.

### IRVING SCHWEIGER, UNIVERSITY OF CHICAGO

These matching studies have been of considerable value. The contributing organizations and individuals should be congratulated

[3] Maurice Liebenberg and Hyman Kaitz, "An Income Size Distribution from Tax and Survey Data, 1944," in Volume Thirteen (1951) of Studies in Income and Wealth, pp. 426–429.

[4] Income Distribution in the United States," Supplement to *Survey of Current Business,* 1953, pp. 50–51.

for an important job well done. As a result of these studies some questions have been brought into much sharper focus.

The problem of "coverage" has been considerably clarified. Far more is now known than before on how many and which types of dwelling units, family members, and income recipients tend to be missed with various field procedures. Progress has been made in distinguishing and measuring differences in the quality of income information furnished by various family members.

These carefully matched studies have highlighted the magnitude of a rather neglected type of reporting error, variability in the reporting of individual incomes in field surveys. Only about half of all units placed themselves consistently in the same broad income bracket (intervals of $500 or larger) in successive interviews a few weeks to a few months apart. For example, of the consumer units that reported incomes of $7,500 to $9,999 in the Census Quality Check just under half reported incomes within this same broad $2,500 class interval in the Survey of Consumer Finances. Of the $7,500–$9,999 CQC group 10 per cent reported incomes of less than $5,000 in the SCF, and 4 per cent reported less than $2,000 of income. Such variability in reporting income information has implications for both reports on income levels and distributions and for any analysis related to income. If consumers reporting incomes of $4,000 to $4,999 in a field survey, for example, really have incomes ranging from $2,000 to $10,000 with only half actually receiving $4,000 to $4,999, then any analysis relating expenditures, savings, family characteristics, and so on to reported income level is almost certainly subject to serious error and distortions.

An illustration of these difficulties appears in the paper by Eleanor M. Snyder, who found that economic status, which is based on relatively long-term factors, was frequently not closely related to reports of current income level. Such a disparity can result from any of a number of socio-economic factors. However it is also bound to develop when persons with incomes of $2,000 report incomes of $5,000 and vice versa. Indeed, the validity of Miss Snyder's indexes of economic status may be verified by her finding of imperfect correlation between income level and economic status. While there are valid reasons why current income may differ from economic status, measurement of the phenomenon is confused by the variability of income reports and tends to be exaggerated by it.

The implications of these methodological findings appear even more serious for the field reporting of items other than income. There are few props to aid in recalling expenditures for food and clothing, increases and decreases in liquid funds, consumer debt, and so forth. Saving, for example, may be subject to wide margins of error because of its many forms, of irregularity in depositing or withdrawing, and lack of independent summations such as income withholding statements. Evidence from a small sample study in which reports on individual savings accounts were matched against bank records indicates that large errors in holdings are quite frequent both in their amounts and changes.[1]

Results of these matching studies of income and of savings accounts warn us that financial and possibly other data obtained in field studies using current methods are subject to serious error in level, distribution, slope of regression, and almost any other calculated statistic. Much variation offset for the entire population is not offset for subgroups. To discover that much of the difficulty in micro-economic analysis lies in variability in reporting is a valuable contribution.

The Sirken, Maynes, and Frechtling paper shows that, for income, variability was lowest (although still present) when first quality respondents were interviewed (heads of spending units in the SCF and individual income recipients in the CQC).

Authors of the analyses in this volume differ on the merits of many versus few questions for reducing random errors: Miller, Pritzker, and Sands believe that a few questions give about as good results as many in determining level; Sirken, Maynes, and Frechtling suggest that more detailed questions will reveal more supplementary and miscellaneous types of income. Data for entrepreneurial incomes are inconclusive; there is a suggestion that use of few questions may lead to greater variation in results. Mrs. Goldsmith's analysis indicates that shortening the farm questionnaire in the 1954 SCF led to a much greater deviation from estimates of aggregate farm income than in previous years.

A new approach to learning how to obtain valid and reliable information seems to be called for. In the long run it should be more productive and less expensive to invest funds in experimental designs that would furnish reliable evidence of the effect of variations in type, phrasing, and number of questions, and of sources of information (respondents, records). The Census Bureau's test of one versus two income questions was a beginning, but far more experimentation of this type is required. Increasing reliance on surveys for information used in formulating government and business policy

[1] See my paper, "Some Factors Affecting Saving of Different Groups," pp. 1–2, given at the Conference on Consumption and Economic Development of the Universities-National Bureau Committee for Economic Research in October 1955, mimeographed, for a brief description of the magnitude of these errors.

underscores the importance of improving current inadequate survey methodology. These papers have made important contributions by showing how to overcome certain deficiencies in technique and by indicating the magnitudes of other hitherto unappreciated problems.

# PART III

## Examples of Uses of Census Income Data

# An Appraisal of the Data for Farm Families

D. GALE JOHNSON, UNIVERSITY OF CHICAGO

Compared with any of its predecessors, the 1950 census is a landmark in the search for more adequate data on the income and other characteristics of farm families. The people who are the Bureau of the Census can be justly proud of what their labors accomplished, recognizing as they do that a better job can be done next time, Congress and money permitting. It is the purpose of this paper to contribute a few small suggestions that might lead to improvement and to make a few comments about the accuracy of the data.

Anyone who uses or appraises the income data for farm families is greatly indebted to the Departments of Agriculture and Commerce for their cooperative publication, *Farms and Farm People.*[1] In this pioneering effort, the matching of approximately 11,000 schedules from the censuses of agriculture and population permitted certain interrelations between farms and farm people to be seen. Among several able analyses of the underlying data, Ernest W. Grove's "Income of Farm-Operator Families in 1949" is especially relevant here. In fact, I have taken this chapter as part of my text for this essay—one way to put one's discussant on the defensive from the very start.

## *Some Basic Features of the Data*

Some special problems arise from three characteristics of the income data: (1) the significant income-receiving unit is the family and not the individual, (2) the income data collected relate only to money income, and (3) incomes of individual farm receiving units vary much more from year to year than do the incomes of nonfarm income-receiving units.

### FARM FAMILIES AS INCOME UNITS

Taking the family as the income-receiving unit has peculiar significance for procedures and findings. Its basis is a fundamental characteristic of the farm population.

The 1950 census enumerated a total of 6,834,000 workers in

[1] *Farms and Farm People: Population, Income, and Housing Characteristics by Economic Class of Farm,* Bureau of the Census, 1953.

farm occupations; of these 919,000 were unpaid family workers. The unpaid family workers on farms constituted 83 per cent of all unpaid family workers enumerated by the census. A little more than 13 per cent of the farm labor force fell in this category. The income representing the productivity of their labor on a farm was undoubtedly attributed to the head of the family, who would normally be classified as a farm operator. Most of the unpaid family workers received no money income from any source.[2]

The problem arising here is that, for rural farm people, the distributions of income for persons and cross tabulations between income and other characteristics for persons are subject to serious limitations and distortions. For example, a cross-classification of income by age will be distorted; while farm operators tend to be older than unpaid family workers, some of the latter will report income and so be included in such distributions.

Also distributions of income of persons living on farms will appear more unequal than they are. Many unpaid family workers who have some money income will be included at low income levels while farm operators will be credited income that is used to increase the level of consumption of the unpaid family workers.

In general, it is usually better to work with distributions of family income data than with individual data. This means, of course, that certain kinds of analyses are not appropriate. Thus interrelations between income and age or education can be discovered only for farm operators, and these relationships may be affected by age or education selectivity among farm operators. Only the most capable young persons or those with the best access to capital can be farm operators, resulting in an overestimate of the "true" income for the younger groups.

### EXCLUSION OF NONMONEY INCOME

The exclusion of nonmoney income has two important consequences. First, farm incomes are seriously underestimated relative to nonfarm incomes. For 1949, the Agricultural Marketing Service estimates that the net money income of the farm population was $16,408 million; if changes in the value of farm inventories are excluded, $17,215 million. The nonmoney income (other than change in inventories) was $3,443 million, or 21 per cent of the

[2] There were 892 thousand unpaid family workers living in rural farm areas; of these 324 thousand reported the receipt of money income and 41 thousand fell in the category "income not reported" leaving 527 thousand without money income (*1950 Census of Population,* Vol. II, *Characteristics of the Population,* Part I, Table 142). It may also be noted that there were 979 thousand persons without income who reported work in 1949. Of these farm persons more than half (494 thousand) reported fifty to fifty-two weeks of work and another 156 thousand reported twenty-seven to forty-nine weeks of work (*ibid.,* Table 141).

net money income, including inventory change in total net income. Of course, nonfarm persons have some nonmoney income, particularly from the value of owned housing, but the relative amount is much less important.

Second, the farm income distribution is made to appear more unequal than it in fact is. As Margaret G. Reid has shown,[3] nonmoney income of farm families is much more equally distributed than is the money income. This is true not only for persons or families within a region but also from one region to another.

I shall here consider only the implications of the underestimation of the real income of farm people. In general, distributions of income combining farm and nonfarm personal incomes should not be presented, certainly not without indicating their serious limitations.

One limitation appears in attempts to correlate education with income. This point can be illustrated by reference to an exceptionally detailed presentation of data relating income to age, education, sex, color, and region.[4] As indicated in Table 11 of the same publication, farm people of any age have less education than do nonfarm people of the same age. For example, the median number of years' schooling for male farm operators thirty-five to forty-four years old is 8.4; for the nonfarm male population of this age group, 10.1. Farm persons thus tend to be concentrated in the lower education levels for any age group. Since the real earnings of farm people are understimated, if farm and nonfarm incomes are combined, the slope of the regression of income on education is steeper than its true value. Since there is little information on the relation between income and education for farm people, one cannot estimate the true value of the regression coefficient.

Even if estimates of the money value of the nonmoney income of the farm population were obtainable, the usual procedure of valuing such items as home-produced food at farm sales prices will still result in too low an estimate of the real value of the nonmoney income to farm families. And economists do not agree on how to correct for this underestimation. Thus it seems appropriate that, regardless of the income concept used, farm and nonfarm income distributions should be kept separate.

### VARIABILITY OF FARM INCOME

The third of the basic features of farm income, the year-to-year variability, is something a decennial census can do little or nothing

[3] Margaret G. Reid, "Distribution of Nonmoney Income," in *Volume Thirteen* (1951) of Studies in Income and Wealth, pp. 124–179.

[4] *1950 Census of Population,* Vol. IV, *Special Reports,* Part 1, Chap. C, Table 12.

about in the collection of data. It is possible to obtain data for one year and one year only. However, to compensate for this variability, I have a suggestion about the presentation of income data for farm persons. Income should never be shown as the independent or the classificatory variable; that is, the mean or median of other variables should not be presented for a given income level or a series of income levels without a distribution of the second variable also.

I have not found a presentation of income data in the census of population where this rule is not followed. However, in *Farms and Farm People,* an otherwise admirable study, there are several. For example, median age of farm operator, average size of family, and number of persons per room are calculated by net income level. Such material tells us little because for most farm families any one year's income varies so from their average or normal income.

The data on the average age of farm operators may be used as an example. For the North and West the following results were obtained: [5]

| *Net Income* | *Median Age* |
|---|---|
| Under $1,000 | 56.8 |
| $1,000– 1,999 | 47.1 |
| 2,000– 2,999 | 44.3 |
| 3,000– 3,999 | 44.8 |
| 4,000– 4,999 | 45.6 |
| 5,000– 9,999 | 46.9 |

It is hard to say what this tabulation tells us about the interrelation between age of farm operator and income. Age declines as income increases from less than $1,000 to the $2,000–2,999 bracket; then as income increases so does age, at least slightly. But except for the lowest income group, the income-age relationship seems flat, and the regression of age on income would probably have a regression coefficient around zero.

The relationship between age and income for rural farm males is exhibited better in the *1950 Census of Population:* [6]

| *Age* | *Median Net Income* |
|---|---|
| 14–19 | $ 356 |
| 20–24 | 1,090 |
| 25–34 | 1,719 |
| 35–44 | 1,850 |
| 45–54 | 1,697 |
| 55–64 | 1,354 |
| 65 and over | 789 |

The age-income relationship for rural farm persons is difficult to estimate accurately because of the importance of unpaid family

[5] *Farms and Farm People,* Chap. 5, Table 4.

[6] Vol. II, *Characteristics of the Population,* Part 1, Table 139.

workers in the lower age groups, yet when income is classified by age rather than vice versa, a more meaningful relationship emerges. The reason is obvious; while income is subject to errors of misreporting and other large random components, the age variable is subject only to errors of misreporting.

Though the following tabulation does not refer to net income, it is a striking illustration of the problem. In the first part of Table 1, the ratio of value of farm products to the value of land and buildings is shown for farms when the value of land and buildings is classified by the value of products. Here there seems to be a definite implication that, as the value of farm products increases, output per unit of this one input increases, and quite dramatically. In the second part of the table, the value of land and buildings has been used as the independent variable. The result as indicated by the ratio of value of products to value of land and buildings is the

TABLE 1

Value of Farm Products and Value of Land and Buildings for Iowa, 1945, and Effect of Criteria of Classification Upon Ratio Between These Values

| *Value of Products* (1) | *Value of Land and Buildings* (2) | *Ratio of (1) to (2)* (3) |
|---|---|---|
| Farms Classified by Value of Products | | |
| $ 147 | $ 6,088 | 0.02 |
| 316 | 4,372 | 0.07 |
| 495 | 4,585 | 0.10 |
| 783 | 5,615 | 0.14 |
| 1,251 | 7,780 | 0.16 |
| 2,014 | 9,492 | 0.21 |
| 3,251 | 12,927 | 0.25 |
| 4,975 | 17,465 | 0.28 |
| 7,673 | 22,903 | 0.34 |
| 15,435 | 34,313 | 0.44 |
| 70,514 | 61,777 | 1.44 |
| Farms Classified by Value of Land and Buildings | | |
| $ 535 | $ 750 | 0.71 |
| 1,357 | 1,500 | 0.90 |
| 1,689 | 2,500 | 0.68 |
| 1,905 | 4,000 | 0.48 |
| 2,499 | 6,250 | 0.40 |
| 3,492 | 8,500 | 0.41 |
| 4,321 | 12,500 | 0.35 |
| 6,706 | 20,000 | 0.34 |
| 10,350 | 35,000 | 0.29 |
| 18,497 | 70,000 | 0.26 |

Source: Based on 1945 Census of Agriculture, *Farms and Farm Characteristics by Value of Products,* Tables 2 and 17.

opposite of the first result. Since land and buildings constitute only one of several inputs, and other inputs, especially labor, do not increase proportionally as land and buildings increase, the results in the second part of the table are consistent with the observed phenomenon that medium-size farms do compete successfully with large-size farms.

Since estimates of the value of land and buildings are subject to error and some year-to-year variation, and since adjustments to changes in size are not completed at once, the estimate of the regression between the two variables is biased even when the value of land and buildings is used as the independent variable. However, the bias is much smaller than when value of products is used as the independent variable.

### *Income Aggregates Derived from Census Data*

Few economists can resist the urge to try to determine the total of the incomes determined by a sample study, even though the aggregate income derived from such an exercise will always be less than some national income estimator's estimate of what the total income really is. I believe that there are three justifications for the attempt, the wish:

1. To determine the relative underestimation of various income components or of various income groups as a guide for income comparisons of the groups (such as farm and nonfarm residents).
2. To determine if the absolute amount of underestimation is large enough to lead to a suspicion of differential underestimation at the various income levels.
3. To provide an independent estimate of the allocation of certain income components to particular residence groups (such as the allocation of nonagricultural income to farm residents).

Sample surveys are known to suffer from two afflictions, other than sampling problems, both resulting in underestimates of income. People forget income items. Or perhaps they do not answer the income question, or the interviewer forgets to ask it, especially if it is part of a long schedule. In the 1950 census, income was not reported for 4.46 per cent of farm families compared to 4.88 per cent of all families.

In the matched sample reported on in *Farms and Farm People*, the nonreporting problem turned out to be somewhat more serious with approximately 10 per cent of the families not reporting total family incomes. Furthermore, many farm operator households who did report, did not separate the farm income from other income. Data on nonreporting are given in Table 2 for family income and for income from farming.

TABLE 2

Commercial Farm Operator Families Not Reporting Total Family Income and Not Reporting Income from Farming, by Value of Farm Products, 1949

(*per cent*)

| *Value of Farm Products* | *Class* | *Not Reporting Total Family Income* | *Not Reporting Income from Farming* |
|---|---|---|---|
| All commercial farms | | 10.2 | 20.4 |
| $10,000 and over | I and II | 9.2 | 17.0 |
| 5,000–$9,999 | III | 8.0 | 15.4 |
| 2,500– 4,999 | IV | 9.4 | 18.2 |
| 1,200– 2,499 | V | 9.9 | 23.8 |
| 250– 1,199 | VI | 14.0 | 26.6 |

Source: *Farms and Farm People: Population, Income, and Housing Characteristics by Economic Class of Farm,* Bureau of the Census, 1953, pp. 27 and 33.

The importance of the matched sample lies partly in what it tells us about the characteristics of the nonreporting cases. Except for farms with sales between $250 and $1,199, the proportions not reporting family income are about the same for the various classes of commercial farms. There is somewhat greater variation in the proportions reporting income from farming, but for the classes with products valued over $1,200, which included 86 per cent of the farms, the differences are quite small.

DESCRIPTION OF SERIES

Before turning to the estimates of the aggregates of the income of farm people that can be derived from the 1950 census, some description of the available series seems desirable. The following estimates or sets of estimates are available:

1. Incomes of farm operator families resulting from the matched sample of the agriculture and population census schedules (including estimates of family incomes as a total, and estimates of income by sources for the farm operator and members of his family).

2. Family incomes of rural farm families and for unrelated individuals.[7]

3. Individual incomes or incomes of persons, available for the United States as a whole; one group is for rural farm people, the other for persons who have a farm occupation.[8]

Only the incomes for rural farm families and unrelated individuals and the individual income data for rural farm persons relate

[7] *Ibid.,* Table 57.

[8] *Ibid.,* Chap. C.

to the same populations. The following are the total numbers of individuals who had an income or for whom the income was not reported (in thousands):

| | |
|---|---|
| Rural farm residents | 9,207 |
| Experienced civilian labor force in agriculture | 6,009 |
| Experienced civilian labor force with farm type jobs | 5,856 |

The difference between the last two consists of persons who work for firms or farms classified as in agriculture but whose jobs (such as typing or bookkeeping) are not called farm jobs. The difference between the first and the other two results from two partially offsetting factors: many rural farm residents have nonfarm jobs, and some of the experienced agricultural or farm labor force live in nonfarm communities.

## ESTIMATES OF TOTAL FARM INCOMES

Two national-income-type aggregates prepared by the Department of Agriculture can be compared to data derived from the census. One, called the net income of the farm population, should be comparable to an aggregate derived from either the family and unrelated individuals income or the persons income in the census, assuming approximately the same definition of the rural farm population in both sources. The other national series is the estimate of the net farm income of farm operators. The only direct counterpart to this in the census is the estimate of income from farm, business, or profession that resulted from matching the agriculture and population schedules.

### *Miller's Estimate*

An obvious difficulty of using sample survey data with open-end intervals and also relatively wide class intervals, particularly at the higher income levels, is that alternative procedures for estimating aggregate income do not give the same results. Differences of 3, 4, or 5 per cent are not unusual.

One attempt to expand the census data on farm incomes was made by Herman P. Miller.[9] He compared his estimate of farm self-employment income of $7.4 billion with the Department of Commerce's national income estimate of $9.9 billion. The difference implies an underestimate for the farm group of about 25 per cent and an underestimate for all United States income receivers of slightly less than 9 per cent, suggesting that underestimation of at

[9] Herman P. Miller, "An Appraisal of the 1950 Census Income Data," *Journal of the American Statistical Association,* March 1953, p. 34.

least the self-employment component of farm family income is greater than it is of the national income as a whole.

But one cannot be certain that the 25 per cent underestimate applies to what the farmers had in mind when they answered the question: "Last year, how much money did he earn working in his own business, professional practice, or farm?" Many farmers still operating on a cash basis may have deducted capital expenditures rather than depreciation charges, and the former exceeded the latter by $2,104 million for all farming in 1949 according to calculations of the Department of Agriculture. On the other hand, farmers who reported income on an accrual basis may have deducted inventory losses (net inventory losses were $807 million in 1949). Both of these actions would have been inconsistent with the instructions, and misunderstandings in both cases would operate in the same direction. Though no single respondent should have erred on both scores, many may have erred because of one or the other.

*Grove's Estimate*

Grove (in *Farms and Farm People*) attempted to adjust for the "no report" cases in two ways. (1) He adjusted the data for the failure to report income from self-employment when family income was reported by assuming that such income was equal to the average self-employment income for operators in Classes I through IV (see my Table 2) and was zero for the two smaller classes of commercial farms and for the noncommercial farms. (2) He assumed that the average income of the farm operator families who did not report income was equal to the average for the farm class in which each fell.

On the whole the adjustments seem reasonable, though one could argue that the assumption of zero self-employment income for those not reporting such income in Classes V and VI is somewhat arbitrary. However the effect of this assumption would not have been significant, involving an increase of $320 million or about 4 per cent of self-employment income and slightly more than 2 per cent of total income.

Grove's estimate of the total income of farm operator families ($14,252 million) cannot be compared directly with estimates derived from the population census data for rural farm residents. The census data include hired workers who live on farms, and Grove's data include farm operator families who live in urban areas. About 5 per cent of all farm operators do not live on the farms they operate, and some farms are actually in urban areas. In 1950, 2.8 per cent of employed farm managers and farm operators resided in urban areas, and 5.6 per cent in rural nonfarm areas.[10] However, the persons living in rural nonfarm areas who live on farms are included in the census farm population and present no problem.

Nor can Grove's estimates be compared directly with those of the Department of Agriculture for the net income of the farm population, which include the income of hired farm workers who reside on farms but are not in farm operator households. However, despite these inconsistencies, some comparisons are attempted below.

*Comparability of Estimates*

By the use of quite unrefined techniques I estimated the aggregate incomes from the census individual income data and from the family and unrelated income data.[11] Without any adjustment for no reporting, the individual income data imply a total of $13,970 million,[12] while the family and unrelated individual data give a total of $12,824 million.[13] The reason for the smaller estimate from the latter source has been adequately explained, at least to my satisfaction, by Miller.[14]

It is not evident how an adjustment for the no-report group in the individual income data should be made. Of a total of 15,817,315 persons fourteen years old and over, 6,609,410 were without income, 8,360,380 reported income, and 847,525 were in the income-not-reported category. Over half of the no-report group were not in the experienced labor force and possibly had zero income. However I made the assumption that this no-report group that was not shown in the experienced labor force in the census could be distributed into classes of work according to the percentages of no-report cases in the experienced labor force shown in the census in the various classes. I then attributed to the resulting no-report cases in each class of work the average income shown for that class by those reporting income. The results indicate that the total income of individuals should be increased by about 5 per cent or to approximately $14,670 million.

Special tabulations indicate that urban farms number about 96,000 or 1.78 of all farms.[15] The difference from the previously noted 2.8 per cent of employed farm managers and operators re-

[10] *1950 Census of Population,* Vol. II, *Characteristics of the Population,* Part 1, Table 126.

[11] The estimates were made by assuming the average income in each income interval was equal to the midpoint of that interval and $15,000 as the average income of the open-end income class.

[12] *Ibid.,* Table 142. [13] *Ibid.,* Table 57. [14] *Op. cit.*

[15] *Farms and Farm People,* p. 67.

siding in urban areas may be accounted for by the number of farm operators not residing on the farms operated but living in urban areas, or in part by differences between the various censuses. However, on the assumption that the individual income data for rural persons do not include that for the 2.8 per cent of operators and managers living in urban areas, and that such operators have an income from agriculture equal to the average for all farm operators as estimated by Grove, or $1,575, an increase of $239 million is implied in the estimate of individual incomes.

To achieve a further degree of comparability, it is necessary to add the income of the farm population not residing in farm operator households to Grove's estimate, or to subtract it from the individual income estimate. This is a difficult task since so little is known about the hired farm labor force and particularly about the proportion living in farm operator households. (The 1950 census definition of the rural farm population, counting hired workers living on farms and paying rent in the rural nonfarm population, is ignored here.)

The only hint of the proportion of those living in farm operator households is from the 1940 Census of Population, which listed 567,940 rural farm households with employed heads classified as farm workers, about 750,000 employed workers in these households, and 1,429,000 hired workers living on rural farms. If it is assumed that employed workers living in households headed by a farm laborer were employed as farm wage workers, these workers would account for 53 per cent of all hired farm workers living in rural farm areas.[16] A less extreme assumption would be that no more than 50 per cent of these workers come from such households.

The aggregate income of all individuals who reported hired farm work as their major occupation in 1950 was $1,713 million, after adjustments for no-report cases (5 per cent) and for underreporting.[17] The Department of Agriculture assumes that 59 per cent of the total cash wages paid by farm operators goes to farm resident workers.[18] If we assume that 50 per cent of this amount goes to members of farm operator families, then 30 per cent of the above total ($514 million) should be added to Grove's total (or, alternatively, subtracted from the total income of the farm population) in

[16] *1940 Census of Population and Housing, Characteristics of Rural-Farm Families,* Table 7, and *1940 Census of Population,* Vol. III, *The Labor Force,* Part I, Table 59.

[17] The adjustment for underreporting assumes that all income was wages and salaries (see below for the adjustment for underreporting).

[18] *The Farm Income Situation,* Dept. of Agriculture, October 31, 1955.

order to make the two series comparable. If this is added to Grove's estimate, the total for the farm population becomes $14,766 million; if $239 million is added to the total of individual incomes to account for self-employment incomes on urban farms, that total is $14,909 million. The astonishing agreement indicates to me that the adjustments made in the data from *Farms and Farm People* were quite reasonable.

However, the closeness of these two semi-independently derived estimates of the income of the farm population says nothing about underestimation of income by the respondents who supplied information. The Department of Agriculture's estimate of money income of the farm population, on a basis of inclusiveness quite comparable to the above two estimates is $17,215 million or about 15 per cent more than the highest of the two estimates (see Table 3).

Can anything further be said about the sources of the underestimate, at least by types of income? According to the distributions of

TABLE 3

Net Money and Total Income of Farm Operators and Farm Population Based on Department of Agriculture Estimates, 1949

(*millions of dollars*)

| | |
|---|---|
| **A. Net Money Income of Farm Operators from Farm Operations** | |
| 1. Total net income of farm operators | 12,866 |
| 2. Realized nonmoney income | 3,085 |
| 3. Value of inventory change | —807 |
| 4. Rent to farm landlords | 531 |
| 5. Total [1 — (2 + 3 + 4)] | 10,057 |
| **B. Net Money Income of Farm Population** | |
| 1. Net money income of farm operators from farm operations (A5) | 10,057 |
| 2. Money wages of farm resident hired workers | 1,427 |
| 3. Rent to farm landlords (A4) | 531 |
| 4. Income from nonfarm sources | 5,200 |
| 5. Total (1 + 2 + 3 + 4) | 17,215 |
| **C. Total Net Income of Farm Population** | |
| 1. Total net money income (B5) | 17,215 |
| 2. Realized nonmoney income | 3,443 |
| 3. Value of inventory change (A3) | —807 |
| 4. Total (1 + 2 + 3) | 19,851 |

Source: *Farm Income Situation,* Dept. of Agriculture, October 31, 1955 for: A1 (Table 2, includes government payments as do all other estimates); A2 (Tables 11 and 17); A3 (Table 14); B2 (Table 17); B4 (Table 3); and C2 (Tables 11 and 17). *Agricultural Statistics,* Dept. of Agriculture, 1953, p. 617 for A4, adjusted by subtracting $17 million of interest payments that had been counted as an expense of farm opertors.

income by source in *Farms and Farm People,* $1,506 million of the underestimate is due to the difference in the estimates of farm operator income, leaving $943 million to be attributed to the other sources of income. Miller estimates that census figures for salaries and wages for the nation as a whole were low by the reciprocal of 1.028, while other sources of income were low by the reciprocal of 1.855 if the individual income data are compared with the National Income Division estimates.[19] The estimates in *Farms and Farm People* for other sources of income and for wages and salaries have apparently been adjusted somewhat: for other sources the aggregate estimate is $1,568 million, and my estimate from the published distribution is $1,462 million; the estimate of wages and salaries is $4,133 million against my estimate of $3,792 million. My adjustments, noted above, were use of $15,000 instead of $14,000 as the value for the open-end class, of the middle value of each income interval to estimate aggregate income in that interval; and the addition of $514 million to cover the incomes of hired workers who are farm residents but not members of farm operator families (see Table 4).

If Miller's estimates of underreporting are applied to the income distributions (not Grove's estimates) given in *Farms and Farm People* for salaries and wages and for other income (assuming that all the income of hired farm workers who are not members of farm operator households is wage and salary income), the total for wages and salaries is $4,412 million and for other income is $2,712 million.[20] Adding this to the net farm income of farm operators as estimated by the Department of Agriculture, after adjustment for comparability, gives a total net money income of the farm population of $17,181 million. This is nearly equal to the $17,215 million adjusted estimate of the Department of Agriculture.

A rough check made by subtracting rent paid to farm landlords and wages paid to farm residents, as estimated by the Department of Agriculture from the excess of the total income of the farm population over the net operator income, gives an estimate of income from nonfarm sources of $5,166 million or nearly the same as that given in *The Farm Income Situation* for 1949 (B4 of Table 3).

I will conclude this rough survey of the income aggregates with the statement that, if one uses the individual earner data and adjusts for the no-report cases, the income data for the farm population

[19] *Op. cit.,* pp. 34–35.

[20] It should be noted that the estimate of income for farm residents who are not members of farm households has also been included.

TABLE 4

Total Money Income of Farm Operators and Farm Population Based on Estimates in *Farms and Farm People,* 1949

(*millions of dollars*)

| | | |
|---|---|---|
| **A. Estimates of Income of Farm Operator Families** | | |
| As adjusted by Grove: [a] | | |
| From farm operations | | 8,551 |
| Wages and salaries | | 4,133 |
| Operators | 2,850 | |
| Other family members | 1,283 | |
| Other income | | 1,568 |
| Operators | 998 | |
| Other family members | 570 | |
| Total | | 14,252 |
| Derived from income distributions: [b] | | |
| Wages and salaries | | 3,792 |
| Operators | 2,679 | |
| Other family members | 1,113 | |
| Other income | | 1,462 |
| Operators | 951 | |
| Other family members | 511 | |
| Derived from income distributions and adjusted for underreporting: [c] | | |
| Wages and salaries (1.028) | | 3,898 |
| Other income (1.855) | | 2,712 |
| Total | | 6,610 |
| **B. Estimate of Income of Farm Resident Hired Farm Workers Not Members of Farm Operator Families** | | |
| As adjusted for underreporting [d] | | 514 |
| **C. Estimate of Income of Farm Population** | | |
| As adjusted for underreporting and a further adjustment to raise income from farm operations to Dept. of Agriculture estimate: | | |
| Income from farm operations | | 10,057 |
| Wages and salaries and other income: | | |
| Farm operator families | | 6,610 |
| Farm resident hired workers not members of farm operator families | | 514 |
| Total | | 17,181 |

[a] *Farms and Farm People: Population, Income, and Housing Characteristics by Economic Class of Farm,* Bureau of the Census, 1953, pp. 27–30.

[b] *Ibid.,* pp. 31–34. Midpoint of each income range assumed to equal average income. Open-end class estimated at $15,000.

[c] Adjustments made on basis of results derived from Herman P. Miller, "An Appraisal of the 1950 Census Income Data," *Journal of the American Statistical Association,* March 1953, p. 34.

[d] See text, pp. 292–299.

is underestimated by something of the order of 15 per cent. If the same adjustments are made in data for the rest of the population the underestimate is probably of the order of 5 per cent.

For many purposes of analysis family income data are more useful than individual data, especially for rural farm areas. For the United States as a whole, Miller found that, when the same value was used for the open-end class of individual and family data, the family data aggregate was 5.4 per cent smaller than the individual earner aggregate.[21] For the rural farm families the difference is larger—8.2 per cent. Thus use of the family income data may result in underestimation of rural farm family incomes, after adjustment for the no-report cases, by about 22 per cent compared with an underestimation for the rest of the population of a probable 10 per cent.

### *Area Differences in Aggregates Derived from Individual Earner and Family Income Data*

As indicated above, the nature of the farm enterprise and the significance of unpaid family labor in agriculture means that family income data are frequently more useful than individual earner data in economic analyses of rural farm income. However, family income data include a smaller fraction of total income than do individual earner data. The relative completeness of the family data, may also vary according to certain conditions that are not randomly distributed among the various states or economic areas. To indicate the general nature of the problem, in Table 5, I show the relative differences in totals derived from family and from individual income data in seven states (selected, I should point out, on the basis of whim, fancy, and scholarly insights).

Total individual income is smaller in proportion to total family income in each of the four southern states than in the three north central states. The extremes are 86.7 per cent in Mississippi to 94.1 per cent in Iowa.

The other data presented in the table represent information on items that I thought might help to explain the observed differences. But there seem to be no systematic differences in these characteristics that are associated with the differences in the two income aggregates. A comparison of Iowa and Mississippi, for example, reveals nothing to me that would explain the relatively large difference in the income estimates. Though it is possible that the individual income responses were more complete in Mississippi than in Iowa, I

[21] *Op. cit.*, p. 40.

TABLE 5

Various Characteristics of Rural Farm Population Income, 1949, and of Rural Farm Labor Force, 1950, Selected States

| | *Mis-sissippi* | *South Carolina* | *Ala-bama* | *Ar-kansas* | *Ohio* | *Wis-consin* | *Iowa* |
|---|---|---|---|---|---|---|---|
| Total income (millions): | | | | | | | |
| Family | $265 | $204 | $270 | $268 | $592 | $465 | $669 |
| Individual | 306 | 232 | 304 | 296 | 634 | 497 | 711 |
| Various characteristics: | | | | | | | |
| Family income as % of individual income | 86.7% | 87.6% | 88.9% | 90.7% | 93.3% | 93.4% | 94.1% |
| No income report: | | | | | | | |
| Family | 3.7 | 4.8 | 3.9 | 4.0 | 6.1 | 3.6 | 4.3 |
| Individual | 6.1 | 9.9 | 8.6 | 9.4 | 13.1 | 8.1 | 9.5 |
| Rural farm labor force: | | | | | | | |
| Engaged in agriculture | 81.0 | 70.3 | 72.4 | 77.5 | 56.8 | 80.0 | 87.1 |
| Wage or salary workers | 25.4 | 36.5 | 31.7 | 31.5 | 45.9 | 29.0 | 22.0 |
| Unpaid family workers | 15.0 | 19.8 | 15.6 | 10.4 | 7.0 | 18.0 | 12.1 |

Source: *1950 Census of Population,* Vol. II, *Characteristics of the Population,* Chaps. B and C in state volumes.

can think of no reason why this would be so; and on the basis of the evidence at hand, I have been unable to check the relative accuracy of the state estimates of individual earner income data for the rural farm population. In terms of my original expectations, Ohio should have exhibited the largest differences between the two income estimates.[22] However, this exercise leads me to the conclusion that, in the use of the family income data for rural farm areas, some adjustment for interarea comparability may be required.

## COMMENT

ERNEST W. GROVE, DEPARTMENT OF AGRICULTURE

Since D. Gale Johnson based part of his paper on my chapter in *Farms and Farm People* and in general treated it with respect, it would be unseemly for me to disagree with this part of his paper. And I do not find fault with the other parts either. On the whole, Johnson has provided us with a reasonable and valuable appraisal of the 1950 census income data for farm families. However, in two places he implies some objection to my methods of estimation.

[22] I had expected that the states with the greatest proportion of nonfarm workers in the rural population would have the largest underestimate of family income. I had assumed that, as the number of income sources and income earners increased, there would be a tendency to forget some of the sources in reporting family income.

UNREPORTED TOTAL INCOME

In section A of his Table 4, Johnson compares estimates derived from my summary tables of the total money income received by farm operator families with estimates of his own derived from the original distributions. Because my totals are higher than his unadjusted totals, he suggests that I must have made some unspecified adjustment to the data.

This is correct, but the adjustment made was a very simple one to allow for the nonreporting of income. No allowance is made for the no-report cases in most of the tables in *Farms and Farm People*. For example, the number of farm operators not reporting any income from wages or salaries includes not only those who reported they received no such income but also those from whom no report on it was obtained. Working more with average incomes for each economic class of farm than with income totals, the only way I could make some allowance for the no-report cases was to divide the income totals in each economic class not by the total number of farms in that class but by the number of farms reporting total family income. For all economic classes combined about 10 per cent of the farms did not report total family income. My procedure, therefore, raised the totals of wages and salaries and other income by about 10 per cent, which accounts for the discrepancies found by Johnson.

UNREPORTED SELF-EMPLOYMENT INCOME

The only other place where Johnson may imply some criticism of my methods is his discussion of the adjustments for farm-operator families who reported total family income but failed to include in it any income from farm, business, or profession. For farms in Classes I through IV (commercial) I assumed the omitted income to be equal to the class average of reported self-employment income; for farms in Classes V and VI (commercial) and all noncommercial farms, to be zero. Johnson apparently disagrees with the assumption of zero unreported farm income for Classes V and VI.

Assuming that unreported farm income was zero in these classes may be open to some question, especially for the lower classes of commercial farms, but it is not entirely unreasonable. Also in defense of my assumption, I did everything I could within reason to hold down the averages of farm income for these classes in an only partly successful attempt to reconcile them with agricultural census data.

## RECONCILIATION OF POPULATION AND AGRICULTURAL CENSUS DATA

The matched sample of schedules from the 1950 Census of Population and Housing and from the 1950 Census of Agriculture combined income data from the population census with data on value of farm products sold and on certain farm production expenditures from the agricultural census. For the higher economic classes of farms, the income data from the population census were low relative to the corresponding information on value of sales and expenditures from the agricultural census. This raised no problem, as substantial understatement of incomes is to be expected in any field survey of income.

But the data for the four lowest economic classes presented a serious problem of reconciliation. Self-employment income for each of the lowest classes calculated from the population census averaged considerably higher than the agricultural census could justify. As the person designated to analyze and report on these matched data, I was in the rather unpleasant position of a referee obliged to render a decision on their comparative accuracy. I had some qualms about the income averages derived from the population census, but all previous experience with income surveys suggested that exaggeration of farm income by the smaller farmers in their reports to the census enumerators did not seem at all likely. Consequently, I argued that the value of farm products sold as reported to the agricultural census must have been greatly understated for the lower economic classes of farms.

This view seemed reasonable enough at the time to all parties concerned—except the Agriculture Division of the Census Bureau, which naturally was reluctant to agree that the results of its census were of such poor quality. A compromise was finally reached which served more or less as a basis for the report. The published report does not state that the value of farm products sold was understated for the lower classes as much as I then thought it *was* understated. Nevertheless, the onus of the discrepancy was left almost entirely on the agricultural census.

I am not so sure now that I was right in this judgment, and some of the papers in this volume provide reasons for my uncertainty. Toward the end of his useful summary of the Census Bureau's experience with income questions, Edwin D. Goldfield admits rather casually that some self-employed persons tend to report their total gross receipts instead of their net income. Presumably this includes farmers, and chiefly the lower-income farmers. Relatively few reports involving such an error would distort both the averages and the distribution of farm income. For example, if a fourth of all Class VI farmers reported their gross value of sales instead of their net income, this alone might account for most of the discrepancy in Class VI between the population and agricultural census data for 1949.[1]

The results of the Post-Enumeration Survey, as reported by Leon Pritzker and Alfred Sands, are not at all reassuring on this point. The PES did not obtain information specifically on farm income, but it modified the census procedure on self-employment income by asking first for gross income and then for net income. This one important change in the questionnaire resulted in lowering the median income from self-employment by $160 for males and $170 for females, and in raising by more than 10 per cent the number reporting self-employment income of less than $500.

Could it be that farm income at the lower levels was seriously exaggerated in the 1950 census? I do not know, and I am more inclined now than I was in 1953 to reserve judgment. The general conclusion then was that the 1950 census income data were more reliable at the lower income levels than the agricultural census data on the value of farm products sold. I still think that the value of farm products sold may be relatively more understated for the lower than for the higher economic classes of farms, but I would no longer put all of the blame for the discrepancy on the agricultural census.

There was also a tendency to assume that the size distribution of farm income obtained from the 1950 census for the year 1949 was more reliable than that obtained by the then Bureau of Agricultural Economics (now the Agricultural Marketing Service) in its survey for the year 1946.[2] I am now inclined to question this view also. In fact, I do not think we know which, if any, survey distribution of farm income is correct.

[1] By agricultural census definition, Class VI farms are those with sales varying from $250 to $1,199, and with all other family income less than the value of sales. Adapted from page 33 of *Farms and Farm People* is the distribution of Class VI operators reporting income from farm, business, or profession by size of such income:

| | |
|---|---|
| Under $ 500 | 46.5 |
| $ 500– 999 | 33.6 |
| 1,000– 1,499 | 12.1 |
| 1,500 and over | 7.8 |
| Total | 100.0 |

[2] Nathan M. Koffsky and Jeanne E. Lear, *The Size Distribution of Farm Operators' Income in 1946,* Dept. of Agriculture, September 1950. A preliminary report appears in Volume Thirteen (1951) of Studies in Income and Wealth.

In this connection, I can heartily agree with Monroe G. Sirken, E. Scott Maynes, and John A. Frechtling, in their comparison of the Survey of Consumer Finances with the Census Quality Check, when they state that "The inconclusive results of our examination of entrepreneurial incomes underlines again the need for the experiments on income reporting by farmers and businessmen." I think this is true, so I find it rather disturbing when they report abandonment of the separate farm schedule previously used in the SCF. The issue admittedly remains unresolved, but those in charge of the SCF have apparently decided to act as though it *had* been resolved.

# The Size Distribution of Farm Income

ERNEST W. GROVE, DEPARTMENT OF AGRICULTURE

Near the end of his interesting introductory paper, Thomas Atkinson concludes that we are not yet out of the woods in determining how much of a redistribution of total income has occurred in the United States over the past two decades. My conclusion on farm income is that we are not yet out of the woods in determining for sure what its size distribution is or was at any one time, let alone determining what changes in the distribution may have taken place over time.

The two accompanying tables were constructed in part to assemble the available information relevant to the size distribution of farm income. They also provide a basis for appraising the Current Population Survey farm income data in the light of one or two of the tests applied to the 1950 census data by D. Gale Johnson in his paper in this volume.

Table 1 shows the distribution of farm-operator families and unrelated individuals by size class of net cash farm income for all available years from 1945 through 1954. In addition to the regular annual CPS distributions of farm self-employment income, the table includes for comparison the original and adjusted distributions from the 1946 survey by the then Bureau of Agricultural Economics (now the Agricultural Marketing Service) and the unadjusted distribution of farm operators by income from farm, business, or profession as reported in *Farms and Farm People*.[1]

Table 2 shows the distribution of rural farm families and unrelated individuals by size class of total net cash income for all years from 1944 through 1954 except 1946. In addition to the regular CPS distributions, this table includes the 1950 census distribution for the year 1949.

In both tables the distributions are supplemented by:

1. Estimates of median income taken usually from published sources
2. Estimates of mean income derived from the distributions
3. Computed totals of income obtained by multiplying numbers reporting by the calculated arithmetic means of the income distributions

[1] *Farms and Farm People*, Bureau of the Census, 1953.

TABLE 1

Distribution of Farm-operator Families and Unrelated Individuals by Size of Net Cash Farm Income, 1945–1946 and 1949–1954

| NET CASH FARM INCOME | | *1945* | *1946* BAE | | *1949* | | *1950* | *1951* | *1952* | *1953* | *1954* |
|---|---|---|---|---|---|---|---|---|---|---|---|
| | | CPS | *As Re-ported* | *Ad-justed* [a] | CPS | *1950 Census* [b] | CPS | CPS | CPS | CPS | CPS |
| | | | | | (*number in thousands*) | | | | | | |
| Total reporting [c] | | 4,100 | 5,859 | 5,859 | 4,897 | 3,643 | 4,707 | 4,331 | 3,923 | 4,385 | 4,018 |
| | | | | | (*per cent*) | | | | | | |
| Income class: | Class mean: [d] | | | | | | | | | | |
| Under $ 500 | $ 20 | 46.9 | 56.5 | 51.3 | 44.0 | 23.9 | 38.8 | 34.2 | 32.5 | 43.1 | 42.8 |
| $ 500– 999 | 750 | 17.5 | 13.5 | 10.6 | 15.6 | 18.6 | 12.4 | 15.3 | 14.2 | 13.2 | 15.3 |
| 1,000– 1,999 | 1,480 | 18.4 | 13.3 | 13.2 | 16.5 | 23.6 | 16.3 | 19.3 | 15.8 | 15.6 | 16.8 |
| 2,000– 2,999 | 2,450 | 10.0 | 6.3 | 6.9 | 10.1 | 13.6 | 12.1 | 12.8 | 13.9 | 11.6 | 11.2 |
| 3,000– 3,999 | 3,450 | 2.5 | 3.5 | 4.7 | 6.1 | 8.2 | 8.2 | 7.3 | 9.3 | 4.4 | 5.1 |
| 4,000– 4,999 | 4,450 | 2.2 | 2.4 | 3.6 | 2.2 | 4.3 | 4.2 | 3.0 | 5.4 | 4.1 | 3.5 |
| 5,000– 5,999 | 5,450 | 1.0 | 1.2 | 2.4 | 1.5 | 2.4 | 2.5 | 1.8 | 2.8 | 2.4 | 1.9 |
| 6,000– 9,999 | 7,630 | 1.2 | 2.0 | 3.3 | 2.7 | 3.7 | 2.8 | 3.5 | 3.9 | 4.0 | 1.8 |
| 10,000 and over | 17,000 | 0.3 | 1.3 | 4.0 | 1.3 | 1.7 | 2.7 | 2.8 | 2.2 | 1.6 | 1.6 |
| | | | | | (*dollars*) | | | | | | |
| Median income [e] | | 591 | 353 | 476 | 691 | 1,260 | 948 | 1,021 | 1,217 | 758 | 737 |
| Mean income [f] | | 1,039 | 1,130 | 1,839 | 1,435 | 2,003 | 1,917 | 1,947 | 2,073 | 1,665 | 1,491 |

continued on next page

TABLE 1, continued

| NET CASH FARM INCOME | 1945 CPS | 1946 BAE As Reported | 1946 BAE Adjusted [a] | 1949 CPS | 1949 1950 Census [b] | 1950 CPS | 1951 CPS | 1952 CPS | 1953 CPS | 1954 CPS |
|---|---|---|---|---|---|---|---|---|---|---|
| | | | | (billions of dollars) | | | | | | |
| Computed total | 4.3 | 6.6 | 10.8 | 7.0 | 7.3 | 9.0 | 8.4 | 8.1 | 7.3 | 6.0 |
| AMS total | 9.3 | 11.0 | 11.0 | 10.1 | 10.1 | 9.3 | 10.8 | 9.9 | 9.6 | 8.2 |
| | | | | (per cent) | | | | | | |
| Computed as % of AMS total | 46 | 60 | 98 | 69 | 72 | 97 | 78 | 82 | 76 | 73 |

AMS = Agricultural Marketing Service, BAE = Bureau of Agricultural Economics (now Agricultural Marketing Service), and CPS = Current Population Survey.

[a] Adjusted to account for an earlier version of the AMS total for 1946.

[b] The unadjusted distribution of farm operators by income from farm, business, or profession as given on page 33 of *Farms and Farm People,* Bureau of the Census, 1953.

[c] The BAE survey number for 1946 was expanded to the 1945 Census of Agriculture number of farms. Numbers for other years are expanded sample numbers.

[d] To allow for net losses in net cash farm income, the average for the lowest class was taken at only $20. Means assumed for the thousand-dollar classes, a little below the midpoints, were designed to give as nearly as possible the same results as would the use of midpoints of five-hundred-dollar classes. For the class from $6,000 to $9,999, an attempt was made to approximate the actual mean of the cases. An average of $17,000 was assumed for the open-end class above $10,000.

[e] Medians were derived from five-hundred-dollar classes.

[f] Means were derived on the basis of the assumed class means shown above.

4. Corresponding Agricultural Marketing Service income totals, derived as Johnson derived his 1949 totals in his Table 3
5. The computed totals (3) as percentages of the AMS totals (4)

Johnson found that aggregates computed from distributions of income of persons were larger than those computed from distributions of families and unrelated individuals. Similar calculations for the CPS rural farm distributions also indicated somewhat the same tendency, although the differences were far less than those in the 1950 census. However, for farm self-employment income alone there has been no consistent difference in the aggregates computed from the two types of distribution. Tables 1 and 2 are based on distributions for families and unrelated individuals because in Table 1 only this sort of distribution of farm self-employment income may properly be compared with the BAE distributions for 1946 and with the 1950 census distribution from *Farms and Farm People*. The class intervals used in the tables are the least common denominator for the surveys included.

### *Farm Income Totals and Their Relative Coverage*

The AMS totals of Table 1 are conceptually the same as the census and CPS data on farm self-employment income—insofar as the latter may be said to be conceptually fixed in the single-question approach. Doubts and uncertainties derive from the possibility that gross receipts may be reported instead of net income; respondents to a single question on farm income may or may not include the value of inventory changes; all legitimate deductions, including depreciation, may not have been taken into account; and finally, as Johnson notes, capital expenditures may be deducted instead of depreciation.

The AMS totals of farm income, themselves subject to an unknown margin of error, are, however, as accurate as thirty years of continuous work can make them. During that time the Department of Agriculture's crop and livestock reporting system, its monthly price reports, the quinquennial agricultural census, and other statistical reporting systems have been developed in part to provide data necessary for the estimation of aggregate farm income and expenditures. These reporting systems are far from perfect, and the estimates of farm income based on them are in no sense absolute in their reliability. But they are unquestionably more reliable than the Census Bureau's survey data on farm income. These data, subject to the uncertainties noted above, are also subject to the underreporting and the other response errors typical of income surveys

TABLE 2

Distribution of Rural Farm Families and Unrelated Individuals by Size of Net Cash Total Income, 1944–1945 and 1947–1954

| NET CASH TOTAL INCOME | | 1944 CPS | 1945 CPS | 1947 CPS | 1948 CPS | 1949 CPS | 1949 1950 Census | 1950 CPS | 1951 CPS | 1952 CPS | 1953 CPS | 1954 CPS |
|---|---|---|---|---|---|---|---|---|---|---|---|---|
| | | | | | | *(number in thousands)* | | | | | | |
| Total reporting | | 6,516 | 6,496 | 7,468 | 7,589 | 6,340 | 6,058 | 6,358 | 6,374 | 6,122 | 5,747 | 5,840 |
| | | | | | | *(per cent)* | | | | | | |
| Income class: | Class mean: | | | | | | | | | | | |
| Under $ 500 | $ 200 | 24.4 | 23.2 | 15.9 | 17.0 | 22.5 | 20.1 | 19.9 | 14.1 | 15.8 | 19.5 | 19.1 |
| $ 500– 999 | 750 | 20.7 | 18.9 | 15.1 | 13.9 | 15.0 | 15.4 | 12.9 | 13.4 | 13.4 | 12.6 | 12.4 |
| 1,000– 1,999 | 1,480 | 25.4 | 27.4 | 25.1 | 23.0 | 25.4 | 23.8 | 21.5 | 23.5 | 20.6 | 19.2 | 23.5 |
| 2,000– 2,999 | 2,450 | 14.9 | 16.6 | 16.6 | 18.2 | 16.5 | 16.7 | 18.2 | 17.5 | 16.8 | 14.3 | 14.0 |
| 3,000– 3,999 | 3,450 | 7.1 | 6.1 | 9.8 | 12.8 | 9.8 | 10.1 | 12.5 | 12.4 | 12.2 | 11.1 | 11.1 |
| 4,000– 4,999 | 4,450 | 2.9 | 3.8 | 5.0 | 5.4 | 4.0 | 5.3 | 5.7 | 7.6 | 8.1 | 7.9 | 7.4 |
| 5,000– 5,999 | 5,450 | 1.5 | 1.5 | 4.4 | 3.3 | 2.5 | 3.1 | 3.2 | 3.6 | 4.7 | 5.9 | 3.8 |
| 6,000– 9,999 | 7,630 | 1.6 | 2.0 | 5.5 | 4.2 | 3.1 | 3.9 | 4.2 | 6.0 | 6.1 | 7.3 | 6.8 |
| 10,000 and over | 17,000 | 1.5 | 0.5 | 2.6 | 2.2 | 1.2 | 1.6 | 1.9 | 1.9 | 2.3 | 2.2 | 1.9 |
| | | | | | | *(dollars)* | | | | | | |
| Median income | | 1,157 | 1,291 | 1,752 | 1,814 | 1,462 | 1,567 | 1,785 | 1,953 | 2,011 | 1,915 | 1,760 |
| Mean income | | 1,778 | 1,699 | 2,585 | 2,481 | 2,031 | 2,240 | 2,403 | 2,648 | 2,743 | 2,755 | 2,583 |
| | | | | | | *(billions of dollars)* | | | | | | |
| Computed total | | 11.6 | 11.0 | 19.3 | 18.8 | 12.9 | 13.6 | 15.3 | 16.9 | 16.8 | 15.8 | 15.1 |
| AMS total | | 15.1 | 15.4 | 20.0 | 19.0 | 17.2 | 17.2 | 16.6 | 18.5 | 18.3 | 17.7 | 16.0 |
| | | | | | | *(per cent)* | | | | | | |
| Computed as % of AMS total | | 77 | 71 | 97 | 99 | 75 | 79 | 92 | 91 | 92 | 89 | 94 |

The notes to Table 1 on class means and the distribution medians and means apply here also, except that, for the lowest class, $200 rather than $20 was assumed as the mean on the grounds that other sources of income would at least partly offset any losses.

but perhaps more serious for farm income than for other types of income. And finally, the farm operator sample in the CPS has never been large enough to assure consistent results from one year to the next. Thus, since there can be no question of the superior reliability of the AMS estimates of farm income, both in absolute level and in year-to-year change, it is quite legitimate to use the AMS totals to check the adequacy of the census data, as in Johnson's appraisal and in the last line of Table 1.

The CPS coverage of farm self-employment income was relatively poor in 1945, the first year shown, but not much worse than that of the unadjusted BAE survey results for the following year. The CPS and the census provided about the same coverage of total farm income in 1949, despite marked differences in practically all other aspects of the income distribution for that year. The best coverage of all was provided by the CPS distribution for 1950, which accounted for 97 per cent of the AMS total. Since 1950, the CPS coverage of farm income has tended to decline in percentage terms. However, the actual dollar shortage has remained somewhere around $2 billion, and this fairly constant amount has been an increasing percentage of the declining total of farm income.

The percentage coverage in the last line of the table depends just as much on the number reported in the top line as it does on the computed average of farm income. The number obtained in 1945 was much too low, but from 1949 or 1950 to 1954 the number reporting farm self-employment income to the CPS declined about in line with the number of farms found in the 1950 and 1954 agricultural censuses. The CPS numbers are on a lower level than those of the agricultural census, however, approximately 700,000 farms having apparently been missed by the CPS. The decline in the CPS number was also rather erratic. For example, the increase in number from 1952 to 1953 was probably not a real increase, but simply the result of the new sample design first adopted in 1953.

So much for the aggregates of farm income and their relative coverage. What about the size distribution of farm income? Table 1 illustrates the uncertainties in this area better than Table 2 because the size distribution of farm self-employment income is the main issue.

### *Comparison of Census and CPS Size Distributions*

The census distribution for 1949, taken from *Farms and Farm People,* seems entirely out of line with all the other distributions of net cash farm income. A single question was used in all the surveys shown in Table 1 except the BAE survey for 1946, which used a detailed questionnaire. But the question asked in the 1950 census was less satisfactory than that asked in the CPS in most years, and it was asked by comparatively untrained enumerators. The divergence in the 1950 census distribution, therefore, probably should be taken as a reason for rejecting it entirely, not for preferring it to all the others (a conclusion contrary to the concensus at the time *Farms and Farm People* was first published).

The CPS distributions, with some exceptions, tend to change from year to year about as one would expect. Since some recipients of farm income are regularly omitted, if the distributions could be adjusted for these omissions, they might tie in fairly well with the adjusted BAE distribution for 1946.

This is just a guess—not a firm conclusion. We still do not know the true size distribution of farm income, and I think we are past the point where we can continue to ignore our ignorance.

The comparison of census and AMS income totals in Table 2 provides only a rough check for consistency between the two sets of data. In fact, the percentages in the last line of Table 2 are not nearly so good a test of the adequacy of the census data as those in Table 1, because the AMS totals in Table 2 are neither exactly comparable with the census data nor are they entirely independent of them.

### *Limitations of AMS Estimates*

Three steps are required to translate the Table 1 data on net cash farm income to the Table 2 concept of net cash total income of rural farm families:

1. Subtraction of farm income from urban farms and farm income received by nonresident operators of rural farms
2. Addition of cash farm wages and net farm rents received by rural farm residents
3. Addition of total money income received by rural farm residents from nonagricultural sources, including transfer payments

There is not enough information available to separate and deduct item 1 from the AMS totals, but the amount is probably relatively small. The AMS totals also do not include transfer payments (item 3). The exclusion of transfer payments originated in the historical requirements for the measurement of income parity for agriculture, but in recent years inadequate information has been the main reason for not including them.

The total of transfer payments received by the farm population may be fairly large, and their omission from the AMS totals seems to have more than offset the continued inclusion of nonresident farm income. The net result is that the dollar discrepancies between computed and AMS totals are generally smaller in Table 2 than in Table 1, even though Table 2 represents the more comprehensive income totals. If transfer payments could be added to the AMS totals in Table 2, the absolute differences in the totals might then be of about the same order of magnitude as those shown in Table 1 for farm income alone. This probability brings out the second weakness in the AMS totals—their partial dependence on census, CPS, and other survey-type sources of information.

The AMS estimates of income of the farm population from nonfarm sources are based on various survey benchmarks. For one of these the census income data from *Farms and Farm People* and the CPS income data for 1950 (when more questions than usual were asked) were actually combined to provide a benchmark estimate for the AMS series. Estimates of farm wages are based mainly on the agricultural census, but the fraction estimated to have been received by farm residents is based on CPS information also. To repeat, Table 2 does not provide any test of CPS coverage of off-farm income comparable to that provided for farm income in Table 1. Such income may be understated in both the AMS and CPS income data for rural farm families, but in the absence of independent-check data there is no way of proving it.

Despite these difficulties, some interest still attaches to the percentages in the last line of Table 2. The decline in recent years shown in Table 1 is not duplicated in Table 2, apparently because of the higher totals of income involved and of the stabilizing influence of off-farm income. Thus a fairly constant dollar discrepancy in both tables represents an increasing percentage of a declining total in Table 1, but a fairly steady percentage of a somewhat more stable total in Table 2.

## *Limitations of Census Data*

The CPS surveys for 1947 and 1948 used fewer questions than those for other years,[2] apparently as an experiment, and the procedure was followed in the 1950 census. Self-employment income was not obtained separately as farm and nonfarm income. And for these

[2] See the table provided by Edwin D. Goldfield in this volume on the characteristics of the various CPS income surveys.

two years the CPS coverage of total rural farm money income was better than for any other year before or since. There is considerable evidence that a single question on farm income obtains "more total income" than a detailed questionnaire covering both gross income and expenses. The CPS results for 1947 and 1948 carry the matter a step further and suggest that even more total income may be obtained if no separate question on farm self-employment income is asked.

There has been a tendency to accept the Census Bureau's results on farm income without too much scrutiny, probably on the simple assumption that a gift horse should not be examined too closely. In view of the new information made available by the Bureau in this volume, and in view of the comparisons presented in Tables 1 and 2, I am inclined to agree with Leon Pritzker and Alfred Sands when they argue that the best procedure is not necessarily the one that produces the most income. In fact, aside from the cost, I would now favor use of a much more detailed questionnaire on farm income. For the 1960 census, I think the minimum requirement is for a separate question on farm self-employment income, preceded by one on gross income.

Another noteworthy aspect of Table 2 is the relatively poor CPS coverage of rural farm income in 1949. It is hard to say what may have gone wrong in the April 1950 survey for the year 1949, but I am convinced that something did, and that the 1949 results are not at all comparable with the CPS farm income data for other years.

In view of these problems, I think the Census Bureau was remiss in allowing the recent publication of a time series chart showing annual CPS median incomes of rural farm families in both current and constant dollars from 1947 through 1954.[3] The text of the release contains no explicit discussion of the reliability of the annual medians of rural farm family income plotted in the chart, which follow:

| | | | |
|---|---|---|---|
| 1947 | $1,963 | 1951 | $2,131 |
| 1948 | 2,036 | 1952 | 2,226 |
| 1949 | 1,587 | 1953 | 2,131 |
| 1950 | 1,970 | 1954 | 1,973 |

These are for families alone, excluding unrelated individuals, so they are uniformly higher than the medians given in Table 2. However, they are directly related to the CPS distributions of Table 2, and the year-to-year change in the medians is similar to that in Table 2.

On the whole, I think these figures are probably fairly good, and

[3] *Current Population Reports—Consumer Income,* Bureau of the Census, December 1955, Series P-60, No. 20, Figure 2.

in any case I am not in a position to prove them definitely in error. If it is assumed that only money income is reported to the CPS, with all inventory changes excluded, and if it is further assumed that medians change from one year to the next in the same direction as arithmetic means do, then the direction of year-to-year median change seems to be in error for only two of the seven years shown in the chart—1947 to 1948 and 1949 to 1950. A look at Table 2, however, shows that from 1947 to 1948 the arithmetic mean of incomes calculated from the CPS distributions actually declined, whereas the median income rose. The rising median has to be taken on faith in such a situation, which leaves only the change from 1949 to 1950 in definite conflict with changes in economic conditions in those years.

My criticism is directed not so much at the figures themselves as at their publication as a time series in both current and constant dollars without any directly associated discussion of their reliability. Near the end of the same report appears one of the customary illustrative calculations of standard errors for the included median incomes. Use for the first time in such calculations of the median for rural farm families as an illustration provides, apparently by chance, the standard error for the 1954 median shown in the chart.

The Census Bureau usually uses the criterion of twice the standard error as a test for its textual statements about changes in income from one year to the next.[4] Twice the reported standard error for the 1954 median income of rural farm families provides an income range which includes all the medians shown in the chart from 1947 through 1954, except those for 1949 and 1952. A range of three standard errors would include 1952 as well; as previously indicated, I think the median for 1949 belongs in a different universe. What is actually needed, of course, is some measure of the reliability of the differences between medians, not of the medians themselves.[5]

The Census Bureau's reports usually include a routine statement to the effect that "the sampling variability of a difference between two estimates depends upon the sampling variability of each of the

[4] *Current Population Reports—Consumer Income,* December 1953, Series P-60, No. 14, p. 8.

[5] Herman P. Miller defends the Census Bureau practice in his comment on this paper. But there is a simple device for indicating both the existence and size of sampling errors on a line chart. This is to add two dotted lines, one above and one below the solid line of medians, to indicate the range for one or two standard errors above and below the median for each year. The Census Bureau might well consider adopting this as standard practice. On this particular chart, however, the spread between dotted lines would have been so wide as to put the chart itself in question.

estimates and the correlation between them." Even if the ordinary lay reader understands this statement, he has no way of interpreting the correlation factor involved, and so the statement is simply another form of lip service to the formulas of the sampling specialists. I suspect that the standard error of the difference between any two of the medians shown in the chart is larger than that for either median.

A bill introduced in the Congress early in 1956 requiring the Census Bureau to develop annual data on farm income by economic class of farm would, if enacted, require the Census Bureau to do every year what has been done only once before, in *Farms and Farm People*. A greatly expanded farm sample which this bill would require may be the best possible answer to some of the problems I have been discussing. The experiments that would also be necessary before this bill could be satisfactorily implemented might well provide the basis for a proper evaluation of the relative merits of the global versus the detailed approach in the collection of farm income data.

Given a little more time, perhaps we can even provide a definite answer to the question: What *is* the size distribution of farm income?

## COMMENT

HERMAN P. MILLER, BUREAU OF THE CENSUS

In his concluding paragraphs, Ernest W. Grove criticizes the Census Bureau for publishing a chart showing the median income of rural-farm families for 1947–1954 without an "explicit discussion of the reliability of the annual medians." He amplifies this remark by adding that in his opinion publication of a time series based on sample data should provide the reader with "some measure of the reliability of the differences between medians, not of the medians themselves."

Since Grove is familiar with the fact that all statements in Census Bureau releases are thoroughly checked for statistical significance, I assume he makes this criticism because he thinks that each reader should be enabled to make such checks for himself, perhaps even to test comparisons not shown in the published report, though for this the Census Bureau would have to present measures of reliability of the differences between all possible combinations of medians. The Census Bureau does attempt to aid the reader by pointing out significant relationships based on its interpretation of the reliability of the results, and it presents tables and specific illustrations providing a general indication of the reliability of the data. Although the Bureau has not published as much information on this subject as Grove (and many Census Bureau officials) would like to see, it probably has gone further in this area than any other organization, and looks forward to expanding its output of such information in the near future with the aid of electronic computing equipment.

Although I agree with Grove that more data on reliability are desirable, I am convinced that the informed user of census data can make his own tests of significance from the measures of reliability already appearing regularly. The established way to present estimates of reliability is in general tables which show the standard errors for a range of numbers and percentages. Such tables, permitting users to test comparisons based on any of the information shown in a report, and therefore more valuable than illustrative estimates of the standard errors for specific characteristics, appear in each of the family income reports (except in the most recent one, for which the data were not available because of expansion of the Current Population Survey sample). I suspect that Grove is searching for a simple device which would enable the "ordinary lay reader" to make his own tests of significance. The Census Bureau tries to assist people in the use of its data. But if such a reader wants to make tests of significance, he must learn some of the rudiments of statistics.

Grove may be right in his assertion that AMS farm income aggregates are more reliable than those prepared from census estimates. However, since he admits that "the AMS totals of farm income [are] themselves subject to an unknown margin of error," he cannot logically conclude that "they are unquestionably more reliable than the Census Bureau's survey data on farm income."

At one point Grove says that "the farm operator sample in the CPS has never been large enough to assure consistent results from one year to the next." Since the size of the sample affects only the standard error of the estimates and not the consistency of the results, what Grove actually means is that he thinks the standard error of the estimated median income of farm families in the CPS is too large. In view of the sizeable reporting errors which undoubtedly exist in the CPS farm income estimates, it is difficult to understand the insistence upon the further reduction of the relatively small sampling errors. In 1954 and earlier years the standard error of the estimated median income of rural farm families was only about $100. In 1955 and later years the standard error will be reduced because of the sample expansion from about 21,000 to about 35,000 interviewed households. As Grove well knows, income estimates derived from sample surveys are subject to response errors as well as sampling errors. With limited funds, these two types of errors can be dealt with only by striving for an optimum position, not necessarily reached by increasing the size of the sample.

# A Method of Identifying Chronic Low-Income Groups from Cross-Section Survey Data

ELEANOR M. SNYDER, BUREAU OF LABOR STATISTICS,
DEPARTMENT OF LABOR

## *An Estimate of the Size of the Urban Population with Low Economic Status in 1950*

### MEASUREMENT OF ECONOMIC STATUS

The continuing prevalence of poverty during the twentieth century, despite the rapid industrial expansion and the rise in national income and standards of living throughout the Western world, has led to numerous studies of low-income groups. These studies have brought about a general recognition of the fact that some people are poor primarily as a result of the operations of the economic system rather than because of any individual failure or inadequacy.

But present statistics do not provide reliable estimates of the size of the group whose low income has come to be considered a matter of public concern. A distribution of the population by economic status would be extremely helpful in determining public policy,[1] evaluating current welfare programs, and assessing current unmet needs. Existing empirical data on family income, however, do not permit a direct measure of economic status, since none of the comprehensive field surveys obtained income histories of identical families for more than two successive years. And, "It is now generally recognized that the incomes of individuals and families in a particular year may deviate considerably from the averages over a number of years. The distribution for one year includes individuals with incomes below their average in the lower part of the income range and individuals with incomes above their average in the higher income brackets." [2]

Classification of the population by economic status, however,

[1] Economic status may be defined as annual income averaged over a period long enough to eliminate the effect of the transitory factors that cause a family's income in any one year to deviate significantly from customary levels. Milton Friedman and Dorothy S. Brady conclude from entirely different models that the period may be as short as three years for nonfarm families. An analysis of continuous records of farm families' income indicates that the required time span may be longer than four years for farm families, and may vary by type of farm.

[2] Dorothy S. Brady, preface to Herman P. Miller, *Income of the American People,* Wiley, 1955.

would not in itself identify those whose income is "too low" or "inadequate" and who therefore are entitled to public or private aid. The dividing line between adequacy and inadequacy is not fixed. Adequacy has most frequently been measured crudely by the standards prevailing during the period of investigation; if poverty is defined as a position below the average, poverty will always exist. At present some families and individuals are considered poor simply because they possess less than others. But in absolute terms, their resources may be equal to or greater than the resources of those classified as moderately well off in an earlier period.

Many methods of scaling have been devised in the past, chiefly by sociologists interested in the measurement of social status and other aspects of social behavior. Until recent years economists devoted little attention to the problems of measuring economic status. This paper discusses the conceptual and methodological framework underlying estimates of the size of the 1950 urban population with low economic status contained in a recent study sponsored by the Franklin D. Roosevelt Foundation.[3]

The study used a concept developed in England more than fifty years ago. In identifying the poor, Booth and Rountree defined the dividing line between adequacy and inadequacy as the cost of a minimum standard budget.[4] Such a definition of poverty is in es-

[3] This study, now being readied for publication, was conducted by the author under the direction of Isador Lubin, Chairman of the Executive Committee of the Franklin D. Roosevelt Foundation. Excerpts from the report are contained in "Characteristics of the Low-Income Population and Related Federal Programs," in *Selected Materials Assembled by the Staff of the Subcommittee on Low-Income Families,* Joint Committee on the Economic Report, Joint Committee print, 84th Cong., 1st sess., pp. 43–51.

See also "The Aged Low-Income Population," mimeographed, a brief statement prepared for the use of the Federal–State Conference on Aging, in Washington, D. C., June 5–7, 1956.

Estimates of the portion of the low-income urban population whose economic status is also low were based on special tabulations of the Bureau of Labor Statistics 1950 Survey of Consumer Expenditures.

[4] In three surveys conducted in York, Rountree measured the extent of poverty in 1900, 1936, and 1950 in this way, and studied the characteristics of the population living at substandard levels. For each period, the "poverty line" was redefined in terms of current prices. The 1950 report was primarily a study of the extent to which the various government welfare and income security programs put into effect chiefly after 1936 had succeeded in reducing the number of poor families. He concluded that the 3 per cent of the working class population classified as poor in 1950 would be raised to 22 per cent if the welfare measures were eliminated. (See the following sources: B. Seebohm Rountree, *Poverty: A Study of Town Life,* London, Macmillan, 1901, and *Poverty and Progress: A Second Social Survey of York,* London, Longmans, 1942; B. Seebohm Rountree and G. R. Lavers, *Poverty and the Welfare State: A Third Social Survey of York,* London, Longmans, 1951; and Charles Booth, *Labour and the Life of the People,* London, Williams & Norgate, 1889.)

sence subjectively determined; the contents and therefore the costs vary from one "standard" budget to another. Yet most definitions of poverty are in fact based on a concept of income inadequacy. As Rountree said: [5]

"To say that a family is in poverty may mean that they have not enough available income to provide the essential needs of physical efficiency, no matter how wisely and economically they spend their money. On the other hand, it may mean that they are obviously living in want and squalor, notwithstanding the fact that their income is sufficient to maintain them in a state of physical efficiency."

Most studies of the poor imply the use of a definition of poverty similar to Rountree's first sentence. In the eighteenth and nineteenth centuries "essential needs of physical efficiency" generally were literally construed to include only purely physical requirements, without regard to social or cultural needs. During the last half-century or so budget makers have come to recognize that physical efficiency, in a productive sense, is dependent on meeting at least a minimum level of social needs also. In the United States today, minimum-level budgets, such as state-prepared budgets for working women developed to assist minimum wage boards in fixing wage rates for women, include a modest amount for recreation, contributions, reading matter, and so forth. Similarly, the Bureau of Labor Statistics "city worker's family budget," as described by its technical advisory committee, defines the necessary minimum in terms of items needed "for health, efficiency, social participation, and the maintenance of self-respect and the respect of others." [6]

The Roosevelt Foundation study adopted this broader concept of the necessary minimum. Poverty was said to exist among families unable in the long run to obtain the necessary minimum, the minimum being defined as the dollar cost of a specified budget. The poor thus are described as families whose economic resources are less than a specified minimum for a continuing period of years, and who therefore possess low economic status. Such a definition is not based on the personal opinions of the families classified as "poor," some of whom would be chagrined at being so labeled.

Families and individuals with current resources (income plus other assets) below the cost of a minimum-level budget, however, do not necessarily have low economic status, since the inadequacy of their resources may be merely temporary. In the identification

[5] Foreword by B. Seebohm Rountree to *Labor, Life and Poverty,* by F. Zweig, London, Gollancz, 1948.

[6] Report of the technical advisory committee (Hazel Kyrk, Chairman), published in *Workers' Budgets in the United States,* Bureau of Labor Statistics, Bull. 927, 1948.

of low-status families, the first step taken in the study was to eliminate all families with current income above the cost of a minimum standard budget. This procedure introduces a downward bias in the estimate since it automatically excludes from the low-status group all families whose incomes were temporarily above the budget position. The income cut-off points used were based on 1950 dollar costs of the goods and services included in two minimum budgets, a city worker's family budget and a companion budget for an elderly couple.[7] Comparable costs for families of different sizes were calculated by applying the equivalent-income scale developed by Dorothy S. Brady.[8]

### IDENTIFICATION OF LOW-INCOME-STATUS FAMILIES

Identification of families whose long-term (as well as current) incomes lie below the budget line could not be achieved by direct measurement because the data were limited to a one-year period, so known relationships between current family income and expenditures for consumption goods and services were used for this purpose. Analyses of family expenditures in relation to income have shown that subsistence levels can be identified and described by such correlations.[9] The progressive levels of living are manifested in the correlations of current income and expenditures by a changing composition of the necessities of life. Engel pointed out about seventy-five years ago that the poorer the family, the greater is the proportion of its total expenditures used for food. At successively higher levels more types of goods and services are added to the list of "essentials" and a correspondingly smaller proportion of income is spent on food and housing.

Families living at the lowest level of income who lack any ap-

[7] The worker's family budget was developed by the BLS in response to a Congressional request "to find out what it costs a worker's family to live in the large cities of the United States" (see *Worker's Budgets in the United States: City Families and Single Persons,* BLS Bull. 927, 1948; and *Family Budget of City Worker, October 1950,* BLS, Bull. 1021, 1951).

The "elderly couples' " budget was designed by the Federal Security Administration to provide a means of evaluating the adequacy, in terms of need, of OASI retirement benefits and assistance programs (see "A Budget for the Elderly Couple," *Social Security Bulletin,* February 1948).

Both budgets were developed to measure the cost of a modest but adequate level of living, and have been rather extensively used by welfare agencies dispensing funds to those in need.

[8] The Brady scale is based on the correlation of family income and saving. The relationship by size of family can be described by logarithmic straight lines which are approximately parallel. The scale and its derivation are given in *Worker's Budgets in the United States: City Families and Single Persons.*

[9] R. G. D. Allen and A. L. Bowley, *Family Expenditure: A Study of Its Variation,* London, King, 1935.

preciable savings or access to credit are compelled to live within their means. But, when families are arrayed by current income, all cross-section expenditure surveys have shown that, on the average, the lowest-income groups incurred some dissaving. The average dissaving of the low-income group as a whole may be explained by the inclusion of families whose current incomes have temporarily fallen below customary levels but who did not lower their expenditures correspondingly. This typically limited response to temporary income reverses is found at both the lower and higher ends of the income distribution, producing the characteristic S-shaped income-consumption curve from cross-section studies.

Thus at the lower end of the income distribution there are differences in the patterns of consumption expenditures of families located at their customary income position and of those who expect that their low income is of relatively short duration, for example, because of short-run illness or unemployment of the chief earner. The latter group also includes younger families in which the chief earner is just commencing his working career and receiving limited earnings, but whose economic background, training, and capacities normally will lead to increasingly higher levels of income. In addition, families with low money income who possess savings or other resources that enable them to maintain an adequate level of consumption, such as the aged living on savings, should not be included in the group with low economic status.

On the average, families with customarily low incomes (that is, with low economic status) apparently do not incur substantial debts; those who dissave represent chiefly the older groups. Moreover, low-income-status families spend a substantial portion of income on the basic essentials, food and housing. On the other hand, families whose economic resources permit an adequate level of living display a higher and more diversified spending pattern and are more prone to go into debt.

Various criteria can be selected as a means of splitting the lower end of the income distribution into these two major groups. In the Roosevelt Foundation study, if one or more of the following criteria was satisfied, it was accepted as an indication that the economic status of the individual family or single consumer was adequate (all criteria applying to 1950), although current income was below the budget level.

1. Home equipment and furnishings expenditures above 10 per cent of current income
2. Purchase of a car

3. Combined food and housing expenditures above current income
4. Purchase of a home

The first criterion, which relates to a consumption category characterized by a high income elasticity, set a limit higher than the average level of expenditures of urban families on this category in 1950 (8 per cent of income) and substantially above the average level of spending of families at the lower end of the income scale. The second and fourth criteria involved relatively large outlays on items whose purchase can be deferred. The third indicated that the family was able to incur debts or dissaving equal to expenditures on items other than food or housing.

The families and single consumers not eliminated by these criteria comprised the group with low economic status as well as low current money income. It would be of some interest to test the stability of the derived distributions in this study by reclassifying on the basis of other possible criteria.

Of the four applied, greater-than-average expenditures on home equipment and furnishings was found to have the greatest relative importance. Over 43 per cent of all consumer units of two or more persons, with incomes below the budget line but excluded from the low-income-status group, were rejected on this account. Among single consumers with below-budget incomes, almost one-half were not included in the group with low economic status because their expenditures on food and housing alone was greater than their total current money income. Table 1 gives the distribution of units with low current income but not with low economic status, by criteria for classification.

According to the findings of the study, over 50 per cent of urban families and single consumers with 1950 incomes under $2,000 also possessed economic resources too limited to maintain an adequate level of living. Across the entire income distribution, almost 19 per cent had low economic status. Cumulated income distributions are shown graphically in Chart 1 for all urban units, for units with adequate economic status, and for units whose economic status was estimated to be low. The following table compares the income distribution of all urban consumer units and of urban units with low economic status in 1950: [10]

In terms of economic welfare, the distribution of a population by current income consists of three components: units with in-

[10] Based on unpublished tabulations from the 1950 BLS Survey of Consumer Expenditures. The distribution of all consumer units was calculated by the author and based on preliminary data. It is expected that the final distribution being

TABLE 1

Urban Consumer Units with Low Current Incomes but Not Low Economic Status, by Criteria for Classification, 1950

| CRITERION | TWO OR MORE PERSONS: Total | Husband-Wife [a] | One Parent | Other [b] | ONE PERSON |
|---|---|---|---|---|---|
| | *(per cent)* | | | | |
| Home equipment and furnishings expenditures above 10% of current income | 43.3 | 40.5 | 62.5 | 51.9 | 28.9 |
| Purchase of a car | 23.4 | 25.6 | 6.1 | 17.5 | 4.5 |
| Combined food and housing expenditures above current income | 6.6 | 6.1 | 9.6 | 8.3 | 44.3 |
| Purchase of a home | 2.1 | 1.9 | 0 | 2.7 | 0.2 |
| Combinations: | | | | | |
| Two criteria | 21.0 | 22.3 | 17.7 | 16.3 | 20.4 |
| Three or more criteria | 3.6 | 3.6 | 4.1 | 3.3 | 1.7 |
| Total: | | | | | |
| Per cent | 100.0 | 100.0 | 100.0 | 100.0 | 100.0 |
| Number, in thousands | 5,338 | 3,573 | 134 | 921 | 710 |

[a] Couples, and families with children.

[b] Doubled-up consumer units.

Source: Unless otherwise noted, the data used in this table and in all succeeding tables and charts are from unpublished tabulations derived from the 1950 Survey of Consumer Expenditures of the Bureau of Labor Statistics. These tabulations were prepared for the Franklin D. Roosevelt Foundation.

comes large enough to provide an adequate level of family living; those with current incomes below the specified standard but with customary incomes above the standard; and the group with usual as well as current incomes below the standard, that is, with low economic status. The modal income class of the three groups shifted

prepared by the BLS, as well as the estimate of the total number of consumer units, will not agree precisely with the estimate given here.

| INCOME CLASS | *All Units* | *Units with Low Economic Status* |
|---|---|---|
| | *(per cent)* | |
| Under $1,000 | 6.3 | 17.8 |
| $ 1,000– 1,999 | 12.4 | 37.2 |
| 2,000– 2,999 | 18.8 | 27.4 |
| 3,000– 3,999 | 23.9 | 14.7 |
| 4,000– 4,999 | 16.9 | 2.6 |
| 5,000– 5,999 | 9.4 | 0.3 |
| 6,000– 7,499 | 6.4 | 0 |
| 7,500– 9,999 | 3.5 | 0 |
| 10,000 and over | 2.4 | 0 |
| Total: | | |
| Per cent | 100.0 | 100.0 |
| Number, in thousands | 33,900 | 6,380 |

Chart 1
Cumulated Income Distribution of All Urban Consumer Units, by Economic Status, 1950

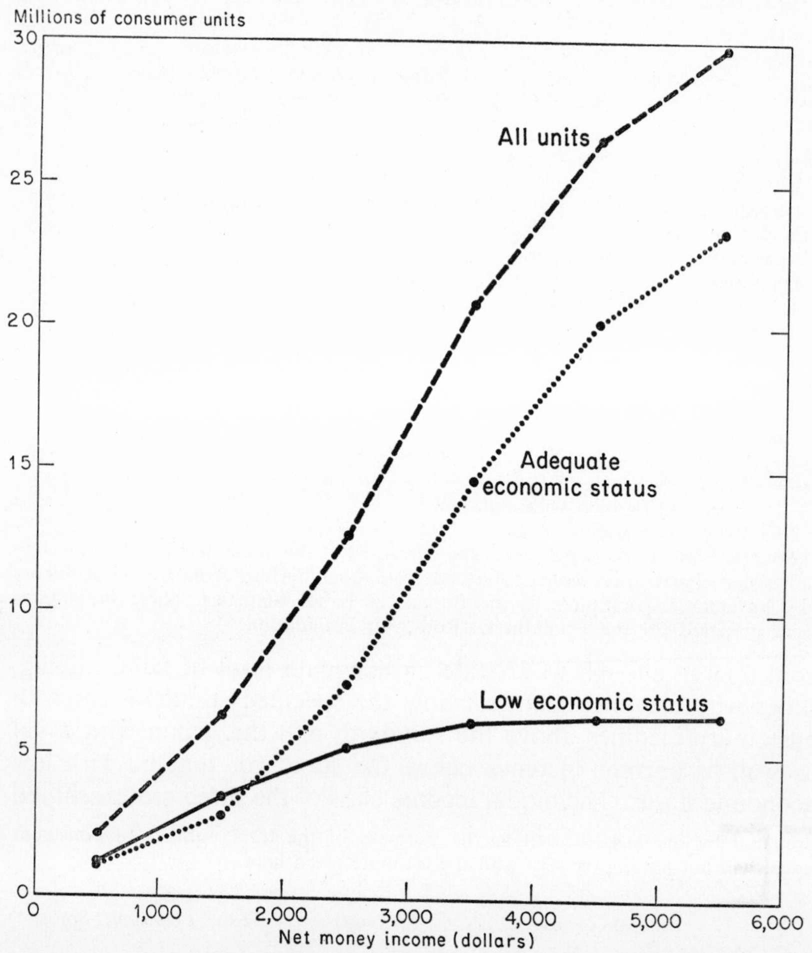


down the income scale, moving from the highest to the lowest economic welfare classification, as Chart 2 illustrates. By definition, the economic status of the third group alone was classified as low. (In Chart 1, the first and second groups were combined and identified as units with adequate economic status.)

The separate distributions by income of single consumers and of consumer units consisting of two or more persons both display a smaller concentration in the lowest income class (under $1,000) for the groups with low economic status compared to the groups

**Chart 2**

**Components of the Total Income Distribution of All Urban Consumer Units, 1950**

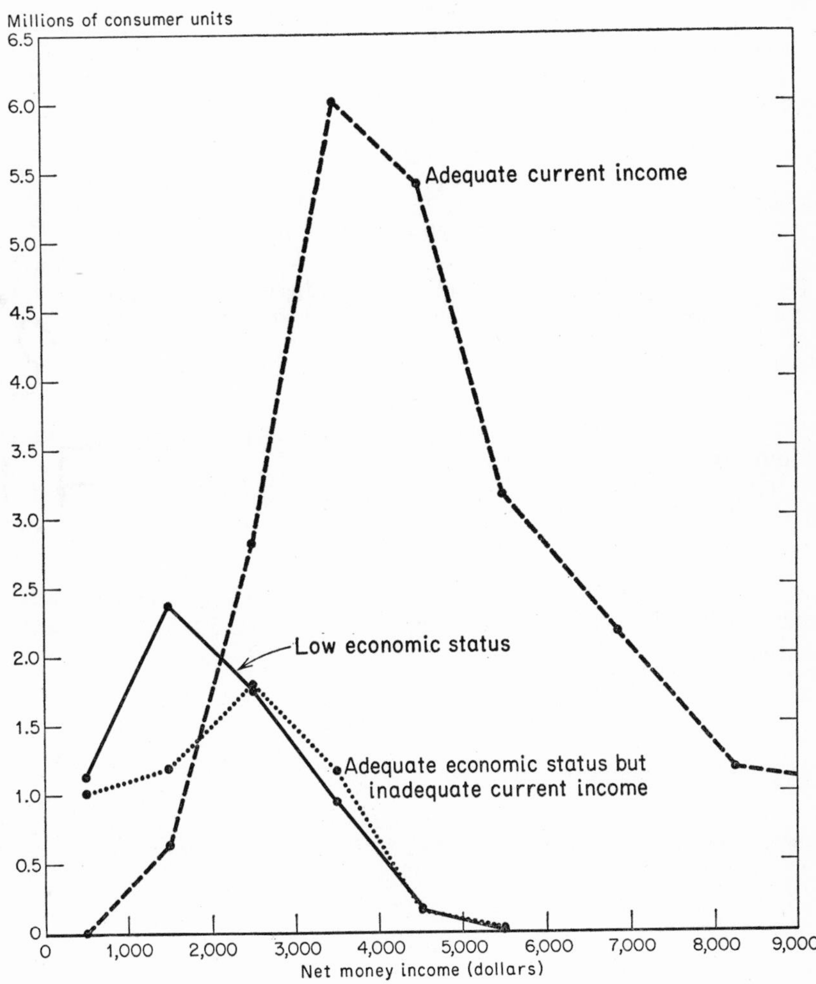


Note: The three separate distributions when combined equal the distribution of all urban units.

with low current income but not low status (see Table 2). The comparison indicates a concentration in the under $1,000 class of families and single persons who possessed economic assets in addition to current income. While 65 per cent of the single individuals with incomes under $1,000 were included in the group estimated to possess low economic status, only 44 per cent of the units of two or more persons with incomes below the budget line were esti-

TABLE 2

Urban Consumer Units with Current Incomes below the Budget Line, by Income Class, 1950

| INCOME CLASS | TWO OR MORE PERSONS: *Low Economic Status* | TWO OR MORE PERSONS: *Adequate Economic Status* | ONE PERSON: *Low Economic Status* | ONE PERSON: *Adequate Economic Status* |
|---|---|---|---|---|
| | | (*per cent*) | | |
| Under $1,000 | 6.2 | 10.8 | 53.1 | 72.3 |
| $1,000– 1,999 | 34.0 | 21.4 | 46.9 | 27.7 |
| 2,000– 2,999 | 36.4 | 38.8 | 0 | 0 |
| 3,000– 3,999 | 19.5 | 25.2 | 0 | 0 |
| 4,000– 4,999 | 3.5 | 3.3 | 0 | 0 |
| 5,000 and over | 0.4 | 0.5 | 0 | 0 |
| Total: | | | | |
| Per cent | 100.0 | 100.0 | 100.0 | 100.0 |
| Number, in thousands | 4,800 | 4,600 | 1,600 | 700 |

mated to have low status. In the next higher income class ($1,000–2,000) 62 per cent of the families with incomes below the budget line, and 81 per cent of the single consumers were classified as substandard.

Adequacy of economic resources was found to vary substantially by type of family; over one-half of broken families (only one parent present) had low economic status, compared to less than 15 per cent of the husband-wife families (see Table 3). It was estimated that, in all, 6.4 million urban consumer units had low economic status.[11]

TABLE 3

Urban Consumer Units, by Economic Status, 1950

| ECONOMIC STATUS | TOTAL: *Number, in thousands* | TOTAL: *Per cent* | TWO OR MORE PERSONS: *Husband-Wife* [a] | TWO OR MORE PERSONS: *One Parent* | TWO OR MORE PERSONS: *Other* [b] | ONE PERSON |
|---|---|---|---|---|---|---|
| | | | | (*per cent*) | | |
| Adequate economic resources | 22,200 | 65.5 | 70.9 | 22.8 | 59.8 | 51.1 |
| Low current income but adequate economic status | 5,300 | 15.7 | 15.6 | 22.0 | 16.1 | 15.2 |
| Low economic status | 6,400 | 18.8 | 13.5 | 55.2 | 24.1 | 33.7 |
| Total: | | | | | | |
| Per cent | | 100.0 | 100.0 | 100.0 | 100.0 | 100.0 |
| Number, in thousands | 33,900 | | 22,900 | 600 | 5,700 | 4,700 |

[a] Couples, and families with children.
[b] Doubled-up consumer units.

[11] Preliminary family size distributions, derived from the BLS Survey of Consumer Expenditures, were applied to preliminary 1950 census population estimates to obtain an estimate of the total number of urban consumer units.

CURRENT EXPENDITURES OF LOW-INCOME FAMILIES

If the procedure described in the previous section effectively identifies those with low economic status within the low-income population, one would expect significant differences in the income-consumption relationships displayed by this group and by the group with low current income but not low economic status, as well as differences in general characteristics. When spending patterns of low-income families with and without low economic status are compared, significant differences emerge. Charts 3 through 5 show

**Chart 3**

**Total Consumption Expenditures and Net Money Income: Husband-Wife Families with Inadequate Current Income in Large Cities, North Central–Northeast Region, by Economic Status, 1950**

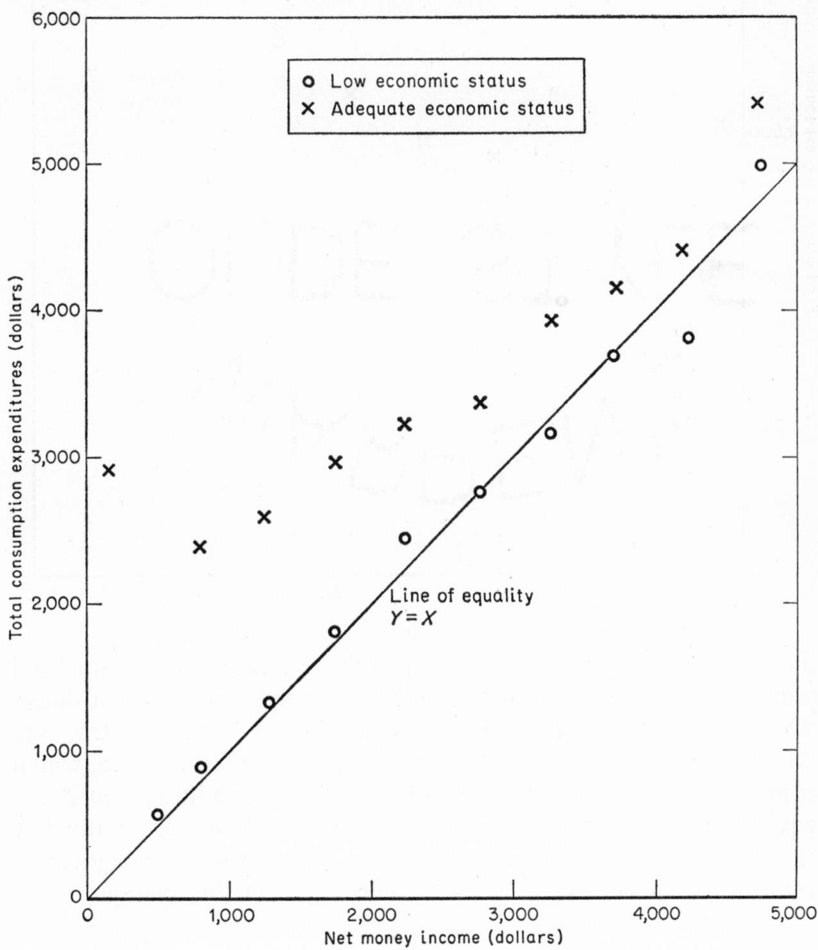

Chart 4

Food and Housing Expenditures and Net Money Income: Husband-Wife Families with Inadequate Current Income in Large Cities, North Central–Northeast Region, by Economic Status, 1950

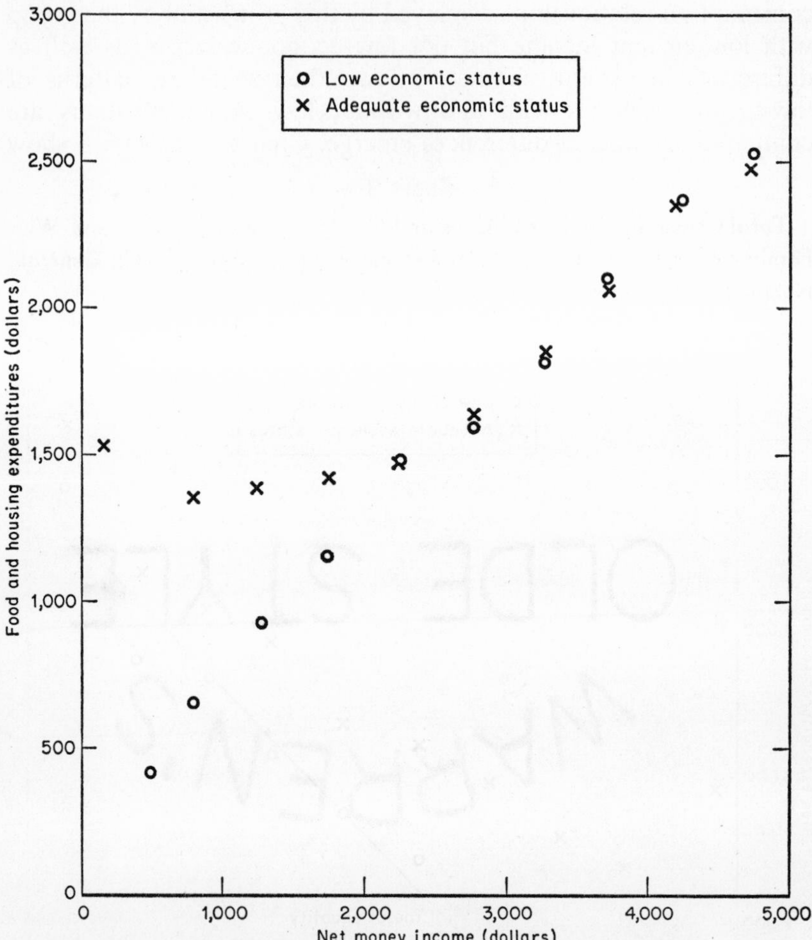


the level of total consumption expenditures, expenditures on food plus housing, and expenditures on home equipment and furnishings of husband-wife families in large cities in the North Central and Northeast regions. The greatest variation is shown in Chart 5, which compares, by income class, average family expenditures on home equipment and furnishings. Families were excluded from the low status group if their expenditures on this consumption category exceeded 10 per cent of current income, and, on the average, those in the total group with low current income but not low economic status spent considerably above this limit (first criterion). Families classified as having low economic status, on the other hand, spent less than 5 per cent on these items. The difference reflects in part significant differences in the age distribution; the low-status group contains substantially fewer younger families, normally heavy purchasers of household durables and furnishings. For 6.7 million urban husband-wife families (including couples, and families with children) with incomes below the budget line, the following tables show (1) the proportion with low or adequate economic status in classes determined by the age of the head:

| AGE OF HEAD (*years*) | *Low Economic Status* (*per cent*) | *Adequate Economic Status* (*per cent*) |
|---|---|---|
| Under 25 | 37.2 | 62.8 |
| 25–34 | 34.6 | 65.4 |
| 35–49 | 47.8 | 52.2 |
| 50–64 | 53.5 | 46.5 |
| 65 and over | 59.7 | 40.3 |
| Total: | | |
| Per cent | 46.3 | 53.7 |
| Number, in thousands | 3,100 | 3,600 |

and (2) the distribution of all these families by the age of the head:

| AGE OF HEAD (*years*) | *Low Economic Status* (*per cent*) | *Adequate Economic Status* (*per cent*) |
|---|---|---|
| Under 25 | 4.7 | 6.9 |
| 25–34 | 20.5 | 33.4 |
| 35–49 | 33.9 | 31.9 |
| 50–64 | 23.5 | 17.6 |
| 65 and over | 17.4 | 10.2 |
| Total: | | |
| Per cent | 100.0 | 100.0 |
| Number, in thousands | 3,100 | 3,600 |

The comparison of food and housing expenditures of the two groups indicates that the third criterion is useful only when applied to the lowest-income families. On the average, there are no significant intergroup differences in the level of spending of families with incomes above $2,500. As shown in Table 1, relatively few families were excluded from the low-economic-status group on this account alone, although it was the most important criterion when applied to single consumers.

## Chart 5

**Home Equipment and Furnishings Expenditures and Net Money Income: Husband-Wife Families with Inadequate Current Income in Large Cities, North Central–Northeast Region, by Economic Status, 1950**

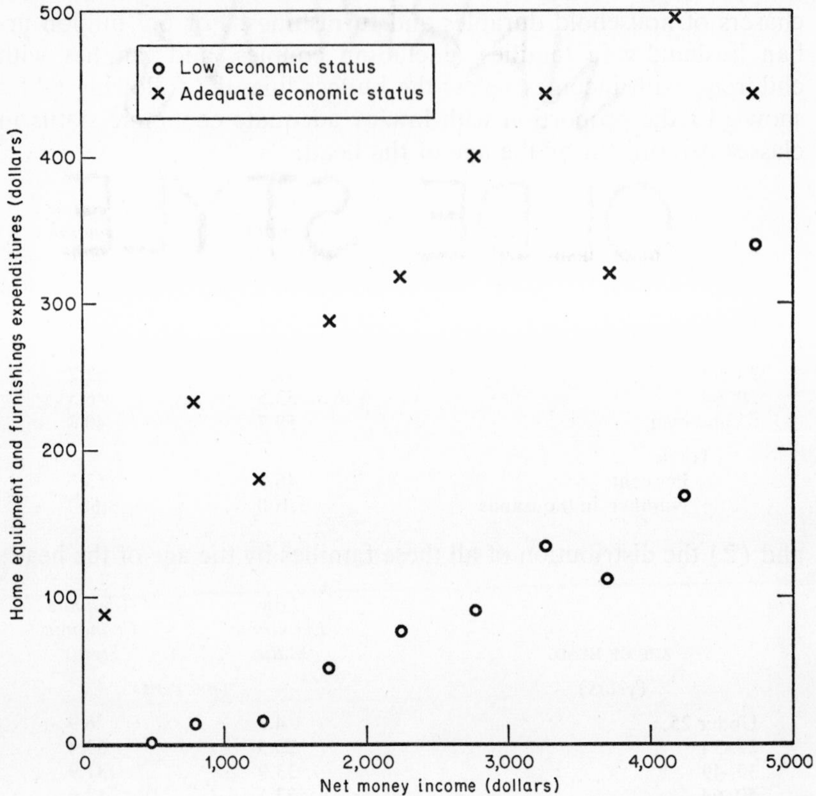


Chart 3 illustrates that expenditures of families with adequate status on the average substantially exceeded current income; this group thus drew on previously accumulated savings or incurred sizeable debts. Families with low economic status spent little if anything beyond the level of their current income; overspending is a luxury in which the "permanently poor" cannot indulge.

### EFFECT OF WORKING DEFINITIONS ON ESTIMATES

Estimates of the size of the group with low economic status in any given population will vary according to the way in which the population is counted: by households, by natural families, by economic units, and so forth.[12] The Roosevelt Foundation study, since it was based primarily on data from the BLS Survey of Consumer Expenditures, used the BLS definition of "consumer unit." The BLS defines a consumer unit as a group of persons who live together and pool income; they live as a single economic unit and in most cases are related by blood or marriage. Most consumer units consist of natural families living alone, but a small proportion are doubled-up families, such as those where aged parents live with married sons or daughters. Some instances of doubling include component families who are being supported by other members of the unit. To the extent that this is true, any measure of the number of families (or single individuals) with either low economic status or low income is biased downward if the estimate being made is based on the distribution of economic units. A detailed examination thus was made of all doubled-up units, regardless of income level, to determine the current income of each of the component families.

In 14 per cent of doubled-up urban units in 1950 there was no indication that the doubling-up was due to economic necessity; every family and single individual in these consumer units had sufficient income to enable them to live alone at an adequate level of income. In another 46 per cent, the combined income of all component families, when pooled, was high enough to provide an adequate level of living for all, although in each unit the income of one or more components was below the budget line. (In relatively few instances, 3 per cent, the economics of joint living arrangements made possible a higher level of living for all components of the group.) In the remaining 40 per cent of doubled-up consumer units, the combined income of all members was below the budget line set for each size of unit. Tables 4 and 5 show the distributions of families and single persons living in doubled-up consumer units.

Husband-wife families represent about 43 per cent of all separate components (families and single persons) of doubled-up units. It seems apparent that husband-wife families also constitute the economic core of the combined unit and provide the largest contribution to its total income.[13] Of all husband-wife families living with others, 71 per cent had incomes adequate to support the family, if not the total unit; whereas only 19 per cent of the one-parent fami-

[12] See, for example, Dorothy S. Brady, "Measurement and Interpretation of the Income Distribution in the United States," mimeographed, International Association for Research in Income and Wealth, Fourth Conference, 1955.

[13] Considering only doubled-up units with low economic status, husband-wife families represented about 30 per cent of the total number of components but contributed 55 per cent of the income of the unit. Single persons (primarily the aged), on the other hand, were 37 per cent of all components but contributed less than 10 per cent of the unit income.

TABLE 4

Components of Doubled-up Urban Consumer Units, by Economic Status of the Unit and Adequacy of Current Income of Components, 1950

| INCOME AND ECONOMIC STATUS | COMPONENTS OF UNIT | |
|---|---|---|
| | *Families* | *Single Individuals* |
| | (*per cent*) | |
| *Adequate unit income and adequate unit economic status* | | |
| Incomes of components: | | |
| All adequate | 13.3 | 10.8 |
| Some inadequate | 47.3 | 51.7 |
| Adequate | 35.3 | 9.7 |
| Inadequate | 12.0 | 42.0 |
| *Inadequate unit income but adequate unit economic status* | | |
| Incomes of components: | | |
| All inadequate | 12.2 | 10.0 |
| Some adequate | 5.8 | 5.6 |
| Adequate | 4.7 | 0.6 |
| Inadequate | 1.1 | 5.0 |
| *Inadequate unit income and low unit economic status* | | |
| Incomes of components: | | |
| All inadequate | 15.5 | 15.8 |
| Some adequate | 5.9 | 6.1 |
| Adequate | 4.0 | 1.4 |
| Inadequate | 1.9 | 4.7 |
| All components: | | |
| Adequate income | 57.3 | 22.5 |
| Inadequate income | 42.7 | 77.5 |
| Total: | | |
| Per cent | 100.0 | 100.0 |
| Number, in thousands | 4,530 | 3,896 |

Note: "Adequate income" is income above the budget line; "inadequate income," below it.

lies with young children, and 23 per cent of the individuals had adequate personal incomes. A distribution within units (classified by economic status) of the separate components indicates which are the dependent groups (see Table 6).

While the BLS survey data permit an estimate of the annual income of each component family and single individual living in doubled-up consumer units, economic status can be measured only on the basis of whole units.[14] A rough estimate was made, however, of the total number of families and single persons with low economic status, including all those in doubled-up units where personal income was below the budget standard. Assuming that of those with current income below the budget line, the proportion

[14] It is not possible to determine consumption expenditures of the individual components of the doubled-up consumer unit; expenditures relate to the unit as a whole.

TABLE 5

Composition of Doubled-up Urban Consumer Units, by Economic Status of the Unit and Adequacy of Current Income of the Components, 1950

| INCOME AND ECONOMIC STATUS | COMPONENTS OF UNIT | | | |
|---|---|---|---|---|
| | *Families* | | | |
| | *Husband-Wife* [a] | *One Parent* | *Other* | *Single Individuals* |
| | *(per cent)* | | | |
| *Adequate unit income and adequate unit economic status* | | | | |
| Incomes of components: | | | | |
| Adequate | 65.4 | 7.6 | 0.4 | 26.6 |
| Inadequate | 15.4 | 9.4 | 0.1 | 75.1 |
| *Inadequate unit income but adequate unit economic status* | | | | |
| Incomes of components: | | | | |
| Adequate | 81.2 | 8.5 | [a] | 10.3 |
| Inadequate | 35.3 | 13.0 | 1.1 | 50.6 |
| *Inadequate unit income and low unit economic status* | | | | |
| Incomes of components: | | | | |
| Adequate | 62.1 | 14.6 | [a] | 23.3 |
| Inadequate | 30.5 | 17.6 | 2.1 | 49.8 |

[a] Less than 0.1 per cent.

Note: "Adequate income" is income above the budget line; "inadequate income," below it.

TABLE 6

Doubled-up Urban Consumer Units: Components with Inadequate Current Income, by Income Class, 1950

| FAMILY INCOME BEFORE TAXES | COMPONENTS OF UNIT | | | | | | | |
|---|---|---|---|---|---|---|---|---|
| | *Total* | | *Families* | | | | *Single Individuals* | |
| | | | | *One Parent, with Children* | | | | |
| | *Number, in thousands* | *Per cent* | *Husband-Wife* | *All under 18 yrs.* | *Oldest 18 yrs. or over* | *Other* | *Men* | *Women* |
| | | | *(per cent)* | | | | | |
| None | 1,012 | 28.8 | 4.7 | 21.1 | 0 | 0 | 32.0 | 48.0 |
| $ 1–$ 999 | 1,231 | 35.0 | 13.4 | 30.8 | 15.1 | 48.8 | 53.2 | 42.2 |
| 1,000– 1,999 | 691 | 19.7 | 30.7 | 26.0 | 38.2 | 42.8 | 14.8 | 9.8 |
| 2,000– 2,999 | 381 | 10.9 | 28.8 | 16.8 | 35.8 | 8.4 | 0 | 0 |
| 3,000– 3,999 | 168 | 4.8 | 18.8 | 5.3 | 9.6 | 0 | 0 | 0 |
| 4,000– 4,999 | 20 | 0.6 | 2.7 | 0 | 1.1 | 0 | 0 | 0 |
| 5,000 and over | 6 | 0.2 | 0.9 | 0 | 0.2 | 0 | 0 | 0 |
| Total: | | | | | | | | |
| Per cent | | 100.0 | 100.0 | 100.0 | 100.0 | 100.0 | 100.0 | 100.0 |
| Number, in thousands | 3,500 | | 580 | 381 | 408 | 49 | 617 | 1,474 |

with low economic status is the same for families living with others as the proportion which was ascertained for families living alone, the study estimated that over one-fifth of all urban families and individuals had low economic status in 1950.[15] Differences in the estimated distribution of the urban population with low economic status which result from shifting from a count by consumer units (including units of two or more families) to a count of families and single individuals regardless of living arrangement, are shown in Table 7.

TABLE 7

Percentage of Urban Population with Low Economic Status; Consumer Units, and Families and Single Individuals, 1950

| | CONSUMER UNITS | | FAMILIES & INDIVIDUALS [a] | |
|---|---|---|---|---|
| TYPE OF UNIT | *Total Number, in thousands* | *Percentage with low economic status* | *Total Number, in thousands* | *Percentage with low economic status* |
| Husband-wife [b] | 22,900 | 13.5 | 26,400 | 13.9 |
| One parent [b] | 600 | 55.2 | 1,200 | 56.7 |
| Other [a] | 5,700 [c] | 24.1 | 1,900 [d] | 24.5 |
| Single individuals | 4,700 | 33.7 | 8,600 | 42.7 |
| Total | 33,900 | 18.8 | 38,100 | 22.3 |

[a] Families and single individuals living in doubled-up units counted separately.
[b] Including all children under eighteen years old.
[c] Includes one-parent consumer units with adult children, units consisting of 2 or more families, and other combinations of adults.
[d] Includes same types as listed in note c with the exception of doubled-up units.

## *Comparison of Income Size Distributions from Field Survey Data*

While estimates of income distributions of the urban population vary according to the source, "all sources confirm the fact that, now as in times past, the lower income population is heavily concentrated among those whose current earning capacity is low relative to the rest of the population. The very aged, the infirm or incapacitated, the widow with dependent children, and the uneducated thus comprise the greater part of the low-income group." [16]

Estimates of the size of the urban population with low economic

[15] This assumption undoubtedly results in a downward bias in the estimate of the number of natural families with low economic status, in the face of available evidence that urban families double-up primarily because of economic factors.

[16] Selma F. Goldsmith, "Comparisons of Family-Income Distributions, Family Income Data from Field Surveys, Technical Note," pp. 40–43 in *Characteristics of the Low-Income Population and Related Federal Programs,* Selected Materials Assembled by the Staff of the Subcommittee on Low-Income Families, Joint Committee on the Economic Report, 84th Cong., 1st sess., 1955.

status will show some variation, depending upon which of the available distributions by current income are used. For example, in a comparison of the BLS and Census Bureau 1950 family income distributions, the greatest difference is in the "under $1,000" class. The following table gives the distribution by 1950 money income before taxes of urban consumer units (BLS) and urban families and unrelated individuals (census): [17]

Selma F. Goldsmith and others have described and explained basic differences in income distributions obtained from field surveys. This section describes in somewhat more detail the extent to which some elements of the urban population were underrepresented in the 1950 BLS Survey of Consumer Expenditures. Although only limited data are available, there is evidence that complete coverage of the urban civilian population would have yielded a larger proportion at the lower end of the income distribution than was obtained in the survey.

One major source of variation in the income distribution obtained in the BLS survey and in the census estimates of 1950 family income is the difference in the method of handling units whose composition altered between the beginning of the survey period and the date of personal interview. A comparison of BLS and census income distributions of families whose composition remained unchanged could be of value in assessing the magnitude of variation due to other factors.

### POPULATION COVERAGE, 1950 BLS SURVEY OF CONSUMER EXPENDITURES

The BLS defined its coverage as follows: [18]

"This survey was designed to record the 1950 income, expendi-

[17] "Income of Families and Persons in the United States, 1950," *Current Population Reports,* Consumer Income, Bureau of the Census, Series P-60, No. 9, March 25, 1952.

| | BLS | *Census* |
|---|---|---|
| | *(per cent)* | |
| Under $1,000 | 6.2 | 14.8 |
| $ 1,000– 1,999 | 11.5 | 12.4 |
| 2,000– 2,999 | 16.6 | 16.6 |
| 3,000– 3,999 | 21.7 | 20.4 |
| 4,000– 4,999 | 17.1 | 13.4 |
| 5,000– 5,999 | 10.5 | 8.7 |
| 6,000– 7,499 | 8.2 | 10.7 |
| 7,500– 9,999 | 5.0 | |
| 10,000 and over | 3.2 | 3.1 |
| Total | 100.0 | 100.0 |

[18] Helen Humes Lamale, "Methodology and Appraisal of Consumer Expenditure Studies," paper presented at the 115th Annual Meeting of the American Statistical Association in New York City, December 28, 1955.

tures, and savings of all non-institutional consumer units residing in United States' cities. Persons living in military camps, posts, or reservations, and inmates of private or public institutions were excluded from the survey. The *'consumer unit'* was defined as either (1) a *family* of two or more persons dependent upon a common or pooled income for their major items of expense, and usually living in the same household, or (2) a *single consumer*—a person who is financially independent of any family group, living either in a separate household or as a roomer in a private home, lodging house, or hotel. In deciding the classification of consumer units, related persons living in one household were considered as forming one consumer unit unless it was very clear that some of the group, such as married children living with parents, kept their household finances separate. Never-married children living in the household were always considered as members of the family. Also, family members temporarily living away from home, such as children at school, were included in the family. . . . In most cases, the membership of families did not change during the year; but many families were found to have had part-year family members—that is, persons who joined or left the family in 1950. Income and expenditures for part-year family members were recorded for that portion of the year when they were in the family, and these data were combined with the data for the rest of the family."

The information recorded in the survey relates to consumer units as they existed during 1950, the survey year, rather than at the time of interview in the spring of 1951. Various procedures could be devised to take account of consumer units newly formed in 1950 and units that changed in composition during the survey. An examination of the eligibility rules adopted in the 1950 BLS survey indicates that some bias was introduced into the sample. These rules automatically excluded some individuals as well as some consumer units from full representation in the expenditure study. The rules were as follows:

*One Consumer Unit Split into Two or More New Units*

Only one of the newly formed units was included. The units to be excluded were determined as follows:

1. If divorce or separation caused the split, the new unit with the male ex-head was excluded.

2. If divorce or separation had not caused the split, and the new units were of equal size, the new unit with the younger head was excluded.

3. If divorce or separation had not caused the split, and the new units were of unequal size, the smaller new unit was excluded. Individual members of excluded units were represented on a part-year basis if the other unit formed as a result of the split fell in the sample. In the latter case, full information was recorded for this new unit and for all members of the original doubled-up unit for the duration of its existence during the survey year.

*Two or More Consumer Units Combined into One New Unit*

Consumer units (and the members thereof) did not provide income-expenditure data relating to the period prior to the formation of the new unit in the following situations:

1. If two single consumers married, data relating to the husband were not recorded for the preceding period.
2. If two other types of consumer units combined in marriage, data relating to members of the former unit headed by the husband were not recorded for the preceding period.
3. If two or more units of equal size combined, not in marriage, data relating to members of the former unit with the younger head were not recorded for the preceding period.
4. If two or more units of unequal size combined, not in marriage, data relating to members of the former smaller unit were not recorded for the preceding period.

*Individual Left Still-Existing Unit to Become New Single Consumer*

In this case no data were recorded. However, if the unit from which he came was drawn in the sample, complete data relating to him were recorded for the period of his membership in the unit.

Approximately 2.5 per cent of the total sample was excluded from the survey on the basis of the eligibility requirements. The following table shows the distribution of consumer units excluded from the BLS survey because of ineligibility: [19]

| | *(per cent)* |
|---|---|
| Part-year unit in 1950, due to: | |
| Undoubling | 5.8 |
| Divorce or separation | 16.3 |
| Marriage | 29.9 |
| New single consumer unit formed | 11.5 |
| Other reasons | 19.2 |
| Unit formed in 1951 | 17.3 |
| Total | 100.0 |

[19] Data based on a sample of eighteen survey cities in the North Central-Northeastern region.

Having ascertained that a person or consumer unit was ineligible for representation in the survey, the BLS field agent was not required to obtain any further information. In slightly over 50 per cent of the cases, however, an estimate of annual money income was obtained.[20] A comparison of the income size distribution of ineligible units reporting an annual income and of all eligible units indicated that ineligible units were concentrated at the lower income levels. This hypothesis is strengthened by the fact that 40 per cent of the ineligible units consisted of newly married couples and newly formed single consumer units. The following table shows that 64 per cent of the ineligible units had incomes in 1950 of less than $3,000, compared to 35 per cent of the eligible units for whom usable schedules were obtained: [21]

| | *Eligible Units* | *Ineligible Units* |
|---|---|---|
| | (*per cent*) | |
| Under $1,000 | 6 | 14 |
| $ 1,000– 1,999 | 11 | 25 |
| 2,000– 2,999 | 18 | 25 |
| 3,000– 3,999 | 23 | 21 |
| 4,000– 4,999 | 17 | 7 |
| 5,000– 5,999 | 11 | 4 |
| 6,000– 7,499 | 7 | 2 |
| 7,500– 9,999 | 4 | 0 |
| 10,000 and over | 3 | 2 |

Underrepresentation of certain groups in the BLS survey undoubtedly explains some of the differences between the aggregate income distributions derived from these data and from the Current Population Surveys (CPS) of the Bureau of the Census.[22] Some of the units excluded from the BLS distribution but included in the CPS data undoubtedly are located at the lower income levels. Some of the units formed during the survey year or in the period between the end of the year and the date of interview consist of individuals who may not have been earners during the entire year, such as young single consumers, newly married young couples, and so forth. Unpublished tabulations of the April 1951 CPS, for example,

[20] On this point instructions given by the field supervisors apparently differed, since reporting on this question varies between cities. It is not known, of course, whether the ineligible units reporting income represent an unbiased sample in terms of the income distribution.

[21] Only 50 per cent of the ineligible units reported annual income. Both distributions are based on survey cities in the North Central-Northeastern region.

[22] For discussion on basic differences in these two sources see: *Income Distribution in the United States, Supplement, 1953, Survey of Current Business,* Dept. of Commerce; Robert Wasson, Abner Hurwitz, and Irving Schweiger, "Field Surveys of Consumer Income: An Appraisal," in Volume Thirteen (1951) of Studies in Income and Wealth; and Goldsmith, *op. cit.*

which obtained 1950 annual income data, shows the following distribution of urban families and unrelated individuals with incomes under $500:

| | Total | Families | Individuals |
|---|---|---|---|
| | | (per cent) | |
| Negative income | 4.6 | 9.0 | 2.2 |
| Zero income | 36.6 | 33.4 | 38.3 |
| $1–$499 | 58.8 | 57.6 | 59.5 |
| Total: | | | |
| Per cent | 100.0 | 100.0 | 100.0 |
| Number, in thousands | 2,432 | 851 | 1,581 |

It would be of some interest to compare the BLS and CPS urban income distributions of units which had no change in composition during the survey year. Since the Bureau of the Census obtains information on changes in family composition, presumably it would be possible to identify those units in which no change in composition had occurred. The sampling design, however, permits construction of an income distribution derived from only 50 per cent of the sample of units supplying income data (that is, two-thirds of the full CPS sample).

In the BLS survey, 14 per cent of the families furnishing usable schedules changed in composition during the survey year. Births accounted for one-half of all changes; changes resulting from the presence of a person with no earnings who was in the unit for only part of the year were about 20 per cent of all changes. Such changes in family composition had no effect on the aggregate income distribution, but changes due to other causes presumably would. The following table compares the distribution by money income after taxes of consumer units of two or more persons whose change in composition was not due to births or to the part-year presence of other members with no earnings with the distribution of all other consumer units of two or more persons:

| | Changed Units | All Other Units |
|---|---|---|
| | (per cent) | |
| Under $1,000 | 2.2 | 2.6 |
| $ 1,000– 1,999 | 5.8 | 7.5 |
| 2,000– 2,999 | 17.3 | 16.5 |
| 3,000– 3,999 | 16.6 | 25.1 |
| 4,000– 4,999 | 15.1 | 19.6 |
| 5,000– 5,999 | 12.2 | 12.3 |
| 6,000– 7,499 | 8.6 | 8.4 |
| 7,500– 9,999 | 4.3 | 4.8 |
| 10,000 and over | 17.9 | 3.2 |
| Total | 100.0 | 100.0 |

It appears that a larger proportion of the units with changes may have been concentrated at the upper end of the income distribution, 43 per cent compared to 29 per cent. Further study is required to explain the differences in the two distributions. The BLS is currently undertaking a comprehensive analysis of the variations in the distributions of the urban population, by income and by other factors, which appear in the cross-section data compared to those given in the CPS. It is to be hoped that as a result of this study, apparent divergences in the two sources of data can be explained in greater detail than is now possible.

## COMMENT

JENNY PODOLUK, DOMINION BUREAU STATISTICS

The preliminary findings of the Roosevelt Foundation project on low income urban families, as released in materials assembled for the Senate Subcommittee on Low Income Families and in Eleanor M. Snyder's paper, represent one of the most interesting studies of low economic status as it exists at the present time. The study departs from what Dorothy S. Brady has called "the notion of a measurable boundary marking off the range on the lower part of the income scale that can be designated substandard,"[1] a boundary now commonly set at a family income of $2,000. By the criteria of the present study only 55 per cent of urban consumer units with low economic status had incomes below $2,000, and some 3 per cent had incomes above $4,000.

The need for some definition of low economic status other than in terms of low current income is urgent since existing income distribution data tend to obscure significant changes and, on occasion, lead to absurd conclusions. Canadian experience in recent years illustrates the problem of assessing income changes from global income distributions.

### CANADIAN PENSIONS AND UNDOUBLING OF FAMILY UNITS

From the late twenties until 1951 the Canadian provincial governments administered payment of monthly pensions to persons aged seventy and over who could demonstrate need. In 1951 slightly more than 300,000 of approximately 650,000 aged persons were receiving provincial old age pensions. In January 1952, under new

[1] Dorothy S. Brady, "Research on the Size Distribution of Income" in Volume Thirteen (1951) of Studies in Income and Wealth, p. 30.

legislation, the federal government began payment of monthly pensions ($40) to all those seventy and over who had fulfilled a specified period of residence in Canada regardless of their economic status. By 1954, 98 per cent of persons seventy and over were receiving these monthly payments, which were also extended to persons aged sixty-five to sixty-nine who could meet a means test.

The effect of this change becomes clear when the income distribution in 1951, the last year before the universal pension plan, is compared with that of 1954, the third years of the plan's operation. Between these years the population aged sixty-five and over increased from 1,085,000 with 300,000 receiving old age pensions to 1,180,000 with approximately 800,000 receiving them.

During this period the total number of family units in the country increased by 320,000. (The definition of family unit in Canadian income statistics is identical with that of the Bureau of the Census and includes unattached individuals.) A classification of families by major source of income indicated that three-quarters received their incomes from wages and salaries or self-employment. The remaining 80,000 family units derived their incomes from unearned sources such as investments, pensions, and transfer payments, the last predominating. Thus, the increase in the number of families reporting transfer payments as a source of income was almost as great as the increase in the number of persons aged sixty-five and over.

These statistics indicate that the liberalization of social security payments to the aged has led in Canada as elsewhere to undoubling family units. The impact on the income distribution is most evident at the lower levels: of all family units with incomes under $1,500, 38 per cent had incomes originating in pensions, investments, and transfer payments in 1951, 43 per cent in 1954. The changes in the composition of income at the lower income levels were more striking. In 1951 approximately 50 per cent of the aggregate income of family units with incomes below $500 came from government transfer payments; by 1954 this ratio was 68 per cent. For incomes of $500 to $1,000 the ratio increased from 29 to 39 per cent; and for incomes of $1,000 to $1,500 the change was from 18 to 27 per cent. In fact transfer payments became a significant component of income for family units with income up to $3,000, although the percentage of aggregate cash income originating in transfer payments only increased from 5.2 to 5.8 per cent.

Such an undoubling of family units may change the economic status of both the new family units and of the units with whom they previously resided. Miss Snyder has pointed out that in 60 per cent of all doubled-up consumer units, incomes were high enough to provide an adequate level of living for all, and that in a significant portion of cases, doubling up did not appear to be a matter of economic necessity. Our own estimate for Canada, for 1954, indicated that the average income of doubled-up family units was higher than the incomes reported by other families consisting of married couples and single children; about 50 per cent of doubled-up family units reported incomes of $5,000 or more. These statistics suggest that the majority of doubled-up families in Canada may be attaining an adequate standard of living.

This three-year period was also characterized by substantial increases in earnings and little change in prices; the proportion of families with low incomes in 1954 was lower than in 1951. Probably the decline would have been greater if undoubling had not been occurring, but it is difficult to isolate the effects of rising real incomes from the effects of the extension of social security payments.

## MINOR COMMENTS ON MISS SNYDER'S PRESENTATION

Miss Snyder's contribution in presenting the problems of identifying low economic status in a new and original context demonstrates that equating low incomes with low economic status is unjustified, although without studies such as Miss Snyder's general users of income data will undoubtedly continue to do so.

It would be useful to have more details of the methods employed in the study. Miss Snyder might also have assessed the methods employed and commented on whether, now that the study is nearing completion, changes in approach could be usefully incorporated into future studies.

The original Bureau of Labor Statistics survey collected data from some 11,000 families, and my impression is that the estimates in her paper are based upon a subsample of these 11,000 schedules. One cannot help wondering, for example, about consumer units with incomes above $5,000 classified as having a low economic status. It would be useful to have more detail on the characteristics of families with low economic status and those with low current income but not low economic status, and further analysis by family size, age group, occupation, and so forth, cross-classified by income size.

Perhaps the most important problem is that data of the type collected by the BLS in the 1950 survey become available at only infrequent intervals, and the 1950 data are available only for urban families. Continuation of this work would necessitate the regular collection of such data.

PETER O. STEINER, UNIVERSITY OF WISCONSIN

The Roosevelt Foundation study is open to two basic questions. First, are the data on the lowest groups in the income distribution subject to biases significantly different from those affecting the income distribution as a whole? Second, can data collected for low-income groups properly be held to reflect the group with low economic status?

While Miss Snyder has chosen to discuss only the second point, I will begin with a few comments on special biases in the data for low-income groups.

### BIASES IN THE DATA

Field survey data measuring income are subject to errors whose systematic effect is to understate the true aggregate of incomes. Do such biases operate with special force at the low end of the income scale? While missed income might not affect the percentage distribution by size of income, evidence presented in other papers at this conference strongly suggests that it does.[1] The size of the lowest-income group appears to be significantly overstated in census income distributions, for several reasons.

Given a pervasive tendency of reporting units to understate their incomes, it is a matter of simple logic that this tendency will be most pronounced at the extremes of the income distribution. Intermediate class intervals will gain frequency from the class intervals above and lose frequency to the classes below, but the lowest-income class will have a net gain.

A second source of special bias is the relatively greater importance of unearned income for low-income groups. At least for the aged,[2] the absence of earnings is the strongest correlative of low income. But underreporting of income other than earnings is significantly greater than underreporting of earnings.[3] Therefore low-income groups will be subject to an additional downward bias

[1] See especially Selma F. Goldsmith's paper in this volume, Table 4.

[2] The aged are the only low income group on which I can claim competence. Lest this be regarded as too damaging a limitation, it may be recalled that in 1954 some 46 per cent of the unrelated individuals with income under $1,000 were sixty-five and over, and 31 per cent of the families in this income bracket had heads sixty-five or over.

[3] Evidence to this effect is found in other papers in this volume. See Selma F. Goldsmith's Table 2; also the paper by Pritzker and Sands, who consider that "Perhaps the most striking finding of the PES is that the deficiency of income recipients reported in the census was caused primarily by the failure to record income from sources other than earnings" (p. 231). Evidence from other sources is consistent with this finding.

in their reported total incomes, and to further exaggeration of their size.

These two factors are probably the most important, but two others may be briefly mentioned. While any definition of income must be to some extent arbitrary, differences between the census definition and those used by taxing authorities and by state and local welfare authorities lead to honest confusion about what is income. The census distinctions between regular and irregular contributions, between direct and indirect contributions, and between use of savings and use of the interest on savings add to the difficulties. Since much of the income of low-income groups is at or near the definitional margins, a further special bias may be operative. Finally there is the question of deliberate underreporting. Incentives exist for this at all income levels, but the low-income recipient of public assistance or relief may feel especially reluctant to give information which may jeopardize his eligibility.

Whether or not these factors suffice to explain the apparent overstatement of the size of low-income groups in field survey data, I hesitate to interpret income data for low-income groups as if they had the same order of accuracy as those for the population as a whole.

### MEASURING LOW ECONOMIC STATUS

Miss Snyder's concern about the data on low-income groups, if I understand it correctly, is that the size of the group with low economic status is overstated because of year-to-year variation of income. Her definition of low status involves income below specified budget levels in *each* of a series of years. (I will accept for the sake of argument both this conception of low economic status and the particular budget levels she has chosen, though I have reservations about both.) Is her procedure for measuring the size of the group with low economic status by reducing the number below budget levels according to the four criteria listed in her paper satisfactory? I think not.

Particularly disturbing is her third discriminant, the exclusion from low economic status of those whose combined food and housing expenditures were above total reported current family income. This is indeed "an indication that the family was able to incur debts or dissaving equal to expenditures on items other than food or housing." Miss Snyder appears to believe that this procedure serves to eliminate from the "hard core" low-income groups those whose current money income is low over a period longer than a year or so, but who possess *adequate* economic resources of other types such as savings. But will it not also eliminate those with dissaving whose total level of expenditures is inadequate, that is, that falls below the prescribed budget levels? In fact, many of the aged living in part on savings are doing so at levels of consumption less than adequate, and Miss Snyder's procedure eliminates from the low-status group many of those with the very lowest status.

I have been supposing above that income is adequately measured. If however, there is any systematic tendency for understatement of income, small amounts of "apparent dissaving" to meet living expenses can result merely from errors in reporting income and can result in a classification of "not low status" on purely synthetic grounds.

A more sensible procedure for identifying the group whose incomes are temporarily low, and who are relying on non-income sources to maintain an adequate level of consumption, would be to compare the appropriate budget level with the level of total expenditures, and to eliminate from the low-status group only those whose expenditures exceeded the specified levels of adequacy. (This is based on the hypothesis of consumer behavior that those with temporarily low incomes maintain their consumption levels at or above the budget level; it also substitutes a single discriminant about the *level* of consumption for a series of discriminants concerning the *kind* of consumption expenditure.)

In the follow-up survey of the aged [4] intended to gather data for such an appraisal, including especially a measurement of the amount of dissaving for meeting living expenses, findings on the use of savings (dissaving) do not conform to the pattern assumed by Miss Snyder. While the practice was frequent among the aged (about 15 per cent), its distribution was J-shaped, with 20 to 25 per cent in amounts under $200 and more than half under $500. Typically the amounts were small in relation to total income, but even those for whom it was the principal source of income had small total expenditures, frequently well below budget levels.[5]

In the following comparison I chose a group of the aged in urbanized areas closely similar to Miss Snyder's and used a budget level directly comparable with hers. I computed the percentage with *incomes* below the budget level and then recomputed for the percentage with *expenditures* (including those financed by dissaving) below that level. This procedure, followed separately for couples, for unrelated males, and for unrelated females, shows in

[4] For a description of the survey see Peter O. Steiner and Robert Dorfman, *The Economic Status of the Aged,* University of California Press, 1957, Appendix A.
[5] Cf. Steiner and Dorfman, *op. cit.,* pp. 115–119.

each group that only 5 to 6 per cent of those with incomes below budget levels had total expenditures above the same budget levels. Compare this with Miss Snyder's table on page 333 which shows 40 per cent of the class with head aged sixty-five and over and with incomes below budget levels ranked as having adequate economic status. This is a difference in kind. To assume that use of savings relieves the economic distress of many of those with low incomes is not safe.

Miss Snyder's procedure errs (if my criticism is valid) in the right direction; it compensates for errors that tend to overstate the size of the low income group. It does so, however, in a way that introduces a systematic bias into the makeup of the low-status group. A cruder, but probably more satisfactory procedure would be to reduce budget levels arbitrarily to allow for understatement of incomes.

ROBERT SUMMERS, YALE UNIVERSITY

Miss Snyder attempts to distinguish between households which ordinarily enjoyed an adequate plane of living but had temporarily depressed incomes in the survey year and households which typically had low incomes. Since her income data covered only one year, she resorted to the expedient of classifying households on the basis of their spending behavior. Information about household stocks rather than flows might provide a better guide, but as she has pointed out, there are many variables that conceivably could be used and we should not expect her paper to exhaust the subject.

Of her four criteria for splitting off temporarily low income households from hard core ones, the third, in which expenditures on food and shelter are compared with income, is probably best. It surely selects out the low-income households which had higher incomes before the survey year. Whether or not the higher incomes were above the minimum budget levels is not determinable, of course, but except for one-person households, the criterion does not seem to be significant.

The other three criteria bear discussion. The purchase of a home in the survey year by low-income households was uncommon, so it provides very little discrimination. If the purchase of a home should disqualify a household from membership in the hard core, then house ownership would also be a good disqualifying attribute conceptually, and it would provide better discrimination because it is more common. Data on home ownership were collected in the survey so this alternative variable could easily be used.

Similarly, possession of an automobile is as good, or as bad, a variable as automobile purchase. Cars are no longer a luxury and models providing transportation, if not comfort, are available at very low prices. In fact, in 1950 around 40 per cent of the cars households bought cost less than $500. This amount is not formidable to households with access to auto finance credit. Such access depends primarily upon the income, debts, and past credit worthiness of the household, and only incidentally upon the number of dependents in it. A household may be categorized low because of the substantial needs inherent in a large family and still qualify for credit. Thus the purchase of a car is within the reach of hard-core households but whether or not they really buy is an empirical question. Ruth P. Mack reported in her 1948 *Review of Economics and Statistics* article that at any income level, households that previously had higher incomes spent more on cars and their upkeep than households that had had steady incomes. This supports Miss Snyder's criterion, though Mrs. Mack referred to amounts spent. Instead of using the criterion $0 paid for a car versus some positive number of dollars, it would be better to use a more reasonable breaking point, even if it had to be guessed at arbitrarily.

The criterion involving a household's spending more or less than 10 per cent of its income on household furnishings and equipment is satisfactory in principle since it takes into account the dollar amount spent.

Perhaps the problem of identifying hard-core households by means of criteria like these can be attacked with the relatively sophisticated technique of discriminant analysis. The technique requires data on low-income households whose hard-core status is known, however. The Survey Research Center's reinterview samples which contain brief income histories would be suitable. Using Miss Snyder's income criteria as well as I could, I sorted out of a 1951–1952 reinterview deck the data cards for households with low income status for the two years. I did not apply discriminant analysis to the reinterview deck, but I did check the proportion of two-year low income households, practically hard core households, which spent more than 20 per cent of their disposable incomes on cars and consumer durables. The outlays were net of trade-in values. The proportion I found, about 12 per cent, suggests that Miss Snyder's cut-off figure of 10 per cent for household furnishings may be low. With more complete information about the reinterview households, one could check on her other criteria.

IRWIN WOLKSTEIN AND MARIE M. DELANEY,
BUREAU OF OLD-AGE AND SURVIVORS INSURANCE

Miss Snyder's use of certain types of expenditures for the classification of consumer units by economic status was based on Allen and Bowley's study published in 1935, which showed that subsistence levels of living can be identified and described by relationships existing between current family income and expenditures for consumption goods and services. The purchases involved in her discriminants 1 and 3 are spread fairly evenly over a calendar year and hence can conceivably be related to a current year's family income. However automobiles and houses (discriminants 2 and 4) are items purchased relatively infrequently (certainly not annually), and we therefore feel that they do not necessarily have any direct correlation with current family income but rather with assets or expected future income.

Assets and expected future income are obviously significant in determining economic status. Unfortunately, the two discriminants employed are very inadequate measures of them. The *ownership* of a car or house and their value seem superior in this respect to their actual purchase. Also these discriminants may be more critical in rural than in urban areas since a car may be a vital means of transportation in the country, not a deferrable purchase as Miss Snyder states.

As defined we feel the discriminants indicate expenditure status for the year 1950, not economic status. They have a tendency to place consumer units with high savings rates into the inadequate economic status group. They do not give sufficient weight to assets, both tangible and intangible, a particularly important consideration if the income data is necessarily limited to one year.

Despite these shortcomings her criteria may be satisfactory if they discriminate as well as or better than equally available alternatives. However, we recommend that the stability of the distributions obtained on the basis of these discriminants be tested by reclassifying the consumer units on the basis of alternative ones which take into account the points we have raised.

GEORGE GARVY, FEDERAL RESERVE BANK OF NEW YORK

By Miss Snyder's technique units with low economic status whose income was temporarily higher in 1950, perhaps because of a windfall, would not be included in her estimate. No doubt techniques similar to those used in the Roosevelt Foundation study could be developed to identify units with a current income above the budget minimum but with low income status. One important difficulty is finding discriminants to separate units that have permanently moved from a low to a higher status from those that are expected to revert to a low income status. To make this distinction, discriminants based on the budget structure of low-income units might prove unreliable because there is usually a lag before units that have emerged from a low-income status adjust their spending patterns. Even though the number of low status families in any particular period receiving income above the minimum budget cost is probably relatively small, it might increase in periods of full and more-than-full employment when marginal members of the labor force and retired workers are temporarily drawn into full or part-time employment.

Miss Snyder's technique for identifying low status units is incomplete. Also, the validity of the discriminants 2 and 4 is questionable because two types of specific spending actions are used in isolation. Purchase of a car or a home is considered sufficient to disqualify a family from being considered as having a low income status because they involve "relatively large outlays on items whose purchase could be deferred." This is not necessarily so. Consider, for instance, a home-owning family whose head has retired. In making adjustments to a low income status, such a family may sell its home, now too expensive to maintain, and buy a smaller one. The discriminant used does not distinguish between purchases of homes by renting families and purchases by units already home owners. Even this distinction would not be sufficient; one would have also to know whether a family was moving to a less or more expensive house.

An analogous case exists with respect to cars. Since a car is a necessity for most families, the mere replacement of one jalopy by another can hardly be considered as an act suggesting an above-low-income status. Perhaps distinction between the purchase of a new and a used car would help. However, I am not even sure that the purchase of a car by a family not previously owning one could be justified as a discriminant if the cost of the car is low.

The use of more refined discriminants may have been precluded by the nature of the source data used in the Roosevelt Foundation Study. However, this should not have prevented Miss Snyder from discussing the limitations of her discriminants. The use of the purchase of homes and cars as criteria raises the question of the interpretation of low income status when it is combined with relatively large holdings of consumer capital. It also raises the broader question of whether low income status can be defined without reference to assets.

Normally ownership of assets is reflected in income since most types of assets are income producing, so that the pairing of low income with large assets will occur only in those exceptional cases in which assets are held uninvested (for instance, as demand deposits). Accumulation of relatively large amounts of consumer capital (including housing) before retirement is not unusual, and disregarding the ownership of such assets (which reduces current expenditures) may lead to biased estimates of the low-income-status population.

My remarks concern, however, the methodology developed by Miss Snyder and not her substantive findings. Modification of discriminants 2 and 4 in the sense suggested would presumably add relatively few families to the low-status classifications. And I do not believe that many additional such families would be shifted to that part of the population which has a current income exceeding the budget minimum.

# Changes in the Industrial Distribution of Wages in the United States, 1939–1949

HERMAN P. MILLER, BUREAU OF THE CENSUS

Wages are among the most stable components of aggregate income.[1] They are generally less subject to the fluctuations characterizing earnings from "riskier" activities like the operation of a farm or a business, or receipts from other sources like dividends, rents, and royalties. This fact, perhaps, explains why income analysts have tended to overlook the vast body of 1940 census data on the distribution of wage income as well as some of the information provided by the 1950 census.

The present study attempts to remedy this oversight. It is based largely on wage data tabulated from the past two decennial censuses and on data obtained in the annual income surveys conducted by the Bureau of the Census. It aims to identify some of the variable as well as the stable elements of the distribution of wage income. Recently available data indicate that between 1939 and 1949 there was a marked decrease of inequality in this distribution. What are the underlying forces responsible for the change? What general lessons can be learned from the changes for specific industry groups? These are two questions which the present study attempts to answer.

## *Changes in the Distribution of Wages*

Between 1939 and 1949 total wages increased from $46 billion to $134 billion. This threefold increase was accompanied by a marked change in their level and distribution.

In 1939 the average wage earner received about $800 during the entire year. By 1949 this figure rose to $2,000 (Table 1). In 1939 only 1 per cent of the wage earners had incomes of $5,000 or more and 60 per cent had incomes below $1,000. By 1949 the proportion in the higher classes increased fourfold, and the proportion in the lowest class was cut by one-half. For men alone, typically the primary income recipients in their families and likely to be full-time workers, the changes are even more striking.

The changes in the level of wage income and in the frequency distribution of the earners were accompanied by a marked change

[1] Because wages and salaries are not distinguished in this paper, "wages" and "wage income" will be used to include both types of income.

TABLE 1

Wage Income of Persons, by Income Class and Sex, 1939, 1945, and 1949

| INCOME CLASS | Both Sexes | | | Male | | | Female | | |
|---|---|---|---|---|---|---|---|---|---|
| | *1939* [a] | *1945* | *1949* | *1939* [a] | *1945* | *1949* | *1939* [a] | *1945* | *194* |
| | | | | | (*per cent*) | | | | |
| Total | 100.0 | 100.0 | 100.0 | 100.0 | 100.0 | 100.0 | 100.0 | 100.0 | 100 |
| $ 1–$ 999 | 60.0 | 32.9 | 27.6 | 52.8 | 23.0 | 19.6 | 79.0 | 49.0 | 44 |
| 1,000– 1,999 | 29.2 | 28.4 | 21.8 | 33.4 | 21.8 | 18.1 | 18.1 | 39.3 | 29. |
| 2,000– 2,499 | 5.3 | 13.2 | 13.2 | 6.8 | 16.4 | 12.9 | 1.6 | 7.8 | 13 |
| 2,500– 2,999 | 2.0 | 9.7 | 11.0 | 2.6 | 14.1 | 13.3 | 0.5 | 2.4 | 6. |
| 3,000– 4,999 | 2.4 | 13.6 | 22.0 | 3.1 | 20.8 | 30.0 | 0.6 | 1.5 | 5. |
| 5,000 and over | 1.0 | 2.4 | 4.2 | 1.4 | 3.8 | 6.1 | 0.1 | — | 0. |
| | | | | | (*dollars*) | | | | |
| Median income | 789 | 1,617 | 2,016 | 939 | 2,157 | 2,476 | 555 | 1,023 | 1,20 |

Note: In this and the following tables, figures do not always add to totals because of roun ing.

[a] Include receipts from public emergency work.

Source: *Current Population Reports—Consumer Income,* Bureau of the Census, Series P-6 No. 7, 1951, Table 23 (for 1939 and 1949) and P-60, No. 2, 1948, Table 22 (for 1945).

in the dispersion (or "inequality") in the distribution of this type of income. Table 2 shows the relative distribution of wage income for several years between 1939 and 1949.

The substantial changes in the relative distribution of wage income took place during the war years. Between 1939 and 1945 the share received by the highest fifth of the recipients decreased from 49 per cent to 44 per cent. In contrast, the years immediately following World War II (1947–1949) did not see any change in the relative distribution. This suggests that something about the expansion of economic activities stimulated by World War II resulted in a decrease in the concentration of wage income. However,

TABLE 2

Percentage of Total Wage Income Received by Persons Ranked by Amount Received, Selected Years, 1939–1949

| RANK | *1939* | *1945* | *1947* | *1948* | *1949* |
|---|---|---|---|---|---|
| Total | 100.0 | 100.0 | 100.0 | 100.0 | 100.0 |
| Lowest fifth | 3.4 | 2.9 | 2.9 | 2.9 | 2.6 |
| Second fifth | 8.4 | 10.1 | 10.3 | 10.2 | 10.1 |
| Middle fifth | 15.0 | 17.4 | 17.8 | 18.6 | 18.7 |
| Fourth fifth | 23.9 | 25.7 | 24.7 | 25.5 | 26.2 |
| Highest fifth | 49.3 | 43.9 | 44.3 | 42.8 | 42.4 |

Source: Herman P. Miller, *Income of the American People,* Wiley, 1955, p. 104.

during the immediate postwar period, when employment levels were high, there was relatively little change in income concentration. This should be kept in mind when the data for detailed industries are considered.

Tables 1 and 2 clearly indicate a marked equalization in the distribution of wage income between 1939 and 1949. To what extent can this be explained by census wage data for separate industries? This paper will consider the relationship between the equalization of wages and salaries between 1939 and 1949 and (1) changes in the industrial distribution of the labor force, (2) change in the relative earnings position of industries, (3) decrease in the wage spread between high-paid and low-paid industries, and (4) decrease in the wage spread between high-paid and low-paid workers within industries.

## *Impact of Changes in the Labor Force*

The frequency distribution of all workers classified by the amount of wage income is the weighted sum of a large number of component distributions. Conceivably this distribution could have changed even if all of the component groups retained their initial distributions and only their associated weights changed. For example, each of the 117 industries examined in this report might have had exactly the same distribution of wage income in 1949 as it had ten years earlier, but changes in the industrial distribution of the labor force (the proportion of workers in each industry) might have caused a change in the distribution of total wages.

The decline in the importance of agricultural activities and the increasing importance of manufacturing, evident for many decades, appear in the data for the two most recent decennial censuses. Table 3 shows that between 1940 and 1950 the proportion of persons employed in agriculture dropped by about one-third (from 19 to 13 per cent), but the proportion employed in manufacturing, particularly in durable goods manufacturing, increased significantly (from 11 to 13 per cent). How are these changes related to equalization in the distribution of total wages?

An attempt is made to answer this question in Table 4. On the assumption that each industry had exactly the same number of male workers in 1949 as it had ten years earlier and that the only variable was the frequency distribution of workers by wage income, the separate distributions were combined to obtain a single distribution based on 1939 weights and 1949 frequencies, shown in fifths.

TABLE 3

Employed Persons, by Major Industry Group, 1940 and 1950

| INDUSTRY GROUP [a] | *1940* | *1950* |
|---|---|---|
| | (*number in thousands*) | |
| Total | 44,888 | 55,843 |
| | (*per cent*) | |
| Agriculture | 18.7 | 12.8 |
| Mining | 2.0 | 1.7 |
| Construction | 4.6 | 6.2 |
| Manufacturing | 23.6 | 25.3 |
| Durable goods | 11.4 | 13.2 |
| Nondurable goods | 11.8 | 11.8 |
| Not specified manufacturing | 0.4 | 0.3 |
| Transportation, communication, and other public utilities | 6.9 | 7.6 |
| Wholesale and retail trade | 16.8 | 18.6 |
| Service industries | 22.5 | 21.6 |
| All other industries | 3.4 | 4.7 |
| Industry not reported | 1.5 | 1.5 |

[a] The industry in which the person was employed (or the industry of his last job, if unemployed) at the time of the census.

Source: *1950 Census of Population, Employment and Income in the United States, by Regions, 1950,* Series PC-7, No. 2, Table 8.

TABLE 4

Percentage of Total Wage Income Received by Male Workers Ranked by Amount Received; Actual, 1939 and 1949, and Standardized, 1949

| RANK OF WORKERS | *1939* *Actual* [a] | *1949* *Actual* [a] | *Standardized* [b] |
|---|---|---|---|
| Total | 100.0 | 100.0 | 100.0 |
| Lowest fifth | 3.8 | 5.2 | 4.9 |
| Second fifth | 9.2 | 13.3 | 12.8 |
| Middle fifth | 16.2 | 18.2 | 18.2 |
| Fourth fifth | 23.3 | 23.3 | 23.5 |
| Highest fifth | 46.6 | 39.8 | 40.6 |

[a] Based on Appendix Tables B-1 and B-2.

[b] The standardized distribution was obtained by multiplying the actual distributions in Table B-1 by the numbers of workers in Table B-2 and summing the results.

The standardized distribution shows the changes associated with variations in the component frequency distributions, assuming no changes in the weights associated with each distribution.

Apparently most of the equalization of wages and salaries between 1939 and 1949 can be explained *without* reference to changes in the industrial distribution of the labor force. The share of aggregate wage income received by the top fifth of the male workers decreased from 47 per cent in 1939 to 40 per cent in 1949. This fifth would have received 41 per cent of the aggregate in 1949 if there had been no change in the industrial distribution of the labor force. Therefore by far the greatest part of the equalization of wages during the decade is attributable to changes in the component distributions rather than to changes in the weights associated with those distributions.

### *Changes in the Dispersion of Wages within Industries*

To what extent does the change in the over-all distribution reflect a decrease in the dispersion of wages between high-paid and low-paid workers within specific industries?

An examination of the changes in the dispersion of wage income for men indicates that there was a narrowing of wage differentials in all but five of the 117 industries examined. In fifty-four industries the share of the aggregate wages received by the highest paid fifth of the workers in the industry decreased by less than 10 per cent; in an additional fifty-four industries the share received by the top fifth decreased by between 10 and 20 per cent, and in four industries the decrease was over 20 per cent (Table 5). Decreases in

TABLE 5

Industries Ranked by 1949 Mean Wage Income of Male Workers, by Change in Dispersion of Income between 1939 and 1949

| | | CHANGE IN SHARE OF TOTAL RECEIVED BY HIGHEST-PAID FIFTH OF WORKERS, 1939 TO 1949 | | | |
|---|---|---|---|---|---|
| | | *Decrease* | | | |
| RANK OF INDUSTRY | TOTAL | *20.0% or More* | *10.0 to 19.9%* | *Less than 10.0%* | *Increase* |
| Total | 117 | 4 | 54 | 54 | 5 |
| Lowest tenth | 5 | — | — | 5 | — |
| Second tenth | 13 | — | 3 | 8 | 2 |
| Third tenth | 12 | 1 | 5 | 5 | 1 |
| Fourth tenth | 11 | — | 4 | 7 | — |
| Fifth tenth | 11 | — | 6 | 3 | 2 |
| Sixth tenth | 18 | — | 11 | 7 | — |
| Seventh tenth | 19 | 1 | 13 | 5 | — |
| Eighth tenth | 8 | — | 3 | 5 | — |
| Ninth tenth | 4 | 1 | — | 3 | — |
| Highest tenth | 16 | 1 | 9 | 6 | — |

Changes in dispersion are defined here in terms of changes in the share of aggregate wage income received by the highest-paid fifth of the workers.

Source: Derived from Appendix Table B-4.

dispersion were somewhat greater in the high-paid industries than in those with relatively low average incomes. Thus, fourteen of the twenty-eight industries in the highest three tenths (ranked by median wage or salary income in 1949) had decreases in dispersion of 10 per cent or more, whereas only nine of the thirty industries in the lowest three tenths had decreases this great.

Some factors affecting the distribution of wages within an industry can be brought into sharper focus by examining the changes in average wages for specific occupations within it. Data available from the past two censuses permit the analysis of changes in average wage income for the following groups of male workers within eleven manufacturing industries, which include about one-fourth of all wage workers: laborers (not elsewhere classified or n.e.c.); operatives (n.e.c.); and all other workers. Although these data are extremely useful, they are defective in several important ways.

In the first place, they do not show separate income distributions for *all* laborers and for *all* operatives within each industry, but only for those who were not classified in specific occupations. This defect can be roughly adjusted for by the procedure discussed below. A second and more important defect, which cannot be adjusted for, stems from the fact that the residual category "other workers" does not distinguish between craftsmen and the other occupations. For this reason the data cannot be regarded as showing the differential income gains of unskilled, semiskilled, and skilled workers within each industry but rather of unskilled, semiskilled, and "higher-paid" workers, since about three-fourths of the "other workers" category in most industries is composed of professional and managerial workers and craftsmen.

The unadjusted data, summarized in Table 6, show that in each of the industries studied, the lowest-paid workers made the greatest relative gains and the highest-paid workers made the smallest. For example, in the iron and steel industry the increase in average wages between 1939 and 1949 was 152 per cent for laborers, 133 per cent for operatives, and 112 per cent for "other workers." The increase in the food manufacturing industry was 149 per cent for laborers, 123 per cent for operatives, and 109 per cent for "other workers."

As previously indicated, the data require adjustment. It is known from a tabulation of industry by occupation (but without a further classification by wage income) that there were 376,000 male operatives and 46,000 male laborers in the motor vehicle and motor vehicle equipment manufacturing industry in 1950.[2] However, 279,-000 operatives and 45,000 laborers were not classified in specific

[2] *1950 Census of Population,* Vol. IV, *Special Reports,* Part 1, Chap. C.

Mean Wages of Male Laborers, Operatives, and "Other Workers" in Selected Manufacturing Industries, 1939 and 1949

| INDUSTRY | 1939 | | | | 1949 | | | | PERCENTAGE INCREASE, 1939 TO 1949 | | | |
|---|---|---|---|---|---|---|---|---|---|---|---|---|
| | | | "Other Workers" | | | | "Other Workers" | | | | "Other Workers" | |
| | Laborers [a] | Operatives [a] | Unadjusted [b] | Adjusted [c] | Laborers [a] | Operatives [a] | Unadjusted [b] | Adjusted [c] | Laborers [a] | Operatives [a] | Unadjusted [b] | Adjusted [c] |
| Food and kindred products | $ 853 | $1,119 | $1,662 | $1,842 | $2,128 | $2,491 | $3,481 | $3,762 | 149 | 123 | 109 | 104 |
| Textiles, textile products and apparel | 675 | 878 | 1,609 | 1,718 | 1,913 | 2,452 | 3,606 | 3,791 | 183 | 179 | 124 | 121 |
| Furniture, lumber, and wood products [d] | 573 | 852 | 1,033 | 1,447 | 1,585 | 1,906 | 2,364 | 3,531 | 177 | 124 | 129 | 144 |
| Paper, paper products, and printing | 871 | 1,160 | 1,896 | 1,950 | 2,325 | 2,775 | 3,746 | 3,838 | 167 | 139 | 98 | 97 |
| Chemicals, petroleum, and coal products | 912 | 1,345 | 2,188 | 2,299 | 2,444 | 3,053 | 4,362 | 4,556 | 168 | 127 | 99 | 98 |
| Stone, clay, and glass products | 815 | 1,114 | 1,745 | 1,872 | 2,213 | 2,684 | 3,497 | 3,691 | 172 | 141 | 100 | 97 |
| Iron and steel and not specified metal industries | 924 | 1,162 | 1,670 | 1,778 | 2,325 | 2,711 | 3,543 | 3,762 | 152 | 133 | 112 | 99 |
| Nonferrous metals and their products | 990 | 1,110 | 1,671 | 1,827 | 2,307 | 2,602 | 3,523 | 3,833 | 133 | 134 | 111 | 110 |
| Machinery | 943 | 1,177 | 1,817 | 1,898 | 2,318 | 2,797 | 3,757 | 3,895 | 146 | 138 | 107 | 105 |
| Motor vehicles and motor vehicle equipment | 1,074 | 1,227 | 1,695 | 1,825 | 2,621 | 2,876 | 3,793 | 4,074 | 144 | 134 | 124 | 123 |
| Transportation equipment, except motor vehicles | 866 | 1,112 | 1,577 | 1,647 | 2,262 | 2,910 | 3,575 | 3,653 | 161 | 162 | 127 | 122 |

[a] The distributions of mean wages shown for laborers and operatives are assumed to be the same whether they include or exclude laborers and operatives classified as "other workers" in the census (see text for explanation).

[b] Includes some laborers and operatives (see text).

[c] Excludes all laborers and operatives (see text).

[d] Changes in the income differentials between operatives and "other workers" are difficult to measure for this industry. In the 1940 census sawyers were classified as craftsmen; in the 1950 census, as operatives. Also adjusted means in this industry are subject to considerably greater errors of estimation than those for other industries because more than one-half of the "other workers" category contained operatives and laborers, as well as because of the change in classification of sawyers.

Source: Derived from Appendix Tables B-1 and B-2 and from Herman P. Miller, *Income of the American People,* Wiley, 1955, Tables C1 and C3.

occupations within their respective major groups. Thus, about 97,000 operatives (largely welders and painters) and 1,000 laborers were included in the category of "other workers," which is comprised for the most part of craftsmen and white-collar workers. These workers can be separated from the "other workers" group by assuming that they have the same distribution by wage income as operatives (n.e.c.) and laborers (n.e.c.). The addition of the former groups to operatives (n.e.c.) and laborers (n.e.c.) does not change the mean for the combined group since identical distributions were assumed for both. However, their removal from "other workers" raises the mean for the latter group from $3,793 to $4,074. Similar adjustments were made for each industry and the revised results for "other workers" are presented in the "adjusted" columns. In every case, with the exception of the furniture, lumber, and wood products industry, the adjustment tended to reduce the relative gain in average wage income for this group.

TABLE 7

Relationship of Mean Wages of Laborers, Operatives, and "Other Workers," in Selected Manufacturing Industries, 1939 and 1949

| | *Mean Wage of:* | | | |
|---|---|---|---|---|
| | *"Other Workers" as % of Laborers'* | | *Operatives as % of Laborers'* | |
| INDUSTRY | *1939* | *1949* | *1939* | *1949* |
| Food and kindred products | 216 | 177 | 131 | 117 |
| Textiles, textile products, and apparel | 255 | 198 | 130 | 128 |
| Furniture, lumber, and wood products | 253 | 223 | 149 | 120 |
| Paper, paper products, and printing | 224 | 165 | 133 | 119 |
| Chemicals, petroleum, and coal products | 252 | 186 | 147 | 125 |
| Stone, clay, and glass products | 230 | 167 | 137 | 121 |
| Iron and steel and not specified metal industries | 192 | 162 | 126 | 117 |
| Nonferrous metals and their products | 185 | 166 | 112 | 113 |
| Machinery | 201 | 168 | 125 | 121 |
| Motor vehicles and motor vehicle equipment | 170 | 155 | 114 | 110 |
| Transportation equipment, except motor vehicles | 190 | 161 | 128 | 129 |

Source: Derived from Table 6.

Another way of viewing the differential gains of unskilled, semi-skilled, and "other workers" within specified manufacturing industries is presented in Table 7. The average wage income of laborers is expressed first in relation to the average for high-paid workers within each industry for 1939 and 1949, and then in relation to the average for operatives. In every industry there was a marked reduction in income differentials between high-paid workers and laborers, it being greatest in the stone, clay, and glass products industry. In this industry, high-paid workers made 2.3 times as much as laborers in 1939 but only 1.7 times as much in 1949. The wage differentials were most stable in the motor vehicle and motor vehicle equipment industry; high-paid workers made 1.7 times as much as laborers in 1939 and 1.6 times as much in 1949.

Because of the heterogeneous nature of the "other workers" category, changes in differentials between only unskilled workers (laborers) and semiskilled workers (operatives) within each industry may be more significant. Here again, Table 7 shows a reduction in wage differentials within most industries. In 1939, for example, operatives in the food processing industry; the paper and printing industry; and the stone, clay and glass industry made about one-third more than laborers. In 1949, they made only one-fifth more. In the chemicals, petroleum, and coal products industries the differential between operatives and laborers was reduced from nearly one-half to one-fourth.

It could be argued that these decreases are in some measure attributable to the reduction in unemployment, which had the greatest impact on the earnings of low-paid workers. While there is some justification for this view, it may unduly minimize the importance of reductions in wage rate differentials, which are not affected by variations in the extent of employment. Evidence on this point is presented in Table 8, which shows the average wage or salary income in 1939 and 1949 of operatives and laborers who were full-year workers in specified manufacturing industries. A full-year worker is defined in this table as a person who worked fifty weeks or more during the year. Weeks worked, as defined in the 1950 census, includes all weeks in 1949 during which work was performed. Accordingly, full-year workers for 1949 are persons who did any paid work (not necessarily full-time) in fifty weeks or more. Persons who worked regularly on a part-time basis were thus counted as full-year workers in 1949. In contrast, the 1940 census enumerators were instructed to convert part-time work to equivalent full-time weeks. Accordingly, a full-year worker for 1939 is a person who worked full-time during the entire year. This change tended to understate the decrease in wage differentials because the inclusion of regular part-time workers in the 1939 data would have probably reduced the average income for laborers proportionately more than the average income for operatives.

Despite this, it is apparent from Table 8 that there was a reduction in wage differentials between unskilled and semiskilled workers in most of the industries. The greatest reductions were in food processing; furniture, lumber, and wood products; chemicals,

TABLE 8

Relationship of Mean Wages of Full-Year Laborers and Operatives in Selected Manufacturing Industries, 1939 and 1949

| INDUSTRY | 1939 | | | 1949 | | |
|---|---|---|---|---|---|---|
| | *Mean Wage of:* | | | *Mean Wage of:* | | |
| | *Operatives*[a] (1) | *Laborers*[a] (2) | *(1) as % of (2)* (3) | *Operatives*[a] (4) | *Laborers*[a] (5) | *(4) as % of (5)* (6) |
| Food and kindred products | $1,323 | $1,097 | 121 | $2,834 | $2,549 | 111 |
| Textiles, textile products, and apparel | 1,061 | 852 | 125 | 2,771 | 2,235 | 124 |
| Furniture, lumber, and wood products | 1,056 | 736 | 143 | 2,301 | 1,902 | 121 |
| Paper, paper products, and printing | 1,350 | 1,073 | 126 | 3,098 | 2,616 | 118 |
| Chemicals, petroleum, and coal products | 1,540 | 1,169 | 132 | 3,353 | 2,793 | 120 |
| Stone, clay, and glass products | 1,355 | 1,030 | 132 | 2,986 | 2,575 | 116 |
| Iron and steel and not specified metal industries | 1,411 | 1,209 | 117 | 3,040 | 2,652 | 115 |
| Nonferrous metals and their products | 1,359 | 1,230 | 110 | 3,016 | 2,727 | 111 |
| Machinery | 1,447 | 1,202 | 120 | 3,180 | 2,768 | 115 |
| Motor vehicles and motor vehicle equipment | 1,555 | 1,393 | 112 | 3,311 | 3,063 | 108 |
| Transportation equipment, except motor vehicles | 1,476 | 1,164 | 127 | 3,301 | 2,671 | 124 |

[a] Not elsewhere classified.

Source: Herman P. Miller, *Income of the American People,* Wiley, 1955, Tables C2 and C4

petroleum, and coal products; and stone, clay, and glass products. In most of the other industries there were small, but persistent, reductions.

The preceding tables are based entirely on census results and are subject to all of the biases inherent in the household survey technique as well as difficulties of interpretation. For this reason, it is particularly important to refer to independent data on the same subject as a check. Table 9 presents estimates derived from the Bureau of Labor Statistics index of urban wage rates. They show the percentage increase in wage rates for skilled, semiskilled, and unskilled workers by industry groups from October 1943 to April 1947. These data support the conclusions based on census results. In almost all of the industries the greatest relative gains in wage rates were made by unskilled workers and the smallest by skilled workers.

### *Changes in the Level of Wages among Industries*

The decade which ended in 1949 was a period of rapid increase in average earnings for practically all industries. The increases, how-

TABLE 9

Percentage Increase in Urban Wage Rates, by Industry, October 1943–April 1947

| INDUSTRY | *Total* | *Skilled Workers* | *Semiskilled Workers* | *Unskilled Workers* |
|---|---|---|---|---|
| Total | 32.3 | 27.7 | 34.5 | 35.7 |
| Food and kindred products | 34.3 | 28.3 | 35.1 | 38.8 |
| Tobacco manufactures | 41.3 | 30.1 | 40.2 | 48.8 |
| Textile mill products | 51.5 | 45.3 | 58.5 | 52.3 |
| Apparel and allied products | 47.9 | 34.2 | 49.5 | 42.4 |
| Furniture and finished lumber products | 44.9 | 40.9 | 44.3 | 55.3 |
| Paper and allied products | 35.3 | 28.0 | 34.4 | 40.9 |
| Printing, publishing, and allied industries | 46.9 | 45.0 | 49.6 | 51.4 |
| Chemicals and allied products | 37.8 | 34.7 | 37.3 | 40.7 |
| Products of petroleum and coal | 31.7 | 28.8 | 31.7 | 34.7 |
| Rubber products | 34.0 | 30.9 | 34.1 | 38.5 |
| Leather and leather products | 46.9 | 47.9 | 45.1 | 54.0 |
| Basic iron and steel | 25.2 | 21.4 | 22.7 | 38.8 |
| Shipbuilding | 18.8 | 15.9 | — | 24.4 |
| Metal working, excluding basic iron and steel and shipbuilding | 27.5 | 23.2 | 29.0 | 31.2 |

Source: Harry Ober, "Occupational Wage Differentials, 1907–1947," *Monthly Labor Review,* Dept. of Labor, August 1948, p. 131.

ever, were by no means uniform. Out of 117 industries examined, eighteen had increases in average wage income of less than 100 per cent, forty-seven of 100 to 125 per cent, thirty-eight of 125 to 150 per cent, and fourteen of 150 per cent or more (Table 10).

TABLE 10

Industries Ranked by 1949 Mean Wage Income of All Workers, by Increase in Mean Income between 1939 and 1949

| | | INCREASE IN MEAN INCOME, 1939 TO 1949 | | | |
|---|---|---|---|---|---|
| RANK OF INDUSTRY | TOTAL | *Less than 100.0%* | *100.0 to 124.9%* | *125.0 to 149.9%* | *150.0% or More* |
| Total | 117 | 18 | 47 | 38 | 14 |
| Lowest tenth | 5 | — | 3 | 1 | 1 |
| Second tenth | 13 | 1 | 4 | 6 | 2 |
| Third tenth | 12 | 1 | 3 | 6 | 2 |
| Fourth tenth | 11 | 1 | 4 | 4 | 2 |
| Fifth tenth | 11 | 2 | 3 | 3 | 3 |
| Sixth tenth | 18 | 2 | 10 | 4 | 2 |
| Seventh tenth | 19 | 3 | 8 | 8 | — |
| Eighth tenth | 8 | 3 | 2 | 3 | — |
| Ninth tenth | 4 | 1 | 3 | — | — |
| Highest tenth | 16 | 4 | 7 | 3 | 2 |

Source: Derived from Appendix Table B-4.

These different gains could have had an important impact on the distribution of total wage income.

There was a marked difference between the gains of high-paid and low-paid industries (Table 10). Among the thirty lowest-paid industries, eighteen had gains in average earnings of 125 per cent or more, and only two failed to double their average wage incomes. In contrast, of the twenty-eight highest-paid industries, only eight had increases of 125 per cent or more, and an equal number failed to double their average earnings. These data lend support to the hypothesis that the greater relative gains of the lower-paid industries are a factor in the general reduction in the dispersion of wage income during the decade.

An examination of the particular industries involved quickly dispels the notion that the greater relative gains of the low-paid groups can be entirely explained by a single factor such as the increase in union membership during the decade. For example, included among the lowest third of the industries with income gains of 125 per cent or more are agriculture, restaurants, logging, sawmills, taxicab service, gasoline service stations, drug stores, laundries, and many others in which the impact of the union has been relatively slight. Probably most of the relatively greater wage increases in the low-paid industries resulted from the pressure for workers exerted by the other industries in the expanding defense program during the early 1940's. Industries losing workers were forced to raise wages to hold their existing labor force or to attract people outside the labor market. This increase in wages tended to change the wage relationships which prevailed in 1940. During the war, the revised wage differentials, established early during the defense program, were more or less stabilized by regulation. As a result, the postwar period inherited a wage structure which differed significantly from that of 1940. The relatively full-employment conditions during the postwar period have served to maintain the differentials.

Despite the differential gains in average earnings among industries, there were comparatively few changes in the relative position of industries. When ranked by mean wage income in 1949, ninety-four of the 117 industries studied remained either in the same tenths or in tenths adjacent to the ones they had been in 1939 (Appendix Table B-5). However, welfare and religious services dropped from the seventh tenth in 1939 to the third in 1949; educational services, from the eighth to the fourth; telephone and state and local public administration, from the highest to the sixth; and postal services and credit agencies, from the highest to the eighth.

About one-third of the workers in these industries were in government or education.

### *Reasons for the Decrease in Differentials*

The statistical data clearly show that the decrease in the dispersion of wages during the decade which ended in 1949 is primarily attributable to decreases in wage differentials between skilled and unskilled workers within each industry and between high-paid and low-paid industries. What forces operated to produce these changes?

The decrease in differentials between skilled and unskilled workers can perhaps best be understood as part of a historical process observed in the United States since the turn of the century.[3] In 1907, for example, the median earnings of skilled workers in manufacturing industries was about twice that received by unskilled workers. By the end of World War I it was only 75 per cent greater, and by the end of World War II, only about 55 per cent greater (Table 11). Thus, during a forty-year period, the differential between skilled and unskilled workers was reduced by about 50 per cent, or by an average of about 1 per cent per year.

TABLE 11

Relationship between Earnings of Skilled and Unskilled Occupations in Manufacturing Industries, 1907–1947

(*average earnings for representative unskilled occupations = 100*)

| PERIOD | *Median* | *Range* [a] |
|---|---|---|
| 1907 | 205 | 180 – 280 |
| 1918–1919 | 175 | 150 – 225 |
| 1931–1932 | 180 | 160 – 220 |
| 1937–1940 | 165 | 150 – 190 |
| 1945–1947 | 155 | 145 – 170 |

[a] Middle half of all indexes.

Source: Harry Ober "Occupational Wage Differentials, 1907–1947," *Monthly Labor Review,* Dept. of Labor, August 1948, p. 130.

Many factors, of course, contributed to the reduction, and there is disagreement on the importance of specific factors. One student has explained the decrease during this period largely in terms of forces affecting the supply of workers for unskilled jobs.[4] He points

[3] The tendency for occupational wage differentials to narrow has also been observed in Great Britain. The British experience is analyzed in a study by K. G. C. Knowles and D. J. Robertson, "Differences between the Wages of Skilled and Unskilled Workers, 1880–1950," *Bulletin of Oxford University Institute of Statistics,* April 1951, pp. 109–127.

[4] See particularly Harry M. Douty, "Union Impact on Wage Structures," *Proceedings of Sixth Annual Meeting of Industrial Relations Research Association,* 1953.

out that the restriction of immigration and a declining birth rate up to the 1940's tended to reduce the supply of unskilled workers relative to that of skilled workers and thereby to increase the relative price of the former. Also the extension of the minimum legal age for leaving school both delayed the entrance of many young people into the labor force and increased the numbers eligible for the more skilled jobs. But the increase in the productivity of unskilled labor by its combination with larger quantities of capital may also have made it economically feasible to raise wages.

Wage differentials since the depression have probably continued to be affected by the relative supply of skilled and unskilled workers. As previously indicated, the lowest paid, least organized industries are among those which made the greatest relative gains during the 1940's. Workers in these industries undoubtedly benefited from the pressures for higher wages exerted by organized workers. In addition, however, many employers in these industries doubtless raised wages because they were afraid of losing workers to the higher paying defense industries. So the relative labor supply was probably important in the decrease of wage differentials even during the past decade.

At the same time, however, two powerful forces, the federal government and the unions, have influenced wage regulation and wage determination to an unprecedented extent during the past twenty years. Before the depression of the 1930's the government exercised little direct control over wages. Even the unions played a relatively minor role during this period.[5]

Since the 1930's, however, the federal government has assumed an increasingly prominent role. Aside from its direct influence as the employer of an ever-growing proportion of the labor force, it has attempted to regulate wage differentials under a minimum wage law and by the policies and decisions of the various wage control and stabilization boards beginning with the National War Labor Board in 1942. Each of these has tended to affect wage structures differently.

The past twenty years have also witnessed a tremendous growth in union membership, from 2.9 million in 1933, mostly craftsmen concentrated in a few industries like construction, railroads, and printing, to about 17 million in 1952 scattered throughout the econ-

[5] It has been pointed out that "as late as 1934, union-management contracts fixed the wages and working conditions for some three or four million workers and were confined, to a great extent, to the so-called sheltered trades such as printing, construction, or bakeries, or to regulated industries like railroads." (see Everett M. Kassalow, "New Patterns of Collective Bargaining," *Insights into Labor Issues*, ed. by R. A. Lester and J. Shister, Macmillan, 1948, p. 117).

omy.[6] Most economists agree that the growth of the big union, like the growth of big government, has had some impact on wage structures. Some, like Milton Friedman, believe that the efficacy of union pressure has been exaggerated. But even Friedman concedes that between 10 and 20 per cent of the labor force "can be supposed to have had their wages significantly affected by the existence of unions." [7]

One cannot separate the impact of government and union policy on wage differentials from those of other forces. The fact that the policies of both of these major institutions generally coincided with the changes in wage dispersion does not signify that they *caused* these changes.

### FAIR LABOR STANDARDS ACT

Federal minimum wage regulation began in 1938 with the passage of the Fair Labor Standards Act. The statutory minimum wage set was 25 cents an hour. Subsequently the minimum was raised to 30 cents (1939), 35 cents (1941), 40 cents (1944) and 75 cents (1950). By 1955 about 24 million of the 44 million workers in private firms were covered by the law.[8]

The law could theoretically have reduced dispersion in the distribution of wages by raising the average level in low-paid industries more than in high-paid industries and of low-paid workers more than of high-paid workers. Actually, however, it has probably had little impact because it was enacted at the beginning of a relatively long period of high employment during which wage rates, even in covered industries, were substantially above the minimum. It was estimated in 1954, for example, that an increase in the minimum wage rate for workers covered by the Fair Labor Standards Act from 75 cents an hour to $1.00 an hour would affect less than 2 million workers out of the total of 44 million.[9] However, there is some evidence that it influenced the wage structure within at least one industry—the southern lumber industry.[10] This may provide important clues to the impact of an effective minimum wage law on the average level and dispersion of wages within industries. The

[6] *Statistical Abstract of the United States, 1954,* Bureau of the Census, p. 235.

[7] Milton Friedman, "Some Comments on the Significance of Labor Unions for Economic Policy," *Impact of the Union,* ed. by David McC. Wright, Harcourt, Brace, 1951.

[8] *Economic Report of the President,* January 1955, p. 58.

[9] Clarence D. Long, "The Minimum Wage," mimeographed, May 6, 1954.

[10] J. F. Walker and Harry M. Douty, "Effects of Minimum Wage in Southern Sawmills," and J. F. Walker, "Earnings in the Southern Lumber Industry," in the September 1950 and October 1953 issues, respectively, of the *Monthly Labor Review,* Dept. of Labor.

trend of wages in the southern lumber industry has been summarized as follows: "When the first FLSA minimum of 25 cents became effective in October 1938, the average in the industry rose almost immediately from about 27 cents to 31 cents. The 5-cent raise in the minimum a year later increased the average 3 cents, from 32 to 35 cents an hour. The next 5-cent increase in the minimum (to 35 cents) in November 1941 raised the industry average from 39 to 42 cents per hour. . . . The 75-cent minimum, effective January 25, 1950, had the immediate result of raising the average 11 cents to 80 cents an hour by March 1950."[11]

Both the timing and the magnitude of these changes suggest that this average is very responsive to changes in the statutory minimum hourly wage. In view of this fact, it is reasonable to assume that the minimum wage law tends to raise the average level of wages in the low-paid industries. The law may account in some measure for the fact that average annual earnings of laborers in the furniture, lumber, and wood products industry rose proportionately more between 1939 and 1949 than those of laborers in every other industry for which data are shown, with the exception of the textile and apparel industry (Table 6).

Although the minimum wage law appears to have had a direct impact on the average level of wages in the southern lumber industry, apparently it has had only a negligible effect on the dispersion of wages within the industry. The available evidence is presented in Table 12, where the relationship in average hourly earnings for six

TABLE 12

Relationship of Average Hourly Earnings of Six Occupations in the Southern Lumber Industry, 1949, 1950, and 1953

(*average earnings of machine off-bearers = 100*)

| OCCUPATION | *October–December 1949* | *March 1950*[a] | *April 1953* |
|---|---|---|---|
| Teamsters, logging | 105 | 103 | 104 |
| Truck drivers, logging | 106 | 103 | 106 |
| Fallers and buckers, hand | 117 | 114 | 111 |
| Circular head-saw operators | 170 | 153 | 164 |
| Band-head-saw operators | 216 | 195 | 206 |

[a] The minimum hourly wage was raised to 75 cents on January 25, 1950.

Source: James F. Walker, "Earnings in the Southern Lumber Industry," *Monthly Labor Review*, October 1953, p. 1080.

different types of jobs are examined for a period just preceding an increase in the statutory minimum wage, immediately after an increase, and three years after the increase.

[11] Walker, *op. cit.*, p. 1078.

The immediate effect of the increase in the minimum wage to 75 cents an hour was a reduction in wage differentials. The average hourly earnings of machine off-bearers, a low-paying job, rose relative to the average for each of the other five types of higher-paying jobs. Three years later, however, the wage differentials before the increase in the minimum wage had been largely re-established. Although the data indicate that after three years machine off-bearers had made a slight net gain relative to three of the other skills, the minimum wage law apparently did not permanently affect the dispersion of wages within this industry to any significant degree.

## NATIONAL WAR LABOR BOARD

One month after our entry into World War II, the National War Labor Board (NWLB) was established and given general responsibility for "settling labor disputes which threatened to impede the effective prosecution of the war." The NWLB still did not then have authority to regulate wages, only to "resolve issues in dispute by mediation, voluntary arbitration, or arbitration under rules of its own making." Nearly one year later, in October 1942, it was given complete jurisdiction over all wage rate adjustments, with the stipulation that it could grant increases in wage rates prevailing in September 1942 only "to correct maladjustments or inequalities, to eliminate substandards of living, to correct gross inequities, or to aid in the effective prosecution of the war." [12]

Thus, at the very inception of the wartime regulation, provision was made for wage adjustments consistent with the established government policy of raising the lower end of the income curve. Even before the authority for wartime wage controls was officially turned over to the NWLB, President Roosevelt stated in his anti-inflation message to Congress on April 27, 1942, that "the existing machinery for labor disputes will . . . continue to give due consideration to inequalities and to the elimination of substandards of living." [13]

The NWLB used three major administrative techniques in deciding whether or not to grant wage increases: (1) the "Little Steel Formula"; (2) the bracket system; and (3) the substandard policy.

### *The Little Steel Formula*

Superficially, the Little Steel Formula appears to have tended to maintain wage differentials existing at the outbreak of the war—

[12] *Termination Report of the National War Labor Board,* Dept. of Labor, 1947, Vol. 1, pp. 7 and 8.

[13] *Ibid.,* p. 211.

and it has been so interpreted by some authors [14]—since it permitted an increase in straight-time hourly earnings of 15 per cent over the January 1941 levels. However, "One of the fundamental concepts of the Little Steel Formula was that it should be applied to combined occupational groups rather than to individual employees or to individual job classifications in order that all workers in the unit should receive the same wage or salary adjustment in cents per hour, and, that, percentagewise, the unskilled relatively low-paid workers should receive greater increases than the skilled, high-paid workers." [15]

The Little Steel Formula provided a basis for compensating workers for increases in the cost of living and for stabilizing the general level of wages. It did not provide an effective basis for adjusting wage rates in new plants or in plants converting to the manufacture of new products. And it was not suitable for adjusting problems associated with wage differentials between plants in an industry or an area. To deal with "interplant inequities," the wage rate bracket approach was adopted.

### *Wage Brackets*

The wage bracket was defined as "a band of rates or rate ranges from minimum to maximum representing the sound, tested, and stable rates paid by employers for a particular job classification in a particular industry and labor market area." [16] This range was then converted to a single rate bracket minimum,[17] and rates below the minimum could be raised to it. However rates within the bracket could not be increased on the basis of comparisons with other plants.

The effect was to reduce the dispersion of wages by raising the wage level for the lowest-paid workers. Within each occupation in a given industry and locality, most wage rates of the lowest-paid workers were raised to a point 10 per cent below the average for that group. About 60 per cent of the approvals of wage rate increases by the NWLB were made on the basis of the bracket system.[18] This procedure, therefore, was very important in the general reduction in the dispersion of wages during the war.

[14] David R. Roberts, "The Meaning of Recent Wage Changes," *Insights into Labor Issues,* p. 201.

[15] *Termination Report of the National War Labor Board,* Vol. 1, p. 201.

[16] *Ibid.,* p. 230.

[17] Two methods were employed to convert the range of rates to a single rate. The procedure recommended by the NWLB and the one most commonly used established the single-rate bracket minimum at 10 per cent below the weighted average of rates for the given occupation, industry, and area. The other method was to set the single-rate bracket minimum at the first substantial cluster of rates for the occupation, industry, and area.

[18] Roberts, *op. cit.,* p. 227.

*Substandard Rates*

Wage increases granted by the NWLB for "eliminating substandards of living" were specifically designed to raise the incomes of the lowest-paid workers. In general, the Board interpreted its task as one of determining "an appropriate minimum up to which wage adjustments could voluntarily be made to correct substandards of living."[19] In accordance with this policy, the NWLB decided in February 1943 that wage rates could be raised up to 40 cents an hour without obtaining approval.[20] The permissive minimum was raised to 50 cents an hour in November 1944 and, finally, to 55 cents an hour in August 1945. To make its substandard policy consistent with its wage rate brackets, the NWLB permitted wages below the substandard rate to be increased to that level. However, increases at higher wage rates had to be tapered progressively to zero at 70 cents per hour. In other words, no wage rate increases were permitted on the basis of the substandard policy for rates of 70 cents an hour or more. The net effect of this procedure, as in the case of the Little Steel Formula and the wage-rate bracket policy, was to raise the level of the lowest paid workers relative to others.

## UNION POLICY

During recent years, labor unions have increasingly demanded higher wages in terms of uniform cents-per-hour increases. Such increases, of course, tend to reduce the dispersion of wages since they result in greater relative gains for lower-paid workers. This inclination on the part of organized labor was manifested even before the outbreak of World War II. However, its greatest actual impact on the distribution of wages began with the cessation of hostilities.

About six months after the end of World War II, the United States experienced some of the greatest strikes in its history. Among the first and the most important, because they set the pattern for later demands and settlements, were the steel strike (750,000 workers), the electrical workers (200,000), the automobile workers (200,000), the meat packers (125,000), and the oil workers (35,000). Altogether, about 1,750,000 workers were idled by strikes in January 1946 alone.

What were the wage demands of these strikes? The United Steel Workers of America (CIO) and the United Electrical, Radio and Machine Workers of America (CIO) both demanded an increase of $2 per day.[21] In the meat-packing industry, the United Packinghouse Workers (CIO) initially demanded a wage increase of 25 cents per hour; the Amalgamated Meat Cutters and Butcher Work-

[19] *Ibid.*, p. 211.
[20] *Ibid.*, p. 212.
[21] *Monthly Labor Review*, March 1946, pp. 426 ff.

men of North America (AFL) a minimum wage rate of $36 per week, but were willing later to accept a straight increase of 15 cents per hour. At some point in each of these strikes the unions demanded a uniform cents-per-hour increase. Only the United Automobile Workers (CIO) and the Oil Workers International (CIO) stated their demands in percentage terms, both demanding a 30 per cent increase. (Ultimately the automobile workers settled for a uniform cents-per-hour increase of 18½ cents and the oil workers received an 18 per cent increase.) In addition, numerous other disputes during the first year after VJ Day were settled on a uniform cents-per-hour basis.

Since the early postwar strikes, organized labor has shifted its major emphasis to demands for pension and welfare and other funds. However, many unions have continued to press for uniform cents-per-hour increases; and some contracts, particularly in the motor vehicle industry, feature automatic uniform changes in wage rates for annual increases in productivity or for changes in the cost of living.

## *Appendix A: Definitions and Explanations*

### DEFINITIONS

#### *Money Wages*

This is the total money earnings received for work performed as an employee during the calendar year preceding the date of the census. Thus, in the 1950 census, the money wages refer to earnings during 1949. They include wages, salaries, Armed Forces pay, commissions, tips, piece-rate payments, and cash bonuses earned, before deductions were made for taxes, bonds, pensions, union dues, and so forth. They do not include the value of free meals, board, or other wages "in kind," or earnings from the operation of a farm, business, or professional practice.

#### *Occupation, Industry and Class of Worker*

The data on industry, occupation, and class of worker refer to the job held during the survey week. Persons employed at two or more jobs were reported in the job at which they worked the greatest number of hours during the week. Persons who were unemployed during the survey week were classified according to their last civilian job.

Wage workers are persons who worked as employees for wages or salaries. They include not only factory operatives, laborers, clerks, and so forth, who worked for wages, but also other persons working for tips or for room or board, salesmen, and other employees working for commissions, and salaried business managers, corporation executives, and government officials.

The industrial and occupational classification systems used in the

1940 census are basically the same as those used in 1950. An attempt was made to make each group as comparable as possible for 1940 and 1950. There are, however, a number of differences in the specific content of particular groups. The industry data shown for 1940 have not been entirely adjusted for comparability with the 1950 classification system. But available evidence indicates that the 1940–1950 relationships shown by the data are not significantly affected by these differences. The 1940 classification by class of worker is similar to the 1950 classification.

## METHOD OF ESTIMATING AGGREGATE WAGE OR SALARY INCOME

An estimate of the number of persons at each income level was obtained by distributing those not reporting on income among all the income levels in the same proportion as those that did report. A mean income was then selected for each wage income level, and estimates of aggregate wages were obtained by multiplying the number of persons at each income level by the mean for that level.

For income levels under $10,000, the midpoint of each level was assumed to be the mean. The open-end interval in the 1950 census was "$10,000 and over." The Current Population Survey for April 1951 and other sources indicated that $20,000 was a reasonable estimate of the mean wage income for this interval. The open-end interval in the wage data for 1939 was "$5,000 and over." Income tax returns for that year and data obtained in the income surveys indicated that $9,000 was a reasonable estimate of the mean wage or salary income for this interval.

## METHOD OF CLASSIFYING INDUSTRIES BY DECILES

Table B-5 shows industries classified by level of wage income in 1939 and 1949 and Table B-6 shows a similar classification by dispersion of wage income. The procedure described below was used to prepare Table B-5. A similar procedure was used for Table B-6.

A listing of industries ranked from lowest to highest by mean wage income was prepared for 1939 and a separate listing for 1949. Each listing showed the name of the industry, the average income, and the proportion of all wage workers included in the industry. On the basis of these listings, the industries were grouped into tenths.

## COMPARABILITY OF CENSUS RESULTS WITH OTHER DATA

One method of appraising the accuracy of the wage or salary data obtained for specific industries in the 1940 and 1950 decennial censuses is to compare them with similar information from other sources. All the comparisons attempted in this paper must be regarded as rough approximations because they are subject to a wide range of error attributable to differences in definition. However the data may indicate the probable direction and magnitude of error in the census results for specific industries.

Table A-1 shows the mean wage income in 1949 for workers in seven-

TABLE A-1

Estimates of 1949 Mean Wage Income for Workers in Seventeen Manufacturing Industries, Census of Population, National Income Division, and Survey of Manufactures

| INDUSTRY | *Census of Population* [a] (1) | *National Income Division* [b] (2) | *Survey of Manufactures* [c] (3) | *Difference:* (2)–(1) as % of (2) (4) | *Difference:* (3)–(1) as % of (3) (5) |
|---|---|---|---|---|---|
| Food and kindred products | $2,680 | $2,926 | $2,870 | 8.4 | 6.6 |
| Tobacco manufactures | 1,960 | 2,089 | 2,063 | 6.2 | 5.0 |
| Textile mill products | 2,279 | 2,565 | 2,542 | 11.2 | 10.3 |
| Apparel and related products | 2,026 | 2,383 | 2,341 | 15.0 | 13.5 |
| Lumber and furniture products | 2,083 | 2,463 | 2,382 | 15.4 | 12.6 |
| Paper and allied products | 2,858 | 3,230 | 3,174 | 11.5 | 10.0 |
| Printing and publishing | 3,210 | 3,653 | 3,629 | 12.1 | 11.5 |
| Chemicals and allied products | 3,313 | 3,529 | 3,418 | 6.1 | 3.1 |
| Petroleum and coal products | 4,058 | 4,179 | 3,936 | 2.9 | −3.1 |
| Rubber products | 3,033 | 3,225 | 3,208 | 6.0 | 5,5 |
| Leather and leather products | 2,143 | 2,410 | 2,376 | 11.1 | 9.8 |
| Stone, clay, and glass products | 2,759 | 3,014 | 2,920 | 8.5 | 5.5 |
| Metals | 3,021 | 3,366 | 3,361 | 10.2 | 10.1 |
| Machinery, except electrical | 3,248 | 3,478 | 3,520 | 6.6 | 7.7 |
| Electrical machinery | 2,950 | 3,247 | 3,234 | 9.1 | 8.8 |
| Transportation equipment | 3,251 | 3,604 | 3,595 | 9.8 | 9.6 |
| Miscellaneous manufacturing industries | 2,692 | 2,961 | 2,983 | 9.1 | 9.8 |

[a] Derived from Appendix Table B-4.

[b] Derived from *National Income and Product of the United States, 1929–1950,* Dept. of Commerce, 1951, Table 14 (wages and salaries by industry) and Table 25 (average number of full-time and part-time employees by industry).

[c] Derived from *Annual Survey of Manufactures, 1949 and 1950,* Bureau of the Census, 1952, Table 4, p. 17.

teen manufacturing industry groups. These data were obtained from the National Income Division (NID) of the Department of Commerce, the 1950 Survey of Manufactures (SM) conducted by the Bureau of the Census, and the 1950 Census of Population. Table A-2 shows the mean wage income for all industries and is based on information obtained from the NID and the 1950 census. Several important conceptual differences underly these data. In the SM each plant was asked to report the total wages and salaries paid to all employees. Average employment was reported by each plant for the four pay periods nearest the 15th of March, May, August, and November. The NID data for manufacturing industries are based largely on the quarterly reports filed by each employer with the Bureau of Employment Security. These reports contain a list of all employees and the taxable earnings paid to each employee. The estimates prepared from the SM and from the NID data are conceptually very similar since they are based largely on reported payroll information taken from the accounting records of establishments. In contrast, the 1950 census averages for each industry represent the wages and salaries paid to persons employed in that industry in April 1950 or who were then unemployed but worked in that industry at their last job. Thus the wages of individuals who left the labor force during the year would not appear in the census data by industry, but they would be reflected in the series based on establishment reports. Many people who do some work during a given year are not in the labor force in a particular month. In January 1952, for example, about one-third of the men and one-sixth of the women who were not in the labor force did some work during the preceding year.[22] In addition, the wages and salaries of workers who changed jobs during the year or who had more than one job at the time of the survey were all attributed to the industry at which most time was spent during the survey week in the census data. In contrast, in the establishment reports all such earnings were allocated to the industry in which the earnings were actually made.

One can only speculate about the net effect of these conceptual differences. There can be little question that the census aggregates tend to be lower than those derived from establishment reports because of the exclusion of the wages of persons who left the labor force. The impact of these differences on the averages, however, is more difficult to determine. The census averages tend to be higher than those based on establishment reports because of the exclusion of workers who left the labor force and who typically have lower earnings. The impact of multiple job holders (either at a given time or throughout the year) on the averages for both series is indeterminate because it tends to raise some averages and depress others.

Table A-1 indicates that the census averages are below those derived from the NID in all of the seventeen manufacturing industries for which data are shown. The difference was between $200 and $300 (6 and 10 per cent) in most cases. Only in two industries (apparel and lumber) was the difference between the estimates as great as 15 per cent. One possible explanation is that in 1949 these two industries had a considerably larger proportion of part-year workers than most other manufacturing industries.[23] Conversely, the similarity of the estimates for the petroleum and coal products industry may be related to the fact that this industry had the largest proportion of full-year workers in 1949.

Census and NID estimates of mean wage income for all industries for 1939 and 1949 are shown in Table A-2. These figures again emphasize the tendency for the census estimates to be lower than those based on establishment reports. The census estimates in 1949 exceeded NID in only nine industries. In seven of these industries, however, the census estimates for 1939 were also higher than those based on NID figures. This fact is significant because it suggests that there is a certain degree of stability in the relationship between the two sets of data. In the manufacturing

[22] *Current Population Reports–Labor Force,* Bureau of the Census, Series P-50, No. 43, 1953, Table 5.

[23] Derived from *1950 Census of Population,* Vol. II, *Characteristics of the Population,* Part 1, United States Summary, Table 135.

## TABLE A–2

Estimates of 1939 and 1949 Mean Wage Income for Workers, by Industry, 1950 Census of Population and National Income Division

| INDUSTRY | CENSUS OF POPULATION [a] | | | NATIONAL INCOME DIVISION [b] | | | DIFFERENCE: NID–CENSUS | | | |
|---|---|---|---|---|---|---|---|---|---|---|
| | | | | | | | *1939* | | *1949* | |
| | *1939* | *1949* | *Percentage Increase* | *1939* | *1949* | *Percentage Increase* | *Absolute* | *As % of* NID | *Absolute* | *As % of* NID |
| Agriculture, forestry, and fisheries: | | | | | | | | | | |
| Agriculture | $ 382 | $1,156 | 203 | $ 393 | $1,304 | 232 | $ 11 | 3 | $148 | 11 |
| Forestry | 700 | 2,073 | 196 | 440 | 2,000 | 355 | —260 | —1 | —73 | —4 |
| Fisheries | 852 | 2,286 | 168 | 1,000 | 2,767 | 177 | 148 | 15 | 481 | 17 |
| Mining: | | | | | | | | | | |
| Metal mining | 1,282 | 3,065 | 139 | 1,515 | 3,411 | 125 | 233 | 15 | 346 | 10 |
| Coal mining | 909 | 2,505 | 176 | 1,237 | 2,920 | 136 | 328 | 27 | 415 | 14 |
| Crude petroleum and natural gas products | 1,658 | 3,697 | 123 | 1,684 | 3,735 | 122 | 26 | 2 | 38 | 1 |
| Nonmetallic mining and quarrying | 932 | 2,663 | 186 | 1,178 | 3,021 | 156 | 246 | 21 | 358 | 12 |
| Contract construction | 967 | 2,649 | 174 | 1,268 | 3,235 | 155 | 301 | 24 | 586 | 18 |
| Manufacturing: | | | | | | | | | | |
| Food and kindred products | 1,250 | 2,680 | 114 | 1,372 | 2,926 | 113 | 122 | 9 | 246 | 8 |
| Tobacco manufactures | 835 | 1,960 | 135 | 916 | 2,089 | 128 | 81 | 9 | 129 | 6 |
| Textile mill products | 858 | 2,279 | 166 | 960 | 2,565 | 167 | 102 | 11 | 286 | 11 |
| Apparel and other finished fabricated products | 830 | 2,026 | 144 | 1,025 | 2,383 | 132 | 195 | 19 | 357 | 15 |
| Lumber, furniture, and wood products | 837 | 2,083 | 149 | 1,042 | 2,463 | 136 | 205 | 20 | 380 | 15 |
| Paper and allied products | 1,251 | 2,858 | 128 | 1,414 | 3,230 | 128 | 163 | 12 | 372 | 12 |
| Printing, publishing, and allied industries | 1,585 | 3,210 | 103 | 1,718 | 3,653 | 113 | 133 | 8 | 443 | 12 |
| Chemicals and allied products | 1,524 | 3,313 | 117 | 1,611 | 3,529 | 119 | 87 | 5 | 216 | 6 |
| Products of petroleum and coal | 1,886 | 4,058 | 115 | 1,852 | 4,179 | 126 | —34 | —2 | 121 | 3 |
| Rubber products | 1,410 | 3,033 | 115 | 1,548 | 3,225 | 108 | 138 | 9 | 192 | 6 |

continued on next page

TABLE A–2, continued

| INDUSTRY | CENSUS OF POPULATION [a] | | | NATIONAL INCOME DIVISION [b] | | | DIFFERENCE: NID–CENSUS | | | |
|---|---|---|---|---|---|---|---|---|---|---|
| | | | | | | | *1939* | | *1949* | |
| | *1939* | *1949* | *Percentage Increase* | *1939* | *1949* | *Percentage Increase* | *Absolute* | *As % of* NID | *Absolute* | *As % of* NID |
| Leather and leather products | 910 | 2,143 | 135 | 1,038 | 2,410 | 132 | 128 | 12 | 267 | 11 |
| Stone, clay, and glass products | 1,184 | 2,759 | 133 | 1,359 | 3,014 | 122 | 175 | 13 | 255 | 8 |
| Iron and steel and their products | $1,344 | $3,029 | 125 | $1,549 | $3,390 | 119 | $205 | 13 | $316 | 11 |
| Nonferrous metals and their products | 1,330 | 2,978 | 124 | 1,521 | 3,271 | 115 | 191 | 13 | 293 | 9 |
| Machinery, except electrical | 1,480 | 3,248 | 119 | 1,681 | 3,478 | 107 | 201 | 12 | 230 | 7 |
| Electrical machinery | 1,465 | 2,950 | 101 | 1,601 | 3,247 | 103 | 136 | 8 | 297 | 9 |
| Transportation equipment except automobile | 1,380 | 3,265 | 137 | 1,667 | 3,600 | 116 | 287 | 17 | 335 | 9 |
| Automobile and automobile equipment | 1,414 | 3,246 | 130 | 1,762 | 3,607 | 105 | 348 | 20 | 361 | 10 |
| Miscellaneous manufacturing industries | 1,196 | 2,692 | 125 | 1,337 | 2,961 | 121 | 141 | 11 | 269 | 9 |
| Wholesale and retail trade: | | | | | | | | | | |
| Wholesale trade | 1,579 | 3,213 | 103 | 1,718 | 3,559 | 107 | 139 | 8 | 346 | 10 |
| Retail trade and automobile service | 972 | 2,185 | 125 | 1,076 | 2,362 | 120 | 104 | 10 | 177 | 7 |
| Finance, insurance, and real estate: | | | | | | | | | | |
| Banking, credit agencies, and commercial brokers | 2,017 | 3,187 | 58 | 1,961 | 3,243 | 65 | –56 | –3 | 56 | 2 |
| Insurance and real estate | 1,574 | 2,903 | 84 | 1,473 | 2,706 | 84 | –101 | –7 | –197 | –7 |
| Transportation: | | | | | | | | | | |
| Railroads | 1,617 | 3,199 | 98 | 1,877 | 3,704 | 97 | 260 | 14 | 505 | 14 |
| Local railways, bus lines, and highway passenger transportation | 1,391 | 2,735 | 97 | 1,563 | 2,960 | 89 | 172 | 11 | 225 | 8 |
| Highway freight transportation and warehouses | 1,120 | 2,757 | 146 | 1,271 | 2,963 | 133 | 151 | 12 | 206 | 7 |
| Water transportation | 1,259 | 3,113 | 147 | 1,473 | 3,938 | 167 | 214 | 15 | 825 | 21 |

continued on next page

TABLE A–2, concluded

| Industry | Census of Population [a] | | | National Income Division [b] | | | Difference: NID–Census | | | |
|---|---|---|---|---|---|---|---|---|---|---|
| | | | | | | | *1939* | | *1949* | |
| | *1939* | *1949* | *Percentage Increase* | *1939* | *1949* | *Percentage Increase* | *Absolute* | *As % of NID* | *Absolute* | *As % of NID* |
| Air transportation | 1,783 | 3,862 | 117 | 2,267 | 3,870 | 71 | 484 | 21 | 8 | — |
| Pipe-line transportation | 1,579 | 3,750 | 137 | 1,955 | 4,172 | 113 | 376 | 19 | 422 | 10 |
| Services allied to transportation | 1,321 | 3,028 | 129 | 1,127 | 2,586 | 129 | −194 | −17 | −442 | −17 |
| Communications and public utilities: | | | | | | | | | | |
| Telephone, telegraph, and related services | $1,574 | $2,810 | 79 | $1,600 | $2,907 | 82 | $ 26 | 2 | $ 97 | 3 |
| Radio broadcasting and television | 2,167 | 4,183 | 93 | 2,261 | 4,056 | 79 | 94 | 4 | −127 | −3 |
| Utilities and public services | 1,685 | 3,085 | 83 | 1,739 | 3,340 | 92 | 54 | 3 | 255 | 8 |
| Services: | | | | | | | | | | |
| Hotels and other lodging places | 738 | 1,616 | 119 | 891 | 1,817 | 104 | 153 | 17 | 201 | 11 |
| Personal services | 825 | 1,836 | 123 | 941 | 2,038 | 117 | 116 | 12 | 202 | 10 |
| Private households | 354 | 788 | 123 | 466 | 1,263 | 171 | 112 | 24 | 475 | 38 |
| Educational services (including commercial trade schools) | 1,416 | 2,484 | 75 | 1,234 | 2,378 | 93 | −182 | −15 | −106 | −4 |
| Business services | 1,599 | 3,273 | 105 | 1,525 | 3,057 | 100 | −74 | −5 | −216 | −7 |
| Miscellaneous repair services | 1,000 | 2,513 | 151 | 1,257 | 2,734 | 118 | 257 | 20 | 221 | 8 |
| Motion pictures, amusement, and recreation | 1,251 | 2,385 | 91 | 1,379 | 2,245 | 63 | 128 | −9 | −140 | −6 |
| Medical and other health services | 926 | 1,970 | 113 | 907 | 1,995 | 120 | −19 | −2 | 25 | 1 |
| Legal, engineering, and other professional service | 1,741 | 3,271 | 88 | 1,301 | 2,747 | 111 | −440 | −34 | −524 | −19 |
| Religious organizations and nonprofit organizations | 1,327 | 2,276 | 72 | 1,183 | 2,249 | 90 | −144 | −12 | −27 | −1 |

[a] Derived from Appendix Table B-4.
[b] Derived from *National Income and Product of the United States, 1929–1950,* Dept. of Commerce, 1951, Tables 14 and 25.

industries, there was considerable improvement in the consistency of the results between 1939 and 1949. In all but four of the manufacturing industries the percentage difference between the census and NID averages were reduced between 1939 and 1949. The lumber and apparel industries, which showed the greatest relative differences among manufacturing industries in 1949, were also among those with the greatest relative differences in 1939. Similarly, the petroleum and coal industry, which showed the smallest relative difference in 1949, also showed the smallest relative difference in 1939. The most striking changes in the relationships between the two series were found in transportation. In the automobile manufacturing industry the percentage difference between the census and NID average was reduced from 20 per cent in 1939 to 10 per cent in 1949 and in industries which manufactured transportation equipment other than automobiles the differential was reduced from 17 to 9 per cent.

Among nonmanufacturing industries, there appears to be a wide variation in the consistency of the results produced by the two series. The estimates tended to be most consistent in the following industry groups: wholesale and retail trade; banking, insurance, and real estate; and communications and public utilities. Only two of the specific industries within these groups showed differences as great as 10 per cent in 1939 or 1949. The group of service industries was the only one in which the census estimates were typically greater than NID ones. One-half of all industries in in which the census average exceeded NID one were in the service trades. The contract construction industry showed widely divergent averages in the census and NID in 1939 and 1949. In 1939, the NID average was 24 per cent greater than the census one, in 1949, 18 per cent greater. The census and NID estimates for the mining industry also differed markedly in 1939 and 1949. Within this group, only the crude petroleum and natural gas production industry produced census and NID averages which did not differ significantly in 1939 or 1949. The averages for other mining industries ranged from a minimum of 10 per cent for metal mining in 1949 to a maximum of 27 per cent for coal mining in 1939. In transportation, as in mining and construction, wide differences between the census and NID estimates were typical.

# Appendix B: Statistical Tables Relating to Industries

**TABLE B-1**

Wage Workers, by Industry in 1950, by Wage Income in 1949, and by Sex

| INDUSTRY | NUMBER WITH $1 OR MORE (*thousands*) (1) | PERCENTAGE DISTRIBUTION BY INCOME CLASS: Under $500 (2) | $500 to $999 (3) | $1,000 to $1,499 (4) | $1,500 to $1,999 (5) | $2,000 to $2,499 (6) | $2,500 to $2,999 (7) | $3,000 to $3,499 (8) | $3,500 to $3,999 (9) | $4,000 to $4,499 (10) | $4,500 to $4,999 (11) | $5,000 to $5,999 (12) | $6,000 to $6,999 (13) | $7,000 to $9,999 (14) | $10,000 and Over (15) | INCOME AT QUARTILE POSITION: $Q_1$ (16) | *Median* $Q_2$ (17) | $Q_3$ (18) | ARITHMETIC MEAN (19) | MEASURES OF DISPERSION: $1-\frac{Q_1}{Q_2}$ (20) | $\frac{Q_3}{Q_2}-1$ (21) | $\frac{Q_3-Q_1}{Q_2}$ (22) | |
|---|---|---|---|---|---|---|---|---|---|---|---|---|---|---|---|---|---|---|---|---|---|---|---|
| *PART 1: MALES* | | | | | | | | | | | | | | | | | | | | | | | |
| 1. Total | 30,675 | 6.2 | 7.0 | 7.9 | 9.5 | 13.9 | 13.4 | 14.8 | 9.3 | 6.3 | 3.4 | 4.2 | 1.7 | 1.5 | 1.0 | $1,705 | $2,705 | $3,623 | $2,942 | 0.370 | 0.339 | 0.709 | 1. |
| 2. Agriculture, forestry, & fisheries | 1,403 | 26.1 | 25.5 | 17.8 | 12.6 | 8.0 | 3.8 | 2.6 | 1.2 | 0.8 | 0.4 | 0.5 | 0.2 | 0.2 | 0.1 | 478 | 968 | 1,722 | 1,244 | 0.506 | 0.777 | 1.283 | 2. |
| 3. Agriculture | 1,326 | 27.0 | 25.9 | 17.9 | 12.6 | 7.9 | 3.6 | 2.2 | 1.0 | 0.6 | 0.3 | 0.4 | 0.2 | 0.2 | 0.1 | 462 | 944 | 1,666 | 1,203 | 0.510 | 0.765 | 1.275 | 3. |
| 4. Forestry | 37 | 11.4 | 20.6 | 18.0 | 9.8 | 7.0 | 6.5 | 8.4 | 4.9 | 4.2 | 3.7 | 3.3 | 1.1 | 0.9 | 0.3 | 830 | 1,500 | 3,101 | 2,116 | 0.447 | 1.067 | 1.514 | 4. |
| 5. Fisheries | 40 | 10.6 | 14.4 | 14.1 | 13.0 | 12.6 | 8.2 | 8.5 | 4.5 | 5.5 | 1.9 | 2.9 | 1.4 | 1.7 | 0.7 | 1,000 | 1,919 | 3,123 | 2,351 | 0.479 | 0.627 | 1.106 | 5. |
| 6. Mining, extract., & quarry. | 883 | 3.6 | 5.1 | 7.3 | 10.1 | 19.0 | 16.3 | 13.6 | 9.1 | 5.8 | 3.3 | 3.6 | 1.7 | 1.0 | 0.5 | 1,945 | 2,650 | 3,500 | 2,871 | 0.266 | 0.320 | 0.586 | 6. |
| 7. Metals | 91 | 1.9 | 2.8 | 5.5 | 7.6 | 14.9 | 18.0 | 22.2 | 12.9 | 5.9 | 3.2 | 2.4 | 1.1 | 0.6 | 0.8 | 2,241 | 2,980 | 3,581 | 3,080 | 0.248 | 0.201 | 0.449 | 7. |
| 8. Coal | 497 | 4.4 | 6.0 | 8.6 | 12.3 | 24.5 | 19.4 | 11.4 | 4.4 | 2.9 | 1.6 | 2.4 | 1.3 | 0.4 | 0.3 | 1,743 | 2,381 | 2,994 | 2,508 | 0.268 | 0.257 | 0.525 | 8. |
| 9. Crude petroleum & nat. gas | 209 | 2.5 | 3.6 | 3.7 | 4.3 | 8.0 | 8.9 | 14.9 | 19.2 | 12.9 | 7.2 | 7.5 | 3.5 | 2.9 | 1.0 | 2,662 | 3,606 | 4,383 | 3,760 | 0.262 | 0.215 | 0.477 | 9. |
| 10. Nonmetals, exc. fuel | 86 | 3.6 | 6.4 | 9.8 | 13.6 | 17.7 | 14.7 | 14.0 | 7.2 | 5.3 | 3.4 | 2.4 | 0.7 | 0.6 | 0.6 | 1,691 | 2,468 | 3,328 | 2,680 | 0.316 | 0.348 | 0.664 | 10. |
| 11. Construction | 2,817 | 6.5 | 9.0 | 10.4 | 11.7 | 14.3 | 11.3 | 11.8 | 7.4 | 6.2 | 4.0 | 4.6 | 1.4 | 0.9 | 0.4 | 1,456 | 2,433 | 3,500 | 2,666 | 0.402 | 0.438 | 0.840 | 11. |
| 12. Manufacturing | 10,733 | 3.8 | 4.8 | 6.1 | 8.4 | 14.2 | 15.5 | 17.6 | 10.2 | 6.9 | 3.6 | 4.3 | 1.7 | 1.5 | 1.1 | 2,066 | 2,909 | 3,725 | 3,127 | 0.290 | 0.280 | 0.570 | 12. |
| 13. Durable goods | 6,420 | 3.3 | 5.0 | 6.2 | 7.9 | 13.7 | 16.4 | 19.1 | 10.7 | 6.7 | 3.4 | 3.9 | 1.5 | 1.3 | 0.9 | 2,094 | 2,923 | 3,658 | 3,091 | 0.284 | 0.251 | 0.535 | 13. |
| 14. Lumber & wood prod., exc. furn. | 741 | 11.7 | 17.0 | 17.6 | 14.2 | 11.3 | 8.6 | 8.1 | 4.3 | 2.8 | 1.3 | 1.5 | 0.6 | 0.5 | 0.4 | 891 | 1,630 | 2,686 | 1,965 | 0.454 | 0.647 | 1.101 | 14. |
| 15. Logging | 147 | 15.8 | 21.0 | 17.5 | 12.0 | 8.9 | 6.2 | 6.6 | 4.5 | 2.8 | 1.4 | 1.9 | 0.7 | 0.3 | 0.3 | 719 | 1,377 | 2,488 | 1,800 | 0.478 | 0.807 | 1.285 | 15. |
| 16. Saw & planing mills, & mill work | 515 | 11.3 | 16.9 | 18.0 | 14.4 | 11.1 | 8.8 | 8.3 | 4.2 | 2.8 | 1.3 | 1.4 | 0.5 | 0.5 | 0.4 | 905 | 1,631 | 2,687 | 1,963 | 0.446 | 0.646 | 1.092 | 16. |
| 17. Misc. wood prod. | 79 | 6.2 | 10.3 | 15.4 | 17.3 | 17.4 | 11.9 | 9.4 | 5.0 | 2.4 | 1.1 | 1.4 | 0.6 | 0.8 | 0.7 | 1,275 | 2,022 | 2,852 | 2,278 | 0.370 | 0.410 | 0.780 | 17. |
| 18. Furniture & fixtures | 259 | 4.7 | 7.5 | 10.6 | 15.1 | 18.3 | 14.9 | 12.6 | 6.3 | 4.0 | 1.6 | 2.1 | 0.6 | 0.8 | 0.8 | 1,572 | 2,330 | 3,154 | 2,560 | 0.326 | 0.353 | 0.679 | 18. |
| 19. Stone, clay, & glass prod. | 373 | 2.8 | 4.6 | 6.9 | 10.0 | 17.8 | 17.4 | 16.4 | 9.4 | 5.8 | 2.7 | 3.2 | 1.2 | 1.0 | 0.9 | 2,019 | 2,727 | 3,472 | 2,961 | 0.260 | 0.273 | 0.533 | 19. |
| 20. Glass & glass prod. | 107 | 2.7 | 4.2 | 5.7 | 7.9 | 16.5 | 16.6 | 16.0 | 12.2 | 7.3 | 3.4 | 4.1 | 1.7 | 0.9 | 0.9 | 2,136 | 2,891 | 3,721 | 3,117 | 0.262 | 0.286 | 0.548 | 20. |
| 21. Cement, concrete, gypsum, & plaster prod. | 96 | 3.1 | 5.5 | 7.3 | 9.8 | 17.3 | 18.8 | 16.9 | 8.4 | 5.1 | 2.4 | 3.2 | 1.0 | 0.9 | 0.5 | 1,964 | 2,686 | 3,390 | 2,830 | 0.269 | 0.262 | 0.531 | 21. |
| 22. Structural clay prod. | 68 | 2.9 | 5.6 | 9.6 | 13.2 | 21.9 | 17.0 | 13.8 | 6.4 | 4.0 | 1.3 | 1.6 | 0.9 | 1.0 | 0.8 | 1,761 | 2,426 | 3,173 | 2,672 | 0.275 | 0.307 | 0.582 | 22. |
| 23. Pottery & rel. prod. | 35 | 2.5 | 3.7 | 7.0 | 11.9 | 17.6 | 18.0 | 16.4 | 8.7 | 5.9 | 3.3 | 3.1 | 0.7 | 0.8 | 0.4 | 1,995 | 2,702 | 3,435 | 2,851 | 0.262 | 0.271 | 0.533 | 23. |
| 24. Misc. nonmet. min. & stone prod. | 67 | 2.3 | 3.7 | 5.2 | 9.7 | 16.3 | 16.8 | 18.8 | 10.0 | 6.1 | 3.2 | 3.6 | 1.2 | 1.5 | 1.6 | 2,125 | 2,880 | 3,610 | 3,217 | 0.263 | 0.253 | 0.516 | 24. |
| 25. Metal industries | 1,798 | 2.1 | 3.2 | 4.6 | 7.3 | 16.4 | 19.6 | 20.1 | 10.3 | 6.2 | 3.2 | 3.5 | 1.4 | 1.2 | 0.9 | 2,237 | 2,918 | 3,582 | 3,143 | 0.234 | 0.227 | 0.461 | 25. |
| 26. Iron & steel & their prod. | 1,513 | 2.0 | 3.1 | 4.5 | 7.2 | 16.4 | 19.8 | 20.2 | 10.3 | 6.2 | 3.2 | 3.4 | 1.4 | 1.2 | 0.9 | 2,250 | 2,924 | 3,587 | 3,142 | 0.231 | 0.226 | 0.457 | 26. |
| 27. Blast furn., steel wks., & roll. mills | 645 | 1.4 | 2.2 | 3.4 | 5.7 | 16.8 | 22.3 | 21.6 | 10.7 | 6.2 | 3.1 | 3.4 | 1.4 | 1.1 | 0.7 | 2,366 | 2,959 | 3,574 | 3,179 | 0.201 | 0.207 | 0.408 | 27. |
| 28. Oth. prim. iron, steel, & fab. steel prod. | 868 | 2.4 | 3.8 | 5.4 | 8.4 | 16.1 | 17.9 | 19.2 | 10.1 | 6.1 | 3.3 | 3.5 | 1.4 | 1.2 | 1.1 | 2,155 | 2,888 | 3,589 | 3,127 | 0.254 | 0.242 | 0.496 | 28. |
| 29. Nonferrous metals & their prod. | 274 | 2.6 | 3.5 | 4.7 | 7.4 | 16.1 | 18.8 | 19.4 | 10.4 | 6.5 | 3.2 | 3.8 | 1.3 | 1.4 | 0.9 | 2,211 | 2,917 | 3,620 | 3,141 | 0.243 | 0.240 | 0.483 | 29. |
| 30. Not spec. metal ind. | 11 | 3.2 | 5.3 | 5.3 | 8.2 | 19.6 | 13.2 | 14.3 | 9.4 | 9.4 | 3.2 | 3.2 | 1.8 | 1.2 | 2.9 | 2,076 | 2,818 | 3,813 | 3,405 | 0.264 | 0.353 | 0.617 | 30. |
| 31. Machinery, exc. elec. | 1,107 | 1.9 | 3.1 | 4.1 | 5.8 | 12.5 | 16.7 | 21.1 | 12.5 | 8.4 | 4.1 | 4.8 | 1.9 | 1.8 | 1.3 | 2,404 | 3,139 | 3,892 | 3,428 | 0.235 | 0.239 | 0.474 | 31. |
| 32. Agri. mach. & tractors | 161 | 1.6 | 2.5 | 4.5 | 5.6 | 13.0 | 20.6 | 23.8 | 12.8 | 7.2 | 3.1 | 2.8 | 0.9 | 1.1 | 0.6 | 2,415 | 3,046 | 3,632 | 3,168 | 0.208 | 0.192 | 0.400 | 32. |
| 33. Office & store mach. & devices | 82 | 1.2 | 3.2 | 3.2 | 5.3 | 11.4 | 13.1 | 18.2 | 14.8 | 11.4 | 5.3 | 6.3 | 2.1 | 2.7 | 1.9 | 2,526 | 3,346 | 4,201 | 3,751 | 0.245 | 0.255 | 0.500 | 33. |
| 34. Misc. mach. | 864 | 1.9 | 3.0 | 4.1 | 6.2 | 13.0 | 16.8 | 21.1 | 12.4 | 7.9 | 4.0 | 4.9 | 1.8 | 1.7 | 1.3 | 2,376 | 3,118 | 3,858 | 3,409 | 0.238 | 0.237 | 0.475 | 34. |
| 35. Electrical machinery, equip., & supp. | 501 | 2.1 | 3.4 | 4.1 | 5.4 | 11.6 | 15.9 | 20.7 | 12.4 | 9.1 | 4.4 | 5.2 | 2.4 | 2.1 | 1.4 | 2,431 | 3,181 | 3,975 | 3,508 | 0.236 | 0.249 | 0.485 | 35. |
| 36. Transportation equip. | 1,242 | 1.7 | 2.8 | 3.5 | 5.1 | 10.1 | 16.1 | 24.7 | 14.5 | 8.5 | 4.3 | 4.9 | 1.8 | 1.3 | 0.7 | 2,555 | 3,216 | 3,879 | 3,377 | 0.206 | 0.206 | 0.412 | 36. |
| 37. Motor vehicles & motor veh. equip. | 790 | 1.7 | 2.7 | 3.4 | 5.0 | 9.7 | 16.4 | 26.0 | 13.6 | 8.5 | 4.3 | 4.8 | 1.9 | 1.3 | 0.7 | 2,576 | 3,213 | 3,871 | 3,382 | 0.199 | 0.204 | 0.403 | 37. |
| 38. Aircraft & parts | 233 | 1.5 | 2.2 | 2.8 | 3.7 | 8.9 | 15.2 | 22.7 | 16.8 | 9.9 | 5.1 | 6.2 | 2.2 | 1.7 | 0.8 | 2,694 | 3,345 | 4,060 | 3,557 | 0.195 | 0.213 | 0.408 | 38. |
| 39. Ship & boat bldg. & repair. | 158 | 2.7 | 4.0 | 4.8 | 7.4 | 13.0 | 15.1 | 21.7 | 15.6 | 6.7 | 3.2 | 3.3 | 1.1 | 0.7 | 0.6 | 2,234 | 3,069 | 3,701 | 3,093 | 0.272 | 0.206 | 0.478 | 39. |
| 40. Railroad & misc. transp. equip. | 61 | 1.1 | 2.5 | 3.9 | 6.2 | 11.9 | 17.3 | 22.2 | 14.2 | 8.4 | 3.7 | 4.7 | 1.7 | 1.2 | 0.8 | 2,474 | 3,159 | 3,848 | 3,340 | 0.217 | 0.217 | 0.434 | 40. |
| 41. Other durable goods | 399 | 3.4 | 4.8 | 5.5 | 8.9 | 14.9 | 15.6 | 16.6 | 9.7 | 7.2 | 3.7 | 4.5 | 2.0 | 2.0 | 1.4 | 2,080 | 2,900 | 3,773 | 3,245 | 0.283 | 0.300 | 0.583 | 41. |
| 42. Professional & photo. equip. & supp. | 112 | 1.6 | 3.0 | 3.6 | 5.8 | 11.4 | 15.7 | 19.5 | 12.3 | 8.8 | 5.3 | 5.9 | 2.9 | 2.8 | 1.4 | 2,482 | 3,228 | 4,119 | 3,613 | 0.232 | 0.276 | 0.508 | 42. |
| 43. Watches, clocks, & misc. mfg. ind. | 287 | 4.1 | 5.5 | 6.3 | 10.1 | 16.3 | 15.6 | 15.5 | 8.6 | 6.5 | 3.0 | 3.9 | 1.6 | 1.7 | 1.3 | 1,950 | 2,746 | 3,593 | 3,070 | 0.290 | 0.308 | 0.598 | 43. |
| 44. Nondurable goods | 4,313 | 4.5 | 4.5 | 6.0 | 9.3 | 15.1 | 14.3 | 15.4 | 9.5 | 7.2 | 3.9 | 5.1 | 2.0 | 1.8 | 1.4 | 2,023 | 2,870 | 3,810 | 3,207 | 0.296 | 0.327 | 0.623 | 44. |
| 45. Food & kindred prod. | 1,051 | 3.7 | 5.3 | 6.4 | 8.9 | 15.3 | 15.7 | 17.2 | 10.1 | 6.8 | 3.3 | 3.9 | 1.4 | 1.1 | 0.8 | 2,022 | 2,831 | 3,623 | 3,003 | 0.286 | 0.279 | 0.565 | 45. |
| 46. Meat prod. | 218 | 2.7 | 4.1 | 5.1 | 7.8 | 16.8 | 19.5 | 18.9 | 9.8 | 6.2 | 3.0 | 3.2 | 1.3 | 0.8 | 0.7 | 2,157 | 2,846 | 3,505 | 3,008 | 0.242 | 0.231 | 0.473 | 46. |
| 47. Dairy prod. | 128 | 3.4 | 5.1 | 6.1 | 9.0 | 15.1 | 15.8 | 18.8 | 11.1 | 6.5 | 3.2 | 3.2 | 1.0 | 1.0 | 0.8 | 2,046 | 2,857 | 3,576 | 2,996 | 0.284 | 0.251 | 0.535 | 47. |
| 48. Can. & preserv. fruit, veg. & sea food | 95 | 7.4 | 11.9 | 10.3 | 11.7 | 16.3 | 11.8 | 12.0 | 6.8 | 4.3 | 2.2 | 2.8 | 0.9 | 0.7 | 0.8 | 1,276 | 2,266 | 3,233 | 2,496 | 0.437 | 0.426 | 0.863 | 48. |
| 49. Grain mill prod. | 96 | 3.6 | 4.8 | 8.0 | 11.2 | 17.8 | 15.3 | 15.1 | 8.8 | 6.2 | 2.4 | 2.9 | 1.4 | 1.2 | 1.2 | 1,883 | 2,650 | 3,473 | 2,953 | 0.290 | 0.310 | 0.600 | 49. |
| 50. Bakery prod. | 196 | 3.7 | 4.9 | 5.5 | 7.4 | 14.0 | 15.1 | 16.8 | 10.4 | 8.5 | 4.5 | 5.9 | 1.7 | 1.1 | 0.5 | 2,125 | 2,980 | 3,865 | 3,114 | 0.287 | 0.297 | 0.584 | 50. |
| 51. Confectionery & rel. prod. | 38 | 4.2 | 5.4 | 7.2 | 10.0 | 17.7 | 16.9 | 14.9 | 6.9 | 5.7 | 2.9 | 3.4 | 1.5 | 1.9 | 1.5 | 1,910 | 2,662 | 3,456 | 3,048 | 0.283 | 0.298 | 0.581 | 51. |
| 52. Beverage ind. | 170 | 3.3 | 3.8 | 5.6 | 7.7 | 12.7 | 13.6 | 19.8 | 13.4 | 8.4 | 3.6 | 4.0 | 1.6 | 1.5 | 1.0 | 2,181 | 3,083 | 3,817 | 3,226 | 0.293 | 0.237 | 0.530 | 52. |
| 53. Misc. food prep. & not spec. food ind. | 110 | 3.2 | 5.4 | 7.3 | 10.9 | 15.2 | 15.5 | 15.6 | 9.5 | 6.0 | 3.1 | 3.8 | 1.4 | 1.6 | 1.2 | 1,917 | 2,758 | 3,600 | 3,040 | 0.305 | 0.305 | 0.610 | 53. |
| 54. Tobacco manufactures | 46 | 6.2 | 7.5 | 10.5 | 18.0 | 20.7 | 12.9 | 10.3 | 4.7 | 2.8 | 1.5 | 1.8 | 0.8 | 1.0 | 1.2 | 1,522 | 2,188 | 2,968 | 2,515 | 0.305 | 0.356 | 0.661 | 54. |

continued on next page

TABLE B-1, males, continued

| | INDUSTRY | NUMBER WITH $1 OR MORE (*thousands*) (1) | PERCENTAGE DISTRIBUTION BY INCOME CLASS: *Under $500* (2) | *$500 to $999* (3) | *$1,000 to $1,499* (4) | *$1,500 to $1,999* (5) | *$2,000 to $2,499* (6) | *$2,500 to $2,999* (7) | *$3,000 to $3,499* (8) | *$3,500 to $3,999* (9) | *$4,000 to $4,499* (10) | *$4,500 to $4,999* (11) | *$5,000 to $5,999* (12) | *$6,000 to $6,999* (13) | *$7,000 to $9,999* (14) | *$10,000 and Over* (15) | INCOME AT QUARTILE POSITION: $Q_1$ (16) | *Median* $Q_2$ (17) | $Q_3$ (18) | ARITH-METIC MEAN (19) | MEASURES OF DISPERSION: $1-\frac{Q_1}{Q_2}$ (20) | $\frac{Q_3}{Q_2}-1$ (21) | $\frac{Q_3-Q_1}{Q_2}$ (22) | |
|---|---|---|---|---|---|---|---|---|---|---|---|---|---|---|---|---|---|---|---|---|---|---|---|---|
| 55. | Textile mill prod. | 719 | 3.4 | 5.0 | 8.4 | 15.6 | 23.1 | 16.5 | 12.3 | 5.3 | 3.6 | 1.7 | 2.3 | 0.9 | 0.9 | 1.1 | 1,762 | 2,380 | 3,121 | 2,711 | 0.260 | 0.311 | 0.571 | 55. |
| 56. | Knitting mills | 73 | 3.7 | 4.7 | 8.8 | 13.7 | 16.2 | 12.0 | 12.1 | 7.2 | 7.3 | 4.1 | 6.0 | 1.7 | 1.3 | 1.2 | 1,784 | 2,620 | 3,763 | 3,048 | 0.320 | 0.436 | 0.756 | 56. |
| 57. | Dyeing & fin. tex. exc. knit goods | 46 | 3.2 | 3.9 | 5.5 | 10.3 | 22.8 | 20.5 | 15.5 | 6.1 | 4.0 | 1.6 | 2.4 | 1.1 | 1.7 | 1.6 | 2,046 | 2,604 | 3,283 | 3,009 | 0.215 | 0.260 | 0.475 | 57. |
| 58. | Carpets, rugs, & oth. floor cov. | 46 | 2.0 | 3.3 | 3.6 | 8.0 | 17.5 | 17.7 | 19.4 | 10.2 | 7.1 | 3.3 | 4.0 | 1.3 | 1.3 | 1.3 | 2,231 | 2,940 | 3,671 | 3,241 | 0.242 | 0.248 | 0.490 | 58. |
| 59. | Yarn, thread, & fabric mills | 521 | 3.5 | 5.3 | 9.1 | 17.2 | 24.8 | 16.6 | 11.3 | 4.5 | 2.6 | 1.2 | 1.6 | 0.7 | 0.7 | 1.0 | 1,706 | 2,300 | 2,954 | 2,574 | 0.259 | 0.284 | 0.543 | 59. |
| 60. | Misc. tex. mill prod. | 33 | 3.3 | 4.4 | 6.8 | 11.9 | 19.2 | 16.9 | 15.8 | 6.4 | 5.2 | 2.7 | 3.4 | 0.9 | 1.6 | 1.5 | 1,941 | 2,630 | 3,395 | 3,015 | 0.262 | 0.290 | 0.552 | 60. |
| 61. | Apparel & oth. fab. tex. prod. | 291 | 3.7 | 5.5 | 8.2 | 12.2 | 16.2 | 12.5 | 13.1 | 7.8 | 6.0 | 2.8 | 5.4 | 2.1 | 2.3 | 2.0 | 1,811 | 2,668 | 3,730 | 3,210 | 0.322 | 0.398 | 0.720 | 61. |
| 62. | Apparel & access. | 257 | 3.6 | 5.3 | 8.1 | 12.3 | 15.6 | 12.3 | 13.2 | 8.0 | 6.2 | 2.9 | 5.6 | 2.1 | 2.4 | 2.2 | 1,825 | 2,707 | 3,787 | 3,273 | 0.326 | 0.398 | 0.724 | 62. |
| 63. | Misc. fab. tex. prod. | 34 | 4.4 | 6.4 | 8.8 | 11.9 | 20.9 | 13.8 | 11.9 | 6.6 | 4.5 | 2.2 | 4.5 | 1.4 | 1.6 | 0.8 | 1,726 | 2,442 | 3,369 | 2,791 | 0.294 | 0.379 | 0.673 | 63. |
| 64. | Paper & all. prod. | 356 | 2.7 | 3.6 | 5.0 | 7.6 | 16.2 | 18.2 | 18.4 | 10.5 | 6.6 | 3.4 | 3.6 | 1.5 | 1.5 | 1.1 | 2,188 | 2,909 | 3,657 | 3,171 | 0.248 | 0.257 | 0.505 | 64. |
| 65. | Pulp, paper, & paperboard mills | 200 | 2.5 | 3.3 | 4.7 | 6.8 | 15.9 | 19.8 | 19.7 | 11.0 | 6.6 | 3.1 | 3.1 | 1.4 | 1.2 | 0.8 | 2,242 | 2,924 | 3,604 | 3,115 | 0.234 | 0.232 | 0.466 | 65. |
| 66. | Paperboard cont. & boxes | 74 | 3.5 | 4.3 | 6.4 | 9.8 | 16.7 | 15.7 | 15.6 | 9.9 | 6.3 | 3.5 | 3.5 | 1.7 | 1.6 | 1.4 | 2,029 | 2,796 | 3,651 | 3,131 | 0.275 | 0.305 | 0.580 | 66. |
| 67. | Misc. paper & pulp prod. | 82 | 2.4 | 3.7 | 4.5 | 7.7 | 16.4 | 16.7 | 17.6 | 9.8 | 6.7 | 4.1 | 5.0 | 1.5 | 2.2 | 1.6 | 2,204 | 2,958 | 3,806 | 3,351 | 0.255 | 0.286 | 0.541 | 67. |
| 68. | Printing, publ., & all. ind. | 593 | 13.3 | 4.4 | 4.0 | 5.3 | 9.0 | 8.3 | 10.7 | 8.4 | 9.2 | 6.4 | 10.9 | 4.5 | 3.5 | 2.1 | 1,811 | 3,266 | 4,687 | 3,607 | 0.446 | 0.435. | 0.881 | 68. |
| 69. | Chemicals & all. prod. | 523 | 2.3 | 3.5 | 4.4 | 6.5 | 11.6 | 14.6 | 19.3 | 12.3 | 8.1 | 5.0 | 5.4 | 2.5 | 2.5 | 2.0 | 2,357 | 3,183 | 4,030 | 3,605 | 0.260 | 0.265 | 0.525 | 69. |
| 70. | Synthetic fibers | 42 | 1.0 | 3.3 | 2.8 | 5.2 | 13.4 | 23.4 | 26.3 | 9.8 | 5.2 | 2.7 | 4.0 | 1.4 | 1.0 | 0.5 | 2,473 | 3,017 | 3,492 | 3,165 | 0.181 | 0.157 | 0.338 | 70. |
| 71. | Paints, varn., & rel. prod. | 47 | 2.9 | 3.0 | 4.4 | 5.7 | 13.7 | 18.5 | 19.9 | 10.7 | 6.0 | 3.6 | 4.4 | 2.3 | 2.7 | 2.0 | 2,328 | 3,045 | 3,822 | 3,496 | 0.236 | 0.255 | 0.491 | 71. |
| 72. | Drugs, med., & misc. chem. & all. prod. | 434 | 2.3 | 3.5 | 4.6 | 6.8 | 11.2 | 13.3 | 18.5 | 12.7 | 8.7 | 5.4 | 5.6 | 2.7 | 2.6 | 2.1 | 2,348 | 3,224 | 4,120 | 3,654 | 0.272 | 0.277 | 0.549 | 72. |
| 73. | Petroleum & coal prod. | 260 | 1.1 | 1.7 | 2.0 | 2.7 | 6.0 | 7.8 | 15.8 | 17.1 | 18.0 | 10.1 | 8.7 | 4.0 | 3.2 | 1.9 | 3,117 | 3,877 | 4,638 | 4,227 | 0.197 | 0.196 | 0.393 | 73. |
| 74. | Petro. refining | 234 | 1.0 | 1.4 | 1.7 | 2.3 | 5.2 | 6.6 | 15.0 | 17.9 | 19.3 | 10.8 | 9.2 | 4.3 | 3.4 | 2.0 | 3,226 | 3,969 | 4,712 | 4,339 | 0.188 | 0.187 | 0.375 | 74. |
| 75. | Misc. petro. & coal prod. | 26 | 1.7 | 4.2 | 4.1 | 6.3 | 13.7 | 18.7 | 22.8 | 9.9 | 6.0 | 3.3 | 4.9 | 1.7 | 1.5 | 1.2 | 2,317 | 3,028 | 3,676 | 3,291 | 0.235 | 0.214 | 0.449 | 75. |
| 76. | Rubber prod. | 181 | 1.6 | 2.3 | 3.4 | 5.6 | 11.9 | 18.0 | 22.6 | 13.8 | 8.6 | 3.8 | 4.4 | 1.6 | 1.7 | 0.8 | 2,505 | 3,159 | 3,847 | 3,373 | 0.207 | 0.217 | 0.424 | 76. |
| 77. | Leather & leather prod. | 211 | 3.7 | 6.0 | 9.6 | 15.4 | 20.9 | 17.0 | 13.0 | 5.7 | 3.0 | 1.1 | 2.3 | 0.6 | 0.8 | 1.0 | 1,685 | 2,366 | 3,092 | 2,631 | 0.288 | 0.306 | 0.594 | 77. |
| 78. | Leather: tanned, curried, & fin. | 42 | 1.9 | 4.1 | 6.4 | 11.3 | 19.5 | 20.4 | 18.0 | 7.7 | 3.9 | 1.4 | 2.4 | 0.8 | 0.9 | 1.2 | 2,033 | 2,666 | 3,316 | 2,919 | 0.238 | 0.243 | 0.481 | 78. |
| 79. | Footwear, exc. rubber | 135 | 4.1 | 6.6 | 10.3 | 17.2 | 22.1 | 16.1 | 11.4 | 5.1 | 2.5 | 0.9 | 1.6 | 0.5 | 0.7 | 1.0 | 1,616 | 2,266 | 2,956 | 2,520 | 0.288 | 0.304 | 0.592 | 79. |
| 80. | Leather prod., exc. footwear | 34 | 4.0 | 6.1 | 10.8 | 13.4 | 17.7 | 16.3 | 12.9 | 6.2 | 3.2 | 1.5 | 5.0 | 0.5 | 1.4 | 1.2 | 1,652 | 2,443 | 3,259 | 2,797 | 0.324 | 0.333 | 0.657 | 80. |
| 81. | Not spec. mfg. ind. | 82 | 4.2 | 5.8 | 7.0 | 9.1 | 15.4 | 15.3 | 16.2 | 9.0 | 5.8 | 2.6 | 3.5 | 1.8 | 2.2 | 2.1 | 1,939 | 2,777 | 3,611 | 3,218 | 0.302 | 0.299 | 0.601 | 81. |
| 82. | Transportation, commun., & oth. pub. util. | 3,568 | 2.7 | 4.0 | 5.2 | 7.1 | 13.3 | 14.6 | 19.4 | 12.4 | 8.7 | 4.7 | 4.8 | 1.6 | 1.0 | 0.5 | 2,225 | 3,079 | 3,850 | 3,168 | 0.278 | 0.250 | 0.528 | 82. |
| 83. | Transportation | 2,632 | 2.8 | 4.3 | 5.6 | 7.4 | 13.4 | 14.5 | 19.7 | 12.5 | 8.4 | 4.5 | 4.3 | 1.4 | 0.8 | 0.5 | 2,182 | 3,050 | 3,792 | 3,114 | 0.285 | 0.242 | 0.527 | 83. |
| 84. | Railroads & railway exp. serv. | 1,347 | 1.9 | 2.8 | 4.2 | 6.1 | 13.1 | 15.0 | 20.7 | 13.9 | 9.3 | 5.3 | 5.3 | 1.6 | 0.5 | 0.3 | 2,381 | 3,166 | 3,902 | 3,231 | 0.248 | 0.232 | 0.480 | 84. |
| 85. | St. railways & bus lines | 298 | 2.3 | 3.6 | 3.5 | 4.7 | 9.8 | 14.7 | 28.9 | 17.0 | 9.0 | 3.4 | 2.1 | 0.5 | 0.4 | 0.3 | 2,537 | 3,197 | 3,720 | 3,146 | 0.207 | 0.163 | 0.370 | 85. |
| 86. | Trucking serv. | 437 | 4.7 | 6.5 | 7.1 | 8.8 | 13.4 | 13.8 | 17.8 | 10.8 | 7.9 | 3.9 | 3.3 | 0.9 | 0.6 | 0.4 | 1,880 | 2,844 | 3,634 | 2,859 | 0.339 | 0.277 | 0.616 | 86. |
| 87. | Warehousing & storage | 79 | 5.1 | 5.8 | 8.3 | 11.4 | 18.4 | 17.9 | 15.3 | 6.9 | 4.9 | 2.0 | 2.0 | 0.8 | 0.5 | 0.5 | 1,754 | 2,527 | 3,264 | 2,629 | 0.306 | 0.291 | 0.597 | 87. |
| 88. | Taxicab serv. | 135 | 6.0 | 10.3 | 13.6 | 18.5 | 22.2 | 14.6 | 8.1 | 3.0 | 1.7 | 0.8 | 0.6 | 0.1 | 0.2 | 0.1 | 1,319 | 2,036 | 2,650 | 2,049 | 0.352 | 0.301 | 0.653 | 88. |
| 89. | Water transp. | 209 | 3.5 | 6.2 | 8.7 | 9.8 | 14.4 | 12.0 | 14.8 | 8.5 | 6.8 | 4.1 | 5.4 | 2.5 | 2.4 | 1.1 | 1,836 | 2,808 | 3,829 | 3,156 | 0.346 | 0.363 | 0.709 | 89. |
| 90. | Air transp. | 78 | 1.4 | 2.9 | 3.3 | 4.7 | 10.7 | 13.5 | 16.2 | 13.2 | 10.5 | 6.0 | 6.5 | 3.6 | 3.9 | 3.6 | 2,574 | 3,416 | 4,433 | 4,156 | 0.247 | 0.297 | 0.544 | 90. |
| 91. | Petro. & gas. pipe lines | 19 | 1.7 | 3.0 | 3.7 | 3.7 | 5.5 | 7.0 | 12.5 | 18.8 | 20.9 | 10.1 | 7.6 | 3.2 | 1.8 | 0.7 | 3,016 | 3,843 | 4,456 | 3,852 | 0.216 | 0.159 | 0.375 | 91. |
| 92. | Serv. incid. to transp. | 30 | 3.3 | 5.2 | 5.5 | 7.2 | 16.9 | 14.9 | 18.9 | 9.8 | 6.3 | 3.3 | 4.5 | 1.3 | 1.5 | 1.6 | 2,112 | 2,899 | 3,658 | 3,217 | 0.272 | 0.261 | 0.533 | 92. |
| 93. | Telecommunications | 250 | 2.0 | 2.4 | 2.9 | 4.3 | 10.2 | 13.1 | 15.3 | 11.3 | 12.2 | 8.2 | 9.7 | 4.1 | 3.3 | 1.0 | 2,622 | 3,493 | 4,579 | 3,833 | 0.250 | 0.310 | 0.560 | 93. |
| 94. | Telephone, wire & radio | 221 | 1.2 | 2.0 | 2.3 | 4.1 | 10.7 | 13.5 | 15.2 | 11.0 | 12.5 | 8.4 | 10.1 | 4.4 | 3.6 | 1.0 | 2,674 | 3,545 | 4,648 | 3,914 | 0.246 | 0.311 | 0.557 | 94. |
| 95. | Telegraph, wire & radio | 29 | 8.0 | 5.7 | 6.9 | 5.8 | 7.0 | 10.0 | 15.6 | 13.2 | 10.1 | 7.0 | 6.7 | 2.0 | 1.3 | 0.4 | 1,879 | 3,211 | 4,138 | 3,135 | 0.415 | 0.288 | 0.703 | 95. |
| 96. | Utilities & sanitary serv. | 686 | 2.2 | 3.4 | 4.7 | 7.1 | 13.8 | 15.8 | 19.6 | 12.5 | 8.4 | 4.5 | 4.6 | 1.6 | 1.1 | 0.6 | 2,275 | 3,076 | 3,836 | 3,206 | 0.261 | 0.246 | 0.507 | 96. |
| 97. | Elec. light, power, gas, & oth. util. | 418 | 1.8 | 2.6 | 3.4 | 5.3 | 11.8 | 14.0 | 19.5 | 14.5 | 10.8 | 6.0 | 5.9 | 2.0 | 1.5 | 0.8 | 2,503 | 3,284 | 4,097 | 3,473 | 0.238 | 0.247 | 0.485 | 97. |
| 98. | Gas & steam supply systems | 101 | 1.8 | 2.7 | 3.8 | 6.6 | 12.9 | 17.5 | 22.3 | 13.8 | 7.8 | 3.6 | 3.7 | 1.8 | 1.1 | 0.6 | 2,391 | 3,105 | 3,768 | 3,238 | 0.230 | 0.213 | 0.443 | 98. |
| 99. | Water supply & san. serv. | 167 | 3.6 | 5.8 | 8.4 | 11.9 | 19.5 | 19.6 | 18.0 | 6.7 | 2.7 | 1.4 | 1.6 | 0.5 | 0.3 | 0.2 | 1,802 | 2,520 | 3,172 | 2,547 | 0.285 | 0.258 | 0.543 | 99. |
| 100. | Wholesale & retail trade | 5,052 | 7.1 | 7.7 | 8.5 | 10.7 | 15.0 | 12.7 | 13.0 | 7.9 | 5.5 | 2.9 | 4.1 | 1.7 | 1.8 | 1.4 | 1,579 | 2,539 | 3,518 | 2,915 | 0.379 | 0.385 | 0.764 | 100. |
| 101. | Wholesale trade | 1,329 | 3.5 | 4.8 | 6.0 | 8.6 | 13.8 | 13.2 | 15.0 | 9.9 | 7.0 | 4.0 | 5.8 | 2.7 | 3.0 | 2.6 | 2,076 | 3,003 | 4,014 | 3,559 | 0.309 | 0.336 | 0.645 | 101. |
| 102. | Motor vehicles & equip. | 41 | 1.9 | 4.4 | 4.1 | 7.1 | 13.9 | 14.1 | 17.9 | 10.0 | 8.3 | 5.5 | 5.3 | 3.2 | 2.5 | 1.8 | 2,269 | 3,125 | 4,096 | 3,556 | 0.274 | 0.310 | 0.584 | 102. |
| 103. | Drugs, chem., & all. prod. | 56 | 2.6 | 3.0 | 5.2 | 6.7 | 12.8 | 13.1 | 14.6 | 10.2 | 7.2 | 5.6 | 8.3 | 4.3 | 4.2 | 2.2 | 2,292 | 3,226 | 4,472 | 3,821 | 0.290 | 0.386 | 0.676 | 103. |
| 104. | Dry goods & apparel | 65 | 3.6 | 3.6 | 4.5 | 6.2 | 12.4 | 11.1 | 10.5 | 8.2 | 7.5 | 4.1 | 9.7 | 5.2 | 5.4 | 7.9 | 2,286 | 3,409 | 5,340 | 4,857 | 0.330 | 0.566 | 0.896 | 104. |
| 105. | Food & rel. prod. | 396 | 4.2 | 5.7 | 7.1 | 9.6 | 14.2 | 14.1 | 15.9 | 10.2 | 6.9 | 3.3 | 4.5 | 1.5 | 1.5 | 1.1 | 1,916 | 2,826 | 3,705 | 3,059 | 0.322 | 0.311 | 0.633 | 105. |
| 106. | Elec. goods, hardware, & plumb. equip. | 114 | 2.2 | 3.7 | 4.4 | 8.1 | 13.4 | 13.8 | 16.1 | 10.8 | 7.0 | 4.4 | 6.3 | 3.1 | 3.8 | 2.8 | 2,246 | 3,136 | 4,178 | 3,776 | 0.284 | 0.332 | 0.616 | 106. |
| 107. | Machinery, equip., & supp. | 98 | 2.3 | 3.2 | 4.4 | 6.9 | 12.0 | 12.4 | 15.1 | 11.0 | 7.8 | 4.8 | 8.1 | 4.3 | 4.2 | 3.5 | 2,341 | 3,291 | 4,493 | 4,061 | 0.289 | 0.365 | 0.654 | 107. |
| 108. | Petro. prod. | 122 | 2.2 | 2.2 | 4.2 | 5.9 | 12.4 | 12.3 | 17.2 | 12.7 | 10.7 | 5.7 | 6.5 | 2.8 | 3.0 | 2.3 | 2,423 | 3,313 | 4,275 | 3,810 | 0.269 | 0.290 | 0.559 | 108. |
| 109. | Farm prod. & raw materials | 60 | 5.3 | 6.0 | 7.0 | 12.2 | 17.3 | 14.4 | 14.1 | 7.1 | 4.8 | 2.8 | 3.1 | 2.0 | 1.7 | 2.3 | 1,774 | 2,576 | 3,453 | 3,111 | 0.312 | 0.340 | 0.652 | 109. |
| 110. | Misc. wholesale | 340 | 4.0 | 5.9 | 6.8 | 9.4 | 14.2 | 12.5 | 13.6 | 8.7 | 6.0 | 3.6 | 5.7 | 2.7 | 3.6 | 3.2 | 1,941 | 2,888 | 3,994 | 3,596 | 0.328 | 0.383 | 0.711 | 110. |
| 111. | Not spec. wholesale | 37 | 3.9 | 5.3 | 5.8 | 9.6 | 15.4 | 13.6 | 14.1 | 7.7 | 4.9 | 3.4 | 6.1 | 2.8 | 3.9 | 3.6 | 2,012 | 2,867 | 3,974 | 3,696 | 0.299 | 0.385 | 0.684 | 111. |
| 112. | Retail trade, stores | 3,723 | 8.4 | 8.7 | 9.4 | 11.5 | 15.4 | 12.5 | 12.2 | 7.2 | 4.9 | 2.5 | 3.4 | 1.4 | 1.3 | 1.0 | 1,420 | 2,389 | 3,372 | 2,677 | 0.406 | 0.411 | 0.817 | 112. |

continued on next page

## TABLE B-1, males, continued

| | INDUSTRY | NUMBER WITH $1 OR MORE (thousands) (1) | PERCENTAGE DISTRIBUTION BY INCOME CLASS: Under $500 (2) | $500 to $999 (3) | $1,000 to $1,499 (4) | $1,500 to $1,999 (5) | $2,000 to $2,499 (6) | $2,500 to $2,999 (7) | $3,000 to $3,499 (8) | $3,500 to $3,999 (9) | $4,000 to $4,499 (10) | $4,500 to $4,999 (11) | $5,000 to $5,999 (12) | $6,000 to $6,999 (13) | $7,000 to $9,999 (14) | $10,000 and Over (15) | INCOME AT QUARTILE POSITION: $Q_1$ (16) | Median $Q_2$ (17) | $Q_3$ (18) | ARITHMETIC MEAN (19) | MEASURES OF DISPERSION: $1-\frac{Q_1}{Q_2}$ (20) | $\frac{Q_3}{Q_2}-1$ (21) | $\frac{Q_3-Q_1}{Q_2}$ (22) | |
|---|---|---|---|---|---|---|---|---|---|---|---|---|---|---|---|---|---|---|---|---|---|---|---|---|
| 113. | Food, exc. dairy prod. | 664 | 12.3 | 9.8 | 9.2 | 10.4 | 14.4 | 12.2 | 12.1 | 7.3 | 5.1 | 2.3 | 2.7 | 0.9 | 0.9 | 0.4 | 1,157 | 2,288 | 3,276 | 2,417 | 0.495 | 0.432 | 0.927 | 113. |
| 114. | Dairy prod. & milk retail | 99 | 5.8 | 5.3 | 4.7 | 6.1 | 10.3 | 11.6 | 16.2 | 14.2 | 12.5 | 5.7 | 4.8 | 1.5 | 0.8 | 0.4 | 2,150 | 3,191 | 4,032 | 3,141 | 0.327 | 0.263 | 0.590 | 114. |
| 115. | Genl. merchandise | 281 | 6.3 | 6.9 | 7.8 | 11.4 | 15.5 | 13.0 | 12.3 | 7.5 | 5.1 | 2.9 | 4.6 | 2.1 | 2.2 | 2.5 | 1,675 | 2,580 | 3,620 | 3,182 | 0.351 | 0.402 | 0.753 | 115. |
| 116. | Five & ten cent | 26 | 14.1 | 10.3 | 8.8 | 9.6 | 11.8 | 8.1 | 10.0 | 5.4 | 4.6 | 3.8 | 4.9 | 2.3 | 2.8 | 3.6 | 1,034 | 2,305 | 3,712 | 3,159 | 0.552 | 0.610 | 1.162 | 116. |
| 117. | Apparel & acc., exc. shoe | 141 | 6.9 | 6.6 | 7.3 | 9.4 | 13.6 | 11.5 | 13.4 | 8.2 | 5.8 | 3.1 | 6.0 | 2.6 | 2.8 | 3.0 | 1,723 | 2,769 | 3,884 | 3,418 | 0.378 | 0.402 | 0.780 | 117. |
| 118. | Shoe | 50 | 8.9 | 7.8 | 6.9 | 7.7 | 13.3 | 11.0 | 13.8 | 9.6 | 7.1 | 3.2 | 5.4 | 1.9 | 1.6 | 1.6 | 1,590 | 2,745 | 3,791 | 3,042 | 0.421 | 0.381 | 0.802 | 118. |
| 119. | Furniture & housefurn. | 155 | 4.9 | 6.6 | 8.4 | 11.8 | 15.9 | 13.0 | 12.8 | 7.5 | 5.1 | 3.2 | 5.1 | 2.2 | 2.2 | 1.3 | 1,716 | 2,592 | 3,606 | 3,025 | 0.339 | 0.391 | 0.730 | 119. |
| 120. | Household appl. & radio | 125 | 6.9 | 7.0 | 8.2 | 9.8 | 15.4 | 12.8 | 13.7 | 7.8 | 6.6 | 2.8 | 5.0 | 1.8 | 1.5 | 0.7 | 1,647 | 2,605 | 3,576 | 2,853 | 0.368 | 0.372 | 0.740 | 120. |
| 121. | Motor vehicles & acc. | 378 | 3.3 | 4.9 | 6.9 | 9.0 | 14.6 | 14.3 | 14.6 | 10.0 | 7.1 | 3.8 | 5.3 | 2.4 | 2.2 | 1.8 | 2,030 | 2,895 | 3,870 | 3,336 | 0.299 | 0.336 | 0.635 | 121. |
| 122. | Gas. serv. stations | 266 | 11.9 | 12.5 | 13.6 | 15.4 | 17.2 | 11.7 | 9.3 | 4.1 | 2.0 | 0.9 | 0.9 | 0.2 | 0.3 | 0.1 | 1,022 | 1,889 | 2,688 | 1,963 | 0.460 | 0.422 | 0.882 | 122. |
| 123. | Drug | 114 | 16.7 | 13.2 | 8.9 | 9.4 | 9.8 | 7.6 | 9.0 | 6.3 | 6.1 | 3.7 | 5.5 | 2.0 | 1.2 | 0.6 | 814 | 2,091 | 3,531 | 2,464 | 0.611 | 0.688 | 1.299 | 123. |
| 124. | Eating & drinking places | 558 | 10.2 | 12.8 | 13.8 | 14.5 | 16.5 | 11.7 | 10.0 | 4.5 | 2.4 | 1.1 | 1.4 | 0.5 | 0.3 | 0.2 | 1,072 | 1,955 | 2,807 | 2,063 | 0.452 | 0.435 | 0.887 | 124. |
| 125. | Hardware & farm impl. | 131 | 4.7 | 5.5 | 7.6 | 13.6 | 21.2 | 16.4 | 14.0 | 6.2 | 3.8 | 2.0 | 2.1 | 1.1 | 1.4 | 0.6 | 1,764 | 2,438 | 3,214 | 2,684 | 0.277 | 0.318 | 0.595 | 125. |
| 126. | Lumber & bldg. material retail | 256 | 3.9 | 6.1 | 8.4 | 12.0 | 16.6 | 13.5 | 14.0 | 8.5 | 5.5 | 2.8 | 4.1 | 1.8 | 1.6 | 1.1 | 1,775 | 2,611 | 3,529 | 2,954 | 0.321 | 0.351 | 0.672 | 126. |
| 127. | Liquor | 38 | 4.7 | 6.7 | 8.8 | 10.8 | 20.0 | 16.3 | 13.6 | 6.0 | 5.7 | 2.1 | 2.5 | 0.9 | 0.9 | 0.9 | 1,722 | 2,475 | 3,283 | 2,720 | 0.305 | 0.326 | 0.631 | 127. |
| 128. | Florists | 21 | 12.7 | 9.3 | 11.2 | 13.7 | 16.5 | 14.1 | 10.0 | 5.3 | 2.4 | 1.4 | 2.1 | 0.3 | 0.8 | 0.2 | 1,133 | 2,093 | 2,911 | 2,175 | 0.459 | 0.390 | 0.849 | 128. |
| 129. | Jewelry | 42 | 5.5 | 7.9 | 7.6 | 8.9 | 13.5 | 11.7 | 13.7 | 10.2 | 4.7 | 2.9 | 6.0 | 3.1 | 2.3 | 2.0 | 1,724 | 2,782 | 3,803 | 3,241 | 0.381 | 0.367 | 0.748 | 129. |
| 130. | Fuel & ice | 108 | 6.5 | 7.3 | 9.4 | 12.3 | 17.9 | 14.2 | 13.2 | 7.0 | 4.4 | 2.6 | 2.5 | 0.9 | 1.0 | 0.8 | 1,573 | 2,405 | 3,280 | 2,640 | 0.346 | 0.363 | 0.709 | 130. |
| 131. | Misc. retail | 195 | 8.3 | 8.0 | 9.0 | 11.3 | 14.5 | 12.1 | 11.9 | 7.8 | 4.9 | 2.6 | 4.2 | 1.6 | 2.3 | 1.4 | 1,483 | 2,462 | 3,495 | 2,871 | 0.398 | 0.419 | 0.817 | 131. |
| 132. | Not spec. retail | 75 | 9.1 | 8.1 | 9.4 | 11.0 | 16.2 | 11.5 | 11.1 | 6.5 | 5.4 | 2.7 | 2.8 | 1.7 | 1.8 | 2.8 | 1,414 | 2,382 | 3,436 | 3,014 | 0.407 | 0.442 | 0.849 | 132. |
| 133. | Finance, insurance, & real estate | 904 | 3.6 | 4.7 | 6.4 | 8.6 | 12.6 | 11.1 | 12.5 | 9.1 | 7.7 | 4.9 | 7.6 | 3.9 | 3.9 | 3.5 | 2,067 | 3,120 | 4,415 | 3,874 | 0.338 | 0.415 | 0.753 | 133. |
| 134. | Bank. & cred. agenc. & commod. brok. | 295 | 2.5 | 3.6 | 4.4 | 7.8 | 12.1 | 11.8 | 13.8 | 10.0 | 7.8 | 4.6 | 7.6 | 4.0 | 4.7 | 5.2 | 2,276 | 3,282 | 4,630 | 4,312 | 0.307 | 0.410 | 0.717 | 134. |
| 135. | Insurance | 354 | 2.6 | 2.9 | 4.1 | 5.6 | 9.0 | 9.3 | 13.8 | 10.9 | 10.3 | 7.1 | 10.7 | 5.2 | 4.9 | 3.7 | 2,543 | 3,623 | 4,957 | 4,351 | 0.299 | 0.368 | 0.667 | 135. |
| 136. | Real estate, incl. real est. ins. law off. | 255 | 6.1 | 8.5 | 11.7 | 13.6 | 18.2 | 12.7 | 9.3 | 5.4 | 3.9 | 2.1 | 3.4 | 2.0 | 1.7 | 1.3 | 1,444 | 2,277 | 3,225 | 2,713 | 0.366 | 0.416 | 0.782 | 136. |
| 137. | Business & repair serv. | 840 | 5.5 | 7.0 | 8.5 | 11.0 | 15.9 | 14.2 | 14.6 | 8.5 | 5.3 | 2.7 | 3.1 | 1.2 | 1.3 | 1.2 | 1,681 | 2,573 | 3,441 | 2,859 | 0.347 | 0.337 | 0.684 | 137. |
| 138. | Advertising | 61 | 4.4 | 5.6 | 5.2 | 5.5 | 8.1 | 9.4 | 10.5 | 8.4 | 9.1 | 4.1 | 9.1 | 4.7 | 7.1 | 8.7 | 2,265 | 3,577 | 5,516 | 5,042 | 0.367 | 0.542 | 0.909 | 138. |
| 139. | Account. audit., bookkeep., & misc. bus. serv. | 151 | 5.2 | 6.7 | 6.0 | 7.8 | 12.2 | 11.2 | 14.1 | 10.3 | 7.3 | 4.6 | 6.4 | 3.0 | 3.1 | 2.2 | 1,955 | 3,031 | 4,102 | 3,481 | 0.356 | 0.353 | 0.709 | 139. |
| 140. | Auto. repair serv. & garages | 485 | 5.5 | 7.2 | 9.5 | 12.6 | 18.4 | 15.5 | 15.0 | 7.9 | 4.2 | 1.9 | 1.5 | 0.5 | 0.3 | 0.2 | 1,611 | 2,413 | 3,210 | 2,480 | 0.333 | 0.330 | 0.663 | 140. |
| 141. | Misc. repair serv. | 143 | 6.3 | 7.3 | 9.5 | 11.4 | 14.8 | 14.9 | 15.5 | 8.5 | 5.1 | 2.8 | 2.8 | 0.6 | 0.4 | 0.2 | 1,583 | 2,523 | 3,348 | 2,570 | 0.373 | 0.326 | 0.699 | 141. |
| 142. | Personal serv. | 815 | 13.3 | 13.3 | 14.2 | 15.0 | 15.6 | 10.1 | 8.2 | 4.1 | 2.4 | 1.1 | 1.6 | 0.6 | 0.4 | 0.3 | 939 | 1,806 | 2,678 | 1,997 | 0.480 | 0.482 | 0.962 | 142. |
| 143. | Private households | 188 | 28.2 | 21.3 | 16.7 | 14.1 | 10.9 | 4.4 | 2.4 | 1.0 | 0.4 | 0.2 | 0.2 | 0.2 | 0.1 | 0.1 | 443 | 1,014 | 1,812 | 1,246 | 0.564 | 0.785 | 1.349 | 143. |
| 144. | Hotels & lodging places | 226 | 10.4 | 14.3 | 16.1 | 17.0 | 16.6 | 9.1 | 7.1 | 3.6 | 2.2 | 0.9 | 1.4 | 0.5 | 0.5 | 0.3 | 1,009 | 1,770 | 2,532 | 1,969 | 0.430 | 0.430 | 0.860 | 144. |
| 145. | Laund., clean., & dyeing | 233 | 6.3 | 7.4 | 11.3 | 14.4 | 17.2 | 13.4 | 13.0 | 6.6 | 4.0 | 1.8 | 2.7 | 1.0 | 0.4 | 0.4 | 1,500 | 2,308 | 3,192 | 2,473 | 0.351 | 0.383 | 0.734 | 145. |
| 146. | Dress & shoe rep. shops & misc. pers. serv. | 168 | 10.1 | 11.3 | 13.3 | 14.1 | 17.3 | 13.1 | 9.3 | 4.7 | 2.5 | 1.2 | 1.8 | 0.7 | 0.4 | 0.2 | 1,135 | 2,034 | 2,839 | 2,132 | 0.443 | 0.395 | 0.838 | 146. |
| 147. | Entertain. & recr. | 352 | 15.1 | 11.5 | 10.5 | 9.9 | 10.2 | 7.6 | 7.7 | 5.8 | 4.8 | 3.2 | 5.2 | 2.6 | 3.1 | 2.8 | 930 | 2,147 | 3,715 | 2,969 | 0.567 | 0.730 | 1.297 | 147. |
| 148. | Radio broad. & television | 45 | 3.6 | 4.5 | 4.6 | 6.2 | 8.6 | 8.5 | 11.6 | 10.1 | 7.2 | 6.1 | 9.4 | 5.5 | 7.5 | 6.7 | 2,354 | 3,618 | 5,425 | 4,839 | 0.350 | 0.499 | 0.849 | 148. |
| 149. | Theaters & motion pict. | 126 | 12.5 | 9.9 | 8.9 | 7.8 | 8.5 | 6.8 | 8.3 | 6.8 | 6.6 | 4.7 | 7.8 | 3.4 | 4.0 | 4.1 | 1,146 | 2,676 | 4,416 | 3,570 | 0.572 | 0.650 | 1.222 | 149. |
| 150. | Bowl. all., bill. & pool parl., & misc. ent. | 181 | 19.7 | 14.4 | 13.1 | 12.4 | 11.7 | 8.0 | 6.4 | 4.1 | 2.9 | 1.4 | 2.3 | 1.4 | 1.4 | 0.9 | 684 | 1,612 | 2,731 | 2,089 | 0.576 | 0.693 | 1.269 | 150. |
| 151. | Professional & rel. serv. | 1,443 | 6.3 | 8.4 | 9.7 | 10.7 | 13.8 | 11.2 | 10.9 | 7.6 | 5.9 | 3.9 | 5.5 | 2.5 | 2.3 | 1.2 | 1,528 | 2,549 | 3,763 | 2,981 | 0.401 | 0.476 | 0.877 | 151. |
| 152. | Medical & oth. health | 340 | 6.0 | 8.7 | 12.8 | 14.7 | 19.3 | 13.5 | 9.1 | 4.9 | 2.5 | 1.6 | 2.3 | 1.2 | 2.0 | 1.5 | 1,402 | 2,202 | 3,000 | 2,639 | 0.364 | 0.362 | 0.726 | 152. |
| 153. | Educational | 708 | 6.3 | 7.7 | 8.1 | 8.8 | 12.0 | 10.9 | 12.2 | 9.1 | 7.8 | 5.2 | 6.6 | 2.7 | 2.0 | 0.7 | 1,664 | 2,825 | 3,994 | 3,063 | 0.411 | 0.413 | 0.824 | 153. |
| 154. | Welfare, relig., & nonprofit | 294 | 7.3 | 10.8 | 11.9 | 12.2 | 13.6 | 10.4 | 10.4 | 6.7 | 4.5 | 2.9 | 4.3 | 2.3 | 1.9 | 0.9 | 1,289 | 2,286 | 3,423 | 2,699 | 0.436 | 0.496 | 0.932 | 154. |
| 155. | Legal, eng., arch. & misc. prof. | 101 | 4.7 | 5.5 | 5.3 | 6.6 | 9.0 | 7.4 | 8.8 | 9.2 | 8.9 | 5.3 | 12.2 | 6.1 | 6.6 | 4.6 | 2,161 | 3,646 | 5,352 | 4,450 | 0.408 | 0.467 | 0.875 | 155. |
| 156. | Public administration | 1,865 | 2.5 | 3.1 | 4.3 | 5.9 | 12.3 | 16.4 | 19.4 | 16.5 | 7.6 | 3.9 | 4.0 | 1.8 | 1.6 | 0.6 | 2,373 | 3,141 | 3,836 | 3,264 | 0.245 | 0.221 | 0.466 | 156. |
| 157. | Postal serv. | 410 | 2.1 | 2.3 | 2.8 | 3.3 | 7.4 | 16.8 | 19.2 | 33.3 | 8.3 | 2.7 | 1.4 | 0.3 | 0.1 | 0.1 | 2,711 | 3,398 | 3,816 | 3,222 | 0.203 | 0.123 | 0.326 | 157. |
| 158. | Federal pub. admin. | 693 | 2.5 | 3.1 | 4.4 | 5.5 | 12.6 | 15.7 | 17.3 | 11.6 | 7.6 | 5.7 | 6.5 | 3.4 | 3.3 | 0.9 | 2,376 | 3,179 | 4,151 | 3,526 | 0.253 | 0.305 | 0.558 | 158. |
| 159. | State & local pub. admin. | 762 | 2.7 | 3.5 | 5.0 | 7.8 | 14.7 | 16.8 | 21.4 | 11.9 | 7.3 | 2.9 | 3.1 | 1.2 | 1.0 | 0.6 | 2,204 | 2,985 | 3,630 | 3,068 | 0.262 | 0.216 | 0.478 | 159. |

continued on next page

TABLE B-1, continued

| | INDUSTRY | NUMBER WITH $1 OR MORE (thousands) (1) | Under $500 (2) | $500 to $999 (3) | $1,000 to $1,499 (4) | $1,500 to $1,999 (5) | $2,000 to $2,499 (6) | $2,500 to $2,999 (7) | $3,000 to $3,499 (8) | $3,500 to $3,999 (9) | $4,000 to $4,499 (10) | $4,500 to $4,999 (11) | $5,000 to $5,999 (12) | $6,000 to $6,999 (13) | $7,000 to $9,999 (14) | $10,000 and Over (15) | INCOME AT QUARTILE POSITION $Q_1$ (16) | Median $Q_2$ (17) | $Q_3$ (18) | ARITHMETIC MEAN (19) | MEASURES OF DISPERSION $1-\frac{Q_1}{Q_2}$ (20) | $\frac{Q_3}{Q_2}-1$ (21) | $\frac{Q_3-Q_1}{Q_2}$ (22) | |
|---|---|---|---|---|---|---|---|---|---|---|---|---|---|---|---|---|---|---|---|---|---|---|---|---|
| | | | | | | | | | PERCENTAGE DISTRIBUTION BY INCOME CLASS | | | | | | | | | | | | | | | |
| | PART 2: FEMALES | | | | | | | | | | | | | | | | | | | | | | | |
| 1. | Total | 13,120 | 16.2 | 15.2 | 15.8 | 17.7 | 16.9 | 9.2 | 5.0 | 1.8 | 1.0 | 0.5 | 0.4 | 0.1 | 0.1 | 0.1 | 789 | 1,579 | 2,298 | 1,648 | 0.501 | 0.455 | 0.956 | 1. |
| 2. | Agriculture, forestry, & fisheries | 128 | 63.0 | 18.4 | 6.9 | 5.3 | 3.3 | 1.4 | 0.8 | 0.2 | 0.2 | — | 0.2 | 0.1 | 0.2 | 0.1 | 199 | 398 | 826 | 684 | 0.500 | 1.075 | 1.575 | 2. |
| 3. | Agriculture | 122 | 64.5 | 18.3 | 6.8 | 5.1 | 2.8 | 0.9 | 0.7 | 0.1 | 0.2 | — | 0.2 | 0.1 | 0.2 | 0.1 | 193 | 387 | 786 | 650 | 0.500 | 1.029 | 1.529 | 3. |
| 4. | Forestry | 4 | 13.4 | 20.6 | 5.2 | 12.4 | 18.6 | 18.6 | 7.2 | 3.1 | — | — | 1.0 | — | — | — | 781 | 1,935 | 2,629 | 1,805 | 0.597 | 0.358 | 0.955 | 4. |
| 5. | Fisheries | 2 | 43.9 | 20.0 | 20.0 | 4.0 | 6.0 | 6.0 | — | — | — | — | — | — | — | — | 284 | 652 | 1,277 | 879 | 0.564 | 0.957 | 1.521 | 5. |
| 6. | Mining, extract., & quarry. | 21 | 5.4 | 5.7 | 8.3 | 12.1 | 25.0 | 18.5 | 14.3 | 5.4 | 2.7 | 0.7 | 0.9 | 0.6 | 0.3 | 0.3 | 1,731 | 2,370 | 3,000 | 2,432 | 0.270 | 0.265 | 0.535 | 6. |
| 7. | Metals | 2 | 5.0 | 5.0 | 5.0 | 16.7 | 23.3 | 10.0 | 25.0 | 8.3 | 1.7 | — | — | — | — | — | 1,799 | 2,392 | 3,200 | 2,400 | 0.248 | 0.337 | 0.585 | 7. |
| 8. | Coal | 4 | 4.5 | 8.0 | 13.0 | 15.6 | 25.3 | 18.2 | 7.1 | 3.9 | 1.3 | 0.6 | — | 1.9 | — | 0.6 | 1,480 | 2,175 | 2,736 | 2,280 | 0.320 | 0.257 | 0.577 | 8. |
| 9. | Crude petroleum & nat. gas | 12 | 5.9 | 4.0 | 6.7 | 8.8 | 24.4 | 19.8 | 17.4 | 6.4 | 3.2 | 1.1 | 1.3 | 0.3 | 0.3 | 0.3 | 1,977 | 2,505 | 3,155 | 2,546 | 0.211 | 0.259 | 0.470 | 9. |
| 10. | Nonmetals, exc. fuel | 3 | 4.7 | 9.4 | 9.4 | 16.5 | 28.2 | 18.8 | 5.9 | 1.2 | 3.5 | — | 1.2 | — | 1.2 | — | 1,545 | 2,177 | 2,680 | 2,193 | 0.291 | 0.231 | 0.522 | 10. |
| 11. | Construction | 82 | 9.9 | 8.9 | 11.9 | 17.7 | 22.1 | 14.1 | 8.9 | 2.8 | 1.3 | 0.6 | 0.9 | 0.4 | 0.2 | 0.3 | 1,260 | 2,036 | 2,659 | 2,065 | 0.381 | 0.306 | 0.687 | 11. |
| 12. | Manufacturing | 3,557 | 8.8 | 11.9 | 17.6 | 22.3 | 22.1 | 10.4 | 4.5 | 1.2 | 0.6 | 0.3 | 0.3 | 0.1 | 0.1 | 0.1 | 1,122 | 1,762 | 2,325 | 1,787 | 0.364 | 0.319 | 0.683 | 12. |
| 13. | Durable goods | 1,195 | 7.7 | 9.5 | 12.5 | 19.9 | 26.5 | 14.7 | 6.4 | 1.5 | 0.6 | 0.3 | 0.2 | 0.1 | 0.1 | 0.1 | 1,312 | 2,007 | 2,479 | 1,945 | 0.347 | 0.234 | 0.581 | 13. |
| 14. | Lumber & wood prod., exc. furn. | 36 | 14.6 | 15.8 | 19.8 | 19.1 | 15.2 | 8.7 | 3.9 | 1.5 | 0.4 | 0.1 | 0.4 | 0.2 | 0.1 | 0.2 | 829 | 1,494 | 2,187 | 1,606 | 0.446 | 0.463 | 0.909 | 14. |
| 15. | Logging | 1 | 10.9 | 19.6 | 21.7 | 13.0 | 15.2 | 13.0 | 4.3 | 2.2 | — | — | — | — | — | — | 860 | 1,449 | 2,322 | 1,595 | 0.406 | 0.602 | 1.008 | 15. |
| 16. | Saw & planing mills, & mill work | 20 | 13.4 | 13.1 | 15.4 | 19.0 | 19.5 | 10.2 | 5.0 | 2.0 | 0.7 | 0.2 | 0.7 | 0.3 | 0.2 | 0.3 | 942 | 1,713 | 2,361 | 1,787 | 0.450 | 0.378 | 0.828 | 16. |
| 17. | Misc. wood prod. | 15 | 16.4 | 18.8 | 24.8 | 19.8 | 10.2 | 6.4 | 2.6 | 0.8 | 0.2 | — | — | — | — | — | 729 | 1,298 | 1,879 | 1,367 | 0.438 | 0.448 | 0.886 | 17. |
| 18. | Furniture & fixtures | 49 | 11.7 | 12.7 | 17.4 | 22.5 | 20.4 | 8.2 | 4.1 | 1.3 | 0.6 | 0.3 | 0.3 | 0.3 | 0.1 | — | 1,017 | 1,682 | 2,262 | 1,686 | 0.396 | 0.344 | 0.740 | 18. |
| 19. | Stone, clay, & glass prod. | 76 | 8.4 | 10.6 | 15.7 | 24.9 | 24.4 | 9.2 | 4.2 | 1.3 | 0.6 | 0.3 | 0.3 | — | — | — | 1,191 | 1,807 | 2,315 | 1,776 | 0.341 | 0.281 | 0.622 | 19. |
| 20. | Glass & glass prod. | 34 | 7.3 | 9.6 | 16.4 | 24.6 | 25.3 | 9.9 | 4.4 | 1.1 | 1.1 | 0.2 | 0.1 | — | — | 0.1 | 1,246 | 1,839 | 2,337 | 1,833 | 0.323 | 0.270 | 0.593 | 20. |
| 21. | Cement, concrete, gypsum, & plaster prod. | 4 | 6.8 | 12.3 | 11.0 | 14.4 | 26.0 | 15.1 | 6.8 | 3.4 | — | 1.4 | 2.0 | 0.7 | — | — | 1,268 | 2,105 | 2,649 | 2,069 | 0.398 | 0.257 | 0.655 | 21. |
| 22. | Structural clay prod. | 7 | 11.6 | 12.8 | 13.6 | 23.6 | 26.0 | 5.0 | 3.7 | 2.9 | — | — | 0.8 | — | — | — | 1,022 | 1,754 | 2,257 | 1,703 | 0.418 | 0.286 | 0.704 | 22. |
| 23. | Pottery & rel. prod. | 19 | 9.0 | 13.3 | 19.2 | 31.1 | 17.8 | 4.7 | 3.6 | 0.5 | 0.3 | 0.3 | — | — | — | — | 1,070 | 1,636 | 2,067 | 1,599 | 0.347 | 0.263 | 0.610 | 23. |
| 24. | Misc. nonmet. min. & stone prod. | 12 | 9.2 | 7.4 | 11.8 | 21.3 | 30.0 | 14.4 | 3.8 | 1.3 | 0.3 | 0.3 | 0.3 | — | — | — | 1,355 | 2,005 | 2,421 | 1,885 | 0.324 | 0.207 | 0.531 | 24. |
| 25. | Metal industries | 217 | 6.1 | 7.7 | 10.8 | 21.2 | 30.0 | 14.7 | 6.3 | 1.6 | 0.6 | 0.3 | 0.2 | 0.1 | 0.1 | 0.1 | 1,509 | 2,070 | 2,486 | 2,008 | 0.271 | 0.201 | 0.472 | 25. |
| 26. | Iron & steel & their prod. | 171 | 5.9 | 7.1 | 10.4 | 21.4 | 30.7 | 15.0 | 6.2 | 1.6 | 0.6 | 0.3 | 0.2 | 0.2 | 0.1 | 0.1 | 1,537 | 2,084 | 2,491 | 2,029 | 0.263 | 0.195 | 0.458 | 26. |
| 27. | Blast furn., steel wks., & roll. mills | 35 | 4.0 | 3.4 | 7.2 | 18.5 | 35.8 | 19.1 | 7.9 | 2.3 | 0.7 | 0.4 | 0.3 | 0.1 | 0.4 | — | 1,781 | 2,236 | 2,659 | 2,228 | 0.204 | 0.189 | 0.393 | 27. |
| 28. | Oth. prim. iron, steel, & fab. steel prod. | 136 | 6.4 | 8.0 | 11.3 | 22.2 | 29.4 | 13.9 | 5.8 | 1.5 | 0.6 | 0.3 | 0.2 | 0.2 | 0.1 | 0.1 | 1,469 | 2,035 | 2,460 | 1,986 | 0.279 | 0.208 | 0.487 | 28. |
| 29. | Nonferrous metals & their prod. | 44 | 6.8 | 9.8 | 12.4 | 19.7 | 27.9 | 13.6 | 6.8 | 1.7 | 0.5 | 0.1 | 0.3 | 0.1 | 0.1 | 0.1 | 1,338 | 2,023 | 2,471 | 1,954 | 0.339 | 0.221 | 0.560 | 29. |
| 30. | Not spec. metal ind. | 2 | 8.2 | 12.3 | 9.6 | 31.5 | 19.2 | 13.7 | 4.1 | 1.4 | — | — | — | — | — | — | 1,234 | 1,815 | 2,348 | 1,778 | 0.321 | 0.293 | 0.614 | 30. |
| 31. | Machinery, exc. elec. | 173 | 5.1 | 7.3 | 9.6 | 20.1 | 30.0 | 16.6 | 7.6 | 2.2 | 0.6 | 0.3 | 0.4 | 0.1 | 0.1 | 0.1 | 1,574 | 2,131 | 2,587 | 2,097 | 0.262 | 0.213 | 0.475 | 31. |
| 32. | Agri. mach. & tractors | 19 | 4.0 | 5.4 | 7.7 | 16.7 | 31.8 | 21.1 | 10.5 | 1.5 | 0.5 | 0.3 | 0.2 | 0.2 | — | 0.2 | 1,736 | 2,254 | 2,722 | 2,231 | 0.230 | 0.207 | 0.437 | 32. |
| 33. | Office & store mach. & devices | 26 | 4.5 | 6.3 | 8.2 | 16.6 | 32.6 | 17.6 | 9.4 | 3.0 | 0.6 | 0.2 | 0.7 | — | 0.1 | — | 1,680 | 2,220 | 2,693 | 2,169 | 0.244 | 0.212 | 0.456 | 33. |
| 34. | Misc. mach. | 128 | 5.4 | 7.7 | 10.1 | 21.3 | 29.3 | 15.8 | 6.8 | 2.1 | 0.6 | 0.3 | 0.4 | 0.1 | 0.1 | 0.1 | 1,542 | 2,093 | 2,537 | 2,060 | 0.264 | 0.212 | 0.476 | 34. |
| 35. | Electrical machinery, equip., & supp. | 258 | 8.9 | 10.2 | 11.9 | 18.3 | 29.2 | 13.8 | 5.6 | 1.1 | 0.4 | 0.2 | 0.1 | 0.1 | — | — | 1,247 | 2,011 | 2,440 | 1,866 | 0.380 | 0.212 | 0.592 | 35. |
| 36. | Transportation equip. | 158 | 4.4 | 5.9 | 7.2 | 12.6 | 26.2 | 27.4 | 12.3 | 2.2 | 1.0 | 0.5 | 0.2 | — | — | — | 1,797 | 2,379 | 2,841 | 2,268 | 0.245 | 0.193 | 0.438 | 36. |
| 37. | Motor vehicles & motor veh. equip. | 108 | 4.7 | 5.8 | 7.7 | 12.6 | 25.8 | 27.1 | 12.5 | 2.1 | 0.9 | 0.4 | 0.1 | — | — | — | 1,769 | 2,372 | 2,839 | 2,245 | 0.254 | 0.197 | 0.451 | 37. |
| 38. | Aircraft & parts | 34 | 3.9 | 5.7 | 5.9 | 12.5 | 26.6 | 29.1 | 11.4 | 2.6 | 1.1 | 0.6 | 0.4 | — | 0.1 | — | 1,880 | 2,413 | 2,850 | 2,317 | 0.221 | 0.181 | 0.403 | 38. |
| 39. | Ship & boat bldg. & repair. | 9 | 2.7 | 2.7 | 6.3 | 12.0 | 26.7 | 31.0 | 14.7 | 2.3 | 0.3 | 0.7 | 0.7 | — | — | — | 2,024 | 2,492 | 2,896 | 2,417 | 0.188 | 0.162 | 0.350 | 39. |
| 40. | Railroad & misc. transp. equip. | 7 | 4.1 | 11.9 | 6.8 | 13.7 | 29.7 | 18.7 | 9.6 | 1.8 | 1.4 | 0.9 | 0.9 | — | — | 0.5 | 1,580 | 2,227 | 2,735 | 2,238 | 0.291 | 0.228 | 0.519 | 40. |
| 41. | Other durable goods | 228 | 9.7 | 12.5 | 17.4 | 23.5 | 21.3 | 9.8 | 3.9 | 1.0 | 0.4 | 0.2 | 0.2 | — | 0.1 | — | 1,080 | 1,721 | 2,279 | 1,705 | 0.373 | 0.324 | 0.697 | 41. |
| 42. | Professional & photo. equip. & supp. | 48 | 5.7 | 7.3 | 10.6 | 19.9 | 30.1 | 17.9 | 5.5 | 2.0 | 0.3 | 0.4 | 0.2 | 0.1 | — | — | 1,535 | 2,107 | 2,539 | 2,022 | 0.272 | 0.204 | 0.476 | 42. |
| 43. | Watches, clocks, & misc. mfg. ind. | 180 | 10.8 | 13.9 | 19.1 | 24.4 | 19.0 | 7.6 | 3.4 | 0.7 | 0.4 | 0.1 | 0.2 | — | 0.2 | 0.1 | 1,007 | 1,627 | 2,178 | 1,640 | 0.381 | 0.339 | 0.720 | 43. |
| 44. | Nondurable goods | 2,362 | 9.3 | 13.1 | 20.1 | 23.5 | 19.8 | 8.2 | 3.5 | 1.1 | 0.5 | 0.3 | 0.3 | 0.1 | 0.1 | 0.1 | 1,064 | 1,659 | 2,227 | 1,697 | 0.359 | 0.342 | 0.701 | 44. |
| 45. | Food & kindred prod. | 320 | 13.8 | 15.8 | 16.0 | 19.4 | 20.5 | 8.9 | 3.4 | 0.9 | 0.5 | 0.2 | 0.2 | 0.1 | 0.1 | 0.1 | 854 | 1,613 | 2,243 | 1,619 | 0.471 | 0.390 | 0.861 | 45. |
| 46. | Meat prod. | 54 | 7.6 | 11.0 | 12.8 | 18.6 | 28.9 | 13.5 | 5.5 | 1.0 | 0.6 | 0.1 | 0.2 | 0.1 | 0.1 | 0.1 | 1,250 | 2,000 | 2,432 | 1,901 | 0.375 | 0.216 | 0.591 | 46. |
| 47. | Dairy prod. | 26 | 11.5 | 13.5 | 15.8 | 23.1 | 20.9 | 10.9 | 2.5 | 0.8 | 0.5 | 0.1 | — | — | 0.1 | 0.3 | 1,000 | 1,699 | 2,265 | 1,707 | 0.412 | 0.333 | 0.745 | 47. |
| 48. | Can. & preserv. fruit, veg. & sea food | 68 | 28.6 | 28.3 | 17.1 | 11.4 | 8.4 | 3.6 | 1.7 | 0.3 | 0.2 | — | 0.1 | 0.1 | 0.2 | — | 437 | 878 | 1,543 | 1,089 | 0.503 | 0.758 | 1.261 | 48. |
| 49. | Grain mill prod. | 15 | 5.6 | 8.8 | 11.0 | 22.4 | 27.7 | 14.8 | 4.3 | 2.8 | 1.3 | 0.4 | — | 0.2 | 0.2 | 0.4 | 1,481 | 2,039 | 2,490 | 2,068 | 0.274 | 0.221 | 0.495 | 49. |
| 50. | Bakery prod. | 56 | 10.0 | 12.3 | 17.5 | 23.2 | 24.3 | 8.1 | 2.6 | 0.8 | 0.6 | 0.2 | 0.2 | 0.1 | — | 0.1 | 1,077 | 1,719 | 2,246 | 1,698 | 0.374 | 0.306 | 0.680 | 50. |
| 51. | Confectionery & rel. prod. | 38 | 11.2 | 16.1 | 21.0 | 23.0 | 18.0 | 6.4 | 3.1 | 0.4 | 0.3 | 0.3 | 0.2 | 0.1 | 0.1 | — | 928 | 1,536 | 2,102 | 1,563 | 0.396 | 0.368 | 0.764 | 51. |
| 52. | Beverage ind. | 25 | 7.8 | 10.0 | 13.5 | 19.4 | 26.4 | 13.1 | 4.8 | 2.3 | 0.8 | 0.5 | 0.5 | 0.4 | 0.3 | 0.1 | 1,266 | 1,981 | 2,460 | 1,956 | 0.361 | 0.241 | 0.602 | 52. |
| 53. | Misc. food prep. & not spec. food ind. | 38 | 13.0 | 13.0 | 15.4 | 22.5 | 19.8 | 9.5 | 4.2 | 1.1 | 0.4 | 0.3 | 0.4 | 0.2 | 0.2 | — | 961 | 1,691 | 2,280 | 1,684 | 0.432 | 0.348 | 0.780 | 53. |
| 54. | Tobacco manufactures | 54 | 12.6 | 15.0 | 22.8 | 26.1 | 17.0 | 5.2 | 0.5 | 0.3 | 0.1 | 0.1 | 0.1 | 0.1 | 0.1 | 0.1 | 913 | 1,491 | 1,971 | 1,488 | 0.388 | 0.321 | 0.709 | 54. |
| 55. | Textile mill prod. | 518 | 7.7 | 12.2 | 19.8 | 26.9 | 22.5 | 7.5 | 2.2 | 0.5 | 0.2 | 0.1 | 0.1 | — | 0.1 | 0.1 | 1,128 | 1,691 | 2,186 | 1,679 | 0.333 | 0.292 | 0.625 | 55. |
| 56. | Knitting mills | 119 | 9.8 | 16.0 | 25.1 | 24.5 | 15.6 | 5.9 | 1.9 | 0.6 | 0.3 | 0.1 | 0.1 | — | 0.1 | 0.1 | 975 | 1,482 | 1,991 | 1,536 | 0.343 | 0.343 | 0.686 | 56. |

continued on next page

TABLE B-1, females, continued

| | INDUSTRY | NUMBER WITH $1 OR MORE (thousands) (1) | Under $500 (2) | $500 to $999 (3) | $1,000 to $1,499 (4) | $1,500 to $1,999 (5) | $2,000 to $2,499 (6) | $2,500 to $2,999 (7) | $3,000 to $3,499 (8) | $3,500 to $3,999 (9) | $4,000 to $4,499 (10) | $4,500 to $4,999 (11) | $5,000 to $5,999 (12) | $6,000 to $6,999 (13) | $7,000 to $9,999 (14) | $10,000 and Over (15) | $Q_1$ (16) | Median $Q_2$ (17) | $Q_3$ (18) | ARITHMETIC MEAN (19) | $1-\frac{Q_1}{Q_2}$ (20) | $\frac{Q_3}{Q_2}-1$ (21) | $\frac{Q_3-Q_1}{Q_2}$ (22) | |
|---|---|---|---|---|---|---|---|---|---|---|---|---|---|---|---|---|---|---|---|---|---|---|---|---|
| | | | PERCENTAGE DISTRIBUTION BY INCOME CLASS | | | | | | | | | | | | | | INCOME AT QUARTILE POSITION | | | | MEASURES OF DISPERSION | | | |
| 57. | Dyeing & fin. tex. exc. knit goods | 9 | 6.2 | 5.9 | 14.5 | 27.7 | 29.8 | 12.8 | 2.4 | 0.7 | — | — | — | — | — | — | 1,444 | 1,922 | 2,347 | 1,852 | 0.249 | 0.221 | 0.470 | 57. |
| 58. | Carpets, rugs, & oth. floor cov. | 16 | 7.4 | 8.2 | 13.6 | 16.5 | 28.2 | 16.7 | 6.8 | 1.6 | 0.8 | — | 0.2 | — | 0.2 | — | 1,345 | 2,076 | 2,532 | 1,975 | 0.352 | 0.219 | 0.571 | 58. |
| 59. | Yarn, thread, & fabric mills | 355 | 7.0 | 11.2 | 18.4 | 28.2 | 24.6 | 7.5 | 2.1 | 0.4 | 0.2 | 0.1 | 0.1 | 0.1 | 0.1 | — | 1,184 | 1,737 | 2,207 | 1,701 | 0.319 | 0.270 | 0.589 | 59. |
| 60. | Misc. tex. mill prod. | 19 | 8.5 | 12.9 | 21.7 | 27.9 | 18.4 | 6.8 | 2.0 | 0.7 | 0.3 | 0.3 | 0.3 | 0.2 | — | 0.2 | 1,082 | 1,623 | 2,108 | 1,666 | 0.334 | 0.298 | 0.632 | 60. |
| 61. | Apparel & oth. fab. tex. prod. | 736 | 9.6 | 15.3 | 26.4 | 23.4 | 15.1 | 5.6 | 2.6 | 0.8 | 0.4 | 0.2 | 0.2 | 0.1 | 0.1 | 0.1 | 1,001 | 1,475 | 2,009 | 1,559 | 0.321 | 0.362 | 0.683 | 61. |
| 62. | Apparel & access. | 692 | 9.7 | 15.3 | 26.6 | 23.4 | 15.0 | 5.6 | 2.6 | 0.8 | 0.4 | 0.2 | 0.2 | 0.1 | 0.1 | 0.1 | 1,000 | 1,469 | 2,000 | 1,559 | 0.320 | 0.360 | 0.680 | 62. |
| 63. | Misc. fab. tex. prod. | 44 | 9.4 | 16.2 | 23.7 | 22.9 | 17.8 | 5.6 | 2.9 | 0.7 | 0.2 | 0.1 | 0.3 | 0.1 | 0.1 | — | 981 | 1,515 | 2,078 | 1,561 | 0.353 | 0.371 | 0.724 | 63. |
| 64. | Paper & all. prod. | 109 | 7.4 | 9.2 | 16.1 | 25.8 | 25.3 | 10.2 | 3.6 | 1.0 | 0.4 | 0.3 | 0.4 | 0.1 | 0.1 | 0.1 | 1,260 | 1,835 | 2,326 | 1,832 | 0.313 | 0.267 | 0.580 | 64. |
| 65. | Pulp, paper, & paperboard mills | 27 | 6.2 | 7.6 | 11.8 | 24.0 | 28.3 | 14.6 | 5.1 | 1.1 | 0.4 | 0.2 | 0.6 | 0.1 | — | — | 1,474 | 2,007 | 2,448 | 1,951 | 0.266 | 0.220 | 0.486 | 65. |
| 66. | Paperboard cont. & boxes | 39 | 7.9 | 9.4 | 20.0 | 27.3 | 22.1 | 8.2 | 2.6 | 1.0 | 0.4 | 0.3 | 0.3 | — | 0.3 | 0.1 | 1,192 | 1,732 | 2,235 | 1,756 | 0.312 | 0.290 | 0.602 | 66. |
| 67. | Misc. paper & pulp prod. | 43 | 7.8 | 10.1 | 15.3 | 25.5 | 26.3 | 9.3 | 3.6 | 0.9 | 0.4 | 0.3 | 0.2 | 0.1 | 0.1 | 0.1 | 1,232 | 1,829 | 2,309 | 1,808 | 0.327 | 0.262 | 0.589 | 67. |
| 68. | Printing, publ., & all. ind. | 203 | 9.2 | 9.5 | 12.4 | 21.3 | 21.3 | 12.0 | 6.8 | 2.7 | 1.8 | 1.0 | 1.1 | 0.3 | 0.4 | 0.3 | 1,254 | 1,943 | 2,554 | 2,051 | 0.355 | 0.314 | 0.669 | 68. |
| 69. | Chemicals & all. prod. | 129 | 6.5 | 7.6 | 9.0 | 18.4 | 27.6 | 17.4 | 8.4 | 2.5 | 1.1 | 0.6 | 0.5 | 0.3 | 0.2 | 0.1 | 1,551 | 2,153 | 2,669 | 2,133 | 0.280 | 0.239 | 0.519 | 69. |
| 70. | Synthetic fibers | 12 | 4.7 | 5.9 | 6.4 | 14.7 | 32.4 | 24.8 | 9.1 | 1.7 | — | 0.2 | — | — | — | — | 1,772 | 2,282 | 2,719 | 2,173 | 0.224 | 0.191 | 0.415 | 70. |
| 71. | Paints, varn., & rel. prod. | 9 | 3.4 | 7.7 | 11.1 | 20.5 | 32.7 | 16.8 | 5.1 | 1.3 | 0.3 | 0.3 | — | 0.3 | — | 0.3 | 1,568 | 2,111 | 2,493 | 2,082 | 0.258 | 0.180 | 0.438 | 71. |
| 72. | Drugs, med., & misc. chem. & all. prod. | 107 | 7.0 | 7.8 | 9.1 | 18.6 | 26.5 | 16.6 | 8.6 | 2.7 | 1.2 | 0.6 | 0.6 | 0.3 | 0.2 | 0.1 | 1,529 | 2,141 | 2,680 | 2,117 | 0.286 | 0.251 | 0.537 | 72. |
| 73. | Petroleum & coal prod. | 31 | 1.7 | 4.8 | 5.3 | 10.3 | 24.2 | 19.5 | 20.2 | 7.4 | 2.7 | 1.7 | 1.1 | 0.5 | 0.5 | 0.1 | 2,059 | 2,594 | 3,227 | 2,652 | 0.207 | 0.243 | 0.450 | 73. |
| 74. | Petro. refining | 29 | 1.7 | 4.1 | 5.0 | 10.2 | 23.7 | 19.8 | 20.9 | 7.8 | 2.9 | 1.8 | 1.1 | 0.6 | 0.6 | — | 2,084 | 2,633 | 3,251 | 2,684 | 0.209 | 0.234 | 0.443 | 74. |
| 75. | Misc. petro. & coal prod. | 2 | 2.0 | 15.7 | 9.8 | 13.7 | 33.3 | 15.7 | 7.8 | — | — | — | — | — | — | 2.0 | 1,372 | 2,132 | 2,515 | 2,319 | 0.357 | 0.179 | 0.536 | 75. |
| 76. | Rubber prod. | 59 | 5.6 | 7.9 | 11.9 | 20.7 | 33.4 | 13.2 | 5.3 | 0.9 | 0.4 | 0.3 | 0.2 | — | 0.2 | 0.1 | 1,483 | 2,058 | 2,432 | 1,984 | 0.280 | 0.181 | 0.461 | 76. |
| 77. | Leather & leather prod. | 166 | 9.2 | 14.2 | 26.7 | 28.2 | 15.1 | 4.6 | 1.1 | 0.4 | 0.2 | 0.1 | 0.2 | 0.1 | — | 0.1 | 1,029 | 1,498 | 1,941 | 1,524 | 0.313 | 0.295 | 0.608 | 77. |
| 78. | Leather: tanned, curried, & fin. | 6 | 5.7 | 9.0 | 17.1 | 24.2 | 25.6 | 15.6 | 0.9 | 1.4 | — | — | 0.5 | — | — | — | 1,301 | 1,876 | 2,371 | 1,833 | 0.307 | 0.263 | 0.570 | 78. |
| 79. | Footwear, exc. rubber | 129 | 8.9 | 13.4 | 27.4 | 29.4 | 15.0 | 4.0 | 1.0 | 0.4 | 0.2 | 0.1 | 0.1 | 0.1 | — | 0.1 | 1,049 | 1,505 | 1,930 | 1,520 | 0.303 | 0.282 | 0.585 | 79. |
| 80. | Leather prod., exc. footwear | 31 | 11.1 | 18.9 | 25.6 | 23.7 | 13.1 | 4.7 | 1.5 | 0.3 | 0.3 | — | 0.4 | 0.1 | — | 0.1 | 867 | 1,390 | 1,909 | 1,449 | 0.377 | 0.372 | 0.749 | 80. |
| 81. | Not spec. mfg. ind. | 38 | 9.6 | 12.7 | 16.2 | 21.8 | 20.4 | 9.3 | 4.8 | 2.4 | 1.3 | 0.4 | 0.3 | 0.5 | 0.1 | 0.1 | 1,083 | 1,763 | 2,360 | 1,815 | 0.386 | 0.338 | 0.724 | 81. |
| 82. | Transportation, commun., & oth. pub. util. | 660 | 5.3 | 6.7 | 8.4 | 17.3 | 27.9 | 17.6 | 11.1 | 3.2 | 1.2 | 0.5 | 0.4 | 0.1 | 0.1 | 0.1 | 1,632 | 2,220 | 2,767 | 2,195 | 0.265 | 0.246 | 0.511 | 82. |
| 83. | Transportation | 179 | 6.5 | 7.3 | 8.3 | 13.4 | 22.4 | 19.5 | 15.7 | 4.2 | 1.2 | 0.5 | 0.4 | 0.2 | 0.1 | 0.1 | 1,608 | 2,323 | 2,938 | 2,255 | 0.308 | 0.264 | 0.572 | 83. |
| 84. | Railroads & railway exp. serv. | 72 | 2.6 | 3.3 | 5.0 | 7.6 | 21.7 | 24.2 | 26.4 | 6.5 | 1.8 | 0.5 | 0.3 | 0.1 | — | — | 2,149 | 2,702 | 3,200 | 2,605 | 0.205 | 0.184 | 0.389 | 84. |
| 85. | St. railways & bus lines | 25 | 9.6 | 11.0 | 11.3 | 16.4 | 21.6 | 15.7 | 9.3 | 3.2 | 0.6 | 0.6 | 0.3 | 0.4 | — | — | 1,194 | 2,039 | 2,662 | 1,971 | 0.415 | 0.305 | 0.720 | 85. |
| 86. | Trucking serv. | 27 | 8.7 | 9.2 | 11.7 | 21.1 | 23.8 | 14.6 | 6.2 | 1.8 | 0.5 | 0.7 | 0.7 | 0.2 | 0.4 | 0.4 | 1,303 | 1,983 | 2,517 | 2,032 | 0.343 | 0.269 | 0.612 | 86. |
| 87. | Warehousing & storage | 13 | 12.9 | 18.2 | 15.5 | 18.7 | 16.5 | 10.9 | 4.6 | 1.2 | 0.5 | 0.2 | 0.2 | 0.2 | — | 0.2 | 832 | 1,590 | 2,293 | 1,650 | 0.477 | 0.441 | 0.918 | 87. |
| 88. | Taxicab serv. | 7 | 19.0 | 20.5 | 16.7 | 17.6 | 12.9 | 7.1 | 4.3 | 1.0 | 0.5 | — | 0.5 | — | — | — | 646 | 1,314 | 2,046 | 1,429 | 0.509 | 0.557 | 1.066 | 88. |
| 89. | Water transp. | 12 | 5.2 | 3.6 | 6.8 | 16.2 | 31.0 | 19.2 | 10.4 | 4.4 | 2.0 | 0.8 | 0.3 | 0.3 | — | — | 1,790 | 2,293 | 2,817 | 2,296 | 0.220 | 0.228 | 0.448 | 89. |
| 90. | Air transp. | 16 | 3.8 | 4.8 | 5.0 | 11.8 | 27.7 | 26.5 | 13.6 | 3.6 | 1.4 | 0.6 | 0.8 | — | 0.2 | 0.2 | 1,983 | 2,444 | 2,913 | 2,432 | 0.189 | 0.191 | 0.380 | 90. |
| 91. | Petro. & gas. pipe lines | 1 | 3.7 | 7.4 | — | 18.5 | 25.9 | 14.8 | 14.8 | 7.4 | 3.7 | — | 3.7 | — | — | — | 1,875 | 2,393 | 3,158 | 2,497 | 0.217 | 0.319 | 0.536 | 91. |
| 92. | Serv. incid. to transp. | 6 | 11.5 | 7.7 | 8.6 | 17.2 | 21.5 | 17.2 | 10.5 | 3.8 | 0.5 | 0.5 | — | 0.5 | 0.5 | — | 1,337 | 2,116 | 2,747 | 2,055 | 0.369 | 0.298 | 0.667 | 92. |
| 93. | Telecommunications | 387 | 4.9 | 6.4 | 8.6 | 18.5 | 30.4 | 16.9 | 9.4 | 2.5 | 1.2 | 0.5 | 0.4 | 0.1 | 0.1 | — | 1,637 | 2,190 | 2,683 | 2,151 | 0.253 | 0.224 | 0.477 | 93. |
| 94. | Telephone, wire & radio | 371 | 5.0 | 6.6 | 8.7 | 18.9 | 30.7 | 16.7 | 8.8 | 2.3 | 1.2 | 0.5 | 0.4 | 0.1 | 0.1 | 0.1 | 1,624 | 2,175 | 2,652 | 2,155 | 0.254 | 0.219 | 0.473 | 94. |
| 95. | Telegraph, wire & radio | 16 | 3.2 | 2.6 | 5.5 | 11.3 | 23.3 | 21.1 | 21.5 | 7.1 | 2.4 | 1.0 | 0.8 | — | 0.2 | — | 2,051 | 2,597 | 3,186 | 2,574 | 0.211 | 0.226 | 0.437 | 95. |
| 96. | Utilities & sanitary serv. | 94 | 4.7 | 6.6 | 7.9 | 19.8 | 27.9 | 17.1 | 9.7 | 3.9 | 1.0 | 0.6 | 0.5 | 0.1 | 0.1 | 0.1 | 1,646 | 2,197 | 2,736 | 2,199 | 0.251 | 0.245 | 0.496 | 96. |
| 97. | Elec. light, power, gas, & oth. util. | 70 | 4.2 | 6.0 | 8.3 | 19.5 | 28.3 | 17.4 | 9.6 | 4.2 | 1.2 | 0.5 | 0.5 | — | — | 0.1 | 1,666 | 2,212 | 2,750 | 2,207 | 0.247 | 0.243 | 0.490 | 97. |
| 98. | Gas & steam supply systems | 15 | 4.9 | 8.5 | 6.6 | 19.0 | 25.1 | 17.9 | 11.5 | 4.3 | 0.2 | 0.6 | 0.6 | — | 0.6 | — | 1,631 | 2,219 | 2,804 | 2,204 | 0.265 | 0.263 | 0.528 | 98. |
| 99. | Water supply & san. serv. | 9 | 8.0 | 8.0 | 7.2 | 23.5 | 29.5 | 13.1 | 7.2 | 0.8 | 0.8 | 0.8 | 0.4 | 0.4 | — | 0.4 | 1,538 | 2,055 | 2,479 | 2,069 | 0.252 | 0.206 | 0.458 | 99. |
| 100. | Wholesale & retail trade | 2,839 | 18.5 | 17.9 | 19.9 | 18.9 | 13.5 | 5.7 | 2.9 | 1.0 | 0.5 | 0.3 | 0.3 | 0.2 | 0.2 | 0.1 | 681 | 1,341 | 1,994 | 1,454 | 0.493 | 0.486 | 0.979 | 100. |
| 101. | Wholesale trade | 358 | 9.4 | 11.7 | 12.9 | 20.3 | 22.7 | 11.6 | 6.5 | 1.9 | 1.0 | 0.6 | 0.7 | 0.3 | 0.2 | 0.2 | 1,151 | 1,894 | 2,455 | 1,926 | 0.393 | 0.296 | 0.689 | 101. |
| 102. | Motor vehicles & equip. | 8 | 7.1 | 7.4 | 11.3 | 24.5 | 26.6 | 11.0 | 8.5 | 1.1 | 1.1 | 0.7 | — | — | 0.4 | 0.4 | 1,464 | 1,993 | 2,464 | 2,055 | 0.266 | 0.235 | 0.501 | 102. |
| 103. | Drugs, chem., & all. prod. | 23 | 9.0 | 8.3 | 10.5 | 20.5 | 27.0 | 14.6 | 5.9 | 1.5 | 0.8 | 0.8 | 0.4 | 0.4 | — | 0.3 | 1,366 | 2,031 | 2,494 | 2,011 | 0.328 | 0.227 | 0.555 | 103. |
| 104. | Dry goods & apparel | 40 | 5.7 | 7.7 | 14.9 | 21.1 | 22.4 | 12.8 | 7.5 | 1.9 | 1.4 | 1.1 | 1.8 | 0.6 | 0.8 | 0.4 | 1,389 | 2,013 | 2,625 | 2,196 | 0.310 | 0.303 | 0.613 | 104. |
| 105. | Food & rel. prod. | 105 | 15.2 | 18.6 | 16.1 | 19.6 | 16.3 | 7.6 | 3.9 | 1.2 | 0.8 | 0.1 | 0.4 | 0.2 | 0.1 | — | 763 | 1,502 | 2,168 | 1,551 | 0.492 | 0.443 | 0.935 | 105. |
| 106. | Elec. goods, hardware, & plumb. equip. | 32 | 5.4 | 9.2 | 11.8 | 22.1 | 29.0 | 12.0 | 6.0 | 1.9 | 0.7 | 0.6 | 0.5 | 0.2 | 0.2 | 0.3 | 1,440 | 2,025 | 2,456 | 2,041 | 0.289 | 0.212 | 0.501 | 106. |
| 107. | Machinery, equip. & supp. | 23 | 5.3 | 7.0 | 8.9 | 19.4 | 31.7 | 15.1 | 7.7 | 2.2 | 1.2 | 0.1 | 0.4 | 0.4 | 0.4 | — | 1,597 | 2,148 | 2,589 | 2,115 | 0.257 | 0.205 | 0.462 | 107. |
| 108. | Petro. prod. | 19 | 4.6 | 6.0 | 7.6 | 15.0 | 26.2 | 18.4 | 14.8 | 4.6 | 2.1 | 0.3 | — | 0.2 | 0.2 | 0.2 | 1,726 | 2,320 | 2,923 | 2,336 | 0.256 | 0.259 | 0.515 | 108. |
| 109. | Farm prod. & raw materials | 11 | 16.1 | 11.5 | 13.3 | 20.2 | 21.0 | 8.6 | 4.0 | 2.3 | 0.6 | 1.4 | 0.9 | — | — | — | 886 | 1,725 | 2,330 | 1,713 | 0.486 | 0.351 | 0.837 | 109. |
| 110. | Misc. wholesale | 81 | 7.9 | 10.6 | 12.1 | 20.8 | 23.8 | 12.4 | 6.9 | 2.0 | 1.0 | 0.9 | 0.7 | 0.3 | 0.2 | 0.3 | 1,268 | 1,966 | 2,495 | 2,010 | 0.355 | 0.269 | 0.624 | 110. |
| 111. | Not spec. wholesale | 16 | 3.7 | 6.1 | 9.3 | 22.4 | 25.2 | 15.2 | 9.8 | 3.9 | 1.2 | 1.0 | 1.4 | 0.4 | 0.4 | — | 1,631 | 2,168 | 2,773 | 2,248 | 0.248 | 0.278 | 0.526 | 111. |
| 112. | Retail trade, stores | 2,481 | 19.9 | 18.8 | 20.9 | 18.7 | 12.2 | 4.9 | 2.4 | 0.9 | 0.5 | 0.2 | 0.3 | 0.1 | 0.2 | 0.1 | 635 | 1,270 | 1,911 | 1,391 | 0.500 | 0.504 | 1.004 | 112. |
| 113. | Food, exc. dairy prod. | 358 | 16.9 | 16.4 | 18.1 | 20.0 | 15.9 | 6.4 | 3.5 | 1.2 | 0.5 | 0.3 | 0.3 | 0.3 | 0.2 | 0.1 | 746 | 1,461 | 2,113 | 1,542 | 0.489 | 0.446 | 0.935 | 113. |
| 114. | Dairy prod. & milk retail | 15 | 21.0 | 15.4 | 18.1 | 16.7 | 15.8 | 8.7 | 2.7 | 1.2 | 0.2 | — | — | — | — | — | 629 | 1,375 | 2,120 | 1,422 | 0.543 | 0.541 | 1.084 | 114. |

continued on next page

TABLE B-1, females, concluded

| | INDUSTRY | NUMBER WITH $1 OR MORE (thousands) (1) | Under $500 (2) | $500 to $999 (3) | $1,000 to $1,499 (4) | $1,500 to $1,999 (5) | $2,000 to $2,499 (6) | $2,500 to $2,999 (7) | $3,000 to $3,499 (8) | $3,500 to $3,999 (9) | $4,000 to $4,499 (10) | $4,500 to $4,999 (11) | $5,000 to $5,999 (12) | $6,000 to $6,999 (13) | $7,000 to $9,999 (14) | $10,000 and Over (15) | $Q_1$ (16) | Median $Q_2$ (17) | $Q_3$ (18) | ARITHMETIC MEAN (19) | $1 - \frac{Q_1}{Q_2}$ (20) | $\frac{Q_3}{Q_2} - 1$ (21) | $\frac{Q_3 - Q_1}{Q_2}$ (22) | |
|---|---|---|---|---|---|---|---|---|---|---|---|---|---|---|---|---|---|---|---|---|---|---|---|---|
| | | | PERCENTAGE DISTRIBUTION BY INCOME CLASS | | | | | | | | | | | | | | INCOME AT QUARTILE POSITION | | | | MEASURES OF DISPERSION | | | |
| 115. | Genl. merchandise | 491 | 16.1 | 14.6 | 22.9 | 23.2 | 14.0 | 4.9 | 2.1 | 0.8 | 0.5 | 0.3 | 0.2 | 0.1 | 0.2 | 0.1 | 804 | 1,421 | 1,961 | 1,480 | 0.434 | 0.379 | 0.813 | 115. |
| 116. | Five & ten cent | 129 | 32.9 | 19.4 | 26.2 | 13.4 | 5.2 | 1.5 | 0.6 | 0.1 | 0.1 | — | 0.2 | — | 0.1 | 0.1 | 379 | 940 | 1,433 | 1,015 | 0.597 | 0.523 | 1.120 | 116. |
| 117. | Apparel & acc., exc. shoe | 254 | 15.1 | 14.7 | 21.2 | 21.4 | 14.5 | 6.3 | 3.3 | 1.3 | 0.7 | 0.3 | 0.6 | 0.2 | 0.3 | 0.2 | 836 | 1,476 | 2,089 | 1,598 | 0.434 | 0.415 | 0.849 | 117. |
| 118. | Shoe | 19 | 21.4 | 13.7 | 19.4 | 18.9 | 13.8 | 6.4 | 3.1 | 1.3 | 0.7 | 0.5 | 0.5 | — | 0.3 | — | 631 | 1,384 | 2,057 | 1,472 | 0.544 | 0.486 | 1.030 | 118. |
| 119. | Furniture & housefurn. | 47 | 14.0 | 13.1 | 16.4 | 22.5 | 19.8 | 6.3 | 3.9 | 1.5 | 0.7 | 0.3 | 0.7 | 0.5 | 0.3 | 0.1 | 919 | 1,644 | 2,227 | 1,694 | 0.441 | 0.354 | 0.795 | 119. |
| 120. | Household appl. & radio | 29 | 13.7 | 12.8 | 18.5 | 21.9 | 18.8 | 7.9 | 3.7 | 0.7 | 1.0 | 0.3 | 0.2 | — | 0.4 | — | 941 | 1,614 | 2,215 | 1,633 | 0.417 | 0.372 | 0.789 | 120. |
| 121. | Motor vehicles & acc. | 55 | 7.0 | 9.3 | 13.6 | 22.3 | 24.0 | 12.1 | 6.0 | 2.7 | 1.1 | 0.6 | 0.8 | 0.1 | 0.3 | 0.2 | 1,319 | 1,950 | 2,475 | 2,007 | 0.324 | 0.268 | 0.592 | 121. |
| 122. | Gas. serv. stations | 8 | 23.3 | 19.0 | 15.5 | 16.8 | 13.8 | 5.6 | 3.9 | 0.9 | 0.4 | — | 0.4 | — | 0.4 | — | 544 | 1,248 | 2,014 | 1,386 | 0.564 | 0.613 | 1.177 | 122. |
| 123. | Drug | 106 | 23.7 | 20.0 | 23.3 | 18.0 | 8.0 | 3.7 | 2.1 | 0.4 | 0.4 | 0.2 | 0.1 | — | 0.1 | — | 532 | 1,135 | 1,722 | 1,221 | 0.531 | 0.517 | 1.048 | 123. |
| 124. | Eating & drinking places | 664 | 25.9 | 28.5 | 21.7 | 12.9 | 6.5 | 2.3 | 1.2 | 0.3 | 0.2 | 0.1 | 0.2 | — | 0.1 | — | 482 | 922 | 1,474 | 1,068 | 0.477 | 0.597 | 1.074 | 124. |
| 125. | Hardware & farm impl. | 29 | 12.6 | 11.9 | 18.7 | 27.3 | 18.8 | 5.4 | 3.3 | 0.8 | 0.5 | 0.1 | 0.2 | 0.1 | 0.2 | — | 1,013 | 1,624 | 2,119 | 1,601 | 0.377 | 0.304 | 0.681 | 125. |
| 126. | Lumber & bldg. material retail | 34 | 8.8 | 10.4 | 14.1 | 23.3 | 20.3 | 12.4 | 4.9 | 2.8 | 1.1 | 0.9 | 0.6 | 0.2 | 0.1 | 0.1 | 1,205 | 1,858 | 2,453 | 1,910 | 0.352 | 0.320 | 0.672 | 126. |
| 127. | Liquor | 6 | 14.0 | 18.1 | 16.0 | 19.2 | 19.7 | 5.2 | 3.6 | 3.1 | 0.5 | 0.5 | — | — | — | — | 803 | 1,549 | 2,195 | 1,571 | 0.482 | 0.416 | 0.898 | 127. |
| 128. | Florists | 15 | 25.4 | 15.4 | 18.5 | 16.6 | 15.0 | 6.4 | 0.9 | 0.7 | 0.9 | 0.2 | — | — | — | — | 492 | 1,248 | 1,972 | 1,317 | 0.606 | 0.579 | 1.185 | 128. |
| 129. | Jewelry | 28 | 16.5 | 14.0 | 17.9 | 22.4 | 13.2 | 6.9 | 4.5 | 1.8 | 0.8 | 0.4 | 0.6 | 0.4 | 0.1 | 0.5 | 803 | 1,535 | 2,159 | 1,683 | 0.477 | 0.405 | 0.882 | 129. |
| 130. | Fuel & ice | 14 | 7.9 | 9.3 | 12.1 | 24.0 | 24.4 | 12.1 | 5.3 | 2.8 | 1.4 | — | 0.2 | 0.2 | 0.2 | — | 1,322 | 1,931 | 2,444 | 1,920 | 0.316 | 0.265 | 0.581 | 130. |
| 131. | Misc. retail | 93 | 18.9 | 15.8 | 18.3 | 19.8 | 15.1 | 6.3 | 2.9 | 1.1 | 0.4 | 0.2 | 0.4 | 0.2 | 0.2 | 0.3 | 693 | 1,418 | 2,072 | 1,528 | 0.512 | 0.461 | 0.973 | 131. |
| 132. | Not spec. retail | 87 | 19.1 | 14.3 | 20.9 | 21.2 | 12.8 | 6.2 | 3.0 | 0.8 | 0.5 | 0.3 | 0.3 | 0.1 | 0.2 | 0.2 | 706 | 1,397 | 1,988 | 1,488 | 0.495 | 0.423 | 0.918 | 132. |
| 133. | Finance, insurance, & real estate | 712 | 7.2 | 10.1 | 13.0 | 25.7 | 24.6 | 11.0 | 5.1 | 1.5 | 0.8 | 0.4 | 0.4 | 0.1 | 0.1 | 0.1 | 1,296 | 1,883 | 2,386 | 1,894 | 0.312 | 0.266 | 0.578 | 133. |
| 134. | Bank. & cred. agenc. & commod. brok. | 273 | 5.3 | 7.9 | 11.9 | 26.6 | 27.2 | 12.4 | 5.7 | 1.5 | 0.6 | 0.3 | 0.3 | 0.1 | 0.1 | 0.1 | 1,495 | 1,968 | 2,428 | 1,972 | 0.240 | 0.233 | 0.473 | 134. |
| 135. | Insurance | 314 | 6.1 | 9.1 | 11.8 | 27.9 | 25.6 | 11.1 | 4.9 | 1.5 | 0.9 | 0.4 | 0.4 | 0.1 | 0.1 | 0.1 | 1,415 | 1,912 | 2,392 | 1,930 | 0.260 | 0.251 | 0.511 | 135. |
| 136. | Real estate, incl. real est. ins. law off. | 125 | 14.3 | 17.3 | 18.4 | 18.4 | 16.2 | 7.5 | 4.0 | 1.5 | 0.7 | 0.5 | 0.6 | 0.2 | 0.2 | 0.2 | 809 | 1,500 | 2,203 | 1,631 | 0.461 | 0.469 | 0.930 | 136. |
| 137. | Business & repair serv. | 146 | 10.0 | 11.1 | 12.9 | 18.6 | 21.0 | 11.9 | 6.8 | 3.0 | 1.5 | 0.8 | 1.1 | 0.6 | 0.4 | 0.3 | 1,151 | 1,930 | 2,558 | 2,023 | 0.404 | 0.325 | 0.729 | 137. |
| 138. | Advertising | 36 | 8.1 | 9.7 | 10.0 | 14.8 | 21.7 | 14.3 | 8.9 | 3.3 | 2.7 | 1.2 | 2.6 | 1.3 | 0.8 | 0.7 | 1,360 | 2,170 | 2,874 | 2,378 | 0.374 | 0.324 | 0.698 | 138. |
| 139. | Account. audit., bookkeep., & misc. bus. serv. | 82 | 11.1 | 11.2 | 12.6 | 18.6 | 21.1 | 11.5 | 6.9 | 3.2 | 1.3 | 0.9 | 0.7 | 0.3 | 0.3 | 0.2 | 1,107 | 1,905 | 2,517 | 1,951 | 0.420 | 0.320 | 0.740 | 139. |
| 140. | Auto. repair serv. & garages | 17 | 8.6 | 10.8 | 19.7 | 25.0 | 19.7 | 9.7 | 3.2 | 1.7 | 0.4 | 0.2 | 0.2 | 0.6 | 0.4 | — | 1,142 | 1,718 | 2,276 | 1,774 | 0.336 | 0.325 | 0.661 | 140. |
| 141. | Misc. repair serv. | 11 | 11.1 | 14.9 | 14.9 | 20.7 | 20.4 | 10.2 | 4.7 | 2.3 | — | 0.3 | — | — | 0.6 | — | 966 | 1,719 | 2,328 | 1,731 | 0.439 | 0.353 | 0.792 | 141. |
| 142. | Personal serv. | 1,893 | 36.7 | 27.4 | 17.2 | 10.9 | 4.8 | 1.5 | 0.7 | 0.2 | 0.2 | 0.1 | 0.1 | 0.1 | 0.1 | — | 340 | 742 | 1,316 | 916 | 0.542 | 0.772 | 1.314 | 142. |
| 143. | Private households | 1,250 | 47.0 | 29.9 | 13.1 | 6.4 | 2.1 | 0.6 | 0.3 | 0.1 | 0.1 | — | 0.1 | 0.1 | 0.1 | — | 265 | 550 | 968 | 719 | 0.517 | 0.759 | 1.276 | 143. |
| 144. | Hotels & lodging places | 199 | 18.1 | 26.1 | 25.0 | 17.3 | 8.5 | 2.6 | 1.4 | 0.3 | 0.3 | — | 0.2 | — | 0.1 | — | 632 | 1,116 | 1,667 | 1,215 | 0.434 | 0.494 | 0.928 | 144. |
| 145. | Laund., clean., & dyeing | 317 | 15.4 | 21.8 | 27.9 | 21.0 | 9.3 | 2.9 | 1.0 | 0.3 | 0.2 | — | 0.1 | — | 0.1 | — | 720 | 1,229 | 1,735 | 1,273 | 0.415 | 0.411 | 0.826 | 145. |
| 146. | Dress & shoe rep. shops & misc. pers. serv. | 127 | 16.9 | 18.3 | 19.4 | 20.0 | 13.9 | 5.6 | 3.0 | 1.1 | 0.8 | 0.3 | 0.4 | 0.2 | 0.1 | 0.1 | 721 | 1,381 | 2,014 | 1,489 | 0.478 | 0.458 | 0.936 | 146. |
| 147. | Entertain. & recr. | 124 | 24.3 | 19.9 | 14.4 | 12.4 | 11.6 | 6.7 | 4.4 | 2.1 | 1.2 | 0.6 | 1.0 | 0.3 | 0.5 | 0.6 | 517 | 1,201 | 2,172 | 1,590 | 0.570 | 0.808 | 1.378 | 147. |
| 148. | Radio broad. & television | 15 | 9.7 | 10.4 | 10.4 | 18.5 | 23.8 | 10.6 | 5.9 | 3.1 | 2.0 | 1.1 | 2.2 | 0.9 | 0.9 | 0.7 | 1,235 | 2,021 | 2,603 | 2,224 | 0.389 | 0.288 | 0.677 | 148. |
| 149. | Theaters & motion pict. | 67 | 27.1 | 21.4 | 14.4 | 11.9 | 8.9 | 5.6 | 4.2 | 2.2 | 1.3 | 0.5 | 0.8 | 0.2 | 0.6 | 0.8 | 461 | 1,052 | 2,011 | 1,536 | 0.562 | 0.911 | 1.473 | 149. |
| 150. | Bowl. all., bill. & pool parl., & misc. ent. | 42 | 24.8 | 21.0 | 15.8 | 11.2 | 11.6 | 7.1 | 4.1 | 1.6 | 0.8 | 0.6 | 0.7 | 0.2 | 0.2 | 0.3 | 504 | 1,132 | 2,094 | 1,453 | 0.555 | 0.849 | 1.404 | 150. |
| 151. | Professional & rel. serv. | 2,351 | 11.9 | 13.5 | 13.5 | 15.1 | 17.3 | 11.8 | 8.0 | 3.9 | 2.4 | 1.2 | 0.9 | 0.2 | 0.1 | 0.1 | 985 | 1,867 | 2,656 | 1,934 | 0.473 | 0.422 | 0.895 | 151. |
| 152. | Medical & oth. health | 880 | 12.4 | 14.9 | 17.4 | 17.4 | 18.4 | 10.3 | 5.4 | 1.9 | 0.8 | 0.4 | 0.3 | 0.1 | 0.1 | 0.1 | 922 | 1,652 | 2,350 | 1,713 | 0.442 | 0.422 | 0.864 | 152. |
| 153. | Educational | 1,174 | 11.2 | 12.1 | 10.4 | 12.9 | 16.4 | 13.2 | 10.2 | 5.8 | 3.8 | 2.1 | 1.4 | 0.2 | 0.1 | 0.1 | 1,081 | 2,103 | 2,954 | 2,135 | 0.486 | 0.404 | 0.890 | 153. |
| 154. | Welfare, relig., & nonprofit | 195 | 16.5 | 18.1 | 15.6 | 15.6 | 15.7 | 8.4 | 5.2 | 2.3 | 1.3 | 0.6 | 0.5 | 0.2 | 0.1 | 0.1 | 734 | 1,493 | 2,292 | 1,637 | 0.509 | 0.535 | 1.044 | 154. |
| 155. | Legal, eng., arch. & misc. prof. | 102 | 7.6 | 9.1 | 10.7 | 19.6 | 22.3 | 14.9 | 9.4 | 2.9 | 1.7 | 0.5 | 0.6 | 0.3 | 0.3 | 0.2 | 1,387 | 2,067 | 2,691 | 2,103 | 0.329 | 0.301 | 0.630 | 155. |
| 156. | Public administration | 607 | 6.7 | 6.1 | 7.0 | 12.9 | 21.5 | 23.0 | 13.3 | 5.1 | 2.1 | 0.9 | 0.7 | 0.3 | 0.1 | 0.1 | 1,701 | 2,402 | 2,952 | 2,334 | 0.292 | 0.228 | 0.520 | 156. |
| 157. | Postal serv. | 51 | 10.5 | 10.4 | 11.7 | 11.9 | 11.7 | 15.1 | 12.7 | 12.5 | 2.2 | 0.5 | 0.5 | 0.2 | — | — | 1,175 | 2,235 | 3,145 | 2,176 | 0.475 | 0.407 | 0.882 | 157. |
| 158. | Federal pub. admin. | 305 | 6.3 | 4.2 | 4.7 | 7.6 | 18.6 | 30.6 | 16.9 | 5.5 | 2.6 | 1.3 | 1.0 | 0.5 | 0.2 | — | 2,059 | 2,640 | 3,088 | 2,531 | 0.221 | 0.169 | 0.390 | 158. |
| 159. | State & local pub. admin. | 251 | 6.6 | 7.6 | 8.9 | 19.5 | 26.9 | 15.4 | 9.0 | 3.1 | 1.5 | 0.5 | 0.5 | 0.2 | 0.1 | 0.1 | 1,548 | 2,137 | 2,678 | 2,120 | 0.276 | 0.253 | 0.529 | 159. |

Source: Unpublished data of the Bureau of the Census. See Appendix A for description of method used to estimate arithmetic mean.

## TABLE B-2

### Wage Workers, by Industry in 1940, by Wage Income in 1939, and by Sex

| INDUSTRY | NUMBER WITH $1 OR MORE (thousands) (1) | PERCENTAGE DISTRIBUTION BY INCOME CLASS: Under $100 (2) | $100 to $199 (3) | $200 to $399 (4) | $400 to $599 (5) | $600 to $799 (6) | $800 to $999 (7) | $1,000 to $1,199 (8) | $1,200 to $1,399 (9) | $1,400 to $1,599 (10) | $1,600 to $1,999 (11) | $2,000 to $2,499 (12) | $2,500 to $2,999 (13) | $3,000 to $4,999 (14) | $5,000 and Over (15) | INCOME AT QUARTILE POSITION: $Q_1$ (16) | Median $Q_2$ (17) | $Q_3$ (18) | ARITHMETIC MEAN (19) | MEASURES OF DISPERSION: $1-\frac{Q_1}{Q_2}$ (20) | $\frac{Q_3}{Q_2}-1$ (21) | $\frac{Q_3-Q_1}{Q_2}$ (22) | |
|---|---|---|---|---|---|---|---|---|---|---|---|---|---|---|---|---|---|---|---|---|---|---|---|
| PART I: MALES | | | | | | | | | | | | | | | | | | | | | | | |
| 1. Total | 25,718 | 2.4 | 4.9 | 11.1 | 9.8 | 10.7 | 9.4 | 9.4 | 9.7 | 8.0 | 9.7 | 7.4 | 2.8 | 3.4 | 1.4 | $ 534 | $1,036 | $1,590 | $1,279 | 0.484 | 0.534 | 1.018 | 1. |
| 2. Agriculture, forestry, & fisheries | 2,186 | 9.3 | 22.3 | 36.5 | 15.1 | 7.7 | 3.4 | 1.9 | 1.5 | 0.8 | 0.7 | 0.4 | 0.1 | 0.2 | 0.1 | 170 | 300 | 491 | 401 | 0.434 | 0.633 | 1.067 | 2. |
| 3. Agriculture | 2,110 | 9.5 | 22.6 | 36.6 | 15.2 | 7.7 | 3.3 | 1.8 | 1.4 | 0.7 | 0.6 | 0.3 | 0.1 | 0.2 | 0.1 | 168 | 297 | 482 | 393 | 0.434 | 0.621 | 1.055 | 3. |
| 4. Forestry | 49 | 3.8 | 14.5 | 37.0 | 11.2 | 8.0 | 4.0 | 3.1 | 3.1 | 3.2 | 4.6 | 3.5 | 2.1 | 1.2 | 0.3 | 236 | 371 | 825 | 699 | 0.364 | 1.221 | 1.585 | 4. |
| 5. Fisheries | 27 | 3.1 | 6.9 | 21.3 | 15.3 | 12.5 | 9.3 | 8.9 | 7.9 | 5.1 | 5.0 | 2.8 | 0.7 | 1.0 | 0.3 | 340 | 654 | 1,148 | 839 | 0.480 | 0.754 | 1.234 | 5. |
| 6. Mining, extract., & quarry. | 957 | 1.4 | 3.2 | 9.9 | 11.3 | 13.1 | 14.2 | 12.0 | 10.0 | 7.3 | 9.4 | 4.4 | 1.4 | 1.6 | 0.6 | 585 | 956 | 1,398 | 1,107 | 0.388 | 0.461 | 0.849 | 6. |
| 7. Metals | 116 | 1.1 | 2.6 | 6.6 | 8.1 | 9.0 | 11.2 | 11.8 | 14.2 | 12.8 | 12.7 | 5.4 | 1.8 | 1.9 | 0.8 | 746 | 1,193 | 1,562 | 1,282 | 0.375 | 0.309 | 0.684 | 7. |
| 8. Coal | 570 | 1.6 | 3.6 | 11.3 | 13.2 | 15.9 | 17.8 | 14.4 | 10.2 | 5.0 | 3.6 | 2.0 | 0.6 | 0.6 | 0.2 | 528 | 849 | 1,161 | 911 | 0.378 | 0.366 | 0.744 | 8. |
| 9. Crude petroleum & natl. gas | 184 | 1.0 | 1.7 | 5.1 | 5.2 | 5.6 | 6.0 | 6.1 | 8.2 | 12.0 | 26.8 | 12.0 | 3.7 | 4.7 | 1.5 | 1,013 | 1,585 | 1,959 | 1,668 | 0.361 | 0.236 | 0.597 | 9. |
| 10. Nonmetals, exc. fuel | 87 | 2.0 | 3.8 | 15.3 | 16.2 | 16.5 | 12.1 | 9.5 | 8.3 | 5.5 | 4.9 | 3.0 | 0.8 | 1.4 | 0.5 | 448 | 753 | 1,191 | 931 | 0.406 | 0.580 | 0.986 | 10. |
| 11. Construction | 2,100 | 2.5 | 5.3 | 15.0 | 14.9 | 13.9 | 10.8 | 8.9 | 7.9 | 6.0 | 6.4 | 4.7 | 1.7 | 1.5 | 0.3 | 429 | 776 | 1,293 | 968 | 0.448 | 0.664 | 1.112 | 11. |
| 12. Manufacturing | 8,544 | 1.3 | 2.7 | 7.5 | 8.8 | 11.1 | 10.5 | 11.7 | 11.7 | 9.8 | 10.7 | 7.1 | 2.6 | 3.1 | 1.5 | 684 | 1,138 | 1,597 | 1,354 | 0.399 | 0.403 | 0.802 | 12. |
| 13. Durable goods | 4,724 | 1.1 | 2.6 | 8.0 | 8.9 | 10.1 | 10.2 | 11.8 | 12.4 | 10.6 | 11.3 | 6.8 | 2.3 | 2.7 | 1.2 | 687 | 1,154 | 1,586 | 1,321 | 0.405 | 0.374 | 0.779 | 13. |
| 14. Lumber & wood prod., exc. furn. | 700 | 2.8 | 6.9 | 20.8 | 19.7 | 15.2 | 9.3 | 7.5 | 6.1 | 4.2 | 3.7 | 2.0 | 0.6 | 0.8 | 0.4 | 347 | 597 | 1,008 | 783 | 0.420 | 0.685 | 1.105 | 14. |
| 15. Logging | 144 | 4.9 | 9.9 | 27.1 | 20.2 | 12.8 | 8.5 | 5.2 | 3.9 | 2.7 | 2.8 | 1.0 | 0.3 | 0.4 | 0.1 | 275 | 480 | 802 | 620 | 0.427 | 0.670 | 1.097 | 15. |
| 16. Saw & planing mills, & mill work | 438 | 2.5 | 6.7 | 20.9 | 20.6 | 15.8 | 8.4 | 7.1 | 6.3 | 4.3 | 3.7 | 1.9 | 0.5 | 0.7 | 0.4 | 351 | 593 | 1,002 | 774 | 0.408 | 0.690 | 1.098 | 16. |
| 17. Misc. wood prod. | 118 | 1.4 | 3.7 | 12.5 | 15.5 | 15.6 | 13.5 | 11.7 | 8.3 | 5.7 | 5.1 | 3.4 | 1.0 | 1.6 | 0.9 | 495 | 819 | 1,226 | 1,014 | 0.396 | 0.497 | 0.893 | 17. |
| 18. Furniture & fixtures | 206 | 1.4 | 2.6 | 9.0 | 12.5 | 20.1 | 14.5 | 12.5 | 9.5 | 6.5 | 5.4 | 2.9 | 1.1 | 1.3 | 0.8 | 592 | 860 | 1,250 | 1,040 | 0.313 | 0.452 | 0.765 | 18. |
| 19. Stone, clay, & glass prod. | 307 | 1.0 | 2.2 | 7.0 | 9.9 | 12.8 | 13.6 | 14.9 | 12.1 | 8.1 | 8.3 | 4.8 | 1.8 | 2.2 | 1.3 | 676 | 1,046 | 1,437 | 1,240 | 0.354 | 0.372 | 0.726 | 19. |
| 20. Glass & glass prod. | 89 | 0.8 | 1.6 | 5.2 | 7.2 | 10.2 | 12.4 | 15.2 | 13.7 | 9.8 | 10.9 | 6.7 | 2.5 | 2.0 | 1.6 | 800 | 1,165 | 1,577 | 1,369 | 0.314 | 0.353 | 0.667 | 20. |
| 21. Cement, concrete, gypsum, & plaster prod. | 67 | 1.0 | 2.1 | 6.5 | 9.4 | 12.8 | 14.6 | 14.6 | 12.0 | 8.5 | 7.6 | 4.3 | 2.0 | 3.3 | 1.3 | 693 | 1,049 | 1,447 | 1,272 | 0.339 | 0.378 | 0.717 | 21. |
| 22. Structural clay prod. | 69 | 1.1 | 3.0 | 10.3 | 15.5 | 18.8 | 15.7 | 13.3 | 9.3 | 3.9 | 3.8 | 2.1 | 1.0 | 1.6 | 0.7 | 536 | 816 | 1,159 | 982 | 0.343 | 0.419 | 0.762 | 22. |
| 23. Pottery & rel. prod. | 29 | 1.3 | 2.0 | 5.9 | 6.3 | 10.0 | 13.0 | 17.4 | 16.2 | 9.3 | 10.3 | 4.5 | 1.1 | 1.5 | 0.9 | 790 | 1,132 | 1,462 | 1,239 | 0.303 | 0.291 | 0.594 | 23. |
| 24. Misc. nonmet. min. & stone prod. | 53 | 0.8 | 2.3 | 6.8 | 9.6 | 11.1 | 11.8 | 15.3 | 10.8 | 9.8 | 9.9 | 5.6 | 2.0 | 2.3 | 2.0 | 699 | 1,099 | 1,532 | 1,343 | 0.365 | 0.394 | 0.759 | 24. |
| 25. Metal industries | 1,469 | 0.7 | 1.9 | 6.1 | 7.1 | 9.0 | 10.4 | 13.5 | 14.7 | 11.6 | 11.7 | 6.7 | 2.3 | 2.7 | 1.3 | 803 | 1,217 | 1,600 | 1,376 | 0.340 | 0.313 | 0.653 | 25. |
| 26. Iron & steel & their prod. | 1,251 | 0.7 | 1.8 | 6.2 | 7.2 | 9.1 | 10.7 | 13.4 | 14.3 | 11.4 | 11.8 | 6.9 | 2.4 | 2.7 | 1.3 | 800 | 1,212 | 1,606 | 1,380 | 0.341 | 0.325 | 0.666 | 26. |
| 27. Blast furn., steel wks., & roll mills | 571 | 0.6 | 1.6 | 6.3 | 6.5 | 7.6 | 9.1 | 12.2 | 15.5 | 12.6 | 14.3 | 7.2 | 2.5 | 3.0 | 1.1 | 852 | 1,278 | 1,683 | 1,421 | 0.334 | 0.316 | 0.650 | 27. |
| 28. Oth. prim. iron, steel, & fab. steel prod. | 680 | 0.8 | 2.1 | 6.1 | 7.8 | 10.4 | 12.1 | 14.4 | 13.4 | 10.4 | 9.7 | 6.7 | 2.2 | 2.4 | 1.5 | 757 | 1,148 | 1,551 | 1,348 | 0.341 | 0.351 | 0.692 | 28. |
| 29. Nonferrous metals & their prod. | 183 | 0.8 | 2.0 | 5.6 | 6.2 | 8.0 | 9.9 | 14.5 | 17.5 | 12.8 | 11.2 | 5.6 | 2.2 | 2.5 | 1.3 | 848 | 1,234 | 1,564 | 1,380 | 0.313 | 0.267 | 0.580 | 29. |
| 30. Not spec. metal ind. | 35 | 1.1 | 2.9 | 6.7 | 8.3 | 10.4 | 13.1 | 13.1 | 13.4 | 9.4 | 9.8 | 5.1 | 2.1 | 1.8 | 2.7 | 715 | 1,114 | 1,527 | 1,380 | 0.359 | 0.370 | 0.729 | 30. |
| 31. Machinery, exc. elec. | 648 | 0.9 | 1.8 | 4.5 | 5.6 | 7.6 | 9.4 | 12.4 | 13.5 | 12.6 | 14.1 | 9.0 | 3.1 | 3.7 | 1.8 | 897 | 1,315 | 1,790 | 1,534 | 0.318 | 0.360 | 0.678 | 31. |
| 32. Agri. mach. & tractors | 88 | 0.8 | 1.2 | 3.9 | 5.8 | 8.3 | 9.5 | 12.1 | 15.8 | 14.3 | 16.0 | 7.3 | 2.0 | 2.1 | 0.9 | 905 | 1,306 | 1,682 | 1,411 | 0.308 | 0.287 | 0.595 | 32. |
| 33. Office & store mach. & devices | 50 | 0.4 | 1.0 | 2.7 | 4.4 | 6.1 | 8.0 | 11.3 | 12.2 | 12.2 | 17.6 | 12.1 | 4.2 | 5.5 | 2.3 | 1,042 | 1,463 | 1,979 | 1,743 | 0.288 | 0.352 | 0.640 | 33. |
| 34. Misc. mach. | 510 | 0.9 | 1.9 | 4.8 | 5.7 | 7.6 | 9.5 | 12.5 | 13.3 | 12.3 | 13.5 | 9.0 | 3.2 | 3.9 | 1.9 | 886 | 1,306 | 1,792 | 1,540 | 0.322 | 0.371 | 0.693 | 34. |
| 35. Electrical machinery, equip., & supp. | 280 | 0.8 | 1.8 | 5.0 | 5.1 | 6.1 | 8.0 | 10.5 | 12.2 | 12.0 | 14.9 | 10.5 | 4.5 | 6.1 | 2.6 | 955 | 1,408 | 1,962 | 1,718 | 0.322 | 0.393 | 0.715 | 35. |
| 36. Transportation equip. | 855 | 0.7 | 1.6 | 5.0 | 5.8 | 7.7 | 8.6 | 11.1 | 13.8 | 14.1 | 16.3 | 9.2 | 2.7 | 2.5 | 0.8 | 897 | 1,337 | 1,761 | 1,437 | 0.329 | 0.317 | 0.646 | 36. |
| 37. Motor vehicles & motor veh. equip. | 553 | 0.5 | 1.4 | 4.2 | 5.1 | 6.8 | 8.4 | 11.4 | 14.7 | 16.0 | 17.6 | 8.0 | 2.7 | 2.5 | 0.8 | 966 | 1,365 | 1,747 | 1,463 | 0.293 | 0.279 | 0.572 | 37. |
| 38. Aircraft & parts | 104 | 1.3 | 2.3 | 6.4 | 8.2 | 9.2 | 9.8 | 11.4 | 13.1 | 11.4 | 12.5 | 8.0 | 2.7 | 2.6 | 1.0 | 747 | 1,221 | 1,660 | 1,356 | 0.388 | 0.359 | 0.747 | 38. |
| 39. Ship & boat bldg. & repair. | 153 | 1.0 | 1.5 | 5.7 | 5.9 | 8.7 | 7.9 | 10.0 | 11.7 | 10.5 | 15.5 | 15.3 | 3.3 | 2.4 | 0.5 | 855 | 1,358 | 1,912 | 1,455 | 0.371 | 0.407 | 0.778 | 39. |
| 40. Railroad & misc. transp. equip. | 45 | 1.3 | 3.5 | 9.3 | 9.8 | 12.7 | 11.1 | 10.8 | 10.5 | 9.0 | 11.0 | 5.4 | 1.3 | 2.9 | 1.3 | 617 | 1,042 | 1,533 | 1,250 | 0.408 | 0.470 | 0.878 | 40. |
| 41. Other durable goods | 259 | 1.1 | 2.8 | 6.4 | 7.7 | 10.6 | 11.5 | 12.8 | 11.1 | 9.7 | 10.2 | 7.7 | 2.8 | 3.7 | 1.9 | 732 | 1,154 | 1,650 | 1,423 | 0.366 | 0.429 | 0.795 | 41. |
| 42. Professional & photo. equip. & supp. | 60 | 0.8 | 1.4 | 3.6 | 4.0 | 6.7 | 8.4 | 11.0 | 11.2 | 12.6 | 16.8 | 12.1 | 3.9 | 5.3 | 2.1 | 1,001 | 1,446 | 1,964 | 1,694 | 0.308 | 0.358 | 0.666 | 42. |
| 43. Watches, clocks, & misc. mfg. ind. | 199 | 1.2 | 3.2 | 7.2 | 8.9 | 11.8 | 12.4 | 13.3 | 11.1 | 8.8 | 8.1 | 6.4 | 2.5 | 3.3 | 1.8 | 676 | 1,079 | 1,534 | 1,340 | 0.374 | 0.420 | 0.794 | 43. |
| 44. Nondurable goods | 3,820 | 1.4 | 2.7 | 6.8 | 8.6 | 12.3 | 11.0 | 11.5 | 10.8 | 9.0 | 10.1 | 7.4 | 3.0 | 3.5 | 1.8 | 689 | 1,125 | 1,635 | 1,387 | 0.388 | 0.453 | 0.841 | 44. |
| 45. Food & kindred prod. | 927 | 1.3 | 2.5 | 6.7 | 7.4 | 9.2 | 10.0 | 12.2 | 13.7 | 11.0 | 11.9 | 7.7 | 2.5 | 2.7 | 1.4 | 754 | 1,210 | 1,633 | 1,383 | 0.377 | 0.349 | 0.726 | 45. |
| 46. Meat prod. | 187 | 0.9 | 1.8 | 4.3 | 5.4 | 6.6 | 9.2 | 14.9 | 18.4 | 13.8 | 11.8 | 7.0 | 2.1 | 2.6 | 1.2 | 930 | 1,275 | 1,595 | 1,421 | 0.271 | 0.251 | 0.522 | 46. |
| 47. Dairy prod. | 97 | 1.1 | 2.3 | 5.5 | 6.6 | 8.7 | 11.0 | 13.1 | 13.8 | 11.0 | 12.8 | 8.1 | 2.0 | 2.4 | 1.5 | 814 | 1,224 | 1,659 | 1,400 | 0.335 | 0.354 | 0.689 | 47. |
| 48. Can. & preserv. fruit, veg. & sea food | 72 | 3.3 | 6.9 | 16.7 | 14.8 | 13.6 | 10.4 | 8.7 | 7.5 | 5.2 | 4.8 | 3.7 | 1.3 | 1.9 | 1.2 | 377 | 722 | 1,216 | 985 | 0.478 | 0.684 | 1.162 | 48. |

continued on next page

| | INDUSTRY | NUMBER WITH $1 OR MORE (thousands) (1) | PERCENTAGE DISTRIBUTION BY INCOME CLASS: Under $100 (2) | $100 to $199 (3) | $200 to $399 (4) | $400 to $599 (5) | $600 to $799 (6) | $800 to $999 (7) | $1,000 to $1,199 (8) | $1,200 to $1,399 (9) | $1,400 to $1,599 (10) | $1,600 to $1,999 (11) | $2,000 to $2,499 (12) | $2,500 to $2,999 (13) | $3,000 to $4,999 (14) | $5,000 and Over (15) | INCOME AT QUARTILE POSITION: $Q_1$ (16) | Median $Q_2$ (17) | $Q_3$ (18) | ARITHMETIC MEAN (19) | MEASURES OF DISPERSION: $1 - \frac{Q_1}{Q_2}$ (20) | $\frac{Q_3}{Q_2} - 1$ (21) | $\frac{Q_3 - Q_1}{Q_2}$ (22) | |
|---|---|---|---|---|---|---|---|---|---|---|---|---|---|---|---|---|---|---|---|---|---|---|---|---|
| 49. | Grain mill prod. | 79 | 1.0 | 2.0 | 7.9 | 8.8 | 11.2 | 13.0 | 12.1 | 12.4 | 9.1 | 9.9 | 5.7 | 2.1 | 3.1 | 1.8 | 694 | 1,100 | 1,545 | 1,347 | 0.369 | 0.403 | 0.772 | 49. |
| 50. | Bakery prod. | 210 | 1.3 | 2.0 | 4.9 | 5.7 | 8.8 | 10.3 | 12.9 | 14.5 | 12.7 | 13.2 | 8.6 | 2.6 | 1.8 | 0.7 | 844 | 1,256 | 1,657 | 1,359 | 0.328 | 0.319 | 0.647 | 50. |
| 51. | Confectionery & rel. prod. | 37 | 1.7 | 2.9 | 9.1 | 9.0 | 10.6 | 11.5 | 13.9 | 13.5 | 7.9 | 7.6 | 5.4 | 2.6 | 2.6 | 1.7 | 643 | 1,074 | 1,470 | 1,288 | 0.402 | 0.368 | 0.779 | 51. |
| 52. | Beverage ind. | 149 | 1.0 | 2.0 | 5.1 | 6.5 | 8.3 | 8.4 | 9.5 | 11.4 | 10.3 | 16.5 | 11.2 | 3.9 | 4.2 | 1.8 | 850 | 1,361 | 1,903 | 1,578 | 0.376 | 0.397 | 0.773 | 52. |
| 53. | Misc. food prep. & not spec. food ind. | 96 | 1.3 | 3.3 | 8.8 | 9.7 | 11.4 | 8.7 | 10.4 | 12.0 | 9.8 | 9.8 | 6.9 | 2.4 | 3.1 | 2.2 | 633 | 1,130 | 1,591 | 1,375 | 0.440 | 0.407 | 0.847 | 53. |
| 54. | Tobacco manufactures | 55 | 1.3 | 4.4 | 11.9 | 14.1 | 15.6 | 12.7 | 9.6 | 7.6 | 6.3 | 5.6 | 4.7 | 2.0 | 2.8 | 1.3 | 504 | 842 | 1,342 | 1,126 | 0.401 | 0.592 | 0.993 | 54. |
| 55. | Textile mill prod. | 739 | 1.1 | 2.9 | 8.7 | 14.3 | 24.0 | 15.4 | 11.2 | 6.8 | 4.8 | 4.2 | 2.7 | 1.2 | 1.5 | 1.2 | 572 | 791 | 1,153 | 1,030 | 0.278 | 0.457 | 0.735 | 55. |
| 56. | Knitting mills | 92 | 1.0 | 2.5 | 7.3 | 10.8 | 16.5 | 13.9 | 11.8 | 8.4 | 8.3 | 9.1 | 5.3 | 1.9 | 2.0 | 1.1 | 641 | 971 | 1,467 | 1,198 | 0.340 | 0.510 | 0.850 | 56. |
| 57. | Dyeing & fin. tex. exc. knit goods | 44 | 1.0 | 2.6 | 7.5 | 11.7 | 20.7 | 16.6 | 15.6 | 7.9 | 4.8 | 3.9 | 2.8 | 1.5 | 2.5 | 0.8 | 621 | 878 | 1,191 | 1,072 | 0.293 | 0.356 | 0.649 | 57. |
| 58. | Carpets, rugs, & oth. floor cov. | 35 | 0.5 | 1.4 | 4.8 | 7.7 | 11.4 | 14.7 | 17.0 | 13.9 | 10.8 | 7.4 | 4.6 | 2.3 | 2.0 | 1.6 | 785 | 1,111 | 1,466 | 1,321 | 0.294 | 0.319 | 0.613 | 58. |
| 59. | Yarn, thread, & fabric mills | 530 | 1.1 | 3.1 | 9.4 | 15.9 | 27.2 | 15.8 | 10.1 | 5.6 | 3.7 | 2.9 | 1.9 | 0.9 | 1.2 | 1.1 | 543 | 750 | 1,049 | 951 | 0.277 | 0.397 | 0.674 | 59. |
| 60. | Misc. tex. mill prod. | 38 | 1.0 | 2.2 | 7.5 | 10.3 | 13.5 | 14.0 | 15.7 | 10.7 | 7.1 | 6.9 | 4.7 | 2.2 | 2.6 | 1.7 | 659 | 1,019 | 1,402 | 1,264 | 0.354 | 0.376 | 0.730 | 60. |
| 61. | Apparel & oth. fab. tex. prod. | 272 | 1.1 | 2.5 | 8.1 | 10.2 | 15.3 | 11.9 | 11.5 | 9.5 | 7.9 | 7.5 | 6.4 | 2.8 | 3.4 | 1.7 | 640 | 1,015 | 1,524 | 1,307 | 0.370 | 0.500 | 0.870 | 61. |
| 62. | Apparel & access. | 254 | 1.0 | 2.4 | 8.0 | 10.2 | 15.3 | 12.0 | 11.6 | 9.6 | 8.0 | 7.5 | 6.6 | 2.8 | 3.4 | 1.6 | 644 | 1,018 | 1,522 | 1,307 | 0.368 | 0.494 | 0.862 | 62. |
| 63. | Misc. fab. tex. prod. | 18 | 2.2 | 4.0 | 10.4 | 10.9 | 15.6 | 11.2 | 10.3 | 9.0 | 6.8 | 8.1 | 4.2 | 2.2 | 2.9 | 2.4 | 554 | 923 | 1,441 | 1,267 | 0.400 | 0.560 | 0.960 | 63. |
| 64. | Paper & all. prod. | 266 | 0.7 | 2.0 | 5.3 | 6.6 | 9.2 | 12.7 | 17.3 | 14.5 | 9.9 | 9.1 | 5.4 | 2.3 | 2.9 | 1.9 | 818 | 1,156 | 1,535 | 1,393 | 0.292 | 0.328 | 0.620 | 64. |
| 65. | Pulp, paper, & paperboard mills | 187 | 0.7 | 1.9 | 4.8 | 6.4 | 8.7 | 13.0 | 17.9 | 15.4 | 10.4 | 9.3 | 5.2 | 2.1 | 2.7 | 1.5 | 838 | 1,162 | 1,519 | 1,365 | 0.279 | 0.307 | 0.586 | 65. |
| 66. | Paperboard cont. & boxes | 47 | 1.1 | 2.7 | 7.2 | 8.1 | 12.4 | 12.6 | 16.3 | 12.3 | 8.1 | 7.6 | 4.2 | 2.0 | 2.5 | 2.7 | 695 | 1,072 | 1,456 | 1,356 | 0.352 | 0.358 | 0.710 | 66. |
| 67. | Misc. paper & pulp prod. | 32 | 0.8 | 1.5 | 5.3 | 5.5 | 7.6 | 11.1 | 14.8 | 12.6 | 10.1 | 10.7 | 8.9 | 3.5 | 4.5 | 3.2 | 877 | 1,253 | 1,813 | 1,634 | 0.301 | 0.445 | 0.746 | 67. |
| 68. | Printing, publ., & all. ind. | 481 | 3.7 | 4.1 | 5.4 | 5.0 | 7.0 | 7.1 | 8.0 | 8.7 | 8.3 | 11.1 | 13.6 | 7.8 | 7.7 | 2.7 | 794 | 1,424 | 2,242 | 1,759 | 0.443 | 0.574 | 1,017 | 68. |
| 69. | Chemicals & all. prod. | 374 | 1.0 | 2.4 | 7.0 | 6.6 | 7.4 | 7.7 | 10.4 | 12.6 | 11.6 | 13.3 | 8.5 | 3.5 | 5.0 | 3.2 | 815 | 1,319 | 1,849 | 1,646 | 0.382 | 0.402 | 0.784 | 69. |
| 70. | Synthetic fibers | 41 | 0.8 | 1.2 | 3.0 | 4.1 | 5.2 | 10.9 | 17.0 | 21.0 | 14.3 | 12.8 | 5.2 | 1.8 | 2.0 | 0.9 | 996 | 1,274 | 1,565 | 1,398 | 0.219 | 0.228 | 0.447 | 70. |
| 71. | Paints, varn., & rel. prod. | 38 | 0.6 | 1.2 | 3.4 | 3.9 | 5.6 | 7.6 | 11.4 | 13.9 | 14.1 | 14.4 | 8.8 | 4.0 | 6.2 | 4.9 | 1,047 | 1,434 | 1,969 | 1,913 | 0.270 | 0.373 | 0.643 | 71. |
| 72. | Drugs, med., & misc. chem. & all. prod. | 295 | 1.1 | 2.7 | 8.0 | 7.3 | 7.9 | 7.2 | 9.4 | 11.2 | 10.9 | 13.2 | 8.9 | 3.7 | 5.2 | 3.3 | 749 | 1,314 | 1,881 | 1,642 | 0.430 | 0.431 | 0.861 | 72. |
| 73. | Petroleum & coal prod. | 196 | 0.4 | 0.8 | 2.5 | 3.0 | 4.2 | 5.5 | 6.6 | 10.6 | 12.8 | 23.6 | 16.6 | 4.5 | 6.2 | 2.9 | 1,237 | 1,661 | 2,150 | 1,936 | 0.255 | 0.294 | 0.549 | 73. |
| 74. | Petro. refining | 172 | 0.3 | 0.6 | 2.1 | 2.3 | 3.3 | 4.6 | 5.9 | 9.9 | 12.9 | 25.4 | 18.1 | 4.9 | 6.6 | 3.0 | 1,319 | 1,727 | 2,212 | 2,003 | 0.237 | 0.280 | 0.517 | 74. |
| 75. | Misc. petro. & coal prod. | 24 | 0.7 | 2.1 | 5.3 | 7.5 | 10.1 | 11.4 | 11.6 | 15.7 | 11.5 | 10.9 | 5.6 | 2.2 | 3.4 | 2.1 | 786 | 1,216 | 1,584 | 1,442 | 0.354 | 0.302 | 0.656 | 75. |
| 76. | Rubber prod. | 129 | 0.6 | 1.6 | 4.0 | 5.3 | 6.6 | 8.9 | 12.2 | 12.8 | 12.6 | 16.1 | 10.9 | 2.9 | 3.5 | 1.9 | 955 | 1,368 | 1,858 | 1,582 | 0.303 | 0.357 | 0.660 | 76. |
| 77. | Leather & leather prod. | 243 | 1.2 | 2.8 | 7.8 | 11.4 | 16.8 | 16.5 | 15.2 | 10.4 | 6.3 | 4.9 | 2.8 | 1.3 | 1.4 | 1.3 | 621 | 921 | 1,263 | 1,108 | 0.326 | 0.371 | 0.697 | 77. |
| 78. | Leather: tanned, curried, & fin. | 51 | 0.5 | 1.6 | 4.2 | 7.3 | 12.0 | 15.2 | 20.3 | 16.1 | 10.5 | 6.6 | 2.5 | 1.2 | 1.0 | 1.0 | 790 | 1,090 | 1,372 | 1,200 | 0.276 | 0.258 | 0.534 | 78. |
| 79. | Footwear, exc. rubber | 155 | 1.3 | 2.9 | 8.8 | 13.0 | 18.5 | 17.8 | 14.0 | 8.6 | 4.8 | 4.2 | 2.6 | 1.1 | 1.3 | 1.1 | 584 | 861 | 1,181 | 1,039 | 0.322 | 0.370 | 0.692 | 79. |
| 80. | Leather prod., exc. footwear | 37 | 1.6 | 4.1 | 8.3 | 10.2 | 16.0 | 13.0 | 13.1 | 10.0 | 7.0 | 5.8 | 4.1 | 2.5 | 2.0 | 2.4 | 610 | 950 | 1,374 | 1,252 | 0.359 | 0.445 | 0.804 | 80. |
| 81. | Not. spec. mfg. ind. | 138 | 1.2 | 2.6 | 7.1 | 8.8 | 10.6 | 11.0 | 13.3 | 12.2 | 10.1 | 9.5 | 6.0 | 2.5 | 2.9 | 2.0 | 700 | 1,130 | 1,562 | 1,370 | 0.381 | 0.381 | 0.762 | 81. |
| 82. | Transportation, commun., & oth. pub. util. | 2,730 | 0.8 | 1.9 | 5.3 | 6.3 | 8.0 | 8.1 | 8.4 | 10.0 | 10.5 | 17.1 | 12.6 | 5.2 | 4.9 | 0.9 | 866 | 1,422 | 1,967 | 1,570 | 0.391 | 0.382 | 0.773 | 82. |
| 83. | Transportation | 2,062 | 0.9 | 2.1 | 5.9 | 7.0 | 9.1 | 9.0 | 9.0 | 9.9 | 10.1 | 16.4 | 11.6 | 4.4 | 4.0 | 0.6 | 800 | 1,341 | 1,892 | 1,471 | 0.404 | 0.410 | 0.814 | 83. |
| 84. | Railroads & railway exp. serv. | 1,170 | 0.5 | 1.4 | 4.1 | 5.3 | 7.6 | 8.6 | 8.4 | 9.4 | 9.8 | 17.8 | 14.6 | 6.2 | 5.5 | 0.6 | 941 | 1,495 | 2,071 | 1,626 | 0.371 | 0.385 | 0.756 | 84. |
| 85. | St. railways & bus lines | 199 | 0.3 | 0.8 | 2.1 | 3.2 | 4.2 | 5.0 | 7.5 | 12.4 | 18.1 | 29.3 | 12.7 | 2.3 | 1.6 | 0.4 | 1,230 | 1,560 | 1,892 | 1,589 | 0.212 | 0.212 | 0.424 | 85. |
| 86. | Trucking serv. | 304 | 1.9 | 4.0 | 10.4 | 10.8 | 11.8 | 10.2 | 10.6 | 10.7 | 9.9 | 10.9 | 5.7 | 1.5 | 1.1 | 0.6 | 561 | 1,016 | 1,492 | 1,134 | 0.449 | 0.467 | 0.916 | 86. |
| 87. | Warehousing & storage | 61 | 2.0 | 4.4 | 14.0 | 11.6 | 11.8 | 9.2 | 9.6 | 9.4 | 9.5 | 9.7 | 4.8 | 1.6 | 1.6 | 0.7 | 479 | 934 | 1,463 | 1,096 | 0.488 | 0.565 | 1.053 | 87. |
| 88. | Taxicab serv. | 65 | 1.3 | 3.3 | 11.0 | 15.8 | 22.2 | 15.6 | 14.5 | 9.3 | 3.6 | 1.9 | 0.8 | 0.3 | 0.3 | 0.3 | 518 | 767 | 1,080 | 847 | 0.324 | 0.407 | 0.731 | 88. |
| 89. | Water transp. | 199 | 1.2 | 3.0 | 8.7 | 11.5 | 14.2 | 11.5 | 9.6 | 9.4 | 6.8 | 9.4 | 7.4 | 2.9 | 3.4 | 1.0 | 608 | 998 | 1,573 | 1,262 | 0.391 | 0.576 | 0.967 | 89. |
| 90. | Air transp. | 21 | 1.6 | 2.9 | 4.9 | 5.4 | 6.3 | 8.3 | 8.5 | 8.6 | 9.7 | 15.4 | 12.1 | 5.1 | 6.4 | 4.5 | 893 | 1,472 | 2,140 | 1,867 | 0.393 | 0.453 | 0.846 | 90. |
| 91. | Petro. & gas. pipe lines | 18 | 0.5 | 2.5 | 6.0 | 6.3 | 6.3 | 4.7 | 4.2 | 7.1 | 7.9 | 29.0 | 16.9 | 5.1 | 3.2 | 0.4 | 944 | 1,662 | 2,014 | 1,603 | 0.432 | 0.212 | 0.644 | 91. |
| 92. | Serv. incid. to transp. | 25 | 1.3 | 3.1 | 7.6 | 8.2 | 8.6 | 6.9 | 9.7 | 15.0 | 11.4 | 15.1 | 6.4 | 2.7 | 3.2 | 1.0 | 711 | 1,261 | 1,684 | 1,372 | 0.436 | 0.335 | 0.771 | 92. |
| 93. | Telecommunications | 170 | 1.1 | 2.0 | 4.0 | 4.1 | 4.3 | 3.4 | 4.7 | 6.1 | 6.7 | 11.0 | 18.5 | 14.6 | 16.4 | 3.0 | 1,245 | 2,070 | 2,811 | 2,270 | 0.399 | 0.358 | 0.757 | 93. |
| 94. | Telephone, wire & radio | 130 | 0.3 | 0.8 | 2.3 | 1.8 | 2.8 | 3.0 | 4.1 | 5.8 | 6.8 | 10.6 | 20.7 | 17.4 | 20.0 | 3.7 | 1,520 | 2,282 | 2,959 | 2,554 | 0.334 | 0.296 | 0.630 | 94. |
| 95. | Telegraph, wire & radio | 40 | 3.7 | 5.7 | 9.5 | 11.6 | 9.3 | 4.9 | 6.9 | 6.9 | 6.5 | 12.6 | 11.3 | 5.5 | 4.6 | 0.9 | 505 | 1,153 | 1,917 | 1,366 | 0.563 | 0.662 | 1.225 | 95. |
| 96. | Utilities & sanitary serv. | 498 | 0.6 | 1.0 | 3.3 | 3.8 | 4.9 | 6.0 | 7.5 | 11.6 | 13.5 | 22.0 | 14.4 | 5.0 | 5.0 | 1.4 | 1,144 | 1,567 | 2,027 | 1,738 | 0.271 | 0.293 | 0.564 | 96. |
| 97. | Elec. light, power, gas, & oth. util. | 299 | 0.4 | 0.7 | 2.3 | 2.8 | 3.6 | 4.9 | 6.6 | 10.6 | 13.1 | 22.3 | 17.7 | 6.6 | 6.5 | 1.8 | 1,269 | 1,689 | 2,217 | 1,901 | 0.249 | 0.312 | 0.561 | 97. |
| 98. | Gas & steam supply systems | 80 | 0.7 | 1.1 | 3.2 | 3.5 | 4.6 | 6.0 | 7.9 | 13.4 | 16.4 | 23.7 | 11.1 | 3.5 | 3.5 | 1.3 | 1,149 | 1,517 | 1,907 | 1,652 | 0.243 | 0.257 | 0.500 | 98. |
| 99. | Water supply & san. serv. | 119 | 1.0 | 1.7 | 5.8 | 6.6 | 8.1 | 8.4 | 9.5 | 12.9 | 12.5 | 19.9 | 8.6 | 2.1 | 2.3 | 0.5 | 842 | 1,337 | 1,770 | 1,391 | 0.371 | 0.323 | 0.694 | 99. |
| 100. | Wholesale & retail trade | 4,066 | 2.4 | 3.9 | 9.0 | 9.7 | 12.2 | 10.8 | 10.8 | 10.9 | 8.3 | 8.8 | 6.4 | 2.4 | 3.0 | 1.3 | 600 | 1,037 | 1,527 | 1,264 | 0.422 | 0.473 | 0.895 | 100. |
| 101. | Wholesale trade [a] | 870 | 1.1 | 2.2 | 5.9 | 6.7 | 8.9 | 8.9 | 9.4 | 10.9 | 9.2 | 11.7 | 10.3 | 4.5 | 6.8 | 3.4 | 804 | 1,326 | 2,004 | 1,724 | 0.394 | 0.511 | 0.905 | 101. |

[a] No breakdown of wholesale trade available for 1939.

continued on next page

TABLE B-2, males, continued

| | INDUSTRY | NUMBER WITH $1 OR MORE (thousands) (1) | Under $100 (2) | $100 to $199 (3) | $200 to $399 (4) | $400 to $599 (5) | $600 to $799 (6) | $800 to $999 (7) | $1,000 to $1,199 (8) | $1,200 to $1,399 (9) | $1,400 to $1,599 (10) | $1,600 to $1,999 (11) | $2,000 to $2,499 (12) | $2,500 to $2,999 (13) | $3,000 to $4,999 (14) | $5,000 and Over (15) | $Q_1$ (16) | Median $Q_2$ (17) | $Q_3$ (18) | ARITHMETIC MEAN (19) | $1-\frac{Q_1}{Q_2}$ (20) | $\frac{Q_3}{Q_2}-1$ (21) | $\frac{Q_3-Q_1}{Q_2}$ (22) | |
|---|---|---|---|---|---|---|---|---|---|---|---|---|---|---|---|---|---|---|---|---|---|---|---|---|
| | | | PERCENTAGE DISTRIBUTION BY INCOME CLASS | | | | | | | | | | | | | | INCOME AT QUARTILE POSITION | | | | MEASURES OF DISPERSION | | | |
| 112. | Retail trade, stores | 3,196 | 2.7 | 4.3 | 9.8 | 10.5 | 13.1 | 11.3 | 11.2 | 11.0 | 8.2 | 8.0 | 5.3 | 1.9 | 1.9 | 0.8 | 556 | 969 | 1,426 | 1,135 | 0.427 | 0.471 | 0.898 | 112. |
| 113. | Food, exc. dairy prod. | 654 | 4.1 | 5.5 | 11.0 | 10.5 | 13.4 | 11.5 | 11.7 | 10.7 | 7.8 | 7.3 | 4.1 | 1.3 | 0.9 | 0.3 | 483 | 895 | 1,336 | 1,000 | 0.460 | 0.492 | 0.952 | 113. |
| 114. | Dairy prod. & milk retail | 128 | 2.1 | 2.7 | 5.6 | 6.1 | 7.1 | 7.2 | 9.3 | 11.5 | 11.6 | 14.8 | 14.5 | 5.4 | 1.5 | 0.5 | 838 | 1,372 | 1,918 | 1,438 | 0.389 | 0.398 | 0.787 | 114. |
| 115. | Genl. merchandise | 252 | 2.4 | 3.1 | 6.8 | 7.9 | 11.4 | 12.0 | 11.9 | 12.6 | 9.1 | 8.1 | 6.3 | 2.2 | 3.6 | 2.6 | 684 | 1,107 | 1,551 | 1,410 | 0.383 | 0.400 | 0.783 | 115. |
| 116. | Five & ten cent | 16 | 3.6 | 3.7 | 8.3 | 7.3 | 10.9 | 11.2 | 10.3 | 10.6 | 6.3 | 8.2 | 5.8 | 4.1 | 5.7 | 4.1 | 638 | 1,097 | 1,736 | 1,579 | 0.418 | 0.582 | 1,000 | 116. |
| 117. | Apparel & acc., exc. shoe | 139 | 1.8 | 3.1 | 7.9 | 8.9 | 12.2 | 10.1 | 11.7 | 10.6 | 9.4 | 9.1 | 7.1 | 3.0 | 3.5 | 1.7 | 654 | 1,102 | 1,585 | 1,356 | 0.407 | 0.437 | 0.844 | 117. |
| 118. | Shoe | 47 | 2.4 | 3.8 | 6.2 | 7.5 | 10.5 | 10.4 | 11.6 | 11.5 | 10.8 | 11.3 | 8.0 | 2.3 | 3.1 | 0.6 | 697 | 1,158 | 1,610 | 1,293 | 0.399 | 0.390 | 0.789 | 118. |
| 119. | Furniture & housefurn. | 113 | 1.3 | 2.6 | 7.1 | 8.1 | 12.4 | 11.0 | 11.0 | 12.0 | 9.4 | 10.1 | 6.9 | 2.7 | 3.3 | 2.2 | 695 | 1,136 | 1,603 | 1,411 | 0.389 | 0.411 | 0.800 | 119. |
| 120. | Household appl. & radio | 61 | 1.8 | 2.5 | 7.0 | 8.6 | 9.8 | 10.2 | 11.5 | 14.0 | 9.9 | 10.8 | 6.8 | 2.9 | 3.7 | 0.6 | 704 | 1,175 | 1,593 | 1,315 | 0.402 | 0.355 | 0.757 | 120. |
| 121. | Motor vehicles & acc. | 246 | 0.9 | 1.8 | 5.6 | 6.8 | 9.6 | 10.1 | 10.9 | 13.8 | 10.7 | 12.6 | 8.6 | 3.3 | 4.0 | 1.2 | 805 | 1,262 | 1,752 | 1,450 | 0.362 | 0.388 | 0.750 | 121. |
| 122. | Gas. serv. stations | 249 | 3.8 | 6.5 | 13.9 | 15.0 | 16.9 | 12.8 | 10.2 | 9.4 | 5.0 | 3.8 | 1.8 | 0.5 | 0.4 | 0.2 | 410 | 727 | 1,119 | 827 | 0.436 | 0.538 | 0.974 | 122. |
| 123. | Drug | 129 | 4.8 | 5.9 | 12.0 | 9.8 | 12.4 | 9.7 | 8.5 | 8.7 | 7.7 | 10.3 | 6.6 | 1.9 | 1.5 | 0.3 | 446 | 905 | 1,483 | 1,065 | 0.507 | 0.638 | 1.145 | 123. |
| 124. | Eating & drinking places | 480 | 2.9 | 5.5 | 14.1 | 15.5 | 17.4 | 12.9 | 11.0 | 8.7 | 5.6 | 3.6 | 1.7 | 0.5 | 0.5 | 0.2 | 432 | 737 | 1,121 | 840 | 0.415 | 0.520 | 0.935 | 124. |
| 125. | Hardware & farm impl. | 90 | 1.2 | 2.7 | 6.5 | 9.0 | 13.6 | 13.7 | 12.6 | 14.0 | 9.2 | 8.8 | 4.5 | 1.5 | 1.8 | 0.8 | 682 | 1,052 | 1,436 | 1,191 | 0.352 | 0.365 | 0.717 | 125. |
| 126. | Lumber & bldg. material retail | 175 | 1.0 | 2.8 | 6.9 | 9.4 | 11.5 | 10.7 | 11.7 | 12.5 | 10.0 | 9.7 | 7.1 | 2.4 | 3.1 | 1.2 | 685 | 1,131 | 1,570 | 1,322 | 0.395 | 0.387 | 0.782 | 126. |
| 127. | Liquor | 27 | 0.9 | 2.4 | 6.5 | 7.8 | 11.3 | 10.1 | 13.0 | 17.6 | 11.0 | 9.0 | 5.5 | 2.1 | 2.0 | 0.7 | 730 | 1,169 | 1,498 | 1,255 | 0.375 | 0.281 | 0.656 | 127. |
| 128. | Florists | 16 | 4.0 | 4.4 | 9.3 | 11.1 | 15.8 | 11.9 | 12.7 | 11.9 | 7.7 | 4.8 | 4.6 | 0.9 | 0.9 | 0.1 | 531 | 890 | 1,297 | 979 | 0.404 | 0.456 | 0.860 | 128. |
| 129. | Jewelry | 27 | 1.0 | 3.4 | 6.4 | 6.4 | 8.0 | 8.4 | 8.2 | 11.4 | 10.0 | 13.3 | 12.2 | 4.3 | 5.3 | 1.8 | 795 | 1,343 | 1,954 | 1,582 | 0.409 | 0.454 | 0.863 | 129. |
| 130. | Fuel & ice | 128 | 2.6 | 5.0 | 12.1 | 12.5 | 13.1 | 9.9 | 10.7 | 10.2 | 7.9 | 7.4 | 4.2 | 1.7 | 1.9 | 0.8 | 484 | 894 | 1,378 | 1,079 | 0.459 | 0.540 | 0.999 | 130. |
| 131. | Misc. retail | 142 | 2.1 | 3.4 | 8.4 | 9.6 | 13.0 | 11.3 | 11.6 | 11.1 | 8.8 | 9.1 | 5.6 | 2.6 | 2.5 | 1.1 | 623 | 1,037 | 1,502 | 1,236 | 0.400 | 0.447 | 0.847 | 131. |
| 132. | Not spec. retail | 77 | 3.3 | 5.3 | 10.0 | 10.6 | 13.2 | 10.4 | 11.4 | 9.0 | 7.3 | 7.6 | 5.5 | 2.2 | 2.4 | 1.7 | 520 | 946 | 1,449 | 1,200 | 0.450 | 0.531 | 0.981 | 132. |
| 133. | Finance, insurance, & real estate | 883 | 0.8 | 1.7 | 4.3 | 5.1 | 7.4 | 7.6 | 8.6 | 10.7 | 8.8 | 11.4 | 11.8 | 6.1 | 10.1 | 5.7 | 950 | 1,486 | 2.364 | 2,082 | 0.361 | 0.590 | 0.951 | 133. |
| 134. | Bank. & cred. agenc. & commod. brok. | 319 | 0.5 | 1.0 | 2.4 | 2.4 | 4.8 | 6.0 | 7.0 | 10.5 | 10.0 | 15.1 | 14.2 | 6.1 | 11.8 | 8.1 | 1,217 | 1,743 | 2,590 | 2,432 | 0.302 | 0.485 | 0.787 | 134. |
| 135. | Insurance | 290 | 0.5 | 1.1 | 2.5 | 3.4 | 4.4 | 5.5 | 6.6 | 9.1 | 8.1 | 11.7 | 15.5 | 10.1 | 14.9 | 6.8 | 1,221 | 1,900 | 2,826 | 2,464 | 0.358 | 0.487 | 0.845 | 135. |
| 136. | Real estate, incl. real est. ins. law off. | 274 | 1.5 | 3.0 | 8.4 | 9.8 | 13.5 | 11.5 | 12.7 | 12.6 | 8.3 | 6.8 | 5.1 | 1.9 | 3.1 | 1.8 | 634 | 1,036 | 1,448 | 1,280 | 0.389 | 0.397 | 0.786 | 136. |
| 137. | Business & repair serv. | 557 | 2.2 | 3.8 | 9.5 | 10.5 | 13.3 | 10.9 | 11.5 | 11.8 | 9.1 | 8.1 | 4.6 | 1.6 | 1.9 | 1.3 | 580 | 996 | 1,432 | 1,181 | 0.417 | 0.438 | 0.855 | 137. |
| 138. | Advertising | 47 | 2.3 | 2.8 | 5.6 | 6.3 | 8.2 | 6.4 | 7.1 | 8.7 | 7.8 | 9.0 | 9.9 | 5.4 | 10.3 | 10.3 | 795 | 1,466 | 2,583 | 2,349 | 0.458 | 0.761 | 1.219 | 138. |
| 139. | Account. audit., bookkeep., & misc. bus. serv. | 73 | 1.8 | 3.4 | 7.4 | 8.1 | 10.0 | 9.3 | 9.4 | 10.0 | 9.0 | 11.0 | 9.0 | 3.5 | 5.2 | 2.9 | 686 | 1,212 | 1,840 | 1,556 | 0.434 | 0.518 | 0.952 | 139. |
| 140. | Auto. repair serv. & garages | 374 | 2.2 | 3.8 | 10.0 | 11.4 | 14.7 | 11.8 | 12.6 | 12.8 | 9.3 | 7.4 | 3.0 | 0.8 | 0.3 | 0.1 | 557 | 933 | 1,332 | 991 | 0.403 | 0.427 | 0.830 | 140. |
| 141. | Misc. repair serv. | 63 | 3.2 | 5.2 | 11.3 | 11.3 | 12.7 | 10.6 | 11.1 | 10.3 | 9.0 | 8.0 | 5.0 | 1.1 | 1.0 | 0.2 | 493 | 918 | 1,386 | 1,019 | 0.463 | 0.508 | 0.971 | 141. |
| 142. | Personal serv. | 874 | 3.8 | 6.7 | 14.9 | 14.3 | 14.9 | 11.3 | 9.7 | 9.1 | 5.8 | 4.7 | 2.7 | 0.9 | 0.8 | 0.4 | 394 | 738 | 1,187 | 884 | 0.466 | 0.608 | 1.074 | 142. |
| 143. | Private households | 286 | 6.6 | 11.7 | 20.6 | 15.7 | 13.6 | 9.1 | 6.3 | 7.1 | 4.2 | 3.1 | 1.4 | 0.3 | 0.2 | 0.1 | 265 | 541 | 949 | 675 | 0.511 | 0.753 | 1,264 | 143. |
| 144. | Hotels & lodging places | 250 | 2.7 | 5.2 | 15.4 | 16.0 | 16.6 | 12.5 | 9.3 | 8.3 | 5.0 | 4.2 | 2.4 | 0.8 | 1.0 | 0.5 | 421 | 728 | 1,141 | 885 | 0.423 | 0.566 | 0.989 | 144. |
| 145. | Laund., clean., & dyeing | 182 | 2.0 | 3.0 | 8.2 | 10.3 | 14.0 | 12.3 | 12.8 | 11.7 | 9.1 | 8.2 | 4.8 | 1.8 | 1.2 | 0.6 | 621 | 1,003 | 1,415 | 1,126 | 0.381 | 0.410 | 0.791 | 145. |
| 146. | Dress & shoe rep. shops & misc. pers. serv. | 156 | 2.8 | 4.2 | 11.2 | 13.8 | 16.0 | 12.4 | 12.7 | 10.7 | 6.2 | 4.1 | 3.1 | 1.1 | 1.2 | 0.5 | 498 | 832 | 1,235 | 972 | 0.401 | 0.484 | 0.885 | 146. |
| 147. | Entertain. & recr. | 317 | 4.0 | 5.7 | 11.6 | 11.1 | 11.5 | 9.4 | 7.8 | 7.1 | 5.7 | 6.4 | 6.4 | 3.8 | 6.2 | 3.1 | 466 | 929 | 1,668 | 1,420 | 0.499 | 0.794 | 1.293 | 147. |
| 148. | Radio broad. & television | 19 | 0.9 | 1.7 | 3.4 | 4.7 | 5.3 | 6.3 | 6.5 | 9.3 | 9.0 | 11.7 | 13.2 | 7.4 | 12.1 | 8.5 | 1,083 | 1,699 | 2,702 | 2,418 | 0.363 | 0.590 | 0.953 | 148. |
| 149. | Theaters & motion pict. | 128 | 2.8 | 3.6 | 7.3 | 7.6 | 9.6 | 8.2 | 7.6 | 6.9 | 6.2 | 8.4 | 9.9 | 6.4 | 10.7 | 4.8 | 677 | 1,295 | 2,343 | 1,883 | 0.478 | 0.808 | 1.286 | 149. |
| 150. | Bowl. all., bill. & pool parl., misc. ent. | 170 | 5.2 | 7.8 | 15.8 | 14.5 | 13.7 | 10.7 | 8.1 | 7.0 | 5.0 | 4.3 | 3.0 | 1.5 | 2.2 | 1.1 | 351 | 697 | 1,180 | 954 | 0.496 | 0.691 | 1.187 | 150. |
| 151. | Professional & rel. serv. | 1,050 | 1.3 | 2.5 | 6.9 | 8.8 | 10.2 | 9.7 | 8.7 | 10.7 | 7.5 | 9.8 | 8.7 | 4.7 | 7.7 | 2.8 | 707 | 1,235 | 1,955 | 1,636 | 0.428 | 0.582 | 1.010 | 151. |
| 152. | Medical & oth. health | 203 | 1.9 | 3.7 | 9.4 | 13.5 | 16.3 | 11.5 | 9.9 | 11.6 | 5.6 | 5.5 | 3.7 | 1.8 | 3.5 | 2.0 | 548 | 890 | 1,351 | 1,215 | 0.385 | 0.518 | 0.903 | 152. |
| 153. | Educational | 546 | 1.1 | 2.1 | 6.0 | 7.5 | 8.1 | 9.6 | 8.5 | 10.3 | 8.1 | 11.5 | 10.2 | 5.7 | 9.0 | 2.4 | 804 | 1,337 | 2,107 | 1,720 | 0.399 | 0.575 | 0.974 | 153. |
| 154. | Welfare, relig., & nonprofit | 227 | 1.4 | 2.8 | 7.6 | 8.9 | 11.2 | 9.3 | 8.7 | 12.0 | 8.2 | 9.4 | 8.1 | 3.7 | 6.4 | 2.2 | 676 | 1,201 | 1,808 | 1,516 | 0.437 | 0.504 | 0.941 | 154. |
| 155. | Legal, eng., arch., & misc. prof. | 74 | 1.3 | 1.7 | 4.7 | 5.3 | 5.9 | 6.1 | 6.4 | 7.6 | 6.8 | 10.0 | 12.7 | 7.9 | 14.1 | 9.6 | 1,000 | 1,768 | 2,911 | 2,522 | 0.435 | 0.646 | 1.081 | 155. |
| 156. | Public administration | 1,454 | 1.1 | 1.9 | 8.6 | 5.6 | 6.0 | 5.2 | 5.4 | 8.2 | 7.4 | 14.6 | 21.2 | 6.0 | 7.2 | 1.8 | 869 | 1,616 | 2,259 | 1,777 | 0.463 | 0.397 | 0.860 | 156. |
| 157. | Postal serv. | 281 | 0.4 | 0.9 | 2.6 | 2.2 | 2.9 | 2.8 | 3.5 | 6.8 | 4.5 | 14.6 | 49.0 | 7.0 | 2.4 | 0.2 | 1,528 | 2,089 | 2,344 | 1,932 | 0.269 | 0.122 | 0.391 | 157. |
| 158. | Federal pub. admin. | 502 | 2.2 | 3.6 | 19.3 | 9.9 | 8.9 | 5.6 | 5.0 | 6.8 | 5.7 | 9.8 | 8.0 | 4.8 | 7.7 | 2.7 | 398 | 1,020 | 1,926 | 1,494 | 0.609 | 0.888 | 1.497 | 158. |
| 159. | State & local pub. admin. | 671 | 0.6 | 1.2 | 3.1 | 3.8 | 5.1 | 5.8 | 6.4 | 9.7 | 9.8 | 18.1 | 19.2 | 6.6 | 8.8 | 1.8 | 1,168 | 1,699 | 2,296 | 1,915 | 0.313 | 0.351 | 0.664 | 159. |

continued on next page

| | INDUSTRY | NUMBER WITH $1 OR MORE (thousands) (1) | PERCENTAGE DISTRIBUTION BY INCOME CLASS Under $100 (2) | $100 to $199 (3) | $200 to $399 (4) | $400 to $599 (5) | $600 to $799 (6) | $800 to $999 (7) | $1,000 to $1,199 (8) | $1,200 to $1,399 (9) | $1,400 to $1,599 (10) | $1,600 to $1,999 (11) | $2,000 to $2,499 (12) | $2,500 to $2,999 (13) | $3,000 to $4,999 (14) | $5,000 and Over (15) | INCOME AT QUARTILE POSITION $Q_1$ (16) | Median $Q_2$ (17) | $Q_3$ (18) | ARITHMETIC MEAN (19) | MEASURES OF DISPERSION $1-\frac{Q_1}{Q_2}$ (20) | $\frac{Q_3}{Q_2}-1$ (21) | $\frac{Q_3-Q_1}{Q_2}$ (22) | |
|---|---|---|---|---|---|---|---|---|---|---|---|---|---|---|---|---|---|---|---|---|---|---|---|---|
| | *PART 2: FEMALES* | | | | | | | | | | | | | | | | | | | | | | | |
| 1. | Total | 9,797 | 7.0 | 10.1 | 17.2 | 14.9 | 16.2 | 11.5 | 7.7 | 5.7 | 3.4 | 3.2 | 1.7 | 0.6 | 0.6 | 0.1 | $ 291 | $ 609 | $ 966 | $ 716 | 0.522 | 0.585 | 1.107 | 1. |
| 2. | Agriculture, forestry, & fisheries | 125 | 41.5 | 31.6 | 16.5 | 3.8 | 2.6 | 1.7 | 0.7 | 0.8 | 0.4 | 0.3 | — | — | — | — | 60 | 126 | 223 | 199 | 0.526 | 0.757 | 1.283 | 2. |
| 3. | Agriculture | 124 | 41.9 | 31.8 | 16.5 | 3.7 | 2.5 | 1.6 | 0.7 | 0.7 | 0.3 | 0.3 | — | — | — | — | 59 | 125 | 215 | 195 | 0.525 | 0.719 | 1.244 | 3. |
| 4. | Forestry | 1 | 11.5 | 17.3 | 21.2 | 3.8 | 9.6 | 5.8 | 3.8 | 13.5 | 9.6 | 3.8 | — | — | — | — | 178 | 400 | 1,229 | 633 | 0.555 | 2.074 | 2.629 | 4. |
| 5. | Fisheries | — | — | — | — | — | — | — | — | — | — | — | — | — | — | — | — | — | — | — | — | — | — | 5. |
| 6. | Mining, extract., & quarry. | 12 | 2.5 | 4.8 | 9.9 | 6.1 | 9.4 | 13.2 | 10.6 | 15.0 | 12.1 | 9.6 | 4.6 | 0.8 | 1.2 | 0.2 | 636 | 1,077 | 1,457 | 1,110 | 0.410 | 0.353 | 0.763 | 6. |
| 7. | Metals | 1 | 1.5 | 6.2 | 9.2 | 4.6 | 10.8 | 4.6 | 6.2 | 23.1 | 15.4 | 10.8 | 6.2 | 1.5 | — | — | 664 | 1,259 | 1,514 | 1,152 | 0.473 | 0.201 | 0.674 | 7. |
| 8. | Coal | 4 | 3.4 | 5.3 | 19.3 | 10.6 | 12.6 | 15.4 | 12.6 | 9.2 | 4.8 | 3.4 | 1.9 | 1.4 | — | — | 368 | 780 | 1,133 | 820 | 0.528 | 0.451 | 0.979 | 8. |
| 9. | Crude petroleum & natl. gas | 6 | 1.9 | 3.4 | 4.2 | 2.3 | 6.4 | 13.2 | 9.8 | 16.6 | 18.1 | 15.5 | 6.0 | 0.4 | 1.9 | 0.4 | 903 | 1,306 | 1,590 | 1,325 | 0.309 | 0.217 | 0.526 | 9. |
| 10. | Nonmetals, exc. fuel | 1 | 3.3 | 8.3 | 5.0 | 8.3 | 11.7 | 13.3 | 11.7 | 18.3 | 6.7 | 3.3 | 6.7 | — | 3.3 | — | 601 | 1,001 | 1,346 | 1,081 | 0.400 | 0.344 | 0.744 | 10. |
| 11. | Construction | 37 | 3.5 | 6.2 | 12.5 | 12.5 | 15.0 | 13.6 | 10.6 | 10.2 | 6.2 | 5.3 | 2.2 | 1.2 | 0.6 | 0.2 | 444 | 804 | 1,221 | 900 | 0.448 | 0.518 | 0.966 | 11. |
| 12. | Manufacturing | 2,466 | 2.9 | 5.9 | 16.3 | 19.6 | 23.0 | 14.0 | 8.6 | 4.5 | 2.2 | 1.6 | 0.7 | 0.2 | 0.2 | 0.1 | 398 | 646 | 904 | 697 | 0.383 | 0.399 | 0.782 | 12. |
| 13. | Durable goods | 586 | 2.6 | 5.3 | 11.6 | 13.6 | 20.0 | 17.8 | 13.5 | 7.6 | 3.6 | 2.5 | 1.1 | 0.3 | 0.3 | 0.1 | 480 | 769 | 1,060 | 812 | 0.375 | 0.379 | 0.754 | 13. |
| 14. | Lumber & wood prod., exc. furn. | 33 | 3.2 | 6.7 | 17.8 | 17.5 | 19.8 | 13.4 | 8.8 | 6.0 | 3.2 | 2.2 | 1.0 | 0.2 | 0.2 | 0.1 | 369 | 648 | 949 | 719 | 0.430 | 0.463 | 0.893 | 14. |
| 15. | Logging | 1 | 1.4 | 8.5 | 25.4 | 21.1 | 18.3 | 8.5 | 5.6 | 4.2 | 4.2 | 2.8 | — | — | — | — | 318 | 539 | 807 | 629 | 0.409 | 0.496 | 0.905 | 15. |
| 16. | Saw & planing mills, & mill work | 10 | 3.6 | 6.1 | 15.1 | 12.1 | 16.5 | 13.4 | 11.3 | 10.0 | 5.4 | 4.6 | 1.5 | — | 0.4 | — | 403 | 758 | 1,145 | 820 | 0.469 | 0.509 | 0.978 | 16. |
| 17. | Misc. wood prod. | 22 | 3.2 | 6.9 | 18.6 | 19.6 | 21.4 | 13.7 | 7.9 | 4.2 | 2.1 | 1.0 | 0.8 | 0.3 | 0.1 | 0.2 | 360 | 615 | 877 | 678 | 0.416 | 0.424 | 0.840 | 17. |
| 18. | Furniture & fixtures | 22 | 2.8 | 5.0 | 12.2 | 16.3 | 24.1 | 18.0 | 8.8 | 6.4 | 3.6 | 1.3 | 0.6 | 0.2 | 0.1 | 0.7 | 461 | 713 | 962 | 801 | 0.354 | 0.348 | 0.702 | 18. |
| 19. | Stone, clay, & glass prod. | 46 | 2.1 | 4.4 | 11.2 | 14.4 | 24.9 | 19.6 | 12.4 | 5.7 | 2.4 | 1.3 | 0.9 | 0.2 | 0.2 | 0.3 | 501 | 744 | 984 | 795 | 0.327 | 0.323 | 0.650 | 19. |
| 20. | Glass & glass prod. | 21 | 2.0 | 4.2 | 12.2 | 16.2 | 23.6 | 18.7 | 13.2 | 5.3 | 1.6 | 1.1 | 1.1 | 0.2 | 0.1 | 0.2 | 480 | 729 | 978 | 769 | 0.341 | 0.341 | 0.682 | 20. |
| 21. | Cement, concrete, gypsum, & plaster prod. | 3 | 0.7 | 3.7 | 7.2 | 7.2 | 12.3 | 18.1 | 19.6 | 16.7 | 4.3 | 5.8 | 2.9 | 0.7 | — | 0.7 | 700 | 1,008 | 1,274 | 1,061 | 0.305 | 0.263 | 0.568 | 21. |
| 22. | Structural clay prod. | 4 | 0.5 | 3.8 | 9.8 | 13.7 | 25.1 | 21.9 | 14.2 | 4.4 | 3.8 | 1.1 | 0.5 | — | 1.1 | — | 559 | 776 | 1,002 | 822 | 0.281 | 0.290 | 0.571 | 22. |
| 23. | Pottery & rel. prod. | 11 | 3.0 | 5.0 | 11.6 | 14.8 | 34.8 | 20.3 | 5.7 | 2.4 | 1.5 | 0.4 | — | 0.2 | — | 0.4 | 472 | 689 | 857 | 709 | 0.315 | 0.242 | 0.557 | 23. |
| 24. | Misc. nonmet min. & stone prod. | 7 | 2.5 | 4.9 | 10.1 | 11.3 | 17.8 | 20.6 | 16.9 | 8.6 | 4.3 | 1.5 | 0.9 | — | 0.3 | 0.3 | 533 | 833 | 1,092 | 854 | 0.360 | 0.311 | 0.671 | 24. |
| 25. | Metal industries | 122 | 2.0 | 4.8 | 9.4 | 11.0 | 20.2 | 19.4 | 14.6 | 8.5 | 4.2 | 3.4 | 1.4 | 0.3 | 0.4 | 0.2 | 560 | 826 | 1,112 | 876 | 0.323 | 0.345 | 0.668 | 25. |
| 26. | Iron & steel & their prod. | 97 | 1.9 | 4.6 | 9.2 | 10.9 | 19.9 | 19.9 | 14.6 | 8.9 | 4.3 | 3.6 | 1.5 | 0.2 | 0.4 | 0.2 | 570 | 835 | 1,117 | 887 | 0.317 | 0.338 | 0.655 | 26. |
| 27. | Blast furn., steel wks., & roll mills | 20 | 1.7 | 3.4 | 6.8 | 7.5 | 10.7 | 15.6 | 18.7 | 14.5 | 8.4 | 8.1 | 3.0 | 0.4 | 0.6 | 0.4 | 704 | 1,045 | 1,346 | 1,083 | 0.327 | 0.287 | 0.614 | 27. |
| 28. | Oth. prim. iron, steel, & fab. steel prod. | 77 | 2.0 | 4.9 | 9.8 | 11.8 | 22.2 | 21.0 | 13.6 | 7.5 | 3.2 | 2.4 | 1.1 | 0.2 | 0.3 | 0.2 | 540 | 793 | 1,048 | 839 | 0.319 | 0.321 | 0.640 | 28. |
| 29. | Nonferrous metals & their prod. | 20 | 2.6 | 5.6 | 10.1 | 10.5 | 22.2 | 18.4 | 15.1 | 6.3 | 4.0 | 3.4 | 0.8 | — | 0.8 | 0.1 | 527 | 790 | 1,074 | 841 | 0.333 | 0.357 | 0.690 | 29. |
| 30. | Not spec. metal ind. | 5 | 2.7 | 6.7 | 12.1 | 15.6 | 18.3 | 15.2 | 11.6 | 10.3 | 2.7 | 0.9 | 0.4 | 2.7 | 0.4 | 0.4 | 444 | 740 | 1,075 | 844 | 0.400 | 0.451 | 0.851 | 30. |
| 31. | Machinery, exc. elec. | 63 | 2.3 | 4.0 | 7.1 | 7.4 | 17.2 | 20.9 | 18.6 | 11.0 | 5.3 | 3.6 | 1.7 | 0.3 | 0.4 | — | 648 | 914 | 1,173 | 928 | 0.291 | 0.282 | 0.573 | 31. |
| 32. | Agri. mach. & tractors | 5 | 1.2 | 2.7 | 5.4 | 6.2 | 15.2 | 23.3 | 17.9 | 15.2 | 5.8 | 4.7 | 1.2 | 1.2 | — | — | 725 | 965 | 1,240 | 994 | 0.250 | 0.284 | 0.534 | 32. |
| 33. | Office & store mach. & devices | 12 | 1.5 | 2.6 | 7.6 | 7.8 | 21.6 | 21.8 | 20.5 | 8.7 | 4.8 | 1.5 | 1.3 | 0.2 | — | 0.2 | 650 | 881 | 1,118 | 904 | 0.262 | 0.268 | 0.530 | 33. |
| 34. | Misc. mach. | 46 | 2.7 | 4.6 | 7.2 | 7.5 | 16.2 | 20.4 | 18.1 | 11.2 | 5.4 | 4.1 | 1.9 | 0.3 | 0.6 | — | 637 | 915 | 1,181 | 938 | 0.305 | 0.289 | 0.594 | 34. |
| 35. | Electrical machinery, equip., & supp. | 109 | 2.3 | 5.4 | 11.2 | 12.7 | 18.1 | 18.6 | 16.6 | 7.7 | 3.7 | 2.5 | 0.7 | 0.3 | 0.2 | — | 496 | 803 | 1,080 | 815 | 0.383 | 0.345 | 0.728 | 35. |
| 36. | Transportation equip. | 66 | 1.5 | 3.3 | 10.1 | 10.4 | 13.9 | 17.6 | 18.5 | 12.8 | 5.4 | 4.1 | 1.7 | 0.5 | 0.3 | 0.1 | 594 | 922 | 1,196 | 941 | 0.357 | 0.296 | 0.653 | 36. |
| 37. | Motor vehicles & motor veh. equip. | 55 | 1.3 | 3.1 | 10.0 | 10.7 | 14.9 | 18.3 | 18.9 | 12.7 | 4.9 | 3.1 | 1.2 | 0.4 | 0.3 | 0.1 | 598 | 909 | 1,176 | 919 | 0.343 | 0.294 | 0.637 | 37. |
| 38. | Aircraft & parts | 5 | 2.6 | 3.8 | 13.6 | 10.2 | 8.9 | 16.6 | 15.3 | 14.9 | 5.1 | 3.8 | 3.8 | 0.9 | — | 0.4 | 498 | 931 | 1,253 | 963 | 0.466 | 0.346 | 0.812 | 38. |
| 39. | Ship & boat bldg. & repair. | 3 | 0.6 | 2.3 | 7.0 | 4.7 | 7.6 | 12.3 | 12.3 | 14.6 | 11.1 | 19.9 | 5.3 | 1.8 | 0.6 | — | 845 | 1,243 | 1,650 | 1,254 | 0.321 | 0.326 | 0.647 | 39. |
| 40. | Railroad & misc. transp. equip. | 3 | 3.8 | 6.0 | 11.3 | 10.5 | 11.3 | 12.0 | 22.6 | 7.5 | 8.3 | 3.8 | 3.0 | — | — | — | 474 | 918 | 1,177 | 890 | 0.484 | 0.282 | 0.766 | 40. |
| 41. | Other durable goods | 125 | 3.6 | 6.7 | 15.4 | 18.1 | 24.3 | 15.2 | 8.6 | 4.2 | 1.9 | 1.1 | 0.6 | 0.1 | 0.2 | 0.1 | 390 | 651 | 890 | 686 | 0.400 | 0.368 | 0.768 | 41. |
| 42. | Professional & photo. equip. & supp. | 23 | 2.1 | 4.4 | 6.8 | 10.3 | 20.8 | 20.5 | 18.0 | 10.0 | 3.3 | 2.0 | 1.1 | 0.3 | 0.5 | 0.2 | 613 | 854 | 1,112 | 894 | 0.283 | 0.301 | 0.584 | 42. |
| 43. | Watches, clocks, & misc. mfg. ind. | 102 | 3.9 | 7.1 | 17.3 | 19.7 | 25.0 | 14.0 | 6.5 | 2.9 | 1.7 | 0.9 | 0.5 | 0.1 | 0.1 | 0.1 | 361 | 616 | 828 | 641 | 0.413 | 0.344 | 0.757 | 43. |
| 44. | Nondurable goods | 1,880 | 3.1 | 6.2 | 17.7 | 21.6 | 23.9 | 12.7 | 6.9 | 3.5 | 1.8 | 1.4 | 0.6 | 0.2 | 0.2 | 0.1 | 377 | 611 | 839 | 663 | 0.384 | 0.372 | 0.756 | 44. |
| 45. | Food & kindred prod. | 215 | 5.7 | 9.1 | 18.3 | 14.7 | 18.0 | 14.7 | 9.5 | 4.8 | 2.3 | 1.6 | 0.7 | 0.2 | 0.3 | 0.1 | 311 | 624 | 925 | 675 | 0.502 | 0.481 | 0.983 | 45. |
| 46. | Meat prod. | 33 | 3.1 | 4.7 | 11.7 | 11.7 | 15.6 | 23.6 | 16.8 | 6.8 | 2.8 | 2.0 | 0.8 | 0.2 | 0.1 | 0.1 | 494 | 827 | 1,054 | 811 | 0.403 | 0.275 | 0.678 | 46. |
| 47. | Dairy prod. | 17 | 5.2 | 7.5 | 14.7 | 12.4 | 18.2 | 16.4 | 12.3 | 6.0 | 4.0 | 1.9 | 0.7 | 0.1 | 0.2 | 0.2 | 367 | 712 | 1,009 | 746 | 0.485 | 0.417 | 0.902 | 47. |
| 48. | Can. & preserv. fruit, veg. & sea food | 43 | 13.4 | 18.0 | 32.0 | 13.6 | 9.7 | 6.3 | 3.2 | 2.2 | 0.9 | 0.4 | 0.3 | 0.1 | 0.1 | — | 164 | 316 | 570 | 420 | 0.481 | 0.803 | 1.284 | 48. |
| 49. | Grain mill prod. | 8 | 2.4 | 3.9 | 8.9 | 11.1 | 15.2 | 20.3 | 16.7 | 10.9 | 5.8 | 2.9 | 1.0 | 0.2 | — | 0.7 | 576 | 883 | 1,158 | 933 | 0.348 | 0.310 | 0.658 | 49. |
| 50. | Bakery prod. | 39 | 3.4 | 6.0 | 14.4 | 15.2 | 28.1 | 17.0 | 8.2 | 3.7 | 1.9 | 1.3 | 0.5 | 0.1 | 0.2 | 0.1 | 415 | 678 | 892 | 700 | 0.388 | 0.316 | 0.704 | 50. |

continued on next page

## TABLE B-2, females, continued

| | INDUSTRY | NUMBER WITH $1 OR MORE (thousands) (1) | Under $100 (2) | $100 to $199 (3) | $200 to $399 (4) | $400 to $599 (5) | $600 to $799 (6) | $800 to $999 (7) | $1,000 to $1,199 (8) | $1,200 to $1,399 (9) | $1,400 to $1,599 (10) | $1,600 to $1,999 (11) | $2,000 to $2,499 (12) | $2,500 to $2,999 (13) | $3,000 to $4,999 (14) | $5,000 and Over (15) | $Q_1$ (16) | Median $Q_2$ (17) | $Q_3$ (18) | ARITHMETIC MEAN (19) | $1-\frac{Q_1}{Q_2}$ (20) | $\frac{Q_3}{Q_2}-1$ (21) | $\frac{Q_3-Q_1}{Q_2}$ (22) | |
|---|---|---|---|---|---|---|---|---|---|---|---|---|---|---|---|---|---|---|---|---|---|---|---|---|
| | | | PERCENTAGE DISTRIBUTION BY INCOME CLASS | | | | | | | | | | | | | | INCOME AT QUARTILE POSITION | | | | MEASURES OF DISPERSION | | | |
| 51. | Confectionery & rel. prod. | 40 | 4.5 | 10.6 | 20.5 | 20.0 | 20.5 | 12.9 | 6.0 | 2.8 | 1.0 | 0.6 | — | 0.4 | 0.1 | 0.1 | 296 | 544 | 789 | 591 | 0.455 | 0.450 | 0.905 | 51. |
| 52. | Beverage ind. | 17 | 3.4 | 6.2 | 14.2 | 14.3 | 15.3 | 13.3 | 14.0 | 8.0 | 3.6 | 4.1 | 1.6 | 0.6 | 1.1 | 0.4 | 416 | 755 | 1,118 | 870 | 0.449 | 0.480 | 0.929 | 52. |
| 53. | Misc. food prep. & not spec. food ind. | 18 | 4.1 | 7.2 | 15.5 | 14.8 | 18.0 | 13.6 | 10.5 | 6.5 | 4.3 | 3.2 | 1.2 | 0.2 | 0.7 | 0.1 | 376 | 693 | 1,034 | 773 | 0.457 | 0.491 | 0.948 | 53. |
| 54. | Tobacco manufactures | 66 | 2.5 | 6.3 | 19.9 | 27.1 | 24.2 | 11.4 | 5.2 | 2.0 | 0.8 | 0.3 | 0.1 | — | 0.1 | — | 362 | 557 | 758 | 584 | 0.349 | 0.361 | 0.710 | 54. |
| 55. | Textile mill prod. | 503 | 2.2 | 5.5 | 17.2 | 24.8 | 30.6 | 12.0 | 4.5 | 1.6 | 0.8 | 0.4 | 0.1 | — | — | 0.1 | 400 | 601 | 765 | 607 | 0.335 | 0.271 | 0.606 | 55. |
| 56. | Knitting mills | 137 | 2.3 | 4.7 | 16.8 | 25.1 | 29.3 | 13.3 | 5.6 | 1.7 | 0.7 | 0.3 | 0.1 | — | — | 0.1 | 409 | 607 | 778 | 619 | 0.326 | 0.280 | 0.606 | 56. |
| 57. | Dyeing & fin. tex. exc. knit goods | 9 | 2.8 | 3.7 | 15.1 | 19.3 | 29.2 | 17.9 | 5.6 | 3.0 | 1.9 | 0.5 | 0.7 | — | — | 0.5 | 435 | 662 | 854 | 713 | 0.343 | 0.290 | 0.633 | 57. |
| 58. | Carpets, rugs, & oth. floor cov. | 12 | 2.2 | 3.3 | 12.4 | 17.1 | 22.9 | 17.9 | 14.0 | 5.3 | 2.2 | 1.7 | 0.5 | 0.2 | 0.2 | — | 483 | 731 | 991 | 761 | 0.340 | 0.355 | 0.695 | 58. |
| 59. | Yarn, thread, & fabric mills | 326 | 2.1 | 6.0 | 17.6 | 25.3 | 31.9 | 10.9 | 3.7 | 1.3 | 0.7 | 0.4 | 0.1 | — | — | — | 392 | 592 | 750 | 588 | 0.338 | 0.267 | 0.605 | 59. |
| 60. | Misc. tex. mill prod. | 19 | 2.7 | 6.4 | 18.5 | 22.5 | 23.6 | 13.6 | 5.1 | 3.0 | 2.1 | 1.5 | 0.5 | 0.2 | 0.1 | 0.1 | 371 | 599 | 819 | 649 | 0.380 | 0.367 | 0.747 | 60. |
| 61. | Apparel & oth. fab. tex. prod. | 559 | 3.4 | 6.7 | 21.7 | 26.2 | 22.7 | 9.3 | 5.2 | 2.1 | 1.2 | 0.8 | 0.4 | 0.2 | 0.2 | 0.1 | 337 | 538 | 749 | 598 | 0.375 | 0.391 | 0.766 | 61. |
| 62. | Apparel & access. | 531 | 3.3 | 6.6 | 21.7 | 26.4 | 22.5 | 9.3 | 5.2 | 2.2 | 1.2 | 0.8 | 0.4 | 0.2 | 0.2 | 0.1 | 339 | 539 | 751 | 599 | 0.372 | 0.392 | 0.764 | 62. |
| 63. | Misc. fab. tex. prod. | 28 | 5.1 | 7.9 | 21.3 | 22.9 | 25.7 | 10.1 | 4.0 | 1.4 | 0.7 | 0.2 | 0.2 | — | 0.1 | 0.2 | 312 | 537 | 738 | 566 | 0.418 | 0.374 | 0.792 | 63. |
| 64. | Paper & all. prod. | 76 | 2.1 | 5.1 | 13.4 | 17.4 | 24.6 | 19.8 | 8.9 | 4.1 | 1.7 | 1.6 | 0.6 | 0.2 | 0.2 | 0.4 | 450 | 697 | 925 | 754 | 0.355 | 0.326 | 0.681 | 64. |
| 65. | Pulp, paper, & paperboard mills | 28 | 2.0 | 3.7 | 11.9 | 13.9 | 22.4 | 23.9 | 10.0 | 5.2 | 2.3 | 2.2 | 0.8 | 0.1 | 0.3 | 0.5 | 506 | 765 | 976 | 819 | 0.339 | 0.276 | 0.615 | 65. |
| 66. | Paperboard cont. & boxes | 27 | 2.1 | 6.6 | 16.6 | 22.0 | 26.9 | 14.0 | 6.4 | 2.7 | 1.0 | 0.8 | 0.3 | 0.2 | 0.1 | 0.2 | 396 | 620 | 811 | 654 | 0.361 | 0.308 | 0.669 | 66. |
| 67. | Misc. paper & pulp prod. | 21 | 2.1 | 4.9 | 11.4 | 16.1 | 24.6 | 21.8 | 9.7 | 4.3 | 1.8 | 1.9 | 0.7 | 0.2 | 0.1 | 0.4 | 481 | 726 | 945 | 776 | 0.337 | 0.302 | 0.639 | 67. |
| 68. | Printing, publ., & all. ind. | 134 | 3.2 | 4.6 | 9.4 | 9.6 | 18.2 | 17.4 | 12.7 | 9.0 | 5.5 | 4.7 | 3.0 | 1.1 | 1.1 | 0.3 | 562 | 857 | 1,198 | 961 | 0.345 | 0.397 | 0.742 | 68. |
| 69. | Chemicals & all. prod. | 78 | 2.1 | 4.4 | 9.0 | 10.1 | 16.7 | 21.3 | 14.9 | 9.2 | 5.3 | 3.9 | 1.5 | 0.8 | 0.5 | 0.4 | 588 | 872 | 1,153 | 938 | 0.326 | 0.321 | 0.647 | 69. |
| 70. | Synthetic fibers | 13 | 1.3 | 2.5 | 7.0 | 9.4 | 15.4 | 33.3 | 20.7 | 5.6 | 3.0 | 0.6 | 0.6 | 0.2 | — | 0.3 | 662 | 886 | 1,058 | 882 | 0.253 | 0.194 | 0.447 | 70. |
| 71. | Paints, varn., & rel. prod. | 5 | 1.4 | 2.5 | 7.1 | 8.9 | 11.7 | 22.0 | 15.6 | 14.1 | 6.4 | 7.1 | 1.8 | 0.7 | 0.4 | 0.4 | 687 | 967 | 1,282 | 1,040 | 0.290 | 0.325 | 0.615 | 71. |
| 72. | Drugs, med., & misc. chem. & all. prod. | 60 | 2.3 | 4.9 | 9.6 | 10.4 | 17.5 | 18.5 | 13.6 | 9.5 | 5.7 | 4.3 | 1.7 | 0.9 | 0.6 | 0.4 | 557 | 857 | 1,173 | 937 | 0.350 | 0.368 | 0.718 | 72. |
| 73. | Petroleum & coal prod. | 15 | 1.2 | 1.8 | 3.3 | 4.5 | 6.7 | 10.5 | 14.8 | 22.8 | 10.6 | 16.8 | 5.0 | 0.8 | 1.0 | 0.3 | 942 | 1,263 | 1,577 | 1,299 | 0.254 | 0.248 | 0.502 | 73. |
| 74. | Petro. refining | 14 | 1.1 | 1.9 | 3.1 | 4.0 | 5.9 | 9.7 | 14.9 | 23.6 | 10.7 | 17.7 | 5.4 | 0.9 | 0.9 | 0.3 | 985 | 1,279 | 1,602 | 1,320 | 0.230 | 0.252 | 0.482 | 74. |
| 75. | Misc. petro. & coal prod. | 1 | 1.9 | — | 5.7 | 11.3 | 17.0 | 20.8 | 13.2 | 13.2 | 9.4 | 5.7 | — | — | 1.9 | — | 671 | 935 | 1,277 | 1,017 | 0.282 | 0.365 | 0.647 | 75. |
| 76. | Rubber prod. | 37 | 1.8 | 3.7 | 11.2 | 13.3 | 22.5 | 20.5 | 14.0 | 8.0 | 2.4 | 1.3 | 0.5 | 0.5 | 0.2 | 0.1 | 524 | 777 | 1,028 | 807 | 0.326 | 0.322 | 0.648 | 76. |
| 77. | Leather & leather prod. | 147 | 3.0 | 6.1 | 21.5 | 25.7 | 25.2 | 10.9 | 4.5 | 1.7 | 0.7 | 0.4 | 0.2 | 0.1 | — | 0.1 | 347 | 550 | 748 | 583 | 0.369 | 0.358 | 0.727 | 77. |
| 78. | Leather: tanned, curried, & fin. | 5 | 2.7 | 5.4 | 10.2 | 15.6 | 24.5 | 20.7 | 10.2 | 5.1 | 2.4 | 2.7 | 0.3 | — | — | — | 485 | 731 | 960 | 745 | 0.336 | 0.312 | 0.648 | 78. |
| 79. | Footwear, exc. rubber | 112 | 2.9 | 5.8 | 21.2 | 26.6 | 25.8 | 10.8 | 4.3 | 1.5 | 0.6 | 0.3 | 0.1 | — | — | 0.1 | 353 | 551 | 743 | 577 | 0.359 | 0.348 | 0.707 | 79. |
| 80. | Leather prod., exc. footwear | 30 | 3.4 | 7.4 | 24.8 | 24.3 | 22.9 | 9.4 | 4.2 | 2.0 | 0.6 | 0.4 | 0.1 | 0.2 | 0.1 | 0.1 | 314 | 518 | 731 | 562 | 0.394 | 0.411 | 0.805 | 80. |
| 81. | Not. spec. mfg. ind. | 50 | 2.4 | 5.7 | 13.7 | 16.8 | 21.6 | 15.8 | 10.3 | 5.7 | 2.8 | 2.8 | 1.1 | 0.5 | 0.3 | 0.4 | 438 | 705 | 987 | 794 | 0.380 | 0.399 | 0.779 | 81. |
| 82. | Transportation, commun., & oth. pub. util. | 347 | 1.7 | 3.0 | 6.0 | 6.8 | 11.8 | 14.8 | 16.8 | 15.7 | 11.0 | 8.6 | 2.7 | 0.5 | 0.5 | 0.1 | 727 | 1,070 | 1,379 | 1,085 | 0.321 | 0.289 | 0.610 | 82. |
| 83. | Transportation | 80 | 1.8 | 2.9 | 6.3 | 6.5 | 9.9 | 11.0 | 12.1 | 15.2 | 14.3 | 14.7 | 3.7 | 0.8 | 0.7 | 0.2 | 751 | 1,191 | 1,530 | 1,186 | 0.370 | 0.283 | 0.653 | 83. |
| 84. | Railroads & railway exp. serv. | 39 | 0.9 | 1.9 | 4.1 | 4.3 | 6.9 | 7.3 | 9.3 | 16.6 | 19.3 | 22.0 | 5.3 | 1.0 | 0.9 | 0.2 | 989 | 1,384 | 1,680 | 1,355 | 0.286 | 0.213 | 0.499 | 84. |
| 85. | St. railways & bus lines | 8 | 1.2 | 1.2 | 6.0 | 6.7 | 9.0 | 11.2 | 19.2 | 15.7 | 13.7 | 12.4 | 3.0 | 0.7 | — | — | 816 | 1,153 | 1,470 | 1,148 | 0.293 | 0.274 | 0.567 | 85. |
| 86. | Trucking serv. | 14 | 2.5 | 3.5 | 7.9 | 10.1 | 15.7 | 17.3 | 14.6 | 10.7 | 8.6 | 5.8 | 1.8 | 0.6 | 0.6 | 0.4 | 612 | 919 | 1,263 | 996 | 0.334 | 0.374 | 0.708 | 86. |
| 87. | Warehousing & storage | 5 | 6.4 | 8.3 | 14.0 | 8.3 | 14.8 | 14.4 | 11.0 | 9.8 | 5.7 | 4.2 | 2.7 | — | — | 0.4 | 347 | 775 | 1,160 | 838 | 0.553 | 0.495 | 1.048 | 87. |
| 88. | Taxicab serv. | 2 | 1.4 | 8.1 | 13.5 | 12.2 | 18.9 | 23.0 | 13.5 | 5.4 | 4.0 | — | — | — | — | — | 432 | 756 | 981 | 732 | 0.428 | 0.297 | 0.725 | 88. |
| 89. | Water transp. | 6 | 2.4 | 3.5 | 6.3 | 9.1 | 8.4 | 9.1 | 12.2 | 23.0 | 9.1 | 11.5 | 2.8 | 1.4 | 1.4 | — | 688 | 1,183 | 1,421 | 1,145 | 0.419 | 0.201 | 0.620 | 89. |
| 90. | Air transp. | 2 | 2.0 | 5.9 | 7.9 | 7.9 | 6.9 | 12.9 | 15.8 | 15.8 | 14.9 | 6.9 | 2.0 | — | 1.0 | — | 637 | 1,082 | 1,398 | 1,049 | 0.411 | 0.292 | 0.703 | 90. |
| 91. | Petro. & gas. pipe lines | 1 | — | — | 22.2 | — | — | 5.6 | — | 22.2 | 22.2 | 22.2 | 5.6 | — | — | — | 900 | 1,400 | 1,650 | 1,264 | 0.358 | 0.178 | 0.536 | 91. |
| 92. | Serv. incid. to transp. | 3 | 2.2 | 2.2 | 5.8 | 5.8 | 14.5 | 18.8 | 15.9 | 15.2 | 10.1 | 6.5 | 0.7 | 1.4 | 0.7 | — | 724 | 1,008 | 1,328 | 1,044 | 0.283 | 0.317 | 0.600 | 92. |
| 93. | Telecommunications | 210 | 2.0 | 3.4 | 6.7 | 7.5 | 13.5 | 16.2 | 18.0 | 14.8 | 9.3 | 5.9 | 1.8 | 0.3 | 0.3 | 0.1 | 680 | 1,007 | 1,304 | 1,009 | 0.326 | 0.293 | 0.619 | 93. |
| 94. | Telephone, wire & radio | 194 | 2.0 | 3.6 | 6.9 | 7.6 | 13.7 | 15.7 | 18.3 | 14.9 | 9.3 | 5.7 | 1.7 | 0.3 | 0.3 | 0.1 | 671 | 1,005 | 1,296 | 1,006 | 0.333 | 0.289 | 0.622 | 94. |
| 95. | Telegraph, wire & radio | 16 | 1.4 | 1.9 | 4.8 | 6.5 | 11.8 | 21.2 | 15.2 | 14.0 | 9.8 | 8.8 | 3.0 | 1.0 | 0.6 | — | 776 | 1,031 | 1,374 | 1,097 | 0.248 | 0.332 | 0.580 | 95. |
| 96. | Utilities & sanitary serv. | 57 | 0.7 | 1.6 | 3.4 | 4.5 | 8.3 | 15.1 | 18.8 | 19.7 | 12.3 | 9.7 | 4.4 | 0.6 | 0.7 | 0.1 | 886 | 1,174 | 1,447 | 1,203 | 0.246 | 0.232 | 0.478 | 96. |
| 97. | Elec. light, power, gas, & oth. util. | 43 | 0.6 | 1.7 | 3.3 | 3.9 | 8.1 | 15.5 | 19.0 | 20.9 | 12.3 | 9.2 | 4.0 | 0.6 | 0.8 | 0.1 | 895 | 1,177 | 1,432 | 1,206 | 0.240 | 0.216 | 0.456 | 97. |
| 98. | Gas & steam supply systems | 10 | 1.4 | 1.2 | 3.9 | 6.2 | 9.5 | 15.9 | 18.2 | 15.9 | 12.2 | 9.5 | 5.0 | 0.4 | 0.4 | — | 835 | 1,130 | 1,445 | 1,155 | 0.262 | 0.278 | 0.540 | 98. |
| 99. | Water supply & san. serv. | 4 | 0.5 | 1.4 | 2.7 | 6.4 | 7.3 | 9.6 | 18.3 | 17.4 | 12.8 | 15.1 | 6.4 | 1.4 | 0.5 | 0.5 | 939 | 1,243 | 1,578 | 1,318 | 0.245 | 0.268 | 0.513 | 99. |
| 100. | Wholesale & retail trade | 1,746 | 6.7 | 8.8 | 16.5 | 16.2 | 20.6 | 13.8 | 8.0 | 4.5 | 2.1 | 1.5 | 0.7 | 0.3 | 0.3 | 0.1 | 315 | 617 | 889 | 665 | 0.490 | 0.441 | 0.931 | 100. |
| 101. | Wholesale trade [a] | 182 | 2.8 | 6.4 | 12.0 | 10.4 | 16.0 | 16.7 | 13.4 | 10.2 | 5.0 | 4.0 | 1.6 | 0.7 | 0.4 | 0.3 | 473 | 828 | 1,159 | 886 | 0.430 | 0.399 | 0.829 | 101. |
| 112. | Retail trade, stores | 1,564 | 7.1 | 9.1 | 17.1 | 16.9 | 21.1 | 13.5 | 7.4 | 3.8 | 1.8 | 1.2 | 0.6 | 0.2 | 0.2 | 0.1 | 302 | 597 | 854 | 637 | 0.494 | 0.430 | 0.924 | 112. |

[a] No breakdown of wholesale trade available for 1939.

continued on next page

TABLE B-2, females, continued

| | INDUSTRY | NUMBER WITH $1 OR MORE (thousands) (1) | Under $100 (2) | $100 to $199 (3) | $200 to $399 (4) | $400 to $599 (5) | $600 to $799 (6) | $800 to $999 (7) | $1,000 to $1,199 (8) | $1,200 to $1,399 (9) | $1,400 to $1,599 (10) | $1,600 to $1,999 (11) | $2,000 to $2,499 (12) | $2,500 to $2,999 (13) | $3,000 to $4,999 (14) | $5,000 and Over (15) | $Q_1$ (16) | Median $Q_2$ (17) | $Q_3$ (18) | ARITHMETIC MEAN (19) | $1 - \frac{Q_1}{Q_2}$ (20) | $\frac{Q_3}{Q_2} - 1$ (21) | $\frac{Q_3 - Q_1}{Q_2}$ (22) | |
|---|---|---|---|---|---|---|---|---|---|---|---|---|---|---|---|---|---|---|---|---|---|---|---|
| | | | PERCENTAGE DISTRIBUTION BY INCOME CLASS | | | | | | | | | | | | | | INCOME AT QUARTILE POSITION | | | | MEASURES OF DISPERSION | | | |
| 113. | Food, exc. dairy prod. | 141 | 7.2 | 10.0 | 17.4 | 18.9 | 20.7 | 12.8 | 6.9 | 3.0 | 1.5 | 0.7 | 0.4 | 0.1 | 0.1 | 0.1 | 289 | 562 | 812 | 600 | 0.486 | 0.443 | 0.929 | 113. |
| 114. | Dairy prod. & milk retail | 15 | 5.5 | 5.9 | 12.1 | 13.9 | 18.4 | 16.8 | 10.3 | 7.7 | 4.4 | 2.1 | 2.3 | 0.4 | — | 0.1 | 421 | 736 | 1,046 | 786 | 0.428 | 0.420 | 0.848 | 114. |
| 115. | Genl. merchandise | 440 | 6.6 | 7.5 | 11.8 | 12.9 | 25.8 | 18.1 | 9.0 | 3.9 | 1.7 | 1.2 | 0.7 | 0.3 | 0.3 | 0.2 | 384 | 686 | 914 | 708 | 0.440 | 0.332 | 0.772 | 115. |
| 116. | Five & ten cent | 64 | 13.5 | 11.6 | 16.1 | 23.8 | 24.5 | 7.4 | 1.8 | 0.6 | 0.5 | 0.2 | 0.1 | — | 0.1 | — | 199 | 473 | 681 | 474 | 0.580 | 0.438 | 1.018 | 116. |
| 117. | Apparel & acc., exc. shoe | 176 | 4.9 | 6.7 | 14.0 | 14.7 | 23.6 | 15.5 | 9.9 | 4.8 | 2.4 | 1.6 | 0.9 | 0.3 | 0.4 | 0.2 | 391 | 682 | 943 | 731 | 0.427 | 0.382 | 0.809 | 117. |
| 118. | Shoe | 11 | 7.7 | 7.7 | 12.6 | 11.9 | 23.2 | 15.1 | 9.2 | 7.5 | 2.9 | 1.5 | 0.4 | 0.2 | — | 0.2 | 352 | 687 | 957 | 712 | 0.488 | 0.393 | 0.881 | 118. |
| 119. | Furniture & housefurn. | 28 | 3.7 | 6.3 | 9.4 | 13.0 | 21.0 | 17.0 | 12.7 | 8.7 | 3.4 | 2.5 | 1.2 | 0.2 | 0.7 | 0.3 | 486 | 767 | 1,072 | 840 | 0.367 | 0.397 | 0.764 | 119. |
| 120. | Household appl. & radio | 10 | 4.4 | 6.7 | 12.7 | 11.1 | 17.0 | 18.6 | 12.7 | 9.7 | 3.2 | 2.0 | 1.2 | 0.6 | 0.2 | — | 421 | 777 | 1,070 | 793 | 0.458 | 0.376 | 0.834 | 120. |
| 121. | Motor vehicles & acc. | 29 | 2.7 | 3.7 | 7.1 | 9.0 | 17.0 | 20.4 | 15.5 | 12.8 | 5.6 | 4.2 | 1.4 | 0.4 | 0.1 | 0.1 | 629 | 902 | 1,194 | 927 | 0.303 | 0.323 | 0.626 | 121. |
| 122. | Gas. serv. stations | 6 | 6.1 | 9.6 | 17.9 | 15.5 | 16.8 | 10.3 | 7.6 | 6.5 | 3.4 | 3.8 | 1.4 | 0.3 | 0.7 | — | 303 | 610 | 976 | 714 | 0.503 | 0.599 | 1.102 | 122. |
| 123. | Drug | 47 | 6.0 | 7.9 | 15.4 | 19.6 | 24.3 | 14.5 | 6.2 | 2.9 | 1.2 | 0.7 | 0.8 | — | 0.2 | — | 344 | 609 | 824 | 622 | 0.435 | 0.354 | 0.789 | 123. |
| 124. | Eating & drinking places | 404 | 8.8 | 12.8 | 28.3 | 22.9 | 14.9 | 6.6 | 3.1 | 1.3 | 0.6 | 0.4 | 0.2 | — | 0.1 | — | 224 | 400 | 629 | 462 | 0.442 | 0.570 | 1.012 | 124. |
| 125. | Hardware & farm impl. | 13 | 3.6 | 5.6 | 12.2 | 12.0 | 19.5 | 18.6 | 11.1 | 9.1 | 3.9 | 2.8 | 0.8 | 0.3 | 0.3 | 0.2 | 460 | 770 | 1,063 | 816 | 0.403 | 0.380 | 0.783 | 125. |
| 126. | Lumber & bldg. material retail | 22 | 3.0 | 4.5 | 6.2 | 10.8 | 16.4 | 19.7 | 14.9 | 11.6 | 6.4 | 3.5 | 1.9 | 0.6 | 0.5 | 0.1 | 606 | 892 | 1,193 | 934 | 0.321 | 0.337 | 0.658 | 126. |
| 127. | Liquor | 2 | 1.7 | 5.2 | 14.7 | 15.5 | 7.8 | 16.4 | 10.3 | 11.2 | 7.8 | 3.4 | 1.7 | — | 4.3 | — | 443 | 862 | 1,260 | 979 | 0.486 | 0.462 | 0.948 | 127. |
| 128. | Florists | 7 | 8.0 | 8.7 | 16.4 | 16.1 | 18.9 | 13.3 | 9.3 | 5.6 | 1.5 | 1.2 | 0.6 | 0.3 | — | — | 301 | 608 | 904 | 587 | 0.505 | 0.487 | 0.992 | 128. |
| 129. | Jewelry | 12 | 3.6 | 3.9 | 11.9 | 12.0 | 23.1 | 18.6 | 11.7 | 6.3 | 4.2 | 2.7 | 1.0 | 0.2 | 0.7 | 0.2 | 493 | 761 | 1,032 | 828 | 0.352 | 0.356 | 0.708 | 129. |
| 130. | Fuel & ice | 12 | 2.8 | 3.5 | 8.7 | 8.0 | 16.3 | 16.6 | 18.0 | 12.3 | 6.2 | 5.0 | 1.6 | 0.7 | 0.3 | — | 624 | 928 | 1,217 | 944 | 0.328 | 0.310 | 0.638 | 130. |
| 131. | Misc. retail | 57 | 6.2 | 7.8 | 12.9 | 13.6 | 19.3 | 15.3 | 10.7 | 7.1 | 3.2 | 2.1 | 1.0 | 0.3 | 0.4 | 0.1 | 370 | 698 | 998 | 745 | 0.470 | 0.429 | 0.899 | 131. |
| 132. | Not spec. retail | 68 | 8.4 | 9.7 | 14.3 | 15.2 | 23.9 | 13.4 | 7.1 | 3.6 | 1.6 | 1.2 | 0.7 | 0.2 | 0.4 | 0.3 | 296 | 620 | 852 | 660 | 0.522 | 0.374 | 0.896 | 132. |
| 133. | Finance, insurance, & real estate | 438 | 1.8 | 3.1 | 7.1 | 7.9 | 14.5 | 17.6 | 16.8 | 14.8 | 7.6 | 5.3 | 2.2 | 0.5 | 0.6 | 0.2 | 670 | 977 | 1,283 | 1,018 | 0.315 | 0.313 | 0.628 | 133. |
| 134. | Bank. & cred. agenc. & commod. brok. | 152 | 1.0 | 1.9 | 4.0 | 5.4 | 11.0 | 16.2 | 18.9 | 20.0 | 10.1 | 7.0 | 2.8 | 0.7 | 0.8 | 0.2 | 820 | 1,111 | 1,366 | 1,142 | 0.262 | 0.229 | 0.491 | 134. |
| 135. | Insurance | 187 | 1.5 | 2.7 | 5.2 | 5.3 | 14.0 | 21.1 | 19.1 | 14.7 | 7.6 | 5.4 | 2.1 | 0.6 | 0.5 | 0.2 | 747 | 1,002 | 1,282 | 1,048 | 0.255 | 0.280 | 0.535 | 135. |
| 136. | Real estate, incl. real est. ins. law off. | 99 | 3.6 | 5.9 | 15.4 | 16.7 | 20.5 | 13.2 | 9.2 | 6.9 | 3.7 | 2.6 | 1.3 | 0.3 | 0.5 | 0.2 | 401 | 681 | 995 | 771 | 0.412 | 0.459 | 0.871 | 136. |
| 137. | Business & repair serv. | 66 | 3.7 | 5.5 | 9.8 | 10.8 | 17.1 | 16.4 | 12.1 | 10.0 | 4.5 | 4.8 | 3.0 | 0.9 | 1.0 | 0.4 | 511 | 837 | 1,193 | 946 | 0.390 | 0.424 | 0.814 | 137. |
| 138. | Advertising | 18 | 3.9 | 4.3 | 7.7 | 8.3 | 12.1 | 13.1 | 11.6 | 15.6 | 6.8 | 6.4 | 5.9 | 1.7 | 1.8 | 0.7 | 613 | 1,010 | 1,379 | 1,137 | 0.394 | 0.365 | 0.759 | 138. |
| 139. | Account. audit., bookkeep., & misc. bus. serv. | 34 | 3.5 | 5.8 | 9.6 | 10.4 | 17.7 | 19.6 | 12.6 | 7.9 | 4.0 | 4.9 | 2.0 | 0.7 | 0.8 | 0.4 | 517 | 830 | 1,133 | 913 | 0.378 | 0.364 | 0.742 | 139. |
| 140. | Auto. repair serv. & garages | 11 | 2.6 | 6.8 | 11.6 | 14.6 | 22.2 | 15.0 | 12.2 | 7.4 | 3.3 | 2.6 | 1.5 | — | — | 0.2 | 454 | 729 | 1,036 | 788 | 0.377 | 0.419 | 0.796 | 140. |
| 141. | Misc. repair serv. | 3 | 7.7 | 5.8 | 16.9 | 15.6 | 22.1 | 7.1 | 9.7 | 8.4 | — | 2.6 | 1.9 | 0.6 | 1.3 | — | 336 | 636 | 994 | 733 | 0.472 | 0.562 | 1.034 | 141. |
| 142. | Personal serv. | 2,473 | 14.9 | 22.0 | 28.6 | 16.0 | 10.7 | 4.5 | 1.7 | 0.8 | 0.3 | 0.2 | 0.1 | 0.1 | 0.1 | — | 145 | 291 | 518 | 367 | 0.500 | 0.778 | 1.278 | 142. |
| 143. | Private households | 1,944 | 17.4 | 25.6 | 30.7 | 14.5 | 7.4 | 2.7 | 0.8 | 0.4 | 0.1 | 0.1 | 0.1 | — | — | — | 129 | 245 | 417 | 307 | 0.472 | 0.701 | 1.173 | 143. |
| 144. | Hotels & lodging places | 174 | 6.3 | 11.3 | 26.0 | 21.7 | 18.6 | 7.4 | 4.0 | 2.4 | 0.9 | 0.6 | 0.4 | 0.2 | 0.1 | 0.1 | 256 | 458 | 704 | 530 | 0.441 | 0.534 | 0.975 | 144. |
| 145. | Laund., clean., & dyeing | 208 | 4.0 | 6.8 | 19.7 | 24.8 | 27.3 | 10.7 | 3.8 | 1.5 | 0.7 | 0.3 | 0.2 | 0.1 | — | 0.1 | 344 | 557 | 744 | 576 | 0.383 | 0.335 | 0.718 | 145. |
| 146. | Dress & shoe rep. shops & misc. pers. serv. | 147 | 6.2 | 8.2 | 16.5 | 17.5 | 20.8 | 15.1 | 8.2 | 3.9 | 1.5 | 1.2 | 0.4 | 0.1 | 0.1 | 0.1 | 328 | 615 | 876 | 643 | 0.467 | 0.424 | 0.891 | 146. |
| 147. | Entertain., & recr. | 82 | 5.8 | 8.0 | 16.4 | 15.4 | 15.7 | 10.2 | 9.1 | 5.9 | 4.2 | 3.0 | 2.7 | 1.4 | 1.1 | 1.1 | 336 | 656 | 1,076 | 878 | 0.487 | 0.641 | 1.128 | 147. |
| 148. | Radio broad. & television | 5 | 2.0 | 4.8 | 10.8 | 7.6 | 13.3 | 13.3 | 16.5 | 10.0 | 4.0 | 6.0 | 5.2 | 2.4 | 2.0 | 2.0 | 595 | 973 | 1,334 | 1,214 | 0.388 | 0.371 | 0.759 | 148. |
| 149. | Theaters & motion pict. | 48 | 5.7 | 7.5 | 16.0 | 15.3 | 16.5 | 9.7 | 8.9 | 5.8 | 4.4 | 2.7 | 3.0 | 1.7 | 1.4 | 1.3 | 347 | 666 | 1,096 | 916 | 0.479 | 0.644 | 1.123 | 149. |
| 150. | Bowl. all., bill. & pool parl., misc. ent. | 29 | 6.5 | 9.4 | 18.1 | 17.0 | 14.7 | 10.5 | 8.2 | 5.3 | 3.8 | 3.0 | 1.7 | 0.7 | 0.5 | 0.5 | 300 | 588 | 977 | 747 | 0.490 | 0.661 | 1.151 | 150. |
| 151. | Professional & rel. serv. | 1,643 | 2.7 | 3.9 | 10.7 | 11.9 | 13.9 | 14.2 | 9.9 | 9.0 | 6.2 | 7.6 | 5.5 | 2.0 | 2.3 | 0.2 | 529 | 897 | 1,373 | 1,069 | 0.410 | 0.530 | 0.940 | 151. |
| 152. | Medical & oth. health | 488 | 4.6 | 5.6 | 13.1 | 15.2 | 17.2 | 15.2 | 9.9 | 8.7 | 4.4 | 4.1 | 1.4 | 0.3 | 0.3 | 0.1 | 422 | 733 | 1,082 | 806 | 0.425 | 0.475 | 0.900 | 152. |
| 153. | Educational | 958 | 1.6 | 2.7 | 9.4 | 10.4 | 12.1 | 14.1 | 9.6 | 8.9 | 7.0 | 9.6 | 7.9 | 3.0 | 3.6 | 0.2 | 614 | 995 | 1,577 | 1,242 | 0.383 | 0.583 | 0.966 | 153. |
| 154. | Welfare, relig., & nonprofit | 109 | 3.7 | 6.8 | 14.7 | 13.5 | 14.6 | 10.6 | 9.8 | 8.9 | 5.8 | 5.7 | 3.1 | 1.3 | 1.1 | 0.3 | 397 | 754 | 1,229 | 940 | 0.474 | 0.628 | 1.102 | 154. |
| 155. | Legal, eng., arch., & misc. prof. | 88 | 2.9 | 3.9 | 7.8 | 9.8 | 15.2 | 12.8 | 13.0 | 12.6 | 8.7 | 7.3 | 3.9 | 1.2 | 0.9 | 0.2 | 607 | 962 | 1,352 | 1,075 | 0.369 | 0.404 | 0.773 | 155. |
| 156. | Public administration | 362 | 1.7 | 2.6 | 5.4 | 5.4 | 8.7 | 11.5 | 12.1 | 15.2 | 13.5 | 8.0 | 7.0 | 6.2 | 1.3 | 1.1 | 820 | 1,234 | 1,583 | 1,386 | 0.335 | 0.283 | 0.618 | 156. |
| 157. | Postal serv. | 35 | 3.6 | 5.8 | 12.4 | 11.6 | 16.4 | 8.3 | 6.8 | 5.8 | 3.3 | 6.4 | 17.5 | 1.5 | 0.5 | 0.2 | 455 | 804 | 1,662 | 1,156 | 0.435 | 1.065 | 1.500 | 157. |
| 158. | Federal pub. admin. | 115 | 1.3 | 1.8 | 3.9 | 3.8 | 6.2 | 9.2 | 9.3 | 11.9 | 20.3 | 23.7 | 5.5 | 1.7 | 1.3 | 0.2 | 973 | 1,425 | 1,723 | 1,401 | 0.317 | 0.208 | 0.525 | 158. |
| 159. | State & local pub. admin. | 212 | 1.6 | 2.6 | 5.1 | 5.3 | 8.8 | 13.2 | 14.5 | 18.5 | 11.5 | 11.7 | 4.8 | 1.1 | 1.2 | 0.2 | 824 | 1,184 | 1,493 | 1,232 | 0.305 | 0.260 | 0.565 | 159. |

Source: Derived from the 1940 census report, *The Labor Force* (*Sample Statistics*): *Wage or salary income in 1939*, Table 8.

TABLE B-3

Percentage of Total Wage Income Received by Each Fifth of Wage Workers, by Industry and by Sex, 1939 and 1949

| | INDUSTRY | 1939 | | | | | 1949 | | | | | |
|---|---|---|---|---|---|---|---|---|---|---|---|---|
| | | *Lowest Fifth* (1) | *Second Fifth* (2) | *Middle Fifth* (3) | *Fourth Fifth* (4) | *Highest Fifth* (5) | *Lowest Fifth* (6) | *Second Fifth* (7) | *Middle Fifth* (8) | *Fourth Fifth* (9) | *Highest Fifth* (10) | |
| | | | | | | *PART 1: MALES* | | | | | | |
| 1. | Total | 3.8 | 9.8 | 16.2 | 23.3 | 46.6 | 5.2 | 13.3 | 18.2 | 23.3 | 39.8 | 1. |
| 2. | Agriculture, forestry, & fisheries | 5.1 | 10.6 | 14.9 | 20.8 | 48.3 | 4.0 | 9.6 | 15.4 | 24.3 | 46.5 | 2. |
| 3. | Agriculture | 5.2 | 10.6 | 15.2 | 20.9 | 47.9 | 4.1 | 9.5 | 15.4 | 24.5 | 46.2 | 3. |
| 4. | Forestry | 4.1 | 8.5 | 9.9 | 20.1 | 57.2 | 4.3 | 8.9 | 14.2 | 25.9 | 46.4 | 4. |
| 5. | Fisheries | 4.9 | 9.2 | 15.3 | 24.8 | 45.6 | 4.1 | 9.7 | 16.5 | 23.9 | 45.6 | 5. |
| 6. | Mining, extract., & quarry. | 5.7 | 11.7 | 17.5 | 23.4 | 41.6 | 7.2 | 14.6 | 18.2 | 23.2 | 36.5 | 6. |
| 7. | Metals | 5.9 | 13.0 | 18.6 | 23.2 | 39.0 | 8.9 | 15.7 | 19.3 | 22.2 | 33.5 | 7. |
| 8. | Coal | 6.3 | 13.2 | 18.5 | 23.8 | 38.0 | 7.2 | 15.6 | 18.7 | 22.8 | 35.4 | 8. |
| 9. | Crude petroleum & natl. gas | 5.7 | 13.8 | 19.6 | 22.1 | 38.5 | 7.6 | 15.5 | 19.1 | 22.1 | 35.4 | 9. |
| 10. | Nonmetals, exc. fuel | 5.2 | 11.0 | 16.3 | 23.3 | 43.9 | 6.8 | 14.2 | 18.4 | 23.2 | 37.2 | 10. |
| 11. | Construction | 4.7 | 10.2 | 16.1 | 24.1 | 44.6 | 5.2 | 12.4 | 18.3 | 24.7 | 39.1 | 11. |
| 12. | Manufacturing | 5.1 | 11.5 | 16.9 | 22.4 | 43.9 | 6.8 | 14.3 | 18.7 | 22.3 | 37.7 | 12. |
| 13. | Durable goods | 5.2 | 11.9 | 17.6 | 22.9 | 42.2 | 7.1 | 14.7 | 19.0 | 22.3 | 36.7 | 13. |
| 14. | Lumber & wood prod., exc. furn. | 5.4 | 10.0 | 15.2 | 22.9 | 46.2 | 4.6 | 10.5 | 16.2 | 24.8 | 43.7 | 14. |
| 15. | Logging | 5.3 | 9.6 | 15.5 | 23.5 | 45.9 | 3.9 | 9.2 | 15.4 | 24.5 | 46.7 | 15. |
| 16. | Saw & planing mills, & mill work | 5.6 | 10.2 | 15.3 | 22.8 | 45.8 | 4.7 | 10.6 | 16.2 | 24.8 | 43.4 | 16. |
| 17. | Misc. wood prod. | 5.4 | 11.2 | 16.0 | 22.4 | 44.8 | 5.9 | 12.7 | 17.7 | 23.0 | 40.4 | 17. |
| 18. | Furniture & fixtures | 6.4 | 12.3 | 16.2 | 22.5 | 42.4 | 6.4 | 13.5 | 18.3 | 23.2 | 38.4 | 18. |
| 19. | Stone, clay, & glass prod. | 5.9 | 12.4 | 16.6 | 21.7 | 43.1 | 7.6 | 14.4 | 18.3 | 22.6 | 36.8 | 19. |
| 20. | Glass & glass prod. | 6.6 | 12.7 | 17.1 | 21.8 | 41.5 | 7.6 | 14.8 | 18.6 | 22.5 | 36.3 | 20. |
| 21. | Cement, concrete, gypsum, & plaster prod. | 6.0 | 12.2 | 16.2 | 21.3 | 44.0 | 7.4 | 14.8 | 18.9 | 22.8 | 35.8 | 21. |
| 22. | Structural clay prod. | 6.5 | 12.2 | 16.5 | 21.9 | 42.7 | 7.5 | 14.7 | 18.1 | 22.4 | 37.1 | 22. |
| 23. | Pottery & rel. prod. | 6.8 | 13.8 | 18.4 | 22.2 | 38.6 | 8.4 | 14.8 | 18.8 | 23.1 | 34.6 | 23. |
| 24. | Misc. nonmet. min. & stone prod. | 5.6 | 11.8 | 16.3 | 21.4 | 44.7 | 7.8 | 14.2 | 18.0 | 21.3 | 38.5 | 24. |
| 25. | Metal industries | 6.2 | 13.0 | 17.6 | 22.3 | 40.6 | 8.8 | 15.3 | 18.5 | 21.7 | 35.5 | 25. |
| 26. | Iron & steel & their prod. | 6.2 | 12.9 | 17.5 | 22.3 | 40.9 | 8.9 | 15.4 | 18.6 | 21.7 | 35.2 | 26. |

continued on next page

TABLE B-3, males, continued

| | INDUSTRY | 1939 Lowest Fifth (1) | 1939 Second Fifth (2) | 1939 Middle Fifth (3) | 1939 Fourth Fifth (4) | 1939 Highest Fifth (5) | 1949 Lowest Fifth (6) | 1949 Second Fifth (7) | 1949 Middle Fifth (8) | 1949 Fourth Fifth (9) | 1949 Highest Fifth (10) | |
|---|---|---|---|---|---|---|---|---|---|---|---|---|
| 27. | Blast furn., steel wks., & roll. mills | 6.2 | 13.4 | 17.8 | 22.8 | 39.6 | 10.2 | 15.8 | 18.5 | 21.4 | 33.8 | 27. |
| 28. | Oth. prim. iron, steel, & fab. steel prod. | 6.1 | 12.3 | 17.2 | 21.7 | 42.4 | 7.9 | 15.0 | 18.5 | 21.8 | 36.6 | 28. |
| 29. | Nonferrous metals & their prod. | 6.4 | 13.7 | 17.8 | 21.6 | 40.3 | 8.3 | 15.2 | 18.6 | 21.8 | 35.9 | 29. |
| 30. | Not spec. metal ind. | 5.3 | 11.6 | 16.2 | 20.7 | 46.0 | 6.5 | 12.9 | 16.6 | 20.9 | 42.9 | 30. |
| 31. | Machinery, exc. elec. | 6.1 | 13.0 | 17.2 | 21.8 | 41.7 | 8.6 | 14.9 | 18.3 | 21.4 | 36.5 | 31. |
| 32. | Agri. mach. & tractors | 7.1 | 14.2 | 18.5 | 23.0 | 37.0 | 9.7 | 16.2 | 19.2 | 21.8 | 32.9 | 32. |
| 33. | Office & store mach. & devices | 7.0 | 13.0 | 16.7 | 21.7 | 41.4 | 8.5 | 14.4 | 17.9 | 21.2 | 37.8 | 33. |
| 34. | Misc. mach. | 6.0 | 12.8 | 16.9 | 21.7 | 42.4 | 8.6 | 14.9 | 18.3 | 21.3 | 36.7 | 34. |
| 35. | Electrical machinery, equip., & supp. | 5.6 | 12.3 | 16.3 | 21.6 | 44.0 | 8.2 | 14.7 | 18.1 | 21.5 | 37.3 | 35. |
| 36. | Transportation equip. | 6.6 | 13.8 | 18.8 | 23.2 | 37.4 | 9.2 | 15.9 | 19.2 | 21.8 | 33.7 | 36. |
| 37. | Motor vehicles & motor veh. equip. | 7.2 | 14.4 | 18.7 | 22.8 | 36.6 | 9.3 | 16.0 | 19.2 | 21.6 | 33.6 | 37. |
| 38. | Aircraft & parts | 5.6 | 12.5 | 17.8 | 23.3 | 40.4 | 9.6 | 16.2 | 18.6 | 21.9 | 33.3 | 38. |
| 39. | Ship & boat bldg. & repair. | 6.2 | 13.2 | 18.8 | 24.6 | 37.0 | 8.1 | 15.8 | 19.8 | 22.8 | 33.3 | 39. |
| 40. | Railroad & misc. transp. equip. | 5.0 | 11.1 | 16.6 | 23.0 | 44.1 | 9.5 | 15.6 | 19.0 | 21.7 | 33.9 | 40. |
| 41. | Other durable goods | 5.3 | 11.4 | 16.4 | 21.8 | 44.9 | 6.8 | 13.8 | 18.0 | 21.7 | 39.5 | 41. |
| 42. | Professional & photo. equip. & supp. | 6.5 | 12.8 | 16.9 | 22.1 | 41.4 | 8.5 | 14.4 | 17.8 | 21.6 | 37.5 | 42. |
| 43. | Watches, clocks, & misc. mfg. ind. | 5.1 | 11.5 | 16.0 | 21.4 | 45.8 | 6.5 | 13.6 | 17.8 | 22.2 | 39.6 | 43. |
| 44. | Nondurable goods | 5.1 | 11.2 | 16.2 | 22.1 | 45.1 | 6.4 | 13.4 | 18.1 | 22.1 | 39.7 | 44. |
| 45. | Food & kindred prod. | 5.5 | 12.4 | 17.4 | 22.5 | 42.0 | 6.9 | 14.3 | 19.0 | 22.8 | 36.7 | 45. |
| 46. | Meat prod. | 6.9 | 14.3 | 17.8 | 21.8 | 39.0 | 8.1 | 15.5 | 18.9 | 22.4 | 34.9 | 46. |
| 47. | Dairy prod. | 6.0 | 12.9 | 17.3 | 22.5 | 41.0 | 7.2 | 14.6 | 19.2 | 22.8 | 36.0 | 47. |
| 48. | Can. & preserv. fruit, veg. & sea food | 4.2 | 8.7 | 14.8 | 22.3 | 49.9 | 4.6 | 12.0 | 18.2 | 24.1 | 40.8 | 48. |
| 49. | Grain mill prod. | 5.4 | 11.7 | 16.3 | 21.5 | 44.9 | 7.0 | 13.9 | 17.7 | 22.6 | 38.6 | 49. |
| 50. | Bakery prod. | 6.5 | 13.8 | 18.2 | 23.5 | 37.7 | 7.0 | 14.9 | 19.1 | 23.2 | 35.6 | 50. |
| 51. | Confectionery & rel. prod. | 4.9 | 11.4 | 16.5 | 21.3 | 45.6 | 6.4 | 13.6 | 17.3 | 21.7 | 40.8 | 51. |
| 52. | Beverage ind. | 5.6 | 12.1 | 17.3 | 22.6 | 42.2 | 7.2 | 14.9 | 19.1 | 22.2 | 36.4 | 52. |
| 53. | Misc. food prep. & not spec. food ind. | 4.7 | 10.5 | 16.4 | 21.9 | 46.2 | 6.9 | 13.6 | 18.1 | 22.5 | 38.6 | 53. |
| 54. | Tobacco manufactures | 4.8 | 10.3 | 14.6 | 21.8 | 48.2 | 5.9 | 13.0 | 17.4 | 22.1 | 41.3 | 54. |
| 55. | Textile mill prod. | 6.5 | 12.2 | 15.3 | 20.5 | 45.2 | 7.6 | 14.3 | 17.4 | 21.7 | 38.8 | 55. |
| 56. | Knitting mills | 6.0 | 11.7 | 16.3 | 22.3 | 43.5 | 6.6 | 12.9 | 17.0 | 23.0 | 40.2 | 56. |
| 57. | Dyeing & fin. tex. exc. knit goods | 6.6 | 12.5 | 16.1 | 21.2 | 43.3 | 7.8 | 14.4 | 17.3 | 20.5 | 39.8 | 57. |

continued on next page

TABLE B-3, males, continued

| | INDUSTRY | 1939 Lowest Fifth (1) | 1939 Second Fifth (2) | 1939 Middle Fifth (3) | 1939 Fourth Fifth (4) | 1939 Highest Fifth (5) | 1949 Lowest Fifth (6) | 1949 Second Fifth (7) | 1949 Middle Fifth (8) | 1949 Fourth Fifth (9) | 1949 Highest Fifth (10) | |
|---|---|---|---|---|---|---|---|---|---|---|---|---|
| 58. | Carpets, rugs, & oth. floor cov. | 7.1 | 12.7 | 16.9 | 20.9 | 42.1 | 8.7 | 14.7 | 18.1 | 21.3 | 36.9 | 58. |
| 59. | Yarn, thread, & fabric mills | 6.8 | 12.7 | 15.4 | 20.4 | 44.5 | 7.7 | 14.5 | 17.5 | 22.0 | 38.1 | 59. |
| 60. | Misc. tex. mill prod. | 5.7 | 11.7 | 16.0 | 20.7 | 45.6 | 7.3 | 13.8 | 17.3 | 21.4 | 40.0 | 60. |
| 61. | Apparel & oth. fab. tex. prod. | 5.3 | 10.8 | 15.4 | 21.7 | 46.5 | 6.1 | 12.5 | 16.4 | 21.7 | 43.0 | 61. |
| 62. | Apparel & access. | 5.4 | 10.9 | 15.4 | 21.7 | 46.3 | 6.1 | 12.3 | 16.4 | 21.5 | 43.4 | 62. |
| 63. | Misc. fab. tex. prod. | 4.3 | 9.8 | 14.6 | 20.7 | 50.3 | 6.3 | 14.0 | 17.4 | 22.5 | 39.6 | 63. |
| 64. | Paper & all. prod. | 6.4 | 12.8 | 16.6 | 20.7 | 43.2 | 8.0 | 14.9 | 18.4 | 21.8 | 36.8 | 64. |
| 65. | Pulp, paper, & paperboard mills | 6.8 | 13.4 | 17.0 | 20.8 | 41.7 | 8.6 | 15.5 | 18.7 | 22.0 | 34.9 | 65. |
| 66. | Paperboard cont. & boxes | 5.3 | 11.5 | 15.6 | 20.1 | 47.2 | 7.1 | 13.7 | 18.0 | 22.0 | 39.0 | 66. |
| 67. | Misc. paper & pulp prod. | 5.7 | 11.9 | 15.1 | 20.3 | 46.7 | 7.8 | 14.2 | 17.6 | 21.2 | 39.0 | 67. |
| 68. | Printing, publ., & all. ind. | 3.5 | 10.5 | 16.4 | 23.4 | 46.0 | 2.6 | 11.8 | 18.1 | 24.3 | 43.0 | 68. |
| 69. | Chemicals & all. prod. | 4.8 | 11.3 | 16.0 | 20.6 | 47.1 | 7.6 | 14.1 | 17.6 | 21.2 | 39.3 | 69. |
| 70. | Synthetic fibers | 8.5 | 14.9 | 18.2 | 21.5 | 36.6 | 10.3 | 16.4 | 19.0 | 21.2 | 32.8 | 70. |
| 71. | Paints, varn., & rel. prod. | 6.2 | 11.9 | 14.8 | 19.4 | 47.5 | 7.8 | 14.3 | 17.4 | 20.4 | 39.9 | 71. |
| 72. | Drugs, med., & misc. chem. & all. prod. | 4.3 | 10.8 | 16.0 | 21.1 | 47.6 | 7.4 | 13.9 | 17.5 | 21.4 | 39.6 | 72. |
| 73. | Petroleum & coal prod. | 7.3 | 13.7 | 17.6 | 20.9 | 40.3 | 9.4 | 15.5 | 18.4 | 21.0 | 35.4 | 73. |
| 74. | Petro. refining | 7.9 | 14.0 | 17.6 | 20.8 | 39.4 | 9.9 | 15.7 | 18.3 | 20.6 | 35.2 | 74. |
| 75. | Misc. petro. & coal prod. | 6.0 | 12.0 | 16.8 | 21.0 | 43.9 | 8.5 | 15.1 | 18.4 | 21.0 | 36.8 | 75. |
| 76. | Rubber prod. | 6.6 | 13.1 | 17.4 | 21.8 | 40.9 | 9.5 | 15.5 | 18.8 | 21.5 | 34.4 | 76. |
| 77. | Leather & leather prod. | 6.2 | 12.0 | 16.8 | 21.3 | 43.4 | 7.0 | 14.3 | 17.9 | 22.3 | 38.3 | 77. |
| 78. | Leather: tanned, curried, & fin. | 8.0 | 14.0 | 18.1 | 21.9 | 37.7 | 8.5 | 14.7 | 18.2 | 21.6 | 36.7 | 78. |
| 79. | Footwear, exc. rubber. | 6.3 | 12.3 | 16.4 | 21.4 | 43.4 | 6.9 | 14.0 | 17.8 | 22.4 | 38.6 | 79. |
| 80. | Leather prod., exc. footwear | 4.9 | 10.5 | 15.4 | 20.3 | 48.7 | 6.4 | 13.3 | 17.5 | 21.7 | 40.9 | 80. |
| 81. | Not spec. mfg. ind. | 5.2 | 11.6 | 16.6 | 21.5 | 44.8 | 6.0 | 13.0 | 17.3 | 21.2 | 42.3 | 81. |
| 82. | Transportation, commun., & oth. pub. util. | 5.7 | 12.5 | 18.1 | 23.9 | 39.6 | 7.8 | 15.4 | 19.4 | 22.8 | 34.4 | 82. |
| 83. | Transportation | 5.7 | 12.3 | 18.2 | 24.0 | 39.5 | 7.6 | 15.4 | 19.5 | 22.8 | 34.4 | 83. |
| 84. | Railroads & railway exp. serv. | 6.4 | 13.1 | 18.6 | 24.0 | 37.6 | 9.2 | 15.7 | 19.6 | 22.9 | 32.4 | 84. |
| 85. | St. railways & bus lines | 9.2 | 16.5 | 20.0 | 22.6 | 31.5 | 9.2 | 17.0 | 20.6 | 22.6 | 30.3 | 85. |
| 86. | Trucking serv. | 4.9 | 11.2 | 17.8 | 24.6 | 41.2 | 6.2 | 14.4 | 20.1 | 24.1 | 34.9 | 86. |
| 87. | Warehousing & storage | 4.4 | 10.5 | 16.9 | 24.6 | 43.4 | 6.6 | 15.0 | 19.2 | 23.4 | 35.6 | 87. |

continued on next page

TABLE B-3, males, continued

| | INDUSTRY | 1939 | | | | | 1949 | | | | | |
|---|---|---|---|---|---|---|---|---|---|---|---|---|
| | | *Lowest Fifth* (1) | *Second Fifth* (2) | *Middle Fifth* (3) | *Fourth Fifth* (4) | *Highest Fifth* (5) | *Lowest Fifth* (6) | *Second Fifth* (7) | *Middle Fifth* (8) | *Fourth Fifth* (9) | *Highest Fifth* (10) | |
| 88. | Taxicab serv. | 7.1 | 13.8 | 18.0 | 23.7 | 37.1 | 6.7 | 14.6 | 19.9 | 24.2 | 34.4 | 88. |
| 89. | Water transp. | 5.2 | 10.6 | 15.8 | 23.2 | 44.9 | 6.0 | 12.9 | 17.8 | 22.6 | 40.4 | 89. |
| 90. | Air transp. | 4.4 | 10.8 | 15.9 | 21.3 | 47.3 | 7.7 | 13.2 | 16.5 | 20.1 | 42.2 | 90. |
| 91. | Petro. & gas. pipe lines | 5.3 | 14.2 | 21.4 | 23.9 | 34.9 | 8.5 | 16.6 | 20.0 | 22.4 | 32.3 | 91. |
| 92. | Serv. incid. to transp. | 4.9 | 12.4 | 18.1 | 23.5 | 40.8 | 6.8 | 14.0 | 18.1 | 21.4 | 39.3 | 92. |
| 93. | Telecommunications | 4.7 | 12.5 | 18.3 | 22.9 | 41.3 | 8.4 | 14.7 | 18.2 | 22.7 | 35.7 | 93. |
| 94. | Telephone, wire & radio | 6.7 | 13.4 | 17.8 | 23.2 | 38.7 | 9.0 | 14.8 | 18.0 | 22.6 | 35.5 | 94. |
| 95. | Telegraph, wire & radio | 3.2 | 8.7 | 16.8 | 26.0 | 45.1 | 4.5 | 14.2 | 20.3 | 25.1 | 35.6 | 95. |
| 96. | Utilities & sanitary serv. | 7.0 | 14.2 | 18.6 | 22.2 | 37.7 | 8.4 | 15.4 | 19.1 | 22.5 | 34.4 | 96. |
| 97. | Elec. light, power, gas, & oth. util. | 7.8 | 14.3 | 18.1 | 21.9 | 37.6 | 9.0 | 15.2 | 18.9 | 22.6 | 34.0 | 97. |
| 98. | Gas & steam supply systems | 7.5 | 14.8 | 18.6 | 21.7 | 37.0 | 9.3 | 15.7 | 19.2 | 21.9 | 33.6 | 98. |
| 99. | Water supply & san. serv. | 6.3 | 13.6 | 19.3 | 24.4 | 36.1 | 7.6 | 15.7 | 19.7 | 23.7 | 32.9 | 99. |
| 100. | Wholesale & retail trade | 4.5 | 10.7 | 16.3 | 22.6 | 45.7 | 4.8 | 12.4 | 17.3 | 22.9 | 42.4 | 100. |
| 101. | Wholesale trade [a] | 4.8 | 10.6 | 15.4 | 21.6 | 47.4 | 6.1 | 12.6 | 16.8 | 21.1 | 43.1 | 101. |
| 102. | Motor vehicles & equip. | | | | | | 7.5 | 13.8 | 17.5 | 21.5 | 39.5 | 102. |
| 103. | Drugs, chem., & all. prod. | | | | | | 6.9 | 13.0 | 16.8 | 21.7 | 41.3 | 103. |
| 104. | Dry goods & apparel | | | | | | 5.1 | 10.2 | 14.0 | 20.0 | 50.5 | 104. |
| 105. | Food & rel. prod. | | | | | | 6.3 | 13.6 | 18.6 | 22.7 | 38.5 | 105. |
| 106. | Elec. goods, hardware, & plumb. equip. | | | | | | 7.0 | 13.0 | 16.4 | 20.6 | 42.7 | 106. |
| 107. | Machinery, equip., & supp. | | | | | | 6.8 | 12.4 | 16.3 | 20.6 | 43.7 | 107. |
| 108. | Petro. prod. | | | | | | 7.9 | 13.6 | 17.5 | 21.1 | 39.7 | 108. |
| 109. | Farm prod. & raw materials | | | | | | 5.6 | 12.7 | 16.4 | 21.1 | 44.0 | 109. |
| 110. | Misc. wholesale | | | | | | 5.4 | 11.6 | 16.2 | 20.6 | 45.9 | 110. |
| 111. | Not spec. wholesale | | | | | | 5.6 | 11.5 | 15.7 | 19.8 | 47.1 | 111. |
| 112. | Retail trade, stores | 4.6 | 11.0 | 17.2 | 23.4 | 43.5 | 4.5 | 12.2 | 18.0 | 23.5 | 41.6 | 112. |
| 113. | Food, exc. dairy prod. | 4.1 | 11.6 | 17.8 | 24.7 | 41.5 | 3.6 | 11.7 | 19.0 | 25.1 | 40.3 | 113. |
| 114. | Dairy prod. & milk retail | 5.3 | 13.2 | 19.2 | 24.9 | 37.1 | 5.9 | 15.2 | 20.0 | 24.8 | 33.9 | 114. |
| 115. | Genl. merchandise | 4.5 | 11.0 | 15.7 | 20.7 | 47.8 | 4.7 | 12.0 | 16.0 | 21.3 | 45.7 | 115. |
| 116. | Five & ten cent | 3.4 | 9.2 | 13.8 | 19.7 | 53.6 | 2.5 | 8.2 | 14.6 | 21.6 | 52.9 | 116. |

[a] No breakdown available for wholesale trade for 1939.

continued on next page

TABLE B-3, males, continued

| | INDUSTRY | 1939 Lowest Fifth (1) | 1939 Second Fifth (2) | 1939 Middle Fifth (3) | 1939 Fourth Fifth (4) | 1939 Highest Fifth (5) | 1949 Lowest Fifth (6) | 1949 Second Fifth (7) | 1949 Middle Fifth (8) | 1949 Fourth Fifth (9) | 1949 Highest Fifth (10) | |
|---|---|---|---|---|---|---|---|---|---|---|---|---|
| 117. | Apparel & acc., exc. shoe | 4.8 | 10.9 | 16.2 | 22.1 | 45.8 | 4.3 | 11.5 | 16.2 | 21.1 | 46.7 | 117. |
| 118. | Shoe | 4.9 | 12.3 | 18.0 | 23.8 | 40.9 | 4.0 | 12.3 | 18.0 | 23.2 | 42.3 | 118. |
| 119. | Furniture & housefurn. | 5.1 | 11.1 | 16.1 | 21.5 | 46.0 | 5.5 | 12.9 | 16.9 | 22.4 | 42.0 | 119. |
| 120. | Household appl. & radio | 5.2 | 12.2 | 18.0 | 23.0 | 41.4 | 5.1 | 13.3 | 17.9 | 23.8 | 39.7 | 120. |
| 121. | Motor vehicles & acc. | 6.0 | 12.4 | 17.2 | 22.7 | 41.5 | 6.5 | 13.0 | 17.5 | 21.6 | 41.2 | 121. |
| 122. | Gas. serv. stations | 4.9 | 11.2 | 17.8 | 24.6 | 41.3 | 4.6 | 12.1 | 19.5 | 25.3 | 38.4 | 122. |
| 123. | Drug | 3.6 | 10.2 | 16.9 | 25.4 | 43.5 | 2.6 | 8.3 | 17.0 | 26.3 | 45.5 | 123. |
| 124. | Eating & drinking places | 5.2 | 11.7 | 17.7 | 24.3 | 40.7 | 4.7 | 12.1 | 19.0 | 24.8 | 39.0 | 124. |
| 125. | Hardware & farm impl. | 6.1 | 12.9 | 17.4 | 22.9 | 40.4 | 6.9 | 14.6 | 18.1 | 22.5 | 37.7 | 125. |
| 126. | Lumber & bldg. material retail | 5.4 | 11.8 | 17.1 | 22.4 | 43.0 | 6.3 | 13.4 | 17.4 | 22.8 | 39.8 | 126. |
| 127. | Liquor | 6.3 | 13.0 | 18.7 | 22.3 | 39.4 | 6.2 | 14.4 | 18.1 | 22.5 | 38.5 | 127. |
| 128. | Florists | 4.9 | 12.4 | 18.1 | 24.6 | 39.7 | 3.9 | 12.5 | 19.0 | 25.0 | 39.2 | 128. |
| 129. | Jewelry | 4.8 | 11.5 | 17.0 | 23.1 | 43.4 | 4.7 | 12.2 | 17.1 | 21.9 | 43.8 | 129. |
| 130. | Fuel & ice | 4.3 | 10.7 | 16.5 | 23.7 | 44.6 | 5.6 | 13.5 | 18.2 | 23.1 | 39.3 | 130. |
| 131. | Misc. retail | 5.0 | 11.3 | 16.6 | 22.7 | 44.3 | 4.4 | 11.8 | 17.2 | 22.9 | 43.5 | 131. |
| 132. | Not spec. retail | 3.8 | 10.1 | 15.7 | 22.0 | 48.1 | 3.9 | 10.9 | 15.9 | 21.2 | 47.9 | 132. |
| 133. | Finance, insurance, & real estate | 4.7 | 10.3 | 14.5 | 20.6 | 49.7 | 5.6 | 11.7 | 15.9 | 21.3 | 45.4 | 133. |
| 134. | Bank & cred. agenc. & commod. brok. | 5.7 | 10.7 | 14.2 | 19.7 | 49.3 | 6.0 | 11.5 | 15.2 | 20.0 | 47.0 | 134. |
| 135. | Insurance | 5.4 | 10.7 | 15.7 | 21.3 | 46.5 | 6.5 | 12.9 | 16.6 | 21.6 | 42.3 | 135. |
| 136. | Real estate, incl. real est. ins. law off. | 5.1 | 11.1 | 15.9 | 21.3 | 46.4 | 5.3 | 11.7 | 16.9 | 21.9 | 43.9 | 136. |
| 137. | Business & repair serv. | 4.8 | 10.9 | 16.8 | 22.8 | 44.4 | 5.5 | 13.4 | 17.8 | 22.9 | 40.1 | 137. |
| 138. | Advertising | 3.1 | 8.0 | 12.7 | 19.8 | 56.1 | 4.0 | 10.1 | 14.2 | 19.7 | 51.7 | 138. |
| 139. | Account. audit., bookkeep., & misc. bus. serv. | 4.1 | 10.0 | 15.5 | 21.6 | 48.4 | 5.0 | 12.4 | 17.3 | 22.0 | 43.1 | 139. |
| 140. | Auto. repair serv. & garages | 5.7 | 12.6 | 18.9 | 25.0 | 37.6 | 6.4 | 14.7 | 19.5 | 24.4 | 34.9 | 140. |
| 141. | Misc. repair serv. | 4.3 | 11.5 | 18.0 | 25.2 | 40.7 | 5.8 | 14.0 | 19.5 | 24.5 | 35.9 | 141. |
| 142. | Personal serv. | 4.5 | 10.1 | 17.0 | 24.5 | 43.6 | 4.1 | 10.8 | 18.3 | 24.6 | 41.8 | 142. |
| 143. | Private households | 3.8 | 9.2 | 16.4 | 25.0 | 45.5 | 4.0 | 8.7 | 16.2 | 25.5 | 45.4 | 143. |
| 144. | Hotels & lodging places | 5.1 | 10.7 | 16.7 | 23.4 | 43.9 | 4.9 | 11.4 | 18.1 | 24.2 | 41.1 | 144. |
| 145. | Laund., clean., & dyeing | 5.6 | 12.2 | 17.7 | 23.6 | 40.6 | 6.0 | 13.2 | 18.8 | 24.2 | 37.5 | 145. |

continued on next page

TABLE B-3, males, continued

| | INDUSTRY | 1939 Lowest Fifth (1) | 1939 Second Fifth (2) | 1939 Middle Fifth (3) | 1939 Fourth Fifth (4) | 1939 Highest Fifth (5) | 1949 Lowest Fifth (6) | 1949 Second Fifth (7) | 1949 Middle Fifth (8) | 1949 Fourth Fifth (9) | 1949 Highest Fifth (10) | |
|---|---|---|---|---|---|---|---|---|---|---|---|---|
| 146. | Dress & shoe rep. shops & misc. pers. serv. | 5.1 | 11.9 | 16.8 | 23.9 | 42.0 | 4.6 | 12.6 | 19.0 | 24.5 | 39.1 | 146. |
| 147. | Entertain. & recr. | 2.9 | 7.9 | 13.0 | 21.1 | 54.9 | 2.5 | 7.7 | 14.4 | 22.6 | 52.6 | 147. |
| 148. | Radio broad. & television | 4.5 | 9.9 | 14.2 | 20.5 | 50.6 | 4.8 | 11.0 | 14.9 | 20.5 | 48.7 | 148. |
| 149. | Theaters & motion pict. | 3.1 | 8.3 | 13.8 | 22.4 | 52.2 | 2.4 | 8.0 | 15.1 | 22.6 | 51.7 | 149. |
| 150. | Bowl. all., bill. & pool parl., misc. ent. | 3.6 | 8.6 | 14.6 | 22.3 | 50.7 | 2.4 | 8.5 | 15.1 | 23.7 | 50.0 | 150. |
| 151. | Professional & rel. serv. | 4.4 | 9.8 | 15.0 | 21.9 | 48.7 | 4.8 | 11.8 | 16.9 | 23.5 | 42.8 | 151. |
| 152. | Medical & oth. health | 4.9 | 10.1 | 14.6 | 20.7 | 49.5 | 5.5 | 11.8 | 16.6 | 21.5 | 44.4 | 152. |
| 153. | Educational | 4.7 | 10.5 | 15.5 | 22.5 | 46.5 | 4.8 | 12.5 | 18.4 | 24.3 | 39.7 | 153. |
| 154. | Welfare, relig., & nonprofit | 4.5 | 10.2 | 15.6 | 21.6 | 47.9 | 4.5 | 11.1 | 17.0 | 23.5 | 43.7 | 154. |
| 155. | Legal, eng., arch., & misc. prof. serv. | 3.7 | 9.0 | 14.3 | 21.9 | 50.9 | 4.4 | 11.0 | 16.4 | 22.3 | 45.7 | 155. |
| 156. | Public administration | 4.3 | 11.7 | 18.4 | 24.2 | 41.1 | 8.6 | 15.6 | 19.2 | 22.3 | 34.1 | 156. |
| 157. | Postal serv. | 8.5 | 17.3 | 23.0 | 23.2 | 27.7 | 10.5 | 17.8 | 21.1 | 23.2 | 27.1 | 157. |
| 158. | Federal pub. admin. | 3.2 | 6.6 | 13.6 | 23.4 | 52.9 | 7.9 | 14.4 | 17.8 | 22.1 | 37.5 | 158. |
| 159. | State & local pub. admin. | 6.4 | 13.3 | 17.9 | 22.6 | 39.6 | 8.2 | 15.6 | 19.4 | 22.5 | 34.0 | 159. |

continued on next page

TABLE B-3, continued

| | INDUSTRY | 1939 Lowest Fifth (1) | 1939 Second Fifth (2) | 1939 Middle Fifth (3) | 1939 Fourth Fifth (4) | 1939 Highest Fifth (5) | 1949 Lowest Fifth (6) | 1949 Second Fifth (7) | 1949 Middle Fifth (8) | 1949 Fourth Fifth (9) | 1949 Highest Fifth (10) | |
|---|---|---|---|---|---|---|---|---|---|---|---|---|
| | *PART 2: FEMALES* | | | | | | | | | | | |
| 1. | Total | 3.8 | 9.9 | 16.9 | 24.4 | 44.7 | 4.1 | 11.7 | 19.0 | 25.8 | 39.2 | 1. |
| 2. | Agriculture, forestry, & fisheries | 5.0 | 5.0 | 14.2 | 20.2 | 55.4 | 7.3 | 7.3 | 7.3 | 19.8 | 58.3 | 2. |
| 3. | Agriculture | 5.1 | 5.1 | 14.3 | 20.2 | 55.1 | 7.6 | 7.6 | 7.6 | 19.6 | 57.3 | 3. |
| 4. | Forestry | 2.7 | 7.0 | 13.9 | 31.4 | 44.7 | 4.5 | 10.1 | 21.7 | 27.6 | 35.8 | 4. |
| 5. | Fisheries | — | — | — | — | — | 5.6 | 5.6 | 14.8 | 26.2 | 47.5 | 5. |
| 6. | Mining, extract., & quarry. | 4.6 | 13.3 | 19.3 | 24.9 | 37.6 | 7.0 | 16.1 | 19.2 | 23.6 | 33.9 | 6. |
| 7. | Metals | 4.6 | 13.7 | 22.0 | 24.9 | 34.6 | 8.3 | 16.3 | 19.7 | 26.0 | 29.5 | 7. |
| 8. | Coal | 5.3 | 10.5 | 19.2 | 25.4 | 39.4 | 7.2 | 14.1 | 19.4 | 22.7 | 36.4 | 8. |
| 9. | Crude petroleum & natl. gas | 6.8 | 14.8 | 19.7 | 23.5 | 34.9 | 7.3 | 16.6 | 19.6 | 23.6 | 32.6 | 9. |
| 10. | Nonmetals, exc. fuel | 4.2 | 12.6 | 18.5 | 23.7 | 40.7 | 7.1 | 15.1 | 20.5 | 23.2 | 34.0 | 10. |
| 11. | Construction | 4.6 | 11.7 | 17.8 | 25.0 | 40.6 | 5.1 | 14.3 | 19.7 | 24.0 | 36.6 | 11. |
| 12. | Manufacturing | 6.2 | 12.8 | 18.7 | 23.6 | 38.4 | 5.9 | 14.2 | 19.5 | 25.0 | 35.2 | 12. |
| 13. | Durable goods | 5.7 | 14.0 | 18.9 | 24.3 | 36.9 | 6.4 | 15.4 | 20.6 | 24.1 | 33.2 | 13. |
| 14. | Lumber & wood prod., exc. furn. | 5.8 | 11.7 | 18.0 | 24.0 | 40.2 | 4.7 | 12.3 | 18.6 | 25.1 | 39.1 | 14. |
| 15. | Logging | 6.9 | 11.0 | 17.0 | 23.9 | 41.0 | 6.0 | 12.4 | 17.6 | 27.1 | 36.9 | 15. |
| 16. | Saw & planing mills, & mill work | 5.0 | 11.7 | 18.6 | 25.6 | 38.8 | 4.6 | 12.1 | 19.0 | 24.9 | 39.2 | 16. |
| 17. | Misc. wood prod. | 6.1 | 12.1 | 18.1 | 23.6 | 39.7 | 5.0 | 12.7 | 18.3 | 25.7 | 38.3 | 17. |
| 18. | Furniture & fixtures | 5.6 | 13.4 | 17.4 | 22.7 | 40.6 | 5.4 | 13.5 | 20.2 | 25.4 | 35.4 | 18. |
| 19. | Stone, clay, & glass prod. | 6.6 | 14.6 | 18.4 | 23.5 | 36.9 | 6.3 | 15.5 | 19.8 | 25.3 | 32.9 | 19. |
| 20. | Glass & glass prod. | 6.7 | 14.3 | 18.6 | 24.1 | 36.0 | 7.0 | 15.4 | 19.6 | 24.5 | 33.2 | 20. |
| 21. | Cement, concrete, gypsum, & plaster prod. | 6.7 | 14.8 | 18.9 | 22.8 | 36.5 | 5.8 | 14.4 | 20.6 | 24.0 | 35.0 | 21. |
| 22. | Structural clay prod. | 7.8 | 15.1 | 18.7 | 23.1 | 35.0 | 5.4 | 13.9 | 20.5 | 25.9 | 34.1 | 22. |
| 23. | Pottery & rel. prod. | 6.4 | 15.6 | 19.7 | 22.7 | 35.3 | 6.5 | 14.9 | 21.4 | 24.2 | 32.8 | 23. |
| 24. | Misc. nonmet. min. & stone prod. | 6.0 | 14.3 | 19.5 | 24.1 | 36.0 | 6.4 | 16.3 | 21.2 | 23.9 | 32.0 | 24. |
| 25. | Metal industries | 6.3 | 14.3 | 18.8 | 23.5 | 36.9 | 7.4 | 16.2 | 20.9 | 23.4 | 31.8 | 25. |
| 26. | Iron & steel & their prod. | 6.4 | 14.2 | 18.8 | 23.3 | 37.1 | 7.6 | 16.4 | 20.9 | 23.2 | 31.6 | 26. |
| 27. | Blast furn., steel wks., & roll. mills | 6.2 | 14.7 | 19.2 | 23.3 | 36.3 | 9.8 | 17.2 | 20.1 | 22.6 | 30.0 | 27. |

continued on next page

TABLE B-3, females, continued

| | INDUSTRY | 1939 Lowest Fifth (1) | 1939 Second Fifth (2) | 1939 Middle Fifth (3) | 1939 Fourth Fifth (4) | 1939 Highest Fifth (5) | 1949 Lowest Fifth (6) | 1949 Second Fifth (7) | 1949 Middle Fifth (8) | 1949 Fourth Fifth (9) | 1949 Highest Fifth (10) | |
|---|---|---|---|---|---|---|---|---|---|---|---|---|
| 28. | Oth. prim. iron, steel, & fab. steel prod. | 6.4 | 14.6 | 18.8 | 23.4 | 36.5 | 7.3 | 16.1 | 20.6 | 23.3 | 32.4 | 28. |
| 29. | Nonferrous metals & their prod. | 5.7 | 14.5 | 18.7 | 23.9 | 37.0 | 6.8 | 15.6 | 20.8 | 23.8 | 32.8 | 29. |
| 30. | Not spec. metal ind. | 5.1 | 12.1 | 17.6 | 23.5 | 41.4 | 6.1 | 16.6 | 19.6 | 24.8 | 32.6 | 30. |
| 31. | Machinery, exc. elec. | 6.6 | 15.3 | 19.6 | 24.2 | 34.1 | 7.7 | 16.2 | 20.9 | 23.3 | 31.7 | 31. |
| 32. | Agri. mach. & tractors | 8.3 | 15.9 | 19.3 | 23.7 | 32.5 | 8.8 | 17.0 | 20.1 | 23.3 | 30.5 | 32. |
| 33. | Office & store mach. & devices | 7.7 | 15.4 | 19.6 | 23.6 | 33.4 | 8.2 | 17.1 | 20.7 | 23.4 | 30.4 | 33. |
| 34. | Misc. mach. | 6.1 | 14.8 | 19.4 | 24.1 | 35.4 | 7.6 | 16.2 | 20.7 | 23.3 | 32.0 | 34. |
| 35. | Electrical machinery, equip., & supp. | 5.9 | 14.3 | 19.6 | 24.9 | 35.1 | 5.8 | 15.8 | 21.6 | 24.5 | 32.1 | 35. |
| 36. | Transportation equip. | 6.5 | 13.9 | 19.8 | 24.3 | 35.3 | 8.3 | 17.6 | 20.6 | 24.2 | 29.1 | 36. |
| 37. | Motor vehicles & motor veh. equip. | 6.8 | 14.1 | 19.9 | 24.5 | 34.4 | 8.1 | 17.6 | 20.7 | 24.4 | 28.9 | 37. |
| 38. | Aircraft & parts | 4.9 | 12.5 | 19.5 | 24.6 | 38.1 | 8.8 | 17.6 | 20.5 | 23.7 | 29.1 | 38. |
| 39. | Ship & boat bldg. & repair. | 6.8 | 14.8 | 19.6 | 25.4 | 33.1 | 10.3 | 17.8 | 20.5 | 22.7 | 28.4 | 39. |
| 40. | Railroad & misc. transp. equip. | 4.6 | 12.8 | 20.6 | 25.2 | 36.5 | 6.6 | 15.7 | 20.1 | 23.1 | 34.2 | 40. |
| 41. | Other durable goods | 5.9 | 12.9 | 19.2 | 23.8 | 37.9 | 5.9 | 14.1 | 20.5 | 25.4 | 33.9 | 41. |
| 42. | Professional & photo. equip. & supp. | 6.8 | 14.8 | 19.1 | 23.5 | 35.6 | 7.7 | 16.4 | 21.3 | 23.8 | 30.6 | 42. |
| 43. | Watches, clocks, & misc. mfg. ind. | 6.1 | 12.9 | 19.3 | 23.9 | 37.5 | 5.8 | 13.8 | 20.1 | 24.9 | 35.2 | 43. |
| 44. | Nondurable goods | 6.4 | 12.9 | 18.5 | 23.3 | 38.6 | 6.0 | 14.0 | 19.8 | 24.7 | 35.2 | 44. |
| 45. | Food & kindred prod. | 4.7 | 10.9 | 18.4 | 24.9 | 40.9 | 5.0 | 12.4 | 19.8 | 26.2 | 36.4 | 45. |
| 46. | Meat prod. | 5.6 | 14.4 | 20.5 | 24.5 | 34.7 | 6.2 | 15.4 | 21.0 | 23.9 | 33.3 | 46. |
| 47. | Dairy prod. | 4.7 | 11.4 | 19.2 | 25.5 | 38.8 | 5.4 | 13.1 | 20.2 | 25.2 | 35.9 | 47. |
| 48. | Can. & preserv. fruit, veg. & sea food | 3.9 | 10.2 | 14.2 | 23.6 | 47.9 | 4.5 | 9.8 | 15.1 | 25.7 | 44.6 | 48. |
| 49. | Grain mill prod. | 6.1 | 13.6 | 18.9 | 23.4 | 37.7 | 7.2 | 15.6 | 19.8 | 22.8 | 34.4 | 49. |
| 50. | Bakery prod. | 6.0 | 13.4 | 19.9 | 23.6 | 36.8 | 5.8 | 14.1 | 20.6 | 25.6 | 33.7 | 50. |
| 51. | Confectionery & rel. prod. | 5.5 | 11.6 | 18.3 | 24.9 | 39.4 | 6.0 | 13.6 | 19.7 | 25.1 | 35.4 | 51. |
| 52. | Beverage ind. | 4.8 | 11.0 | 17.6 | 23.7 | 42.7 | 6.2 | 15.0 | 20.2 | 23.7 | 34.7 | 52. |
| 53. | Misc. food prep. & not spec. food ind. | 5.0 | 11.1 | 17.7 | 25.0 | 40.9 | 5.0 | 13.0 | 20.3 | 25.5 | 35.9 | 53. |
| 54. | Tobacco manufactures | 7.5 | 14.1 | 18.5 | 23.9 | 35.8 | 5.8 | 14.2 | 20.0 | 24.6 | 35.1 | 54. |
| 55. | Textile mill prod. | 7.6 | 14.8 | 19.8 | 23.0 | 34.6 | 6.6 | 14.9 | 20.8 | 24.8 | 32.6 | 55. |
| 56. | Knitting mills | 7.6 | 14.9 | 19.7 | 23.1 | 34.5 | 6.5 | 14.3 | 19.2 | 24.2 | 35.5 | 56. |
| 57. | Dyeing & fin. tex. exc. knit goods | 6.6 | 13.5 | 19.3 | 22.4 | 37.9 | 8.5 | 17.1 | 20.4 | 24.2 | 29.6 | 57. |
| 58. | Carpets, rugs, & oth. floor cov. | 7.0 | 14.4 | 18.9 | 24.7 | 34.8 | 6.8 | 15.3 | 21.3 | 24.3 | 32.1 | 58. |

continued on next page

TABLE B-3, females, continued

| | INDUSTRY | 1939 Lowest Fifth (1) | 1939 Second Fifth (2) | 1939 Middle Fifth (3) | 1939 Fourth Fifth (4) | 1939 Highest Fifth (5) | 1949 Lowest Fifth (6) | 1949 Second Fifth (7) | 1949 Middle Fifth (8) | 1949 Fourth Fifth (9) | 1949 Highest Fifth (10) | |
|---|---|---|---|---|---|---|---|---|---|---|---|---|
| 59. | Yarn, thread, & fabric mills | 7.7 | 15.0 | 20.0 | 23.7 | 33.3 | 7.2 | 15.6 | 20.5 | 25.0 | 31.4 | 59. |
| 60. | Misc. tex. mill prod. | 6.7 | 13.0 | 18.4 | 23.4 | 38.3 | 6.4 | 14.5 | 20.0 | 23.7 | 35.1 | 60. |
| 61. | Apparel & oth. fab. tex. prod. | 6.9 | 12.7 | 17.3 | 23.3 | 39.5 | 6.5 | 14.4 | 18.8 | 24.1 | 36.0 | 61. |
| 62. | Apparel & access. | 6.9 | 12.8 | 17.3 | 23.3 | 39.5 | 6.5 | 14.4 | 18.7 | 24.0 | 36.2 | 62. |
| 63. | Misc. fab. tex. prod. | 6.2 | 12.6 | 18.6 | 24.7 | 37.7 | 6.5 | 14.2 | 19.4 | 24.9 | 34.8 | 63. |
| 64. | Paper & all. prod. | 6.2 | 13.6 | 18.5 | 23.1 | 38.4 | 7.0 | 15.6 | 19.5 | 24.5 | 33.2 | 64. |
| 65. | Pulp, paper, & paperboard mills | 6.6 | 14.2 | 18.5 | 22.4 | 38.0 | 7.6 | 16.5 | 20.6 | 23.6 | 31.6 | 65. |
| 66. | Paperboard cont. & boxes | 6.8 | 13.6 | 19.1 | 23.1 | 37.1 | 7.0 | 15.0 | 19.9 | 24.3 | 33.6 | 66. |
| 67. | Misc. paper & pulp prod. | 6.5 | 14.2 | 18.2 | 23.1 | 37.7 | 6.7 | 15.7 | 19.7 | 24.8 | 32.9 | 67. |
| 68. | Printing, publ., & all. ind. | 5.2 | 13.1 | 17.6 | 23.4 | 40.4 | 5.3 | 14.3 | 18.9 | 23.4 | 37.8 | 68. |
| 69. | Chemicals & all. prod. | 6.0 | 13.7 | 18.6 | 22.9 | 38.5 | 6.8 | 15.6 | 20.7 | 23.6 | 33.0 | 69. |
| 70. | Synthetic fibers | 8.0 | 16.8 | 20.4 | 22.9 | 31.7 | 8.6 | 18.0 | 20.7 | 24.3 | 28.2 | 70. |
| 71. | Paints, varn., & rel. prod. | 6.8 | 15.0 | 18.5 | 23.2 | 36.3 | 8.5 | 16.2 | 20.9 | 22.7 | 31.5 | 71. |
| 72. | Drugs, med., & misc. chem. & all. prod. | 5.6 | 13.4 | 18.2 | 23.4 | 39.2 | 6.6 | 15.6 | 20.6 | 23.8 | 33.2 | 72. |
| 73. | Petroleum & coal prod. | 8.0 | 15.7 | 19.5 | 23.1 | 33.5 | 9.4 | 16.5 | 19.5 | 23.4 | 31.0 | 73. |
| 74. | Petro. refining | 8.3 | 15.7 | 19.6 | 23.2 | 33.0 | 9.6 | 16.5 | 19.6 | 23.3 | 30.8 | 74. |
| 75. | Misc. petro. & coal prod. | 8.0 | 14.5 | 18.3 | 23.6 | 35.3 | 6.5 | 13.4 | 19.1 | 20.5 | 40.2 | 75. |
| 76. | Rubber prod. | 6.9 | 14.8 | 19.1 | 24.0 | 34.9 | 7.7 | 16.2 | 21.1 | 22.8 | 31.9 | 76. |
| 77. | Leather & leather prod. | 7.4 | 13.5 | 18.3 | 23.9 | 36.6 | 6.8 | 15.2 | 19.6 | 23.5 | 34.7 | 77. |
| 78. | Leather: tanned, curried, & fin. | 6.5 | 15.0 | 19.2 | 24.3 | 34.8 | 8.0 | 15.8 | 20.1 | 24.5 | 31.3 | 78. |
| 79. | Footwear, exc. rubber. | 7.6 | 13.8 | 18.5 | 24.2 | 35.6 | 6.9 | 15.6 | 19.8 | 23.3 | 34.2 | 79. |
| 80. | Leather prod., exc. footwear | 7.1 | 12.2 | 17.8 | 24.8 | 37.9 | 6.5 | 13.7 | 18.7 | 24.3 | 36.5 | 80. |
| 81. | Not spec. mfg. ind. | 5.7 | 12.4 | 17.6 | 23.6 | 40.5 | 5.6 | 13.5 | 19.2 | 24.7 | 36.8 | 81. |
| 82. | Transportation, commun., & oth. pub. util. | 6.8 | 14.8 | 19.5 | 24.4 | 34.3 | 7.4 | 16.3 | 20.4 | 23.7 | 31.9 | 82. |
| 83. | Transportation | 6.2 | 14.1 | 20.1 | 24.3 | 35.0 | 6.5 | 16.0 | 20.4 | 24.9 | 31.9 | 83. |
| 84. | Railroads & railway exp. serv. | 7.5 | 16.2 | 20.4 | 24.2 | 31.5 | 9.9 | 17.2 | 21.0 | 24.1 | 27.5 | 84. |
| 85. | St. railways & bus lines | 7.6 | 15.7 | 20.1 | 24.3 | 32.0 | 5.1 | 14.5 | 20.7 | 25.3 | 34.1 | 85. |
| 86. | Trucking serv. | 6.0 | 13.3 | 18.6 | 23.7 | 38.1 | 5.7 | 14.8 | 19.5 | 23.4 | 36.3 | 86. |
| 87. | Warehousing & storage | 3.7 | 10.5 | 18.6 | 25.4 | 41.5 | 5.1 | 11.7 | 19.2 | 25.6 | 38.1 | 87. |
| 88. | Taxicab serv. | 6.0 | 14.1 | 20.7 | 25.3 | 33.6 | 3.8 | 10.6 | 18.8 | 26.6 | 40.0 | 88. |
| 89. | Water transp. | 5.6 | 13.9 | 20.7 | 23.7 | 35.8 | 8.7 | 17.0 | 19.5 | 23.3 | 31.2 | 89. |

continued on next page

TABLE B-3, females, continued

| | INDUSTRY | 1939 | | | | | 1949 | | | | | |
|---|---|---|---|---|---|---|---|---|---|---|---|---|
| | | *Lowest Fifth* (1) | *Second Fifth* (2) | *Middle Fifth* (3) | *Fourth Fifth* (4) | *Highest Fifth* (5) | *Lowest Fifth* (6) | *Second Fifth* (7) | *Middle Fifth* (8) | *Fourth Fifth* (9) | *Highest Fifth* (10) | |
| 90. | Air transp. | 5.1 | 14.4 | 20.4 | 25.7 | 34.2 | 9.0 | 17.3 | 19.9 | 22.6 | 30.9 | 90. |
| 91. | Petro. & gas. pipe lines | 4.7 | 17.0 | 22.1 | 25.5 | 30.4 | 8.8 | 16.0 | 18.9 | 23.9 | 32.1 | 91. |
| 92. | Serv. incid. to transp. | 7.5 | 15.2 | 19.2 | 23.8 | 34.0 | 4.6 | 15.1 | 20.6 | 25.1 | 34.3 | 92. |
| 93. | Telecommunications | 6.5 | 15.2 | 19.9 | 24.3 | 33.9 | 7.8 | 16.6 | 20.9 | 23.5 | 31.0 | 93. |
| 94. | Telephone, wire & radio | 6.4 | 15.1 | 19.9 | 24.2 | 34.2 | 7.7 | 16.3 | 20.8 | 23.2 | 31.8 | 94. |
| 95. | Telegraph, wire & radio | 8.0 | 15.2 | 18.6 | 23.7 | 34.2 | 9.6 | 16.9 | 20.2 | 23.8 | 29.2 | 95. |
| 96. | Utilities & sanitary serv. | 8.8 | 16.0 | 19.5 | 22.9 | 32.6 | 7.9 | 16.1 | 20.4 | 23.4 | 32.0 | 96. |
| 97. | Elec. light, power, gas, & oth. util. | 9.1 | 16.0 | 19.5 | 22.7 | 32.5 | 8.4 | 16.3 | 20.3 | 23.4 | 31.4 | 97. |
| 98. | Gas & steam supply systems | 8.3 | 15.5 | 19.6 | 23.8 | 32.5 | 7.1 | 16.1 | 20.4 | 24.0 | 32.2 | 98. |
| 99. | Water supply & san. serv. | 8.2 | 15.4 | 18.7 | 23.0 | 34.4 | 6.2 | 16.1 | 20.1 | 22.6 | 34.7 | 99. |
| 100. | Wholesale & retail trade | 4.5 | 11.4 | 18.5 | 24.4 | 41.0 | 3.9 | 11.5 | 18.4 | 25.7 | 40.3 | 100. |
| 101. | Wholesale trade [a] | 4.8 | 12.9 | 18.5 | 24.3 | 39.2 | 5.3 | 14.2 | 19.6 | 24.1 | 36.6 | 101. |
| 102. | Motor vehicles & equip. | | | | | | 6.9 | 15.6 | 19.3 | 22.6 | 35.4 | 102. |
| 103. | Drugs, chem., & all. prod. | | | | | | 5.8 | 15.4 | 20.3 | 23.5 | 34.8 | 103. |
| 104. | Dry goods & apparel | | | | | | 7.0 | 14.0 | 18.3 | 22.3 | 38.2 | 104. |
| 105. | Food & rel. prod. | | | | | | 4.7 | 11.6 | 19.3 | 25.9 | 38.2 | 105. |
| 106. | Elec. goods, hardware, & plumb. equip. | | | | | | 7.3 | 15.5 | 19.9 | 22.6 | 34.4 | 106. |
| 107. | Machinery, equip., & supp. | | | | | | 7.6 | 16.2 | 21.1 | 23.0 | 31.8 | 107. |
| 108. | Petro. prod. | | | | | | 7.8 | 16.4 | 19.3 | 24.0 | 32.3 | 108. |
| 109. | Farm prod. & raw materials | | | | | | 4.0 | 12.3 | 20.1 | 25.9 | 37.4 | 109. |
| 110. | Misc. wholesale | | | | | | 5.8 | 14.7 | 19.5 | 23.5 | 36.2 | 110. |
| 111. | Not spec. wholesale | | | | | | 8.3 | 15.5 | 19.6 | 22.9 | 33.4 | 111. |
| 112. | Retail trade, stores | 4.4 | 11.5 | 18.7 | 24.6 | 40.5 | 3.6 | 11.2 | 18.1 | 25.7 | 41.2 | 112. |
| 113. | Food, exc. dairy prod. | 4.4 | 11.7 | 18.8 | 25.2 | 39.6 | 4.2 | 11.8 | 18.9 | 25.4 | 39.3 | 113. |
| 114. | Dairy prod. & milk retail | 4.7 | 12.4 | 18.8 | 24.7 | 39.1 | 3.5 | 11.4 | 19.5 | 27.6 | 37.8 | 114. |
| 115. | Genl. merchandise | 4.5 | 12.7 | 19.7 | 24.0 | 38.8 | 4.6 | 13.2 | 19.0 | 24.7 | 38.2 | 115. |
| 116. | Five & ten cent | 3.4 | 11.0 | 20.5 | 27.3 | 37.5 | 4.9 | 8.4 | 18.5 | 25.3 | 42.7 | 116. |
| 117. | Apparel & acc., exc. shoe | 5.1 | 12.1 | 19.0 | 23.7 | 39.9 | 4.6 | 12.5 | 18.4 | 24.2 | 40.0 | 117. |
| 118. | Shoe | 4.0 | 11.8 | 19.6 | 24.8 | 39.5 | 3.3 | 11.3 | 18.8 | 26.0 | 40.3 | 118. |

[a] No breakdown available for wholesale trade for 1939.

continued on next page

TABLE B-3, females, continued

| | INDUSTRY | 1939 Lowest Fifth (1) | 1939 Second Fifth (2) | 1939 Middle Fifth (3) | 1939 Fourth Fifth (4) | 1939 Highest Fifth (5) | 1949 Lowest Fifth (6) | 1949 Second Fifth (7) | 1949 Middle Fifth (8) | 1949 Fourth Fifth (9) | 1949 Highest Fifth (10) | |
|---|---|---|---|---|---|---|---|---|---|---|---|---|
| 119. | Furniture & housefurn. | 5.0 | 13.7 | 18.2 | 23.6 | 39.3 | 4.7 | 12.6 | 19.6 | 24.7 | 38.2 | 119. |
| 120. | Household appl. & radio | 4.9 | 12.9 | 19.6 | 25.0 | 37.4 | 4.9 | 13.3 | 19.8 | 25.4 | 36.3 | 120. |
| 121. | Motor vehicles & acc. | 6.5 | 14.6 | 19.4 | 24.7 | 34.6 | 6.6 | 14.9 | 19.3 | 23.3 | 35.6 | 121. |
| 122. | Gas. serv. stations | 4.2 | 10.1 | 17.0 | 24.6 | 43.8 | 3.6 | 9.6 | 17.9 | 27.1 | 41.5 | 122. |
| 123. | Drug | 5.3 | 13.0 | 19.6 | 24.6 | 37.2 | 4.0 | 10.7 | 18.9 | 25.7 | 40.3 | 123. |
| 124. | Eating & drinking places | 4.5 | 12.4 | 17.3 | 24.7 | 40.8 | 4.6 | 11.2 | 16.6 | 25.2 | 42.1 | 124. |
| 125. | Hardware & farm impl. | 5.2 | 13.5 | 18.8 | 24.1 | 38.2 | 5.4 | 14.2 | 20.8 | 24.8 | 34.6 | 125. |
| 126. | Lumber & bldg. material retail | 6.2 | 14.0 | 19.0 | 24.3 | 36.3 | 5.7 | 14.8 | 19.2 | 24.3 | 35.8 | 126. |
| 127. | Liquor | 4.8 | 10.4 | 17.3 | 23.9 | 43.3 | 5.0 | 12.0 | 19.6 | 26.3 | 36.8 | 127. |
| 128. | Florists | 4.2 | 11.5 | 19.0 | 25.6 | 39.6 | 3.7 | 9.3 | 18.9 | 28.1 | 39.8 | 128. |
| 129. | Jewelry | 5.5 | 14.1 | 18.2 | 23.3 | 38.6 | 4.0 | 11.7 | 18.3 | 23.5 | 42.4 | 129. |
| 130. | Fuel & ice | 6.1 | 14.3 | 19.9 | 24.5 | 35.0 | 6.4 | 15.8 | 19.9 | 24.0 | 33.7 | 130. |
| 131. | Misc. retail | 4.3 | 11.5 | 18.6 | 25.4 | 39.9 | 3.6 | 11.5 | 18.6 | 25.2 | 40.9 | 131. |
| 132. | Not spec. retail | 3.7 | 11.3 | 18.9 | 23.7 | 42.2 | 3.6 | 12.2 | 18.7 | 25.0 | 40.3 | 132. |
| 133. | Finance, insurance, & real estate | 6.5 | 14.8 | 19.2 | 23.8 | 35.5 | 6.7 | 15.7 | 19.5 | 23.7 | 34.2 | 133. |
| 134. | Bank & cred. agenc. & commod. brok. | 8.4 | 15.2 | 19.5 | 23.0 | 33.7 | 7.9 | 16.4 | 19.8 | 23.0 | 32.6 | 134. |
| 135. | Insurance | 8.0 | 15.5 | 19.1 | 23.0 | 34.2 | 7.4 | 16.3 | 19.4 | 23.3 | 33.4 | 135. |
| 136. | Real estate, incl. real est. ins. law off. | 5.4 | 11.6 | 17.7 | 24.0 | 41.0 | 4.8 | 11.7 | 18.3 | 25.0 | 40.0 | 136. |
| 137. | Business & repair serv. | 4.7 | 12.7 | 17.5 | 23.5 | 41.4 | 4.9 | 13.5 | 19.1 | 23.8 | 38.5 | 137. |
| 138. | Advertising | 4.5 | 12.2 | 17.6 | 23.2 | 42.2 | 5.0 | 13.0 | 18.3 | 22.5 | 40.9 | 138. |
| 139. | Account. audit., bookkeep., & misc. bus. serv. | 4.8 | 13.2 | 18.1 | 22.8 | 40.8 | 4.8 | 13.5 | 19.6 | 24.4 | 37.5 | 139. |
| 140. | Auto. repair serv. & garages | 5.4 | 13.5 | 18.3 | 24.6 | 37.9 | 6.1 | 14.3 | 19.7 | 24.2 | 35.5 | 140. |
| 141. | Misc. repair serv. | 4.3 | 10.7 | 17.4 | 23.6 | 43.7 | 5.4 | 12.7 | 19.9 | 25.5 | 36.3 | 141. |
| 142. | Personal serv. | 4.1 | 9.4 | 16.3 | 24.1 | 45.9 | 5.4 | 7.2 | 16.3 | 25.0 | 45.8 | 142. |
| 143. | Private households | 4.0 | 9.7 | 18.0 | 23.6 | 44.4 | 6.9 | 6.9 | 15.9 | 23.0 | 47.1 | 143. |
| 144. | Hotels & lodging places | 5.1 | 11.3 | 17.4 | 24.3 | 41.6 | 4.8 | 12.3 | 18.8 | 25.0 | 38.9 | 144. |
| 145. | Laund., clean., & dyeing | 6.9 | 13.7 | 18.9 | 24.2 | 36.0 | 5.7 | 12.8 | 19.6 | 25.4 | 36.2 | 145. |
| 146. | Dress & shoe rep. shops & misc. pers. serv. | 5.0 | 12.1 | 19.1 | 25.1 | 38.6 | 4.3 | 11.6 | 18.5 | 25.3 | 40.0 | 146. |

continued on next page

TABLE B-3, females, concluded

| | INDUSTRY | 1939 | | | | | 1949 | | | | | |
|---|---|---|---|---|---|---|---|---|---|---|---|---|
| | | *Lowest Fifth* (1) | *Second Fifth* (2) | *Middle Fifth* (3) | *Fourth Fifth* (4) | *Highest Fifth* (5) | *Lowest Fifth* (6) | *Second Fifth* (7) | *Middle Fifth* (8) | *Fourth Fifth* (9) | *Highest Fifth* (10) | |
| 147. | Entertain. & recr. | 3.8 | 9.0 | 14.6 | 22.1 | 50.3 | 3.1 | 8.0 | 14.8 | 24.8 | 49.1 | 147. |
| 148. | Radio broad. & television | 4.3 | 10.9 | 16.2 | 20.3 | 48.2 | 4.5 | 13.3 | 18.2 | 21.8 | 42.0 | 148. |
| 149. | Theaters & motion pict. | 3.7 | 8.9 | 14.2 | 21.5 | 51.5 | 3.2 | 7.4 | 13.5 | 23.5 | 52.2 | 149. |
| 150. | Bowl. all., bill. & pool parl., misc. ent. | 3.9 | 9.6 | 15.8 | 23.5 | 46.9 | 3.4 | 8.6 | 15.2 | 26.0 | 46.6 | 150. |
| 151. | Professional & rel. serv. | 4.9 | 11.3 | 16.7 | 23.7 | 43.2 | 4.6 | 11.8 | 19.6 | 25.5 | 38.3 | 151. |
| 152. | Medical & oth. health | 4.9 | 11.9 | 18.4 | 24.5 | 40.0 | 5.1 | 12.4 | 19.0 | 25.6 | 37.6 | 152. |
| 153. | Educational | 5.2 | 11.4 | 16.3 | 24.2 | 42.6 | 4.4 | 12.4 | 19.5 | 25.9 | 37.7 | 153. |
| 154. | Welfare, relig., & nonprofit | 4.4 | 10.1 | 16.8 | 24.6 | 43.9 | 4.1 | 10.8 | 18.2 | 25.7 | 41.0 | 154. |
| 155. | Legal, eng., arch., & misc. prof. serv. | 5.5 | 12.6 | 18.6 | 24.2 | 38.9 | 6.1 | 14.8 | 19.7 | 23.9 | 35.3 | 155. |
| 156. | Public administration | 6.0 | 13.2 | 17.9 | 22.3 | 40.3 | 6.5 | 16.5 | 20.5 | 24.1 | 32.1 | 156. |
| 157. | Postal serv. | 3.9 | 10.1 | 15.1 | 26.4 | 44.3 | 4.4 | 12.9 | 20.5 | 27.2 | 34.7 | 157. |
| 158. | Federal pub. admin. | 7.5 | 15.5 | 20.5 | 24.2 | 32.0 | 7.5 | 17.2 | 21.4 | 23.3 | 30.5 | 158. |
| 159. | State & local pub. admin. | 6.9 | 14.8 | 19.5 | 23.1 | 35.5 | 6.8 | 15.7 | 20.6 | 23.7 | 33.0 | 159. |

Source: Derived from Tables B-1 and B-2.

## TABLE B-4

### Derived Estimates for Wage Workers by Industry, 1939 and 1949

| | INDUSTRY | PERCENTAGE DISTRIBUTION OF ALL WORKERS 1939 (1) | 1949 (2) | MEAN INCOME OF ALL WORKERS 1939 (3) | 1949 (4) | DECILE RANK OF INDUSTRY BY MEAN INCOME 1939 (5) | 1949 (6) | PERCENTAGE CHANGE, 1939 TO 1949: Increase in Mean Income (7) | Decrease in Share of Total Received by Highest-Paid Fifth (+ = increase): Male (8) | Female (9) |
|---|---|---|---|---|---|---|---|---|---|---|
| 1. | Total | 100.0 | 100.0 | $1,124 | $2,554 | — | — | 127 | 15 | 12 |
| 2. | Agriculture, forestry, & fisheries | 6.5 | 3.5 | 396 | 1,197 | — | — | 202 | 4 | +5 |
| 3. | Agriculture | 6.3 | 3.3 | 382 | 1,156 | 1 | 1 | 203 | 4 | +4 |
| 4. | Forestry | 0.1 | 0.1 | 700 | 2,073 | 2 | 3 | 196 | 19 | 20 |
| 5. | Fisheries | 0.1 | 0.1 | 852 | 2,286 | 3 | 4 | 168 | — | — |
| 6. | Mining, extract., & quarry. | 2.6 | 2.0 | 1,106 | 2,861 | — | — | 159 | 12 | 10 |
| 7. | Metals | 0.3 | 0.2 | 1,282 | 3,065 | 6 | 7 | 139 | 14 | 15 |
| 8. | Coal | 1.6 | 1.1 | 909 | 2,505 | 3 | 4 | 176 | 7 | 8 |
| 9. | Crude petroleum & natl. gas | 0.5 | 0.5 | 1,658 | 3,697 | 10 | 10 | 123 | 8 | 7 |
| 10. | Nonmetals, exc. fuel | 0.2 | 0.2 | 932 | 2,663 | 4 | 6 | 186 | 15 | 16 |
| 11. | Construction | 6.0 | 6.6 | 967 | 2,649 | 4 | 5 | 174 | 12 | 10 |
| 12. | Manufacturing | 30.5 | 32.5 | 1,207 | 2,793 | — | — | 131 | 14 | 8 |
| 13. | Durable goods | 14.9 | 17.4 | 1,265 | 2,911 | — | — | 130 | 13 | 10 |
| 14. | Lumber & wood prod., exc. furn. | 2.1 | 1.7 | 780 | 1,949 | — | — | 150 | 5 | 3 |
| 15. | Logging | 0.4 | 0.3 | 621 | 1,804 | 2 | 2 | 190 | +2 | 10 |
| 16. | Saw & planing mills, & mill work | 1.3 | 1.2 | 775 | 1,957 | 2 | 2 | 153 | 5 | +1 |
| 17. | Misc. wood prod. | 0.4 | 0.2 | 986 | 2,138 | 5 | 3 | 117 | 10 | 4 |
| 18. | Furniture & fixtures | 0.6 | 0.7 | 1,018 | 2,422 | 5 | 4 | 138 | 9 | 13 |
| 19. | Stone, clay, & glass prod. | 1.0 | 1.0 | 1,184 | 2,759 | — | — | 133 | 15 | 11 |
| 20. | Glass & glass prod. | 0.3 | 0.3 | 1,255 | 2,809 | 6 | 6 | 124 | 13 | 8 |
| 21. | Cement, concrete, gypsum, & plaster prod. | 0.2 | 0.2 | 1,257 | 2,800 | 6 | 6 | 123 | 19 | 4 |
| 22. | Structural clay prod. | 0.2 | 0.2 | 973 | 2,587 | 5 | 5 | 166 | 13 | 3 |
| 23. | Pottery & rel. prod. | 0.1 | 0.1 | 1,100 | 2,407 | 5 | 4 | 119 | 10 | 7 |
| 24. | Misc. nonmet. min. & stone prod. | 0.2 | 0.2 | 1,283 | 3,025 | 6 | 7 | 136 | 14 | 11 |
| 25. | Metal industries | 4.5 | 4.6 | 1,338 | 3,021 | — | — | 126 | 13 | 14 |

continued on next page

TABLE B-4, continued

| | INDUSTRY | PERCENTAGE DISTRIBUTION OF ALL WORKERS | | MEAN INCOME OF ALL WORKERS | | DECILE RANK OF INDUSTRY BY MEAN INCOME | | PERCENTAGE CHANGE, 1939 TO 1949 | | |
|---|---|---|---|---|---|---|---|---|---|---|
| | | | | | | | | *Increase in Mean Income* | *Decrease in Share of Total Received by Highest-Paid Fifth (+ = increase)* | |
| | | *1939* | *1949* | *1939* | *1949* | *1939* | *1949* | | *Male* | *Female* |
| | | (1) | (2) | (3) | (4) | (5) | (6) | (7) | (8) | (9) |
| 26. | Iron & steel & their prod. | 3.8 | 3.9 | 1,344 | 3,029 | — | — | 125 | 14 | 15 |
| 27. | Blast furn., steel wks., & roll. mills | 1.7 | 1.6 | 1,409 | 3,129 | 7 | 8 | 122 | 15 | 17 |
| 28. | Oth. prim. iron, steel, & fab. steel prod. | 2.1 | 2.3 | 1,297 | 2,972 | 6 | 7 | 129 | 14 | 11 |
| 29. | Nonferrous metals & their prod. | 0.6 | 0.7 | 1,330 | 2,978 | 7 | 7 | 124 | 11 | 11 |
| 30. | Not spec. metal ind. | 0.1 | — | 1,300 | 3,154 | 7 | 8 | 143 | 7 | 21 |
| 31. | Machinery, exc. elec. | 2.1 | 2.9 | 1,480 | 3,248 | — | — | 119 | 12 | 7 |
| 32. | Agri. mach. & tractors | 0.3 | 0.4 | 1,387 | 3,067 | 7 | 7 | 121 | 11 | 6 |
| 33. | Office & store mach. & devices | 0.2 | 0.2 | 1,581 | 3,370 | 9 | 10 | 113 | 9 | 9 |
| 34. | Misc. mach. | 1.6 | 2.3 | 1,489 | 3,235 | 8 | 10 | 117 | 13 | 10 |
| 35. | Electrical machinery, equip., & supp. | 1.1 | 1.7 | 1,465 | 2,950 | 8 | 7 | 101 | 15 | 9 |
| 36. | Transportation equip. | 2.5 | 3.3 | 1,402 | 3,251 | — | — | 132 | 10 | 18 |
| 37. | Motor vehicles & motor veh. equip. | 1.7 | 2.1 | 1,414 | 3,246 | 7 | 10 | 130 | 8 | 16 |
| 38. | Aircraft & parts | 0.3 | 0.6 | 1,339 | 3,401 | 7 | 10 | 154 | 18 | 24 |
| 39. | Ship & boat bldg. & repair. | 0.4 | 0.4 | 1,455 | 3,060 | 8 | 7 | 110 | 10 | 14 |
| 40. | Railroad & misc. transp. equip. | 0.1 | 0.2 | 1,229 | 3,235 | 6 | 10 | 163 | 23 | 6 |
| 41. | Other durable goods | 1.0 | 1.5 | 1,185 | 2,686 | — | — | 127 | 12 | 11 |
| 42. | Professional & photo. equip. & supp. | 0.2 | 0.4 | 1,482 | 3,138 | 8 | 8 | 112 | 9 | 14 |
| 43. | Watches, clocks, & misc. mfg. ind. | 0.8 | 1.1 | 1,103 | 2,518 | 5 | 5 | 128 | 14 | 6 |
| 44. | Nondurable goods | 15.6 | 15.1 | 1,148 | 2,673 | — | — | 133 | 12 | 9 |
| 45. | Food & kindred prod. | 3.0 | 3.2 | 1,250 | 2,680 | — | — | 114 | 13 | 11 |
| 46. | Meat prod. | 0.6 | 0.6 | 1,332 | 2,790 | 7 | 6 | 109 | 11 | 4 |
| 47. | Dairy prod. | 0.3 | 0.4 | 1,307 | 2,773 | 7 | 6 | 112 | 12 | 7 |
| 48. | Can. & preserv. fruit, veg., & sea food | 0.3 | 0.4 | 774 | 1,908 | 2 | 2 | 147 | 18 | 7 |
| 49. | Grain mill prod. | 0.2 | 0.3 | 1,299 | 2,829 | 7 | 6 | 118 | 14 | 9 |
| 50. | Bakery prod. | 0.7 | 0.6 | 1,253 | 2,798 | 6 | 6 | 123 | 6 | 8 |
| 51. | Confectionery & rel. prod. | 0.2 | 0.2 | 935 | 2,303 | 4 | 4 | 146 | 11 | 10 |
| 52. | Beverage ind. | 0.4 | 0.4 | 1,506 | 3.067 | 8 | 7 | 104 | 14 | 19 |
| 53. | Misc. food prep. & not spec. food ind. | 0.3 | 0.3 | 1,281 | 2,689 | 6 | 6 | 110 | 16 | 12 |

continued on next page

TABLE B-4, continued

| | Industry | Percentage Distribution of All Workers 1939 (1) | 1949 (2) | Mean Income of All Workers 1939 (3) | 1949 (4) | Decile Rank of Industry by Mean Income 1939 (5) | 1949 (6) | Percentage Change, 1939 to 1949: Increase in Mean Income (7) | Decrease in Share of Total Received by Highest-Paid Fifth (+ = increase): Male (8) | Female (9) |
|---|---|---|---|---|---|---|---|---|---|---|
| 54. | Tobacco manufactures | 0.2 | 0.2 | 835 | 1,960 | 3 | 2 | 135 | 14 | 2 |
| 55. | Textile mill prod. | 3.4 | 2.7 | 858 | 2,279 | — | — | 166 | 14 | 6 |
| 56. | Knitting mills | 0.6 | 0.4 | 852 | 2,115 | 3 | 3 | 148 | 8 | +3 |
| 57. | Dyeing & fin. tex. exc. knit goods | 0.1 | 0.1 | 1,000 | 2,818 | 5 | 6 | 182 | 8 | 22 |
| 58. | Carpets, rugs, & oth. floor cov. | 0.1 | 0.1 | 1,170 | 2,919 | 6 | 7 | 149 | 12 | 8 |
| 59. | Yarn, thread, & fabric mills | 2.4 | 2.0 | 813 | 2,220 | 3 | 3 | 173 | 14 | 6 |
| 60. | Misc. tex. mill prod. | 0.2 | 0.1 | 1,053 | 2,519 | 5 | 5 | 139 | 12 | 8 |
| 61. | Apparel & oth. fab. tex. prod. | 2.3 | 2.4 | 830 | 2,026 | — | — | 144 | 8 | 9 |
| 62. | Apparel & access. | 2.2 | 2.2 | 828 | 2,023 | 3 | 2 | 144 | 6 | 8 |
| 63. | Misc. fab. tex. prod. | 0.1 | 0.2 | 848 | 2,103 | 3 | 3 | 148 | 21 | 8 |
| 64. | Paper & all. prod. | 0.9 | 1.1 | 1,251 | 2,858 | — | — | 128 | 15 | 14 |
| 65. | Pulp, paper, & paperboard mills | 0.6 | 0.5 | 1,293 | 2,978 | 6 | 7 | 130 | 16 | 17 |
| 66. | Paperboard cont. & boxes | 0.2 | 0.3 | 1,108 | 2,655 | 5 | 6 | 140 | 17 | 9 |
| 67. | Misc. paper & pulp prod. | 0.1 | 0.3 | 1,283 | 2,824 | 6 | 6 | 120 | 16 | 13 |
| 68. | Printing, publ., & all. ind. | 1.7 | 1.8 | 1,585 | 3,210 | 9 | 9 | 103 | 7 | 6 |
| 69. | Chemicals & all. prod. | 1.3 | 1.4 | 1,524 | 3,313 | — | — | 117 | 17 | 14 |
| 70. | Synthetic fibers | 0.2 | 0.1 | 1,259 | 2,891 | 6 | 7 | 130 | 10 | 11 |
| 71. | Paints, varn., & rel. prod. | 0.1 | 0.1 | 1,814 | 3,268 | 10 | 10 | 80 | 16 | 13 |
| 72. | Drugs, med., & misc. chem. & all. prod. | 1.0 | 1.2 | 1,521 | 3,351 | 8 | 10 | 120 | 17 | 15 |
| 73. | Petroleum & coal prod. | 0.6 | 0.7 | 1,886 | 4,058 | — | — | 115 | 12 | 7 |
| 74. | Petro. refining | 0.5 | 0.6 | 1,952 | 4,156 | 10 | 10 | 113 | 11 | 7 |
| 75. | Misc. petro. & coal prod. | 0.1 | 0.1 | 1,440 | 3,250 | 8 | 10 | 126 | 16 | +14 |
| 76. | Rubber prod. | 0.5 | 0.5 | 1,410 | 3,033 | 7 | 7 | 115 | 16 | 9 |
| 77. | Leather & leather prod. | 1.2 | 0.8 | 910 | 2,143 | — | — | 135 | 12 | 5 |
| 78. | Leather: tanned, curried, & fin. | 0.2 | 0.1 | 1,161 | 2,792 | 6 | 6 | 140 | 3 | 10 |
| 79. | Footwear, exc. rubber. | 0.8 | 0.6 | 846 | 2,030 | 3 | 3 | 140 | 11 | 4 |
| 80. | Leather prod., exc. footwear | 0.2 | 0.1 | 940 | 2,154 | 4 | 3 | 129 | 16 | 4 |
| 81. | Not spec. mfg. ind. | 0.5 | 0.3 | 1,218 | 2,775 | 6 | 6 | 128 | 6 | 9 |

continued on next page

| | Industry | Percentage Distribution of All Workers 1939 (1) | 1949 (2) | Mean Income of All Workers 1939 (3) | 1949 (4) | Decile Rank of Industry by Mean Income 1939 (5) | 1949 (6) | Percentage Change, 1939 to 1949: Increase in Mean Income (7) | Decrease in Share of Total Received by Highest-Paid Fifth (+ = increase): Male (8) | Female (9) |
|---|---|---|---|---|---|---|---|---|---|---|
| 82. | Transportation, commun., & oth. pub. util. | 8.9 | 9.6 | 1,515 | 3,016 | — | — | 99 | 13 | 7 |
| 83. | Transportation | 6.2 | 6.3 | 1,460 | 3,059 | — | — | 110 | 13 | 9 |
| 84. | Railroads & railway exp. serv. | 3.4 | 3.2 | 1,617 | 3,199 | 9 | 8 | 98 | 14 | 13 |
| 85. | St. railways & bus lines | 0.6 | 0.7 | 1,570 | 3,056 | 9 | 7 | 95 | 4 | +7 |
| 86. | Trucking serv. | 0.9 | 1.1 | 1,129 | 2,810 | 5 | 6 | 149 | 15 | 5 |
| 87. | Warehousing & storage | 0.2 | 0.2 | 1,076 | 2,489 | 5 | 4 | 131 | 18 | 8 |
| 88. | Taxicab serv. | 0.2 | 0.3 | 836 | 2,007 | 3 | 2 | 140 | 7 | 19 |
| 89. | Water transp. | 0.6 | 0.5 | 1,259 | 3,113 | 6 | 8 | 147 | 10 | 13 |
| 90. | Air transp. | 0.1 | 0.2 | 1,783 | 3,862 | 10 | 10 | 117 | 11 | 10 |
| 91. | Petro. & gas. pipe lines | 0.1 | — | 1,579 | 3,750 | 9 | 10 | 137 | 7 | +6 |
| 92. | Serv. incid. to transp. | 0.1 | 0.1 | 1,321 | 3,028 | 7 | 7 | 129 | 4 | +1 |
| 93. | Telecommunications | 1.1 | 1.5 | 1,574 | 2,810 | — | — | 79 | 14 | 9 |
| 94. | Telephone, wire & radio | 0.9 | 1.4 | 1,627 | 2,813 | 10 | 6 | 73 | 8 | 7 |
| 95. | Telegraph, wire & radio | 0.2 | 0.1 | 1,304 | 2,933 | 7 | 7 | 125 | 21 | 15 |
| 96. | Utilities & sanitary serv. | 1.6 | 1.8 | 1,685 | 3,085 | — | — | 83 | 9 | 2 |
| 97. | Elec. light, power, gas, & oth. util. | 1.0 | 1.1 | 1,813 | 3,291 | 10 | 10 | 82 | 10 | 3 |
| 98. | Gas & steam supply systems | 0.3 | 0.3 | 1,600 | 3,103 | 9 | 7 | 94 | 9 | 1 |
| 99. | Water supply & san. serv. | 0.3 | 0.4 | 1,390 | 2,523 | 7 | 5 | 82 | 9 | +1 |
| 100. | Wholesale & retail trade | 16.5 | 18.5 | 1,084 | 2,389 | — | — | 120 | 7 | 2 |
| 101. | Wholesale trade | 3.0 | 3.9 | 1,579 | 3,213 | 9 | 9 | 103 | 9 | 7 |
| 112. | Retail trade, stores | 13.5 | 14.6 | 971 | 2,163 | — | — | 123 | 4 | +2 |
| 113. | Food, exc. dairy prod. | 2.2 | 2.3 | 930 | 2,111 | 4 | 3 | 127 | 3 | 1 |
| 114. | Dairy prod. & milk retail | 0.4 | 0.3 | 1,371 | 2,912 | 7 | 7 | 112 | 9 | 3 |
| 115. | Genl. merchandise | 1.9 | 1.8 | 964 | 2,100 | 4 | 3 | 118 | 4 | 2 |
| 116. | Five & ten cent | 0.2 | 0.2 | 1,190 | 2,609 | 2 | 1 | 100 | 1 | +14 |
| 117. | Apparel & acc., exc. shoe | 0.9 | 0.9 | 1,006 | 2,248 | 5 | 3 | 123 | +2 | — |
| 118. | Shoe | 0.2 | 0.4 | 688 | 1,374 | 6 | 5 | 119 | +3 | +2 |
| 119. | Furniture & housefurn. | 0.4 | 0.5 | 1,298 | 2,718 | 6 | 6 | 109 | 9 | 3 |

continued on next page

TABLE B-4, continued

| | INDUSTRY | PERCENTAGE DISTRIBUTION OF ALL WORKERS | | MEAN INCOME OF ALL WORKERS | | DECILE RANK OF INDUSTRY BY MEAN INCOME | | PERCENTAGE CHANGE, 1939 TO 1949 | | |
|---|---|---|---|---|---|---|---|---|---|---|
| | | | | | | | | Increase in Mean Income | Decrease in Share of Total Received by Highest-Paid Fifth (+ = increase) | |
| | | 1939 (1) | 1949 (2) | 1939 (3) | 1949 (4) | 1939 (5) | 1949 (6) | (7) | Male (8) | Female (9) |
| 120. | Household appl. & radio | 0.2 | 0.4 | 1,239 | 2,623 | 6 | 5 | 112 | 4 | 3 |
| 121. | Motor vehicles & acc. | 0.8 | 1.0 | **1,396** | **3,166** | 7 | 8 | 127 | 1 | +3 |
| 122. | Gas. serv. stations | 0.7 | 0.6 | 824 | 1,945 | 3 | 2 | 136 | 7 | 5 |
| 123. | Drug | 0.5 | 0.5 | 943 | 1,864 | 4 | 2 | 98 | +5 | +8 |
| 124. | Eating & drinking places | 2.5 | 2.8 | 667 | 1,522 | 2 | 1 | 128 | 4 | +3 |
| 125. | Hardware & farm impl. | 0.3 | 0.4 | 1,146 | 2,488 | 6 | 4 | 117 | 7 | 9 |
| 126. | Lumber & bldg. material retail | 0.6 | 0.7 | 1,279 | 2,831 | 6 | 6 | 121 | 7 | 1 |
| 127. | Liquor | 0.1 | 0.1 | 1,241 | 2,545 | 6 | 5 | 105 | 2 | 15 |
| 128. | Florists | 0.1 | 0.1 | 870 | 1,833 | 3 | 2 | 111 | 1 | +1 |
| 129. | Jewelry | 0.1 | 0.2 | 1,359 | 2,614 | 7 | 5 | 92 | +1 | +10 |
| 130. | Fuel & ice | 0.4 | 0.3 | 1,064 | 2,557 | 5 | 5 | 140 | 12 | 4 |
| 131. | Misc. retail | 0.6 | 0.7 | 1,095 | 2,438 | 5 | 4 | 123 | 2 | +3 |
| 132. | Not spec. retail | 0.4 | 0.4 | 945 | 2,191 | 4 | 3 | 132 | — | 5 |
| 133. | Finance, insurance, & real estate | 3.7 | 3.7 | 1,729 | 3,002 | — | — | 74 | 9 | 4 |
| 134. | Bank & cred. agenc. & commod. brok. | 1.3 | 1.3 | 2,017 | 3,187 | 10 | 8 | 58 | 5 | 3 |
| 135. | Insurance | 1.3 | 1.5 | 1,910 | 3,213 | 10 | 9 | 68 | 9 | 2 |
| 136. | Real estate, incl. real est. ins. law off. | 1.1 | 0.9 | 1,145 | 2,358 | 5 | 4 | 106 | 5 | 2 |
| 137. | Business & repair serv. | 1.8 | 2.2 | 1,156 | 2,735 | — | — | 137 | 10 | 7 |
| 138. | Advertising | 0.2 | 0.2 | 2,000 | 4,062 | 10 | 10 | 103 | 8 | 3 |
| 139. | Account. audit., bookkeep., & misc. bus. serv. | 0.3 | 0.5 | 1,355 | 2,944 | 7 | 7 | 117 | 11 | 8 |
| 140. | Auto. repair serv. & garages | 1.1 | 1.1 | 987 | 2,456 | 5 | 4 | 149 | 7 | 6 |
| 141. | Misc. repair serv. | 0.2 | 0.4 | 1,000 | 2,513 | 5 | 5 | 151 | 12 | 17 |
| 142. | Personal serv. | 9.5 | 6.3 | 502 | 1,242 | — | — | 147 | 4 | — |
| 143. | Private households | 6.3 | 3.3 | 354 | 785 | 1 | 1 | 123 | — | 6 |
| 144. | Hotels & lodging places | 1.2 | 1.0 | 738 | 1,616 | 2 | 1 | 119 | 6 | 6 |
| 145. | Laund., clean., & dyeing | 1.1 | 1.3 | 833 | 1,825 | 3 | 2 | 119 | 8 | +1 |
| 146. | Dress & shoe rep. shops & misc. pers. serv. | 0.9 | 0.7 | 815 | 1,854 | 2 | 2 | 127 | 7 | +4 |

continued on next page

TABLE B-4, concluded

| | Industry | Percentage Distribution of All Workers 1939 (1) | 1949 (2) | Mean Income of All Workers 1939 (3) | 1949 (4) | Decile Rank of Industry by Mean Income 1939 (5) | 1949 (6) | Percentage Change, 1939 to 1949: Increase in Mean Income (7) | Decrease in Share of Total Received by Highest-Paid Fifth (+ = increase): Male (8) | Female (9) |
|---|---|---|---|---|---|---|---|---|---|---|
| 147. | Entertain. & recr. | 1.2 | 1.0 | 1,308 | 2,609 | — | — | 99 | 4 | 2 |
| 148. | Radio broad. & television | 0.1 | 0.1 | 2,167 | 4,183 | 10 | 10 | 93 | 4 | 13 |
| 149. | Theaters & motion pict. | 0.5 | 0.4 | 1,619 | 2,865 | 9 | 7 | 77 | 1 | +1 |
| 150. | Bowl. all., bill. & pool parl., misc. ent. | 0.6 | 0.5 | 925 | 1,969 | 3 | 2 | 113 | 1 | 1 |
| 151. | Professional & rel. serv. | 7.5 | 8.7 | 1,290 | 2,332 | — | — | 81 | 12 | 11 |
| 152. | Medical & oth. health | 1.9 | 2.8 | 926 | 1,970 | 3 | 2 | 113 | 10 | 6 |
| 153. | Educational | 4.2 | 4.3 | 1,416 | 2,484 | 8 | 4 | 75 | 15 | 12 |
| 154. | Welfare, relig., & nonprofit | 0.9 | 1.1 | 1,327 | 2,276 | 7 | 3 | 72 | 9 | 7 |
| 155. | Legal, eng., arch. & misc. prof. serv. | 0.5 | 0.5 | 1,741 | 3,271 | 10 | 10 | 88 | 10 | 9 |
| 156. | Public administration | 5.1 | 5.7 | 1,699 | 3,036 | — | — | 79 | 17 | 20 |
| 157. | Postal serv. | 0.9 | 1.1 | 1,845 | 3,106 | 10 | 8 | 68 | 2 | 22 |
| 158. | Federal pub. admin. | 1.7 | 2.3 | 1,476 | 3,222 | 8 | 9 | 118 | 29 | 5 |
| 159. | State & local pub. admin. | 2.5 | 2.3 | 1,751 | 2,833 | 10 | 6 | 62 | 14 | 7 |

Source: Derived from Tables B-1, B-2, and B-3.

TABLE B-5

Industries Ranked by Mean Wage Income of All Workers, 1939 and 1949

| *1939* | *1949* |
|---|---|
| *Lowest Tenth* | |
| Agriculture (3)<br>Private households (143) | Agriculture (3)<br>Five and ten cent stores (116)<br>Eating and drinking places (124)<br>Private households (143)<br>Hotels and lodging places (144) |
| *Second Tenth* | |
| Forestry (4)<br>Logging (15)<br>Sawmills (16)<br>Canning and preserving (48)<br>Yarn, thread, and fabric mills (59)<br>Five and ten cent stores (116)<br>Eating and drinking places (124)<br>Hotels and lodging places (144)<br>Dressmaking shops (146) | Logging (15)<br>Sawmills (16)<br>Canning and preserving (48)<br>Tobacco manufacturing (54)<br>Apparel and accessories manufacturing (62)<br>Taxicab service (88)<br>Gasoline service stations (122)<br>Drug stores (123)<br>Retail florists (128)<br>Laundering, cleaning (145)<br>Dressmaking shops (146)<br>Bowling alleys and miscellaneous entertainment (150)<br>Medical and other health services (152) |
| *Third Tenth* | |
| Fisheries (5)<br>Coal mining (8)<br>Tobacco manufacturing (54)<br>Knitting mills (56)<br>Apparel and accessories manufacturing (62)<br>Miscellaneous fabricated textile products (63)<br>Footwear excluding rubber (79)<br>Taxicab service (88)<br>Gasoline service stations (122)<br>Retail florists (128)<br>Laundering, cleaning (145)<br>Bowling alleys and miscellaneous entertainment (150)<br>Medicine and other health services (152) | Forestry (4)<br>Miscellaneous wood products (17)<br>Knitting mills (56)<br>Yarn, thread, and fabric mills (59)<br>Miscellaneous fabricated textile products (63)<br>Footwear excluding rubber (79)<br>Leather products, excluding footwear (80)<br>Food stores excluding dairy products (113)<br>General merchandise stores (115)<br>Apparel and accessories stores (117)<br>Not specified retail trade (132)<br>Welfare and related services (154) |
| *Fourth Tenth* | |
| Nonmetallic mining and quarrying excluding fuel (10)<br>Construction (11)<br>Confectionery and related products (51)<br>Leather products, excluding footwear (80) | Fisheries (5)<br>Coal mining (8)<br>Furniture and fixtures (18)<br>Pottery and related products (23)<br>Confectionery and related products (51)<br>Warehousing and storage (87) |

continued on next page

TABLE B-5, continued

| 1939 | 1949 |
|---|---|
| Food stores excluding dairy products (113)<br>General merchandise stores (115)<br>Drug stores (123)<br>Not specified retail trade (132) | Hardware and farm implements (125)<br>Miscellaneous retail stores (131)<br>Real estate (136)<br>Auto repair service and garages (140)<br>Educational services (153) |
| *Fifth Tenth* | |
| Miscellaneous wood products (17)<br>Furniture and fixtures (18)<br>Structural clay products (22)<br>Pottery and related products (23)<br>Watches, clocks, and miscellaneous manufactures (43)<br>Dyeing and finishing textiles (57)<br>Miscellaneous textile mill products (60)<br>Paperboard containers and boxes (66)<br>Trucking service (86)<br>Warehousing and storage (87)<br>Apparel and accessories stores (117)<br>Fuel and ice retailing (130)<br>Miscellaneous retail stores (131)<br>Real estate (136)<br>Auto repair service and garages (140)<br>Miscellaneous repair services (141) | Construction (11)<br>Structural clay products (22)<br>Watches, clocks, and miscellaneous manufactures (43)<br>Miscellaneous textile mill products (60)<br>Water supply and sanitary service (99)<br>Shoe stores (118)<br>Household appliance and radio stores (120)<br>Liquor stores (127)<br>Jewelry stores (129)<br>Fuel and ice retailing (130)<br>Miscellaneous repair services (141) |
| *Sixth Tenth* | |
| Metal mining (7)<br>Glass and glass products (20)<br>Cement, concrete, gypsum and plaster products (21)<br>Miscellaneous nonmetallic mineral and stone products (24)<br>Other primary iron and steel industries and fabricated steel (28)<br>Railroad and miscellaneous transportation equipment (40)<br>Bakery products (50)<br>Miscellaneous food preparation (53)<br>Carpets and rugs (58)<br>Pulp, paper and paperboard mills (65)<br>Miscellaneous paper and pulp products (67)<br>Synthetic fibers (70)<br>Leather; tanned, curried and finished (78)<br>Not specified manufacturing industries (81)<br>Water transportation (89)<br>Shoe stores (118)<br>Furniture and house furnishings stores (119) | Nonmetallic mining and quarrying, excluding fuel (10)<br>Glass and glass products (20)<br>Cement, concrete, gypsum, and plaster products (21)<br>Meat products (46)<br>Dairy products (47)<br>Grain mill products (49)<br>Bakery products (50)<br>Miscellaneous food preparation (53)<br>Dyeing and finishing textiles (57)<br>Paperboard containers and boxes (66)<br>Miscellaneous paper and pulp products (67)<br>Leather; tanned, curried and finished (78)<br>Not specified manufacturing industries (81)<br>Trucking service (86)<br>Telephone (94)<br>Furniture and house furnishings stores (119)<br>Lumber and building material retailing (126)<br>State and local public administration (159) |

continued on next page

TABLE B-5, continued

| *1939* | *1949* |
|---|---|
| Household appliance and radio stores (120) | |
| Hardware and farm implements (125) | |
| Lumber and building material retailing (126) | |
| Liquor stores (127) | |
| *Seventh Tenth* | |
| Blast furnaces, steel works, and rolling mills (27) | Metal mining (7) |
| Nonferrous metals and their products (29) | Miscellaneous nonmetal mining and stone products (24) |
| Not specified metal industries (30) | Other primary iron and steel industries and fabricated steel (28) |
| Agricultural machinery and tractors (32) | Nonferrous metals and their products (29) |
| Motor vehicles and motor vehicle equipment (37) | Agricultural machinery and tractors (32) |
| Aircraft and parts manufacturing (38) | Electrical machine equipment and supplies (35) |
| Meat products (46) | Ship and boat building (39) |
| Dairy products (47) | Beverage industries (52) |
| Grain mill products (49) | Carpets and rugs (58) |
| Rubber products (76) | Pulp, paper, and paperboard mills (65) |
| Services incidental to transportation (92) | Synthetic fibers (70) |
| Telegraph (95) | Rubber products (76) |
| Water supply and sanitary services (99) | Street railways and bus lines (85) |
| Dairy products stores (114) | Telegraph (95) |
| Motor vehicles and accessories retailing (121) | Services incidental to transportation (92) |
| Jewelry stores (129) | Gas and steam supply systems (98) |
| Accounting, auditing, bookkeeping, and miscellaneous business service (139) | Dairy products stores (114) |
| Welfare and related services (154) | Accounting, auditing, bookkeeping and miscellaneous business service (139) |
| | Theaters and motion pictures (149) |
| *Eighth Tenth* | |
| Miscellaneous machinery (34) | Blast furnaces, steel works and rolling mills (27) |
| Electrical machine equipment and supplies (35) | Not specified metal industries (30) |
| Ship and boat building (39) | Professional and photographic equipment (42) |
| Professional and photographic equipment (42) | Railroads and railway express services (84) |
| Beverage industries (52) | Water transportation (89) |
| Drugs, medicines, and miscellaneous chemicals (72) | Motor vehicles and accessories retailing (121) |
| Miscellaneous petroleum and coal products (75) | Banking and credit agencies (134) |
| Educational services (153) | Postal service (157) |
| Federal public administration (158) | |
| *Ninth Tenth* | |
| Office and store machinery and devices (33) | Printing, publishing, and allied industries (68) |

continued on next page

TABLE B-5, concluded

| *1939* | *1949* |
|---|---|
| Printing, publishing, and allied industries (68) | Wholesale trade (101) |
| Railroads and railway express service (84) | Insurance (135) |
| Street railway and bus lines (85) | Federal public administration (158) |
| Petroleum and gas pipe lines (91) | |
| Gas and steam supply systems (98) | |
| Wholesale trade (101) | |
| Theaters and motion pictures (149) | |
| *Highest Tenth* | |
| Crude petroleum and natural gas extraction (9) | Crude petroleum and natural gas extraction (9) |
| Paints, varnishes, and related products (71) | Office and store machinery and devices (33) |
| Petroleum refining (74) | Miscellaneous machinery (34) |
| Air transportation (90) | Motor vehicles and motor vehicle equipment (37) |
| Telephone (94) | Aircraft and parts manufacturing (38) |
| Electric light and power and other utilities (97) | Railroad and miscellaneous transportation equipment manufacturing (40) |
| Banking and credit agencies (134) | Paints, varnish, and related products (71) |
| Insurance (135) | Drugs, medicines, and miscellaneous chemicals (72) |
| Advertising (138) | Petroleum refining (74) |
| Radio broadcasting (148) | Miscellaneous petroleum and coal products (75) |
| Legal, engineering, and architectural services (155) | Air transportation (90) |
| Postal service (157) | Petroleum and gas pipe lines (91) |
| State and local public administration (159) | Electric light and power and other utilities (97) |
| | Advertising (138) |
| | Radio broadcasting (148) |
| | Legal, engineering, and architectural services (155) |

Source: Derived from Table B-4.

TABLE B-6

Industries Ranked by Dispersion [$(Q_3 - Q_1) / Q_2$] of Wage Income of Male Workers, 1939 and 1949

| *1939* | *1949* |
|---|---|
| *Lowest Tenth* | |
| Crude petroleum and natural gas extraction (9) | Blast furnaces, steel works and rolling mills (27) |
| Pottery and related products (23) | Agricultural machinery and tractors (32) |
| Nonferrous metals and their products (29) | Motor vehicle and motor vehicle equipment (37) |
| Agricultural machinery and tractors (32) | Aircraft and parts (38) |
| Motor vehicles and motor vehicle equipment (37) | Railroad and miscellaneous transportation equipment (40) |
| Meat products (46) | Synthetic fibers (70) |
| Carpets, rugs, and other floor coverings (58) | Petroleum refining (74) |
| Pulp, paper, and paperboard mills (65) | Rubber products (76) |
| Synthetic fibers (70) | Street railways and bus lines (85) |
| Petroleum refining (74) | Petroleum and gasoline pipe lines (91) |
| Leather: tanned, curried and finished (78) | Postal service (157) |
| Street railways and bus lines (85) | |
| Electric light and power, electric gas and other not specified utilities (97) | |
| Gas and steam supply systems (98) | |
| Postal service (157) | |
| *Second Tenth* | |
| Glass and glass products (20) | Metal mining (7) |
| Blast furnaces, steel works, and rolling mills (27) | Crude petroleum and natural gas extraction (9) |
| Office and store machines and devices (33) | Miscellaneous machinery (34) |
| Professional and photographic equipment and supplies (42) | Ship and boat building and repairing (39) |
| Bakery products (50) | Meat products (46) |
| Dyeing and finishing textiles, exclusive of knit goods (57) | Dyeing and finishing textiles except knit goods (57) |
| Yarn, thread and fabric mills (59) | Pulp, paper, and paperboard mills (65) |
| Paints, varnishes, and related products (71) | Miscellaneous petroleum and coal products (75) |
| Miscellaneous petroleum and coal products (75) | Gas and steam supply systems (98) |
| Rubber products (76) | State and local public administration (159) |
| Petroleum and gasoline pipe lines (91) | |
| Telephone (wire and radio) (94) | |
| Liquor stores (127) | |
| State and local public administration (159) | |
| *Third Tenth* | |
| Metal mining (7) | Other primary iron and steel and fabricated steel products (28) |
| Cement, and concrete, gypsum, and | |

continued on next page

TABLE B-6, continued

| *1939* | *1949* |
|---|---|
| plaster products (21) | Nonferrous metals and their products (29) |
| Other primary iron and steel and fabricated steel products (28) | Office and store machines and devices (33) |
| Not specified metal industries (30) | Electrical machinery equipment and supplies (35) |
| Miscellaneous machinery (34) | Professional and photographic equipment and supplies (42) |
| Electrical machinery, equipment and supplies (35) | Carpets, rugs, and other floor coverings (58) |
| Dairy products (47) | Paints, varnishes and related products (71) |
| Miscellaneous textile mill products (60) | Leather: tanned, curried, and finished (78) |
| Paperboard containers and boxes (66) | Railroads and railway express service (84) |
| Footwear, except rubber (79) | Electric light and power, electric gas and other not specified utilities (97) |
| Taxicab service (88) | |
| Water supply and sanitary services (99) | |
| Hardware and farm implement stores (125) | |
| *Fourth Tenth* | |
| Coal mining (8) | Coal mining (8) |
| Structural clay products (22) | Glass and glass products (20) |
| Miscellaneous nonmetallic mineral and stone products (24) | Cement, and concrete, gypsum, and plaster products (21) |
| Aircraft and parts (38) | Pottery and related products (23) |
| Miscellaneous paper and pulp products (67) | Miscellaneous nonmetallic mineral and stone products (24) |
| Not specified manufacturing industries (81) | Dairy products (47) |
| Railroads and railway express service (84) | Beverage industries (52) |
| Household appliance and radio stores (120) | Yarn, thread and fabric mills (59) |
| Motor vehicles and accessories retailing (121) | Miscellaneous textile mill products (60) |
| | Miscellaneous paper and pulp products (67) |
| | Drugs, medicine and miscellaneous chemicals and allied products (72) |
| | Air transportation (90) |
| | Services incidental to transportation (92) |
| | Telephone (wire and radio) (94) |
| | Water supply and sanitary services (99) |
| | Federal public administration (158) |
| *Fifth Tenth* | |
| Furniture and fixtures (18) | Structural clay products (22) |
| Ship and boat buildings and repairing (39) | Not specified metal industries (30) |
| Watches, clocks, and miscellaneous manufacturing industries (43) | Watches, clocks, and miscellaneous manufacturing industries (43) |
| Grain-mill products (49) | Grain mill products (49) |
| Confectionery and related products (51) | Bakery products (50) |
| Beverage industries (52) | Confectionery and related products (51) |
| | Miscellaneous food preparations and |

continued on next page

TABLE B-6, continued

| *1939* | *1949* |
|---|---|
| Leather products, except footwear (77) | kindred products and food industries not specified (53) |
| Services incidental to transportation (92) | Paperboard containers and boxes (66) |
| Dairy products stores and milk retailing (114) | Footwear, except rubber (79) |
| General merchandise stores (115) | Not specified manufacturing industries (81) |
| Shoe stores (118) | Trucking service (86) |
| Furniture and housefurnishings stores (119) | Warehousing and storage (87) |
| Lumber and building material retailing (126) | Wholesale trade (101) |
| Banking and credit agencies and security and commodity brokers companies (134) | Dairy products stores and milk retailing (114) |
| Real estate, including real estate insurance-law offices (136) | Motor vehicles and accessories retailing (121) |
| Laundering, cleaning and dyeing service (145) | Hardware and farm implement stores (125) |
| | Liquor stores (127) |
| *Sixth Tenth* | |
| Miscellaneous wood products (17) | Nonmetallic mining and quarrying except fuel (10) |
| Railroads and miscellaneous transportation equipment (40) | Furniture and fixtures (18) |
| Miscellaneous food preparations and kindred products and not specified food industries (53) | Tobacco manufacturers (54) |
| Knitting mills (56) | Miscellaneous fabricated textile products (63) |
| Apparel and accessories (62) | Leather products (77) |
| Drugs, medicine, and miscellaneous chemicals and allied products (72) | Taxicab service (88) |
| Air transportation (90) | Water transportation (89) |
| Apparel and accessories stores, except shoe stores (117) | Telegraph (wire and radio) (95) |
| Retail florists (128) | Lumber and building material retailing (126) |
| Jewelry stores (129) | Fuel and ice retailing (130) |
| Miscellaneous retail stores (131) | Banking and credit agencies and security and commodity brokers companies (134) |
| Insurance (135) | Insurance (135) |
| Automobile repair services and garages (140) | Accounting, auditing, bookkeeping and miscellaneous business services (139) |
| Dressmaking and shoe repair shops and miscellaneous personal services (146) | Automobile repair services and garages (140) |
| Medical and other health services (152) | Miscellaneous repair services (141) |
| *Seventh Tenth* | |
| Trucking service (86) | Miscellaneous wood products (17) |
| Wholesale trade (101) | Knitting mills (56) |
| Food stores, except dairy products (113) | Apparel and accessories (62) |
| Eating and drinking places (124) | General-merchandise stores (115) |
| Welfare and religious services and nonprofit member organizations (154) | Apparel and accessories stores, except shoe stores (117) |
| | Shoe stores (118) |
| | Furniture and house furnishings stores (119) |

continued on next page

TABLE B-6, continued

| 1939 | 1949 |
|---|---|
| | Household appliance and radio stores (120)<br>Jewelry stores (129)<br>Miscellaneous retail stores (131)<br>Real estate, including real estate-insurance-law offices (136)<br>Laundering, cleaning and dyeing services (152)<br>Medical and other health services (153)<br>Educational services (153) |
| *Eighth Tenth* | |
| Nonmetallic mining and quarrying except fuel (10)<br>Tobacco manufactures (54)<br>Miscellaneous fabricated textile products (63)<br>Printing, publishing and allied industries (68)<br>Warehousing and storage (87)<br>Water transportation (89)<br>Five and ten cent stores (116)<br>Gasoline service stations (122)<br>Fuel and ice retailing (130)<br>Not specified retail trade (132)<br>Accounting, auditing, bookkeeping and miscellaneous business services (139)<br>Miscellaneous repair services (141)<br>Hotels and lodging places (144)<br>Radio broadcasting and television (148)<br>Educational services (153) | Construction (11)<br>Dressmaking and shoe repair shops and miscellaneous personal services (146) |
| *Ninth Tenth* | |
| Agriculture (3)<br>Logging (15)<br>Sawmills, planing mills and mill work (16)<br>Legal, engineering and architectural services and miscellaneous professional services (155) | Canning and preserving fruits, vegetables and sea food (48)<br>Printing, publishing, and allied industries (68)<br>Food stores, except dairy products (113)<br>Gasoline service stations (122)<br>Eating and drinking places (124)<br>Retail florists (128)<br>Not specified retail trade (132)<br>Advertising (138)<br>Hotels and lodging places (144)<br>Radio broadcasting and television (148)<br>Legal, engineering and architectural services and miscellaneous professional services (155) |
| *Highest Tenth* | |
| Forestry (4)<br>Fisheries (5) | Agriculture (3)<br>Forestry (4) |

continued on next page

TABLE B-6, concluded

| *1939* | *1949* |
|---|---|
| Construction (11) | Fisheries (5) |
| Canning and preserving fruits, vegetables and sea foods (48) | Logging (15) |
| Telegraph, wire and radio (95) | Sawmills, planing mills, and mill work (16) |
| Drug stores (123) | Five and ten cent stores (116) |
| Advertising (138) | Drug stores (123) |
| Private households (143) | Private households (143) |
| Theaters and motion pictures (149) | Theaters and motion pictures (149) |
| Bowling alleys, billiard and pool parlors and miscellaneous entertainment and recreation services (150) | Bowling alleys, billiard and pool parlors and miscellaneous entertainment and recreation services (150) |
| Federal public administration (158) | Welfare and religious services and nonprofit member organizations (154) |

# COMMENT

PAUL R. KERSCHBAUM, BUREAU OF LABOR STATISTICS

Everyone who has examined earnings or wage statistics will readily agree that income trends, both secular and during the forties, were in the direction of narrowed differentials of all kinds: occupational, interplant, interindustry, and interregional. The difficulty lies in the development of an analysis of the myriad forces that account for it and in placing a value on each factor. An analysis based on aggregates of one sort or another will most likely neglect a variety of forces—forces often contending for supremacy, often indeed in conflict. On the other hand, as data are broken down by occupation, plant size, geographic location, composition of the work force, product classes, and a host of other relevant compartments, the material becomes increasingly meaningful, but unwieldly.

## NARROWING OF INCOME DIFFERENTIALS

I agree with Herman Miller's contention that government action, principally in the form of National War Labor Board policies and procedures, contributed to a narrowing of income differentials. In the forties, however, a combination of many factors was reinforcing the secular trend toward narrowed differentials. It was a period of war-impelled demand for workers, some rise in prices, and advances in both earnings and wage rates. Government action was deliberately designed to ease the burden on low-income recipients, partly because the impact of inflation falls most heavily on this group. The action, however, was also designed as a general anti-inflationary measure.

A second factor was the continuing advance in the level of education. In 1940 one out of seven in the working population had completed high school; the proportion had increased to one in five by 1950. Extension of the schooling period resulted in a relatively smaller supply of unskilled workers, and a larger supply of workers qualified for jobs requiring higher skills. The continued restriction of immigration, which began in the twenties had the same result.

A third factor was the need because of the war effort to draw into the industrial labor force many persons formerly in agriculture, women from their homes, and youths. Special inducements were necessary to redirect their efforts to totally different activities; often they had to move from the country to the city.

A fourth factor was the increasing use of machinery, which tended to expand the job content in relatively unskilled occupations and to reduce the variety of skills required of operatives and craftsmen. In short, for the forties at least, government action and union activity reinforced the effects of strong social forces which by themselves would have produced a narrowing of differentials.

I agree also with Miller's opinion that union activity contributed to the narrowing of wage differentials, but its impact is not similar to that of government action. National unions usually bargain with a single employer, or with local groups of employers, and collective bargaining has been described as "decentralized in the sense that each national union charts its own course. There is a certain amount of informal consultation, emulation, and rivalry among unions in the same or neighboring industries. A pattern established by one union in a particular year may be virtually binding on another union especially if the two are rivals for the same clientele. Apart from competitive emulation, however, there is no central coordination of wage policy by the top federations."[1] Unions may affect workers' attitudes, may have an impact on the hiring and promotion practices of an employer, and may affect the way in which labor is recruited. They may influence wages by controlling the number of workers admitted to particular industries, but neither the closed shop nor union restriction on employment is very important in the United States.

## UNSETTLED PROBLEMS

I would like to comment on several other points concerning Miller's statistics. First, I have already mentioned the difficulty of comparing occupational differentials over a ten year span. The

[1] Lloyd G. Reynolds and Cynthia H. Taft, *The Evolution of Wage Structure,* Yale University Press, 1956, p. 317.

changing content of seemingly comparable jobs poses problems in analyzing occupational differentials.

A second element, not treated by Miller, is the increase in the size of money differentials during the forties. A Bureau of Labor Statistics study of the period from 1939 to 1948,[2] showed generally greater cents-per-hour increases in high-paid than in low-paid industries. To take extreme examples: the 1939 average hourly earnings in the newspaper industry of about $1.00 (the highest among 103 industries for which data were calculated) had risen by 1948 to $1.89 (89 per cent); cotton manufactures, on the other hand, showed the greatest percentage increase, 182 between 1939 and 1948. Nevertheless, the 1939 money differential in favor of the newspaper industry of 62 cents in 1939 had increased to 80 cents by 1948.[3]

A third point, on which there are no authoritative figures, are "fringe benefits," which in recent years have been a major factor in collective bargaining. Their inclusion—wherever these are adopted on a varying industrial basis—would alter the differentials observed by Miller, possibly disclosing differentials greater than those shown by census data. I am inclined to think that well organized workers in higher-paid industries have been more successful in establishing liberal benefit patterns than have workers in lower-paid industries. If this assumption is valid, inclusion of such figures would disclose greater North-South differentials, since organization is more complete and effective and wage rates are higher in the North. I do not suggest that such a widening of differentials will continue over long periods throughout the country, though I think it likely that the North-South differentials will continue to persist.

Finally, the paper does not comment on the reduction in take-home-pay differentials caused by progressive income taxes.

An increase in differentials has been brought about recently in a relatively high proportion of the major collectively bargained wage settlements. A report published by the Bureau of Labor Statistics shows that about one-third of the major agreements in 1955 either maintained percentage differentials between skilled and unskilled workers by giving uniform percentage adjustments or widened them through extra increases for skilled workers (in addition to uniform cents-per-hour or percentage wage changes applicable to all em-

[2] "Wage Trends, 1939–1949," *Wage Movements,* Bureau of Labor Statistics, Series 3, No. 3, 1950, Table 2.

[3] Average hourly earnings for work shirts and cotton seed oil in 1939 were lower than those for cotton manufactures. However, the relative increase, 1939–1948, was less in these industries than in other industries.

ployees in the bargaining unit).[4] Because only larger settlements are included in the data, the latter type of adjustment affects 40 per cent or more of all workers involved in expanded rates. Since the report concerns companies considered to be wage leaders, such as Ford, General Motors, United States Steel, it is conceivable that the trend may spread.

## A. H. LENEVEU, DOMINION BUREAU OF STATISTICS

The main findings of our attempt to measure the trend of industrial earnings in Canada on the basis of our 1941 and 1951 census statistics on wage-earners correspond closely with the results obtained by Herman P. Miller for the United States.

### CANADIAN EARNINGS TREND

A marked rise in wage earnings of workers in Canada took place over the decade 1941 to 1951. The following tabulation of the percentage distribution of wage earners,[1] by amount of earnings and by sex, shows that about 56 per cent of all male wage earners in Canada earned over $2,000 during the census year ended June 1, 1951, compared with just under 10 per cent in 1941. Among female wage earners, 60 per cent earned over $1,000 in 1951 compared with only a little over 11 per cent in 1941. Median annual earnings more than doubled during this decade.

| EARNINGS GROUP | TOTAL | | MALE | | FEMALE | |
|---|---|---|---|---|---|---|
| | *1941* | *1951* [a] | *1941* | *1951* [a] | *1941* | *1951* [a] |
| | | | (*per cent*) | | | |
| Total | 100.0 | 100.0 | 100.0 | 100.0 | 100.0 | 100.0 |
| Under $1,000 | 62.7 | 22.3 | 54.1 | 15.8 | 88.6 | 40.4 |
| $1,000– 1,999 | 30.4 | 32.9 | 37.0 | 28.2 | 10.7 | 45.9 |
| 2,000– 2,999 | 4.9 | 31.4 | 6.4 | 38.2 | 0.6 | 12.3 |
| 3,000– 3,999 | 1.2 | 9.2 | 1.5 | 12.0 | 0.1 | 1.2 |
| 4,000 and over | 0.8 | 4.3 | 1.0 | 5.7 | [b] | 0.2 |
| | | | (*dollars*) | | | |
| Median earnings | 733 | 1,854 | 874 | 2,132 | [c] | 1,191 |

Figures may not add to totals because of rounding.
[a] The 1951 figures are exclusive of Newfoundland.
[b] Less than 0.05 per cent.
[c] Exact median earnings cannot be determined from data available; the average for females in 1941 was $490.

[4] See "Labor-Management Contract Settlements," *Monthly Labor Review,* Bureau of Labor Statistics, May 1956, p. 527.
[1] Cf. Miller's Table 1.

## CHANGE IN DIFFERENTIALS

The following tabulation of percentages of total earnings for each fifth of all wage earners in Canada, ranked by amount of earnings and by sex, 1941 and 1951, shows the same trend as that experienced in the United States over approximately the same period.[2]

| WAGE EARNERS | *1941* | *1951* |
|---|---|---|
| Both sexes | | |
| Lowest fifth | 4.8 | 4.7 |
| Second fifth | 8.2 | 12.6 |
| Middle fifth | 15.0 | 18.8 |
| Fourth fifth | 28.9 | 24.0 |
| Highest fifth | 43.1 | 39.9 |
| Males | | |
| Lowest fifth | 4.2 | 5.9 |
| Second fifth | 9.9 | 13.8 |
| Middle fifth | 17.4 | 19.0 |
| Fourth fifth | 27.3 | 22.8 |
| Highest fifth | 41.1 | 38.6 |
| Females | | |
| Lowest fifth | 8.3 | 4.1 |
| Second fifth | 8.3 | 11.6 |
| Middle fifth | 15.0 | 20.4 |
| Fourth fifth | 25.7 | 26.5 |
| Highest fifth | 42.8 | 37.4 |

The share of total earnings received by the highest fifth of the wage earners in Canada, ranked by amount of earnings, declined between 1941 and 1951 from 43.1 per cent of the aggregate in 1941 to 39.9 per cent in 1951. The lowest fifth of all wage earners received about the same share in 1941 (4.8 per cent) and 1951 (4.7 per cent). The middle fifth increased their share of total earnings from 15 per cent in 1941 to 18.8 per cent in 1951.

The spread between the median annual earnings of Canada's higher and lower socio-economic occupation groups narrowed over the decade 1941–1951.[3] This is shown in the following table comparing the percentage increases in the medians of annual and weekly earnings (per week employed) of males in various occupation groups.

[2] Cf. Miller's Table 2.

[3] Cf. Miller's Table 11.

| OCCUPATIONAL GROUP | MEDIAN EARNINGS 1941 | 1951 | PERCENTAGE INCREASE 1941 to 1951 | MEDIAN WEEKS EMPLOYED 1941 | 1951 | MEDIAN EARNINGS PER WEEK EMPLOYED 1941 | 1951 | PERCENTAGE INCREASE 1941 to 1951 |
|---|---|---|---|---|---|---|---|---|
| Laborers (nonprimary) | $ 566 | $1,552 | 174.2 | 39.58 | 50.04 | $14.30 | $31.02 | 116.9 |
| Semiskilled [a] | 933 | 2,132 | 128.5 | 50.40 | 50.94 | 18.51 | 41.85 | 126.1 |
| Skilled [b] | 1,052 | 2,292 | 117.9 | 50.19 | 50.88 | 20.96 | 45.05 | 114.9 |
| Clerical, commercial and financial | 1,139 | 2,206 | 93.7 | 51.03 | 51.18 | 22.32 | 43.10 | 93.1 |
| Professional | 1,553 | 2,944 | 92.0 | 51.23 | 51.25 | 30.31 | 57.44 | 89.5 |
| Managerial | 2,082 | 3,603 | 73.1 | 51.38 | 51.41 | 40.52 | 70.08 | 73.0 |

This table accounts for about three-quarters of all male wage and salary earners in 1951.
[a] Includes 76 per cent of all male semiskilled workers in 1951.
[b] Includes 86 per cent of all male skilled workers in 1951.

Median annual earnings for all laborers (other than those employed in primary industries) rose by 174.2 per cent over this ten-year period, while the corresponding percentage increases for other groups were: semiskilled workers, 128.5; skilled, 117.9; clerical and commercial, 93.7; professional, 92.0; and managerial, 73.1 per cent. The relatively greater difference that existed in 1941 between the earnings of laborers and other occupation groups was due partly to the considerable amount of short-time experienced by laborers in that year. These relationships expressed as ratios are shown as follows:

| RATIOS OF MEDIAN EARNINGS OF: | MEDIAN ANNUAL EARNINGS 1941 | 1951 | MEDIAN EARNINGS PER WEEK EMPLOYED 1941 | 1951 |
|---|---|---|---|---|
| Managerial to laborers | 3.7 | 2.3 | 2.8 | 2.3 |
| Professional to laborers | 2.7 | 1.9 | 2.1 | 1.9 |
| Clerical, commercial and financial to laborers | 2.0 | 1.4 | 1.6 | 1.4 |
| Skilled workers to laborers | 1.9 | 1.5 | 1.5 | 1.5 |
| Semiskilled workers to laborers | 1.6 | 1.4 | 1.3 | 1.3 |

The drift toward leveling of wage incomes in Canada during the war and postwar period was attributed by the Department of Labour to a general tendency "toward a reduction of both kinds of wage differentials, that between skilled and unskilled labour, and that between high-wage and low-wage industries." [4]

## REASONS FOR CHANGE

During the first two years they were in force, November 1941 to December 1943, the effect of wage controls was not so much to freeze wage rates as to equalize them, by preventing wage increases

[4] "Effects of the War on Canada's Wage Structure," *Canadian Labour Market*, Canadian Dept. of Labour, March 1948.

which would have resulted in increased wage differentials. Under the National War Labour Board the tendency of unions to demand across-the-board increases for whole plants or whole industries, yielding higher percentage increases in the lower wage groups, was encouraged by the inevitable centralization of collective bargaining. Under the Wartime Wages Control Order of December 1943, while wage increases were more strictly limited, the "gross inequality" clause facilitated increases for lower-paid workers more than for the higher-paid. Thus, the narrowing of the difference in annual earnings between unskilled and other groups of workers over the period 1941 to 1951 is largely a reflection of the wartime trends in wage policy, on the part of governments as well as of labor unions. Over the longer period since the beginning of the century, the proportionate decrease of skilled workers with the greater use of machine processes in production has probably also tended to bring about a larger measure of wage equalization.

In Canada, as in the United States, the rate of increase in annual earnings in the lowest-paid group of industries over the period between 1941 and 1951 was greater than in the highest-paid group. The following table groups industries into deciles, according to median annual earnings of workers at the 1951 census, and shows

| INDUSTRIES RANKED BY MEDIAN EARNINGS IN 1951 | TOTAL | PERCENTAGE INCREASE IN MEDIAN EARNINGS BETWEEN 1941 AND 1951 | | | |
|---|---|---|---|---|---|
| | | *Less than 100.0* | *100.0 to 124.9* | *125.0 to 149.9* | *150.0 or more* |
| Total | 153 [a] | 48 | 42 | 33 | 29 |
| Lowest tenth | 12 [a] | 6 | 2 | 1 | 2 |
| Second tenth | 14 | 6 | 3 | 4 | 1 |
| Third tenth | 20 | 3 | 7 | 5 | 5 |
| Fourth tenth | 13 | 3 | 4 | 4 | 2 |
| Fifth tenth | 11 | 1 | 2 | 4 | 4 |
| Sixth tenth | 27 | 6 | 6 | 6 | 9 |
| Seventh tenth | 5 | 3 | 1 | 1 | – |
| Eighth tenth | 27 | 8 | 10 | 4 | 5 |
| Ninth tenth | 11 | 5 | 3 | 3 | – |
| Highest tenth | 13 | 7 | 4 | 1 | 1 |

[a] There was one decrease of one percentage point occurring in the lowest tenth.

the number of industries by percentage increase in median earnings for each decile over the period since the 1941 census.[5]

The figures above are summarized in the following table:

[5] Cf. Miller's Table 10.

| INDUSTRIES RANKED BY MEDIAN EARNINGS IN 1951 | TOTAL | | INCREASE LESS THAN 100% | | INCREASE 100.0% TO 124.9% | | INCREASE 125.0% TO 149.9% | | INCREASE 150.0% OR MORE | |
|---|---|---|---|---|---|---|---|---|---|---|
| | *No.* | *%* | *No.* | *%* | *No.* | *%* | *No.* | *%* | *No.* | *%* |
| A. *Based on Order of Earnings Size for All Workers in 1951* | | | | | | | | | | |
| Total | 153 | 100.0 | 48 | 31.4 | 42 | 27.5 | 33 | 21.6 | 29 | 19.0 |
| Lowest three tenths | 46 | 100.0 | 15 | 32.6 | 12 | 26.1 | 10 | 21.7 | 8 | 17.4 |
| Highest three tenths | 51 | 100.0 | 20 | 39.2 | 17 | 33.3 | 8 | 15.7 | 6 | 11.8 |
| B. *Based on Order of Earnings Size for Male Workers in 1951* | | | | | | | | | | |
| Total | 153 | 100.0 | 49 | 32.0 | 42 | 27.5 | 33 | 21.6 | 29 | 19.0 |
| Lowest three tenths | 34 | 100.0 | 5 | 14.7 | 8 | 23.5 | 8 | 23.5 | 13 | 38.2 |
| Highest three tenths | 38 | 100.0 | 21 | 55.3 | 15 | 39.5 | 1 | 2.6 | 1 | 2.6 |
| C. *Based on Order of Earnings Size for All Workers in 1941* | | | | | | | | | | |
| Total | 153 | 100.0 | 48 | 31.4 | 42 | 27.5 | 34 | 22.2 | 28 | 18.3 |
| Lowest three tenths | 23 | 100.0 | 5 | 21.7 | 4 | 17.4 | 7 | 30.4 | 7 | 30.4 |
| Highest three tenths | 41 | 100.0 | 30 | 73.2 | 10 | 24.4 | 1 | 2.4 | — | — |

The results in Panel A, based on 1951 wages for all workers, show that among the forty-six industry classes composing the lowest three tenths, in terms of median earnings in 1951, some 17.4 per cent showed an increase in earnings of over 150 per cent, while for the top three tenths only 11.8 per cent recorded an equal rate of increase. Similarly, 21.7 per cent of the former increased by 125 to 150 per cent as compared with only 15.7 per cent of the latter group. As Panel B shows, the difference in rate of increase over this decade in median annual earnings for males in the lowest three-tenths as compared with the highest three-tenths of the industry classes was considerably more marked than for both sexes combined. Panel C of the table shows that, on the basis of the order of earnings size in 1941, 30.4 per cent of the lowest three tenths recorded an increase of 150 per cent or more in earnings over the decade; the highest three tenths were not represented in this rate of increase category. The same proportion of the lowest rank showed an increase in earnings of 125 to 150 per cent, while only 2.4 per cent of the highest paid group recorded this rate of increase. It will be seen that over the period the relative gains in earnings of the lowest three tenths compared with the highest three tenths of the industries were greater when 1941 was the basis of arrangement of industries by earnings size than when 1951 was the basis.

United States census statistics on wage and salary income show that, although the level of income in industry rose substantially during the period 1940 to 1950, there was little change in the relative position of individual industries when ranked on the basis of average wage or salary income of workers. The similar experience of Canada is summarized in the following table.[6] By use of census statistics on median annual earnings by workers in industry for 1951 compared with 1941, industry classes were arranged according to earnings of workers rank in both years. It will be seen that 25.5 per cent of the industry classes were in the same decile in both years, and 45.1 per cent had changed position by only one decile over this period.

| | *Number* | *Percentage* |
|---|---|---|
| Total industries | 153 | 100.0 |
| Same rank | 39 | 25.5 |
| Changing rank by 1 decile | 69 | 45.1 |
| Changing rank by: | | |
| more than 1 decile | 45 | 29.4 |
| 2 deciles | 23 | 15.0 |
| 3 deciles | 18 | 11.8 |
| 4 deciles | 2 | 1.3 |
| 5 deciles | 1 | 0.7 |
| 6 deciles | 1 | 0.7 |

A substantial proportion of the industries that declined three deciles or more between 1941 and 1951 were industries, such as trade and finance, in which the percentage of females employed had increased significantly over this decade.

As for earnings distributions by occupation, no detailed study has been made in Canada. Since the range of earnings shown for many occupational classes listed in census tables is affected by the degree of homogeneity of the class, by difficulties in enumerating certain occupations, by editing and coding procedures, and so forth, careful consideration of the occupations selected for such a study would be required even though in the 1951 census an effort was made to improve the quality of occupation reporting.

Finally, with regard to the relationship between occupation and annual earnings, the extent to which the occupation reported on the census date was followed continuously during the preceding twelve months varies from occupation to occupation. Hence the accuracy of the data shown for any occupation class is affected by the rate of movement into and out of that class. The Bureau is presently making a study of changes in jobs reported, month by month, by workers covered in the Sample Survey of the Labour Force.

[6] Cf. Miller's Tables B-4 and B-5.

# The Effect of Multi-Industry Employment on the Industrial Distribution of Wages

LAZARE TEPER, INTERNATIONAL LADIES' GARMENT WORKERS' UNION

Herman P. Miller's paper brings together valuable material on the distributions of annual wage and salary earnings in 1939 and 1949 and on their changing patterns in order to identify "some of the variable as well as the stable elements of the distribution of income," to determine "the underlying forces responsible for the change," and to establish "what general lessons can be learned from the changes for specific industry groups."

## *Extent of Multi-Industry Employment*

In the main, Miller relies on data gathered by the Bureau of the Census in the course of the decennial enumerations. Such data are limited somewhat by how specific and accurate the average respondent can be. Industrial and occupational characteristics of earnings have to be somewhat broader, and unquestionably somewhat vaguer, than those obtainable in an establishment enumeration.[1] As a result, census occupational designations frequently encompass a variety of jobs varying in content and paid on the basis of widely different standards. For example, the occupation of a sewing machine operator includes jobs differing in skill and occupational requirements and paid at substantially different rates. A swing in the relative importance of specific groups within an occupational class may affect the average level for the group even in the absence of wage movement. The effect is apt to be more pronounced for broad occupational groups, such as skilled, semiskilled, and unskilled. It is impossible to determine, in view of the heterogeneity of jobs within such categories, to what extent the particular changes are a result of the changing mix of jobs.

Census data on annual earnings by industry and occupation are collected and classified on the basis of the last job held (whether for

[1] Recognizing this problem, Australia, in connection with its 1954 population census, conducted a sample survey among employers regarding the industrial and occupational classification of their employees (United Nations Statistical Commission, 9th session, Minutes of the 131st meeting, document E/CN.3/SR.131).

hire, unpaid family work, or in self-employment) by persons who are in the labor force during the census week.[2] For those employed it is the job held during that week, or in the case of persons holding more than one job, the one in which most hours were worked during the week. For those unemployed, it is the last job held.[3] In consequence, an individual is not necessarily classified under the industry and occupation in which the greatest portion of his wage and salary income was earned in the preceding year.

Classification of workers by industry and occupation of last employment provides a valuable yardstick for the evaluation of labor force characteristics at a given time. Yet it unavoidably introduces an element of uncertainty when such data are related to annual earnings of individuals in order to trace changes in interindustry or interoccupational relationships of incomes. It is impossible to differentiate, for example, between the effect of the changing earnings opportunities in a given industrial classification from that brought about by work outside the particular industrial subdivision.

Some insight into this problem is provided by sample data gathered by the Bureau of Old-Age and Survivors Insurance on covered workers. But social security taxes are not always paid on the full amount of annual earnings because of the statutory limits on the taxable amount. This affects the amount reported as taxable wages. Averages derived from such data and changes portrayed by them over a period of time are influenced by the changes in the relative importance of annual incomes which exceed taxable limits. Furthermore, earnings in noncovered employment are not reported to the Bureau. As a result, the level of average annual wages and the extent of multi-industry employment tend to be understated.

Table 1 shows that multi-industry employment is both substantial and variable from year to year. Thus in the 1944–1952 period multi-industry employment (in more than one two-digit industry) [4] of male wage and salary earners varied from 23.7 to 34.7 per cent and of females from 16.1 to 31.7 per cent. The prevalence of multi-industry employment would loom even larger, and more variable, if data were available on a more refined industry

[2] The census week is defined as the week preceding the enumerator's visit.

[3] Occupational and industrial information is not collected for persons outside the labor force during the census week even though they may have worked in the preceding year.

[4] The Standard Industrial Classification, prepared by the Bureau of the Budget and used by the Bureau of Old-Age and Survivors Insurance, provides for grouping industrial activities into nine major divisions. These divisions are divided into major groups coded on a two-digit basis; these are then subdivided into groups of closely related industries coded on a three-digit basis, and further subdivided on the basis of a four-digit code.

TABLE 1

Percentage of All Wage and Salary Earners Who Worked in Covered Employment in More than One Two-Digit Industry in the Year, by Sex, 1944–1952

| YEAR | *Males* | *Females* |
|---|---|---|
| 1944 | 34.7 | 31.7 |
| 1945 | 32.9 | 29.1 |
| 1946 | 33.4 | 26.8 |
| 1947 | 28.7 | 21.1 |
| 1948 | 27.6 | 19.4 |
| 1949 | 23.7 | 16.1 |
| 1950 | 26.3 | 17.5 |
| 1951 | 29.8 | 20.3 |
| 1952 | 29.6 | 20.2 |

For an explanation of "two-digit industry" see note 4 in the text.
Source: *Handbook of Old Age and Survivors Insurance Statistics,* Bureau of Old Age and Survivors Insurance, Volumes for 1944 through 1952.

classification, and also, as previously noted, if non-covered jobs were recorded.

The extent of multi-industry employment, furthermore, differs widely from industry to industry. The broad patterns of this variability can be seen from OASI data for the eight major industrial groups presented in Table 2, which shows the extent of multi-industry employment among male workers classified by industry of last employment for the years 1944 through 1949.[5] Such data are not

TABLE 2

Percentage of Male Workers by Industry in Which Last Employed Who Were Also Employed in Other Industries, 1944–1949

| INDUSTRY | *1944* | *1945* | *1946* | *1947* | *1948* | *1949* |
|---|---|---|---|---|---|---|
| Agriculture, forestry, and fishing | 41.7 | 44.5 | 41.9 | 43.7 | 38.7 | 34.6 |
| Mining | 31.9 | 26.6 | 27.5 | 22.3 | 19.2 | 14.4 |
| Contract construction | 58.6 | 55.2 | 48.9 | 50.2 | 44.3 | 42.4 |
| Manufacturing | 28.4 | 28.9 | 31.0 | 25.1 | 21.3 | 17.0 |
| Public utilities | 43.1 | 34.4 | 28.4 | 29.6 | 28.1 | 24.0 |
| Wholesale and retail trade | 38.0 | 31.9 | 32.5 | 27.8 | 30.0 | 25.6 |
| Finance, insurance, and real estate | 31.5 | 23.4 | 29.0 | 21.3 | 24.4 | 21.9 |
| Service industries | 44.6 | 31.3 | 33.9 | 25.3 | 33.3 | 28.6 |

For a definition of "industry in which last employed" see note 5 in the text.
Source: *Handbook of Old-Age and Survivors Insurance Statistics,* Bureau of Old-Age and Survivors Insurance, volumes for 1944 through 1949.

[5] The concept of "last employment" in the OASI and census usage is not the same. The OASI Bureau classifies a worker by the industry of last employment on the basis of the industry of the first employer report tabulated for the last calen-

available for later years, but Table 3 shows the relative importance of multi-industry workers for each major industrial group in which they were actually employed.[6] It is clear that at different times earn-

TABLE 3

Percentage of Male Workers by Industry in Which Actually Employed Who Were Also Employed in Other Industries, 1949–1952

| INDUSTRY | *1949* | *1950* | *1951* | *1952* |
|---|---|---|---|---|
| Agriculture, forestry, and fishing | 59.2 | 60.5 | 43.0 | 44.7 |
| Mining | 27.7 | 30.6 | 37.7 | 39.5 |
| Contract construction | 49.0 | 51.5 | 64.0 | 63.9 |
| Manufacturing | 23.0 | 25.9 | 35.8 | 36.1 |
| Public utilities | 38.5 | 41.7 | 48.9 | 48.2 |
| Wholesale and retail trade | 34.2 | 37.4 | 47.4 | 47.4 |
| Finance, insurance, and real estate | 36.9 | 39.2 | 44.1 | 43.0 |
| Service industries | 45.8 | 49.4 | 54.7 | 54.2 |

For a definition of "industry in which actually employed" see note 6 in the text.
Source: *Handbook of Old-Age and Survivors Insurance Statistics,* Bureau of Old-Age and Survivors Insurance, volumes for 1949 through 1952.

ings outside of a particular industry have a different effect on the total recorded earnings.

### *Effect of Patterns of Employment on Annual Earnings*

A more comprehensive portrayal of the effects of multi-industry employment is seen in Table 4. It shows, for the year 1949, the extent of multi-industry employment among male workers classified both by industry of last employment and by industry of actual employment, and gives the average annual earnings related to the patterns of employment. The range of variation in the proportion of multi-industry work in the different two-digit industries was from 7.8 to 45.8 per cent when employees were classified by industry of last employment, and from 15.1 to 67.6 per cent when classified by industry of actual employment. In ten two-digit industries out of sixty-eight, multi-industry workers (classified by industry of last employment) earned more than those whose employment was con-

dar quarter in which the worker had covered employment during the year (*Handbook of Old-Age and Survivors Insurance Statistics,* Bureau of Old-Age and Survivors Insurance, 1947, p. 23). It is both industry and employment in which wages were earned in the particular year, although not necessarily the industry which gave rise to all of the earnings. The Census Bureau concept of classification relates to a different period from the one in which the particular worker had earnings, and is not limited to work for wages or salaries.

[6] OASI data by industry of actual employment relate to all persons who worked in a given industry in the course of the year. Persons who worked in more than one industry are thus counted in each.

TABLE 4

Multi-Industry Employment Among Male Covered Workers and Their Average Annual Taxable Wages, 1949

| | PERCENTAGE OF MULTI-INDUSTRY WORKERS IN INDUSTRY OF: | | AVERAGE ANNUAL WAGE BY INDUSTRY OF: | | | | RATIO OF AVERAGE ANNUAL WAGES | |
|---|---|---|---|---|---|---|---|---|
| | | | Last Employment | | | Actual Employment | | |
| INDUSTRY | Last Employment (1) | Actual Employment (2) | All Workers (3) | Multi-Industry Workers (4) | Single Industry Workers (5) | All Workers (6) | Col. (6) ÷ Col. (3) (7) | Col. (4) ÷ Col. (5) (8) |
| Agriculture, forestry, and fishing | 34.6 | 59.2 | $1,347 | $1,288 | $1,378 | $ 884 | 0.656 | 0.935 |
| Mining | 14.4 | 27.7 | 2,070 | 1,731 | 2,128 | 1,825 | 0.882 | 0.813 |
| Metal | 15.2 | 31.8 | 2,253 | 1,820 | 2,331 | 1,976 | 0.877 | 0.781 |
| Anthracite | 8.3 | 15.1 | 2,235 | 1,780 | 2,276 | 2,106 | 0.942 | 0.782 |
| Bituminous and other soft-coal | 10.5 | 20.6 | 1,939 | 1,638 | 1,975 | 1,800 | 0.928 | 0.829 |
| Crude petroleum and natural gas | 20.6 | 39.0 | 2,259 | 1,840 | 2,367 | 1,848 | 0.818 | 0.777 |
| Nonmetallic and quarrying | 21.6 | 42.4 | 1,931 | 1,622 | 2,016 | 1,851 | 0.959 | 0.805 |
| Contract construction | 42.4 | 49.0 | 1,680 | 1,730 | 1,644 | 1,323 | 0.788 | 1.052 |
| Building, general contractors | 45.8 | 67.5 | 1,607 | 1,714 | 1,516 | 1,026 | 0.638 | 1.131 |
| General contractors, other than building | 44.6 | 67.6 | 1,534 | 1,626 | 1,460 | 978 | 0.638 | 1.114 |
| Special-trade contractors | 38.2 | 60.3 | 1,831 | 1,818 | 1,839 | 1,220 | 0.666 | 0.989 |
| Manufacturing | 17.0 | 23.0 | 2,190 | 1,740 | 2,282 | 1,989 | 0.908 | 0.762 |
| Ordnance and accessories | 7.8 | 19.5 | 2,582 | 2,210 | 2,613 | 2,374 | 0.919 | 0.846 |
| Food and kindred products | 22.5 | 40.9 | 1,884 | 1,494 | 1,997 | 1,468 | 0.779 | 0.748 |
| Tobacco manufactures | 26.2 | 37.8 | 1,480 | 943 | 1,670 | 1,186 | 0.801 | 0.565 |
| Textile mill products | 11.5 | 21.2 | 2,074 | 1,631 | 2,131 | 1,891 | 0.912 | 0.765 |
| Apparel, fabric products, etc. | 16.5 | 30.6 | 2,083 | 1,532 | 2,192 | 1,831 | 0.879 | 0.699 |
| Lumber and wood products | 20.5 | 37.7 | 1,300 | 1,211 | 1,323 | 1,034 | 0.795 | 0.915 |
| Furniture and fixtures | 23.1 | 42.1 | 1,909 | 1,595 | 2,003 | 1,448 | 0.759 | 0.796 |

continued on next page

TABLE 4, continued

| INDUSTRY | PERCENTAGE OF MULTI-INDUSTRY WORKERS IN INDUSTRY OF: | | AVERAGE ANNUAL WAGE BY INDUSTRY OF: | | | | RATIO OF AVERAGE ANNUAL WAGES | |
|---|---|---|---|---|---|---|---|---|
| | | | *Last Employment* | | | *Actual Employment* | | |
| | *Last Employment* (1) | *Actual Employment* (2) | *All Workers* (3) | *Multi-Industry Workers* (4) | *Single Industry Workers* (5) | *All Workers* (6) | *Col. (6) ÷ Col. (3)* (7) | *Col. (4) ÷ Col. (5)* (8) |
| Paper and allied products | 15.0 | 28.5 | $2,384 | $1,734 | $2,498 | $2,033 | 0.853 | 0.694 |
| Printing, publishing, etc. | 14.7 | 28.1 | 2,272 | 1,691 | 2,372 | 1,988 | 0.875 | 0.713 |
| Chemicals and allied products | 15.3 | 30.2 | 2,385 | 1,753 | 2,500 | 2,028 | 0.850 | 0.701 |
| Petroleum and coal products | 12.7 | 23.7 | 2,680 | 2,141 | 2,758 | 2,399 | 0.895 | 0.776 |
| Rubber products | 12.8 | 26.7 | 2,521 | 2,047 | 2,591 | 2,215 | 0.879 | 0.790 |
| Leather and leather products | 16.9 | 30.8 | 1,946 | 1,460 | 2,044 | 1,673 | 0.860 | 0.714 |
| Stone, clay, and glass products | 19.9 | 37.0 | 2,151 | 1,708 | 2,261 | 1,726 | 0.802 | 0.755 |
| Primary metal industries | 11.5 | 26.5 | 2,426 | 2,023 | 2,479 | 2,145 | 0.884 | 0.816 |
| Fabricated metal products | 21.9 | 40.5 | 2,265 | 1,839 | 2,385 | 1,781 | 0.786 | 0.771 |
| Machinery, except electrical | 13.6 | 31.7 | 2,463 | 2,131 | 2,515 | 2,084 | 0.846 | 0.847 |
| Electrical machinery, etc. | 16.2 | 31.0 | 2,462 | 2,008 | 2,550 | 2,096 | 0.851 | 0.787 |
| Transportation equipment | 17.9 | 34.1 | 2,470 | 2,124 | 2,546 | 2,080 | 0.842 | 0.834 |
| Instruments, etc. | 11.4 | 25.6 | 2,485 | 2,138 | 2,529 | 2,179 | 0.877 | 0.845 |
| Misc. manufacturing | 21.9 | 40.7 | 2,070 | 1,665 | 2,183 | 1,607 | 0.776 | 0.763 |
| Public utilities | 24.0 | 38.5 | 2,147 | 1,750 | 2,272 | 1,710 | 0.796 | 0.770 |
| Local railways and bus lines | 13.3 | 23.9 | 2,657 | 2,366 | 2,701 | 2,391 | 0.900 | 0.876 |
| Trucking and warehousing for hire | 32.3 | 53.6 | 1,885 | 1,636 | 2,004 | 1,275 | 0.676 | 0.816 |
| Other transportation, except water | 25.3 | 46.5 | 1,927 | 1,694 | 2,006 | 1,385 | 0.719 | 0.844 |
| Water transportation | 28.5 | 48.7 | 2,234 | 1,987 | 2,332 | 1,728 | 0.774 | 0.852 |
| Services allied to transportation | 39.7 | 62.7 | 1,840 | 1,783 | 1,878 | 1,173 | 0.637 | 0.949 |
| Communications, telephone, etc. | 10.0 | 21.2 | 2,399 | 1,520 | 2,497 | 2,176 | 0.907 | 0.609 |
| Electric and gas | 14.3 | 25.4 | 2,492 | 1,927 | 2,586 | 2,211 | 0.887 | 0.745 |

continued on next page

TABLE 4, continued

| INDUSTRY | PERCENTAGE OF MULTI-INDUSTRY WORKERS IN INDUSTRY OF: Last Employment (1) | Actual Employment (2) | AVERAGE ANNUAL WAGE BY INDUSTRY OF: Last Employment: All Workers (3) | Last Employment: Multi-Industry Workers (4) | Last Employment: Single Industry Workers (5) | Actual Employment All Workers (6) | RATIO OF AVERAGE ANNUAL WAGES: Col. (6) ÷ Col. (3) (7) | Col. (4) ÷ Col. (5) (8) |
|---|---|---|---|---|---|---|---|---|
| Local utilities and services, n.e.c. | 22.0 | 42.3 | $1,747 | $1,484 | $1,822 | $1,318 | 0.754 | 0.814 |
| Wholesale and retail trade | 25.6 | 34.2 | 1,791 | 1,518 | 1,884 | 1,472 | 0.822 | 0.806 |
| Full and limited-function wholesalers | 23.9 | 44.6 | 2,036 | 1,641 | 2,160 | 1,532 | 0.752 | 0.760 |
| Other wholesalers | 21.3 | 40.3 | 2,214 | 1,786 | 2,329 | 1,731 | 0.782 | 0.767 |
| Wholesale and retail trade, n.e.c. | 30.4 | 54.6 | 1,805 | 1,520 | 1,929 | 1,179 | 0.653 | 0.788 |
| Retail general merchandise | 28.1 | 45.5 | 1,656 | 1,284 | 1,802 | 1,207 | 0.729 | 0.713 |
| Retail food and liquor stores | 21.6 | 39.5 | 1,669 | 1,432 | 1,734 | 1,286 | 0.771 | 0.826 |
| Retail automotive | 25.1 | 43.6 | 2,061 | 1,750 | 2,165 | 1,604 | 0.778 | 0.808 |
| Retail apparel and accessories | 27.2 | 45.5 | 1,728 | 1,414 | 1,846 | 1,259 | 0.729 | 0.766 |
| Retail trade, n.e.c. | 25.9 | 46.0 | 1,699 | 1,512 | 1,764 | 1,241 | 0.730 | 0.857 |
| Eating and drinking places | 29.7 | 51.0 | 1,288 | 1,287 | 1,288 | 885 | 0.687 | 0.999 |
| Retail filling stations | 36.6 | 60.4 | 1,460 | 1,530 | 1,419 | 866 | 0.593 | 1.078 |
| Finance, insurance, and real estate | 21.9 | 36.9 | 2,125 | 1,931 | 2,179 | 1,710 | 0.805 | 0.886 |
| Banks and trust companies | 11.7 | 22.1 | 2,352 | 2,013 | 2,397 | 2,176 | 0.925 | 0.840 |
| Security dealers and investment | 13.0 | 25.3 | 2,391 | 2,160 | 2,426 | 2,108 | 0.882 | 0.890 |
| Finance agencies, n.e.c. | 26.0 | 42.7 | 2,206 | 2,087 | 2,248 | 1,684 | 0.763 | 0.928 |
| Insurance carriers | 16.1 | 26.8 | 2,425 | 2,112 | 2,485 | 2,151 | 0.887 | 0.850 |
| Insurance agents and brokers | 18.2 | 32.8 | 2,200 | 1,960 | 2,254 | 1,849 | 0.840 | 0.870 |
| Real estate | 32.6 | 56.0 | 1,714 | 1,802 | 1,671 | 1,120 | 0.653 | 1.078 |
| Combination offices | 24.7 | 46.0 | 1,963 | 1,966 | 1,961 | 1,460 | 0.744 | 1.003 |
| Holding companies, except real estate | 22.7 | 43.3 | 2,366 | 2,184 | 2,419 | 1,958 | 0.828 | 0.903 |

continued on next page

TABLE 4, concluded

| INDUSTRY | PERCENTAGE OF MULTI-INDUSTRY WORKERS IN INDUSTRY OF: Last Employment (1) | Actual Employment (2) | AVERAGE ANNUAL WAGE BY INDUSTRY OF: Last Employment — All Workers (3) | Last Employment — Multi-Industry Workers (4) | Last Employment — Single Industry Workers (5) | Actual Employment All Workers (6) | RATIO OF AVERAGE ANNUAL WAGES: Col. (6) ÷ Col. (3) (7) | Col. (4) ÷ Col. (5) (8) |
|---|---|---|---|---|---|---|---|---|
| Service industries | 28.6 | 45.8 | $1,555 | $1,541 | $1,561 | $1,118 | 0.719 | 0.987 |
| Hotels and other lodging places | 30.1 | 53.9 | 1,149 | 1,182 | 1,135 | 759 | 0.661 | 1.041 |
| Personal services | 19.8 | 37.2 | 1,694 | 1,409 | 1,765 | 1,346 | 0.795 | 0.798 |
| Other business services | 25.9 | 47.9 | 1,958 | 1,695 | 2,050 | 1,408 | 0.719 | 0.827 |
| Employment agencies, trade schools, etc. | 31.9 | 54.0 | 1,781 | 1,985 | 1,685 | 1,175 | 0.660 | 1.178 |
| Auto repair services and garages | 30.0 | 54.7 | 1,697 | 1,609 | 1,734 | 1,114 | 0.656 | 0.928 |
| Misc. repair services and trade | 32.8 | 58.3 | 1,790 | 1,770 | 1,799 | 1,137 | 0.646 | 0.984 |
| Motion pictures | 28.6 | 50.0 | 1,410 | 1,387 | 1,419 | 1,027 | 0.728 | 0.977 |
| Other amusement and recreation | 34.8 | 59.2 | 1,005 | 1,338 | 827 | 586 | 0.583 | 1.618 |
| Medical and other health services | 22.5 | 42.0 | 1,439 | 1,398 | 1,451 | 1,097 | 0.762 | 0.963 |
| Law offices and related services | 16.3 | 29.3 | 1,952 | <u>1,516</u> | 2,037 | 1,707 | 0.874 | 0.744 |
| Educational institutions and agencies | 27.4 | 51.7 | 1,487 | <u>1,685</u> | 1,413 | 954 | 0.642 | 1.192 |
| Other professional and social service | 23.0 | 44.9 | 1,963 | 1,702 | 2,042 | 1,521 | 0.775 | 0.833 |
| Nonprofit membership organizations | 40.5 | 63.3 | 1,937 | 2,223 | 1,743 | 926 | 0.478 | 1.275 |

Averages computed for sample cells of less than one hundred workers are underlined; n.e.c. = not elsewhere classified.

"Taxable" refers to the amount of total wages covered by OASI.

Source: *Handbook of Old-Age and Survivors Insurance Statistics,* Bureau of Old-Age and Survivors Insurance, 1949.

fined to a single industry, in an extreme case 61.8 per cent more. In the remaining fifty-eight industries, multi-industry workers earned less by as much as 43.5 per cent than single-industry employees. The average annual earnings of workers by industry of actual employment can, of course, be expected to be in all cases lower than those of workers classified by industry of last employment. Here again the differences are extremely variable, with earnings by industry of actual employment ranging from 49.1 to 95.9 per cent of earnings classified by industry of last employment. A comparatively close relationship, however, did exist between the annual earnings of all workers classified by industry of last employment and those whose employment was limited solely to the same industries.

The pattern of changes in annual earnings over a period of time cannot be fully appreciated from the OASI data because of the differences in pressures of incomes against the taxable ceilings imposed by the Social Security Act. However, a short-term comparison, presented in Table 5 for the years 1948 and 1949, highlights some of the possible consequences of the different concepts of annual industrial earnings. On the whole, changes in earnings of all males classified by industry of last employment and those who worked in but a single industry have shown fairly closely related movements. In twenty-six of the sixty-eight industries, divergence was less than 1 percentage point and in fifty-two cases less than 2 percentage points.[7] On the other hand, the difference in movement between the annual earnings of workers who worked in a single industry and the average earnings of all workers who worked in the same industry was more pronounced. In only two industries was the divergence in movements smaller than 1 percentage point, and in only seventeen was it under 5 percentage points. In forty-two industries, divergences ranged from 5 to 10 percentage points, and in seven industries they were 10 to 39 points. Divergencies between earnings of all workers classified by industry of last employment and those classified by industry of actual employment are substantially similar.

## *Employment Patterns Affecting Annual Earnings*

The OASI data suggest that variations in the industrial distribution of annual wage and salary incomes are materially affected by the

[7] To measure divergence in the movement of two series, differences in percentage points between the 1948–1949 ratios of each series were used. Because of the nature of the data, they do not differ materially from similar figures obtainable more laboriously in percentage form.

TABLE 5

Percentage Change in Average Annual Taxable Wages of Male Covered Workers between 1948 and 1949

| INDUSTRY | PERCENTAGE CHANGE IN AVERAGE ANNUAL WAGE BY INDUSTRY OF: | | | |
|---|---|---|---|---|
| | *Last Employment* | | | *Actual Employment* |
| | *All Workers* | *Multi-Industry Workers* | *Single Industry Workers* | *All Workers* |
| Mining: | | | | |
| Metal | +0.2 | −6.2 | +0.1 | +6.2 |
| Anthracite | −13.3 | −19.5 | −12.8 | −13.0 |
| Bituminous and other soft-coal | −14.7 | −13.1 | −15.4 | −12.7 |
| Crude petroleum and natural gas | +4.1 | −3.9 | +4.2 | +9.6 |
| Nonmetallic and quarrying | +2.5 | −5.8 | +3.5 | +42.2 |
| Contract construction: | | | | |
| Building, general contractors | −2.4 | −0.4 | −4.1 | +0.6 |
| General contractors, other than building | +1.7 | +0.6 | +3.6 | +10.8 |
| Special-trade contractors | −0.5 | +1.7 | −2.0 | +1.8 |
| Manufacturing: | | | | |
| Ordnance and accessories | +1.4 | +10.8 | −1.8 | +16.0 |
| Food and kindred products | +4.1 | −1.1 | +4.0 | +12.2 |
| Tobacco manufactures | −5.4 | +4.0 | −6.3 | +0.2 |
| Textile mill products | −3.5 | −1.3 | −4.1 | +0.1 |
| Apparel, fabric products, etc. | −1.7 | −0.3 | −2.7 | +3.5 |
| Lumber and wood products | −0.9 | −3.7 | −0.4 | +3.9 |
| Furniture and fixtures | +2.4 | +1.7 | +0.9 | +12.2 |
| Paper and allied products | +1.3 | −3.8 | 0 | +9.2 |
| Printing, publishing, etc. | +2.4 | +0.9 | +1.7 | +5.7 |
| Chemicals and allied products | +0.4 | −5.8 | −0.2 | +8.3 |
| Petroleum and coal products | +0.6 | −5.6 | +0.2 | +7.7 |
| Rubber products | +1.4 | +6.9 | −0.5 | +7.1 |
| Leather and leather products | −0.2 | +1.7 | −0.5 | +6.2 |
| Stone, clay and glass products | +2.6 | +3.0 | +0.6 | +13.4 |
| Primary metal industries | +0.2 | +4.0 | −1.8 | +9.3 |
| Fabricated metal products | +0.1 | −0.3 | −1.1 | +10.1 |
| Machinery, except electrical | +1.2 | +5.4 | −0.6 | +7.1 |
| Electrical machinery, etc. | +0.3 | +3.0 | −0.9 | +6.7 |
| Transportation equipment | +2.1 | +4.9 | +0.4 | +8.1 |
| Instruments, etc. | +2.3 | +9.7 | −0.8 | +8.5 |
| Misc. manufacturing | +0.5 | +1.4 | −0.8 | +7.9 |
| Public utilities: | | | | |
| Local railways and bus lines | +3.6 | +10.9 | +1.5 | +13.0 |
| Trucking and warehousing for hire | +2.0 | +2.7 | +0.1 | +9.6 |
| Other transportation, except water | 0 | −0.5 | −1.0 | +5.2 |
| Water transportation | +3.7 | −0.4 | +4.9 | +8.2 |
| Services allied to transportation | +5.0 | +9.8 | +2.0 | +12.9 |
| Communication, telephone, etc. | +4.6 | +0.1 | +2.7 | +9.7 |
| Electric and gass | +4.7 | +8.9 | +3.2 | +9.8 |
| Other local utilities and services | −7.3 | −1.1 | −10.0 | −1.2 |

continued on next page

TABLE 5, concluded

| INDUSTRY | PERCENTAGE CHANGE IN AVERAGE ANNUAL WAGE BY INDUSTRY OF: Last Employment All Workers | Last Employment Multi-Industry Workers | Last Employment Single Industry Workers | Actual Employment All Workers |
|---|---|---|---|---|
| Wholesale and retail trade | | | | |
| Full and limited-function wholesalers | +2.1 | −1.1 | +1.2 | +8.7 |
| Other wholesalers | +2.3 | −4.1 | +2.3 | +10.5 |
| Wholesale and retail trade, n.e.c. | +6.1 | +0.7 | +6.4 | +13.9 |
| Retail general merchandise | +4.6 | −2.4 | +5.4 | +11.9 |
| Retail food and liquor stores | +3.3 | −0.8 | +3.6 | +10.9 |
| Retail automotive | +3.4 | +3.5 | +2.3 | +8.8 |
| Retail apparel and accessories | −1.4 | −4.1 | −1.5 | +4.2 |
| Retail trade, n.e.c. | +1.7 | −1.3 | +2.1 | +9.4 |
| Eating and drinking places | −2.4 | −7.4 | +0.2 | +7.7 |
| Retail filling stations | +5.0 | +3.7 | +6.9 | +14.9 |
| Finance, insurance and real estate: | | | | |
| Banks and trust companies | +2.6 | +5.2 | +1.8 | +5.5 |
| Security dealers and investment | +3.5 | +1.6 | +3.3 | +3.1 |
| Finance agencies, n.e.c. | +1.2 | −2.7 | +2.4 | +5.6 |
| Insurance carriers | +1.3 | +6.2 | +0.6 | +4.3 |
| Insurance agents and brokers | +0.2 | −3.2 | +0.5 | +6.8 |
| Real estate | +0.7 | −2.5 | +3.2 | +10.1 |
| Combination offices | +5.7 | +15.9 | +1.9 | +6.9 |
| Holding companies, except real estate | −11.4 | −17.3 | −9.7 | −13.2 |
| Service industries: | | | | |
| Hotels and other lodging places | +0.2 | +2.2 | −0.7 | +8.7 |
| Personal services | +1.8 | +2.0 | +1.1 | +7.8 |
| Other business services | +3.7 | −1.5 | +4.3 | +10.2 |
| Employment agencies, trade schools, etc. | +11.2 | +6.6 | +16.7 | +14.7 |
| Auto repair services and garages | +2.4 | −2.2 | +4.3 | +8.1 |
| Misc. repair services and trades | +0.9 | −3.0 | +3.3 | +12.3 |
| Motion pictures | +3.8 | +8.1 | +1.9 | +7.8 |
| Other amusement and recreation | −2.7 | −4.8 | +2.9 | +7.1 |
| Medical and other health services | −1.9 | +2.9 | −3.7 | +4.2 |
| Law offices and related services | +5.4 | −10.1 | +7.7 | +15.3 |
| Educational institutions and agencies | −0.3 | +12.7 | −5.2 | +2.5 |
| Other professional and social service | −0.5 | −10.3 | +1.7 | +13.0 |
| Nonprofit membership organizations | −0.2 | +0.5 | +2.8 | +6.9 |

n.e.c. = not elsewhere classified.

Source: *Handbook of Old-Age and Survivors Insurance Statistics,* Bureau of Old Age and Survivors Insurance, Volumes for 1948 and 1949.

changing proportion of multi-industry employment and the differences in the earnings of single and multi-industry workers. Many other factors, of course, affect the levels of annual earnings, and hence the industrial distributions, over a period of time. The first of these is the standard by which the basic compensation is determined, such as the hourly or weekly rates for those paid on a time basis, and such as piece rates and minimum wage guarantees for those on incentives. Different standards of compensation are also based on the character of the particular incentive formulas in use, on the length of service in the particular establishments, on the appraisals of workers' capabilities or productivity, and on their age, sex and race. Some of these factors account for interplant differentials in the same industry both within the same as well as among the different localities. Levels of annual earnings may also be affected by the number of hours worked by individuals in the course of the year (whether as a result of personal preferences, the seasonal characteristics of the industry to which attached, the fortunes of the firm in which employed, or the over-all business fluctuations), by the prevalence of work at premium rates (overtime, shift differentials, and so forth), by the existence of various bonus payments (profit sharing, Christmas bonuses, and so forth), and by payments for time not worked (vacations, holidays, sickness, call-in-pay, and so forth). Changes in the occupational make-up of the different industries may also have a decided influence on wage distributions.

Distributions of composite groups are a complex of several distribution curves portraying incomes of the more homogeneous groups—a fact well developed by Miller. To the extent, therefore, that levels of wages are affected by numerous factors, it is important to explore the several composite elements of annual wage distributions on a much larger scale than has been done. The standardization procedure undertaken by Miller in his evaluation of changes in the relative importance of different industries between 1939 and 1949 could well be extended to other determinants of income levels.[8] This in turn suggests a need for many more cross-tabulations of census data. Unquestionably, the main reason why this was not done was a lack of sufficient funds. Yet, additional expenditure of

[8] In *Income of the American People* (Wiley, 1955, pp. 2 f. and pp. 16 ff.), Miller found that for males, income distributions for three major occupational groups, which covered about three-fourths of employed men, were quite symmetrical when viewed separately. These were, of course, broad occupational groupings comprising numerous specific occupational categories. We do not know to what extent the accidental combination of these smaller occupational yet distinct classes of persons in each group, coupled with the many other factors affecting income levels in each subdivision, were responsible for the shape of Miller's distributions. Was the symmetry, in turn, a by-product or combination of several asymetrical distributions or were the symmetries more pronounced in more homogeneous groups? The occupational hourly wage distributions collected for the specific industries by the Bureau of Labor Statistics suggest that the skewness tends to exist when data are taken for the occupations by industry and locality. Is it wiped out for annual incomes comprising both wage and non-wage revenues? Obviously, additional research is needed to provide answers to these questions.

government and private funds in this direction may well be justified.

Household enumerations used by the Census Bureau cannot provide all the information which may have bearing on the patterns of wage and salary incomes. It would be impossible, for example, to obtain information on the relationship between the various wage payment methods found in a given industry and annual earnings except by means of more intensive inquiries conducted in specific industries, combining the establishment and the household approach. The Census Bureau approach could nevertheless provide much more data than it does now both by increasing the detail in its cross tabulations and by exploring further its concept of relating annual incomes to industry and occupation during the census week. More information is needed on the relationship between the occupation and industry during the census week and the occupation and industry which gave rise to the predominant share of wage incomes in the preceding year. More information is also required to determine how seasonal variations in occupational and industrial distribution affect occupational and industrial relationships to income.

Miller's basic conclusions on the narrowing of annual wage differentials probably would not be materially upset were more refined data available, although some of the more detailed observations might possibly have to be modified. His conclusions regarding the relative standing of industries on the basis of the 1939 and 1949 earnings credited to workers would probably be more in question. The very concept of stability used by Miller is not an absolute one. Thus he notes that in only twenty-three out of 117 industries studied, which account for about one-fifth of all workers, did ranks shift by more than one decile. This is, of course, in addition to any change in industry ranking which may have occurred within each decile. It should be noted that deciles referred to by Miller are not those of an array of average annual earnings for the 117 industries. Instead, they are based on a distribution of individual averages into ten approximately equal groups on the basis of the number of workers portrayed by individual averages. The interindustry shifts referred to by Miller are, therefore, a function not only of a change in the relative position of individual industries but of the relative shifts in the size of employment in the different industries as well.

### *Institutional Factors Influencing Wage Differentials*

An entirely different picture of interindustry shifts emerges when the changing pattern of distributions is examined by means of the more conventional form of deciles. To this end, the 117 industries were ranked by their 1939 and 1949 average annual earnings and the positive and negative changes in ranks were arranged in an array on the basis of the relative standing of the individual industries in 1939. The results of this tabulation are shown in Table 6. The

TABLE 6

Change in Ranking of 117 Industries between 1939 and 1949

| DECILES | | | | | | | | | |
|---|---|---|---|---|---|---|---|---|---|
| *1* | *2* | *3* | *4* | *5* | *6* | *7* | *8* | *9* | *10* |
| *Change in Ranking* [a] | | | | | | | | | |
| 0 | +5 | −8 | +30 | −15 | +3 | −3 | −38 | −8 | +6 |
| 0 | −7 | −2 | +6 | −10 | +31 | +22 | +11 | +13 | 0 |
| +3 | −1 | +28 | +5 | +10 | +12 | +2 | +7 | −13 | −38 |
| 0 | +1 | +5 | −10 | +23 | +7 | −17 | −3 | +1 | +5 |
| −2 | +2 | −2 | +13 | −3 | −8 | +7 | +17 | +15 | −2 |
| +14 | +4 | −19 | −6 | +5 | +3 | −46 | −50 | +10 | −5 |
| −2 | +5 | −3 | +2 | +48 | +17 | +2 | +16 | −3 | −22 |
| +3 | +12 | −10 | +4 | −4 | +20 | −19 | −5 | −13 | −14 |
| +4 | −13 | +20 | −4 | −10 | +20 | +32 | −14 | −6 | +2 |
| +18 | +19 | +15 | −9 | +4 | +11 | −4 | +9 | −33 | 0 |
| −2 | −8 | −9 | −12 | +5 | +9 | −31 | 0 | −40 | −20 |
| 0 | | +2 | +17 | | −14 | −9 | +8 | | 0 |
| *Average Change* | | | | | | | | | |
| 4.0 | 11.0 | 10.2 | 9.8 | 12.5 | 12.9 | 16.2 | 14.8 | 14.1 | 9.5 |
| *Number of Changes by Twelve or More Places* | | | | | | | | | |
| 2 | 3 | 4 | 4 | 3 | 6 | 6 | 5 | 6 | 4 |

[a] Industries were ranked on the basis of their 1939 standing and divided sequentially into deciles.
Source: Appendix Table B-4 in the paper by Herman P. Miller in this volume.

largest number of major shifts in the relative standing of individual industries took place in the region of fifth through the ninth decile, although important shifts are scattered throughout the array. This is hardly a portrayal of stability in interindustry location on the basis of annual earnings.[9] Altogether, forty-six industries out of 117 moved up or down by twelve places or more (one decile or more) between 1939 and 1949.

Miller properly notes that the apparent narrowing of wage differentials in the 1939–1949 decade is a continuation of an historical process. Apparently, the phenomenon was not confined to the United States alone but is also evident in many other parts of the

[9] A somewhat different picture emerges if shifts in rank are portrayed by industry standing in the 1949 array. However, such a tabulation also bears out the conclusion that lower displacement of ranks occurred at the extremes of the array and greater ones in its central portion.

world.[10] The institutional forces responsible for this trend are many and varied. Some of them, like trade union activity or governmental intervention, may actively force changes in wage patterns, while others, such as differential changes in the productivity of different industries, may passively permit change. Furthermore, the existence of pressures for change may generate some subsidiary activity. For instance, unions frequently find that employers improve conditions in the same or related lines of work to stave off unionization. Thus, the influence of the union may be felt even when it is numerically weak or even unsuccessful in carrying through unionization. This is why, short of detailed institutional studies of specific industries in relatively small labor market areas, it is difficult to develop empirical explanations for the changes in the patterns of wage distribution. This is probably the basic reason for the comparative sketchiness of Miller's treatment of the causal factors in the narrowing of wage differentials. Essentially, they are not suitable for statistical treatment.[11]

In this connection, the available information on the effects of changing minimum wages under the Fair Labor Standards Act is somewhat more extensive than that relied upon by Miller and is not always in accord with his findings.[12] The data on the wage distributions of workers in Southern sawmills definitely suggests that the effect of the 75 cent minimum wage was to narrow wage differentials and that it persisted for at least four years.[13] The data also show that from 1948 to 1951 increases in hourly earnings in low-wage industries subject to the law were substantially higher than in the high-wage industries also subject to the law, but that changes in hourly earnings in the low-wage nonsubject industries did not differ materially from changes in the high-wage subject industries. Thus, the average increase for high-wage subject industries was 121 per cent during the period, in the low-wage nonsubject industries 125 per cent, but in low-wage subject industries 171 per cent.[14] These conclusions are also supported by a more recent investigation directed at the evaluation of the effects of $1 minimum wage. In the

[10] See, for example, the following papers in *International Labor Review:* John T. Dunlop and Melvin Rothbaum, "International Comparisons of Wage Structures," April 1955, pp. 347 ff.; "Recent Trends in Industrial Wages" May 1955, pp. 516 ff.; Earl E. Muntz, "The Decline in Wage Differentials Based on Skill in the United States," June 1955, pp. 575ff.; "Changing Wage Structures: An International Review" March 1956, pp. 275 ff.; and Lloyd G. Reynolds and Cynthia H. Taft, *The Evolution of Wage Structure,* Yale University Press, 1956.

[11] Cf. Reynolds and Taft, *op. cit.,* pp. 12 f.

[12] *Results of the Minimum-Wage Increase of 1950: Economic Effects in Selected Low-Wage Industries and Establishments,* Dept. of Labor, August 1954.

[13] *Ibid.,* pp. 21 and 24.

[14] *Ibid.,* pp. 109 and 111 ff.

short run, this minimum, which became effective on March 1, 1956, resulted in a general narrowing of wage differentials, in industries surveyed, particularly among regions, occupations, and plants of different sizes. The study also concludes that since the Fair Labor Standards Act became effective in 1938, "average hourly earnings of workers in selected low-wage industries generally subject to the Act have increased by a larger percentage than earnings for selected high-wage industries or for all manufacturing workers combined," while "earnings of workers in selected low-wage industries in which the Act is not generally applicable have lagged behind the other three groups, for the period 1938 to 1956 taken as a whole." [15]

[15] *Studies of the Economic Effects of the $1.00 Minimum Wage,* Department of Labor, March 1957.

# Index of Authors

# Index of Subjects